D1251613

OCT 14 1997
NOV 27 1997
12/12/98
JUL 12 1999

MAR 14 2000
MAR 6 2001

NOV 30 2004

Perceptual and Cognitive Development

Handbook of Perception and Cognition
2nd Edition

Series Editors
Edward Carterette
and **Morton Friedman**

Perceptual and Cognitive Development

Edited by
Rochel Gelman
Terry Kit-Fong Au
Department of Psychology
University of California, Los Angeles
Los Angeles, California

Academic Press

San Diego   New York   Boston
London   Sydney   Tokyo   Toronto

This book is printed on acid-free paper. ∞

Copyright © 1996 by ACADEMIC PRESS, INC.

All Rights Reserved.
No part of this publication may be reproduced or transmitted in any form or by any
means, electronic or mechanical, including photocopy, recording, or any information
storage and retrieval system, without permission in writing from the publisher.

Academic Press, Inc.
A Division of Harcourt Brace & Company
525 B Street, Suite 1900, San Diego, California 92101-4495

United Kingdom Edition published by
Academic Press Limited
24-28 Oval Road, London NW1 7DX

Library of Congress Cataloging-in-Publication Data

Perceptual and cognitive development / edited by Rochel Gelman, Terry
  Kit-Fong Au.
        p.   cm. -- (Handbook of perception and cognition series, 2nd
  edition)
    Includes bibliographical references and index.
    ISBN 0-12-279660-8 : (alk. paper)
    1. Perception.   2. Cognition.   I. Gelman, Rochel.   II. Au, Terry
  Kit-Fong.   III. Series: Handbook of perception and cognition (2nd
  ed.)
  BF311.P354   1996
  153--dc20   95-50891
                                                               CIP

PRINTED IN THE UNITED STATES OF AMERICA
96 97 98 99 00 01 BC 9 8 7 6 5 4 3 2 1

FERNDALE
COLLEGE
LIBRARY

Contents

Perception and Cognition

1 *The Origins of Object Perception*
  Philip J. Kellman

2   *Perceptual Classification and Expertise*

Susan Carey

3 *Early Cognitive Development: Objects and Space*
Elizabeth S. Spelke and Linda Hermer

Cognition and Language

4 *Concepts and Theories*
Susan A. Gelman

8   *Conversation and Cognition*

Michael Siegal

9   *A Theory of Mind Perspective on Social Cognitive Development*

Marjorie Taylor

Models of Development

10 Developmental Cognitive Neuroscience: A Biological Perspective on Cognitive Change

Mark H. Johnson and Rick O. Gilmore

11 Computational Models of Developmental Mechanisms

Domenico Parisi

12 Activity-Dependent Processes in Perceptual and Cognitive Development

Linda B. Smith and Donald B. Katz

Contributors

Numbers in parentheses indicate the pages on which the authors' contributions begin.

Paul Bloom (151)
Department of Psychology
University of Arizona
Tucson, Arizona 85721

Susan Carey (49)
Department of Brain and Cognitive
  Sciences
Massachusetts Institute of Technology
Cambridge, Massachusetts 02139

Susan A. Gelman (117)
Department of Psychology
University of Michigan
Ann Arbor, Michigan 48109

Rick O. Gilmore (333)
Department of Psychology
Carnegie Mellon University
Pittsburgh, Pennsylvania 15213

Linda Hermer (71)
Department of Psychology
Cornell University
Ithaca, New York 14853

Mark H. Johnson (333)
MRC Cognitive Development Unit
London WC1H 0BT, United Kingdom

Annette Karmiloff-Smith (185)
MRC Cognitive Development Unit
University College
London WC1H 0AH, United
  Kingdom

Donald B. Katz (413)
Department of Psychology
Indiana University
Bloomington, Indiana 47405

xiii

Philip J. Kellman (3)
Department of Psychology
University of California, Los Angeles
Los Angeles, California 90095

Kang Lee (185)
Department of Psychology
Queen's University
Kingston, Ontario Canada K7L 3N6

Kevin F. Miller (213)
Department of Psychology and
  Beckman Institute
University of Illinois at Urbana-
  Champaign
Champaign, Illinois 61820

Domenico Parisi (373)
Institute of Psychology
National Research Council
00137 Rome, Italy

Michael Siegal (243)
Department of Psychology
University of Queensland
Brisbane 4072, Australia

Linda B. Smith (413)
Department of Psychology
Indiana University
Bloomington, Indiana 47405

Elizabeth S. Spelke (71)
Department of Psychology
Cornell University
Ithaca, New York 14853

Marjorie Taylor (283)
Department of Psychology
University of Oregon
Eugene, Oregon 97403

Foreword

The problem of perception and cognition is in understanding how the organism transforms, organizes, stores, and uses information arising from the world in sense data or memory. With this definition of perception and cognition in mind, this handbook is designed to bring together the essential aspects of this very large, diverse, and scattered literature and to give a précis of the state of knowledge in every area of perception and cognition. The work is aimed at the psychologist and the cognitive scientist in particular and at the natural scientist in general. Topics are covered in comprehensive surveys in which fundamental facts and concepts are presented, and important leads to journals and monographs of the specialized literature are provided. Perception and cognition are considered in the widest sense. Therefore, the work will treat a wide range of experimental and theoretical work.

The *Handbook of Perception and Cognition* should serve as a basic source and reference work for all in the arts or sciences, indeed for all who are interested in human perception, action, and cognition.

Edward C. Carterette and Morton P. Friedman

Preface

Carterette and Friedman's invitation to include a volume dedicated to developmental approaches to perception and cognition followed several rounds of editing outlines for the updated series. Some of the volumes in the series could appropriately include a chapter or two on developmental topics, for example, language acquisition and problem solving. However, given how much high-quality developmental work could be included in this edition of the *Handbook of Perception and Cognition,* it was clear that there also had to be a separate developmental volume that illustrates how the developmental approach can yield fundamental contributions to our understanding of perception and cognition as a whole. The chapters in this book can be organized in several ways. Although we favor the one presented here, many connections crisscross chapters in the different sections.

One section illustrates the interplay between perception and cognition. Carey deals with the problem of face perception in the context of how development moves one from being a novice to an expert. She expands this case to a more general statement about the acquisition of perceptual expertise. Kellman offers us an account of important variables that contribute to early object perception. Spelke and Hermer relate early object and space perception to a domain-specific account of early cognitive development.

A second set of papers by Bloom, S. Gelman, Lee and Karmiloff-Smith, Miller, Siegal, and Taylor features fundamental problems in cognition and language: the acquisition of a coherent, organized, and shared understanding of concepts and language. These papers offer insights about the human ability to represent different knowledge domains with different theories and/or representational formats. They also thoughtfully puzzle over to what extent knowledge of people, the physical world, mathematics, representations, language, and so on is domain-specific or theory-like. Their concerns about the development of conversational, social, and cultural skills and how such skills interact with the assessment of skill and knowledge offer valuable insights about the development of shared knowledge, assessment of memory, and perspective taking.

A third set of papers—those by Johnson and Gilmore, Parisi, and Smith and Katz—presents models (in more than one sense) of how to relate developmental, comparative, and neurological considerations to early learning, as well as perceptual and cognitive development.

Some might wonder why there are no chapters with titles like learning, memory, and attention. We spent a fair amount of time pondering how this could be. The answer we settled on is straightforward. Discussions of learning, memory, and attention permeate individual chapters. Kellman is much concerned with an account of what object-relevant information infants attend to as a function of development; Carey's chapter is concerned with the development of attention to different levels of perceptual organization; the Smith and Katz chapter is grounded in discussions about learning. Parisi contrasts developmental models that do and do not learn; Gelman takes on the problem of conceptual induction; Bloom focuses on word learning; Siegal's work illustrates current concerns for context effects on the quality of young children's memory performance, and so on. Put differently, the move is to embed discussions of learning, memory, attention, and problem solving within specific accounts, be these about the stimulus, the neurological status of developing minds, the kind of learning that mediates development of conceptual coherence, the nature of the knowledge, different notational formats, or another topic.

Rochel Gelman and Terry Au

Perception and Cognition

The Origins of Object Perception

Philip J. Kellman

I. INTRODUCTION

Two streams of light enter tiny apertures of a child's eyes. Instantly, she is aware, in rich detail, of the objects that furnish her environment. How is this possible?

To explain object perception, we must connect facts of many different kinds. We need facts about the physical world, such as how light is absorbed and reflected by objects, and geometrical facts about how objects' projections change as they move or as the observer moves. We must also know about information processing: what properties and relationships in reflected light carry information about objects? How is information extracted, represented and transformed? We also need to know how this information processing is carried out biologically: facts about the functions of retinal receptors, single cortical cells, cortical areas, and so on. For some purposes, accounts at one level or another may be most important. For building a computer model or robot, information processing is the focus, since once understood in humans it may be simulated on the computer. The details of our biology will not be shared by the computer, which has much different circuitry. For treating pathology of the human visual system, on the other

Perceptual and Cognitive Development
Copyright © 1996 by Academic Press, Inc. All rights of reproduction in any form reserved.

hand, physiology is crucial, whereas knowing an algorithm for recovering shape from motion is irrelevant.

Woven through these multiple levels of understanding is a dimension we have not yet mentioned: Development. Available information, processes that extract it, and their biological substrates are not static. Growth and learning, especially during the first year of life, profoundly change perception. Our purpose in this chapter is to examine these changes, focusing on the question: How does object perception develop? We will emphasize perceptual abilities at or near the beginning of human life, and what is known about their transformation as a person grows and learns. Both early capacities and patterns of change have implications for early cognitive and social development.

Our treatment will necessarily be confined in several ways. Although objects are perceived via several perceptual systems, we will emphasize vision, both because it is primary in giving us spatial information at a distance, and because it has been heavily researched. We will also concentrate on how perceivers get knowledge about properties of the environment; accordingly, we will draw sparingly from the large literature characterizing sensory thresholds, selectively noting those facts about sensory limitations that can be clearly linked to perceptual performance. (For a more detailed discussion of the development of visual mechanisms, the interested reader may refer to Banks & Salapatek, 1983; Banks & Kellman, in press). Finally, in focusing on object perception we will often note its relation to other topics, such as space and motion perception, but we will not discuss them in detail. (For a detailed treatment of the development of space and motion perception, see Kellman, 1995.)

A. What Is an Object?

Much of perception is object perception. Having said that, it might be useful to say what we mean by an "object." Here "object" will mean a coherent, bounded volume of matter. A stick, a hat, or a cupcake is an object; a pile of sand, a loud noise, or a noun following a verb is not. Our usage suits the study of perception of physical objects. Even this straightforward and limited definition conceals many complexities. One worth mentioning is what might be called the *relativity* of objects.

The Relativity of Objects

Take an object to be a coherent physical unit, held together by forces and separable, by an action such as lifting or pushing, from other objects. A chair fits this definition, but what about a hydrogen atom or a spiral nebula? These latter examples are not objects, for us at least. What counts as an object depends on both physics and ecology (Gibson, 1966, 1979). When something is very large relative to the human body (e.g., the earth), we tend to treat it as a surface rather than as an object. When it is very small, we can still think of it as an object, but it is no longer detected by ordinary perception or acted upon by ordinary manipulation. It is interesting to ponder how our scientific understandings of the very small and large may implicitly contain aspects of our perception and representation of objects. However, we will not do so here. Closer to our focus, we may conjecture that the relativity of size may change with growth. To an infant, a table may appear as a terrain feature, like a hill. To an adult who can move the table, it is more objectlike. The point about relativity also involves *time*. Something that coheres, but only for milliseconds, will not be an object of our experience. Likewise, an apple and pencil are fine examples of objects, but they will not likely remain coherent over centuries. Finally, consider *forces*. How strongly or weakly matter must cohere to be a unit or to allow separation is relative to the capacities of the organism.

We have hardly done justice to the complexities of defining objects and elaborating their ecological basis, but we have some basis from which to proceed. Physical coherence and boundedness at the levels of scale and across the transformations most relevant for human functioning are the roots of, and motivations for, object perception.

B. The Function of Object Perception in Early Development

Before we embark on our excursion into early object perception abilities, a word is in order about the special function of object perception in infancy. Ecologically, it is obvious that perceiving objects allows humans and animals to obtain nutrition, avoid obstacles and predators, recognize conspecifics, return tennis serves, and make cellular telephone calls. It is striking that, early in development, human infants do virtually none of these things. By 5 months, an infant may reach for an object; by 7 months, she may crawl, and by 12 months, walk. These milestones, however, do not equip an infant to feed or protect itself (or even make phone calls). Yet this same infant, from its earliest days, possesses sophisticated object perception abilities. These have blossomed by 3–4 months and are adultlike by one year.

It may be argued that the function of these abilities in infancy is different from their function in adulthood. The young infant is not so much doing things with objects as exploring them. Much of what infants do serves primarily the process of learning about the physical and social worlds (Piaget, 1952, 1954). This difference in the task of infant and adult perception may have implications for the priorities of perceiving (Kellman, 1993). The adult may need split-second reactions to sometimes tentative information. The infant is not capable of rapid response, but must acquire *accurate* information. Consequences of misperception may be more profound in infancy, and opportunities for error correction more limited. For this reason I have conjectured that infant perception might be *risk averse* in that it is limited initially to those information sources of highest ecological validity. Of the variety of sources available to adults, we might expect that young perceivers will initially use those with the greatest accuracy in indicating what the world is really like (Kellman, 1993). We will return to this conjecture as we survey early object perception abilities.

C. A Taxonomy of Object Perception Abilities

Seeing an object means knowing something about the physical world. Certain chunks of the physical environment cohere: They function as units through various events. By the same token, they are separable from other objects and surfaces. A toothbrush may rest against the inside of a cup, which in turn rests upon a surface. When the toothbrush is lifted, its handle and bristles all move together, but no part of the cup or underlying surface moves with the toothbrush. We do not have to perform the action of lifting the toothbrush to know this outcome; it is easily *seen* in advance. Predictability about how things will cohere, separate, and function is the remarkable achievement of object perception.[1] It is central to most of behavior and thought.

Central but not simple. Seeing objects seems effortless and immediate, but the phenomenology conceals many mysteries. First, the structure of the physical world is not obvious in the array of energy that reaches the eye. Physical linkages and three-dimensional (3-D) arrangements are not given by simple properties of reflected light. Consider a convenient representation, used in computer graphics, of an array of light projecting from a scene. In a digitized image, we note for each location (pixel) numbers indicating luminance and spectral values. Strikingly, the pixel map contains no explicit information whatsoever about objects. Moving from one pixel to another, there is no indication that we move from one object to another in the scene.

This is not to say that the pixel map or the projection to the eyes does not contain information. If the latter did not, we could not see; if the former did not, computer vision would be a hopeless dream. But there is much work to do to make that information explicit. A first step is *edge detection*. Since objects are often made of different materials, boundaries between objects will often, but not always, produce optical discontinuities in luminance, color, or texture. Discontinuities in depth and in motion also indicate boundaries, even in the absence of other information (Gibson, Kaplan, Reynolds, & Wheeler, 1969; Julesz, 1971). Not all luminance discontinuities correspond to the boundaries of objects. Some are textural markings on a continuous surface; others are shadows, and so on. Likewise, there may be depth discontinuities within a single object, if its visible parts are at different depths and it is partly self-occluding. Movements of a nonrigid object may produce internal motion discontinuities, yet it may still be a physical unit. Therefore, a necessary next step in perceiving objects is *edge classification*. We need to know which luminance, depth, and motion contours specify object edges as opposed to other phenomena. Close on the heels of edge classification arises the issue of *boundary assignment*. Most visible contours mark the boundary of one object against a background that continues behind (Koffka, 1935). An example is a picture hanging on a wall. The visible contour at the edge of the frame is a boundary of the frame, but not of the wall. Important to perceiving objects is the correct assignment of which way each boundary bounds (c.f., Kellman & Shipley, 1991).

Unit Formation

Objects are continuous in space and persistent over time, but their effects on our senses are not. Behind the observation that most boundaries bound in one direction lies perhaps the hardest problem of object perception, what might be called the *fragmentation problem*. This problem is both spatial and temporal. Spatially, when objects continue behind others, they often project to separate locations on the retina. Temporal fragmentation arises from the fact that as objects and/or observers move, parts of objects go out of and come into view. We look briefly at each of these aspects of the fragmentation problem.

a. Spatial Fragmentation: The Problem of Occlusion

If one could solve all the riddles of edge detection and classification, it would be a great achievement, but it would not suffice to explain object perception. Consider a scene projected to an observer's eyes. Its projection contains areas homogeneous in lightness, color, and/or texture. Between these areas are edges. Are the homogeneous patches, encompassed by edges, objects? No. In general, most objects are partly concealed behind others. To get from the regions delimited by edges to perceived edges requires several minor miracles. Figure 1 gives an example. How many objects are in the display shown in A? To an adult observer, the display is immediately seen to contain three large objects of definite shapes (shown in B, C, and D) and a number of thin objects resembling blades of grass. Each of the grasslike objects is also seen effortlessly as a definite, separable object, although some effort is required to count them in this cluttered scene. (There are 12.) A much more difficult task is to count the number of relatively homogeneous regions that are connected to form each object. The object shown in C is perceived in display A by combining 11 regions; object

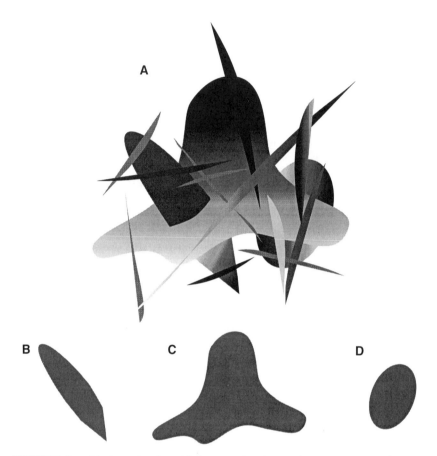

FIGURE 1   (A) Example of spatial fragmentation in unit formation. (B–D) The unoc-cluded objects shown in B, C, and D are readily perceived in A despite the numerous instances of partial occlusion and luminance variation. (See text.)

D is formed from 8 regions; and object B from 5 regions. Strikingly, when we look at the complex display, we take away little information about the shapes of the visible regions.

Figure 1A illustrates many of the perplexities that need to be overcome in unit formation. Technically, few of the regions are homogeneous in the simplest sense, because most contain luminance gradients (gradually chang-ing shades of gray). Parts of single objects appear in separate visible areas. The complete objects are not seen because they are expected or familiar; for example, the shape in C was designed to be novel, yet it is seen effortlessly. Connections form between parts with different luminance, or different gra-dients of luminance, as is true to some degree for objects A, B, and C. Areas of similar luminance are not always seen as connected. The figure contains several examples of cases in which objects are imaged against areas identical in luminance; here, the visual system generates *illusory contours,* such as occurs for the middle portion of the thin, black, vertical object at the top of the display. Thus, spatial gaps in the projections of objects are handled by the visual system by construction of occluded boundaries, behind other objects, and illusory contours, in front of other objects. The object shown in B has an even stranger existence in Figure 1A: Its visible parts are partly in front of and partly behind object C, and these parts connect by *passing through* object C!

Occlusion is pervasive in ordinary environments, and our example in Figure 1A is a simple case, compared to some. The ubiquity of partial occlusion derives from very basic facts: Light moves in straight lines; most objects are opaque, and environments usually contain objects at different distances from the observer. Luckily, human perceivers possess visual processes equal to the physical demands of occlusion: in Figure 1A, they turn the chaos of 45 projected regions into 3 objects and some stray foliage. Below we consider when and how these processes originate.

b. Temporal Fragmentation

Motion of the observer and of objects causes constant changes in patterns of occlusion. Also, because our acuity is relatively poor outside of a small region in the center of the visual field, we register even stationary environments by frequent changes of gaze. Clear views of a given object may be given to our retinas for one or two hundred milliseconds, or even several seconds in some cases, but seldom much longer.

Recovery of linkages and continuity of objects despite spatial and temporal fragmentation in the input to the eyes is called *unit formation.* Sometimes this process is described as *segmentation and grouping.* Either way, a fundamental issue in the perception of objects is how we determine coherent and persisting structures in the environment from intermittent and fragmented stimulation.

Having units in hand (or in sight), we arrive at more familiar object properties. When we do things with objects, when we recognize something as familiar or use them for a particular purpose, *three-dimensional form* and *size* are important properties. Finally, we have so far omitted one of the most important properties of all: perception of the *tangibility* or *substance* of objects.

To summarize, our taxonomy of object perception abilities includes:

1. Edge Detection
2. Edge Classification
3. Boundary Assignment

4. Unit Formation
5. Three-dimensional Form Perception
6. Size Perception
7. Perception of Substance

Our strategy in the remainder of the chapter will be to consider what is known about the developmental course of each of these abilities. For some of these abilities, it will be necessary to say a bit about how they work in adults and about the information available for perception. Most of the findings we will discuss have come in the last two decades. As we will see, more is known about some pieces of the puzzle than others, but on the whole, it is remarkable how complete a picture has been developed in a relatively short period of time.

II. EDGE DETECTION

Do infant perceivers detect edges from the very beginning? If so, how? Of the information used by adults for edge detection, such as luminance, texture, motion, or depth discontinuities, which are available initially and how do others come to function? There has been little explicit research on edge detection. Early performance on pattern and shape perception tasks, however, allows us to make some inferences.

Infants respond to differences among shapes and patterns from birth. For example, Fantz, Fagan, and Miranda (1975) presented patterns in pairs to newborn infants and found reliable fixation preferences. Preference for one of two patterns indicates detection of differences, perhaps implying detection of edges. This interpretation is consistent with another aspect of the data: Outermost contours of patterns were most important in evoking preferential looking. When different patterns were encompassed by a similar surround, such as an enclosing square, preferences were reduced.

Edge detection may not be proven by these results, however. Different patterns might evoke differential interest without their spatial boundaries being detected. Strange as it seems, there is some support for this hypothesis. Early stages of visual processing have been successfully modeled using linear systems analysis (DeValois & DeValois, 1988; Graham, 1989). Any two-dimensional image can be decomposed uniquely into a set of sinusoidally varying luminance components (often called Fourier components, after the mathematician), each having a particular orientation, spatial frequency, and phase. Initial encoding of patterns in the visual cortex involves cells sensitive to such components in local areas of the image. As in the example of the pixel map discussed earlier, this representation in human vision does not make explicit information about object boundaries. This is especially true if *phase* information (spatial relations among components) is left out.

If two patterns are encoded as sets of Fourier components, any detectable difference in their components or amplitudes (contrast) in the two patterns may be sufficient for telling them apart. It has been suggested that infants in the first several weeks of life actually respond on this basis (Banks & Ginsburg, 1983; Braddick, Atkinson, & Wattam-Bell, 1986). Banks and Ginsburg (1983) attempted to account for reported pattern preferences using measures gleaned from the Fourier amplitude spectra of patterns. They obtained good fits of their predictive measures to previously published data on infants' pattern preferences. Their predictive measure included no phase information. Patterns made up of the same spatial frequencies, but with different phase relations, appear radically different to adults, especially in terms of perceived edges. Braddick et al. (1986) carried out explicit tests of infant pattern discrimination for patterns having identical spatial frequency components but differing in phase. They found no evidence of phase sensitivity in infant pattern perception before 2 months of age. Without any phase information, edge detection and classification might be problematic.[2]

Other behavioral evidence, however, casts doubt on the idea that newborns lack edge detection abilities. In an important series of studies, Slater and colleagues (Slater, Mattock, & Brown, 1990; Slater & Morison, 1985) have provided strong evidence for size and shape constancy in newborn infants. Size constancy refers to the ability to detect physical size across variations in retinal size. Shape constancy in this case refers to infants' ability to detect the same planar (two-dimensional) shape across variations in slant toward or away from the observer. (See Section VIB and VII below.) It is hard to invent an explanation for the shape constancy results that does not require detection of boundary orientation in three-dimensional space. The argument from size constancy results is less direct. Detection of object depth is implied by size perception under the circumstances used. If other visible surfaces, as well as the target objects, are assigned depth appropriately, then the object's boundary cannot be a textural marking on a surface. Despite the indirectness of the size argument, these findings taken together suggest that edge detection and classification are possible even for neonates.

It is not clear how to resolve the inconsistency between behavioral evidence on pattern perception in the first 2 months of life and evidence suggesting the early absence of phase information. One possibility is that pattern discrimination in the relatively simple, meaningless, and periodic patterns used by Braddick et al. understates infants' capabilities for using phase information in detection of object boundaries. In particular, it may be the case that particular kinds of phase relations are important. An interesting property of an abrupt luminance edge is that at the location of the edge, many Fourier components of different frequencies will be in the same phase. Marr and Hildreth (1980) proposed that edge detection occurs at several different levels of scale, and that registration of an edge at multiple levels is particularly good information for surface edges. Perhaps infant edge detection abilities are better engaged by edges of ordinary objects than by stimuli composed of two spatial frequency components. Nevertheless, the data are clear in pointing to a conspicuous improvement in phase sensitivity over the first 6–8 weeks.

Other factors limiting the precision of edge detection are orientation selectivity, acuity, and contrast sensitivity. Some research indicates that orientation selectivity is not well developed until about 1 month of age (Atkinson, Hood, Wattam-Bell, Anker, and Tricklebank, et al., 1988; Held, 1993), although it does appear to function to some degree in newborns (Atkinson et al., 1988). Much of the fine detail and many of the low-contrast edges perceptible by adults are not detectable by infants. On the other hand, adult sensitivity far exceeds the minimum required for normal perception of objects and events. As noted by Hofsten (1983), newborn human visual acuity approximates that of an adult cat. Infant sensitivity improves quickly from birth to about 6 months (Banks & Dannemiller, 1987). We can conclude that edges of nearby and large objects may be perceivable quite early, but, in general, luminance edges are registered far less precisely in the first few months than later on.

Another source of information for edges derives from motion relationships. When objects move relative to each other, or when an observer moves while viewing a stationary array, visible texture on more distant objects is progressively *accreted and deleted* as it is revealed or occluded by nearer objects. This form of information supports perception of object boundaries and form by adults, even in the absence of other information, such as in displays comprised of random dots (Gibson et al., 1969; Kaplan, 1969). Kaufmann-Hayoz, Kaufmann, and Stucki (1986) found evidence that 3-month-old infants detected and discriminated shapes based solely on this kind of information. Studies with younger infants would be useful to determine when this ability first arises.

III. EDGE CLASSIFICATION

Evidence for early shape perception implies some capacity to *detect* edges. Implications for edge *classification* are less clear-cut. Detection of a planar object tilted in three-dimensional space may indicate that the shape is seen as an object separate from the background (Slater & Morison, 1985). If so, the edges are not only detected but classified as object boundaries. In this situation, depth discontinuities may provide crucial information. What about perception of figure and ground from luminance or color boundaries alone? Infants detect and discriminate shape from such information. Does this imply that they classify contours as object boundaries? Maybe. But it is also possible that a shape may be seen as a textural marking on a surface rather than as a separate object.

There is some evidence in favor of the latter possibility. Early in life, luminance, color, and texture discontinuities may not indicate object boundaries, a possibility raised by Piaget (1954). Observing his own child, Laurent, at 6 months, 22 days of age, he noted:

> Laurent tries to grasp a box of matches. When he is at the point of reaching it I place it on a book; he immediately withdraws his hand, then grasps the book itself. He remains puzzled until the box slides and thanks to this accident he dissociates it from its support.

When one object rests upon another, differences in luminance, color, and texture at the boundary and possibly the symmetry of each object readily lead adults to perceive object boundaries. Until a relatively late age (Piaget estimated 10 months), infants do not utilize this information, treating adjacent, stationary objects as unitary. In contrast, relative motion, such as the matchbox moving relative to the book, provides information about object boundaries much earlier.

Experimental research has solidified these interpretations. Spelke, Breinlinger, Jacobson, and Phillips (1993) presented displays in which the relationship of two object parts was varied. In homogeneous displays, the two adjacent parts were identical in luminance, color, and texture, and shared a smooth boundary. In heterogeneous displays, the two parts differed in luminance and color, and there were discontinuities (T junctions) where the two parts met. After familiarization with a display, infants viewed an event in which either both parts together or only the top part of the array was lifted. Greater looking time, relative to a baseline condition, to the event in which only the top part moved was interpreted as evidence that the original array was perceived as a single, connected object. Consistent with earlier results, infants at 3 months of age perceived the homogeneous and heterogeneous displays as connected, indicating that neither discontinuities along the outer boundary nor discontinuities of luminance, color, or texture are used for parsing arrays into objects. Results at 5 and 9 months were somewhat ambiguous, but they were consistent with some use of luminance and/or boundary discontinuities as information for object boundaries.

Hofsten and Spelke (1985) carried out experiments using infants' reaching behavior. Five-month-old infants were presented with displays consisting of a small, near object, a larger, further object, and an extended background surface. In some conditions the larger object moved, either rigidly with the background surface or with the smaller object. Infants' reaches were recorded under conditions with different spatial and kinematic relations between the objects. It was assumed that reaches would be directed to perceived boundaries of graspable objects. Much as Piaget (1954) had observed, when the array was stationary and the objects were adjacent, infants reached more to the edges of the larger, further object. This result suggests that infants perceived the two objects as a unit and distinguished the unit from a large extended background surface (as Piaget had also noticed). When the two objects were separated in depth, infants reached more to the nearer, smaller object, suggesting that depth discontinuities provided sufficient information for object segregation. Results of other experiments validated the role of motion in object segregation: when the larger object moved differently from the smaller object, more reaches were directed to the smaller object. Because this effect occurred when the small object was stationary, the findings disconfirmed the idea that infants merely reach for visible moving surfaces. Instead, these results support the idea that motion segregates objects and infants reach for perceived objects (usually the nearest in an array; Yonas & Granrud, 1984).

The informativeness of motion-carried information in infant object segregation was also demonstrated by Granrud et al. (1985). Accretion–deletion of texture, given by observer or object movement, can specify to adults not only contours but object boundaries (Gibson et al., 1969; Kaplan, 1969). Granrud et al. found that infants reached preferentially for the object specified as nearer by the accretion/deletion information.

We can make functional sense of these results. In terms of ecological validity—how well an information source specifies some aspect of the environment—some sources of object boundary information are better than others. Luminance and color changes are ambiguous: They characterize both textural variation on continuous surfaces and boundaries of objects. Depth and motion discontinuities, on the other hand, are unlikely to occur within a unified object. They are thus highly valid indicators of object boundaries. Early edge classification appears to fit the hypothesis that initial perceptual abilities rely on the most valid sources of information (Kellman, 1993). If there is an early stage in development in which luminance/color edges do not mark object boundaries, it remains an important question for future research when adjacent objects begin to be parsed based on their surface qualities, and what brings about this developmental advance.

IV. BOUNDARY ASSIGNMENT

Boundary assignment must occur whenever an object is seen as in front of another object or background. Evidence that infants distinguish shapes, or figures from grounds, might indicate that boundary assignment is occurring. It is not easy, however, to prove that a shape perceived is an object shape, as opposed to a marking on a surface or the shape of a hole.

There is little research that directly addresses this finer distinction relevant to development of boundary assignment. Again, the Slater and Morison (1985) shape constancy result indirectly supports both edge classification and boundary assignment, probably from discontinuities in depth at object edges. Accretion/deletion of texture also seems to determine boundary assignment (Granrud et al., 1985), since infants reached for the surface specified to be nearer by accretion/deletion, presumably indicating it "owned" its boundary. A limitation on reaching evidence is that infants do not achieve consistent, directed reaching until around 5 months of age. By this time infants have had considerable visual experience.

A way to infer younger infants' abilities involves another functionally interpretable behavior: infants' defensive responses to approaching objects. Head withdrawal, eyeblinks, and hand raising have all been reported as defensive behavior to approaching objects, even in the earliest weeks of life (Schiff, 1965; Yonas, 1981). Although there have been interpretive controversies, evidence supports the notion that some observed responses, especially blinking, indicate defensive behavior (Yonas, Arterberry, & Granrud, 1987). Defensive responding to a looming object may imply boundary assignment, but it does not specify much about the relevant information. Carroll and Gibson (1981) attempted to pinpoint effects of accretion/deletion of texture. They presented 3-month-old infants with arrays in which all surfaces were covered with random dot texture. In one condition a textured object approached the infant, whereas in the other condition, an aperture (opening in the surface) approached. This difference in physical events was specified by different accretion/deletion effects. Infants showed defensive behavior more frequently to the approaching objects than to apertures, suggesting that accretion/deletion of texture indicates object boundary ownership even at this early age.

V. UNIT FORMATION

Organizing the world into units is really the defining problem of object perception. Detecting many aspects of objects, for example, shapes, sizes, and familiarity, presupposes the successful operation of unit formation, that is, processes that determine connected regions and their boundaries. Unit formation is thus a foundation of many achievements in cognitive and social development. Some examples are social attachment (Regolin & Vallortigara, 1995), categorization of objects, mathematical skills such as counting, linguistic skills such as naming objects, and many more.

For adults, unit formation occurs routinely and effortlessly. This simplicity masks the fact that it depends on multiple sources of information, which may have different developmental origins. The Gestalt psychologists described a number of influences on unit formation (Michotte, Thines, & Crabbe, 1964; Wertheimer, 1923). The role of motion was expressed as a principle of *common fate*. Things that move together tend to be grouped together. Other principles applied to stationary arrays. By the principle of *good continuation*, things appear connected if their contours continue smoothly instead of changing abruptly. *Good form* refers to a tendency to organize arrays so that simple, symmetrical objects are perceived. The principle of *similarity* suggests a tendency to unify similar parts or areas, and *proximity*, a tendency to group closer things together.

The Gestalt descriptive principles do not permit precise or quantitative predictions. Part of the problem comes from terms that resist clear definition. These include the "goodness" in good continuation and good form, "simplicity," "common fate," and the notorious "similarity." Nevertheless, the principles contain important insights, most of which can be readily illustrated.

A. Two Processes in Unit Formation

Some contemporary work has made progress in giving more precise form to the Gestalt principles. Kellman and Shipley (1991) proposed dividing information for unity into two categories: the *rich* or *edge-sensitive* (ES) process and the *primitive* or *edge-insensitive* (EI) process.

The EI process is an elaboration of what Wertheimer (1923) called *common fate*. The process is edge-insensitive because the positions and orientations of the edges of visible parts play no role in determining their completion behind the occluding object. Certain motion relationships alone indicate connectedness. This information does not specify the exact form of the hidden parts under occlusion. For this reason Kellman and Shipley (1991) labeled it the "primitive process" (c.f., Hebb, 1949).

The ES process depends on edge positions and orientations, both in stationary and moving displays. Many of its formal properties, and some of its neural mechanisms, have been elucidated in recent years (Field, Hayes, & Hess, 1992; Kellman & Shipley, 1991; Polat & Sagi, 1993; Shapley & Gordon, 1987; von der Heydt, Peterhans, & Baumgartner, 1984). The input–output relations in this process may be thought of as a mathematical formalization of the Gestalt principle of good continuation, that is, that segmentation and connection of parts depend on straight lines and smooth curves.[3] Detailed models of the ES process may be found elsewhere (Grossberg, 1994; Kellman & Shipley, 1991, 1992). For our purposes, two points are most important. First, for adults, certain edge relationships support object completion (such edges are termed *relatable* edges), whereas others do not. Figure 2 gives some examples of relatable edges and nonrelatable edges. Second, the boundary interpolation process at work in occlusion cases is the same as in illusory figures (Kellman, Yin, & Shipley, 1995; Shapley &

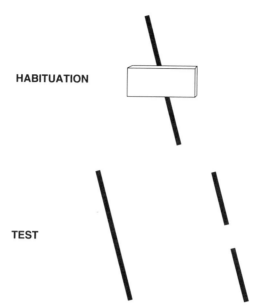

HABITUATION

TEST

FIGURE 2   Relatable and nonrelatable edges. The ES process (see text) connects the visible black parts in each display when the edges are relatable (*top*), but not when the relatability criterion is not met (*bottom*).

Ringach, 1994; Shipley & Kellman, 1992a). This identity allows us to obtain converging evidence on the developmental origins of the ES process.

Perception of object unity and boundaries was studied programmatically by Kellman and Spelke (1983) using habituation/dishabituation of visual attention. If infants perceive a partly occluded object as complete, then after habituation to such a display, they should generalize habituation more to an unoccluded complete object than to an unoccluded display containing separate pieces that correspond to the previously visible parts of the object. Figure 3 illustrates the paradigm. After habituation to a center-occluded display, broken and complete test displays are presented in alternation.

B. Common Motion and Relatable Edges in Combination

To test whether the EI process (common motion) or the ES process (completing relatable edges) functions in early infancy, an occlusion display combining these was constructed. It consisted of two visible, collinear parts of a rod, sharing a common lateral motion. Infants were habituated to this display and tested afterward with alternating presentations of two unoccluded test displays: a moving complete rod and moving broken display, consisting

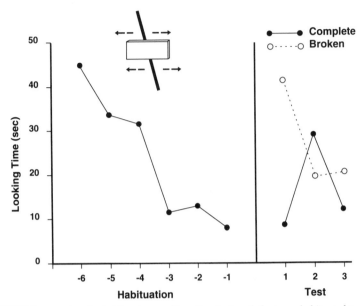

FIGURE 3   Design for habituation studies of occlusion. Infants are habituated to a partly occluded display and tested afterward for generalization of habituation or dishabituation to an unoccluded complete display and an unoccluded "broken" display containing two pieces separated by a gap where the occluder had been. (After Kellman & Spelke, 1983.)

of two rod pieces separated by a gap. Results are shown in Figure 4. After habituation, infants generalized habituation to the complete display and dishabituated to the broken display. This pattern suggests that the occlusion display was perceived as containing a unified object rather than two separate rod pieces. These data alone do not specify whether the EI (common motion), ES process, or both were responsible for unit formation.

C. Common Motion Alone: Revealing the EI Process

To assess the effect of common motion alone, Kellman and Spelke (1983) tested an occlusion display in which edge relationships would not be expected to support boundary completion. One visible piece was a black rod; the other was a red blob with black textural markings constructed randomly within certain constraints (see Figure 5). These two visible parts were not relatable nor similar in surface qualities. They did share a common lateral translation. Results indicated that here, too, infants perceive the visible parts as connected behind the occluder. The broken test stimulus, which included only the parts previously visible in the occlusion display, produced strong recovery of visual attention after habituation. The complete test display, constructed by continuing the rod halfway down and the random blob halfway up, induced little recovery.

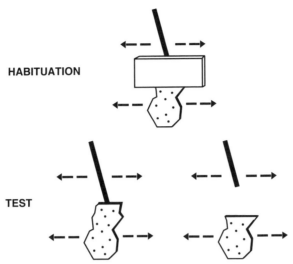

FIGURE 4 Results of experiment testing unity perception from common motion and relatable edges. Infants were habituated to two aligned, visible parts sharing a common lateral translation (*top*). Looking times are shown for the last six habituation trials (with the final one labeled −1 in Figure 3) and the test trials. Test trials consisted of successive presentations of unoccluded complete and broken displays, with half of the subjects seeing the complete display first. (From Kellman & Spelke, 1983.)

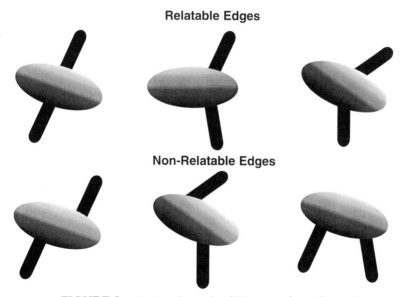

FIGURE 5 Displays for study of EI process alone. (See text.)

The outcome indicates that common motion alone can specify the unity of a partly occluded object to infants. These results occurred despite the fact that the specific form connecting the two visible parts was not specified. Visual attention in this situation seems to be controlled by unity, not specific form, a result confirmed by subsequent research (Craton & Yonas, 1990).

1. Motion Relationships in the EI Process

To say that common motion leads to perceived unity leaves much unsaid. When is motion "common" and what counts as "motion"? Later research addressed both of these questions.

Common motion must include at least the identical lateral translations shared by the object parts in the studies described so far. The class of unifying motions, however, might be larger. Rigid objects can undergo any combination of translations and rotations. One hypothesis, then, is that the two parts will appear connected if related by a rigid motion in three-dimensional space. A different way of thinking about the earlier displays is that each visible part underwent the same visible *event*. Kellman, Spelke, and Short (1986) contrasted these possibilities by testing infants' perception of a rod vertically translating behind an occluder. In this display, the two pieces shared a common translatory motion, but the visible events differed. As one visible part came more into view, the other progressively disappeared. Results supported the rigid motion hypothesis: Infants responded as if a single complete object were perceived in the occlusion display.

Another test of the rigid motion hypothesis involved rigid translation toward and away from the observer in depth. In this case, the stimulus for motion perception is not displacement of the object's projection across the retina, but optical expansion/contraction of the projection (or oculomotor changes in accommodation or convergence as the object moves). If unit formation in the EI process depends on the particular stimulus of optical displacement, then a depth-translating object should not engage the process. In contrast, on the rigid motion hypothesis, such a display should produce unit formation. Kellman et al. (1986) found clear evidence confirming the latter prediction.

A limitation on the class of rigid motions effective in unit formation was reported by Kellman and Short (1987a). Rotation of an object in the frontal plane is a rigid motion, but the two visible parts of the center-occluded object move in opposite directions. This rotation display, as well as others combining rotation and translation, yielded no evidence of unit formation at 16 weeks. A display in which the rotation and translation were phased so that the top and bottom generally always moved in the same direction (looking much like a windshield wiper) did support unit formation. It appears that the class of motions engaging the EI process in the early months is not the full class of rigid motions. In particular, common direction of visible parts seems to be required.

2. What Is Motion?

Motion ordinarily refers to the changing positions of objects in space. In studies of the EI process described so far, moving objects have been involved. Perceptually, motion of an object is detected by means of certain optical events; for example, lateral translation produces optical displacement.

Helmholtz (1885/1910) noted the similarities between optical events produced by motion of an observer and the motion of an object seen by a stationary observer. This similarity leads to the question: Does the EI process depend only on perceived motion of objects or on certain optical events? Could it, for example, be engaged by optical changes given when a moving observer views stationary objects? The question has many implications for perceptual development, only some of which we can consider here. A key question is whether infants can tell the difference between object motion and optical effects generated by observer motion. It has often been asserted (Helmholtz, 1885/1910; James, 1890) that young perceivers cannot distinguish these cases. If so, our question about the basis of the EI process is answered, or moot, at least until infants can tell the difference. J. Gibson (1966, 1979) suggested a more optimistic view of early motion perception. He noted that there is optical information distinguishing the case of observer movement from object motion. When an object moves, there are changes relative to the background that are in general different from what happens when the observer moves while viewing a stationary array. (Discussion of these differences and their role in infant perception may be found in Kellman, 1995.)

Whether unit formation depends on perceived motion or on optical change, and whether infants can tell the difference, were investigated by Kellman, Gleitman, and Spelke (1987). They tested moving infants in two conditions. In a *conjoint motion* condition, the infant's chair and a partly occluded object were rigidly connected beneath the display table, so that they rotated around a vertical axis in between. The conjoint motion condition contained real motion of the object in space, but no physical displacement relative to the subject. If real object motion underlies unit formation, and if it is detectable by a moving observer, this condition was expected to lead to perceived unity. In the other condition, the *observer movement* condition, the observer moved in an arc while viewing a stationary occluded rod. If optical displacement alone can specify unity, infants were expected to perceive a complete object in this condition. Unit formation was assessed, as in earlier studies, by dishabituation patterns following habituation to the occluded displays. Motion characteristics of the object parts were always the same in the test trials as in habituation.

Results were clear. Infants in the conjoint motion condition dishabituated robustly to the broken display, indicating that the occlusion display had been perceived as complete. (Fifteen of sixteen infants in this condition looked at least twice as long at the broken than at the complete test displays on the first test trial.) In the observer movement condition, there was no evidence of unit formation; infants dishabituated equally to the two test objects. Separate analyses, based on looking time differences to moving and stationary displays, indicated that conjoint motion infants perceived object motion during their own motion, whereas observer movement infants accurately perceived their occlusion display as stationary (Kellman et al., 1987).

These findings indicate that the EI process depends on perceived object motion. This outcome has significance for two more general theoretical issues in perceptual development. The first is the idea that early perception depends on sources of information of highest ecological validity. The nature of the EI process confirms this conjecture, for the following reason. The ecological validity of common motion of objects is much superior to that of common optical displacements. The latter occur any time an observer moves and views objects at similar observer-relative distances. It is sometimes the case, but not always, that object parts at similar distances are connected. On the other hand, real motion, such as common rigid translation of visible parts, almost never occurs for unconnected entities. Even when separate objects are subjected to the same force, as when leaves are blown by the wind, their motions virtually never maintain completely rigid relationships. (This situation can, however, be arranged in infant perception laboratories!) The EI process depends on a nearly foolproof principle. When an infant perceives two partly hidden things moving with a rigid relationship as physically connected, they are.

3. Is the EI (Common Motion) Process Innate?

Kellman and Spelke (1983) suggested that the common motion process is an unlearned foundation of object perception. Infants utilize this information at an early age, before other unit formation information operates. The data disconfirm proposals that object perception derives from action- or touch-based learning, because common motion leads to perceived object unity before the onset of skilled reaching or crawling.

Recent research, however, suggests that the common motion principle may not be present at birth. Slater, Morison, Somers, Mattock, Brown, and Taylor (1990) tested infants at 16 weeks and replicated the findings of Kellman and Spelke (1983). Their tests of newborns under identical conditions, however, led to a different result. After habituation to an occlusion display, newborns showed a preference for the complete object compared to a broken display. Newborns consistently showed this pattern after habituation to moving displays in several studies varying the depth separation of the occluder and partly occluded object (Slater, Johnson, Kellman, & Spelke, 1994). Slater et al. (1994) discuss two classes of explanation for this outcome. One possibility is that newborns lack basic visual sensitivity to detect the common motion of the parts. Direction selectivity of cells in visual cortex seems to mature between 1 and 2 months of age (Johnson, 1990; Wattam-Bell, 1991, 1992). It is surprising that before this time there is no behavioral or electrophysiological evidence that infants detect differences in motion direction (Wattam-Bell, 1991, 1992). Therefore, in occlusion situations, newborns may detect motion but not directional coherence of separate parts. If so, perception of separate, bounded fragments is not surprising. Newborns may *segregate* objects by motion at this stage but may not receive the information required for perceived unity.

The second possibility is that infants really do begin with an incorrect perceptual rule, assigning occlusion edges as object boundaries (Slater, Morison, Somers, Mattock, Brown, & Taylor, 1990). The "perceptual inference" (Slater, Morison, Somers, Mattock, Brown, & Taylor, 1990) for connecting visible parts based on common motion might be learned.

These two interpretations cannot be distinguished while infants lack directional sensitivity. The interpretations do make differing predictions about what should happen when directional sensitivity appears. If the EI process is an unlearned basis of unity perception, it should operate as soon as directional sensitivity becomes operative. On the learning account, directional sensitivity would be only the beginning of some learning process. Because the EI process is in place by 16 weeks, we know that if a learning process is involved, it is expeditious and does not require practice at skilled reaching or self-locomotion. These factors may favor a maturational explanation; however, further research would be useful.

D. The Edge-Sensitive Process

Relatability of edges, which underlies the ES process in adult perception (Kellman & Shipley, 1991), does not produce perceived unity for infants in the first half year of life. Typically, after habituation to a stationary, partly occluded rod display, infants show about equal looking times to the complete and broken test displays (Kellman & Spelke, 1983). This often-replicated finding is thought provoking. Greater dishabituation to a complete display might be expected if the visible rod pieces in the initial display were perceived as two separate objects. What might equal looking times, with some dishabituation to both test displays, mean? When infants do not perceive the unity of visible parts emerging from behind an occluder, what might they perceive? Equal dishabituation to both test stimuli suggests that the broken and complete displays are equally consistent with the initial display. A plausible interpretation is that infants at this age are "agnostic" about what happens behind the occluder. They do perceive the fact of occlusion, that the occluding object is nearer than the rod pieces, but their perceptual process renders no verdict on what happens behind the occluder (Kellman & Spelke, 1983). In the absence of the perceptual rules guiding the adult's perception in this situation, being agnostic makes sense. Consider the alternative. Suppose infants start out perceiving visible surfaces as ending where occluding objects intervene. If so, early perception would follow an incorrect perceptual rule: Every stationary, visible part of a partly occluded object would be incorrectly assigned a boundary at the point of occlusion. This chronic misperception would not only handicap early learning about specific objects, but it would impede learning of the correct rule. If rules about object interpolation arise later, whether by learning or maturation, the young perceiver might be better off seeing indeterminately rather than incorrectly.

Infants' inability to use the ES process extends at least through the first half year (Bertenthal, Campos, & Haith, 1980; Schmidt & Spelke, 1984; Spelke et al., 1993). Bertenthal et al. (1980) reported evidence of sensitivity to illusory contours at 7 months of age but not at 5 months. Similar results have been reported for kinetic illusory contours (which depend on relatable edges given sequentially in time) by Kaufmann-Hayoz, Kaufmann, and Walther (1988). Earlier perception of illusory contours was suggested by Ghim (1990), who used a familiarization and preference paradigm with 3- and 4-month-old infants. He predicted that if infants perceived subjective contours, novelty preferences would be greater between a subjective contour display and a display without subjective contours than between two displays with no subjective contours. Some comparisons were consistent with the hypothesis, but at least one predicted outcome failed to occur in each of five experiments. There were also plausible alternative explanations for the preferences that were observed in the studies. To generate control (nonsubjective contour) displays, an illusory square display made from four inducing elements was disrupted by changing the orientation of two or all four elements. This manipulation was elegant in allowing experimental and control display pairs to differ by the same local feature contrasts. Unfortunately, the illusory contour and control stimuli differed in several more global properties that could produce easier discrimination between illusory contour and control displays. For example, the outer perimeter of the illusory contour displays contained only smooth contours, whereas all control displays had either four or eight sharp corners and two or four deep concavities around their outer perimeters. Given these difficulties, these data do not disconfirm indications from other research that the ES process is absent in the first half year of life.

E. Origins of the ES Process

How does the ES process originate? Both neural maturation and learning mechanisms are possible explanations. Noting the onset of a number of pictorial depth cues around 5–7 months of age, Granrud and Yonas (1984) suggested they involve a perceptual module that matures at that time. Likewise, Gunderson, Yonas, Sargent, and Webster-Grant (1993) found that reaching behavior of 7- to 8-week-old macaque monkeys is influenced by pictorial depth cues, suggesting phylogenetic origins of these abilities. Edge-sensitive mechanisms for boundary interpolation might be closely related. In particular, the depth cue of interposition is closely connected to boundary interpolation under occlusion (Kellman and Shipley, 1991). Available evidence suggests that boundary interpolation may arise around this same time (Bertenthal et al., 1980).

Some accounts of the origins of the ES process invoke the traditional empiricist notion that perceiving unity and boundaries depends on experiences with objects (Nakayama & Shimojo, 1992; Spelke et al., 1993; Wallach & Slaughter, 1988). At present, no direct evidence from infant research supports this idea, but it remains a possibility.

There are numerous reasons to believe a contrary hypothesis: that the unit formation phenomena observed by the Gestalt psychologists, and embodied in recent computational models, depend on modular perceptual mechanisms, not recognition processes. Recent neurophysiological work suggests that boundary interpolation processes in occlusion and illusory contour perception are carried out at surprisingly early stages of visual processing, certainly as early as V2 and possibly V1 (von der Heydt et al., 1984). These findings, along with psychophysical results indicating boundary interpolation in cases where no familiar objects are present (Field et al., 1992; Kellman & Shipley, 1991), suggest that computing edge relatability is a basic visual function. It remains possible that effects in V2 or V1 result from some unknown feedback from higher levels, but there is no evidence for this proposition. Other indications that edge-sensitive unit formation is a modular perceptual capacity (c.f., Fodor, 1983) come from evidence indicating that illusory contours and occluded contours are processed by the same mechanisms (Kellman & Shipley, 1991; Kellman et al., 1995; Shapley & Ringach, 1994); local edge relationships override familiarity (Kanizsa, 1979); and the process obeys precise quantitative relationships (Shipley & Kellman, 1992b; Rubin, Shapley & Nakayama, 1995; Lesher & Mingolla, 1993). None of these findings would be expected if object completion depended on familiarity. For example, equivalent strength of boundary completion in illusory and occluded figure cases would not be expected, because occluded boundaries are far more common in ordinary visual experience than are illusory ones. (The latter require an exact visual match of luminance, color, and texture between an object and parts of its background, a situation that is not common.)

Whether or not these considerations are decisive, advancing our understanding of how edge-sensitive unit formation processes arise remains a high priority for future research.

F. Summary: Unit Formation

Unit formation in adult visual perception appears to be governed by two separate processes, what we have labeled EI and ES. The EI process utilizes motion, not edge, relationships, and begins to operate in the early weeks of life. The ES process is richer in specifying not only connectedness of objects but the forms of hidden boundaries, but it is long delayed in development relative to the EI process. The developmental sequence of the two unit formation processes parallels their differing ecological soundness. Coherence in motion is a deep, even defining, property of objects (Spelke, 1985), and if detected with precision, motion relationships are highly diagnostic of unity. Smoothness of object boundaries and connectedness of pieces that bear certain edge relations are common but not nearly universal characteristics of our physical environment. Accordingly, the ES process, sensitive to edge relations given simultaneously or over time, is a robust and useful perceptual process, but not of the highest ecological validity. The development of unit formation, then, fits our characterization of perceptual development as beginning with the most secure information sources and progressing toward more diverse but somewhat less trustworthy sources.

VI. THREE-DIMENSIONAL FORM PERCEPTION

Visual form perception is a great battleground of perceptual theory. Adults perceive three-dimensional (3-D) form from at least three different sources of information (Kellman, 1984), and each of these stands as the canonical example for a theory of form perception. We often perceive—or recognize—the whole form of a familiar object from a single, static view. This ability may depend on seeing a certain 3-D object from various viewpoints. Subsequently, any 2-D view calls up the associated views from memory. This associative account may be taken, as suggested by John Stuart Mill, to define what a 3-D object *is*: It is "the permanent possibilities of sensation." For the visual sense, this view implies that the products of vision are inherently two-dimensional; three-dimensionality can only be realized as the set of possible 2-D views from all vantage points.

The view of an object from a single, stationary point was also emphasized by Gestalt theorists, but for radically different reasons. Even unfamiliar objects could be perceived this way, because the 2-D stimulation sets in motion organizational forces in the nervous system, which in general lead to perception of simple, regular, 3-D forms. Although the Gestalt neurophysiological ideas seem implausible today, form perception might still depend on unlearned organizational tendencies. On the other hand, Brunswik (1956) suggested that laws of perceptual organization might be acquired by experience of object regularities.

Another class of information has become well understood only in the past few decades. Three-dimensional form may be specified by information in continuously changing optical projections, as an object rotates or as an observer walks around an object. It has been argued that this kind of information mathematically specifies object structure without utilizing any assumptions about object symmetry or regularities (Gibson, 1966, 1979; Johansson, 1970; Ullman, 1979).

Each of the several means by which adults perceive 3-D form suggests a developmental account (Kellman, 1984). If 3-D form is a product of accumulated 2-D views, then perceivers may initially have no notion of 3-D form at all. A specific object's form would develop from experience with different views, and perhaps from concurrent, active manipulation of the object (Piaget, 1954). Perceivers would have little competence with, and perhaps no notion of, 3-D form until they had undergone extensive learning. The possibility that perceived 3-D form is a direct response to certain optical transformations is usually linked with the hypothesis of evolved mechanisms sensitive to this kind of information (Fodor, 1983; Gibson, 1966; Shepard, 1984). On this account, perceivers might be sensitive to 3-D form from an early age. Finally, the use of general principles of object completion to derive 3-D form from particular views has been explained in two ways. On the Gestalt view, perceived form results from unlearned, organizational processes rooted in basic neurophysiology. Alternatively, in the position articulated by Brunswik (1949) and anticipated by Helmholtz (1885/1910): rules of perceptual organization might be abstractions from an individual's experience with many objects. These two accounts of how whole form may be gotten from a single view make disparate predictions about development. Gestalt organizational processes should operate as soon as the relevant brain mechanisms are mature, whereas Brunswikian learning has usually been hypothesized to be a protracted process.

A. Kinematic Information in Infant 3-D Form Perception

Which of these accounts of the origins of 3-D form perception is correct? Wallach (1985) raised the interesting possibility that in each perceptual domain (i.e., form, depth, motion), there is some information that is usable innately, whereas other cues are acquired later, perhaps through correlation with the innate process. In form perception, he hypothesized that motion-carried information was the innate foundation. In fact, the motivation for Wallach and O'Connell's classic (1953) studies of the "kinetic depth effect" was to shed light on the development of 3-D form perception. Knowledge of 3-D form seems to be available to congenitally monocular observers despite their having no access to stereoscopic information about 3-D form. Learning might allow 3-D form perception to occur even from pictorial information, but where might the *initial* notion of 3-D form come from? Wallach and O'Connell hypothesized that there must be an unlearned process of 3-D form perception, perhaps based on the optical changes given by motion.

Others have also given theoretical grounds for the primacy of motion-carried information about form. The speed and precision of adult processing of structure from motion (Braunstein, 1976; Johansson, 1975; Ullman, 1979) suggests dedicated neural machinery, especially given the complexity of the information itself. Another reason this information may be the earliest usable by infants is more rooted in developmental considerations. This source of form information has the highest ecological validity. Under reasonable constraints, it can be proven mathematically that perspective transformations contain sufficient information to specify uniquely an object's 3-D form (Ullman, 1979). When a stationary observer views a 3-D object from a single vantage point, its whole form may be predicted on the basis of simplicity, symmetry, or similarity to previously viewed objects. The accuracy of such predictions rests on probabilistic facts about the sorts of objects that exist and vantage points that occur. How often this information signals 3-D form accurately is hard to quantify, but it falls well short of the validity of kinematic information. Early cognitive and social development may be best served by perceivers getting only the most accurate information about 3-D form, even if this information is not obtainable under some circumstances.

These theoretical considerations have been put to empirical test. As predicted by Wallach and O'Connell (1953), evidence suggests that the earliest competence for perceiving overall form appears to be based on kinematic information (Kellman, 1984; Kellman & Short, 1987; Owsley, 1983; Yonas, Arterberry, & Granrud, 1987a).

To test infants' 3-D form perception, one must overcome an intrinsic problem. A viewed 3-D object is seen from a particular vantage point, or a changing sequence of such points. At these vantage points, particular 2-D projections of the object reach the eyes. Perception of 3-D form must somehow be disentangled from responses to these 2-D projections. For example, suppose infants are habituated to a stationary 3-D object from a particular vantage point. After habituation, suppose infants generalize habituation to this same display, but dishabituate to a novel 3-D object. This response pattern might indicate that infants detected the original 3-D form and discriminated it from the novel 3-D form. However, the observed responses could instead be based on differences in the 2-D projections of the original and novel object; 3-D form may not have been perceived at all.

A means of circumventing this problem is based on the geometry of form and motion. Information about a given 3-D form can be provided by rotation around various axes, provided there is some component of rotation in depth. If objects are chosen that are not too symmetric, one can test for detection of invariant 3-D form across rotation sequences that vary and have quite different 2-D appearances.

One experiment of this type (Kellman, 1984) tested 16-week-olds using the two objects depicted in Figure 6. In the kinematic condition, form was tested by habituating infants to videotaped displays of a single object rotating in depth. Two different axes of rotation in depth were used in habituation on alternate trials, so that the only constant from trial to trial was the 3-D form of the object. After habituation, subjects were tested on alternating trials with the same object, now moving around a third (new) axis of rotation, and a different object, rotating around the same new axis. The change to a new axis of rotation in the test period ensured that the particular 2-D views and transformations were novel for both the object shown previously and the new object. Generalization of habituation to the same object would thus reflect extraction of 3-D form, not a response to particular 2-D views.

Besides the kinematic condition, two groups viewed sequential stationary views (photographic slides) taken from the rotation sequences. The two

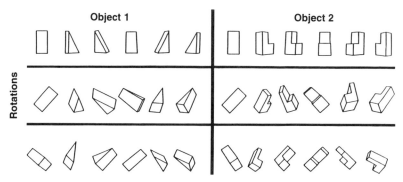

FIGURE 6   Schematic views of 3-D objects and axes of rotation used in a 3-D form perception experiment (Kellman, 1984). Successive views 60° apart are shown. All views in the same column are from the same 3-D object; views in the same row are from the same axis of rotation in depth.

groups differed in the number and spacing of the views. It was possible that infants could detect the 3-D forms of these objects from single views, or sequences of views. Adults can certainly do this; even the line drawings in Figure 6 allow 3-D form to be perceived from most views. If infants detected overall form from single views or sequences of static views, successful performance in the kinematic condition might not indicate use of optical change information; rather, it might indicate that transforming arrays are processed as sequences of static views.

Results indicated that infants perceived 3-D form from kinematic information. Those in the kinematic condition generalized habituation to the same object in a new rotation, but dishabituated to the new object, regardless of the object and particular axes of rotation used in the habituation and test trials. Infants did not appear to acquire 3-D form from static views: they showed no reliable differences in response to new views of an object versus views of a new object.

The finding that young infants have an early ability to perceive 3-D form, but only from continuous optical transformations, is supported by research from several laboratories using a variety of methods (Kellman & Short, 1987b; Owsley, 1983; Yonas et al., 1987a). Additional findings have led to a more precise understanding of this ability.

One interesting prediction was tested by Kellman and Short (1987b). Optical transformations that specify a particular form may be given in principle by either object or observer motion. The specificity of the motion patterns, insofar as 3-D form is concerned, is the same in both cases. Thus, an observer walking in an arc around a stationary object receives the same optical transformations, relevant to that object's form, as those obtained if the object rotates while the observer is stationary. If 3-D form depends on mechanisms sensitive to kinematic information, then moving infants who view stationary objects should detect 3-D form. Kellman and Short (1987b) found that 16-week-old infants did indeed perceive objects' 3-D forms from motion perspective.

1. Isolating Edge Transformations

It is natural to view information about 3-D form as carried by spatiotemporal changes in length and orientation of object edges caused by the object's rotation relative to the observer. However, the transforming optical projection of a rotating (solid) object also contains changes in brightness and texture gradients (Pentland, 1990). Shaw, Roder, and Bushnell (1986) argued that changes in brightness and texture are necessary for infants younger than 24 weeks of age to detect form. To disentangle the contributions of edge transformations from brightness changes during motion, Kellman and Short (1987b) used wire figures similar to those introduced by Wallach and

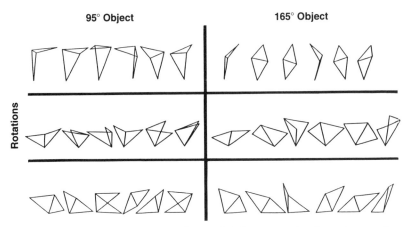

FIGURE 7   Objects and rotations used to test 3-D form perception from edge transformations alone. Successive views 60° apart are shown. (From Kellman & Short, 1987b. Copyright © 1987 by the American Psychological Association. Reprinted with permission.)

O'Connell (1953). Such figures contain thin edges but no surfaces connecting them. In rotation, such objects provide the same geometric transformations of surface boundaries as do solid objects, but without transformations of surface brightness and texture. Lighting was arranged to eliminate visible shading changes even along the thin edges of the figures. The figures used by Kellman and Short (1987b) are shown in Figure 7.

These wire figures allowed an additional way of ruling out contributions from 2-D similarities across axes of rotation. Not only were the two test objects designed to be very similar to each other; their structure virtually guaranteed that static, 2-D information could not give away 3-D form. A theorem of projective geometry states that all triangles are projectively equivalent; that is, any 2-D projection of one triangle could be the (polar) projection of any other triangle in some 3-D orientation and distance. By constructing each 3-D figure from two triangles, the overall structure of the object was minimized in this experiment. The effect of this manipulation was validated in an experiment with adults, whose sorting of static views of the two 3-D objects did not differ from chance (Kellman and Short, 1987b, Experiment 3b).

As shown in Figure 8, infants perceived 3-D forms of the wire figures from edge transformations alone. Two groups are shown, each habituated to one of the wire objects, in two different axes of rotation. Each group generalized habituation to the same 3-D object tested in a novel rotation and dishabituated to the new object. These findings do not rule out the possible informativeness of transformations of shading and texture, but show that the latter are not necessary for early 3-D form perception.

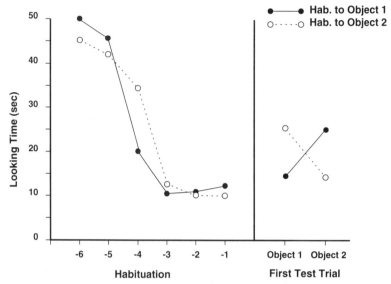

FIGURE 8   Results of experiment on 3-D form perception from edge transformations alone. Looking times are shown for the last six habituation trials (with the final one labeled −1) and the first test trial for each test object. Data are shown separately for infants habituated to each of the two test objects. (From Kellman & Short, 1987b. Copyright © 1987 by the American Psychological Association. Reprinted with permission.

B. Static 3-D Form Perception

In contrast to the infants' early ability to extract 3-D form from motion is their demonstrated inability to perceive whole form from single or multiple static views of objects (Kellman, 1984; Kellman & Short, 1987b; Ruff, 1978).

This failure of static information applies to 2-D stimuli, such as photographic slides, and to stationary views of 3-D objects, as well. Ruff (1978) found that 6-month-old infants failed to apprehend 3-D forms from stationary views of 3-D objects. The objects used were rather complex, however. Kellman and Short (1987b) found the same lack of 3-D form perception from multiple, stationary views of the simpler objects pictured in Figure 6 with infants aged 4 and 6 months, and other work suggests the problem still exists at 8 months (Kellman, 1993). Binocular, static views of objects may allow recognition of 3-D forms that have previously been perceived from kinematic information (Owsley, 1983; Yonas et al., 1987a), but there is no evidence that infants detect the overall form of an object initially from static, binocular views.

Given adult abilities to perceive 3-D form from single views, infants' limitations, persisting into the second half of the first year, are startling. What might be the problem in extracting 3-D form perception from static information? Certainly, some relevant abilities appear to be in place quite early. Earlier we noted that Slater and Morison (1985) tested newborns (mean age: 2 days, 8 hours) for perception of the constant shape of planar objects (e.g., flat rectangles and trapezoids) despite variations in their slant in depth. Results indicated that newborns detect invariant planar shape despite slant variations. Earlier work by Caron, Caron, and Carlson (1979) had found such an ability with 12-week-old infants. Although there is little discussion in these reports of the particular information underlying such performance, it appears that depth information must be combined with projective shape to determine actual planar shape. There are indications that binocular convergence provides the useful depth information in newborn shape and size constancy. (For discussion see Kellman, 1995.)

The results with planar shape perception by newborns make the failure of static 3-D form perception all the more mysterious at 6 months and beyond. By 6 months of age, virtually all infants have stereoscopic depth perception, which should provide extremely accurate information about surface slant. The problem seems to be developing a global 3-D representation. Infants do not appear to do this from successive views from different orientations (Kellman & Short, 1987b) nor from single views. The latter process is not fully understood with adults, but seems to involve symmetry or simplicity in representing unprojected object surfaces (Buffart, Leeuwenberg, & Restle, 1981). This process may be learned. In any case, it occurs relatively late in development. It is likely that the 3-D forms of stationary objects viewed from a stationary position are, to a young infant, indeterminate.

C. Nonrigid Unity and Form

Thus far we have been concerned with perception of objects whose forms are rigid. Some of the most important objects in the infant's world are nonrigid, such as people walking or a hand opening and closing. In this section we consider what is known about unity and form perception in nonrigid objects.

We can define nonrigid objects as those having points whose separations in 3-D space change over time. When we manipulate a glass, all of its points remain in a constant relationship (if it is not dropped), although the object may be rotated or translated in space. Now consider a human hand. When the hand changes from open to a closed fist, the point-to-point distance from a fingertip to the base of the wrist changes a great deal. Human movement can be considered *jointed* motion, because these changes are caused by operation of joints between relatively rigid segments. There are also elastic motions, such as bending, stretching, or squeezing of a rubbery substance (or a jellyfish) in which the nonrigid transformations are quite different. Analytically, it has been harder to describe processing constraints that allow recovery of nonrigid motions from optical information than is the case with rigid motion (Bertenthal, 1993; Cutting, 1981; Hoffman & Flinchbaugh, 1982; Johansson, 1975; Webb & Aggarwal, 1982). Perceptually, the notion of "form" perception must include objects whose forms change. Despite nonrigidity, a jellyfish does not have the same form as a walking person. What remains invariant in a nonrigid form? Some of the answer lies in connectivity: what is connected to what, where are joints located, and so on. These questions bear close relationship to issues of perceived unity in object perception, although they arise within a unit. Since Johansson's pioneering research (1950, 1975), most research on nonrigid motion has used displays comprised of separated points of light in a dark surround. This paradigm involves issues of unity as well as form; accordingly, we consider both below.

Johansson (1975) showed that the human form and its participation in events could be detected from motion information alone. He constructed films of people moving in which the only visible information came from small lights attached to the main joints of the body. Observers rapidly and effortlessly detect a person walking, a couple dancing, and various other events. Recognition of a human form does not occur when these displays are inverted (Sumi, 1984). The developmental origins of this ability have been investigated in programmatic research by Bertenthal, Proffitt, and their associates (Bertenthal, 1993; Bertenthal, Proffitt, & Cutting, 1984; Bertenthal, Proffitt, Kramer, & Spetner, 1987). An early study indicated that both 3- and 5-month-old infants discriminated motion sequences of the upright and inverted point-light walker displays, but did not discriminate static views. These results indicate some perceptual organization of the information that differs between upright and inverted, but they do not indicate whether infants actually perceived a person walking in either display. Some evidence suggests that infants do detect the familiar form of a person in point-light displays, beginning around 5 months of age (Bertenthal, 1993). Two manipulations that disrupt the appearance of a walking person for adult perceivers are phase shifting and inversion. Phase shifting refers to shifting the starting locations in the periodic motions of particular point lights. Both 3- and 5-month-olds discriminate normal from phase-shifted displays when they are upright. When inverted, however, only the 3-month-olds discriminate the two display types (Bertenthal & Davis, 1988). A group of 7-month-olds also showed poorer discrimination with the inverted displays than with upright displays. Although indirect, the results are consistent with the notion that 3-month-olds detect and discriminate certain properties of point-light displays, but do not see a walking person in upright displays. The change in response patterns between 3 and 5 months may reflect the onset of meaningful interpretation of the upright displays, in contrast with the inverted ones (which generally appear meaningless to adults).

D. Summary: 3-D Form Perception

Research on the development of 3-D form perception supports an ecological view (Gibson, 1966, 1979; Shepard, 1984). Recovery of object structure from optical transformations appears to depend on evolved perceptual mechanisms, present at birth or early maturing. Accounts attributing 3-D form perception to learning seem implausible given the developmental order in which kinematic and static information become useful. One might imagine that infants initially encode 2-D optical transformations and later learn their meaning in terms of 3-D form. Since 3-D form is not recoverable from static views, and infants perceive 3-D form from optical change before they attain skilled reaching and manipulation abilities, it is hard to see where initial information about 3-D form might come from (Kellman, 1984; Wallach & O'Connell, 1953).

VII. PERCEPTION OF SIZE

Detecting the physical size of objects requires relational information. The projective size (at the retina) of a given object varies as a function of its distance from the observer. To achieve size constancy (perception of true size despite changes in projective size) in many situations, projective size must be combined with information about viewing distance (Holway & Boring, 1941).

Day and McKenzie (1981) found evidence that 18-week-old infants are capable of perceiving size by taking distance into account. They habituated subjects to an approaching and receding object, and tested after habituation with the same object and another of different size whose retinal projections during its motion fell within the same range of visual angles (projective size) as the habituation object. Infants recovered habituation more to the object of novel size. Slater, Mattock, and Brown (1990) found that newborns also exhibit size constancy. In their design, subjects were familiarized with either a large or a small cube of a constant size, at varied distances across trials. After familiarization, the large and small cubes were presented successively. Distances for the two were selected so that they had identical projective size, and the familiarization object was presented at a novel distance. This arrangement made the (equal) projective sizes of the two objects novel, as well. All subjects looked longer at the object of novel real size.

Other research (Granrud, 1987; Slater & Morison, 1985) has yielded confirming results. Granrud (1987) measured rates of habituation to two kinds of sequences of objects containing identical variations in retinal sizes. Real size varied in one sequence, but did not change in the other. Infants showed slower rates of habituation to the sequence in which real size changed, suggesting that this sequence contained greater novelty.

Research to date thus supports the remarkable idea that size constancy is an innate visual capacity. This conclusion implies that at least one source of egocentric distance information is functional at birth. As yet, there is no direct evidence indicating what this source of distance information might be. A process of elimination along with some indirect evidence suggests that the information may be provided by binocular convergence (Kellman, 1995).

VIII. TANGIBILITY AND SUBSTANCE

It is odd to leave perception of substance for last, because it is so crucial to what an object is. We perceive objects in order to do things with them. We would not grasp, eat, throw, or step out of the way of objects if they did not have substance. We can be forgiven, in part, for our neglect because some considerations of substance are implicit in what we have said already. When a boundary is classified as belonging to one surface, not another, in effect we are determining where the tangible surface lies, that is, a certain shape is a thing, not a hole.

For other aspects of substance, perceiving what an object is made of, more must be said. Most of the research on this important problem has come from Eleanor Gibson and her colleagues. As in other domains, important carriers of information about substance are events. An object made of wood or steel or hard plastic will move rigidly, whereas one made of flesh or rubber will deform in certain characteristic ways as it moves. Gibson, Owsley, and Johnston (1978) tested 5-month-olds' sensitivity to substance from motion information. Infants were habituated to an object undergoing three different rigid motions and tested afterward with a fourth (new) rigid motion and a nonrigid (elastic deformation). Subjects generalized habituation to the novel rigid motion but dishabituated to the nonrigid deformation. Subsequent research (Gibson, Owsley, Walker, & Megaw-Nyce, 1979) showed a similar pattern of results at 3 months of age. A separate experiment (Walker, Owsley, Megaw-Nyce, Gibson, & Bahrick, 1980) produced a complementary result: When habituated to two deforming motions, infants generalized habituation to a new deformation but dishabituated to a rigid motion. These results are consistent with the interpretation that infants perceived a consistent object substance (rigid or nonrigid) in habituation in each case. An alternative interpretation is possible, however; infants might simply categorize the viewed events themselves as rigid motion or nonrigid motion, without attributing some consistent characteristic to the object.

Perception of rigid or nonrigid character of a surface was addressed in a different manner with older infants by Gibson et al. (1987). Crawling and walking infants were presented with narrow enclosed walkways, and their mothers beckoned to them from the far end. Infants' willingness to traverse a walkway varied as a function of visible surface qualities. Static qualities were varied between a homogeneous black velvet surface and a surface with many visible texture elements. Dynamic qualities were varied as well: In one condition, an experimenter pushed on the surface and caused undulations (a waterbed lay beneath the cloth). In another condition, hitting the surface did not lead to any deformation. Walking infants were reluctant to cross homogeneous surfaces and undulating ones. The results suggest that visible texture, as well as lack of deformation from contact events, specify a rigid surface, one that will offer support for locomotion (c.f., Gibson, 1979). Since walking infants have had considerable prior experience with surfaces, the role of learning in these results is not easily assessed.

IX. CONCLUSIONS

Our portrait of the development of object perception, although incomplete in some respects, has recognizable features. These include some understanding of the starting points of components of object perception and later developments.

A. How Object Perception Begins

Forty-three years ago, Piaget wrote about the perceiver's initial state with regard to the perception of objects. To the very young infant, physical objects produce "sensorial images" which:

> only constitute spots which appear, move and disappear without solidity or volume. They are, in short, neither objects, independent images, nor even images charged with extrinsic meaning. (1952, p. 65)

For Piaget, the adult's seemingly direct and immediate perceptual contact with physical objects results from a long process of associative learning:

> Perception of light exists from birth and consequently the reflexes which insure the adaptation of the perception (the pupillary and palpebral reflexes, both to light). All the rest (perception of forms, sizes, positions, distances, prominence, etc.) is acquired through the combination of reflex activity with higher activities. . . . (1952, p. 62)

Piaget's view was novel in his emphasis on action as the core of associative learning about objects. Classic, rather than novel, however, was his belief that perceivers begin with meaningless sensations and construct their meaning·associatively (Berkeley, 1709/1910; Helmholtz, 1885/1910; Locke, 1690/1971; Mill, 1865/1965; Titchener, 1924).

This traditional empiricist view rested on logical considerations and anecdotal observations. Beginning in the late 1950s, systematic experimental research on perceptual development superseded these methods. Results of experimental research have in turn superseded the classical view. It is correct neither about the starting point of perception nor about developmental process.

During this same few decades, an alternative view of perception's origins was articulated, primarily by J. J. and Eleanor Gibson (Gibson & Gibson, 1955; J. Gibson, 1966, 1979; E. Gibson, 1969, 1984; Johansson, 1970). In this *ecological* view, perceptual systems evolved to provide meaningful contact with the environment, not to provide initially meaningless sensations. This view was accompanied by a new emphasis on sources of information that go beyond spatial relationships present in a single, static retinal image. Kinematic information, given by moving observers and objects, and stereoscopic information are less ambiguous indicators about objects and spatial layout than the classical cues, such as pictorial depth cues. Examples of functionally appropriate perceptual behavior by newborns of other species (e.g., Walk & Gibson, 1961; Sperry, 1943) illustrated the plausibility of the notion that perceptual systems are adapted to perceive objects in the same way that fingers and an opposable thumb are adapted to grasp objects.

The ecological premise that perception provides meaningful contact with the world from the start appears to be correct. In each perceptual domain (such as object, depth, and motion perception), there appear to be unlearned capacities to comprehend the environment. In other respects, however, neither the ecological perspective nor the traditional learning-oriented view captures the nuances of findings from the infant perception laboratory. We need a new perspective, one that combines an ecological starting point with later acquired, possibly learned, perceptual abilities.

Object perception begins very early, but the infant's abilities do not match the adult's. In every component of adult object perception, there are multiple sources of information, such as information carried by motion, information related to perceived depth, and information in static spatial (2-D) relationships. Infants in every case respond to a subset of these information sources. They show sensitivity to some information as early as tested but lack competence to use other sources until well into the second half of the first year. The pattern of competence and incompetence is not random. In most domains, kinematic information appears early, whereas information carried in 2-D spatial relationships appears later. Table 1 summarizes these developmental trends in object perception abilities.

Initial stages of visual processing in the human visual system appear to be specialized for edge extraction (DeValois & DeValois, 1988; Marr, 1982). Although maturation of certain mechanisms, such as those sensitive to spatial phase, may occur in the earliest weeks, there is little doubt that edge detection is an unlearned ability. Although the evidence is indirect, it appears that newborns detect edges from discontinuities in luminance and color, motion, and depth. At the same time, limitations are obvious. For

TABLE 1 Developmental Trends in Object Perception Abilities[a]

		Weeks of age					
	0	8	16	24	32	40	48
Edge detection	Luminance, color discontinuities •					Luminance, color discontinuities •	
Edge classification/Boundary assignment		Accretion/deletion of texture • Optical expansion •					
Unit formation		Accretion/deletion of texture Relative motion Depth discontinuities •	Common motion •		Edge relatability • ? Single or multiple static views •		
3-D form perception		Structure-from-motion •		Biological motion •			
Size perception	Depth + projective size •						
Substance perception		Rigid versus nonrigid motions •				Texture •	

[a]Components of object perception are given in the left column. Information sources are given by labels within the chart. Dots indicate that the labeled information can be used by the age shown in that column. Dots do not necessarily indicate the age of onset of an ability, but the earliest age at which competence has been observed. Question marks indicate evidence that the ability is lacking at least as late as the position marked and probably arises later. Some assignments are tentative, based on indirect or incomplete evidence.

example, many sources of depth information are unavailable at this stage, and studies with grating patterns indicate some early limitation in processing spatial phase information.

Edge classification in early infancy depends on information given by motion, such as accretion/deletion of texture and relative motion, and depth discontinuities. Early boundary assignment also appears to be based on motion and depth. Object boundaries are not perceived from luminance and chromatic differences: Infants detect luminance and chromatic differences but do not classify them as object boundaries until as late as 9–10 months.

A similar bifurcation applies to perception of unity of spatially separate visible parts. The EI process (dependent on motion relationships) appears soon after birth, perhaps awaiting only the maturation of direction sensitivity in the visual cortex. But unit formation dependent on the ES process (dependent on spatial relations of edges) is conspicuously absent during the first half year of life.

In 3-D form perception, kinematic information is also primary. During most of the first year, it appears to be the sole source for establishing 3-D object representations. Use of form regularities to go from single views of objects to their whole form seems routine in adult perception, but this ability is a late arrival in the infant's repertoire. Considering both unity and form, we may conclude that stationary environments often appear indeterminate to young infants. A disproportionate share of learning about objects' connections and 3-D forms must come from events in which objects and/or observers move.

Remarkably, evidence indicates innate mechanisms for size constancy. This ability is one of several that implicate early sensitivity to depth information and its use in determining other object properties. (Boundary assignment and planar shape constancy are two others we have considered.) These early competencies go to the heart of centuries-old controversies about the origins of visual perception. Traditional empiricist theories were built on arguments that the third (depth) dimension could not be registered by visual mechanisms, but had to be constructed from experience (Berkeley, 1709/1910). Whereas earlier analyses showed deficiencies in this idea that learning was logically necessary for three-dimensional perception (Gibson, 1966; Johansson, 1970), findings from infant perception research provide stronger evidence of ecological rather than associationist foundations of perceptual knowledge.

B. Is Motion or Ecological Validity Fundamental in Perceptual Development?

The order of appearance of perceptual capacities closely parallels their ecological validity; that is, information that most accurately specifies the environment is usable first, and in some cases exclusively for much of the first year. This arrangement may not be coincidental: It may reflect an adaptation to the requirements of human development. In the infancy period, the task of perception is not to assure immediate survival or effective behavior, but to allow learning about the physical and social worlds. For the adult, failing to attain comprehensive representation of one's environment has severe consequences. Accordingly, adult perceptual systems exploit multiple sources of information for most object properties. Some sources of lesser ecological validity may earn their keep by being available when others are absent. For infants, perceiving comprehensively is not nearly so crucial as perceiving *accurately*. If the infant perceiver is built as risk averse in this sense, we would expect perceptual abilities to appear in order of ecological validity.

Most of the data we have examined fit this conjecture. For edge classification, discontinuities in motion and depth are extremely reliable indicators of boundaries of physical objects in the environment. Luminance discontinuities often mark such boundaries, but arise from numerous other sources as well. That infants *discriminate* shapes given by luminance contours shows that they can detect them. But only motion and depth discontinuities indicate object boundaries.

Size constancy also fits the theme. The optical geometry of size–distance relations is ubiquitous. Even so, it is astonishing that a newborn with striking sensory immaturities in acuity, contrast sensitivity, and phase sensitivity can combine distance information and projective size information to perceive object size. Conversely, it would be just as mind boggling to picture the young infant trying to learn about objects' characteristics in a perceptual world with no reliable size information, or with an erroneous system in which perceived size was based solely on projective size. Here, the key information is not kinematic, but highly ecologically valid and relevant to an object property of great importance.

In unit formation, we saw that common motion is a nearly ironclad indicator of connectedness, whereas continuity of edges is only a good one. In 3-D form, kinematic information was similarly superior to information available in static views. Perceiving unity and 3-D form from motion is possible long before the infant can parse stationary scenes into objects and represent their shapes.

Many, although not all, findings that fit our conjecture about ecological validity also fit the generalization that information carried by moving objects is primary. Its primacy might derive from the relatively early maturation of cortical areas that process temporal patterns relative to those that process spatial detail (Banks & Dannemiller, 1987). It is possible, however, that both the primacy of kinematic information and the early maturation of temporal resolution result from causal factors at an adaptive-evolutionary level. Is motion primary because it is motion or because motion-carried information is generally of high ecological validity (Gibson, 1979; Johansson, 1970; Shepard, 1984)?

There are some clues. One useful comparison involves the roles of object and observer motion in unity perception and in 3-D form perception. Recall that the EI process applies only to moving objects: Common optical change alone, as when the observer moves while viewing object parts at similar depths, does not indicate unity. This pattern might merely reflect a processing advantage for moving objects. Or, it could relate to the greater ecological validity of common object motion for unity over information given by observer motion.

It is instructive that the situation differs in 3-D form perception. Here, the projective geometry underlying structure-from-motion when an object rotates is equivalent to that given to an observer who moves in an arc while viewing a stationary object. If infants are predisposed to use object motion, they might extract the information only when the object moves. But if perception depends on information of highest ecological validity, form should be detectable whether the observer or object moves. As we saw, it turns out not to matter whether the object or observer moves: Infants detect 3-D form. The example suggests that early perceptual skills track informativeness rather than motion, per se.

Our global characterization of early perception has clear elements of conjecture. There is, nonetheless, a pattern in the emergence of perceptual capacities. What we know fits the hypothesis that the priorities of early cognitive and social development, expressed through evolution, have equipped the infant as a risk-averse perceiver. As an adult, she will glean information about objects, some tentative and some definite, from a much wider catalog of sources. As an infant, however, she is restricted to only a few channels of perceptual knowledge. This arrangement leaves much of the world indeterminate, but it ensures that the earliest learning about the physical and social worlds will be based on information that is the most accurate.

Acknowledgments

Preparation of this chapter was supported in part by National Science Foundation Grant SBR-9496112 to Philip J. Kellman. I thank Liana Machado, Laura Kotovsky, and Carol Yin for general assistance, and Rochel Gelman for helpful comments on an earlier draft.

Requests for reprints should be sent to Philip J. Kellman, University of California, Los Angeles, Department of Psychology, Franz Hall, 405 Hilgard Avenue, Los Angeles, CA 90024-1563.

Endnotes

1. There are intermediate cases where an object is not fully separable from other things, such as a tree rooted in the ground. Often this intermediate condition is detectable visually as well.

2. The locations of receptive fields can theoretically provide spatial position information useful in edge detection apart from phase. However, taken at face value, the results of Banks and Ginsburg (1983) and Braddick, Atkinson, and Wattam-Bell (1986) suggest that neonates do not use this information either.
3. The other Gestalt relations do not disappear entirely in recent modeling. *Proximity* is embodied in quantitative variation in strength of boundary interpolation dependent on given edge lengths and gaps between them (Shipley & Kellman, 1992b; Rubin, Shapley, & Nakayama, 1995). *Similarity* does not influence the boundary process, but is important in a complementary process of filling in that operates within interpolated boundaries (Kellman & Shipley, 1991; Yin, Kellman, & Shipley, 1995).

References

Arterberry, M. E., & Yonas, A. (1988). Infants' sensitivity to kinetic information for three-dimensional object shape. *Perception & Psychophysics, 44*(1), 1–6.

Aslin, R. N., Alberts, J., & Petersen, M. (Eds.). (1981). *Development of perception: Psychobiological perspectives: The visual system* (Vol. 2, 313–334). New York: Academic Press.

Atkinson, J., Hood, B., Wattam-Bell, J., Anker, S., & Tricklebank, J. (1988). Development of orientation discrimination in infancy. *Perception, 17*(5), 587–595.

Banks, M. S., & Dannemiller, J. L. (1983). Infant visual psychophysics. In P. Salapatek & L. Cohen (Eds.), *Handbook of infant perception* (Vol. 1). Orlando: Academic Press.

Banks, M. S., & Ginsburg, A. P. (1983). Early visual preferences: A review and a new theoretical treatment. In H. W. Reese (Ed.), *Advances in child development and behavior.* New York: Academic Press.

Banks, M. S., & Salapatek, P. (1983). Infant visual perception. In M. M. Haith & J. Campos (Eds.), *Infancy and biological development* (pp. 435–572). New York: Wiley.

Banks, M. S., & Kellman, P. J. (in press). Infant visual perception. In D. Kuhn & R. Sieglar (Eds.), *Handbook of Child Psychology: Vol. 2. Cognitive Language and Perceptual Development.*

Berkeley, G. (1709/1910). *Essay toward a new theory of vision.* London: Dutton.

Bertenthal, B. I. (1993). Infants' perception of biomechanical motions: Intrinsic image and knowledge-based constraints. In G. Carl (Ed.), *Carnegie Mellon Symposia on Cognition: Visual perception and cognition in infancy* (pp. 175–214). Hillsdale, NJ: Erlbaum.

Bertenthal, B. I., Campos, J. J., & Haith, M. M. (1980). Development of visual organization: The perception of subjective contours. *Child Development, 51*(4), 1072–1080.

Bertenthal, B. I., & Davis, P. (1988). *Dynamic pattern analysis predicts recognition and discrimination of biomechanical motions.* Paper presented at the annual meeting of the Psychonomic Society, Chicago, Ill.

Bertenthal, B. I., Profitt, D. R., & Cutting, J. E. (1984). Infant sensitivity to figural coherence in biomechanical motions. *Journal of Experimental Child Psychology, 37*(2), 213–230.

Bertenthal, B. I., Proffitt, D. R., Kramer, S. J., & Spetner, N. B. (1987). Perception of biomechanical motions by infants: Implementation of various processing constraints. [Special issue: The ontogenesis of perception.] *Journal of Experimental Psychology: Human Perception & Performance, 13*(4), 577–585.

Bertenthal, B. I., Proffitt, D. R., Spetner, N. B., & Thomas, M. A. (1985). The development of infant sensitivity to biomechanical motions. *Child Development, 56*(3), 531–543.

Braddick, O. J., Atkinson, J., & Wattam-Bell, J. R. (1986). Development of the discrimination of spatial phase in infancy. *Vision Research, 26*(8), 1223–1239.

Braunstein, M. (1976). *Depth perception through motion.* New York: Academic Press.

Brunswik, E. (1956). *Perception and the representative design of psychological experiments.* Berkeley: University of California Press.

Buffart, H., Leeuwenberg, E., & Restle, F. (1981). Coding theory of visual pattern completion. *Journal of Experimental Psychology: Human Perception & Performance, 7*(2), 241–274.

Caron, A. J., Caron, R. F., & Carlson, V. R. (1979). Infant perception of the invariant shape of objects varying in slant. *Child Development, 50*(3), 716–721.

Carroll, J. J., & Gibson, E. J. (1981). *Infants' differentiation of an aperature and an obstacle.* Paper presented at the meeting of the Society for Research in Child Development, Boston, MA.

Craton, L. G., & Yonas, A. (1990). The role of motion in infants' perception of occlusion. In T. E. James (Ed.), *Advances in psychology: Vol. 69. The development of attention: Research and theory* (pp. 21–46). Amsterdam: North-Holland.

Cutting, J. E. (1981). Coding theory adapted to gait perception. *Journal of Experimental Psychology: Human Perception & Performance, 7*(1), 71–87.

Day, R. H., & McKenzie, B. E. (1981). Infant perception of the invariant size of approaching and receding objects. *Developmental Psychology, 17*(5), 670–677.

DeValois, R., & DeValois, K. (1988). *Spatial Vision.* New York: Oxford Press.

Fantz, R. L., & Fagan, J. F. (1975). Visual attention to size and number of pattern details by term and preterm infants during the first six months. *Child Development, 46*(1), 3–18.

Fantz, R. L., Fagan, J. F., & Miranda, S. B. (1975). Early visual selectivity. In L. B. Cohen & P. Salapatek (Eds.), *Infant perception: From sensation to cognition.* New York: Academic Press.

Field, D. J., Hayes, A., & Hess, R. F. (1993). Contour integration by the human visual system: Evidence for a local "association field." *Vision Research, 33*(2), 173–193.

Fodor, J. A. (1983). *The modularity of mind: An essay on faculty psychology.* Cambridge, MA: MIT Press.

Ghim, H.-r (1990). Evidence for perceptual organization in infants: Perception of subjective contours by young infants. *Infant Behavior & Development, 13*(2), 221–248.

Gibson, E. J. (1969). *Principles of Perceptual Learning and Development.* New York: Appleton-Century-Crofts.

Gibson, E. J. (1984). Perceptual development from the ecological approach. In M. Lamb, A. Brown & B. Rogoff (Eds.), *Advances in developmental psychology* (Vol. 3, pp. 243–285). Hillsdale, NJ: Erlbaum.

Gibson, E. J., Owsley, C. J., & Johnston, J. (1978). Perception of invariants by five-month-old infants: Differentiation of two types of motion. *Developmental Psychology, 14*(4), 407–415.

Gibson, E. J., Owsley, C. J., Walker, A., & Megaw-Nyce, J. (1979). Development of the perception of invariants: Substance and shape. *Perception, 8*(6), 609–619.

Gibson, E. J., Riccio, G., Schmuckler, M. A., Stoffregen, T. A., Rosenberg, T., & Taormina, J. (1987). Detection of the traversability of surfaces by crawling and walking infants. [Special issue: The ontogenesis of perception.] *Journal of Experimental Psychology: Human Perception & Performance, 13*(4), 533–544.

Gibson, J. J. (1966). *The senses considered as perceptual systems.* Boston: Houghton Mifflin.

Gibson, J. J. (1979). *The ecological approach to visual perception.* Boston: Houghton Mifflin.

Gibson, J. J., & Gibson, E. J. (1955). Perceptual learning: Differentiation or enrichment? *Psychological Review, 62,* 32–41.

Gibson, J. J., Kaplan, G. A., Reynolds, H. N., Jr., & Wheeler, K. (1969). The change from visible to invisible: A study of optical transitions. *Perception & Psychophysics, 5*(2), 113–116.

Graham, N. (1989). *Visual pattern analyzers.* New York: Oxford University Press.

Granrud, C. E. (1987). Size constancy in newborn human infants. *Investigative Ophthalmology and Visual Science, 28 (Suppl.),* 5.

Granrud, C. E., & Yonas, A. (1984). Infants' perception of pictorially specified interposition. *Journal of Experimental Child Psychology, 37*(3), 500–511.

Granrud, C. E., Yonas, A., Smith, I. M., Arterberry, M. E., Glicksman, M. L., & Sorknes, A. (1985). Infants' sensitivity to accretion and deletion of texture as information for depth at an edge. *Child Development, 55,* 1630–1636.

Grossberg, S. (1994). 3-D vision and figure-ground separation by visual cortex. *Perception & Psychophysics, 55*(1), 48–120.

Gunderson, V. M., Yonas, A., Sargent, P. L., & Grant-Webster, K. S. (1993). Infant macaque monkeys respond to pictorial depth. *Psychological Science, 4*(2), 93–98.

Hebb, D. O. (1949). *The organization of behavior.* New York: Wiley.

Held, R. (1993). What can rates of development tell us about underlying mechanisms? In G. Carl (Ed.), *Carnegie Mellon symposia on cognition: Visual perception and cognition in infancy.* (pp. 75–89). Hillsdale, NJ: Erlbaum.

Helmholtz, H. v. (1885/1910). *Handbook of physiological optics* (Vol. 3). New York: Dover.

Hoffman, D. D., & Flinchbaugh, B. E. (1982). The interpretation of biological motion. *Biological Cybernetics, 42*(3).

Holway, A. H., & Boring, E. G. (1941). Determinants of apparent visual size with distance variant. *American Journal of Psychology, 54,* 21–37.

Hood, B., Atkinson, J., Braddick, O., & Wattam-Bell, J. (1992). Orientation selectivity in infancy: Behavioural evidence for temporal sensitivity. *Perception, 21*(3), 351–354.

James, W. (1890). *The principles of psychology* (Vol. 2). New York: Holt.

Johansson, G. (1950). *Configurations in Event Perception.* Uppsala: Almqvist & Wiksell.

Johansson, G. (1970). On theories for visual space perception: A letter to Gibson. *Scandinavian Journal of Psychology, 11*(2), 67–74.

Johansson, G. (1975). Visual motion perception. *Scientific American, 232*(6), 76–88.

Johnson, M. H. (1990). Cortical maturation and the development of visual attention in early infancy. *Journal of Cognitive Neuroscience, 2*(2), 81–95.

Julesz, B. (1971). *Foundations of cyclopean perception.* Chicago: University of Chicago Press.

Kanizsa, G. (1979). *Organization in vision.* New York: Praeger.

Kaplan, G. A. (1969). Kinetic disruption of optical texture: The perception of depth at an edge. *Perception & Psychophysics, 6*(4), 193–198.

Kaufmann-Hayoz, R., Kaufmann, F., & Stucki, M. (1986). Kinetic contours in infants' visual perception. *Child Development, 57*(2), 292–299.

Kaufmann-Hayoz, R., Kaufmann, F., & Walther, D. (1988). *Perception of kinetic subjective contours at 5 and 8 months.* Paper presented at the Sixth International Conference on Infant Studies, Washington, D.C.

Kellman, P. J. (1984). Perception of three-dimensional form by human infants. *Perception & Psychophysics, 36*(4), 353–358.

Kellman, P. J. (1993). Kinematic foundations of infant visual perception. In G. Carl (Ed.), *Carnegie Mellon symposia on cognition: Visual perception and cognition in infancy.* (pp. 121–173). Hillsdale, NJ: Erlbaum.

Kellman, P. J. (1995). Ontogenesis of space and motion perception. In W. Epstein & S. Rogers (Eds.), *Handbook of Perception and Cognition* (Vol. 5, pp. 327–364). New York: Academic Press.

Kellman, P. J., Gleitman, H., & Spelke, E. S. (1987). Object and observer motion in the perception of objects by infants. [Special Issue: The ontogenesis of perception.] *Journal of Experimental Psychology: Human Perception & Performance, 13*(4), 586–593.

Kellman, P. J., & Shipley, T. F. (1991). A theory of visual interpolation in object perception. *Cognitive Psychology, 23*(2), 141–221.

Kellman, P. J., & Shipley, T. F. (1992). Perceiving objects across gaps in space and time. *Current Directions in Psychological Science, 1*(6), 193–199.

Kellman, P. J., & Short, K. R. (1987a). *Infant perception of partly occluded objects: The problem of rotation.* Paper presented at the Third International Conference on Event Perception and Action, Uppsala, Sweden.

Kellman, P. J., & Short, K. R. (1987b). Development of three-dimensional form perception. *Journal of Experimental Psychology: Human Perception & Performance, 13,* 545–557.

Kellman, P. J., & Spelke, E. S. (1983). Perception of partly occluded objects in infancy. *Cognitive Psychology, 15*(4), 483–524.

Kellman, P. J., Spelke, E. S., & Short, K. R. (1986). Infant perception of object unity from translatory motion in depth and vertical translation. *Child Development, 57*(1), 72–86.

Kellman, P. J., Yin, C., & Shipley, T. F. (1995). A common mechanism for occluded and illusory contours: Evidence from hybrid displays. *Investigative Ophthalmology and Visual Science Supplements, 36*(4), S847.

Koffka, K. (1935). *Principles of Gestalt Psychology.* New York: Harcourt, Brace, & World.

Lesher, G. W., & Mingolla, E. (1993). The role of edges and lie-ends in illusory contour formation. *Vision Research, 33*(16), 2253–2270.

Locke, J. (1690/1971). *An essay concerning the human understanding.* New York: World Publishing Co.

Marr, D. (1982). *Vision.* San Francisco: Freeman.

Marr, D., & Hildreth, E. (1980). Theory of edge detection. *Proceedings of the Royal Society of London, B 207,* 187–217.

Marr, D., Poggio, T., & Hildreth, E. (1980). Smallest channel in early human vision. *Journal of the Optical Society of America, 70*(7), 868–870.

Michotte, A., Thines, G., & Crabbe, G. (1964). Les complements amodaux des structures perceptives. *Studia Psychologica.* Louvain: Publications Universitaires de Louvain.

Mill, J. S. (1865/1965). Examination of Sir William Hamilton's philosophy. In R. Herrnstein & E. G. Boring (Eds.), *A source book in the history of psychology.* Cambridge, MA: Harvard University Press.

Nakayama, K., & Shimojo, S. (1992). Experiencing and perceiving visual surfaces. *Science, 257*(5075), 1357–1363.

Owsley, C. (1983). The role of motion in infants' perception of solid shape. *Perception, 12*(6), 707–717.

Pentland, A. (1990). Photometric motion. *Investigative Ophthalmology and Visual Science Supplements, 31* 172.

Piaget, J. (1952). *The origins of intelligence in children.* New York: Norton.

Piaget, J. (1954). *The construction of reality in the child.* New York: Basic Books.

Polat, U., & Sagi, D. (1993). Lateral interactions between spatial channels: Suppression and facilitation revealed by lateral masking experiments. *Vision Research, 33*(7), 993–999.

Regolin, L., & Vallortigara, G. (1995). Perception of partly occluded objects by young chicks. *Perception and Psychophysics, 57*(7), 971–976.

Rubin, N., Shapley, R., & Nakayama, K. (1995). *Rapid propagation speed of signals triggering illusory contours.* Paper presented at the Annual meeting of Investigative Ophthalmology and Visual Science (ARVO), Fort Lauderdale, FL.

Ruff, H. A. (1978). Infant recognition of the invariant form of objects. *Child Development, 49*(2), 293–306.

Schiff, W. (1965). Perception of impending collision: A study of visually directed avoidant behavior. *Psychological Monographs, 79*(Whole No. 604).

Schmidt, H., & Spelke, E. S. (1984). *Gestalt relations and object perception in infancy.* Paper presented at the International Conference on Infant Studies, New York.

Shapley, R., & Gordon, J. (1987). The existence of interpolated illusory contours depends on contrast and spatial separation. In S. Petry & G. E. Meyer (Eds.), (pp. 109–116). New York: Springer-Verlag.

Shapley, R., & Ringach, D. (1994). Similar mechanisms for illusory contours and amodal completion. *Investigative Ophthalmology and Visual Science Supplements, 35*(4), 1490.

Shaw, L., Roder, B., & Bushnell, E. W. (1986). Infants' identification of three-dimensional form from transformations of linear perspective. *Perception & Psychophysics, 40*(5), 301–310.

Shepard, R. N. (1984). Ecological constraints on internal representation: Resonant kinematics of perceiving, imagining, thinking, and dreaming. *Psychological Review, 91*(4), 417–447.

Shipley, T. F., & Kellman, P. J. (1992a). Perception of partly occluded objects and illusory figures: Evidence for an identity hypothesis. *Journal of Experimental Psychology: Human Perception & Performance, 18*(1), 106–120.

Shipley, T. F., & Kellman, P. J. (1992b). Strength of visual interpolation depends on the ratio of physically specified to total edge length. *Perception & Psychophysics, 52*(1), 97–106.

Slater, A., Johnson, S., Kellman, P. J., & Spelke, E. (1994). The role of three-dimensional depth cues in infants' perception of partly occluded objects. *Journal of Early Development and Parenting, 3*(3), 187–191.

Slater, A., Mattock, A., & Brown, E. (1990). Size constancy at birth: Newborn infants' responses to retinal and real size. *Journal of Experimental Child Psychology, 49*(2), 314–322.

Slater, A., & Morison, V. (1985). Shape constancy and slant perception at birth. *Perception, 14*(3), 337–344.

Slater, A., Morison, V., Somers, M., Mattock, A., Brown, E., & Taylor, D. (1990). Newborn and older infants' perception of partly occluded objects. *Infant Behavior & Development, 13*(1), 33–49.

Spelke, E. S. (1985). Perception of unity, persistence and identity: Thoughts on infants' conceptions of objects. In J. Mehler & R. Fox (Eds.), *Neonate cognition* (pp. 89–113). Hillsdale, NJ: Erlbaum.

Spelke, E. S., Breinlinger, K., Jacobson, K., & Phillips, A. (1993). Gestalt relations and object perception: A developmental study. *Perception, 22*(12), 1483–1501.

Sperry, R. W. (1943). Effect of 180 degree rotation of the retinal field on visuomotor coordination. *Journal of Experimental Zoology, 92,* 263–277.

Sumi, S. (1984). Upside-down presentation of the Johansson moving light-spot pattern. *Perception, 13*(3), 283–286.

Titchener, E. B. (1924). *A textbook of psychology.* New York: Macmillan.

Ullman, S. (1979). *The interpretation of visual motion.* Cambridge, MA: MIT Press.

von der Heydt, R., Peterhans, E., & Baumgartner, G. (1984). Illusory contours and cortical neuron responses. *Science, 224*(4654), 1260–1262.

von Hofsten, C. (1983). Foundations for perceptual development. *Advances in Infancy Research, 2,* 241–264.

Walk, R. D., & Gibson, E. J. (1961). A comparative and analytical study of visual depth perception. *Psychological Monographs, 75*(15).

Walker, A. S., Owsley, C. J., Megaw-Nyce, J., Gibson, E. J., & Bahrick, L. B. (1980). Detection of elasticity as an invariant property of objects by young infants. *Perception, 9*(6), 713–718.

Wallach, H. (1985). Learned stimulation in space and motion perception. Meeting of the American Psychological Association (1984, Toronto, Canada). *American Psychologist, 40*(4), 399–404.

Wallach, H., & O'Connell, D. N. (1953). The kinetic depth effect. *Journal of Experimental Psychology, 45,* 205–217.

Wallach, H., & Slaughter, V. (1988). The role of memory in perceiving subjective contours. *Perception & Psychophysics, 43*(2), 101–106.

Wattam-Bell, J. (1991). Development of motion-specific cortical responses in infancy. *Vision Research, 31*(2), 287–297.

Wattam-Bell, J. (1992). The development of maximum displacement limits for discrimination of motion direction in infancy. *Vision Research, 32*(4), 621–630.

Webb, J. A., & Aggarwal, J. K. (1982). Structure from motion of rigid and jointed objects. *Artificial Intelligence, 19,* 107–130.

Wertheimer, M. (1923/1958). Principles of perceptual organization. In D. C. Beardslee & M. Wertheimer (Eds.), *Readings in perception*. Princeton, NJ: Van Nostrand.

Yin, C., Kellman, P. J., & Shipley, T. (1995). A surface spreading process complements boundary interpolation under occlusion. *Investigative Ophthalmology and Visual Science Supplements, 36*(4), S1068.

Yonas, A. (1981). Infants' responses to optical information for collision. In R. N. Aslin, J. Alberts, & M. Petersen (Eds.), *Development of perception: Psychobiological perspectives: the visual system*, (Vol. 2, pp. 313–334). New York: Academic Press.

Yonas, A., Arterberry, M. E., & Granrud, C. E. (1987a). Four-month-old infants' sensitivity to binocular and kinetic information for three-dimensional-object shape. *Child Development, 58*(4), 910–917.

Yonas, A., Arterberry, M. E., & Granrud, C. E. (1987b). Space perception in infancy. *Annals of Child Development, 4*, 1–34.

Yonas, A., & Granrud, C. E. (1984). The development of sensitivity to kinetic, binocular and pictorial depth information in human infants. In D. Ingle, D. Lee, & M. Jeannerod (Eds.), *Brain mechanisms and spatial vision*. Amsterdam: Nijhoff.

Yonas, A., Pettersen, L., & Lockman, J. J. (1979). Young infants' sensitivity to optical information for collision. *Canadian Journal of Psychology, 33*(4), 268–276.

CHAPTER 2

Perceptual Classification and Expertise

Susan Carey

I. INTRODUCTION

Other chapters in this volume cover some key topics in perceptual development, including the maturation of mechanisms underlying face recognition (Johnson and Gilmore), depth and object recognition (Kellman; Spelke and Hermer), and the development of attentional mechanisms (Johnson and Gilmore). This chapter focuses on an aspect of perceptual development that is closely related to cognitive development—the development of the capacity for perceptual classification. Perceptual classification is a kind of categorization; we have the capacity to classify stimuli as members of such categories as cups, cars, dogs, and people. We also have the capacity to recognize *individuals* within such categories; I distinguish my dog Domino from other Labrador Retrievers, and we recognize our mother's face from among others.

There is reason to believe that the processes that allow us to recognize cups differ in important ways from those that allow us to recognize individual dogs or faces. Biederman (1987) has argued convincingly that our capacity to recognize artifacts such as cups and cars relies on representations built from an alphabet of primitive parts (called by him "geons"). For example, the handle of a cup and the handle of a basket are the same geon. Similarly, the body of a cup and the body of a basket (at least a round one) are the same

Perceptual and Cognitive Development
Copyright © 1996 by Academic Press, Inc. All rights of reproduction in any form reserved.

49

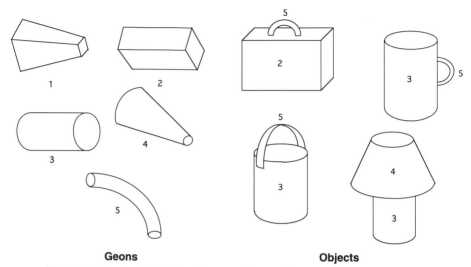

Geons   **Objects**

FIGURE 1   Partial alphabet of geons and some objects constructed from them.

geon. Cups and baskets are distinguished by the relative locations of the handles to the bodies. Figure 1 shows a small subset of the alphabet of geons and some of the objects that can be constructed from them.

Biederman's proposal raises interesting developmental questions that have remained unexplored, at least to my knowledge. Is the alphabet of geons innate? Are there innate constraints on how geons can be combined into representations of objects? Please note, however, that a mechanism that represents objects in terms of the spatial configuration of geons could support the recognition of a face as a face, but it could not underlie the recognition of a particular person, since all people's faces share the same configuration of geons. The present paper explores the nature of representations that individuate members of a category of objects that share a configuration, concentrating on the case that is arguably the most important to humans, and also that presents the hardest problem to a pattern encoder: face recognition.

II. FACE RECOGNITION

We read momentary expression, character, age, sex, and, of course, personal identity from faces. Here, we are concerned with the development of the processes underlying adult expertise at recognition of individual faces. A familiar face is identified in about $\frac{1}{2}$ second, in spite of the large number of faces stored in memory, and in spite of the high degree of similarity among faces. Adults can successfully encode large numbers of new faces from photographs inspected only briefly (e.g., 50 seen for 5 seconds each) and subsequently pick these from distractors at recognition rates of over 90%. Furthermore, once well encoded, representations of faces are not interfered with by newly encoded representations. One demonstration study found above 90% recognition of yearbook photos of schoolmates, independent of class size between 90 and 900, and independent of elapsed time from graduation between 3 months and 35 years (Bahrick, Bahrick, & Wittlinger, 1975)!

A. The Course of Development of Face Recognition

Evolution has provided the baby a running start at face recognition. Neonates preferentially track moving schematic faces, in contrast to other patterns of comparable complexity, including upside-down schematic faces (Goren, Sarty, & Wu, 1975; Johnson et al., 1991; see Johnson and Gilmore, this volume). And, within days, babies have formed representations that support discrimination of their mother's face from a stranger's face (Bushnell, Sai, & Mullin, 1989; Walton & Bower, 1991). During the first half year of life, the baby comes to discriminate young from old faces, male from female faces (e.g., Fagan, 1979). Further, by 5 to 7 months, babies succeed at encoding new faces from minimal exposure, subsequently discriminating these from faces they have not seen before.

In spite of this impressive beginning, face recognition undergoes protracted development. Compared to normal adult levels of skill, young children are profoundly deficient at face encoding. On some clinical tasks, children under 10 perform at a level diagnostic of right hemisphere brain damage, whereas 10-year-olds, while still worse than adults, perform in the normal adult range (Benton & van Allen, 1973; Carey, Diamond, & Woods, 1980). Figure 2 shows the typical developmental function on recognition memory tasks. These data are from a task in which subjects are shown 36 photographs for 5 seconds each and then asked to discriminate these from new photos. Six-year-olds perform just barely better than chance, compared to the ceiling performance of adults. If the size of the set of faces to be encoded is varied, in order to ensure performance levels of 85% or better, children ages 3 and under succeed only at set size 1, whereas by age 10, children can manage sets of 10 or more (Carey, 1981).

Several studies indicate that the improvement over the first decade in life is followed by a decline around age 12 (Figure 2; see also Carey et al., 1980; Flin, 1980). Puberty is implicated in this disruption of performance; two studies have shown that girls in the midst of pubertal change perform worse than prepubescent or postpubescent controls matched for age (Diamond, Carey, & Back, 1983). Of course, this association is consistent with either a biological or a cognitive explanation for the disruption of face encoding at

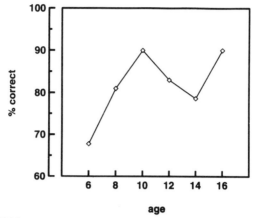

FIGURE 2   Developmental function for a typical face encoding task.

age 12. First (the biological): hormonal changes at puberty may directly affect mental processes. Alternatively (the cognitive): the child's reaction to the bodily changes at puberty might conceivably lead to a new interest in personal appearance and style, which in turn might lead to a reorganization of representations of faces. Flin (1983) found a disruption in performance for recognition of nonface stimuli, as well, militating against any cognitive interpretation specific to the representation of faces. At any rate, the explanation of the decline in performance in early puberty remains to be worked out, and I do not speculate here. Rather, I concentrate on the issues raised by the improvement in face encoding skills during the first decade of life.

B. The Descriptive Problem: *What* Is Developing?

As children get older, we *expect* them to get better at just about anything. This is why the decline in performance at age 12 seems the aspect of the developmental function most in need of explanation. But that we expect children to improve does not mean we are forgiven the task of explaining *why* they do. A first step in providing an explanation is locating the source of improvement. What is it about face recognition in young children that makes them worse at it than older children and adults?

Recognition memory for faces can be broken down into two components—the formation of a representation of a previously unseen face (the initial encoding) and the process of matching a current stimulus with a stored representation (recognition). Several lines of evidence converge on the conclusion that young children's problems concern the *initial encoding* of new faces, rather than the processes of *recognition,* per se. Most straightforwardly, several of the tasks that diagnose subjects' face encoding skills do not involve memory at all, instead requiring a decision of whether two different photographs depict the same person or not. When the faces differ in expression, angle of view, direction of lighting, hair style, clothing, or even size (of photo), young children perform poorly (Benton & van Allen, 1973; Diamond & Carey, 1977; Ellis, 1992; Saltz & Sigel, 1967). Such matches are mediated by representations, of course. Young children have difficulty encoding faces in terms of features that are invariant over such changes. Apparently, children's poor performance on simple recognition memory tasks (e.g., Figure 2) reflects difficulty in encoding faces in terms of features that differentiate one face from another.

The features that distinguish faces one from another must be learned from experience with them. We all have had the experience of encountering a new race of faces and having great difficulty telling people apart. Do children's poor face encoding skills derive from a similar lack of knowledge of faces from their own social group? Alternatively, perhaps the young child is worse than the adult at encoding any complex pattern, and the improvement at face encoding during the first decade of life derives from improvement at pattern encoding in general. We are asking here whether the changes reflected in Figure 2 are domain specific or domain general. The answer to this question is important because it constrains our search for an explanation of the developmental change. If the changes are domain specific, then it is likely that children are bad at face recognition just because they are novices at the task, just as I am bad at bird recognition. If so, there is nothing *developmental* about the function in Figure 2; nothing about being a child contributes to the 6-year-old's poor performance. If the changes are domain general, it is likely that information processing limitations of children contribute to their poor performance at face encoding.

One can see how, in principle, this question should be addressed. One need only compare the developmental course for face encoding with that for some task that places comparable demands on a pattern encoder but for which the adult has no more experience than has the child. In practice, however, it is difficult to meet these desiderata. We have tried twice.

1. Recognition Memory for Inverted Faces

Our first attempt involved comparing the developmental course of recognition memory for upright faces with that for inverted faces. For adults, orientation markedly interferes with encoding success. Moreover, performance on upright faces is not even correlated with performance on inverted faces, suggesting that adults are not able to recruit all their knowledge of faces when encoding inverted faces (Phillips & Rawles, 1979). In terms of pattern complexity, upright and inverted faces are identical, so, as meaningless patterns, both place equal demands on a pattern encoder. Thus, a comparison of the developmental course of encoding upright and inverted faces would help tease apart the contribution of general improvement at pattern encoding skills (applicable to upright *and* inverted faces) from the contribution of acquisition of expertise at face encoding, per se (perhaps applicable to upright faces only). The results from the developmental studies are clear: as long as ceiling and floor effects are controlled for, face encoding is affected by orientation at every age tested, even in infancy (Carey, 1981; Fagan, 1979; Flin, 1983). At least by age 5 months, new faces are being encoded relative to specific knowledge of faces, knowledge better exploited from upright than from inverted stimuli. Equally clear is an age-by-orientation interaction. That is, the magnitude of the inversion effect increases with age (Carey, 1981; Flin, 1983).

What is not so clear is how to interpret this pattern of results with respect to the question at hand. That children improve more on upright faces than on inverted faces shows, I would argue, that *part* of their improvement is due to acquisition of knowledge of faces, per se, knowledge that cannot be applied as efficiently to the encoding of inverted faces. Children's improvement on inverted faces *could* reflect acquisition of general pattern encoding skills that contribute to the emerging expertise at face encoding. But it could also reflect acquisition of knowledge about upright faces that is exploited in the encoding of inverted faces. Thus, while the age-by-orientation interaction indicates that *part* of the development of face encoding in the first decade of life is due to the acquisition of face-specific expertise, these data leave open the question whether *all* is due to this source.

2. Encoding Random Dot Patterns

In our second attempt to address this issue, we studied the developmental course of encoding random dot patterns of the sort first studied by Posner and Keele (1968). Prototypical 9-dot patterns are randomly generated. For each prototype, a set of patterns is created, ranging from small distortions of the prototype to relatively large distortions. The subject is given the task of learning to categorize sets of distortions from a single prototype together, distinguishing them from the patterns derived from different prototypes. Since the patterns are randomly generated, no subject can have had any experience with the features that differentiate them. If the training set consists of large distortions from the prototype, this task places great demands on a pattern encoder. Further, after a training criterion has been met, data from generalization trials allow a characterization of how the patterns have been encoded.

In three separate studies, using several different measures of encoding success, the following pattern emerged: 6- and 10-year-olds did not differ; both groups encoded the patterns less adequately than did 12-year-olds and adults. Between ages 6 and 10, the period of huge changes in face encoding success, the developmental function was totally flat (Diamond & Carey, 1990)! This task requires the subject to extract a prototype, based on the configuration of several points, and to classify novel exemplars in terms of configural similarity to that prototype. All these are certainly aspects of the requirements face encoding places on a pattern encoder. We can tentatively conclude that development of *these* domain-general pattern encoding skills do not underlie improvement at face encoding in the years before age 10. These data are consistent with the conclusion that *all* improvement during these years is due to acquisition of specific expertise about faces. Naturally, the question is still open; future studies will falsify this conclusion if some other general pattern encoding skill applicable to faces is shown to improve over these years and to contribute to increased skill at face encoding.

III. WHAT DO WE KNOW ABOUT THE ACQUISITION OF EXPERTISE AT PERCEPTUAL CLASSIFICATION, INDEPENDENT OF CONSIDERATIONS OF AGE?

We have arrived at a fairly trivial conclusion. Young children are less able than older children and adults to encode new faces in terms of features that support differentiation of that face from others, and this lack derives largely from lack of knowledge of faces, per se. Our task, therefore, is to specify what expertise at face encoding consists of, so as to characterize what the child must acquire. We seek hints about how young children (novices) and adults (experts) differ concerning the encoding of faces.

One indication that children are doing something *different* from adults, rather than just less of what adults do, is the fact that children are less affected by inversion. If we understood the large inversion effect on face encoding, we might begin to grasp what changes with acquisition of expertise.

Encoding individual faces is more affected by inversion than is the encoding of individuals from almost any other class studied to date: houses, bridges, stick figures of men, buildings, landscapes, dogs' faces (Diamond & Carey, 1986; Scapinello & Yarmey, 1970; Yin, 1969, 1970a). In these studies, the stimuli to be encoded are presented in the same orientation both during inspection and recognition; inverted stimuli are first seen upside-down and also presented for recognition upside-down. The difficulty is in forming an adequate representation of an inverted face, not in coping with a mismatch of orientation between test and recognition. Typically, one finds a 20–30% decrement in recognition accuracy for inverted compared to upright faces, whereas one finds only a 0–10% decrement when stimuli from the other classes are inspected and recognized upside-down.

This result has been taken by some to indicate that faces are a unique stimulus class; they pose unique problems to a pattern encoder, and perhaps even have dedicated neural substrate for the solutions to these problems (e.g., Yin, 1970b). No doubt there is dedicated neural underpinnings to the innate representation of faces, and no doubt there are many areas of the brain that subserve face recognition. But evidence for such neural specialization does not show that faces are processed in some ways uniquely. Diamond and Carey (1986) provided an analysis of what it is about faces that makes their encoding so vulnerable to inversion, and supported this analysis by successful prediction of other classes of stimuli that are similarly affected by inversion.

Faces share a basic configuration in a way that can be made precise: each face can be defined in terms of a fixed set of points, such that the average of a set of faces, so defined, is still recognizable as a face. This is not true of a randomly chosen set of bridges, or houses, or buildings, or landscapes (recognition of which is not particularly sensitive to inversion). This is why faces cannot be differentiated on the basis of different geons or geon arrangements. Furthermore, some of the features by which we individuate faces are distinctive variations of that basic configuration. This is seen by the recognizability of line drawings such as those on Figures 3 and 7—these line drawings are all specified in terms of the same 169 points (consider, for now, only those designated "Veridical"; these are produced by locating 169 points on photographs, and instructing the computer to connect the appropriate points, smoothing the curves). Even though these are highly degraded stimuli, they are somewhat recognizable (e.g., subjects familiar with the people depicted recognize on the order of 50–75% of such veridical line drawings; Carey, 1992). Diamond and Carey (1986) dubbed features that are distinctive variations of a shared configuration "second-order relational features." We hypothesized that extracting second-order relational features is particularly affected by inversion, and that the ability to encode individuals in terms of such features requires considerable experience with faces, that is, requires expertise.

Dogs' faces also share a configuration, yet encoding of dogs' faces is affected only minimally by inversion (Scapinello & Yarmey, 1970). But in Scapinello and Yarmey's study, the encoders were not dog experts. Diamond and Carey's analysis predicts that dog experts, encoding individual dogs, should be affected by orientation just as all adults (face experts) are in encoding individual faces. Two studies tested this prediction. American Kennel Club judges inspected a series of individual dogs, shown in profile, and then picked out those individuals from distractors they had not seen before. Nonexperts were tested in two conditions—at the same series size as experts, and at series half the size, so as to equate performance on the upright. Two series of inspection and associated recognition items were prepared, so that each subject could be tested on upright and on inverted

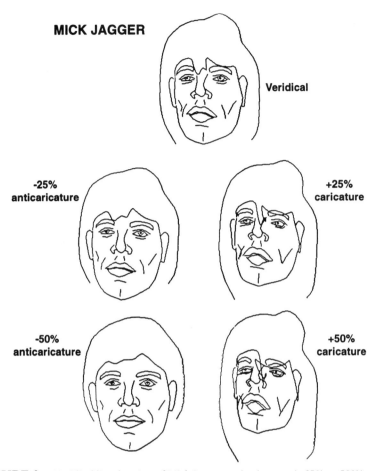

FIGURE 3   Veridical line drawing of Mick Jagger: anticaricatures (−25%, −50%); caricatures (+25%, +50%).

dogs. In the first study, the dog breeds were poodles, setters, Scotties.
Experts were more affected by inversion (12%) than were novices (8% at
the large set size; 3% at the small set size), but not significantly so. However, the experts complained bitterly at the task we had given them—the
three breeds were from different categories of dogs (e.g., sporting dogs,
working dogs), and only "best of show" judges know all breeds. So, in the
second study we used only sporting dogs—setters, retrievers, spaniels—
and only sporting dog experts. These experts were equally affected by
inversion encoding dog profiles (22%) and human faces (20%). Novices
showed the usual stimulus-by-orientation interaction, that is, they were

more affected by orientation at encoding faces (23%) than dogs, at either the large set size (2%) or the small set size (−2%; Diamond & Carey, 1986).

It appears that such perceptual expertise requires about 10 years to develop, whether one is a child or an adult. It is at age 10 that children perform in the normal adult range on face encoding tasks. And the period of apprenticeship for becoming an American Kennel Club judge is 10 years!

Faces are not special in the sense of posing unique problems for a pattern encoder, at least not as reflected in unique sensitivity to inversion. These data support the hypothesis that the inversion effect for faces reflects individuation within a class of patterns that share a configuration in terms of second-order relational features, and that reliance on distinguishing features of this type requires considerable expertise.

IV. THE EFFECT OF ORIENTATION ON CONFIGURAL ENCODING OF FACES

Several sources of data support the importance of configural information in expert face encoding. The relations among features can be directly manipulated on schematic line drawings of faces, and on more realistic faces that can be assembled in Photo-fit type systems (as used by police departments in creating likenesses from witness description). Adults are sensitive to changes in the spatial relations among features, as well as to changes in the features themselves (e.g., Haig, 1984; Sergent, 1984). Furthermore, there is abundant evidence that inversion disproportionately disrupts the processing of configural information of this sort. For example, in a timed task involving same–different judgments of schematic faces, mismatches due to differences in internal spacing of features were processed differently in the upright and inverted conditions, whereas mismatches due to changes of eyes, or changes in overall face contour were processed the same in the two orientations (Sergent, 1984).

Other demonstrations underline the importance of orientation to configural processing of faces. Consider the famous Thatcher illusion (Thompson, 1980). Thompson inverted Thatcher's mouth and the eyes, keeping the rotated features in their normal place within the photograph of her face. The resulting photograph looks grotesque if upright, but does not look particularly unusual if inverted. The grotesque appearance in the upright may be due to violations of constraints on second-order relations among the points that define the shared configuration, constraints that are defined relative to upright faces (e.g., eyes don't slant that way, relative to the nose and forehead).

Others have suggested different interpretations of the difference in monstrosity between the upright and upside-down faces. For example, Parks, Coss, and Coss (1985), showed that inverted mouths, by themselves, look grotesque, so the monstrosity of an upright Thatcherized face may be due to its inverted mouth alone. Most probably there are several distinct sources of the illusion, but a recent demonstration by Bartlett and Searcy (1993) demonstrates that Parks et al.'s alternative cannot explain the whole effect. Bartlett and Searcy created grotesque faces simply by varying the spacing among features that remained in their canonical orientation. Again, monstrosity was much more easily judged from upright than from inverted faces.

Sergent (1984) documented a second sense in which faces are encoded configurally when upright, but not when inverted. The dimensions on which her schematic faces varied were processed interactively in the upright position, but independently when inverted. Others have reported similar results. For example, Maruyama and Endo (1984) showed that perception of eye gaze in schematic faces is more affected by the orientation of the profile when faces are upright than when they are inverted. Faces are processed more holistically when upright. In the course of constructing an integrated representation, one independently manipulated feature influences the contribution other independently manipulated features make to the final representation.

Tanaka and Farah (1993) distinguish between holistic and parts-based representations, and argue that faces are more likely to be encoded holistically than are other classes of stimuli. They further suggest that holistic encoding is more sensitive to inversion than is parts-based encoding.

In their paper, Tanaka and Farah provide two distinct characterizations of holistic encoding. First, holistic representations are those in which the parts of the stimulus are not explicitly represented. In the case of faces, this would mean that a particular face would not be represented in terms of the identities of parts like the nose, eyebrows, mouth, and so on, but rather in terms of a templatelike representation of the whole. In such a representation, individual parts (e.g., Bob's nose) should be harder to recognize in isolation than in the context of the whole face, and indeed, this is what Tanaka and Farah (1993) found. Evidence that holistic representations are sensitive to orientation was provided by the finding that the advantage for recognizing Bob's nose in the whole face disappeared when the stimuli were turned upside-down.

In their second characterization, Tanaka and Farah (1993) state that in holistic representations, the spatial relations among the parts are more important in specifying an individual object than are the representations of the individual parts themselves. Note that this characterization is very different from the first, for in this characterization, there is no claim that the individual parts are not explicitly represented. Indeed, as Farah et al. admit, under this characterization, the distinction between holistic representations and configural representations becomes blurred.

FIGURE 4   Example of composite and noncomposite stimuli (Mr. Spock, top half; Oliver North, bottom half).

Young, Hellawell, and Hay (1987) provided one of the most striking demonstrations that inversion interferes with configural encoding of faces. Here, I describe just one version of the effect they found. Note that the top halves of photographs of famous people, or familiar colleagues, are easily recognizable. Young et al. made two types of displays: composites and noncomposites. In composite photographs the top half of one face (say Mr. Spock) is perfectly aligned with the bottom half of another (say Oliver North), creating a photograph of what seems to be a new person who resembles both Spock and North. In noncomposite photographs, the top half of one face is displayed above, but offset from, the bottom half of another, so the two do not fuse into a new face (see Figure 4). The subject's task is simply to name the person whose face comprises the top part of the composite or noncomposite. Young et al. found that reaction times and errors were markedly greater for composites than for noncomposites, but only when the faces were upright. Performance on inverted composites did not differ from that on inverted noncomposites.

V. ARE FACES PROCESSED LESS AS CONFIGURATIONS BY CHILDREN (NOVICES) THAN BY ADULTS?

All of the results cited in the previous section have been taken as support for the proposition that encoding configural aspects of faces is less efficient if the face is not in its canonical orientation. These results are consistent, then, with the hypothesis that expertise consists of increased reliance on configural features in face encoding. However, the hypothesis requires a direct test. If young children's (novices') poor performance at face encoding reflects lesser reliance on configural features, then children should be less likely to demonstrate all those phenomena that indicate configural encoding of upright faces.

A. The Development of the Composite Effect

Unfortunately for the hypothesis, this does not seem to be true. I know of two attempts to assess the developmental history of the effects of orientation on the tasks that reflect configural encoding reviewed in the previous section. As an example of this research strategy, I will sketch a recent example from Diamond's and my laboratory (Carey & Diamond, 1994). In two studies, we assessed the developmental course of the effects Young et al. documented with composite and noncomposite faces. The patterns of results from both studies were the same; I will present just one here. We prepared composite (aligned) and noncomposite (offset) split-face photographs of children in first grade classes (age 6–7), children in fifth grade classes (age 10–11), and adults in the Department of Brain and Cognitive Sciences at MIT. The study was run at the end of the year; all subjects were very familiar with the people photographed. We then repeated the Young et al. (1987) procedure; subjects named as quickly as possible the faces depicted in the top halves of composite and noncomposite photographs. Each subject saw one series in the upright and one inverted.

The results were totally clear. At each of the three ages, the pattern of results described by Young et al. (1987) obtained. That is, in the upright, the people in composite photographs were named much more slowly, with more errors, than those in noncomposite photographs, whereas composites did not differ from noncomposites if faces were inverted (see Figure 5). There is no developmental increase, at least from age 6 on, in the interference of the bottom half of a composite face to the naming of the top half, and at all ages this interference obtains only when faces are upright. However, there was a second, equally clear result—an overall tendency for older subjects to be affected more by inversion than are younger subjects. That is, 6-year-olds were overall *slower* on upright faces (averaged over composites and noncomposites) than on inverted faces; 10-year-olds processed the upright and inverted faces approximately equally quickly, whereas adults were overall much *faster* on upright than on inverted faces (see Figure 6).

These two effects (composite interference in upright but not inverted faces and the increased sensitivity to inversion with age) were statistically independent of each other. That is, subjects of all ages were slowed by composites when faces were upright but not inverted, and the increased effects of inversion with age were seen equally for composite and noncomposite faces.

This pattern of results supports several conclusions. As far as *this* reflection of configural encoding of faces (Young et al.'s composite effect) is

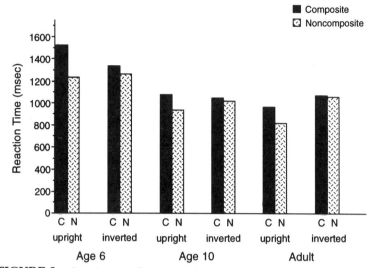

FIGURE 5   Reaction time for correct responses, naming the face in the top half.

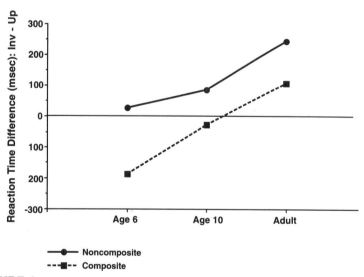

FIGURE 6   Reaction time for inverted faces minus reaction time for upright faces, naming the face in the top half.

concerned, there are no developmental changes over the ages of 6 to adulthood. Therefore, configural encoding in this sense does not underlie the greater sensitivity to inversion that adults (experts) experience. This is shown by the fact that 6-year-olds experience the interference in upright composites, and by the fact that the normal age-related increase in sensitivity to orientation of faces is seen in this study, independent of the composite interference effect. Finally, these data confirm that there are at least two distinct, independent sources of the effect of orientation on face encoding, only one of which requires expertise.

B. The Development of the Tanaka/Farah Holistic Effect

In a second study tracking the development of configural encoding of faces between the ages of 6 and 10, Tanaka charted sensitivity to the whole face advantage in recognizing "Bob's nose" (see above). He found no change in the advantage for whole faces over parts during this age range (Tanaka, personal communication). Thus, his findings corroborate those from Carey and Diamond (1994) on the composite effect. Young et al. (1987) and Tanaka and Farah (1993) have provided interesting demonstrations that configural encoding of faces is sensitive to orientation, but they have not isolated that aspect of face encoding that is sensitive both to inversion and to expertise.

VI. EXPERTISE: THE MYSTERY FACTOR

These data show that 6-year-old children, no less than 10-year-olds and adults, encode upright faces configurally. The composite effect is independent of age, even in the presence of the effect that reflects acquisition of expertise, that is, the increased effect of inversion on face recognition. Similarly, children of age 6 to 10, like adults, are better able to recognize Bob's nose in the context of Bob's face than alone. What these results mean is that the expertise effects are not the result of an increased reliance on holistic/configural encoding. Apparently, there are at least two sources of the inversion effect for faces. First, there is configural encoding, or holistic encoding, as tapped by the composite effect or the Tanaka/Farah whole face superiority effect. This is present throughout the age/expertise range studied here. And then there is something else that is gained with expertise. The something else is the mystery factor.

What is the mystery factor? Up to this point in this chapter, I have treated the hypothesis that experts encode faces in terms of configural features as equivalent to the hypothesis that experts encode faces in terms of second-order relational features. In fact, the two hypotheses are subtly different.

They are related because they both implicate the coding of configural relations, the relations among the parts of a face, as the source of the inversion effect. They are different because the second-order relational feature hypothesis involves norm-based coding (Rhodes, Brennan, & Carey, 1987; Valentine, 1991). The idea is that the *distinctive* configural features are identified by comparing the face to be encoded to a prestored norm. This process of comparison to the norm is sensitive to inversion, because the norm is represented in a canonical orientation. In the remaining two sections of this chapter, I will present evidence for the hypothesis that face encoding is norm based, and argue that the mystery factor is a fuller specification of the norm.

A. Norm-Based Coding of Faces

Consider again the faces in Figures 3 and 7. A set of faces represented by a fixed set of points can be averaged, yielding an average face (Figure 7A). One method is to normalize the faces in the set by aligning the pupils of the two eyes, and then simply average the values of each of the other points. Caricatures can then be created as follows: find the difference between each point on the face to be caricatured with the corresponding point on the

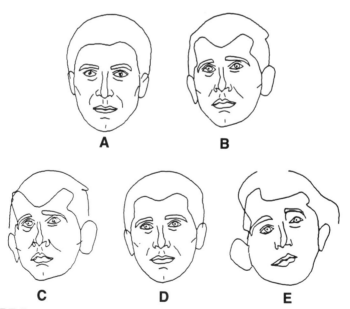

FIGURE 7   Average face (A), veridical line drawing of Oliver North (B), 50% caricature of Oliver North (C), 50% anticaricature of Oliver North (D), 50% lateral caricature of Oliver North (E).

average face, and multiply that difference by a fixed amount (say 50%). This operation has the effect of exaggerating more those aspects of faces that differ more from the average face (50% of a big difference is greater than 50% of a smaller difference). One can also create an anticaricature, by decreasing the difference between the face to be caricatured and the average face. Figure 3 shows a set of anticaricatures and caricatures of Mick Jagger (Brennan, 1985, for a full characterization of the caricature generator).

Distorting faces away from the average face is a nonlinear transformation; it is quite unlike stretching a face along a vertical or horizontal axis. Each point is moved in a unique direction, and by a unique distance. Nonetheless, the caricaturing transformation does not reduce the recognizability of the face; indeed, in some experiments, a 50% caricature is recognized faster than the veridical drawing and a slight caricature is judged the "best likeness" of the person depicted (e.g., Rhodes et al., 1987). This contrasts with the anticaricature transformation, which markedly reduces the recognizability of the face.

The line drawings of Figures 3 and 7 are very degraded representations of faces; it takes much longer to recognize them than to recognize the photograph from which they are traced, and subjects make many errors. Clearly, those aspects of the configuration that define a face captured in such drawings form only a small part of the basis for face recognition. In recent series of studies, Benson and Perrett (1991) created caricatures of full photographs by exaggerating just the same aspects of difference from the norm, leaving information about hair and skin color and texture, eye color, and so on, normally provided by photographs. They, too, found that subjects judged the slight caricature the best representation of the face, and that caricatures were recognized slightly faster. Thus, even in the context of much fuller information about a face, manipulations of the shared configuration depicted in Figure 3 affected recognition similarly to when this configurational information is all subjects had to go by.

An actual caricature advantage is counterintuitive. Our memory representations serve recognition of actual people, their real faces—why should there be an advantage for recognition of caricatures? Since caricatures exaggerate what is distinctive about a face, there could be an advantage in caricaturing the memory representation itself. Alternatively, the caricature advantage could arise in the recognition process, even if memory representations were veridical, because exaggerating what is distinctive decreases the similarity of the target to other faces stored in memory (see Rhodes et al., 1987, for a discussion of these two possibilities; see Tanaka, 1990, for a connectionist model in which a caricature advantage arises, in spite of veridical representations of the stimuli to be recognized).

The lesson I wish to draw from Rhodes et al.'s results does not depend on the actual caricature advantage. Here, I wish to emphasize that in spite of the considerable distortion, caricatures are as well or better recognized than actual faces, much better than anticaricatures that are equally distorted from the veridical. That caricatures are better recognized than anticaricatures is unsurprising, as one can see from Figures 3 and 7—anticaricatures are collapsed toward the average face, so they all begin to resemble the average face, and are very similar to each other. To ensure that the better recognizability of caricatures and veridicals, compared to anticaricatures, is not due only to this fact, we created a set of "lateral caricatures." In a lateral caricature, each point is moved the same distance from its origin as on the caricature or anticaricature, but at a right angle from the vector defined by the relation between the origin and its corresponding point on the average face. The lateral caricatures differ, then, from the veridicals exactly as much as do the caricatures and the anticaricatures, and they are not collapsed toward the average face. Nonetheless, they are not recognizable. Figure 7 includes a lateral caricature of Ollie North. In a study using famous faces, we found that subjects need 1901 ms to recognize the caricatures, 2130 ms for the veridicals (note the actual caricature advantage), 3322 ms the anticaricatures, and 4377 the laterals (Carey, 1992). Whereas 50% of the caricatures and veridicals were recognized, only 12% of the laterals were.

These data support the hypothesis that faces are encoded with respect to a norm. They suggest that there is a privileged vector in face space, originating at the norm, and running through anticaricatures, the veridical representation, and caricatures. All stimuli on this vector, even anticaricatures, respect the relative distinctiveness of feature point in relation to the norm. To see this, imagine a face with very wide set eyes and a very small nose. Caricatures will exaggerate these features—the space between the eyes will become even wider and the nose even smaller. But even in anticaricatures, the eyes will still be set wider than those of the norm and the nose will be smaller than those of the norm. These relations are maintained only on this vector. And, as the experiment with laterals shows, only faces on this vector are recognized.

As we saw above, other classes of stimuli require discrimination within a shared configuration. Rhodes and McLean (1990) recently demonstrated a caricature advantage for recognition of passerines (songbirds) from profile line drawings, but only on the part of expert bird watchers!

B. A More Complete Specification of the Norm: The Mystery Factor

A good candidate for what changes with expertise is the representation of the norm. At all levels of expertise, it crudely reflects the shared overall configuration of faces, but with increasing expertise, it becomes more and more completely specified. A simple metaphor is that it becomes specified in terms of more and more points. Thus, with increasing expertise, norm-based coding will engage many more points, many more spatial relations among points. At all levels of expertise, distinctive configural features are encoded relative to the norm, but these become more adequate to distinguishing among highly similar faces as the norm becomes more fleshed out. Since inversion interferes with norm-based coding of relational distinguishing features, improvement with expertise at encoding upright faces will be greater than improvement at encoding inverted faces (the expertise-by-orientation interaction).

Several well-known phenomena are consistent with this picture. Valentine (1991) showed that inversion interferes more with adult (expert) encoding of typical faces than with atypical faces. On the assumption that typical faces are closer to the norm, and thus that more subtle relational features are required to distinguish among them, typical faces will place higher demands on the norm-based coding mechanism that inversion disrupts. This analysis also predicts a race-by-orientation interaction for subjects who are experts at distinguishing among faces of only one racial group. That is, subjects should show a larger inversion effect for faces they are expert at identifying than for those from other racial groups. Rhodes, Tan, Brake, and Taylor (1989) obtained this finding.[1]

Recent developmental findings from Ellis (1992) bear on the hypothesis that the mystery factor is an increasing specification of the norm—the shared configuration among faces. First, Ellis found a distinctiveness-by-age interaction in a face recognition task. That is, 6- to 7-year-olds showed no recognition advantage for atypical faces, and over the age range from 6 to 14, developmental improvement at encoding atypical faces was greater than that for encoding typical faces. Typicality was determined by adult (expert) ratings. These data show that the youngest children's norm is not adequate to distinguishing faces that adults judge as typical from those adults judge atypical. As the norm becomes more fully specified, distinguishing features from atypical faces are the first to become employable.

VII. A FEW CONCLUDING REMARKS

Locating the source of developmental change is not easy. In this chapter, I have argued that the marked change with age in face recognition ability is not *developmental* at all, in the sense of deriving from general limitations on children. Rather, it reflects acquisition of expertise, exactly of the same sort

[1] Valentine (1991) found the opposite interaction—greater inversion effect for other race faces, but he did not have a full crossover design, so that his findings may reflect differences in difficulty between the two sets of faces. Also, the faces within each race were not as homogeneous as those of Rhodes, Tan, Brake, and Taylor (1989), since Valentine included stimuli with beards, moustaches, and glasses.

as that acquired by adults as they become bird watchers or dog show judges. I have further suggested that all three of these cases of expertise are similar, in that they involve the common problem of distinguishing among stimuli that share a configuration. I have argued that this perceptual problem is solved by norm-based coding, and that expertise consists in a fuller specification of the norm.

References

Bahrick, H. P., Bahrick, O. O., & Wittlinger, R. P. (1975). Fifty years of memory for names and faces: a cross-sectional approach. *Journal of Experimental Psychology: General, 104,* 54–75.

Bartlett, J. C., & Searcy, J. (1993). Inversion and configuration of faces. *Cognitive Psychology, 25,* 281–316.

Benson, P. J., & Perrett, D. I. (1991). Perception and recognition of photographic quality facial caricatures: implications for the recognition of natural images. *European Journal of Cognitive Psychology, 3,* 105–135.

Benton, A. L., & van Allen, M. W. (1973). *Test of facial recognition* (Neurosensory Center Pub. No. 287). Iowa City, IA: University Hospitals, Department of Neurology.

Biederman, I. (1987). Recognition-by-components: A theory of human image understanding. *Psychological Review, 94,* 115–147.

Brennan, S. E. (1985). The caricature generator. *Leonardo, 18,* 170–178.

Bushnell, I. W. R., Sai, F., & Mullin, J. T. (1989). Neonatal recognition of the mother's face. *British Journal of Developmental Psychology, 7,* 3–15.

Carey, S. (1981). The development of face perception. In G. Davies, H. Ellis, & J. Shephard (Eds.), *Perceiving and remembering faces* (pp. 9–38). New York: Academic Press.

Carey, S. (1992). Becoming a face expert. *Philosophical Transactions of the Royal Society of London, 335,* 95–103.

Carey, S., & Diamond, R. (1994). Are faces perceived as configurations more by adults than by children? *Visual Cognition, 1,* 253–274.

Carey, S., Diamond, R., & Woods, B. (1980). The development of face recognition—a maturational component? *Developmental Psychology, 16,* 257–269.

Diamond, R., & Carey, S. (1977). Developmental changes in the representation of faces. *Journal of Experimental Child Psychology, 23,* 1–22.

Diamond, R., & Carey, S. (1986). Why faces are and are not special: an effect of expertise. *Journal of Experimental Psychology: General, 115,* 107–117.

Diamond, R., & Carey, S. (1990). On the acquisition of pattern encoding skills. *Cognition Development, 5,* 345–368.

Diamond, R., Carey, S., & Back, K. (1983). Genetic influences on the development of spatial skills during early adolescence. *Cognition, 13,* 167–185.

Ellis, H. D. (1992). Developmental trends in face recognition. *Philosophical Transactions of the Royal Society of London, 335,* 104–110.

Fagan, J. F. (1979). The origins of facial pattern recognition. In M. H. Bornstein & W. Kessen (Eds.), *Psychological development from infancy: image to intention* (pp. 83–113). Hillsdale, NJ: Erlbaum.

Flin, R. H. (1983). *The development of face recognition.* Unpublished doctoral dissertation, Aberdeen University.

Goren, C. C., Sarty, M., & Wu, P. Y. K. (1975). Visual following and pattern discrimination of face-like stimuli by newborn infants. *Pediatrics, 56,* 544–549.

Haig, N. D. (1984). The effect of feature displacement on face recognition. *Perception, 13,* 505–512.

Johnson, M., Dziurawiec, S., Ellis, H., & Morton, J. (1991). Newborns' preferential tracking of face-like stimuli and its subsequent decline. *Cognition,* p. 3.

Maruyama, K., & Endo, M. (1984). Illusory face dislocation effect and configurational integration in the inverted face. *Tohoku Psychologica Folia, 43,* 150–160.

Parks, T. E., Coss, R. G., & Coss, C. S. (1985). Thatcher and the Cheshire cat: context and the processing of facial features. *Perception, 14,* 747–754.

Phillips, R. J., & Rawles, R. E. (1979). Recognition of upright and inverted faces: a correlational study. *Perception, 8,* 577–583.

Posner, M. I., & Keele, S. W. (1968). On the genesis of abstract ideas. *Journal of Experimental Psychology, 77,* 353–363.

Rhodes, G., Brennan, S., & Carey, S. (1987). Identification and ratings of caricatures: implications for mental representations of faces. *Cognitive Psychology, 19,* 473–479.

Rhodes, G., & McLean, I. G. (1990). Distinctiveness and expertise effects with homogeneous stimuli: towards a model of configural coding. *Perception, 19,* 773–794.

Rhodes, G., Tan, R., Brake, S., & Taylor, K. (1989). Expertise and configural coding in face recognition. *British Journal of Psychology, 80,* 313–331.

Saltz, E., & Sigel, I. E. (1967). Concept overdiscrimination in children. *Journal of Experimental Psychology, 73,* 1–8.

Scapinello, K. F., & Yarmey, A. D. (1970). The role of familiarity and orientation in immediate and delayed recognition of pictorial stimuli. *Psychonomic Science, 21,* 329–330.

Sergent, J. (1984). An investigation into component and configural processes underlying face perception. *British Journal of Psychology, 75,* 221–242.

Tanaka, J. W. (1990). Caricature recognition in a neural network. *Proceedings of the XII Annual Conference of the Cognitive Science Society,* pp. 622–628.

Tanaka, J. W., & Farah, M. J. (1993). Parts and wholes in face recognition. *Quarterly Journal of Experimental Psychology, 46:*225–245.

Thompson, P. (1980). Margaret Thatcher: a new illusion. *Perception, 9,* 483–484.

Valentine, T. (1991). A unified account of the effects of distinctiveness, inversion, and race in face recognition. *Quarterly Journal of Experimental Psychology, 43A,* 161–204.

Walton, G. E., & Bower, T. G. R. (1991). *Newborn preference for familiar faces.* Paper presented at the meeting of the Society for Research in Child Development, Seattle.

Yin, R. K. (1969). Looking at upside-down faces. *Journal of Experimental Psychology, 81,* 141–145.

Yin, R. K. (1970a). *Face recognition: a special process?* Unpublished doctoral dissertation, Massachusetts Institute of Technology.

Yin, R. K. (1970b). Face recognition by brain-injured patients: A dissociable ability? *Neuropsychologia, 8,* 395–402.

Young, A. W., Hellawell, D., & Hay, D. C. (1987). Configural information in face perception. *Perception, 16,* 747–759.

CHAPTER 3

Early Cognitive Development: Objects and Space

Elizabeth S. Spelke
Linda Hermer

Infants and young children face some daunting learning tasks. They must learn to recognize the specific individuals with whom they interact: their friend, their dog, their house, their toy truck (Xu and Carey, in press). They must learn to categorize appropriately the many thousands of kinds of objects that older children and adults pick out at a glance, from cups to telephones to butterflies (S. A. Gelman, this volume). They must become able to keep track of their own position and learn the layout of their surroundings and the locations of objects, so that they can find their way from place to place and locate things that are out of view (see below). They must learn words that refer to surrounding objects, places, and events, while mastering the distinctive ways in which their language allows words to be combined to express thoughts (Bloom, this volume). Perhaps most important, infants and young children must build systems of knowledge that capture the significant regularities in their environment, such as knowledge of the motions of objects, the actions of people and animals, and the structure of social events.

Given these tasks, it is not surprising that infants and young children devote much of their time to exploring and learning about their surroundings. Young infants orient to changes in the environmental layout (Johnson & Gilmore, this volume) and direct their attention to novel objects and events

Perceptual and Cognitive Development
Copyright © 1996 by Academic Press, Inc. All rights of reproduction in any form reserved.

(Kellman, this volume, and below). When an event occurs with regularity in a given context—an object appears at a predictable place and time, a mobile turns with every jostling of the crib—infants are apt to learn the regularity, and they may remember it over weeks or months (e.g., Haith, 1993; Perris, Myers, and Clifton, 1990; Rovee-Collier, 1990). Learning about the external environment begins before birth and continues at a rapid pace: For example, newborn infants already have learned to recognize aspects of the sound pattern of their language (Mehler et al., 1988), and they quickly come to recognize aspects of the face of a parent (Bushnell, Sai, & Mullin, 1989).

I. TWO VIEWS OF COGNITIVE DEVELOPMENT

In light of these tasks, it is perhaps natural to view the infant as a general-purpose learning system that discovers and internalizes whatever regularities the perceptible environment presents (see Helmholtz, 1866; McClelland, 1994, for old and new versions of this position). On this view, infants learn with equal ease about any perceptible regularities. With experience, children's knowledge comes to focus on those entities whose perceptible properties and behavior are experienced most frequently and consistently. As their expertise grows, children gradually move beyond the immediately perceptible properties of such entities and discover the deeper properties that adults take to be central in accounting for an entity's behavior: an object's mass, an animal's motivational state, a person's intentions. The domain-specific systems of abstract knowledge that characterize adults' reasoning therefore would emerge late in development, after children had gained extensive knowledge of their perceptible surroundings.

The view of the infant as a general-purpose learner pervades much of the study of cognitive development, but considerable research suggests it is at least partly wrong. Infants appear predisposed to develop systems of knowledge within specific domains including people, inanimate material objects, and places in the layout (Wellman & Gelman, 1992), although the nature of these learning systems and the boundaries between them remain the subject of some debate (Hirshfeld & Gelman, 1994). Early-developing knowledge does not appear to capture the most obvious features of perceptible entities but some of their most deeply reliable, abstract properties (Simons & Keil, 1995). Finally, early-developing knowledge systems may function only in limited contexts, such that distinct systems guide performance in different problem domains (Karmiloff-Smith, 1992).

The domain and task specificity of early knowledge systems may underlie some of the young child's most striking cognitive limitations. Adults can bring distinct systems of knowledge together to tackle new, unanticipated problems: for example, we may use knowledge of number to understand the motions of objects, or knowledge of fluid flow to understand electricity (Carey & Spelke, 1994; Gentner & Stevens, 1983). Unlike adults, infants may not be able to solve new cognitive problems by relating their existing knowledge systems to one another. Contrary to the first view of cognitive development, general-purpose learning abilities may be a late (and partial) achievement, arising only after the child's initial, domain-specific knowledge systems are well established (Carey & Spelke, 1994; Karmiloff-Smith, 1992; Rozin, 1976).

The latter view of cognitive development is suggested by research on infants' developing knowledge of inanimate object motion, human action, number and arithmetic, and the environmental layout. Because knowledge of human action and number are considered elsewhere in this volume (respectively, in the chapters by Miller and Taylor), we focus here on early-developing knowledge of inanimate objects and the spatial layout.

II. DEVELOPING KNOWLEDGE OF OBJECTS

As Kellman's chapter in this volume attests, infants as young as 2 months, and perhaps younger, perceive their surroundings as a stable, three-dimensional layout furnished with objects. Each object in the layout is perceived as a bounded unit, distinct from other objects and surfaces. Infants perceive objects by detecting the patterns of common and relative motion that provide the most reliable information about objects for adults (Kellman, 1993, and this volume). Infants' perception of objects accords with three highly reliable aspects of object motion: (1) objects move *cohesively,* maintaining their internal connectedness and external boundaries (Figure 1A); (2) objects move *continuously,* tracing a connected path over space and time (Figure 1B); (3) objects influence one another's motion only on *contact* (Figure 1C); (see Spelke & Van de Walle, 1993, for discussion). Although object perception is not our current focus, we will return to these general constraints on object motion.

Given that infants perceive objects under certain conditions, we may ask questions about infants' developing knowledge of objects. First, when do infants begin to represent objects that are not currently visible, and how do object representations change over development? Second, when do infants first apprehend the identity of an object that they encounter at different places and times, and how do their representations of object identity change? Third, when do infants first make inferences about the hidden or future motions of objects, and what knowledge guides their inferences at different ages? Answers to these questions may shed light on a central question about early cognitive development: What are the sources of our mature, commonsense knowledge about the physical world and its behavior?

A. Representing Hidden Objects

Infants appear to represent objects that become invisible as early as they can perceive and act systematically on objects that are visible. Object represen-

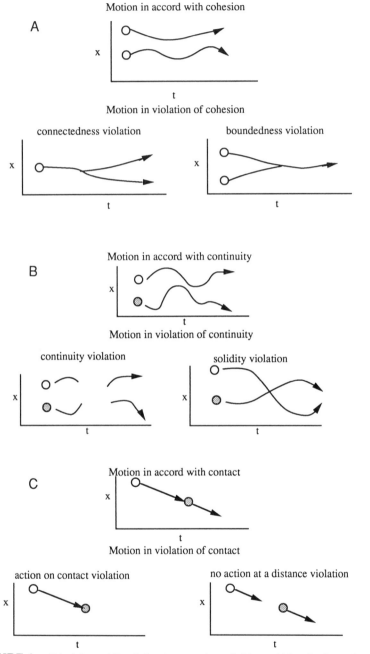

FIGURE 1   Principles guiding infants' perception of objects. (After Spelke and Van de Walle, 1993.)

tations have been revealed by studies of two different kinds of behavior: infants' reaching for objects and their visual attention to events in which objects move from view. We offer one example of each kind of study.

Clifton, Rochat, Litovsky, and Perris (1991) investigated infants' reaching for visible objects and for objects in the dark. Six-month-old infants were presented with objects of two different sizes, a large object similar to a steering wheel and a small object similar to a donut, each with a distinctive sound source at its top (Figure 2). On a series of trials in which the objects were visible, infants had the opportunity to learn the pairing of each object with its sound, and they were allowed to reach for each sounding object. Then the lights were extinguished, the sounds were played, and infants were allowed to reach for the objects in the dark.

Both in the light and in the dark, infants reached differently for the large and small objects: They tended to reach for the donut with one hand directed near the source of the sound, and they tended to reach for the steering wheel with two hands directed to the lateral borders of the object, rather far from the sound source. Infants' reaching in the dark therefore was directed to the now-unseen borders of the object, rather than to the location of the ongoing sound. Infants often reached in the dark by engaging in novel actions, different from those they had performed in the light, that were appropriate to the hidden objects' spatial properties. This experiment and others (Clifton, Rochat, Robin, & Berthier, 1994; Hood & Willats, 1986) provide evidence that infants represent the spatial properties of nonvisible objects, and that such representations inform their reaching.

Further studies of object representations are based on the pervasive finding that infants look longer at novel objects or events (e.g., Bornstein, 1985). In these experiments, infants are presented with a visual display repeatedly until their looking time declines, and then they are presented

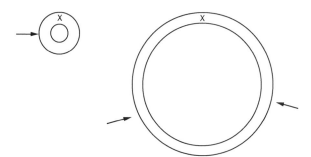

FIGURE 2   Schematic depiction of displays from a study of object-directed reaching in the light and in the dark. Each object was associated with a distinctive sound emanating from the locations marked with **X**s. Characteristic points of contact with an object, during reaching with or without vision, are designated by arrows. (After Clifton, Rochat, Litovsky, and Perris, 1991.)

with changes in that display. Typically, infants look longest at the changed display that they perceive as most different from the original display. Although most studies using preferential looking methods have assessed infants' sensitivity to visible events, a number of studies have used preferential looking methods to probe object representations (see Baillargeon, 1993, for review). An experiment by Craton and Yonas (1990) provides an example.

Six-month-old infants repeatedly watched a disc move behind a screen from a visible position to a hidden position (Figure 3). The object was fully visible or fully hidden only briefly and was otherwise partly occluded. What did infants perceive as this object moved from view: a truncated circle that became narrower and narrower until it disappeared, or a complete disk with a stable, circular shape that moved progressively behind the screen? To address this question, the investigators presented infants whose attention to the original occlusion event had declined with complete and truncated disks in alternation. Infants looked longer at the truncated disk, suggesting they had seen (and become bored by) a complete disk during the occlusion event. This experiment and many others (e.g., Baillargeon, 1987; Hespos & Rochat, 1994; Wilcox, Rosser, & Nadel, 1994, 1995; Wynn, 1992; see also below) provide evidence that infants represent hidden objects.

Preferential looking studies reveal interesting limitations on infants' representations of occluded objects. In particular, infants who are presented with a partly occluded object whose parts are revealed in succession appear to perceive the *unity* of the object but not its specific *shape*. Van de Walle and Spelke (in press) presented 5-month-old infants with a square that moved back and forth behind an occluder such that its two sides alternately were visible on the two sides of an occluder while its center remained hidden (Figure 4A). After looking time to this display had declined, the occluder was removed and infants were presented with a complete square and a broken figure in which the previously visible areas of the square were separated by a gap (Figure 4B). Infants looked longer at the broken square,

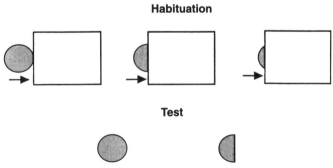

FIGURE 3   Schematic depiction of displays from a study of infants' representations of occluded objects. (After Craton and Yonas, 1990.)

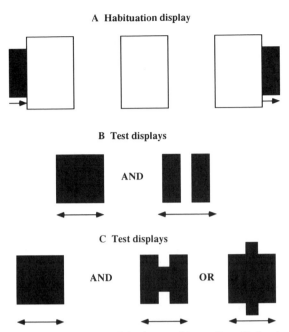

FIGURE 4 Schematic depiction of displays used in studies of infants' perception of the unity and the shape of objects whose parts are revealed over time. (After Van de Walle and Spelke, in press.)

providing evidence that they had perceived the partly occluded square in the occlusion display as one connected object.

In a further experiment, infants were presented repeatedly with the same occlusion display, and then they were shown two fully visible displays with different shapes: a complete square and a more complex form with indentations or protuberances in the previously occluded area (Figure 4C). Adults tested in a separate study reported that the simple square corresponded to the shape of the object in the occlusion event. In contrast, infants looked equally at these two test displays, suggesting that they had failed to perceive the complete shape of the partly occluded square. A number of experiments corroborate the suggestion that young infants fail to perceive the form of an object whose parts are revealed over time (Arterberry, 1993; Kaufmann-Hayoz, Kaufmann, & Walther, 1990; Rose, 1988; Skouteris, McKenzie, & Day, 1992; see Arterberry, Craton, & Yonas, 1993, for discussion). Careful developmental research suggests, moreover, that the ability to perceive the specific shape of such an object develops between 10 and 12 months of age (Arterberry, 1993). We will return to a discussion of this developmental change.

Although the above looking time studies demonstrate that infants represent the unity and stability of occluded objects, young infants have little or no ability to act on objects that are hidden behind visible occluders. If an object is hidden behind an opaque screen or under a cover, infants under 9 months typically fail to reach for it by removing the screen (Piaget, 1954), by directing their hand around the screen (Diamond, 1990b), or even by pressing a button that they used successfully to retrieve a visible object (Munakata, McClelland, Johnson, & Siegler, 1995). Moreover, infants do not track an object that moves behind a stationary occluder or anticipate its re-emergence unless they are given considerable practice (e.g., Moore, Borton, & Darby, 1978; Nelson, 1971). Why do infants fail some tasks involving hidden objects, while succeeding with others? Infants' failures in visual and manual object search tasks have been attributed to the immaturity of action systems (e.g., Baillargeon, Graber, DeVos, & Black, 1990; Diamond, 1990b), insufficiency of memory (e.g., Diamond, 1990a), weakness or instability of object representations (Baillargeon, 1993; Munakata et al., 1995), and aspects of motor history (Thelen & Smith, 1995). Later, we will suggest a different explanation for infants' successes and failures.

B. Apprehending Object Identity

Infants appear to represent objects as persisting, even though their immediate perceptual encounters with any given object typically are brief and sporadic. Do infants also trace the identity of objects that come into view at different places and times, determining whether an object seen at one place and time is the same object that previously appeared at a different place and time? To focus this question, we begin by considering how adults assign identity relations in this situation.

Many philosophers argue that adults' apprehension of object identity relates to our categorization of objects as members of particular kinds (e.g., Geach, 1980; Wiggins, 1980). For example, an object such as a statue can be considered as a statue, a portion of metal, or a symbol of liberty, among many possibilities. Depending on how the object is categorized, the same transformation may lead to different judgments of object persistence and change: melting and remolding, for example, destroys the statue but not the portion of metal. Mature intuitions about object persistence therefore seem to depend on how objects are categorized.

In contrast to these arguments, experiments in visual cognition suggest that perceivers apprehend object identity and object distinctness by virtue of a process that is independent of information for object kind. When visual elements appear at different places and times within a display, relations of identity or distinctness are assigned to the elements in accord with their spatiotemporal properties and irrespective of their categorical identities. A common example occurs when we detect motion at night or in peripheral vision: we often perceive that "a thing" has appeared and moved before we can determine what kind of thing it is (Kahneman & Treisman, 1984). In laboratory studies, adults have been found to represent two distinct alphabetic characters as a single entity when those two characters appear successively within a box that moves continuously across the visual array (Kahneman, Treisman, & Gibbs, 1992). Because this entity is perceived to persist even as it changes both its shape and its category membership (e.g., from an "A" to a "D"), the process that assigns identity relations to the elements evidently does not depend on the process by which the elements are categorized as distinct letters. These disparate studies suggest that adults have multiple processes for tracing persisting objects over time. Studies of infants are beginning to suggest how these processes develop, and how they relate to one another.

A variety of experiments using preferential looking methods provide evidence that infants perceive the identity or distinctness of objects by detecting the spatiotemporal continuity of object motion. In one experiment, for example, infants were familiarized with an object that moved continuously behind two narrow, spatially separated occluders, and then they were presented with fully visible displays containing one versus two objects (Figure 5A). The 4-month-old infants in this experiment looked longer at a fully visible display of two objects, relative to baseline preferences between the displays, suggesting that they perceived a single object in the occlusion event (Spelke, Kestenbaum, Simons, & Wein, 1995). In a further experiment using a similar method, the same finding was obtained at 10 months (Xu & Carey, in press). In a second set of conditions, infants were familiarized with an event involving discontinuous motion: an object moved out of view behind one of the two spatially separated occluders, no motion was

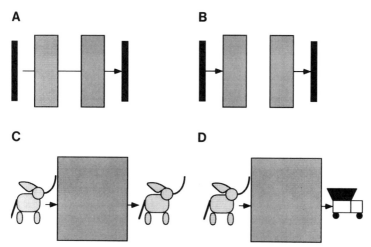

FIGURE 5 Schematic depiction of displays used in studies of infants' apprehension of object identity. (After Spelke, Kestenbaum, Simons, and Wein, 1995; Xu and Carey, in press.)

visible between the occluders, and then an object moved into view from behind the second occluder (Figure 5B). Looking times to the subsequent, fully visible displays provided evidence that both 4- and 10-month-old infants perceived two objects in this occlusion event (Spelke et al., 1995; Xu & Carey, in press). In a third set of conditions, infants were familiarized with an event in which two objects appeared simultaneously on the two sides of a single, wide occluder, and then the objects moved in succession behind the occluder (Figure 5C). Again, 10-month-old infants perceived two distinct objects in this event (Xu & Carey, in press), as did 3- to 5-month-old infants in similar studies (Aguiar & Baillargeon, 1995; Baillargeon & DeVos, 1991; Baillargeon & Graber, 1987).

All these studies suggest that infants apprehend object identity in accord with the principle of continuity: a moving object traces just one connected path over space and time (Spelke & Van de Walle, 1993) (Figure 1B). The continuity principle specifies that a single object participated in the event in Figure 5A, because the occluders were not wide enough to hide two objects occupying distinct locations and moving on distinct paths. This principle specifies that two objects participated in the events in Figure 5B and 5C, because no continuous path can connect the appearances of the objects in these events. The same continuity principle may underlie adults' perception of identity relations in rapidly presented visual displays, independently of the specific categories to which the objects belong (Kahneman et al., 1992).

Further studies by Xu and Carey (in press) suggest surprising limits to infants' apprehension of object identity. In these studies, 10-month-old infants were presented with two featurally distinct objects (e.g., a toy elephant and a toy truck) that appeared in succession behind a single wide screen (Figure 5D). Because the objects moved in succession behind one screen, the continuity principle does not specify whether this event was produced by one or two objects. Adults nevertheless have a strong impression of two objects in this event, because of the evident differences in object properties and kinds: we know that toy elephants do not turn into toy trucks or the reverse. Infants' perception of the distinctness of these objects was tested, as in the above studies, by familiarizing infants with this display and then removing the screen and revealing either both the elephant and the truck or only one of those objects. In contrast to adults, 10-month-old infants showed no preference between these two displays, relative to their baseline preferences between the displays, whereas 12-month-old infants showed the expected preference for the one-object display, relative to baseline. These findings suggest that the younger infants had no determinate perception of the identity or distinctness of the objects, whereas the older infants represented the identity relations as adults do, in accord with information about object properties or kinds.

Subsequent studies by Xu and Carey (1994, 1995, in press; Xu, Carey,

Raphaelidis, & Ginzbursky, 1995; Xu, Carey, & Welch, 1995) and other investigators (Hall & Leslie, 1995; Simon, Hespos, & Rochat, 1995; Wilcox, 1995) eliminate a spectrum of potential explanations for the younger infants' failure to perceive object identity from information about object properties and object kinds. In particular, this failure cannot be explained by a failure to perceive, attend to, or remember the property/kind differences, by limitations of this preferential looking method, or by idiosyncracies in the tested objects. Infants' failure occurs with real artifacts such as cups and books as well as with toys, and it occurs despite independent evidence that infants are able to recognize the objects as familiar (Xu & Carey, in press) and to perceive toy animals and vehicles as members of different categories (Mandler, 1992; Mandler & McDonough, 1993; Xu & Carey, in press, 1995). Experiments probing infants' representations of identity relations for genuinely animate objects and for people have yet to be completed, and such studies may show that the animate–inanimate distinction already guides perception of identity in younger infants (see R. Gelman, Durgin, & Kaufman, 1995; Premack & Premack, 1995, for arguments to this effect). The above research suggests, nevertheless, that infants as old as 10 months trace the identity of inanimate objects by relying on spatiotemporal information, irrespective of the objects' perceptible properties or category membership. In this respect, 10-month-old infants differ from older infants and adults.

What brings about the transformation between 10 and 12 months and leads older infants to trace object identity in new ways? Although existing research does not answer this question decisively, two lines of study suggest that the development of a propensity to trace the identity of inanimate objects in accord with information about object kind is related in some way to the acquisition and use of names for kinds of objects. The first evidence comes from a finding by Xu and Carey (in press). In one study involving highly familiar objects, looking preferences varied systematically as a function of a parent's report as to the particular words in the child's vocabulary: children who, by parental report, understood two or more of the words naming the object kinds used in the study ("ball," "bottle," "book," and "cup") appeared to represent the distinctness of these objects when they appeared in alternation behind a wide screen; children who did not command this vocabulary showed no such ability. Although Xu and Carey caution that the relation between naming and individuation must be tested further, they suggest that the development of names for categories and the development of abilities to use those categories to trace identity somehow are linked together.

The other source of evidence linking language to perception of object identity comes from recent studies of adults by Simons (in press). Simons presented adult subjects with a computer display containing five distinct natural objects (scanned into the computer from color photographs), each placed randomly in one of nine distinct positions. After viewing this display for 2 s, subjects were presented with a dark screen for 1–7 s followed by a second display. Subjects' task was to say whether the second display was identical to the first. On half the trials, the two displays were identical. On the remaining trials, the two displays differed in some way. Two changes from the first display to the second are most relevant to the present discussion: position changes, in which the second display contained the same five objects, but one object appeared in a previously unoccupied location, and category changes, in which the second display contained objects at the same five positions, but one object was new (e.g., a red baseball cap might be replaced by a yellow hair dryer).

In two experiments with photographs of natural objects, subjects detected position changes with accuracy levels of about 95% and detected category changes with about 75–80% accuracy. Because some subjects reported naming the objects in the displays, naming was discouraged in two further experiments by the use of nonsense shapes instead of objects in familiar categories. Performance remained high on position change trials but declined nearly to chance level on category change trials. In a final experiment, familiar objects again were presented, but naming was eliminated by requiring that subjects speak continuously while performing the task (they repeated a long prose passage presented over a tape recorder). Although this "shadowing" task had no effect on subjects' ability to detect position changes, their ability to detect category changes was sharply reduced. These findings, like those of Kahneman et al. (1992), suggest a basic visual process for tracing object identity that depends on spatiotemporal information (where objects are and how they move) and that is independent of information for object properties and kinds. The findings add to the suggestion from Xu and Carey's experiments that language plays some role in extending abilities to perceive object identity.

The limitations on infants' perception of object identity discovered by Xu and Carey (in press) could be related to the previously described limitations on object representation reported by Van de Walle and Spelke (in press), Arterberry (1993), and other investigators (Kaufmann-Hayoz et al., 1990; Rose, 1988; Skouteris et al., 1992). Infants may fail to perceive the shape of an occluded object whose parts appear in succession because of a general inability to relate information about object properties such as shape to information about object motion and persistence over time. Such a limitation would explain why young infants successfully perceive the connectedness of an occluded and disoccluded object in Van de Walle and Spelke's (in press) experiment: object connectedness is a spatiotemporal property that applies to all objects independent of shape or category membership. This limitation also would explain why the transition from failure to success occurs at the same ages in the experiments of Arterberry (1993) and Xu and

Carey (in press), during the period when most children begin to learn names for objects. This account makes two untested predictions: (1) developmental changes in the form integration tasks of Arterberry and others will relate specifically to the emergence of names for kinds of objects; and (2) adults, like young infants, will fail tests of form integration if they are required to engage in a verbal interference task while viewing a partly occluded object.

C. Infants' Inferences about Object Motion

Adults who view a moving object typically can predict the object's future motion. When we reach for a moving object, for example, we extrapolate its motion and aim toward the position the object will occupy when the reach is complete. When an object moves out of view, moreover, we usually can anticipate how its motion will continue and where it will stop. Both abilities have been studied in young infants, who appear to make successful inferences about the future and the hidden motions of objects under an interesting subset of the conditions that are effective for adults.

An experiment by Hofsten, Vishton, Spelke, Feng, and Rosander (1995) investigated infants' predictive reaching. Six-month-old infants were presented with a small graspable object that moved within reach either on a linear path or on a path with an abrupt turn at the center (Figure 6A). Because linear and nonlinear paths were equally frequent and randomly ordered, the behavior of the ball at the display's center was unpredictable. In order to catch the object, however, infants needed to begin their reach before it reached the center and to aim for a position beyond it.

For each trial, aiming movements were categorized as to whether infants aimed for a position on the side of the display to which the object would move if it continued in linear motion ("linear extrapolation") or on the side of the display on which the object began and would remain if it turned ("nonlinear extrapolation"). As Figure 6B indicates, infants aimed for positions on a line with the object's initial motion, whether or not the object turned at the center. The same patterns of aiming were observed in a second study in which infants received blocked trials with each pattern of motion: even when the nonlinear motion occurred repeatedly, infants aimed their predictive reaches in accord with a linear extrapolation of the object's initial motion, consistently missing the object! In a third study (Vishton, Spelke, & von Hofsten, 1996) linear extrapolations occurred when every path of motion in the study was novel, such that infants had no opportunity to learn about the object's motion paths. These findings provide evidence that infants reach predictively by extrapolating linear object motion.

A recent experiment by Huntley-Fenner, Carey, Klatt, and Bromberg (1995) investigated infants' inferences about hidden object motion using a

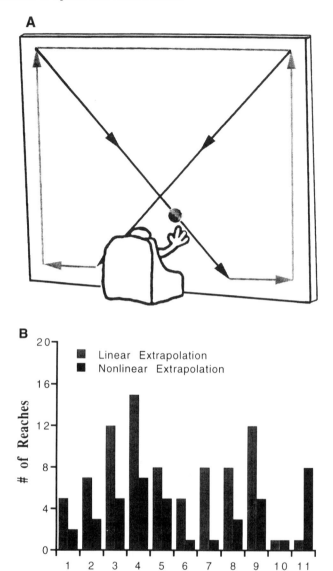

FIGURE 6   (A) Schematic depiction of the four paths of object motion used in the predictive reaching experiments. (B) Numbers of reaches aimed to the linear and nonlinear sides of the display. (After Hofsten, Vishton, Spelke, Feng, and Rosander, 1995; Experiment 1.)

different method. Eight-month-old infants were familiarized with events in which an object was lowered first visibly and then behind a screen to a position on the floor of an open stage (Figure 7). Then a shelf was placed

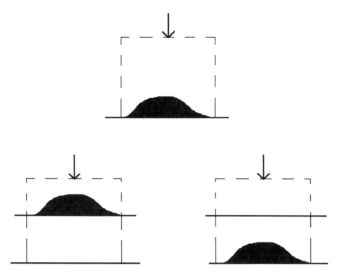

FIGURE 7   Schematic depiction of displays used in a preferential looking study of infants' extrapolation of occluded object motion. (After Huntley-Fenner, Carey, Klatt, and Bromberg, 1995.)

above the stage floor behind the screen, the object again was lowered, and the screen was raised to reveal the object either in a new position on the shelf or in its original position on the floor. When looking times to these outcomes were measured and compared, infants were found to look longer at the outcome in which the object appeared on the floor. This looking preference provides evidence that infants inferred that the hidden object would not pass through the shelf. A considerable number of experiments using preferential looking methods now provide evidence for this inference in infants as young as 3 months (e.g., Baillargeon, 1986, 1987; Baillargeon & DeVos, 1991; Baillargeon et al., 1990; Spelke, Katz, Purcell, Ehrlich, & Breinlinger, 1994; Wilcox et al., 1994, 1995), although some investigators find increases in this ability over the first 8 to 10 months (Lucksinger, Cohen, & Madole, 1992; Sitskoorn & Smitsman, in press) or propose alternative interpretations of some studies (Bogartz, Shinsky, & Speaker, 1995; Cohen, 1995; Thelen & Smith, 1993).[1]

---

[1] Experiments reported by Spelke, Breinlinger, Macomber, and Jacobson (1992), using a method similar to that of Huntley-Fenner, Carey, Klatt, and Bromberg (1995), provided evidence for extrapolations of occluded object motion at $2\frac{1}{2}$ and 4 months of age. A recent attempt to replicate experiment 1 from that series has failed, however (E. S. Spelke, D. A. King, & Y. Munakata, in preparation). Although the reasons for this failure are not clear, we base no conclusions in this chapter on the findings of Spelke, Breinlinger, Macomber, and Jacobson (1992), pending further study.

Given that two methods provide evidence for extrapolations of object motion in infancy, both methods may be used to investigate the principles guiding infants' extrapolations. One might expect that the findings of the studies using the two methods would converge on the same set of principles. Contrary to this expectation, studies using reaching and preferential looking methods suggest that extrapolations are guided by different principles in the two contexts.

In studies of predictive reaching, 6-month-old infants extrapolate motion on paths that are linear (Hofsten et al., 1995), or circular (Hofsten, 1983; Hofsten & Rosander, 1994). When an object moves at different speeds on different trials, the timing of infants' reaches suggests that they extrapolate motion at constant velocity (Hofsten, 1983).

Nevertheless, infants' predictive reaching is perturbed if an occluder screens a portion of the object's motion, even if the occluder is placed out of reach. (Hofsten, Feng, Vishton, & Spelke, 1994). These findings suggest that predictive reaching is guided by the principle that a smoothly moving object will continue in smooth motion (hereafter, "the principle of inertia") but not by the principle that an occluded object exists and moves continuously (an aspect of the principle of continuity).

In contrast, the preferential looking studies cited above suggest that infants extrapolate object motion in accord with the continuity principle, as do other studies using preferential looking methods (e.g., Aguilar & Baillargeon, 1995; Simon et al., 1995; Wilcox et al., 1994, 1995; Wynn, 1992). Preferential looking studies also provide evidence that infants extrapolate object motion in accord with the principle of cohesion (Figure 1A): If an object moves from view successively at two locations and then is revealed either as a single, cohesive body at one location or as two separate bodies at the two locations, infants look longer at the latter outcome, in accord with the principle that objects maintain their connectedness and boundaries as they move (Huntley-Fenner et al., 1995; see also Spelke, Breinlinger, Jacobson, & Phillips, 1993). Finally, preferential looking studies provide evidence that infants extrapolate object motion in accord with the principle of contact: If two objects move in succession behind a single occluder, with timing that evokes for adults an impression of causality (Michotte, 1963), and then the occluder is removed to reveal that the first object either contacts or stops short of the second, infants look longer at the no-contact test event (Ball, 1973; Kotovsky & Baillargeon, 1994; Van de Walle, Woodward, & Phillips, 1994; see also Leslie, 1988; Oakes & Cohen, in press). This preference provides evidence that infants represented the occluded objects as moving into contact, in accord with the constraint that distinct objects influence one another's motion only if they touch.

Preferential looking experiments suggest, nevertheless, that young infants fail to extrapolate occluded object motion in accord with the inertia principle (Spelke et al., 1994). Infants viewed events in which a ball rolled on a straight line behind an occluder and then was revealed, by the removal of the occluder, at a resting position that was either on or off the original line of motion (Figure 8). Although older infants showed weak preferences for the nonlinear outcome under some conditions, 4- and 6-month-old infants showed no such preferences. These negative findings cannot plausibly be attributed to limitations of the preferential looking method, because the method provided positive evidence for inferences about object motion in accord with the continuity principle (Spelke et al., 1994). In preferential looking contexts, infants appear to infer that a hidden object will move in accord with the principles of continuity, cohesion, and contact but not in accord with the principle of inertia.

In brief, infants make inferences about object motions in at least two contexts: when they reach for a moving object and when they watch an object move behind an occluder. As one might expect, infants' inferences in the two situations accord only with a subset of the constraints on object motion that adults recognize. A comparison of the conditions under which

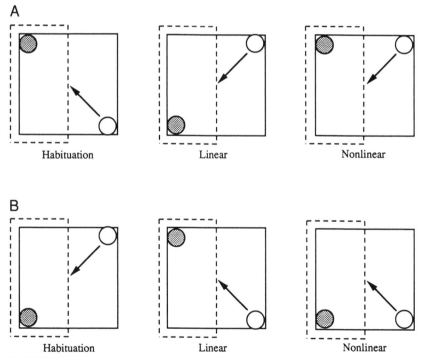

FIGURE 8 Schematic depiction of the displays used in studies of infants' extrapolation of object motion on linear paths. Open and shaded circles indicate the initial and final portions of the object, respectively. (After Spelke, Katz, Purcell, Ehrlich, and Breinlinger, 1994.)

extrapolations occur reveals that the subsets of constraints guiding inferences in the two situations are not the same. In preferential looking experiments, inferences are guided by the principle of continuity but not by the principle of inertia; in predictive reaching experiments, in contrast, inferences are guided by inertia but not by continuity. One interpretation of this "double dissociation" in performance is that infants do not possess a single system of object representation but at least two partly separable systems: a system subserving object-directed reaching (and perhaps other object-directed actions) and a system subserving perception of familiar events and reactions to novelty.

These findings suggest a different interpretation of the discrepant evidence for object representation from the studies reviewed above. Recall that infants steadfastly refuse to retrieve occluded objects until about 9 months (e.g., Piaget, 1954), despite evidence from preferential looking experiments that infants as young as 3 months represent such objects (e.g., Baillargeon & DeVos, 1991). These contrasting findings may stem from differences between infants' two systems for representing objects. Distinct systems subserving object perception and object-directed reaching, residing in distinct cortical visual pathways, have been proposed to exist in adult monkeys and humans (Goodale & Milner, 1992; see Goodale, 1995, for a discussion of the relevant research with humans; see also Ungerleider & Mishkin, 1982). Although these pathways are interconnected and exchange information to some degree in mature animals (DeYoe & Van Essen, 1988; see also below), their functional connections may increase over postnatal life. Thus the perceptual system may represent hidden objects early in development, but its representations may not be available to the system guiding actions on objects.[2]

---

[2] A second potential explanation for the discrepant findings of reaching and preferential looking studies has been proposed by Munakata (in press) and roots infants' inability to act on hidden objects in an inability to maintain representations of objects while they are hidden. In preferential looking experiments, infants must extrapolate the hidden motion of an object but are not constrained as to when they perform this extrapolation. It is possible that infants predict how the object will move before it leaves their view and then compare the predicted with the perceived location of the object after it returns to view. Alternatively, infants may extrapolate the motion of the object backward from its point of reappearance to its point of disappearance, reconstructing the hidden behavior of the object only after the fact. In each of these cases, infants must represent object motion that they do not perceive, but they do not need to keep an object in mind during the time that it is hidden (Spelke, Breinlinger, Macomber, & Jacobson, 1992, p. 620). In studies of reaching for occluded objects, in contrast, infants must act on a representation of an object while it is hidden. Limitations on this ability could explain both infants' failure to reach for stationary objects that are hidden behind occluders and infants' failure to maintain a predictive reach for an object during a brief period of occlusion. Current experiments are attempting to test this explanation by investigating whether, in preferential looking experiments, infants can actively maintain a representation of a hidden object (Munakata, in press).

If systems for perceiving and for acting on objects initially operate in relative independence, then important changes might occur over cognitive development as these systems become intercoordinated. As adults, we are able to draw on all our powers of reasoning in order to locate a hidden object: we mentally retrace our steps, eliminate physically impossible locations, and deduce the set of places the object might occupy. In principle, any knowledge at our disposal may inform this search, giving us flexibility that infants appear to lack. Nevertheless, even adults' object-directed actions show limitations that are reminiscent of the limitations found in infants. When we attempt to catch a rapidly moving object, we are well advised to keep our eyes on it: sudden, brief occlusion or blackout of an object's trajectory impairs the accuracy of mature reaching (e.g., Whiting & Sharp, 1974). Conversely, adults' perception of object properties such as length is prone to distortions that do not hinder reaching and grasping (Aglioti, DeSouza, & Goodale, 1995; Vishton & Cutting, 1995). These findings suggest that systems for perceiving objects and for acting on objects remain partially distinct for adults, and that mature abilities to coordinate these systems are hard-won achievements that are limited in accuracy, slow in execution, and inconsistent in application.

D. Summary: Object Representations in Infancy

The literature reviewed above supports a number of conclusions. First, capacities to represent and reason about objects emerge at an early age and develop synchronously with capacities to perceive and manipulate objects. Early representations of objects accord with three principles capturing general and highly reliable constraints on how objects behave: continuity, cohesion, and contact (Figure 1). These principles also guide infants' perception of objects, suggesting that a common system of representation underlies object perception and physical reasoning (see Spelke & Van de Walle, 1993, for discussion). Finally, the continuity principle guides infants' apprehension of object identity, before the age at which infants trace the identity of inanimate objects by using knowledge of specific object properties and kinds. Nevertheless, the continuity principle does not appear to guide early-developing actions on objects such as object-directed reaching. Comparisons of the extrapolations of object motion revealed by preferential looking tasks and reaching tasks suggest that infants have at least two systems for representing objects and extrapolating object motions: one system guiding their predictive actions on objects and a second system guiding their interpretations of observed events in which objects move from view.

Studies of adults and older children suggest that the processes by which infants represent objects persist over development. Adults who are prevented from naming objects, or who must respond to visual displays rapidly, appear to trace object identity only in accord with spatiotemporal properties of object motion, whereas adults who reach for rapidly moving objects extrapolate object motion in accord with inertia and are perturbed by periods of occlusion. In addition, adults appear to reason most accurately and consistently about the aspects of object motion that guide infants' reasoning in preferential looking experiments. Whereas adults easily and accurately apply the principles of continuity, cohesion, and contact in reasoning about objects, we often have more difficulty, and make more errors, when we must apply the principle of inertia (McCloskey, 1983, discusses errors in adults' reasoning about inertia). This last phenomenon suggests that the principles guiding early object representations remain central to mature reasoning (Spelke, 1994).

Despite these parallels, adults and older children succeed in representing objects, apprehending object identity, and extrapolating object motion under conditions where infants fail. Studies of children and adults converge to suggest two sources of developmental change. First, children and adults are able to consider an object as a member of a kind, and they can use language to single out and remember kinds of individuals. This change may lead children to become increasingly sensitive to object properties that are informative about object kinds, and to use information about those properties to trace identity. Second, children and adults are able to use knowledge of the behavior of objects to guide actions on objects. In particular, they can use knowledge that objects exist continuously to guide their search for an object that has moved from view. Both changes may depend on emerging abilities to relate distinct representational systems to one another, using representations constructed by one system to guide processes normally subserved by a different system. We return to this change in the next section, because it appears to contribute to the development of spatial representation.

III. DEVELOPING KNOWLEDGE OF SPACE

Like many other species, humans construct representations of the surrounding layout and of the locations of objects. Humans and other animals use spatial representations to keep track of where they are, to navigate from place to place, and to guide their search for objects (see Gallistel, 1990; McNaughton, Knierim, & Wilson, 1995, for reviews). Do these accomplishments depend on a unitary representation of the environment that guides all spatial behavior, or do navigation and object localization depend on a number of distinct representations? If distinct representations underlie performance of different spatial tasks, how do the processes that construct these representations interact, and how do their interactions change with development?

In this section, we consider experiments on infants' and young children's developing knowledge of their own spatial position and of the positions of objects. Because the perceptual systems that give rise to our primary awareness of space are discussed in the chapter by Kellman, we focus on children's abilities to represent the locations of hidden objects over the course of their own movement and to reorient themselves after they have lost track of their own position and heading. Studies of these abilities suggest that mechanisms for representing space emerge early in development and capture the information about spatial position that was most reliable in the environments in which humans and other mammals evolved. These studies further suggest that young children have multiple, task-specific systems for representing space, and that developmental changes in spatial representation depend on the child's growing ability to relate these distinct systems to one another.

A. Aspects of Spatial Knowledge

Investigators from many different theoretical perspectives agree that successful navigation depends on processes for extracting the invariant geometric relations among significant locations in the environment, and that these relations become available to humans and other animals as they move about (e.g., Gallistel, 1990; Gibson, 1979; McNaughton et al., 1995). To navigate successfully in the manner of human adults and other animals, a child must come to draw on a number of processes that inform her about her own movements and about the spatial relations among objects. First, she must be able to perceive and represent the spatial locations of objects relative to herself and from a single perspective (see Huttenlocher, Newcombe, & Sandberg, 1994, discussed below). Information about such "egocentric" locations can be derived from vision, audition, and reaching and is often redundantly specified (for a review see Kellman, 1993). As a child moves, she must be able to perceive that environmental locations remain constant despite their changing egocentric directions (Kellman, 1993), she must perceive the direction and extent of her motion, and she must use information about her own motion and about the unchanging positions of objects to compute changes in her own position (see Bremner, Knowles, & Andreasen, 1994, and below). Information for one's own motion is available in changing optic, acoustic, and kinesthetic arrays (Gibson, 1979) and is used by a wide variety of mobile animals to compute accurate representations of their own changing positions (Gallistel, 1990). Finally, the child must form enduring representations of those spatial relations among objects that are independent of her own position and therefore remain invariant as her position changes. These environment-centered or "allocentric" representations are discussed at length in upcoming sections.

B. Infants' Knowledge of the Spatial Locations of Objects

As adult humans and other mammals explore new environments, they form allocentric representations of significant locations (e.g., Loomis et al., 1993; Montgomery, 1952; Morris, 1981; O'Keefe & Nadel, 1978; Rieser, Guth, & Hill, 1986; Tolman, 1948). When in human life do we become able to form and use such representations? Many of the experiments addressing this question with human infants use variations on a method developed by Montgomery (1952), who studied spatial representation in adult rats, and so we begin by summarizing Montgomery's experiments.

Montgomery's studies are based on a behavioral pattern that rats often exhibit in the laboratory: When food is placed at two locations in a maze, rats tend to collect the food by taking alternating trips to the two locations. Because the rats in early studies always began their trips from a single starting position, their "spontaneous alternation" could reflect either a tendency to alternate two responses (i.e., turning left and turning right) or a tendency to alternate visits to two places (i.e., the food stored in the northern and southern end of the maze). In a series of experiments, Montgomery distinguished these possibilities by allowing rats to search for the food from variable starting positions. Her studies clearly showed that rats alternated their visits to the two places, not their performance of the two responses. This and other experiments (e.g., Tolman, 1948; see Gallistel, 1990, for a review) suggest that the rats formed an allocentric representation of their surroundings, and that this representation guided their locomotion through the maze.

In contrast, Piaget suggested that human infants and young children represent the space around them egocentrically, failing to take account of changes in their own positions when they search for hidden objects (Piaget, 1952, 1954). Piaget's conclusion was based on observations that have been amply confirmed by subsequent studies. In one study similar to that of Montgomery (1952), for example, infants watched as a toy was placed in one of two wells standing side by side on a table, the wells were covered, and infants reached for the toy on several familiarization trials (Bremner & Bryant, 1977) (Figure 9). Infants then were moved to the opposite side of the table and again were allowed to reach for the toy, which was hidden in the same well for half the infants and the opposite well for the others. Regardless of where the toy was hidden, 9-month-old infants tended to reach to the new well, repeating the action that had revealed the toy on the familiarization trial. Acredolo (1978) obtained similar results using a paradigm in which 6-, 11-, and 16-month-old infants learned to anticipate with a head turn the appearance of an experimenter in a window to their right or left. After being moved to the opposite side of the room, nearly all the 6-month-old infants and most of the 11-month-old infants turned toward

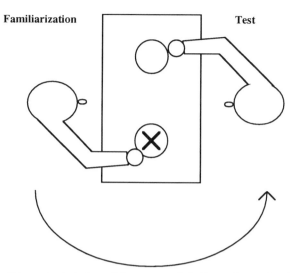

FIGURE 9   Schematic depiction of the setup and findings of a study of infant spatial representation. (After Bremner, 1978.)

the wrong window to look for the experimenter. Only the 16-month-old children searched the allocentrically correct position, as rats would be expected to do.

Although these results suggest that the infants failed to represent the allocentric position of the hidden object, this failure may have occurred in part because the task conditions encouraged young children to learn a particular motor response to bring about a desired result (Bremner, 1978). In further tests using procedures designed to minimize response learning, younger infants were found to form allocentric representations of the locations of events. For example, McKenzie, Day, and Ihsen (1984) trained 6- and 8-month-old infants to anticipate the emergence of a person at one of several locations, over variations in the infant's own heading. On test trials, infants were turned to face in a new direction and were cued that the person was about to appear. Infants tended to look in a novel egocentric direction toward the correct allocentric position. These and other findings (e.g., Bremner, 1978; Keating, McKenzie, & Day, 1986; Landau & Spelke, 1984; Rieser, 1979) suggest that 6- to 9-month-old infants have some ability to represent space in an environment-centered framework. In contrast to adult rats, however, infants are prone to look or reach to egocentric locations when they act repeatedly on an object viewed from a single location and direction (Acredolo, 1990).

When children succeed at responding correctly to an object's allocentric position, what processes underlie their achievement? One solution to the above localization tasks is to (1) perceive and represent the allocentric position of a significant location before one moves; (2) compute the extent of one's own motion; (3) use information about one's motion to update the representation of one's allocentric position; and finally (4) combine knowledge of the allocentric positions of the self and of the significant location to compute the new egocentric position toward which one now 'must move or turn. Rats and other mammals appear to engage in all these processes (see Gallistel, 1990, for review). It is not clear, however, that young children engage in them.

In the above object localization tasks, young children are better able to respond to the allocentric position of an object when that position is perceptually distinct. For example, the infants in Bremner's (1978) experiments were more likely to find the hidden toy in the correct well when the toy was covered by a cloth of a distinctive brightness, and the 11-month-old infants in Acredolo's (1978) experiments were more apt to look at the correct window if it was surrounded by a bright yellow star (see also Acredolo & Evans, 1980; Keating et al., 1986; Rieser, 1979). The borders of the setting in which an object is hidden also appear to mark the object's location for young infants (Keating et al., 1986; Wilcox et al., 1994).

These findings suggest that infants, like other mammals, can use visible landmarks as information for the locations of unseen objects and events. The findings raise further questions, however, about the nature of the representations and processes guiding infants' successful performance in these tasks. For example, do landmarks allow infants to form an allocentric representation of a location, or do they allow the formation of a direct association between themselves and the hidden object, permitting the object to be located by perceptual guidance rather than by spatial knowledge? (See O'Keefe & Nadel, 1978, for extensive discussion of these contrasting strategies for locating objects.) If proximity to a landmark facilitates true spatial knowledge, how much of the environment is incorporated into the infant's spatial representation? Experiments provide evidence that landmarks placed far from a hidden object are less effective as guides to object search (Acredolo & Evans, 1980), suggesting either that the landmark acts as a perceptual beacon or that the infant's spatial representation includes information only in the vicinity of the object. Further experiments could distinguish these possibilities.

As children become adept at independent locomotion in the second year of life, their representations of locations in the environment become more precise, and they become better able to keep track of a hidden object's location in the absence of visible landmarks. For example, Huttenlocher et al. (1994) showed 16- to 24-month-old children a toy being hidden in a long and narrow homogeneous sandbox, smoothed the surface of the sand, called the child's attention away from the display while she remained stationary or turned 180°, and then encouraged her to find the toy. Even the youngest subjects searched for the hidden toy fairly accurately, without any direct landmark indicating its position and independent of the presence of landmarks in the background. By 16 months, children evidently encode and use abstract distance information rather than having to rely on a direct-associative, perceptual guidance strategy. In a further experiment, children were translated to a new position between hiding and search. Even the youngest subjects succeeded in locating the toy, suggesting that they formed allocentric representations of the environment, updated their own position within the environment, and deployed this knowledge to guide their search. Other studies provide converging evidence that 2-year-old children have an allocentric representational capacity (e.g., Acredolo, Adams, & Goodwyn, 1984), although children sometimes have trouble updating their own position (Bremner et al., 1994).

In further studies, young children used allocentric representations to determine the shortest route to a goal. Garino and McKenzie (1988) showed 18- to 24-month-old children an environment containing a chair in which their parent sat behind an L-shaped barrier. After viewing the chair and barrier from overhead or on the ground, the child was placed facing one side of the barrier (such that both the mother and the second side of the barrier were hidden) and was encouraged to move to the mother. Children reliably moved to the mother on the shorter route, avoiding the hidden side of the barrier. The children evidently represented the hidden goal and barrier and used this representation to guide their locomotion.

To locate an object from a novel position in the absence of landmarks, children must represent their own changing position relative to the object. A wide variety of animals accomplish this task through a process of path integration, in which the moving animal updates its position in accord with information about its direction, speed, and acceleration (Mittelstaedt & Mittelstaedt, 1980; Muller & Wehner, 1988; see Gallistel, 1990, for review and discussion). Research with humans provides evidence that path integration is reasonably accurate in adults (e.g., Loomis et al., 1993; Rieser, Guth, & Hill, 1986) and functional in young children (Bremner et al., 1994; Landau, Spelke, & Gleitman, 1984; Lepecq, 1984; Rider & Rieser, 1988) and infants (Lepecq & Lafaite, 1989).

Infants who are tested in the spatial localization tasks described above show higher levels of allocentric localization when they are able to move themselves actively from place to place (Acredolo et al., 1984; see Acredolo, 1990, for discussion) and have prior experience with independent locomotion. Infants who know how to crawl, or who have learned to locomote in a walker, show higher levels of allocentric responding than infants of the same age who have not begun to crawl or use a walker (Bertenthal, Campos, & Barrett, 1984). It is noteworthy that the onset of hands-and-knees crawling correlates with improved allocentric responding when objects in the environment remain in fixed positions but does not correlate with improvement in infants' ability to track changes in the position of a movable object (Bai & Bertenthal, 1992). This dissociation suggests that the increase in allocentric responding by locomoting infants is brought about by the use of path integration or perceptual tracking of fixed environmental positions during self motion, rather than by increased attention to the environment in general.

Studies of young children provide evidence that they update their position without guidance from direct landmarks by means of computations based partly on internal representations of their own movements. For example, Lepecq (1984) familiarized 4- to 6-year-old children with a table in a featureless circular room containing four featurally identical and symmetrically placed buttons, one of which could be pushed to activate a sound (Figure 10). After a child became familiar with the location of the active button, she was blindfolded and walked a variable distance around the table (from $\frac{1}{4}$ turn to more than one complete revolution). The child's ability to represent the extent of her displacement and to compute her new position was assessed by removing the blindfold, encouraging her to activate the button that produced the sound, and then asking her to return to her initial position. At all ages, children tended to press the correct button and to

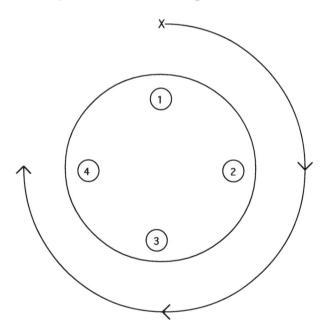

FIGURE 10   Schematic depiction of the display used to test children's path integration abilities. A blindfolded child began at X and walked a variable distance on the path indicated by the arrow. (After Lepecq, 1984.)

return to their starting position with above-chance accuracy, and their two performance measures were highly related. These and other findings (Landau et al., 1984; Lepecq & Lafaite, 1989; Rider & Rieser, 1988) provide evidence that children keep track of the distance and direction in which they move, even in the absence of immediate visual information, and that they use this information to derive the allocentric positions of objects.

C. Spatial Reorientation

We turn now to studies of children's abilities to relocate themselves when they are disoriented. Although animals regularly use path integration and other processes to keep track of their changing positions as they move through the environment, many animals also have systems for re-establishing their position when the path integration system fails and they lose their sense of where they are. To reorient itself in a familiar environment, a disoriented animal must perform some comparison between the environment it now perceives and a representation of the environment it remembers. A variety of studies suggest that this comparison process relies on a representation of the *geometry* of the perceived and remembered environment, a representation of surrounding surfaces, hills, valleys, and enclosures that captures information about the shapes and dispositions of these surfaces (Gallistel, 1990).

The clearest evidence for geometry-based reorientation in animals comes from experiments by Cheng and Gallistel (Cheng, 1986; Margules & Gallistel, 1988; see also Gallistel, 1990). Because their studies are direct precursors to research with young children, we describe one representative experiment in detail (Cheng, 1986) (Figure 11). Cheng and colleagues brought hungry rats into a closed rectangular test chamber, showed them the location of a food supply that was partially buried within the chamber, and then removed the animals, disoriented them, and returned them to the chamber where the food was now fully buried. Based on the studies of rats reviewed above, Cheng assumed that the rats represented the allocentric position of the food during their first encounter with the room (e.g., a rat might

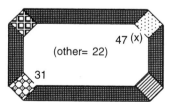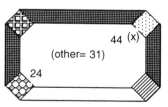

FIGURE 11   Schematic depiction of the testing chambers and the rats' search patterns in an experiment by Cheng (1986).

represent the food as located at the room's northern corner). In order to use this representation to locate the food after disorientation, the rats now needed to re-establish their own sense of orientation (e.g., determining their present heading with respect to north).

Rats were presented with a variety of sources of information that, in principle, could serve to establish their current heading: The corners of the chamber were decorated with distinctive patterns and suffused with distinctive odors, and the brightness of one wall of the chamber contrasted sharply with that of the others. To the investigators' initial surprise, the rats failed to use this information. Instead, rats searched with high and equal frequency at the correct food location and at the geometrically equivalent, opposite location in the room, the two locations that stood in the correct geometric relation to the shape of the test chamber (Figure 11). These findings suggest that the rats reoriented themselves and located the food in accord with the shape of the environment and not in accord with nongeometric properties of the environment.

The failure of rats to reorient by nongeometric information almost certainly did not stem from an inability to detect or attend to that information. Nongeometric properties of an environment such as the brightness of a wall and the quality of an odor are detected by rats in many situations and are used by them in other spatial tasks (see Gallistel, 1990, for a review). Indeed, rats have been shown to learn, over a long series of trials, the locations of stable nongeometric features of the environment (Cheng, 1986; Knierim, Kudrimoti, & McNaughton, in press). These findings suggest that a task-specific system for representing the shape of the environment underlies rats' reorientation in this situation. This system may be used for reorientation in all but the most familiar environments (McNaughton et al., 1995).

Would humans show the same limitations as rats? To address this question, we adapted Cheng and Gallistel's method for studies of human adults and children (Hermer & Spelke, 1994, in press). In our first study, adult subjects were brought into a rectangular room, watched as an experimenter hid an object in one corner, closed their eyes and inertially rotated themselves until they were disoriented, and finally opened their eyes and searched for the hidden object. Adults were tested in a white, rectangular room with no distinctive nongeometric landmarks to break the room's symmetry, and also in a rectangular room with one blue wall (Figure 12A). Like rats, human adults tested in the entirely white room searched with high and equal frequency at the correct corner and at the geometrically equivalent opposite corner. This result indicates that adults were disoriented, that they encoded the shape of the room, and that they used this geometric information to reorient themselves. Unlike rats, human adults searched the correct corner almost exclusively in the room with one blue wall. Adults evidently were able to conjoin geometric with nongeometric information so as to search in a location "to the *left* of the *blue* wall."

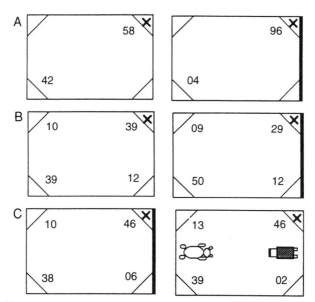

FIGURE 12   Schematic depiction of the rooms and subject search patterns in studies of children's and adults' ability to reorient themselves. (A) The percentage of search in each corner by adults in the all-white room (left) and the room with one blue wall (right). (B) The percentage of search by children 18–24 months in the same two rooms. (C) The percentage of search by children the same age in the room with one blue wall (left) and the room with toy truck and toy bear landmarks (right). (After Hermer and Spelke, 1994.)

We next tested children 18–24 months of age in these two conditions, using a similar procedure. In the all-white room, young children searched equally often at the correct corner and the geometrically equivalent opposite corner (Figure 12B). This search pattern indicated that they, too, were disoriented and that they reoriented in accord with a representation of the shape of their surroundings, like adults and rats. In the room with one blue wall, to our surprise, children continued to search equally at the two correctly shaped corners, irrespective of the location of the blue wall. Children's performance therefore resembled that of rats and contrasted with that of adults.

Further experiments explored a variety of possible reasons for children's failure to reorient in accord with the room's nongeometric properties. For example, we investigated whether children would reorient more effectively if the symmetry of the room were broken by more salient nongeometric information, by testing children in a room containing two distinctive toys of similar global dimensions but different colors, textures, and identities, each placed between two corners flanking a short wall (Figure 12C). We also investigated whether children would reorient by using nongeometric landmarks if they were given several minutes to play with each landmark before the study. These manipulations had no effect on performance: children continued to search equally at the two geometrically appropriate corners, suggesting that they reoriented exclusively in accord with the shape of the room (Hermer & Spelke, 1994) (Figure 12C). Finally, we investigated whether children would reorient in accord with nongeometric information when the relevant information was encountered directly during search for the object. In this study, the object was hidden inside one of two identically shaped containers of different colors, textures, and patterning, placed in symmetrical locations in the rectangular room (Figure 13A). Disoriented children searched these two containers with equal frequency, again failing to use nongeometric information to reorient themselves.

Young children's consistent failure to reorient in accord with nongeometric properties of the room such as the color of a wall, the identity of a nearby object, or the color and texture of the hiding place contrasts with oriented children's successful use of nongeometric information to relocate a hidden object. Recall that infants and young children who change position within an environment are aided in their search for a movable object by landmarks such as a cover of a distinctive brightness (Bremner, 1978) or a window of a distinctive color and pattern (Acredolo, 1978). Because this contrast suggests that reorientation and object search depend on task-specific systems for representing the environment, our next experiments tested that suggestion more directly.

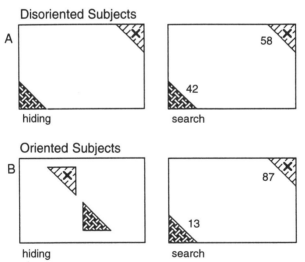

FIGURE 13   Schematic depiction of the rooms and children's search patterns in a study contrasting children's ability to reorient themselves and to locate a moving object. (A) The percentage of search in each container by children who were disoriented. (B) The percentage of search by oriented children who located an object in a movable container. (After Hermer and Spelke, in press.)

In one set of studies, children searched for a toy hidden in one of two distinctive containers in opposite corners of the all-white, rectangular room (Hermer & Spelke, in press) (Figure 13). Children in one condition were given the standard reorientation task: After an object was hidden in one corner, children closed their eyes, were turned until they were disoriented, opened their eyes, and searched for the object. In a second condition, the two containers stood in the center of the room while the object was hidden, children closed their eyes but remained at rest while the containers were placed in the same corners as in the first condition, and then children opened their eyes and searched for the object.

The children in these two conditions faced exactly the same environment at the time of object search, but their tasks were different. Because those in the first condition had lost track of their own position, they needed to reorient themselves in order to find the object. In contrast, children in the second condition were oriented but had lost track of the position of the object, because the object and its container were moved while their eyes were closed. Children's search patterns differed markedly in the two conditions: Whereas disoriented children searched the two containers equally, oriented children preferentially searched the container with the appropriate nongeometric properties (see Figure 13). This finding suggested that distinct representations underlie reorientation and search for movable objects.

A final, double dissociation experiment provided strong support for this suggestion. In this experiment, we again compared object search by children who were disoriented and children who were not. All subjects searched for an object in a distinctively colored and patterned container, after first watching as the object was hidden in one of two containers flanking a short wall of the rectangular room (Figure 14). Then the subjects closed their eyes (and, in one condition, were disoriented) while the two containers were moved quietly across the room to the opposite short wall (Figure 14). This transformation broke the original associations between the geometric and nongeometric properties of the object's hiding location: For example, if the object originally was hidden in a pink container on the left side of a short wall, the pink container now appeared on the right side of a short wall.

Although both disoriented and oriented children viewed exactly the same environment throughout this experiment, the thesis of task-specific systems for reorienting and for locating movable objects predicts that their search performance would differ on the first search trial (before all the children discovered that the toy had moved with one of the containers). Because disoriented children found themselves in a room that was geometrically equivalent to the room in which the toy was hidden, they should not notice that the containers had moved and should confine their search to the corner with appropriate geometry. In contrast, oriented children should infer at

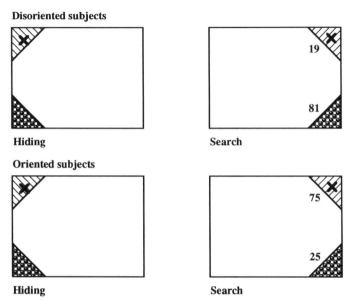

FIGURE 14   Schematic depiction of the room and children's search patterns on their first trial in a study contrasting children's ability to reorient themselves and children's ability to locate a movable object. (After Hermer and Spelke, 1995.)

once that the containers have moved (because, e.g., the two containers previously located to a child's left now appeared to her right). Like the children in the previous experiment, therefore, they should search for the toy in the container with the correct nongeometric properties. As Figure 14 indicates, these predictions were supported: Disoriented subjects searched the geometrically appropriate container, whereas oriented subjects searched the nongeometrically appropriate container.

This last experiment provides evidence that reorientation depends on spatial representations that are task-specific: When children are unsure of their position, they rely on a representation of the shape of the environment to reorient themselves; when they are trying to locate a movable object, they rely on the properties of the container holding it. A similar dissociation has been found in adult rats (Biegler & Morris, 1993). Moreover, these representations are informationally encapsulated: they operate only on a subset of the information that the child has perceived and currently holds in mind. When children closed their eyes before the first search trial, they had no way of knowing whether they would be called on to reorient themselves or to find a displaced object. The subsequent search performance of oriented children therefore provides evidence that all the children encoded the non-geometric properties of the box in which the toy was hidden at the start of the trial. Nevertheless, the disoriented children searched for the object by geometry alone: They appeared unable to conjoin geometric and nongeometric information about the object's location so as to infer that the object had moved. Task-specificity and informational encapsulation are hallmarks of modular cognitive systems (Fodor, 1983). The present findings therefore are consistent with the thesis that reorientation depends on a "geometric module" (Cheng, 1986).

Children and rats may appear unintelligent when they reorient themselves in accord with the shape of the environment. Geometry-based reorientation is not likely to be an adaptive strategy in today's carpentered, symmetrical settings, where distinctive colors and patterns (for humans) and distinctive odors (for rats) might signal orientation more effectively than the shape of the layout. Over the course of mammalian evolution, however, the shape of an animal's surroundings may have been the most reliable kind of information specifying environmental locations and directions. Despite changes in foliage, snowfalls, fires, and other events that occur during an animal's lifetime, the macroscopic shape of the environment, its hills, cliffs, and ravines, would have persisted. Studies of reorientation suggest that young children reorient in accord with the most reliable information available in the environments in which mammals evolved.

Many questions remain concerning the nature of the spatial representations guiding young children's reorientation: For example, are young children's geometric representations egocentric or allocentric? Do these representations include the whole environment or only local views of it, and do they capture movable or only fixed features of the environment? Studies investigating some of these questions are in progress. We close, however, by raising three interrelated questions about the development of spatial reorientation. First, when do children begin to use geometric and nongeometric information more flexibly in reorientation tasks? Second, does the geometric system found in children and rats persist over this developmental change, or is it reorganized as older children begin to orient more flexibly? Finally, what underlies adults' more flexible performance?

In order to approach these questions, we began to investigate developmental changes in spatial representations by repeating the reorientation studies with 3- and 6-year-old children. In the rectangular room with one blue wall, disoriented children searched for an object that was hidden either directly behind the blue fabric or in a corner next to the blue wall. When the object was hidden behind the blue wall, children of both ages succeeded on nearly all trials (Figure 15). When the object was hidden in a corner, children aged 6–6½ years succeeded almost as well as adults, but younger children searched equally at the two geometrically appropriate corners (Hermer, 1994). These findings suggest that the ability to use nongeometric information does not emerge in an all-or-none fashion: children come to use the blue wall to locate an object behind it well before they can use the blue wall to locate an object to its left.

The ages at which children succeeded at each of the above search tasks

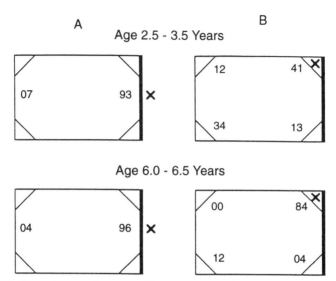

FIGURE 15   Schematic depiction of the rooms and children's search patterns at direct and indirect reorientation tasks.

roughly matched the ages at which a separate group of children, whose conversations were recorded in the CHILDES language database (Mac-Whinney, 1991), began producing phrases that would have uniquely specified object location and orientation. At about 2½–3 years, those children began to produce phrases like "behind the X"; at about 6 years, the children started to produce phrases involving "left" and "right" (Hermer, unpublished data, 1994). Although many factors could explain these roughly converging developments, they raise the possibility that cognitive changes related to the development of spatial language lead to increased flexibility in reorientation tasks.

Further research with adults provides tentative support for this suggestion. We have investigated how adults reorient themselves in a room with distinctive geometric and nongeometric properties while they perform other, concurrent tasks. The same type of verbal shadowing task that disrupted adults' ability to encode object properties in Simons's (in press) experiments, reviewed earlier, was found to disrupt adults' ability to use nongeometric information in the reorientation task. In contrast, shadowing had little or no effect on adults' ability to reorient in accord with the shape of the room (Hermer, Spelke, & Nadel, 1995). These findings suggest that the geometric reorientation process found in rats and children is preserved in adults and is impervious to interference from concurrent language production, whereas the ability to use nongeometric information is vulnerable to such interference.

Finally, the suggestion that language underlies the representation of conjunctions of geometric and nongeometric information is supported by studies comparing memory for such conjunctions by speakers of different languages (Levinson, in press). In a significant minority of the world's languages, spatial relationships between objects are not described egocentrically (e.g., "The cow is *to the left* of the horse") but geocentrically (e.g., "The cow is *to the north* of the horse"). Recent experiments with speakers of such languages, and speakers of left/right languages such as English, have probed how the speakers remember and reproduce spatial relations among objects. Subjects are asked to remember two objects in a given spatial relationship while facing in one direction (e.g., a cow to the left/north of a tree) and then are rotated 180° and asked with neutral language to reproduce the relationship. Speakers of egocentric language tend strongly to reproduce the egocentric relationship between the objects, reversing compass point relations. In contrast, speakers of geocentric languages tend to reproduce the geocentric relationship, reversing left/right relations.

Spatial language thus appears to influence the representation of conjunctions of geometric and nongeometric information. Language may provide an especially useful medium for representing conjunctions of spatial and nonspatial properties of the layout. Whereas systems for representing the environmental layout may be confined to capturing geometric information, and systems for representing movable objects may be confined to capturing local properties of objects or surfaces, language can bring these sources of information together, specifying that an object or surface with one set of properties stands in a particular geometric relationship to another object or surface. As children acquire spatial language, they may come to use their language system to encode information more flexibly in spatial tasks.

D. Summary: Spatial Representations in Infants and Young Children

During the second half of the first year, infants become able to represent spatial locations in an environment-centered framework. Although the capacities of young infants to form allocentric spatial representations are limited, they appear to correspond to the allocentric representations formed by human adults and other mammalian species, as these have been assessed by behavioral studies. Infants also are able to maintain a sense of orientation both by using direct perceptual guides when these are available and by using internally generated information about their own changing position. Finally, young children are able to reorient themselves using a representation of the shape of the environment, as do other mammals. In contrast to older children and adults, however, young children do not reorient in accord with nongeometric information that they perceive, remember, and use in other tasks. In this respect, young children resemble adult rats and differ from older humans.

As in the case of object representation, development appears to bring increases in abilities to represent and use spatial information. In reorientation tasks, increases in the flexibility of children's performance roughly coincides with advances in children's use of spatial language. This finding is reminiscent of Xu and Carey's (in press) studies of developmental changes in object perception, and it suggests a linkage of some kind between the development of language and the development of flexible cognitive performance. In addition, adults' more flexible reorientation processes appear to be vulnerable to interference from simultaneous language tasks, although adults' geometric process for reorientation evidently is not. This finding is reminiscent of Simons's (in press) findings in the domain of object representation. It suggests that the geometric process used by young children is preserved in adults, and that this process operates in relative independence from the processes allowing use of nongeometric information. Finally, adults' abilities to conjoin geometric and nongeometric information appear to vary across people whose languages capture different aspects of these relations. All these findings suggest that children's core processes for representing the environment and using spatial representations to guide behavior are supplemented by later-developing, more flexible processes that are connected in some way to language.

IV. THEMES AND PROSPECTS

Although this chapter has focused on a variety of cognitive abilities with different developmental courses and different internal constraints, common themes emerge from our review. First, core representational capacities appear to develop early in life, allowing infants and young children to gain knowledge of objects and places that are not accessible to immediate perception. Second, early-developing representations appear to be attuned to the information that provides the most reliable and effective guide for action and learning. Third, several distinct, task-specific systems appear to underlie children's earliest representational abilities: The object representations that guide infants' apprehension of object identity, for example, appear to be distinct from those that guide object-directed actions such as reaching, and the spatial representations by which young children relocate hidden, movable objects appear to be distinct from those by which they reorient themselves. Infants' cognitive performance may be limited by the task specificity of their representational systems, leading to errors and inconsistencies that are puzzling to adult observers.

Early-developing systems for representing space and objects appear to persist over the course of later development, but children's cognitive performance becomes increasingly flexible as they grow. It is possible that language and associated memory systems contribute to the growth of flexibility by providing a domain-general medium in which the representations constructed by task-specific systems can be conjoined. Whether or not language plays this role, it now seems clear that cognitive advances occur as children link separate knowledge systems together in novel ways (Carey & Spelke, 1994; Karmiloff-Smith, 1992).

Studies of early cognitive development suggest a number of fruitful directions for further inquiry. First, understanding of human cognition may advance considerably from research in comparative cognition, exploring parallels between early-developing cognitive abilities in children and in other animals. Many of the cognitive problems confronting young children are faced by other animals. Studies of the processes by which animals of various species solve these problems may shed light on the processes by which infants and children solve them, while highlighting those aspects of human problem solving that are unique to us (see Gallistel & Gelman, 1992; Thelen, Bradshaw, & Ward, 1981, for additional examples of this approach).

Understanding of human cognition also may advance through studies exploring parallels between early-developing representations and the representations used by adults in tasks that require rapid decisions and discourage use of language. Where such experiments suggest common processes in the adult and child, investigators may exploit the distinct advantages of the two populations to shed further light on the nature of those processes. In particular, studies of adults allow probes into the nature and limits of representations across a broad range of tasks, whereas studies of infants and young children allow focused investigation of the principles and processes by which representations are constructed by individuals who lack an extensive base of knowledge, and whose knowledge systems interact less extensively than those of adults.

Third, future experiments may fruitfully probe the relation between verbal and nonverbal representations, the changes in cognitive performance that occur as children acquire language, and the cognitive differences that arise between speakers of different languages. Language may function as a common, domain- and task-general medium of representation in which children can conjoin the information that their multiple cognitive systems provide. The processes by which separate representations become conjoined, in language and perhaps in other symbolic systems, provide fertile terrain for research.

Finally, we expect fruitful interactions between investigations of the nature and development of cognitive abilities in the young child and investigations of the nature and development of representational systems in the human brain. The principal themes of this chapter—that cognitive systems begin to function early in development, that distinct systems represent different aspects of objects and environments for different purposes, and that the linkages among these systems increase with development—are supported not only by behavioral studies of infants and children but by anatomical and physiological studies of the brains of humans and other mammals. It is now widely believed that the primate cerebral cortex forms at least two partly distinct systems of object representation (e.g. Goodale, 1995) and multiple systems for representing space (e.g. McNaughton et al., 1995). Functional imaging studies suggest that distinct representations are activated in distinct task contexts, even in the presence of the same stimulating events (e.g., Petersen & Fiez, 1993). Behavioral and neural experiments therefore converge to suggest that human cognition is the product of multiple systems of representation, and that human flexibility results in part from the orchestration of these systems.

The study of the neural basis of early cognitive functioning is itself a nascent field (see Diamond, 1990a; Johnson & Gilmore, this volume; Neville, 1995, for promising beginnings). We have not emphasized specific parallels between brain development and cognitive function in this chapter, because so little is known about the early development of the neural structures underlying humans' representations of objects and the spatial layout. With continued study of early cognitive development, human and animal cognition, and brain function, the outlines of these linkages should emerge, bringing new insights into brain and cognitive development.

Acknowledgments

This research was supported by grants to Elizabeth Spelke from NIH (R37 23103) and NSF (INT 9214114) and by a predoctoral fellowship from NIH to Linda Hermer (MH 10607). We thank Rochel Gelman, Terry Au, and Yuko Munakata for perceptive comments and stimulating discussion, and we offer special thanks to Dan Simons, whose clear thinking and astute editing improved this manuscript immeasurably.

References

Acredolo, L. P. (1978). The development of spatial orientation in infancy. *Developmental Psychology, 14,* 224–234.

Acredolo, L. P. (1990). Behavioral approaches to spatial orientation in infancy. In A. Diamond (Ed.), *The development and neural bases of higher cognitive functions. Annals of the New York Academy of Sciences, 608,* 596–607.

Acredolo, L. P., Adams, A., & Goodwin, S. W. (1984). The role of self-produced movement and visual tracking in infant spatial orientation. *Journal of Experimental Child Psychology, 38,* 312–327.

Acredolo, L. P., & Evans, D. (1980). Developmental changes in the effects of landmarks on infants' spatial behavior. *Developmental Psychology, 16,* 312–318.

Aglioti, S., DeSouza, J. F. X., & Goodale, M. A. (1995). Size-contrast illusions deceive the eye but not the hand. *Current Biology, 5,* 679–685.

Aguiar, A., & Baillargeon, R. (1995). *Reasoning about occlusion events in very young infants.* Paper presented at the meeting of the Society for Research in Child Development, Indianapolis, IN.

Arterberry, M. E. (1993). Development of spatiotemporal integration in infancy. *Infant Behavior and Development, 16,* 343–363.

Arterberry, M. E., Craton, L. G., & Yonas, A. (1993). Infants' sensitivity to motion-carried information for depth and object properties. In C. E. Granrud (Ed.), *Visual perception and cognition in infancy*. Hillsdale, NJ: Erlbaum.

Bai, D. L., & Bertenthal, B. I. (1992). Locomotor status and the development of spatial search skills. *Child Development, 63*, 215–226.

Baillargeon, R. (1986). Representing the existence and the location of hidden objects: Object permanence in 6- and 8-month-old infants. *Cognition, 23*, 21–41.

Baillargeon, R. (1987). Object permanence in 3.5- and 4.5-month-old infants. *Developmental Psychology, 23*, 655–664.

Baillargeon, R. (1993). The object concept revisited: New directions in the investigation of infants' physical knowledge. In C. E. Granrud (Ed.), *Carnegie-Mellon Symposia on Cognition: Vol. 23. Visual perception and cognition in infancy*. Hillsdale, NJ: Erlbaum.

Baillargeon, R., & DeVos, J. (1991). Object permanence in young infants: Further evidence. *Child Development, 62*, 1227–1246.

Baillargeon, R., & Graber, M. (1987). Where's the rabbit? 5.5-month-old infants' representation of the height of a hidden object. *Cognitive Development, 2*, 375–392.

Baillargeon, R., Graber, M., DeVos, J., & Black, J. C. (1990). Why do young infants fail to search for hidden objects? *Cognition, 24*, 255–284.

Ball, W. A. (1973, April). *The perception of causality in the infant*. Paper presented at the meeting of the Society for Research in Child Development, Philadelphia.

Bertenthal, B. I., & Campos, J. J. (1990). A systems approach to the organizing effects of self-produced locomotion during infancy. In C. Rovee-Collier & L. P. Lipsitt (Eds.), *Advances in infancy research* (Vol. 6). Norwood, NJ: Ablex.

Bertenthal, B. I., Campos, J., & Barrett, K. (1984). Self-produced locomotion: An organizer of emotional, cognitive, and social development in infancy. In R. Emde & R. Harmon (Eds.), *Continuities and discontinuities in development*. New York: Plenum.

Biegler, R., & Morris, R. G. M. (1993). Landmark stability is a prerequisite for spatial but not discrimination learning. *Nature, 361*, 631–633.

Bogartz, R. S., Shinsky, J. L., & Speaker, C. (1995). *Interpreting infant looking*. Manuscript submitted for publication.

Bornstein, M. H. (1985). Habituation of attention as a measure of visual information processing in human infants: Summary, systematization, and synthesis. In G. Gottlieb & N. A. Krasnegor (Eds.), *Measurement of audition and vision in the first year of life*. Norwood, NJ: Ablex.

Bremner, J. G. (1978). Egocentric versus allocentric spatial coding in nine-month-old infants: Factors influencing choice of code. *Developmental Psychology, 14*, 346–355.

Bremner, J. G., & Bryant, P. E. (1977). Place versus response as the basis of spatial errors made by young infants. *Journal of Experimental Child Psychology, 23*, 162–171.

Bremner, J. G., Knowles, L., & Andreasen, G. (1994). Processes underlying young children's spatial orientation during movement. *Journal of Experimental Child Psychology, 57*, 355–376.

Bushnell, I. W. R., Sai, F., & Mullin, J. T. (1989). Neonatal recognition of mother's face. *British Journal of Developmental Psychology, 7*, 3–15.

Carey, S., & Spelke, E. S. (1994). Domain-specific knowledge and conceptual change. In L. A. Hirschfeld & S. A. Gelman (Eds.), *Mapping the mind: Domain specificity in cognition and culture*. Cambridge: Cambridge University Press.

Cheng, K. (1986). A purely geometric module in the rat's spatial representation. *Cognition, 23*, 149–178.

Clifton, R. K., Rochat, P., Litovsky, R., & Perris, E. (1991). Object representation guides infants' reaching in the dark. *Journal of Experimental Psychology: Human Perception and Performance, 17*, 323–329.

Clifton, R. K., Rochat, P., Robin, D., & Berthier, N. (1994). Multimodal perception in the control of infant reaching. *Journal of Experimental Psychology: Human Perception and Performance, 20,* 876–886.

Cohen, L. B. (1995). *How solid is infants' understanding of solidity?* Paper presented at the meeting of the Society for Research in Child Development, Indianapolis, IN.

Craton, L. G., & Yonas, A. (1990). The role of motion in infant perception of occlusion. In J. T. Enns (Ed.), *The development of attention: Research and theory.* New York: Elsevier/North-Holland.

DeYoe, E. A., & Van Essen, D. C. (1988). Concurrent processing streams in monkey visual cortex. *Trends in Neuroscience, 11,* 219–226.

Diamond, A. (1990a). The development and neural bases of memory functions as indexed by the AB and delayed response tasks in human infants and infant monkeys. In A. Diamond (Ed.), *The development and neural bases of higher cognitive functions. Annals of the New York Academy of Sciences, 608,* 517–536.

Diamond, A. (1990b). Developmental time course in human infants and infant monkeys, and the neural bases of, inhibitory control in reaching. In A. Diamond (Ed.), *The development and neural bases of higher cognitive functions. Annals of the New York Academy of Sciences, 608,* 637–676.

Fodor, J. (1983). *The modularity of mind.* Cambridge, MA: MIT Press.

Gallistel, C. R. (1990). *The organization of learning.* Cambridge, MA: MIT Press.

Gallistel, C. R., & Gelman, R. (1992). Preverbal and verbal counting and computation. *Cognition, 44* 43–74.

Garino, E., McKenzie, B. E. (1988). The development of inference-based navigation in infancy. *Australian Journal of Psychology, 40,* 391–401.

Geach, P. T. (1980). *Reference and generality: An examination of some medieval and modern theories* (2nd ed.). Ithaca, NY: Cornell University Press.

Gelman, R., Durgin, F., & Kaufman, L. (1995). Distinguishing between animates and inanimates: not by motion alone. In D. Sperber, D. Premack, & A. J. Premack (Eds.), *Causal cognition: A multidisciplinary debate.* Oxford: Clarendon.

Gentner, D., & Stevens, K. (1983). *Mental models.* Hillsdale, NJ: Erlbaum.

Gibson, J. J. (1979). *The ecological approach to visual perception.* Boston: Houghton-Mifflin.

Goodale, M. A. (1995). The cortical organization of visual perception and visuomotor control. In D. Osherson (Ed.), *Invitation to cognitive science* (2nd ed.). Cambridge, MA: Bradford/MIT Press.

Goodale, M. A., & Milner, D. A. (1992). Separate visual pathways for perception and action. *Trends in Neuroscience, 15,* 20–25.

Haith, M. M. (1993). Future-oriented processes in infancy: The case of visual expectations. In C. E. Granrud (Ed.), *Carnegie-Mellon Symposia on Cognition: Vol. 23. Visual perception and cognition in infancy.* Hillsdale, NJ: Erlbaum.

Hall, D. G., & Leslie, A. M. (1995). *Tracing the identity of objects as 12 months of age: The role of shape and color.* Paper presented at the meeting of the Society for Research in Child Development, Indianapolis, IN.

Helmholtz, H. L. F. von (1866). Treatise on physiological optics, Vol. III. (Trans. by J. P. C. Southall, Optical Society of America, 1925.)

Hermer, L. (1994, March). *Increasing flexibility for spatial reorientation in humans linked to emerging language abilities.* Poster presented at the First Annual Meeting of the Cognitive Neuroscience Society, San Francisco.

Hermer, L., & Spelke, E. S. (1994). A geometric process for spatial reorientation in young children. *Nature, 370,* 57–59.

Hermer, L., & Spelke, E. S. (in press). Modularity and development: The case of spatial reorientation. *Cognition.*

Hermer, L., Spelke, E. S., and Nadel, L. (1995, November). *Conservation of a process for spatial representation and reorientation based on environmental shape across human adults, children and adult rats.* Poster presented at the 26th Society for Neuroscience Meeting,

Hespos, S. J., & Rochat, P. (1994). *Spatial anticipation by 4- to 8-month-old infants.* Presented at the International Conference on Infant Studies, Paris.

Hirshfeld, L. A., & Gelman, S. A. (1994). Towards a topography of mind: An introduction to domain specificity. In L. A. Hirshfeld & S. A. Gelman (Eds.), *Mapping the mind: Domain specificity in cognition and culture.* Cambridge: Cambridge University Press.

Hofsten, C. von (1983). Catching skills in infancy. *Journal of Experimental Psychology: Human Perception and Performance, 9,* 75–85.

Hofsten, C. von, Feng, Q., Vishton, P., & Spelke, E. S. (1994). *Predictive reaching and head turning for partly occluded objects.* Poster presented at the International Conference on Infant Studies, Paris.

Hofsten, C. von, & Rosander, K. (1994). *Perturbation of target motion during catching.* Manuscript submitted for publication.

Hofsten, C. von, Vishton, P., Spelke, E. S., Feng, Q., & Rosander, K. (1995). *Predictive action in infancy: Head tracking and reaching for moving objects.* Manuscript submitted for publication.

Hood, B., & Willats, P. (1986). Reaching in the dark to an object's remembered position: Evidence for object permanence in 5-month-old infants. *British Journal of Developmental Psychology, 4,* 57–65.

Huntley-Fenner, G., Carey, S., Klatt, L., & Bromberg, H. (1995). *Physical reasoning in infancy: The distinction between objects and non-solid substances.* Manuscript submitted for publication.

Huttenlocher, J. E., Newcombe, N., & Sandberg, E. H. (1994). The coding of spatial relationships in young children. *Cognitive Psychology, 27,* 115–148.

Kahneman, D., & Treisman, A. (1984). Changing views of attention and automaticity. In R. Parasuraman & D. A. Davies (Eds.), *Varieties of attention.* New York: Academic Press.

Kahneman, D., Treisman, A., & Gibbs, B. J. (1992). The reviewing of object files: Object-specific integration of information. *Cognitive Psychology, 24,* 175–219.

Karmiloff-Smith, A. (1992). *Beyond modularity: A developmental perspective on cognitive science.* Cambridge, MA: MIT Press.

Kaufmann-Hayoz, R., Kaufmann, F., & Walther, D. (1990, April). *Moving figures seen through a narrow slit.* Paper presented at the International Conference on Infant Studies, Montreal.

Keating, M. B., McKenzie, B. E., & Day, R. H. (1986). Spatial localization in infancy: Position constancy in a square and circular room with and without a landmark. *Child Development, 57,* 115–124.

Kellman, P. J. (1993). Kinematic foundations of infant visual perception. In C. E. Granrud (Ed.), *Visual perception and cognition in infancy.* Hillsdale, NJ: Erlbaum.

Knierim, J. J., Kudrimoti, H. S., & McNaughton, B. L. (in press). Hippocampal place fields, the internal compass, and the learning of landmark stability. *Journal of Neuroscience.*

Kotovsky, L., & Baillargeon, R. (1994). Calibration-based reasoning about collision events in 11-month-old infants. *Cognition, 51,* 107–129.

Landau, B., & Spelke, E. S. (1984). Geometric complexity and object search in infancy. *Developmental Psychology, 24,* 512–521.

Landau, B., Spelke, E., & Gleitman, H. (1984). Spatial knowledge in a young blind child. *Cognition, 16,* 225–260.

Lepecq, J. C. (1984). Young children's spatial localization after moving. *International Journal of Behavioral Development, 7,* 375–393.

Lepecq, J. C., & Lefaite, M. (1989). The early development of position constancy in a no-landmark environment. *British Journal of Developmental Psychology, 7,* 289–306.

Leslie, A. M. (1988). The necessity of illusion: Perception and thought in infancy. In L. Weiskrantz (Ed.), *Thought without language.* Oxford: Clarendon.

Levinson, S. (in press). Frames of reference and Molyneux's question: Cross-linguistic evidence. In P. Bloom, M. Peterson, L. Nadel, & M. Garrett (Eds.), *Language and space*. Cambridge, MA: MIT Press.

Loomis, J. M., Klatzky, R. L., Golledge, R. G., Cicinelli, J. G., Pellegrino, J. W., & Fry, P. A. (1993). Nonvisual navigation by blind and sighted: Assessment of path integration ability. *Journal of Experimental Psychology: General, 122,* 73–91.

Lucksinger, K. L., Cohen, L. B., & Madole, K. L. (1992). *What infants infer about hidden objects and events.* Paper presented at the International Conference on Infant Studies, Miami.

MacWhinney, B. (1991). *The CHILDES Project: Tools for analyzing talk.* Hillsdale, NJ: Erlbaum.

Mandler, J. M. (1992). How to build a baby II: Conceptual primitives. *Psychological Review, 99,* 587–604.

Mandler, J. M., & McDonough, L. (1993). Concept formation in infancy. *Cognitive Development, 8,* 291–318.

Margules, J., & Gallistel, C. R. (1988). Heading in the rat: Determination by environmental shape. *Animal Learning and Behavior, 16,* 404–410.

McClelland, J. (1994). The interaction of nature and nurture in development: A parallel distributed processing approach. In P. Bertelson, P. Eelen, & G. d'Ydewalle (Eds.), *Current advances in psychological science: Ongoing research.* Hillsdale, NJ: Erlbaum.

McCloskey, M. (1983). Naive theories of motion. In D. Gentner & A. L. Stevens (Eds.), *Mental models.* Hillsdale, NJ: Erlbaum.

McKenzie, B. E., Day, R. H., & Ihsen, E. (1984). Localization of events in space: Young infants are not always egocentric. *British Journal of Developmental Psychology, 2,* 1–9.

McKenzie, B. E., Keating, B. E., & Day, R. H. (1986). Spatial localization in infancy: position constancy in a square or circular room with or without a landmark. *Child Development, 57,* 115–124.

McNaughton, B. L., Knierim, J. J., and Wilson, M. A. (1995). Vector encoding and the vestibular foundations of spatial cognition: Neurophysiological and computational mechanisms. In M. S. Gazzaniga (Ed.), *The cognitive neurosciences.* Cambridge, MA: Bradford/MIT Press.

Mehler, J., Jusczyk, P. W., Lambertz, G., Halsted, N., Bertoncini, J., & Amiel-Tison, C. (1988). A precursor of language acquisition in young infants. *Cognition, 29,* 143–178.

Michotte, A. (1963). *The perception of causality.* Andover, MA: Methuer.

Mittelstaedt, M. L., & Mittelstaedt, H. (1980). Homing by path integration in a mammal. *Naturwissenschaften, 67,* 566–567.

Montgomery, K. (1952). A test of two explanations of spontaneous alternation. *Journal of Comparative and Physiological Psychology, 45,* 287–293.

Moore, M. K., Borton, R., & Darby, B. L. (1978). Visual tracking in young infants: Evidence for object identity or object permanence? *Journal of Experimental Child Psychology, 25,* 183–198.

Morris, R. G. M. (1981). Spatial localization does not require the preserve of local cues. *Learning and Motivation, 12,* 239–260.

Muller, M., & Wehner, R. (1988). Path integration in desert ants. *Proceedings of the National Academy of Sciences, USA, 85,* 5287–5290.

Munakata, Y. (in press). Task-dependency in infant behavior: Toward an understanding of the processes underlying cognitive development. In F. Lacerta, C. von Hofsten, & J. Heimann (Eds.), *Transitions in perception, cognition, and action in early infancy.*

Munakata, Y., McClelland, J. L., Johnson, M. H., & Siegler, R. S. (1995). *Principles, processes, and infant knowledge: Rethinking successes and failures in object permanence tasks.* Manuscript submitted for publication.

Nelson, K. E. (1971). Accommodation of visual tracking patterns in human infants to object movement patterns. *Journal of Experimental Child Psychology, 12,* 182–196.

Neville, H. J. (1995). Developmental specificity in neurocognitive development in humans. In M. S. Gazzaniga (Ed.), *The cognitive neurosciences*. Cambridge, MA: Bradford/MIT Press.

Oakes, L. M., & Cohen, L. B. (in press). Infant causal perception. In C. Rovee-Collier & L. P. Lipsitt (Eds.), *Advances in infancy research* (Vol. 9). Norwood, NJ: Ablex.

O'Keefe, J. O., & Nadel, L. (1978). *The hippocampus as a cognitive map*. Oxford: Oxford University Press.

Perris, E. E., Myers, N. A., & Clifton, R. K. (1990). Long-term memory for a single infancy experience. *Child Development, 61,* 1796–1807.

Petersen, S. E., & Fiez, J. A. (1993). The processing of single words studied with positron emission tomography. *Annual Review of Neuroscience, 16,* 509–530.

Piaget, J. (1952). *The origins of intelligence in childhood*. New York: International Universities Press.

Piaget, J. (1954). *The construction of reality in the child*. New York: Basic Books.

Premack, D., & Premack, A. J. (1995). Intention as psychological cause. In D. Sperber, D. Premack, & A. J. Premack (Eds.), *Causal cognition: A multidisciplinary debate*. Oxford: Clarendon.

Rider, E. A., & Rieser, J. (1988). Pointing at objects in other rooms: Young children's sensitivity to perspective after walking with and without vision. *Child Development, 59,* 480–494.

Rieser, J. J. (1979). Spatial orientation of six-month-olds. *Child Development, 50,* 1079–1087.

Rieser, J. J., Guth, D. A., & Hill, E. W. (1986). Sensitivity to perspective structure while walking without vision. *Perception, 15,* 173–188.

Rose, S. A. (1988). Shape recognition in infancy: Visual integration of sequential information. *Child Development, 59,* 1161–1176.

Rovee-Collier, C. (1990). The "memory system" of prelinguistic infants. In A. Diamond (Ed.), *The development and neural bases of higher cognitive functions. Annals of the New York Academy of Sciences, 608,* 517–536.

Rozin, P. (1976). The evolution of intelligence and access to the cognitive unconscious. In J. M. Sprague & A. M. Epstein (Eds.), *Progress in psychobiology and physiological psychology*. New York: Academic Press.

Simon, T., Hespos, S., & Rochat, P. (1995). Do infants understand simple arithmetic? A replication of Wynn (1992). *Cognitive Development, 10,* 253–269.

Simons, D. J. (in press). *In sight, out of mind: When object representations fail. Psychological Science*.

Simons, D. J., & Keil, F. C. (1995). An abstract to concrete shift in the development of biological thought: The *insides* story. *Cognition, 56,* 129–163.

Sitskoorn, M., & Smitsman, A. (in press). Infant perception of object relations: Passing through or support? *Child Development*.

Skouteris, H., McKenzie, B. E., & Day, R. H. (1992). Integration of sequential information for shape perception by infants: A developmental study. *Child Development, 63,* 1164–1176.

Spelke, E. S. (1994). Initial knowledge: Six suggestions. *Cognition, 50,* 431–445.

Spelke, E. S., Breinlinger, K., Jacobson, K., & Phillips, A. (1993). Gestalt relations and object perception: A developmental study. *Perception, 22,* 1483–1501.

Spelke, E. S., Breinlinger, K., Macomber, J., & Jacobson, K. (1992). Origins of knowledge. *Psychological Review, 99,* 605–632.

Spelke, E. S., Katz, G., Purcell, S. E., Ehrlich, S. M., & Breinlinger, K. (1994). Early knowledge of object motion: Continuity and inertia. *Cognition, 51,* 131–176.

Spelke, E. S., Kestenbaum, R., Simons, D., & Wein, D. (1995). Spatiotemporal continuity, smoothness of motion, and object identity in infancy. *British Journal of Developmental Psychology, 13,* 113–142.

Spelke, E. S., & Van de Walle, G. A. (1993). Perceiving and reasoning about objects: Insights from infants. In N. Eilan, W. Brewer, & R. McCarthy (Eds.), *Spatial representation*. Oxford: Blackwell.

Thelen, E., Bradshaw, G., & Ward, J. A. (1981). Spontaneous kicking in month-old infants: Manifestation of a human central locomotor program. *Behavioral and Neural Biology, 32,* 45–53.

Thelen, E., & Smith, L. B. (1993). A dynamic systems approach to the development of cognition and action. Cambridge, MA: Bradford/MIT Press.

Thelen, E., & Smith, L. B. (1995, April). *A dynamic systems approach to the object concept.* Paper presented at the meeting of the Society for Research in Child Development, Indianapolis, IN.

Tolman, E. C. (1948). Cognitive maps in rats and men. *Psychological Review, 55,* 189–208.

Ungerleider, L. G., & Mishkin, M. (1982). Two cortical visual systems. In D. J. Ingle, M. A. Goodale, & R. J. W. Mansfield (Eds.), *The analysis of visual behavior.* Cambridge, MA: MIT Press.

Van de Walle, G., & Spelke, E. S. (in press). Spatiotemporal integration and object perception in infancy: Perceiving unity vs. form. *Child Development.*

Van de Walle, G., Woodward, A., & Phillips, A. T. (1994). *Infants' inferences about contact relations in a causal event.* Paper presented at the International Conference on Infant Studies, Paris.

Vishton, P. M., & Cutting, J. E. (1995, March). *Veridical size perception for action: Reaching vs. estimation.* Paper presented at the annual meeting of the Association for Research in Vision and Opthamology, Sarasota, FL.

Vishton, P. M., Spelke, E. S. & Hofsten, C. von (1996, April). *Infant reaching is truly predictive and based on an inertia-like principle at 6 months of age.* Paper presented at the International Conference on Infant Studies, Providence, RI.

Wellman, H. M., & Gelman, S. A. (1992). Cognitive development: Foundational theories of core domains. *Annual Review of Psychology, 43,* 337–375.

Whiting, H. T. A., & Sharp, R. H. (1974). Visual occlusion factors in a discrete ball-catching task. *Journal of Motor Behavior, 6,* 11–16.

Wiggins, D. (1980). *Sameness and substance.* Oxford: Blackwell.

Wilcox, T. (1995). *Reasoning about object identity: Infants' use of featural information.* Paper presented at the meeting of the Society for Research in Child Development, Indianapolis, IN.

Wilcox, T., Rosser, R., & Nadel, L. (1994). Representation of object location in 6.5-month-old infants. *Cognitive Development, 9,* 193–210.

Wilcox, T., Rosser, R., & Nadel, L. (1995). *Location memory in young infants.* Manuscript submitted for publication.

Wynn, K. (1992). Addition and subtraction in infants. *Nature, 358,* 749–750.

Xu, F., & Carey, S. (1994, June). *Infants' ability to individuate and trace identity of objects.* Paper presented at the International Conference on Infant Studies, Paris.

Xu, F., & Carey, S. (1995, April). *Criteria for object individuation: A shift between 10 and 12 months.* Paper presented at the meeting of the Society for Research in Child Development, Indianapolis, IN.

Xu, F., & Carey, S. (in press). Infants' metaphysics: The case of numerical identity. *Cognitive Psychology.*

Xu, F., Carey, S., Raphaelidis, K., & Ginzbursky, A. (1995). Twelve-month-olds have the conceptual resources to support the acquisition of count nouns. *Proceedings of the 26th Stanford Child Language Research Forum.*

Xu, F., Carey, S., & Welch, J. (1995). *Infants' ability to use object kind information in object individuation.* Unpublished manuscript.

Cognition and Language

CHAPTER 4

Concepts and Theories

Susan A. Gelman

I. INTRODUCTION

Concepts are fundamental to all of human experience. Naming objects, recognizing novel instances, generalizing from the known to the unknown, making inferences, and learning new information all make use of concepts. Thus, for decades psychologists have been deeply interested in the structure of concepts and their development (Bruner, Goodnow, & Austin, 1956; Bruner, Olver, & Greenfield, 1966; Inhelder & Piaget, 1964; James, 1890). In recent years, the study of concepts has undergone an important shift: whereas concepts were traditionally treated as isolated, atomic units, it is now recognized that they are interrelated and influenced by larger knowledge systems or theories (Murphy & Medin, 1985). This shift has altered current thinking about the very nature of concepts and their organization.

This chapter reviews recent arguments and evidence demonstrating the links between theories and concepts. Theories do not exist apart from concepts, and (more surprising) in many domains concepts do not exist apart from theories (Barrett, Abdi, Murphy, & Gallagher, 1993; Carey, 1985; S. A. Gelman, Coley, & Gottfried, 1994; Keil, 1989; McCauley, 1987; Murphy, 1993; Murphy & Medin, 1985). Thus, a theory of biology includes abstract concepts such as "alive" or "inheritance" and more particular concepts for individual species such as "dog" or "pterodactyl." At the same time, concepts—both concrete and abstract—are imbued with theory. For

Perceptual and Cognitive Development
Copyright © 1996 by Academic Press, Inc. All rights of reproduction in any form reserved.

example, a child's concept of "alive" will reflect whether she has a mature theory of biology or instead thinks that all things that move (including clouds and bicycles) have intentions and desires (Carey, 1985).

What do we mean by "concept" or "theory"? Both are mental representations that give order to experience. Clark (1983, p. 789) defines *concept* as "a set of properties that are associated with each other in memory and thus form a unit." This unit can refer to either an individual (e.g., Socrates) or a category (e.g., birds), and is often encoded in a single word (e.g., animal, mine, mama). In contrast, theories are larger structures that include interrelated sets of beliefs, causal explanations, and predictions (e.g., a theory of mind; see Taylor, this volume). Thus, theories "are sets of interconnected relations, and concepts are the units connected by these relations" (Murphy, 1993, p. 177). Although traditionally scholars have questioned whether young children are capable of forming either kind of construct (Inhelder & Piaget, 1964; Piaget, 1929), a growing body of evidence suggests that children form a rich and complex set of both concepts and tacit theories, beginning in the first year of life.

The structure of the chapter is as follows. First I discuss concepts, raising the question of which aspects change developmentally and which are fundamentally stable throughout life. Then I turn to theories, illustrating with children's beliefs within the particular domain of biology. In the final section, I consider mutual influences of theories on concepts and of concepts on theories.

II. CONCEPTS

A. Conceptual Functions

Concepts[1] serve many important functions: to organize information efficiently in memory, identify novel entities, solve problems, form analogies, enable inferences that extend knowledge beyond what is already known, embody and pass down ideological beliefs, create figurative images (with metaphor and poetry), and so on (S. A. Gelman & Medin, 1993).

At least two of the basic functions of concepts are present in children even before they begin to speak: that of ordering information efficiently, and that of fostering inferences about the unknown. Efficiency is arguably needed for survival (Bruner et al., 1956; Rosch, Mervis, Gray, Johnson, & Boyes-Braem, 1976). If children were unable to categorize, their experiences would be overflowing with individual beings, objects, properties, sensations, and events too numerous to hold in memory. Fortunately, a child's world is not so chaotic. From earliest infancy children form categories that are strikingly similar to those of adults. In their first few months of life, children form categories of speech sounds (Eimas, Siqueland, Jusczyk, & Vigorito, 1971; Mehler et al., 1988; Kuhl, 1985; Werker, 1989), faces

(Cohen & Strauss, 1979; Fagan & Singer, 1979), emotional expressions (Kestenbaum & Nelson, 1990), colors (Teller & Bornstein, 1987), objects (Baillargeon, 1993; Baillargeon, Spelke, & Wasserman, 1985), and cross-modal mappings (Meltzoff & Borton, 1979; Lewkowicz & Turkewitz, 1981; Rose & Orlian, 1991), all of which preserve distinctions that adults find relevant and important. (See Spelke & Hermer, this volume, for review.) Similarly, preverbal children categorize animal species, both real and artificial (Cohen & Younger, 1983; Quinn & Eimas, 1986; Quinn, Eimas, & Rosenkrantz, 1993), on a variety of tasks including habituation, paired preference, and sequential touching (Mandler, Bauer, & McDonough, 1991). By 18 months of age, most children have begun a naming explosion, adding roughly nine new words each day to their vocabulary (Carey, 1978). Assuming that most new words encode concepts, this suggests that 1- and 2-year-old children are adept at concept acquisition.

Less work has documented the inductive function of categories, although it is equally important. Without the inferential capacity of categories, it would be necessary to determine by trial and error how to interact with every new object—to decide, for example, whether an object was suitable for wearing, reading, sitting upon, and so on. On seeing an apple one would not know whether it was edible—regardless of how many apples one had eaten in the past—because it would be an individual whose characteristics need to be discovered anew.

It is not surprising, then, that the capacity to use categories as the basis of inferences also appears to be available to very young children. Rovee-Collier and colleagues found that under appropriate conditions, 3-month-olds can form a novel category-based inference (Hayne, Rovee-Collier, & Perris, 1987). After a baby learns that one mobile shakes in response to his kicking, he infers that other mobiles also shake in response to kicking, particularly if they are also similar in other respects. Baldwin, Markman, and Melartin (1993) demonstrated that infants between 9 and 16 months of age can make specific inductions about novel actions from one category member to another. Baldwin et al. presented infants with a novel toy that produced a nonobvious and unanticipated effect (e.g., a can that wailed when tilted or shook). The subjects were then shown a second toy that closely resembled the original toy but failed to produce the interesting effect (e.g., a wailing can that had been altered so that it made no sound). In their exploratory play, the infants attempted to produce the original effect (e.g., tilting and shaking the silent can), and showed increased and persistent exploration when the second toy failed to meet their expectations. Control conditions demonstrated that children did not show the same degree of interest or exploration of the second toy when the original toy did not produce the interesting effect; nor did they show increased attention or category-specific actions when the second toy was a different kind of object altogether from the first (e.g., if the first was a wailing can and the second was a toy horn).

Thus, 9-month-olds drew category-specific inferences about nonobvious object properties, based on only a single example.

B. Developmental Dichotomies?

Although category functions of efficiency and induction appear early in infancy and may be unchanging developmentally, the content of concepts and their organization into larger systems are open to developmental change. Just how much change is involved has been a question of intense interest and debate. On many traditional accounts, concepts undergo a fundamental, qualitative shift with development. That is, children and adults are often said to be at opposite end points of various dichotomies, moving from perceptual to conceptual (Bruner et al., 1966), from thematic to taxonomic (Vygotsky, 1962), from syntagmatic to paradigmatic (see Nelson, 1977, for review), from concrete to abstract (Piaget, 1951), or from similarity to theories (Quine, 1977).

These developmental dichotomies are intuitively appealing, in part because each promises to capture a broad array of changes in a simple model. Furthermore, in many contexts children do behave in ways that would support one or another of these distinctions.[2] For example, in the well-known conservation error studied by Piaget, children below age 6 or 7 years of age report that an irrelevant transformation leads to a change in quantity (e.g., the volume of liquid in a container increases when the water is poured into a taller, skinnier container; Piaget, 1952). Children appear to focus on one salient but misleading dimension (e.g., height), forgoing a deeper conceptual analysis. Throughout the past several decades there have been many demonstrations that "the preschool-age child is prone to accept things as they seem to be, in terms of their outer, perceptual, phenomenal, 'on-the-surface' characteristics" (Flavell, 1977, p. 79).

However, as an account of what children are *capable* of doing, developmental dichotomies are inadequate (Bauer & Mandler, 1989; R. Gelman, 1978; Gibson & Spelke, 1983; Markman & Hutchinson, 1984; Nelson, 1977). With appropriately sensitive tasks, children sometimes can display competencies that do not emerge in their everyday performance (S. A. Gelman, 1994). For example, Smiley and Brown (1979) found that although first grade children preferred to group pictures thematically (e.g., putting a spider with a web), they were able to sort taxonomically (e.g., putting a spider with a grasshopper) when asked whether there was a different way of answering. The children even provided sensible justifications for their taxonomic choices.

The past twenty years have yielded a greater understanding of children's concepts not only because of methodological advances, with the development of more sensitive techniques for assessing children's knowledge (R. Gelman & Baillargeon, 1983), but also because of changing assumptions about the nature of concepts. According to most developmental dichotomy positions, children's concepts are uniform across domains and across contexts (e.g., uniformly "concrete" or "perceptual"), and adults' concepts have an abstract, logical structure that is lacking in children. More recently, both of these assumptions have been questioned. Specifically, there is now compelling evidence to suggest that: (1) children's concepts are domain specific and context dependent; (2) the internal structure of children's categories often resembles that of adults' categories; (3) for both children and adults, categories are arranged into hierarchical systems that include abstract as well as specific concepts. Below, I review evidence to support these conclusions.

1. Domain Specificity and Context Dependence

Specialized knowledge in particular domains can exert powerful effects on cognition and cognitive development (R. Gelman & Baillargeon, 1983; Hirschfeld & Gelman, 1994; Wellman & Gelman, 1992). Chase and Simon's (1973) classic studies demonstrated that chess experts have superior memory for the position of pieces on a chessboard, although they are no better than nonexperts in their memory for digits. Chi (1978) has demonstrated the same phenomenon in children: child chess experts even outperform adult chess novices, which is an interesting reversal of the more usual developmental finding. In these examples, experts are not *in general* more intelligent or more skilled than novices. The effects are localized within the domain of expertise.

More specifically regarding concept development, it now seems unlikely that a fundamental, age-related shift could be occurring, given that the child's level of conceptual sophistication varies by content area. A clear demonstration of this point is provided by Keil and Batterman (1984): although children consistently shift over time from using misleading "characteristic" features (e.g., defining grandmothers by their gray hair and penchant for baking cookies) to using appropriate "defining" features (defining grandmothers in terms of biological relations), the shift occurs at different ages for different concepts. For example, a child will define moral terms such as "lie" using defining features but relational terms such as "uncle" using characteristic features. Chi, Feltovich, and Glaser (1981), focusing on the domain of physics, also find strong effects of expertise on the features that a problem solver will consider. Similarly, Chi, Hutchinson, and Robin (1989) find that expertise allows children to generate a richer set of inferences, generate causal explanations, and classify taxonomically—all in the domain of expertise (in this case, dinosaurs).[3]

Conceptual structure varies not only by domain but also by task. Even within a domain, children use different information in different contexts, depending on the task or function at hand. For example, although preschool children show the usual thematic bias in a nonlinguistic sorting task, they demonstrate a taxonomic bias when the task involves generalizing a novel word (Baldwin, 1992; Markman & Hutchinson, 1984; Waxman & Gelman, 1986), or when they are rewarded for responding taxonomically (Bauer & Mandler, 1989; Smiley & Brown, 1979). Analogously, children focus on salient perceptual features when the task requires identifying novel category instances (DeVries, 1969; Keil, 1989), but overlook such features when trained to do so (Deak & Bauer, in press), when provided with a task that minimizes the potential to use spatial cues (e.g., when sorting items into a plastic bag rather than on a tabletop; Markman, Cox & Machida, 1981), or when told the identity of a familiar category and then asked to draw inferences about novel properties (S. A. Gelman, Collman, & Maccoby, 1986). Children consider various kinds of information and flexibly deploy different sorting strategies depending on the task, displaying links between task and strategy that are precise and predictable.[4] There cannot be a single or uniform developmental shift, because children are not limited to any single type of concept.

2. Internal Structure of Categories

Measures of early categorization abilities often required children to figure out or apply a single, explicit rule in a perfectly consistent, exceptionless manner. For example, Inhelder and Piaget (1964) used a classification task in which children were shown a variety of pictures or objects and asked to put the ones together that go together. A child in their studies might see an array of triangles, squares, and half rings of different colors. Inhelder and Piaget had several criteria for "correct" performance, including the requirement that children apply a consistent criterion to govern the entire classification. For example, an appropriate response would be to put all the straight-edged pieces in one group and all the curved pieces in another group.

Children typically fail to sort in this manner. Instead, preschool children often make "graphic collections," in which they make pictures with the objects (e.g., making a house, or laying out the figures in a line), or "complexives," in which items are related by local rather than general rules of grouping. So, instead of coming up with attributes that all category members share, children will make successive links between pairs of items (e.g., a child explains the commonalities among bananas, peaches, potatoes, meat, and milk by saying: "Banana and peach are both yellow, peach and potato are round, potato and meat are served together, meat and milk both come from cows"; Olver & Hornsby, 1966). (See also Bowerman, 1978, and Dromi, 1987, for examples of complexives in children's natural language.)

These sorts of responses were taken as evidence that young children's groupings are not true concepts, in part because they are not clear-cut, logical entities. The underlying assumption was that adult categories have necessary and sufficient conditions for determining category membership (e.g., "bachelors" are unmarried, marriageable men; but see Lakoff, 1987).

This was a pervasive idea in a range of disciplines, including linguistics, philosophy, the anthropological study of kinship, and psychiatry (e.g., in which people debate what are the defining features of depression or schizophrenia; Cantor, Smith, French, & Mezzich, 1980). Indeed, the assumption of defining features appears to be part of our folk theory of language (McNamara & Sternberg, 1983).

Yet, a large body of research over the past twenty years suggests that natural language categories cannot be characterized solely in terms of clear-cut boundaries that are determined by individually necessary and jointly sufficient defining features (e.g., E. E. Smith & Medin, 1981). Although criterial features are undoubtedly important in certain circumstances (e.g., to identify your mother's 2-year-old brother as your uncle; Keil, 1989) and for certain categories (e.g., "triangles" are three-sided geometric figures),[5] there is abundant evidence that such features are inadequate to account for all the uses to which categories are put. Currently there is debate regarding which model best characterizes the structure of human categories (Armstrong, Gleitman, & Gleitman, 1983; W. K. Estes, 1986; Margolis, 1994; Medin & Schaffer, 1978; Nosofsky, 1986; Rey, 1983; E. E. Smith, 1995). This debate is beyond the scope of the present chapter; an excellent treatment of the issues is found in E. E. Smith and Medin (1981). For present purposes, the relevant point is that prototype models capture much of how adults reason with categories (Rosch & Mervis, 1975).

The prototype of a category consists of an abstract summary of the category (E. E. Smith, 1995) to which instances are compared when deciding on category membership. In other words, when identifying items, people often decide whether something belongs in the category on the basis of its similarity to the prototype. During this process, the categorizer does not need to consider clear-cut defining features, and category membership is fuzzy. Prototypes have important consequences for how information is processed, stored, and retrieved (see Mervis & Rosch, 1981; E. E. Smith & Medin, 1981, for more extensive review and discussion). For example, subjects rate prototypical category instances as "better" members of the category than atypical instances (e.g., a robin is a "better" bird than an ostrich), suggesting that category members are not all psychologically equivalent. People are faster at classifying prototypes than nonprototypes (E. E. Smith, Shoben, & Rips, 1974). Prototypes are better recalled, even when they have not been seen and only inferred (Posner & Keele, 1970). Prototypical instances are also learned more readily by children than are atypical instances (Anglin, 1977; Mervis & Pani, 1980; Younger & Cohen, 1983).

What is especially important for the present discussion is that both children and adults make use of prototype structure when reasoning about categories (Hayes & Taplin, 1992; Mervis & Rosch, 1981; Younger, 1985), and often neither children nor adults rely on defining features. Thus, in contrast to a developmental dichotomies position, it is not that children fail to appreciate the one true logical structure that adults developed; rather, for some tasks the adult end point looks rather similar to the structures that children have been described as using all along.[6]

3. Hierarchical Systems of Categories

In the examples used to argue for developmental differences, adult concepts are often implicitly portrayed as abstract and not readily captured in a single image (Inhelder & Piaget, 1964). These abstract mental structures stand apart from the more concrete concepts children can readily represent and manipulate. Yet in many domains, categories for both children and adults are universally organized into hierarchical systems (Atran, 1990; Berlin, Breedlove, & Raven, 1973; Rosch et al., 1976) that include both specific and abstract mental units. That is, categories are hierarchically nested such that a general category includes more specific ones. For example, in English the same entity can be classified at an abstract or superordinate level ("animal"), a specific or subordinate level ("terrier" or "Scotch terrier"), or a basic level in between the two extremes ("dog").[7] Hierarchies have the advantage of enabling deductive inferences (e.g., if all animals have leukocytes in their blood, then all giraffes have leukocytes in their blood; Harris, 1975; C. Smith, 1979; Markman & Callanan, 1984) and inductive inferences (e.g., if giraffes and mice have leukocytes in their blood, then all animals may have leukocytes in their blood; Carey, 1985; Osherson, Smith, Wilkie, Lopez, & Shafir, 1990), and enable children to convey a variety of different sorts of contrasts (Horton, 1983; Waxman & Hatch, 1992).

Because of the hierarchical category systems they are constructing, children are not limited to "concrete" or specific concepts. Even beginning language learners have some ability to learn categories at superordinate levels, especially given linguistic contexts that enhance attention to nonbasic levels (S. A. Gelman, Wilcox, & Clark, 1989; Taylor & Gelman, 1989; Waxman, 1990). Furthermore, children are adept at forming "global" (or ontological) categories, such as animate versus inanimate (Mandler et al., 1991; see also Keil, 1979), although these global categories are distinct from (and in fact more abstract than) superordinate categories.

Nonetheless, basic-level categories are the most widely used concepts for both children and adults. Indeed, children often have special difficulties forming categories at nonbasic levels, particularly the superordinate level (Markman & Callanan, 1984; Rosch et al., 1976). The basic-level advantage obtains even when controlling for the amount of experience a child has with the category or category label (Horton & Markman, 1980). Because many standard classification tasks use superordinate-level items (e.g., Inhelder & Piaget, 1964), they probably underestimate children's classification abilities. In other words, a child who appears deficient on a standard categorization task will probably be impressively skillful when the task requires attention to the basic level (Rosch et al., 1976).

C. Summary of Concepts

The view that children's concepts are qualitatively different from those of adults (the "developmental dichotomy" position) has presupposed that children's concepts can be characterized in a single, homogeneous manner. In contrast, I have reviewed evidence that there are strong domain-specific and context-specific effects on children's concepts, so that it is untenable to contrast children's concepts with those of adults in a global way. The developmental dichotomy position also assumes that children's concepts differ from those of adults by lacking an abstract, logical structure (i.e., necessary and sufficient defining features). In contrast, I have reviewed evidence that adults make use of information that cannot be characterized by defining features; rather, both adults and children use prototype structures to identify category instances. Furthermore, I have summarized findings arguing that both children and adults form both specific and abstract concepts. Overall, then, children's concepts share important similarities with those of adults.

III. THEORIES

Throughout childhood, children are acquiring a vast amount of knowledge. They are learning about their own and others' mental lives, about how animals are born and grow and die, about social groupings such as race and gender, about the workings of bicycles and the movements of clouds and countless other topics. Children's knowledge includes more than isolated bits of information or localized procedures for obtaining results (Hatano & Inagaki, 1994; D. Kuhn, 1989); rather, children are constructing coherent systems of knowledge. These knowledge systems enable children to provide causal explanations of phenomena (Sperber, Premack, & Premack, 1995), form questions about the unknown (Callanan & Oakes, 1992), and make sensible predictions (Au, 1994; Wellman, 1990). These conceptual structures are often referred to as intuitive, folk, naive, or common-sense theories.

Intuitive theories differ from scientific theories (see also Brewer & Samarapungavan, 1991; Carey, 1985; S. A. Gelman et al., 1994; Gopnik & Wellman, 1994; Kaiser, McCloskey, & Proffitt, 1986; Karmiloff-Smith & Inhelder, 1975; Keil, 1989; McCloskey, 1983; Murphy & Medin, 1985). An intuitive theory is not as detailed, explicitly formulated, coherent, or directly tested as a scientific theory. Wellman draws a distinction between framework theories and specific theories: framework theories carve out a domain of interest, but unlike scientific theories do not set forth detailed, formal tests. For example, a behaviorist theory of psychology is a framework theory; the Rescorla–Wagner theory of conditioning is a specific theory. Children's belief systems, he notes, resemble framework theories.

An intuitive theory has at least four characteristics: a distinct ontology, domain-specific causal laws, interrelated beliefs, and appeals to unobservables (Gopnik & Wellman, 1994). Ontology refers to the basic categories of existence—what kinds of things there are. Each theoretical domain has a distinct ontology, for example, mental entities are distinct from physical entities. Theories also make use of causal laws that are specific to the domain in question (e.g., force dynamics and gravity do not apply to mental states).

In order to account for these causal relations, people invent powerful, unobservable constructs. Thus, we appeal to force and energy to explain why one object causes another to move; we appeal to gravitational forces to explain why an object falls from a height. In psychology we refer to beliefs and desires. For living things we refer to genetic dispositions and innate potential. Force, gravity, beliefs, desires, and genes are not visible or easily measured. They are constructions designed to explain events that are more readily and directly perceived.

Unobservable constructs are also important because they can lead to classifications in which category instances differ from one another in salient ways yet share properties relevant to the theory. For example, adults generally classify plants and animals together into a category of living things, largely because of a set of beliefs regarding biological commonalities (e.g., both plants and animals grow, reproduce, take in water and nutrients, and can heal themselves). Without such knowledge, there may be no reason for grouping plants and animals together, and indeed, young children often fail to treat them as a single category of "living things" (Carey, 1985). A related point is that adults refrain from classifying together things that seem superficially the same but differ in theory-relevant properties. For example, adults exclude leaf-insects from the category of leaves; although the two entities have similar appearances, there are important differences between the two (e.g., self-sustained motion in the case of the leaf-insect).

A theory perspective introduces many questions concerning cognitive development. When do children's theories first emerge? How are theories structured for children? How do children's early theories change into adult theories, and how continuous or discontinuous is this transformation? Are there universal tendencies in the kinds of theories children construct in particular domains, and if so, are these tendencies also reflected in the theories adults hold? Conversely, to what extent are theories open to influence from cultural and individual knowledge sources? How does knowledge in different domains interact, that is, how do different content-theories "speak" to one another? What aspects, if any, of children's early theories can be predicted or constrained by domain-general principles? How do theories constrain, influence, or become integrated into children's reasoning, problem solving, and memory processes? Although we cannot answer these questions in more than a sketchy way at the moment, it is valuable to keep these larger issues in mind when reviewing the descriptive evidence on children's theories.

From a practical standpoint, it is important to ask how many theories there are for young children. If there are innumerable domains, then a theory approach to cognitive development ceases to be useful; knowledge about any given theory would tell very little about children's cognition more generally. However, if the number of theories children hold is small, then investigating children's theories will provide insight regarding a broad piece of early cognition. Currently, evidence suggests children develop theories in a handful of domains, including number, physics, and psychology, and perhaps biology and substance kind (Wellman & Gelman, 1992).[8]

In the remainder of this section, I illustrate claims about theories using recent research findings. I focus exclusively on biology as a case example, for three reasons. First, biological understandings are important and wide reaching. They concern the distinction between living and nonliving things, the relation of humans to other species, and the nature of human differences (e.g., why individuals have particular features or traits; the extent to which age, gender, and/or race are viewed as biological properties). Thus, from a purely descriptive standpoint, it is of interest to chart out the nature of children's beliefs in the realm of biology. Second, there is a practical reason to focus on this domain, as it is one area apart from theory of mind (Taylor, this volume; Siegal, this volume) that has been studied extensively. And third, currently there is controversy regarding the extent to which children's knowledge about living things can be said to constitute a theory (Carey & Spelke, 1994; Keil, 1994). The dispute helps highlight what is entailed by proposing that children's knowledge is organized into a theory.

To summarize, my goal in this section is to review children's early biological knowledge in order to examine the claim that this knowledge forms a theory. Important questions regarding developmental change in children's biological thought are not addressed; see Carey (1985) and Solomon, Johnson, Zaitchik, and Carey (1993) for discussion of these issues. I will also not review the work on children's theories in other domains (but see Wellman & Gelman, 1992). Other sources provide excellent treatments of psychology (Gopnik & Wellman, 1994), number (R. Gelman & Gallistel, 1978; Gelman et al., 1991), physics (Spelke & Hermer, this volume; Kaiser et al., McCloskey, & Proffitt, 1986), and substance kind (Carey, 1991; C. Smith, Carey, & Wiser, 1985).

A. Overview of Biology

A framework theory of biology concerns itself with ontological distinctions between living and nonliving things, with biological processes such as growth and inheritance, and with the question of how humans are like and unlike other species. Thinking biologically requires the realization that causal processes or forces can be distinct from humans—neither animistic (derived from psychological states) nor artificialistic (resulting from human actions or interventions from God). There are two classes of suggestions that young children might not treat biology as a distinct domain: children could apply domain-general principles to understand specifically biological phenomena, or children could confuse biology with some other domain, most plausibly psychology (Carey, 1985). I will review evidence suggesting that children's biological knowledge cannot be wholly characterized in either of these ways. There are four sections below: ontology, domain-specific processes, coherence, and unobservables.

1. Ontology

The foundation of any theory is its ontology—those fundamental distinctions that set forth what kinds of entities there are. Preschool children readily distinguish animals from inanimate objects (e.g., R. Gelman, Spelke, & Meck, 1983; Legerstee, 1992), and when doing so focus on biologically relevant properties, such as independence from human actions (S. A. Gelman & Kremer, 1991; Massey & Gelman, 1988). However, the ontological distinction between living and nonliving things, even more basic to biology as a domain, is difficult. Elementary school children make many errors when asked which things are alive (Carey, 1985; Hatano et al., 1993; Richards & Siegler, 1986; Stavy & Wax, 1989) and which properties are crucial for sustaining life (e.g., breathing, eating; Carey, 1985). Much of the difficulty is that living things include plants (Carey, 1985), which are wholly different from animals on every dimension *except* those relevant to biology (e.g., plants and animals have different parts and different shapes, and differ in the capacity for self-generated movement and psychological states). Indeed, the distinction between animals and plants is itself an ontological distinction (Keil, 1979). Given the salient differences between plants and animals, it is striking that even 3- and 4-year-old children distinguish living things (including *both* animals and plants) from human artifacts with respect to important properties such as growth (Hickling & Gelman, 1995) and capacity to heal without human intervention (Backscheider, Shatz, & Gelman, 1993). What seems to be crucial in the studies showing early success is that they appropriately focus children on particular relevant features (e.g., growth) rather than asking about the more abstract concept of life. This suggests that preschool children have a fragile, yet consistent, grasp of plants as biological entities.

Another issue raised by this research concerns the relation between ontology and theory: Can children be said to hold a biological theory even if their ontology differs from that of adults? Although a complete grasp of biology would require treating animals and plants together as a single unit, children appear to have a biological understanding that extends first or more solidly to animals. In other words, children seem to treat animals as biological entities before they treat plants as alive and subject to the same laws. It is useful here to maintain a distinction between the theory-based ontological distinction and its domain of application. By preschool age, children hold the appropriate ontological distinction (there is a fundamental distinction between entities that are subject to biological laws and those that are not), but for years continue to err in its domain of application (precisely which things are biological and which are not).

2. Domain-Specific Processes

When do children begin to appreciate that there are domain-specific biological processes? To qualify as such, children need to appreciate the existence of uniquely *biological* processes, and need to consider *causal* (rather than merely explanatory) mechanisms. More research is needed concerning both these issues, yet initial research findings are suggestive. Young children hold many misconceptions regarding certain biological processes, particularly internal bodily processes that involve specialized structures, such as respiration, digestion, or circulation of the blood. For example, children below age 10 do not think that all living things need to eat and breathe (see Carey, 1985, for more general review). Nonetheless, preschool children make predictions and provide explanations that distinguish biological from psychological processes (Inagaki & Hatano, 1993). For example, 4- and 5-year-olds understand that certain biological processes (e.g., breathing or sleep) and properties (e.g., eye color) cannot be controlled or modified by psychological processes. Similarly, young children say that people cannot prevent an animal from growing, just because they want it to remain small and cute (Inagaki & Hatano, 1987). These findings suggest that children maintain a general framework in which bodily functions are understood as distinct from conscious control,[9] and (given their other errors) that this framework does not follow from a detailed knowledge base.

In addition to this abstract understanding, children have varying degrees of insight regarding particular processes, including movement, growth, and inheritance. Movement, growth, and inheritance are notable for involving the entire animal (in contrast to more obscure processes such as digestion), and perhaps more important, have broader implications for interpreting an animal's behavior and judging its identity. For example, adults rely on movement to make decisions regarding agency and responsibility; use knowledge of growth to track identity of an animal over time; and rely on biological inheritance when predicting or explaining the characteristics of offspring. Somewhat paradoxically, then, children's first insights into domain-specific biological processes involve those arenas that have implications beyond the realm of biology.

Perhaps the earliest understandings concern movement. Even infants appreciate that animals move in certain characteristic ways (Bertenthal, Proffitt, Spetner, & Thomas, 1985). Preschool children also realized that animals undergo self-generated movement, whereas simple artifacts do not (R. Gelman, Durgin, & Kaufman, 1995; Massey & Gelman, 1988). Moreover, children's causal explanations of how movement takes place differs between animals and artifacts. Children aged 3 and 4 years appeal to an "innards principle" for the movement of animals but not simple artifacts (R. Gelman, 1990).

Children also understand several aspects of growth by preschool age. They understand that growth and development are constrained in specific ways: animals get bigger with age but cannot get smaller; animals can take on a more complex form (e.g., caterpillar to butterfly), but not a simpler form (e.g., butterfly to caterpillar; Rosengren, Gelman, Kalish, & McCormick, 1991). Only animals and plants undergo the distinctive process of growth; human artifacts such as toys or machines cannot (Carey, 1985; Rosengren et al., 1991). Similarly, Backscheider et al. (1993) found that 3- and 4-year-old children report that living things are capable of self-healing; artifacts are not. For example, if the fur is removed from a dog or a rose from a rosebush, children report that it will grow back by itself. But if the hair is cut off a doll, children report that it requires human intervention to be restored.

Children appear to reason differently about the natural process of growth than they do about nonbiological processes. With nonbiological processes such as surgical operations, children below age 7 accept a wide range of transformations as possible, including those adults deem impossible. For example, a live cat could become a dog (DeVries, 1969), or a raccoon that was operated on by a physician could be transformed into something that looked like a skunk (Keil, 1989). But for natural transformations, children realize that the changes that can occur are bounded and that identity remains constant across those changes (see S. A. Gelman, 1993, for review). Thus, it seems that children are sensitive to whether the mechanism inducing change is a natural biological one or an artificial one.

Inheritance is a specifically biological process; all and only living things have offspring to which they are capable of passing along inherited characteristics. Although the details of the process certainly require expertise to appreciate, young children have an early grasp of some of the more basic aspects. Mervis (1987) observed that even before the age of two years, her son Ari classified waterfowl based on knowledge about the parents. For example, in one instance Ari referred to a picture of a baby flamingo as "flamingo." When asked why, he said, "Because its mommy is a flamingo" (Mervis, 1987, p. 228). This may mean that Ari had a tacit theory that kinship bonds exist even in the fact of apparent differences (Barrett et al., 1993, p. 1596).

More recent work confirms and extends this insight. Springer (1992; Springer & Keil, 1989, 1991) asked preschool children to predict which features of parents would be inherited by their offspring. For example, they were told that "Mr. and Mrs. Bull . . . were both born with pink hearts inside their chests instead of normal-colored hearts" and were asked to predict whether their children would be born with a normal-colored heart or a pink heart. Subjects more often treated a feature as inherited when it led to biological outcomes (e.g., a particular type of stomach allowed the animal to eat a lot) than when it led to social or psychological outcomes (e.g., a particular type of stomach made the animal feel angry).

Children also have reasonable expectations about the means by which biological properties are transmitted from parent to offspring. Springer and Keil (1991) found that preschool children appeal to internal causal mechanisms to explain how biological kinds get their color (e.g., how a dog gets to be brown or a flower gets to be blue) but not how an artifact does (how a can gets to be red). The children rejected psychological, artificialistic explanations.

Springer (1992) found that preschool children are aware of the biological implications of kinship. They expect animals of the same family to share stable physical features (e.g., hairy ears, tiny bones inside, ability to see in the dark), even in the strong case when perceptual similarity is placed in conflict with kinship. For example, in the absence of kinship information, more similar animals are assumed to share more properties than less similar animals. However, if the less similar animals are related, the results switch.

Related to the notion of inheritance is the understanding that individuals have a certain innate potential that is determined at or before birth and that emerges in a broad array of environmental contexts. For example, a mouse may be genetically programmed to have black and white fur, even though it is hairless at birth. A frog will be good at jumping, even if it is raised as a pet and never observes other frogs jumping. By age 4 years, children appreciate that animals have innate potential of this sort; by $4\frac{1}{2}$ years of age, they apply this understanding to plant seeds, as well. When children are told about infant animals and seeds that are raised in an environment more suited to another species (e.g., a calf raised among pigs; a seed that came from an apple and was planted in a pot full of flowers), they report that the animals and plants will have species-appropriate characteristics (e.g., the adult cow will moo and have a straight tail; S. A. Gelman and Wellman, 1991).

Children believe that this sort of innate potential exists for humans as well as other animals. Taylor (1993) found that young children expect that gender-linked characteristics (e.g., play preferences and aptitudes) are innately determined and unaffected by environmental opportunities. For example, an infant boy raised with only girls and women will, at age 10, be good at playing football and prefer trucks to dolls. Children do not start to acknowledge the importance of environmental influence until middle childhood (roughly age 9 or 10 years; Taylor, 1993). Hirschfeld (1994), using a similar paradigm, has found that preschool-age children believe that race is inherited and unaffected by upbringing. For example, children predict that a newborn baby whose biological parents are white but whose adoptive parents are black, will be white.

3. Coherence

To what extent are children's biological beliefs coherent? Although the issue has rarely been examined, evidence suggests that there is some interrelatedness of children's biological knowledge by late preschool. Backscheider (1993) told preschool children about items that each possessed either a biological or a nonbiological property, then asked children to infer the presence or absence of other biological and nonbiological properties. Children were not permitted to see the item during questioning. For example, they were told on one item, "This is something that grows," and were asked whether it was held together with nails and screws, whether it got a scratch that got better all by itself, and so on. Backscheider's 4-year-old subjects showed different inference patterns, depending on whether they were told that an item possessed biological or nonbiological properties. When told that an item had one biological property, they tended to infer that it had other biological (but not nonbiological) properties; when told that an item had one nonbiological property, they tended to infer that it had other nonbiological (but not biological) properties.

4. Unobservables

As noted earlier, theories involve attributing unseen constructs to account for observable phenomena (e.g., molecules, desires, gravity, DNA). An excellent example can be found in the domain of substance kind. Au, Sidle, and Rollins (1993) demonstrated that preschool and early elementary school children appeal to tiny, invisible particles to explain contamination or the dissolution of sugar in water. Children as young as 3 show some implicit understanding, saying, for example, that a sugar solution that appears completely clear will nonetheless taste sweet. Moreover, a small subset of children between 4 and 7 years of age spontaneously explained the dissolution of sugar in water by appealing to invisible particles. For example, a child who had just turned 4 years said, "It turned into little sugars, so little that you can't see them." A 7-year-old referred to "Sugar trapped inside water, in tinier molecules." When directly asked whether the sugar "broke into tiny pieces of sugar, so tiny that we can't see" or instead "turned into plain water," most 3- to 7-year-olds endorsed the invisible particles explanation. (See also Rosen and Rozin, 1993, for related findings.)

In biology, one important example of unobservables is a category essence

(S. A. Gelman et al., 1994). Medin (1989; Medin & Ortony, 1989) writes about "psychological essentialism" belief in an underlying nature that is responsible for the observable qualities that category members have in common. Recent evidence suggests that preschool children may believe in biological essences, attributing to animals distinctive internal parts (e.g., blood, bones) and innate potential (S. A. Gelman & Wellman, 1991).

A further question is whether understanding unobservables is a prerequisite to other kinds of explanations or understandings. In the domain of matter, for example, the tendency to endorse invisible particles correlates with the ability to conserve matter, demonstrating that it is not an isolated belief, but perhaps foundational to other understandings of substance kind (Au et al., 1993). It is not yet known what role essentialism may play in the development of biological beliefs.

B. Summary of Theories

In order to understand how children organize knowledge, it is necessary to look at how they organize knowledge in specific domains (Carey, 1984). Evidence suggests that children build theories in several realms, including psychology, physics, number, biology, and substance kind. We illustrated from the domain of biology. Preschoolers organize biologically specific beliefs into theory-like structures: they have a distinct ontology, domain-specific causal processes, some evidence for coherence, and appeal to unobservable properties. However, these structures undergo substantial changes over childhood: from a system in which humans are the prototype to one in which humans are one animal among many; from a system in which the mechanics of bodily systems are mysterious to one in which they are understood in detail; from a system in which origins are understood in terms of human actions and limitations to one that incorporates evolutionary theory.

Although the details of each domain need to be worked out separately, there are some general conclusions that reach across the specific content areas. One major point is that fundamental ontological distinctions emerge quite early in development. This claim is in contrast to the traditional argument that children merge categories (e.g., animate and inanimate; object and motion; cause and effect; mental and physical). Infants and young children do not treat the world as undifferentiated, but rather have organized their experiences into sensible and clearly delimited ontological groupings.

Similarly, domain-specific causal understandings also emerge early. Children supply different explanations for biological events than for mechanical events, for example. Such explanations at times include mention of "unobservables"—internal or invisible entities that play a crucial role in understanding a domain (e.g., innate potential for living things; invisible particles for substances). That children are so attentive to causal underpinnings has led some researchers to suggest that children are causal determinists (Brown, 1990; Bullock, Gelman, & Baillargeon, 1982; S. A. Gelman & Kalish, 1993)—children may assume all events and all environmental regularities are caused. This intriguing idea deserves further study.

There is less evidence that children's beliefs are interrelated in a coherent system or even what would constitute coherence. In large part this may be because there is still relatively little work regarding the coherence and consistency of early beliefs. One possibility is that children's beliefs appear inconsistent due to lack of knowledge regarding the domain in question, rather than lack of coherence per se (Au, 1994, p. 109). Another possibility is that children's intuitive theories are coherent but not consistent. "Coherence" implies that various concepts and explanations within a particular domain make reference to other concepts and explanations within that same domain. For example, beliefs, desires, and intentional actions are mutually informative (Bartsch & Wellman, 1989); intentional actions cannot be understood without reference to both beliefs and desires. However, "consistency" would require holding only logically compatible beliefs, in other words, beliefs that do not contradict one another. Children may not have the metacognitive sophistication to notice and resolve such contradictions. For example, children may think that offspring resemble their parents and that caterpillars turn into butterflies, and not resolve the contradiction until explicitly faced with the conflict. In any case, consistency and coherence are in principle independent of one another (see also Wellman & Gelman, 1992, p. 368).

Another area that has intrigued researchers, yet requires more attention, is that of cognitive change. One of the more important implications of a theory approach is that cognitive development is analogous to theory change (Carey, 1985). Given what is known regarding the evolution of scientific theories (e.g., T. S. Kuhn, 1962), the analogy suggests that misconceptions can be deeply entrenched and developmental change can be difficult. Theories have a certain entropy, and it often is difficult to disengage from a particular belief system once it is entrenched. Carey (1985) argues that children undergo radical theory change in the domains of biology and substance kind (see also Vosniadou & Brewer, 1992).

Of course, there are points where the analogy between intuitive and scientific theories breaks down (Brewer & Samarapungavan, 1991; Harris, 1994): scientific theories involve entire research communities and not individuals; thus, it is not even clear that theory revision takes place within an individual scientist. There is some evidence that cultural belief systems may exert effects on theories (e.g., Morris, Nisbett, & Peng, 1995, in the domain of social explanation; Hatano et al., 1993, in the domain of biology). To what extent is theory change driven by external forces (parental input, knowledge, formal teaching), and to what extent is it internally driven (e.g., Karmiloff-Smith, 1991; Karmiloff-Smith & Inhelder, 1975)? More work is needed regarding the kinds of inputs children receive and their potential effects (see also R. Gelman, Massey, and McManus, 1991).

IV. CONCEPTS AND THEORIES

As noted earlier, concepts are not atomic, isolated units, but rather are inextricably linked to theories (Murphy & Medin, 1985). In this section I consider first the influence of theories on concepts, and then briefly speculate about the influence of concepts on theories.

A. Influence of Theories on Concepts

For adults, concepts are influenced by theoretical belief systems (Keil, 1989; Murphy, 1993; Murphy & Medin, 1985; Quine, 1977). Examples from the homely to the exotic make the point that ordinary use of language carries with it theoretical implications. To give one simple example, the classification of an action as either "jump" or "fall" requires a theoretical commitment regarding the mental states or intentions of the actor or target. A less common example can be found in the domain of reproductive technology. Recent experiments make it possible for a woman to be a grandmother without ever having been a mother (*The New York Times,* January 11, 1994). The eggs of a woman's aborted fetus can be artificially inseminated and implanted in another woman, resulting in a newborn baby. Medical ethicists who pondered this scenario referred to the woman who aborted the fetus as the newborn's grandmother, noting that she need not ever have been a mother. This usage illustrates that the concept "grandmother" is open to change as one's theory of reproduction changes. It is simply not possible to provide an atheoretical definition of "grandmother" in terms of fixed features (e.g., "grandmother" = "mother of a mother"; see also Lakoff, 1987). Rather, as knowledge and theory change, the boundaries of the category shift. There may be no theory-neutral description of things or events, in the ordinary language of adults.

These examples from language use are paralleled in the judgments of adult subjects in classification experiments (see Murphy, 1993, for review). For example, Rips (1989; Rips & Collins, 1993) finds a divergence between similarity judgments (which are presumably theory neutral) and classification. When subjects are told about a circular object 3 inches in diameter, they judge it to be more similar to a quarter than a pizza, but more likely to be a pizza than a quarter. Although this particular example need not rely on theories (e.g., subjects may have been using knowledge of the known variability of pizza size vs. quarter size to make their judgments), it poses a problem for a simple model in which categorization is the direct output of a domain-general similarity metric. Other items are more compelling, as when subjects learned about an animal that originally appeared to be a bird (ate seeds and berries, had two wings, two legs, lived in a nest, had feathers), but due to an unfortunate encounter with hazardous waste became transformed so that it looked and acted like an insect (Rips, 1989). Again, subjects' judgments of similarity and category membership diverged: the animal was judged as more similar to an insect but more likely to be a bird. The example suggests that categorization is tied to theoretical beliefs and not reducible to a domain-general similarity metric (but see E. E. Smith & Sloman, 1994, for questions regarding the generality of these findings).

A central developmental question is when and how children begin to incorporate theories into their concepts. Piaget argued that preoperational children do not have the logical capacity to construct either theories or true concepts (Inhelder & Piaget, 1964). Even when such an extreme position is not taken, a long-held view is that children's initial categories are similarity based (Quine, 1977), and only with experience and schooling incorporate theories.[10] Others suggest that the role of theories in children's early categorization is minimal at best (Jones & Smith, 1993).

In contrast, it may be difficult for children to acquire concepts *without* theories. Murphy (1993) notes that theories function to help concept learners, in three respects: (1) theories help identify those features that are relevant to a concept; (2) theories constrain how (e.g., along which dimensions) similarity should be computed; and (3) theories can influence how concepts are stored in memory. The implication here is that concept acquisition may proceed more smoothly with the help of theories. If so, this is reason to expect that theories may play a role in children's concepts, even though the theories themselves are changing developmentally.

Indeed, recent studies provide compelling demonstrations that young children use theoretical knowledge in their classifications. Barrett et al. (1993) note that "Concept learning involves more than simply keeping a running tally of which features are associated with which concept" (p. 1612), and present data suggesting that children's intuitive theories help determine which properties and which feature correlations children attend to in their classifications. For example, in a task that required children to categorize novel birds into one of two novel categories, first and fourth grade children noticed the association between brain size and memory capacity and used that correlation to categorize new members. Specifically, exemplars that preserved the correlation were more often judged to be category members, and to be more typical of the category. The children did not make use of features that correlated equally well but were unsupported by a theory (e.g., the correlation between structure of heart and shape of beak). In a second experiment, Barrett et al. (1993) found that (p. 1605):

"the same set of features is represented differently depending on whether or not the feature pair embodies a theory-based correlation." Third grade children were presented with stimuli that were described as either animals or tools, and then learned five properties about each category. When the category was described as an animal, children selectively focused on correlations between one subset of the properties, for example, "is found in the mountains" and "has thick wool." In contrast, when the category was described as a tool, children selectively focused on correlations between a different subset of properties, for example, "is found in the mountains" and "can crush rocks."

An implication of these results, and one that is often assumed (though not necessarily made explicit), is that errors or limitations in children's theories may constrain or shape children's concepts. For example, errors regarding the concepts of false belief or surprise are thought to reflect children's larger theoretical difficulties regarding theories of mind (Gopnik & Wellman, 1994). Thus, examining children's concepts should be informative regarding their larger theories.

Findings analogous to those of Barrett et al. (1993) can be seen in children's judgments of identity. Keil (1989) asked children to consider animals and objects that had undergone transformations leading them to appear to be something else, for example, a raccoon that underwent an operation so that it looked and acted like a skunk. By second grade, children realized that animal identity was unaffected by superficial transformations (e.g., the animal was judged to be a raccoon despite its skunklike properties). This understanding was specific to animals; children judged that artifacts could be transformed (e.g., a coffeepot could be made into a bird feeder). Even younger children demonstrated a similar understanding when considering objects that were transformed to resemble something from a different ontological category (e.g., preschoolers reported that a porcupine that was transformed to look like a cactus was still a porcupine), or that were transformed by means of a costume. S. A. Gelman and Wellman (1991) similarly found that preschool children appreciated that for some objects, insides are more important than outsides for judgments of identity and functioning (e.g., a dog without its insides cannot bark and is not a dog, whereas a dog without its outsides can bark and is a dog). These data converge to provide a picture of preschool children as attending to theory-relevant properties even when they are subtle and relatively nonobvious.

A related question is whether children consider the ontological status of an object (e.g., as animal or inanimate) in their classifications and word meanings. Currently this question is under serious debate. One proposal is that children have a general shape bias in their interpretations of novel count nouns, such that a new word (e.g., "a dax") is assumed to refer to a set of objects that share a common shape, even when they are taxonomically unrelated (Imai, Gentner, & Uchida, 1994; Landau, Jones, & Smith, 1992; Landau, Smith, & Jones, 1988). This would mean that ontological status is irrelevant (e.g., toy bears and real bears are both "bears" because they have a common shape; Jones & Smith, 1993). In favor of this theory, many studies indicate that shape is an important and salient feature for children, particularly in word-learning contexts (Baldwin, 1989, 1992; L. B. Smith, Jones, & Landau, 1992). However, children may attend to shape not because it is definitive or the basis on which words are extended, but rather because it correlates with and "is often . . . a good source of information about" what kind of thing an object is (Soja, Carey, & Spelke, 1992). Indeed, children override similarity (including shape) when extending novel words at the basic level (Golinkoff, Shuff-Bailey, Olguin, & Ruan, 1995), and make use of information such as object function and syntax to extend new words (Gathercole, Cramer, Somerville, & op de Haar, 1995).

In any case, the shape-bias hypothesis seems incomplete, given that features are either highlighted or downplayed depending on how the child conceptualizes the larger category to which the object belongs. For example, Jones, Smith, and Landau (1991) found that adding eyes to a nonsense figure altered children's classifications. Specifically, when 2- and 3-year-olds were asked to classify simple novel objects (e.g., geometric shapes made of wood, wire, or sponge), children attended primarily to shape, yet when the same items had plastic "eyes" attached, subjects attended to both shape and texture. Apparently, the addition of eyes changed the child's conception of the object's ontological status (from object to animal), which in turn influenced categorization judgments. Similarly, Ward, Becker, Hass, and Vela (1991) found that although children generally rely on shape for classifying and extending novel words, they do not do so when the shape is a temporary one (e.g., a snake curled into a circle). Moreover, Soja *et al.* (1991) demonstrate that, although children use shape when learning words for objects, they do not do so when learning words for substances.

Another set of issues concerns the inductive function of categories, that is, their potential to generate novel inferences. S. A. Gelman and Markman (1986, 1987) noted that, for adults, categories function to extend knowledge beyond what is obvious or already known. For example, after learning that one dog has leukocytes inside it, subjects are likely to infer that other dogs also have leukocytes inside them. Categories that are tied to theories promote especially many inferences concerning novel features (Markman, 1989; Quine, 1977). Gelman and Markman presented preschool children with items in which category membership was put into conflict with superficial appearances, and children were asked to make a series of inductive inferences. For example, on one of Gelman and Markman's items children saw a brontosaurus, a rhinoceros, and a triceratops, which were labeled as "dinosaur," "rhinoceros," and "dinosaur" respectively. Category labels and outward appearances conflicted: the brontosaurus and triceratops are members of the same category, whereas the rhinoceros and triceratops look more alike outwardly. Then children learned a new property of the brontosaurus and the rhinoceros (that they had cold blood and warm blood, respectively), and were asked which property was true of the triceratops. These children reported that the triceratops has cold blood like the brontosaurus, even though it more closely resembled the rhinoceros. The results of this and other related experiments showed that by $2\frac{1}{2}$ years of age, children base inferences on category membership, despite conflicting surface appearances (S. A. Gelman & Coley, 1990).

Control studies showed that these effects were not simply a response bias due to hearing the same word for the two category members. For example, when children learned properties that should not generalize (e.g., accidental properties such as an animal's age), they did not generalize from one category member to another (S. A. Gelman, 1988; S. A. Gelman & Markman, 1986). Furthermore, on some items, preschool children drew category-based inferences even in the absence of labels. For example, even when none of the pictures was named, children drew more inferences from a green leaf-insect to a black beetle, than from a green leaf-insect to a green leaf (S. A. Gelman & Markman, 1987). Subtle properties of the appearance enabled children to determine that the leaf-insect was an insect and not a leaf.

B. Influence of Concepts on Theories

Although a number of studies have begun to examine the influence of theories on early concepts, little work addresses the reverse question, regarding the influence of concepts on early theories. However, it seems plausible that certain concepts may enable or constrain aspects of children's theories. Concepts may *enable* theories in that they make it possible for children to honor appropriate ontological distinctions. To phrase this differently, children could not represent ontologies (nor, by extension, theories) if they were unable to form concepts. Indeed, Inhelder and Piaget (1964) proposed that preoperational children could not form true concepts and that they blurred fundamental ontological distinctions (real vs. apparent; mental vs. physical; animate vs. inanimate). More recent evidence that even infants construct concepts (as reviewed above) makes it plausible that children also honor the appropriate ontological distinctions.

I illustrate how concepts may *constrain* theories, with two brief examples. One example concerns the concept of essentialism (Atran, 1990; Medin & Ortony, 1989). An essentialist assumption is compatible with certain kinds of biological theories more than others (e.g., creationism vs. evolution; Mayr, 1988), and may even encourage the development of such theories. For example, essentialism implies that each category has an unchanging essence, and thus is difficult to reconcile with the changes inherent in evolutionary theory. As Mayr (1988) notes, it is interesting that evolutionary theory appears to have been so difficult for people to construct or discover. Perhaps we are predisposed toward creationist accounts, in part as an extension of essentialist biases from childhood (Evans, 1994).

The second example concerns the mutual exclusivity bias (Markman, 1989), which appears to operate across a variety of domains. According to mutual exclusivity, count nouns refer to nonoverlapping categories (e.g., *cat* and *dog* honor mutual exclusivity; *cat* and *pet,* or *cat* and *animal* do not). Although both children and adults honor some exceptions to this general tendency, it is particularly firm during the early word–learning years (Markman, 1989). It may be that this bias helps structure how children think about a broad set of domains, including beliefs about emotions. For example, a mutual exclusivity bias may be partly responsible for children's assumption that people cannot experience mixed emotions (Harter & Buddin, 1987). It would be interesting to explore if children structure their knowledge in other domains, as well, around this assumption.

V. CONCLUSIONS

From early childhood, children construct adultlike concepts and organize their growing knowledge base into theorylike structures. This chapter explored the interrelations between concepts and theories for children. It is important to keep in mind that concepts are varied, and children are flexible in the kinds of information they use. Children focus on different features, depending on the conceptual function that is called for (S. A. Gelman & Medin, 1993). For example, when rapidly identifying particular instances, children and adults appear to make use of information that is immediate and accessible. However, asking children about inheritance or the causal bases of movement elicits talk about internal or essential features. Thus, domain-general descriptions of children's concepts need to be integrated with the notion that concepts are theory laden, even for children (Keil, 1989). We have only begun to explore the influence of concepts on theories, but this also appears to be a fruitful direction for the future.

Acknowledgments

Preparation of this chapter was supported by NSF Grant 91-00348. I am grateful to Terry Au, Rochel Gelman, Gail Gottfried, Bruce Mannheim, and Marjorie Taylor for helpful comments.

Endnotes

1. The meaning of "concept" varies according to user (Heath, 1967). I will use the terms "concept," "category," and "word meaning" as related but distinct. Specifically, catego-

ries can be mental or nonmental groupings of individuals or individual properties that can be distinguished but are treated as alike. Concepts include mentally represented categories as well as other mental entities (including representations of individuals, collections, thematic associations, scripts, and complexives; Mandler, 1983; Markman, 1989; Vygotsky, 1962). Both concepts and categories are potentially distinct from word meanings. Not all concepts and categories are encoded in single words (e.g., "black-and-white spotted cow"; "the scent of baking bread"; the distinction between "wearing" a hat and "wearing" a ring), and not all words map onto concepts (e.g., the semantic distinction between "beech" and "elm" may have not been known by the language user; see Putnam, 1973; other words, such as "the," do not have isolated meanings in the usual sense). For further discussion of the distinction between concepts and meanings, see Clark (1983). For other uses of the terms concept and category, see Mandler (1988), Margolis (1994), and Murphy and Medin (1985).

2. However, various developmental dichotomies do not uniformly make the same predictions. To give just one example: although the perceptual-to-conceptual shift would predict that younger children would rely more on perceptual similarity than older children, the thematic-to-taxonomic shift would predict that younger children would rely less on perceptual similarity, because thematically related things tend to share fewer perceptual features than do taxonomically related things.

3. Although Chi and others explain domain-specific effects in terms of expertise, there are other accounts of domain specificity, resting on different theoretical frameworks. See Hirschfeld and Gelman (1994).

4. Some theorists question whether concepts are represented in a stable way at all (Barsalou, 1987, 1993; Jones & Smith, 1993; L. B. Smith & Jones, 1993; see S. A. Gelman & Medin, 1993, for some questions regarding this position).

5. Even for such apparent cases, it is not clear that concepts have defining features (see Armstrong, Gleitman, & Gleitman, 1983).

6. I assume that prototypes do not fully characterize conceptual structure, for adults or children; indeed, more than one process is involved in category formation and storage. People store information regarding the predictive validity of learned cues and use this information to make informed guesses about novel cases (as the literature on prototypes amply demonstrates). However, people also readily make use of information at a theoretical (or principled) level, when it is available (R. Gelman, 1990; R. Gelman, Durgin, & Kaufman, 1995; Medin, 1989). This point is elaborated in more detail in Section IV below.

7. In addition, there are more abstract ontological categories (e.g., "living thing," "solid object," "entity"; see Carey, 1983; Keil, 1979), which are discussed in the section on theories.

8. Children also develop complex belief systems about other domains of knowledge that will not be reviewed here, for example: time (Friedman, 1982); astronomy (Vosniadou & Brewer, 1992); morality (Kagan & Lamb, 1987); space (Huttenlocher, Newcombe, & Sandberg, 1994; Pick, 1993); and religion (Boyer, 1994).

9. At some point in development, however, we learn that biological and psychological processes are not wholly distinct, as in the case of psychosomatic illnesses or biofeedback.

10. A potential contradiction in this view is that similarity judgments often have theorylike qualities: they can be domain specific, species specific, and biased in particular ways. For example, even infants perceive categorical distinctions in speech sounds and colors, whereas in physical reality no such boundaries exist (Eimas, Siqueland, Jusczyk, & Vigorito, 1971). As Keil (1989) points out, at no point in development is there a theory-neutral sense of similarity. However, it seems reasonable not to call these perceptual biases "theories," at least not in the sense described above, as they need not entail causal explanatory systems of ontological commitments. More generally, not every bias or domain-

specific tendency in children's categories can be ascribed to theories (see also cases of perceptual learning; Biederman & Shiffrar, 1987).

References

Anglin, J. M. (1977). *Word, object, and conceptual development.* New York: Norton.

Armstrong, S. L., Gleitman, L. R., & Gleitman, H. (1983). What some concepts might not be. *Cognition, 13,* 263–308.

Atran, S. (1990). *Cognitive foundations of natural history.* Cambridge: Cambridge University Press.

Au, T. K. (1994). Developing an intuitive understanding of substance kinds. *Cognitive Psychology, 27,* 71–111.

Au, T. K., Sidle, A. L., & Rollins, K. B. (1993). Developing an intuitive understanding of conservation and contamination: Invisible particles as a plausible mechanism. *Developmental Psychology, 29,* 286–299.

Backscheider, A. G. (1993). *Preschoolers' understanding of living kinds.* Unpublished doctoral dissertation, University of Michigan.

Backscheider, A. G., Shatz, M., & Gelman, S. A. (1993). Preschoolers' ability to distinguish living kinds as a function of self-healing. *Child Development, 64,* 1242–1257.

Baillargeon, R. (1993). The object concept revisited. In C. Granrud (Ed.), *Carnegie-Mellon Symposia on Cognition: Vol. 23. Visual perception and cognition in infancy* (pp. 265–315). Hillsdale, NJ: Erlbaum.

Baillargeon, R., Spelke, E. S., & Wasserman, S. (1985). Object permanence in five-month-olds. *Cognition, 20,* 191–208.

Baldwin, D. A. (1989). Priorities in children's expectations about object label reference: Form over color. *Child Development, 60,* 1289–1306.

Baldwin, D. A. (1992). Clarifying the role of shape in children's taxonomic assumptions. *Journal of Experimental Child Psychology, 54,* 392–416.

Baldwin, D. A., Markman, E. M., & Melartin, R. L. (1993). Infants' ability to draw inferences about nonobvious object properties: Evidence from exploratory play. *Child Development, 64,* 711–728.

Barrett, S. E., Abdi, H., Murphy, G. L., & Gallagher, J. M. (1993). Theory-based correlations and their role in children's concepts. *Child Development, 64,* 1595–1616.

Barsalou, L. W. (1987). The instability of graded structure: Implications for the nature of concepts. In U. Neisser (Ed.), *Concepts and concept development: Ecological and intellectual factors in categorization* (pp. 101–140). Cambridge: Cambridge University Press.

Barsalou, L. W. (1993). Challenging assumptions about concepts. *Cognitive Development, 8,* 169–180.

Bartsch, K., & Wellman, H. M. (1989). Young children's attribution of action to beliefs and desires. *Child Development, 60,* 946–964.

Bauer, P. J., & Mandler J. M. (1989). Taxonomies and triads: conceptual organization in one- to two-year-olds. *Cognitive Psychology, 21,* 156–184.

Berlin, B., Breedlove, D., & Raven, P. (1973). General principles of classification and nomenclature in folk biology. *American Anthropologist, 75,* 212–242.

Bertenthal, B. I., Proffitt, H. D. R., Spetner, N. B., & Thomas, M. A. (1985). The development of infant sensitivity to biomechanical motions. *Child Development, 56,* 531–54.

Biederman, I., & Shiffrar, M. M. (1987). Sexing day-old chicks: A case study and expert systems analysis of a difficult perceptual-learning task. *Journal of Experimental Psychology: Learning, Memory, and Cognition, 13,* 640–645.

Bowerman, M. (1978). The acquisition of word meaning: An investigation into some current conflicts. In N. Waterson & C. Snow (Eds.), *Development of communication*. New York: Wiley.

Boyer, P. (1994). Cognitive constraints on cultural representations: Natural ontologies and religious ideas. In L. A. Hirschfeld & S. A. Gelman (Eds.), *Mapping the mind: Domain specificity in cognition and culture* (pp. 391–411). New York: Cambridge University Press.

Brewer, W. F., & Samarapungavan, A. (1991). Children's theories versus scientific theories: Differences in reasoning or differences in knowledge? In R. Hoffman & D. Palermo (Eds.), *Cognition and the symbolic processes: Applied and ecological perspectives*. Hillsdale, NJ: Erlbaum.

Brown, A. L. (1990). Domain-specific principles affect learning and transfer in children. *Cognitive Science, 14,* 107–133.

Bruner, J. S., Goodnow, J. J., & Austin, G. A. (1956). *A study of thinking*. New York: Wiley.

Bruner, J. S., Olver, R. R., & Greenfield, P. M. (1966). *Studies in cognitive growth*. New York: Wiley.

Bullock, M., Gelman, R., & Baillargeon, R. (1982). The development of causal reasoning. In W. J. Friedman (Ed.), *The developmental psychology of time* (pp. 209–254). New York: Academic Press.

Callanan, M. A., & Oakes, L. M. (1992). Preschoolers' questions and parents' explanations: Causal thinking in everyday activity. *Cognitive Development, 7,* 213–233.

Cantor, N., Smith, E. E., French, R. D., & Mezzich, J. (1980). Psychiatric diagnosis as prototype categorization. *Journal of Abnormal Psychology, 89,* 181–193.

Carey, S. (1978). The child as word learner. In J. Bresnan, G. Miller, & M. Halle (Eds.), *Linguistic theory and psychological reality* (pp. 264–293). Cambridge, MA: MIT Press.

Carey, S. (1983). Constraints on the meanings of natural kind terms. In T. B. Seiler & W. Wannenmacher (Eds.), *Concept development and the development of word meaning* (pp. 126–143). New York: Springer-Verlag.

Carey, S. (1984). Cognitive development: The descriptive problem. In M. S. Gazzaniga (Ed.), *Handbook of cognitive neuroscience* (pp. 37–66). New York: Plenum.

Carey, S. (1985). *Conceptual change in childhood*. Cambridge, MA: MIT Press.

Carey, S. (1991). Knowledge acquisition: Enrichment or conceptual change? In S. Carey & R. Gelman (Eds.), *The epigenesis of mind: Essays on biology and cognition* (pp. 257–291). Hillsdale, NJ: Erlbaum.

Carey, S., & Spelke, E. (1994). Domain-specific knowledge and conceptual change. In L. A. Hirschfeld & S. A. Gelman (Eds.), *Mapping the mind: Domain specificity in cognition and culture* (pp. 169–200). Cambridge: Cambridge University Press.

Chase, W. G., & Simon, H. A. (1973). Perception in chess. *Cognitive Psychology, 4,* 55–81.

Chi, M. T. H. (1978). Knowledge structure and memory development. In R. Siegler (Ed.), *Children's thinking: What develops?* (pp. 73–96). Hillsdale, NJ: Erlbaum.

Chi, M., Feltovich, H. A., & Glaser, R. (1981). Categorization and representation of physics problems by experts and novices. *Cognitive Science, 5,* 121–152.

Chi, M., Hutchinson, J., & Robin, A. (1989). How inference about novel domain-related concepts can be constrained by structured knowledge. *Merrill-Palmer Quarterly, 35,* 27–62.

Clark, E. V. (1983). Meanings and concepts. In J. H. Flavell & E. M. Markman (Eds.), *Handbook of child psychology: Vol. 3. Cognitive development* (4th ed., pp. 787–840). New York: Wiley.

Cohen, L. B., & Strauss, M. S. (1979). Concept acquisition in the human infant. *Child Development, 50,* 419–424.

Cohen, L. B., & Younger, B. A. (1983). Perceptual categorization in the infant. In E. Scholnick (Ed.), *New trends in conceptual representation: Challenges to Piaget's theory?* (pp. 197–220). Hillsdale, NJ: Erlbaum.

Deak, G., & Bauer, P. J. (in press). The effects of task comprehension on preschoolers' and adults' categorization choices. *Journal of Experimental Child Psychology.*

DeVries, R. (1969). Constancy of generic identity in the years three to six. *Monographs of the Society for Research in Child Development, 34*(Whole No. 127).

Dromi, E. (1987). *Early lexical development.* Cambridge: Cambridge University Press.

Eimas, P. D., Siqueland, E., Jusczyk, P. W., & Vigorito, J. (1971). Speech perception in infants. *Science, 171,* 303–306.

Estes, D., Wellman, H. M., & Woolley, J. D. (1989). Children's understanding of mental phenomena. In H. Reese (Ed.), *Advances in child development and behavior* (Vol. 21, pp. 41–87). New York: Academic Press.

Estes, W. K. (1986). Array models for category learning. *Cognitive Psychology, 18,* 500–549.

Evans, M. (1994). *God or Darwin? The development of beliefs about the origin of species.* Unpublished doctoral dissertation, University of Michigan.

Fagan, J. F., III, & Singer, L. T. (1979). The role of simple feature differences in infants' recognition of faces. *Infant Behavior and Development, 2,* 39–45.

Flavell, J. (1977). *Cognitive development.* Englewood Cliffs, NJ: Prentice-Hall.

Friedman, W. J. (Ed.), (1982). *The developmental psychology of time.* New York: Academic Press.

Gathercole, V. C. M., Cramer, L. J., Somerville, S. C., & op de Haar, M. J. (1995). Ontological categories and function: Acquisition of new names. *Cognitive Development, 10,* 225–251.

Gelman, R. (1978). Cognitive development. *Annual Review of Psychology, 29,* 297–332.

Gelman, R. (1990). First principles organize attention to and learning about relevant data: Number and the animate-inanimate distinction as examples. *Cognitive Science, 14,* 79–106.

Gelman, R., & Baillargeon, R. (1983). A review of some Piagetian concepts. In J. H. Flavell & E. M. Markman (Eds.), *Handbook of child psychology* (Vol. 3, pp. 167–230). New York: Wiley.

Gelman, R., Durgin, F., & Kaufman, L. (1995). Distinguishing between animates and inanimates: not by motion alone. In D. Sperber, D. Premack, & A. J. Premack (Eds.), *Causal cognition: A multidisciplinary debate* (pp. 150–184). Oxford: Clarendon Press.

Gelman, R., & Gallistel, C. R. (1978). *The child's understanding of number.* Cambridge, MA: Harvard University Press.

Gelman, R., Massey, C. M., & McManus, M. (1991). Characterizing supporting environments for cognitive development: Lessons from children in a museum. In J. M. Levine, L. B. Resnick, & S. D. Teasley (Eds.), *Perspectives on socially shared cognition* (pp. 226–256). Washington, DC: American Psychological Association.

Gelman, R., Spelke, E. S., & Meck, E. (1983). What preschoolers know about animate and inanimate objects. In D. Rogers & J. A. Sloboda (Eds.), *The acquisition of symbolic skills* (pp. 297–324). New York: Plenum.

Gelman, S. A. (1988). The development of induction within natural kind and artifact categories. *Cognitive Psychology, 20,* 65–95.

Gelman, S. A. (1993). Early conceptions of biological growth. In J. Montangero, A. Cornu-Wells, A. Tryphon, & J. Voneche (Eds.), *Conceptions of change over time* (pp. 197–208). Geneva: Cahiers de la Fondation Archives Jean Piaget No. 13.

Gelman, S. A. (1994). Competence versus performance. In R. J. Sternberg (Ed.), *Encyclopedia of human intelligence* (Vol. 1, pp. 283–286). New York: Macmillan.

Gelman, S. A., & Coley, J. D. (1990). The importance of knowing a dodo is a bird: Categories and inferences in 2-year-old children. *Developmental Psychology, 26,* 796–804.

Gelman, S. A., Coley, J. D., & Gottfried, G. M. (1994). Essentialist beliefs in children: The acquisition of concepts and theories. In L. A. Hirschfeld & S. A. Gelman (Eds.), *Mapping the mind: Domain specificity in cognition and culture* (pp. 341–365). New York: Cambridge University Press.

Gelman, S. A., Collman, P., & Maccoby, E. E. (1986). Inferring properties from categories versus inferring categories from properties: The case of gender. *Child Development, 57,* 396–404.

Gelman, S. A., & Kalish, C. W. (1993). Categories and causality. In R. Pasnak & M. L. Howe (Eds.), *Emerging themes in cognitive development* (Vol. 2, pp. 3–32). New York: Springer-Verlag.

Gelman, S. A., & Kremer, K. E. (1991). Understanding natural cause: Children's explanations of how objects and their properties originate. *Child Development, 62,* 396–414.

Gelman, S. A., & Markman, E. M. (1986). Categories and induction in young children. *Cognition, 23,* 183–209.

Gelman, S. A., & Markman, E. M. (1987). Young children's inductions from natural kinds: The role of categories and appearances. *Child Development, 58,* 1532–1541.

Gelman, S. A., & Medin, D. L. (1993). What's so essential about essentialism? A different perspective on the interaction of perception, language, and conceptual knowledge. *Cognitive Development, 8,* 157–167.

Gelman, S. A., & Wellman, H. M. (1991). Insides and essences: Early understandings of the non-obvious. *Cognition, 38,* 213–244.

Gelman, S. A., Wilcox, S. A., & Clark, E. V. (1989). Conceptual and lexical hierarchies in young children. *Cognitive Development, 4,* 309–326.

Gibson, E. J., & Spelke, E. S. (1983). The development of perception. In J. H. Flavell & E. M. Markman (Eds.), *Handbook of child psychology: Vol. 3. Cognitive development* (4th ed., pp. 1–76). New York: Wiley.

Golinkoff, R. M., Shuff-Bailey, M., Olguin, R., & Ruan, W. (1995). Young children extend novel words at the basic level: Evidence for the principle of categorical scope. *Developmental Psychology, 31,* 494–507.

Gopnik, A., & Wellman, H. M. (1994). The theory theory. In L. A. Hirschfeld, & S. A. Gelman (Eds.), *Mapping the mind: Domain specificity in cognition and culture* (pp. 257–293). New York: Cambridge University Press.

Harris, P. (1975). Inferences and semantic development. *Journal of Child Language, 2,* 143–152.

Harris, P. (1994). Thinking by children and scientists: False analogies and neglected similarities. In L. A. Hirschfeld & S. A. Gelman (Eds.), *Mapping the mind: Domain specificity in cognition and culture* (pp. 294–315). Cambridge, MA: Cambridge University Press.

Harter, S., & Buddin, B. J. (1987). Children's understanding of the simultaneity of two emotions: A five-stage developmental acquisition sequence. *Developmental Psychology, 23,* 388–399.

Hatano, G., & Inagaki, K. (1994). Young children's naive theory of biology. *Cognition, 50,* 171–188.

Hatano, G., Siegler, R. S., Richards, D. D., Inagaki, K., Stavy, R., & Wax, N. (1993). The development of biological knowledge: A multi-national study. *Cognitive Development, 8,* 47–62.

Hayes, B. K., & Taplin, J. E. (1992). Developmental changes in categorization processes: Knowledge and similarity-based modes of categorization. *Journal of Experimental Child Psychology, 54,* 188–212.

Hayne, H., Rovee-Collier, C., & Perris, E. E. (1987). Categorization and memory retrieval by three-month-olds. *Child Development, 58,* 750–767.

Heath, P. L. (1967). Concept. In P. Edwards (Ed.), *The encyclopedia of philosophy* (Vol. 1, pp. 177–180). New York: Macmillan.

Hickling, A. K., & Gelman, S. A. (1995). How does your garden grow? Early conceptualization of seeds and their place in plant growth cycle. *Child Development, 66,* 856–876.

Hirschfeld, L. A. (1994). The child's representation of human groups. In D. Medin (Ed.), *The psychology of learning and motivation: Advances in research and theory* (Vol. 31. pp. 133–185). New York: Academic Press.

Hirschfeld, L. A., & Gelman, S. A. (1994). Toward a topography of mind: An introduction to domain specificity. In L. A. Hirschfeld & S. A. Gelman (Eds.), *Mapping the mind: Domain specificity in cognition and culture* (pp. 3–35). Cambridge: Cambridge University Press.

Horton, M. S. (1983). *The development of hierarchical and contrastive organization in natural category domains.* Paper presented at the meeting of the Society for Research in Child Development, Detroit.

Horton, M. S., & Markman, E. M. (1980). Developmental differences in the acquisition of basic and superordinate categories. *Child Development, 51,* 708–719.

Huttenlocher, J., Newcombe, N., & Sandberg, E. H. (1994). The coding of spatial location in young children. *Cognitive Psychology, 27,* 115–148.

Imai, M., Gentner, D., & Uchida, N. (1994). Children's theories of word meaning: The role of shape similarity in early acquisition. *Cognitive Development, 9,* 45–75.

Inagaki, K., & Hatano, G. (1987). Young children's spontaneous personification as analogy. *Child Development, 58,* 1013–1020.

Inagaki, K., & Hatano, G. (1993). Young children's understanding of the mind-body distinction. *Child Development, 64,* 1534–1549.

Inhelder, B., & Piaget, J. (1964). *The early growth of logic in the child.* New York: Norton.

James, W. (1890). *The principles of psychology.* New York: Dover.

Jones, S. S., & Smith, L. B. (1993). The place of perception in children's concepts. *Cognitive Development, 8,* 113–139.

Jones, S. S., Smith, L. B., & Landau, B. (1991). Object properties and knowledge in early lexical learning. *Child Development, 62,* 499–516.

Kagan, J., & Lamb, S. (Eds.). (1987). *The emergence of morality in young children.* Chicago: University of Chicago.

Kaiser, M. K., McCloskey, M., & Proffitt, D. R. (1986). Development of intuitive theories of motion: Curvilinear motion in the absence of external forces. *Developmental Psychology, 22,* 1–5.

Karmiloff-Smith, A. (1991). Beyond modularity: Innate constraints and developmental change. In S. Carey & R. Gelman (Eds.), *The epigenesis of mind: Essays on biology and cognition* (pp. 171–197). Hillsdale, NJ: Erlbaum.

Karmiloff-Smith, A., & Inhelder, B. (1975). If you want to get ahead, get a theory. *Cognition, 3,* 195–212.

Keil, F. C. (1979). *Semantic and conceptual development.* Cambridge, MA: Harvard University Press.

Keil, F. C. (1989). *Concepts, kinds, and cognitive development.* Cambridge, MA: MIT Press.

Keil, F. C. (1994). The birth and nurturance of concepts by domains: The origins of concepts of living things. In L. A. Hirschfeld & S. A. Gelman (Eds.), *Mapping the mind: Domain specificity in cognition and culture* (pp. 234–254). New York: Cambridge University Press.

Keil, F. C., & Batterman, N. (1984). A characteristic to defining shift in the development of word meaning. *Journal of Verbal Learning and Verbal Behavior, 23,* 221–236.

Kestenbaum, R., & Nelson, C. A. (1990). The recognition and categorization of upright and inverted faces by 7 month old infants. *Infant Behavior and Development, 13,* 497–511.

Kuhl, P. (1985). Categorization of speech by infants. In J. Mehler & R. Fox (Eds.), *Neonate cognition: beyond the blooming, buzzing confusion* (pp. 231–262). Hillsdale, NJ: Erlbaum.

Kuhn, D. (1989). Children and adults as intuitive scientists. *Psychological Review, 96,* 674–689.

Kuhn, T. S. (1962). *The structure of scientific revolutions.* Chicago: University of Chicago Press.

Lakoff, G. (1987). *Women, fire, and dangerous things.* Chicago: University of Chicago Press.

Landau, B., Jones, S., & Smith, L. (1992). Perception, ontology, and naming in young children: Commentary on Soja, Carey, and Spelke. *Cognition, 43,* 85–91.

Landau, B., Smith, L. B., & Jones, S. S. (1988). The importance of shape in early lexical learning. *Cognitive Development, 3,* 299–321.

Legerstee, M. (1992). A review of the animate–inanimate distinction in infancy: Implications for models of social and cognitive knowing. *Early Development and Parenting, 1,* 59–67.

Lewkowicz, D. J., & Turkewitz, G. (1981). Intersensory interaction in newborns: Modification of visual preferences following exposure to sound. *Child Development, 52,* 827–832.

Mandler, J. M. (1983). Representation. In J. H. Flavell & E. M. Markman (Eds.), *Handbook of child psychology* (Vol. 3, pp. 420–494). New York: Wiley.

Mandler, J. M. (1988). How to build a baby: On the development of an accessible representational system. *Cognitive Development, 3,* 113–136.

Mandler, J. M., Bauer, P. J., & McDonough, L. (1991). Separating the sheep from the goats: differentiating global categories. *Cognitive Psychology, 23,* 263–298.

Margolis, E. (1994). A reassessment of the shift from the classical theory of concepts to prototype theory. *Cognition, 51,* 73–89.

Markman, E. M. (1989). *Categorization and naming in children: Problems of induction.* Cambridge, MA: MIT Press.

Markman, E. M., & Callanan, M. A. (1984). An analysis of hierarchical classification. In R. J. Sternberg (Ed.), *Advances in the psychology of human intelligence* (Vol. 2, pp. 325–365). Hillsdale, NJ: Erlbaum.

Markman, E. M., Cox, B., & Machida, S. (1981). The standard object-sorting task as a measure of conceptual organization. *Developmental Psychology, 17,* 115–117.

Markman, E. M., & Hutchinson, J. E. (1984). Children's sensitivity to constraints on word meaning: Taxonomic versus thematic relations. *Cognitive Psychology, 16,* 1–27.

Massey, C., & Gelman, R. (1988). Preschoolers' ability to decide whether a photographed unfamiliar object can move itself. *Developmental Psychology, 24,* 307–317.

Mayr, E. (1988). *Toward a new philosophy of biology: Observations of an evolutionist.* Cambridge, MA: Belknap Press.

McCauley, R. N. (1987). The role of theories in a theory of concepts. In U. Neisser (Ed.), *Concepts and conceptual development: Ecological and intellectual factors in categorization* (pp. 288–309). Cambridge: Cambridge University Press.

McCloskey, M. (1983). Intuitive physics. *Scientific American, 248,* 122–130.

McNamara, T. P., & Sternberg, R. J. (1983). Mental models of word meaning. *Journal of Verbal Learning and Verbal Behavior, 22,* 449–474.

Medin, D. (1989). Concepts and conceptual structure. *American Psychologist, 44,* 1469–1481.

Medin, D., & Ortony, A. (1989). Psychological essentialism. In S. Vosniadou & A. Ortony (Eds.), *Similarity and analogical reasoning* (pp. 179–195). Cambridge: Cambridge University Press.

Medin, D. L., & Schaffer, M. M. (1978). A context theory of classification learning. *Psychological Review, 85,* 207–238.

Mehler, J., Jusczyk, P., Lambertz, G., Halssted, N., Bertoncini, J., & Amiel-Tison, C. (1988). A precursor of language acquisition in young infants. *Cognition, 29,* 143–178.

Meltzoff, A. N., & Borton, R. W. (1979). Intermodal matching by human neonates. *Nature, 282,* 404.

Mervis, C. B. (1987). Child-basic object categories and early lexical development. In U. Neisser (Ed.), *Concepts and conceptual development: Ecological and intellectual factors in categorization* (pp. 201–233). Cambridge: Cambridge University Press.

Mervis, C. B., & Pani, J. R. (1980). Acquisition of basic object categories. *Cognitive Psychology, 12,* 496–522.

Mervis, C. B., & Rosch, E. (1981). Categorization of natural objects. *Annual Review of Psychology, 32,* 89–115.

Morris, M., Nisbett, R., & Peng, K. (1995). Causal attribution across domains and cultures. In D. Sperber, D. Premack, & A. J. Premack (Eds.), *Causal cognition: A multidisciplinary debate* (pp. 577–612). Oxford: Clarendon.

Murphy, G. L. (1993). Theories and concept formation. In *Categories and concepts: Theoretical views and inductive data analysis*. New York: Academic Press.

Murphy, G. L., & Medin, D. L. (1985). The role of theories in conceptual coherence. *Psychological Review, 92*, 289–316.

Nelson, K. (1977). The syntagmatic-paradigmatic shift revisited: A review of research and theory. *Psychological Bulletin, 84*, 93–116.

Nosofsky, R. M. (1986). Attention, similarity, and the identification-categorization relationship. *Journal of Experimental Psychology: General, 115*, 39–57.

Olver, R. R., & Hornsby, J. R. (1966). On equivalence. In J. S. Bruner, R. R. Olver, & P. M. Greenfield, *Studies in cognitive growth* (pp. 68–85). New York: Wiley.

Osherson, D., Smith, E., Wilkie, O., Lopez, A., & Shafir, E. (1990). Category-based induction. *Psychological Review, 97*, 185–200.

Piaget, J. (1929). *The child's conception of the world*. London: Routledge & Kegan Paul.

Piaget, J. (1951). *Play, dreams, and imitation in childhood*. New York: Norton.

Piaget, J. (1952). *The child's concept of number*. New York: Norton.

Pick, H. L., Jr. (1993). Organization of spatial knowledge in children. In N. Eilan, R. McCarthy, & B. Brewer (Eds.), *Spatial representation*. Oxford: Blackwell.

Posner, M. I., & Keele, S. W. (1970). Retention of abstract ideas. *Journal of Experimental Psychology, 77*, 353–363.

Putnam, H. (1973). Meaning and reference. *Journal of Philosophy, 70*, 699–711.

Quine, W. V. (1977). Natural kinds. In S. P. Schwartz (Ed.), *Naming, necessity, and natural kinds* (pp. 155–175). Ithaca, NY: Cornell University Press.

Quinn, P. C., & Eimas, P. D. (1986). On categorization in early infancy. *Merrill-Palmer Quarterly, 32*, 331–363.

Quinn, P. C., Eimas, P. D., & Rosenkrantz, S. L. (1993). Evidence for representations of perceptually similar natural categories by 3-month-old and 4-month-old infants. *Perception, 22*, 463–475.

Rey, G. (1983). Concepts and stereotypes. *Cognition, 15*, 237–262.

Richards, D. D., & Siegler, R. S. (1986). Children's understanding of the attributes of life. *Journal of Experimental Child Psychology, 42*, 1–22.

Rips, L. J. (1989). Similarity, typicality, and categorization. In S. Vosniadou & A. Ortony (Eds.), *Similarity and analogical reasoning* (pp. 23–59). Cambridge: Cambridge University Press.

Rips, L. J., & Collins, A. (1993). Categories and resemblance. *Journal of Experimental Psychology: General, 122*, 468–486.

Rosch, E., & Mervis, C. B. (1975). Family resemblances: Studies in the internal structure of categories. *Cognitive Psychology, 7*, 573–605.

Rosch, E., Mervis, C. B., Gray, W. D., Johnson, D. M., & Boyes-Braem, P. (1976). Basic objects in natural categories. *Cognitive Psychology, 8*, 382–439.

Rose, S. A., & Orlian, E. K. (1991). Asymmetries in infant cross-modal transfer. *Child Development, 62*, 706–718.

Rosen, A. B., & Rozin, P. (1993). Now you see it, now you don't: The preschool child's conception of invisible particles in the context of dissolving. *Developmental Psychology, 29*, 300–311.

Rosengren, K. S., Gelman, S. A., Kalish, C. W., & McCormick, M. (1991). As time goes by: Children's early understanding of growth in animals. *Child Development, 62*, 1302–1320.

Rosengren, K. S., Kalish, C. W., Hickling, A. K., & Gelman, S. A. (1994). Exploring the relation between preschool children's magical beliefs and causal thinking. *British Journal of Developmental Psychology, 12*, 69–82.

Smiley, S. S., & Brown, A. L. (1979). Conceptual preference for thematic or taxonomic relations: A nonmonotonic age trend from preschool to old age. *Journal of Experimental Child Psychology, 28*, 249–257.

Smith, C. (1979). Children's understanding of natural language hierarchies. *Journal of Experimental Child Psychology, 27*, 437–458.

Smith, C., Carey, S., & Wiser, M. (1985). On differentiation: A case study of the development of the concepts of size, weight, and density. *Cognition, 21*, 177–237.

Smith, E. E. (1995). Concepts and categorization. In E. E. Smith & D. Osherson (Eds.), *Invitation to cognitive science. Vol. 3. Thinking* (2nd ed.) (pp. 3–33). Cambridge, MA: MIT Press.

Smith, E. E., & Medin, D. L. (1981). *Categories and concepts.* Cambridge, MA: Harvard University Press.

Smith, E. E., Shoben, E. J., & Rips, L. J. (1974). Structure and process in semantic memory: A featural model for semantic decisions. *Psychological Review, 81*, 214–241.

Smith, E. E., & Sloman, S. A. (1994). Similarity- versus rule-based categorization. *Memory & Cognition, 22*, 377–386.

Smith, L. B., & Jones, S. S. (1993). Cognition without concepts. *Cognitive Development, 8*, 181–188.

Smith, L. B., Jones, S. S., & Landau, B. (1992). Count nouns, adjectives, and perceptual properties in children's novel word interpretations. *Developmental Psychology, 28*, 273–286.

Soja, N. N., Carey, S., & Spelke, E. S. (1991). Ontological categories guide young children's inductions of word meaning: Object terms and substance terms. *Cognition, 38*, 179–211.

Soja, N. N., Carey, S., & Spelke, E. S. (1992). Discussion: Perception, ontology, and meaning. *Cognition, 45*, 101–107.

Solomon, G., Johnson, S., Zaitchik, D., & Carey, S. (1993). *The young child's conception of inheritance.* Paper presented at the meeting of the Society for Research in Child Development, New Orleans, Louisiana.

Sperber, D., Premack, D., & Premack, A. J. (Eds.). (1995). *Causal cognition: A multidisciplinary debate.* Oxford: Clarendon.

Springer, K. (1992). Children's awareness of the biological implications of kinship. *Child Development, 63*, 950–959.

Springer, K., & Keil, F. C. (1989). On the development of biologically specific beliefs: The case of inheritance. *Child Development, 60*, 637–648.

Springer, K., & Keil, F. C. (1991). Early differentiation of causal mechanisms appropriate to biological and nonbiological kinds. *Child Development, 62*, 767–781.

Stavy, R., & Wax, N. (1989). Children's conceptions of plants as living things. *Human Development, 32*, 88–94.

Taylor, M. G. (1993). *Children's beliefs about the biological and social origins of gender differences.* Unpublished doctoral dissertation, University of Michigan.

Taylor, M., & Gelman, S. A. (1989). Incorporating new words into the lexicon: Preliminary evidence for language hierarchies in 2-year-old children. *Child Development, 60*, 625–636.

Teller, D. Y., & Bornstein, M. H. (1987). Infant color vision and color perception. In P. Salapatek & L. B. Cohen (Eds.), *Handbook of infant perception: From sensation to perception* (pp. 185–236). New York: Academic Press.

Vosniadou, S., & Brewer, W. F. (1992). Mental models of the earth: A study of conceptual change in childhood. *Cognitive Psychology, 24*, 535–585.

Vygotsky, L. S. (1962). *Thought and language.* Cambridge, MA: MIT Press.

Ward, T. B., Becker, A. H., Hass, S. D., & Vela, E. (1991). Attribute availability and the shape bias in children's category generalization. *Cognitive Development, 6*, 143–167.

Waxman, S. R. (1990). Linguistic biases and the establishment of conceptual hierarchies: evidence from preschool children. *Cognitive Development, 5*, 123–150.

Waxman, S., & Gelman, R. (1986). Preschoolers' use of superordinate relations in classification and language. *Cognitive Development, 1*, 139–156.

Waxman, S., & Hatch, T. (1992). Beyond the basics: preschool children label objects flexibly at multiple hierarchical levels. *Journal of Child Language, 19,* 153–166.

Wellman, H. M. (1990). *The child's theory of mind.* Cambridge, MA: MIT Press.

Wellman, H. M., & Gelman, S. A. (1992). Cognitive development: Foundational theories of core domains. *Annual Review of Psychology, 43,* 337–375.

Werker, J. (1989). Becoming a native speaker. *American Scientist, 77,* 54–59.

Younger, B. A. (1985). The segregation of items into categories by ten-month-old infants. *Child Development, 56,* 1574–1583.

Younger, B. A., & Cohen, L. B. (1983). Infant perception of correlations among attributes. *Child Development, 54,* 858–867.

CHAPTER 5

Controversies in Language Acquisition: Word Learning and the Part of Speech

Paul Bloom

I. INTRODUCTION

Genuinely new ideas are rare in any field, and the study of word learning is no exception. If Hume, for instance, were to rise from the dead, walk to the nearest university library, and pick up any "state-of-the-art" review on the topic of lexical development, little of what is written would be entirely unfamiliar to him. This is not to deny that there has been progress; it is just that most of this progress has been the development and extension of theories that were proposed long ago. Much current work, for instance, focuses on the nature of children's sensitivity to the intentions of language users, the role of perception in early word learning, and the nature of children's and adults' understanding of names for artifacts and natural kinds. These are the same issues that have occupied scholars since antiquity. There is nothing necessarily wrong about this; perhaps it just shows that one of these traditional perspectives on word learning (Hume's associationism, say, or Plato's nativism) is *right,* and now our task is to find out which and to work out the details.

This chapter is about an exception to the above, as it focuses on something entirely new in the study of word learning. It reviews the status of a proposal first made by Roger Brown in a paper published in 1957 entitled

Perceptual and Cognitive Development
Copyright © 1996 by Academic Press, Inc. All rights of reproduction in any form reserved.

"Linguistic determinism and the part of speech." In the study reported in that paper, Brown showed preschoolers a picture of a strange action performed upon a novel substance with a novel object. One group of children was told, "Do you know what it means to sib? In this picture, you can see sibbing" (verb syntax); another group was told, "Do you know what a sib is? In this picture, you can see a sib" (count noun syntax); and a third group was told, "Have you seen any sib? In this picture, you can see sib" (mass noun syntax). Then the children were shown three pictures, one depicting the same action, another depicting the same object, and a third depicting the same substance. They were asked, according to what they were initially told, either "show me another picture of sibbing" (verb syntax), or "another picture of a sib" (count noun syntax), or "another picture of sib" (mass noun syntax). Brown found that the preschoolers tended to construe the verb as referring to the action, the count noun as referring to the object, and the mass noun as referring to the substance.

Based on these findings, Brown (1957) speculated that "the part-of-speech membership of [a] new word could operate as a filter selecting for attention probably relevant features of the nonlinguistic world" (p. 3) and, more generally, "young English-speaking children take the part-of-speech membership of a new word as a clue to the meaning of the word" (5).

This is a radical claim. Common sense tells us that children learn the meanings of words by somehow drawing upon their understanding of the external world. Under some theories, they use spatiotemporal association to link up words with their referents. For instance, Locke (1690/1964, Book 3.IX.9) proposed that "people ordinarily show [children] the thing whereof they would have them have the idea, and then repeat to them the name that stands for it." Alternatively, more sophisticated cognitive mechanisms, such as children's sensitivity to the intentions of others, are sometimes said to underlie the word learning process. Thus Augustine sees word learning as a highly *inferential* process: "When they [my elders] named any thing, and as they spoke turned towards it, I saw and remembered that they called what they would point out by the name they uttered. And that they meant this thing and no other was plain from the motion of their body, the natural language, as it were, of all nations, expressed by the countenance, glances of the eye, gestures of the limbs, and tones of the voice, indicating the affections of the mind, as it pursues, possesses, rejects, or shuns." (*Confessions* I:8). These otherwise quite different proposals share the assumption that children learn the meaning of a word by attending to information about the external world, such as what the adult is looking toward when the word is being uttered.

Brown's proposal suggests an alternative mechanism, as it shifts the emphasis from the *content* of the situation toward the *form* of the linguistic expression. It may not be entirely by virtue of relating "dogs" to our perception of dogs or "running" to our perception of running that one learns the meaning of such words—perhaps word learning succeeds at least in part because we attend to the grammatical contexts in which the words "dogs" and "running" are used.

I will first review research on the nature and development of the capacity to use syntactic cues to acquire aspects of the meanings of words. Following this, two specific questions will be addressed:

1. Where does the capacity to use syntactic cues to determine word meanings come from?
2. How powerful are syntactic cues; that is, how much of the meanings of words do they provide children? Are they necessary for the acquisition of some word meanings?

This chapter concludes by considering the proper place of syntactic cues to word meaning within the broader context of a theory of early language development.

II. EVIDENCE CONCERNING THE ROLE OF SYNTAX IN WORD LEARNING

Before reviewing the studies that address the role of syntactic cues in the acquisition of word meaning, there are some qualifications that should be made concerning the conclusions that one can draw from this research.

First, a distinction must be made between information conveyed by syntax versus information conveyed by sentence meaning. It is obvious that people can learn aspects of a word's meaning from the meaning of a sentence or a set of sentences without any help of extrasentential information—this is why there are dictionaries. Such a process is likely to play an important role in word learning, even with young children. For instance, hearing the sentence "John prefers to drive a zoop" can tell you a lot about what the new word "zoop" refers to. It is unlikely to be a nightmare, for instance, or a spoon, but it could be a car, a boat, or a plane. This inference is based on our understanding of the sorts of things people drive, and not the syntactic context in which the word "zoop" appears.

The distinction between context and syntax might seem clear enough in principle, but they are often difficult to distinguish in practice. For instance, Fisher, Hall, Rakowitz, and Gleitman (1994) describe children's understanding of the semantic implications of the contrast between "The elephant is zorking the ball to the bunny" versus "The bunny is zorking the ball from the elephant" as evidence for sensitivity to syntax, while Pinker (1994) argues that children are drawing inferences from the semantic properties of the prepositions, and thus such inferences are not syntactically based. There *are* clear cases of syntactic cues (such as sensitivity to transitive vs. intransitive verb frames) and clear cases of nonsyntactic contextual information (such as sensitivity to specific semantic implications of verbs like "drive"), but in some experiments it is hard to tell whether the results bear on children's ability to draw inferences about meaning of words based on their syntax, or on their ability to draw inferences about the meanings of words based on the meanings of other words in the sentences that they appear in.

Second, there is a difference between showing that children understand some mappings between syntax and semantics and showing that this understanding can lead to actual inferences about word meaning. Gathercole (1986) points out, for instance, that the Brown experiment described above does not actually show that children can use syntax to *learn* aspects of word meaning, since they could succeed at this task without attending to the new word at all; all they have to attend to is the syntactic frame of the question: "Show me another picture of _____ing/ of a _____/ of _____". A similar point applies to other studies, such as those reported by Bloom (1994a) and Hirsh-Pasek, Gleitman, Gleitman, Golinkoff, and Naigles (1988). These studies show that children are sensitive to the semantic implications of syntactic structure, which is consistent with, but not the same as, showing that they can use this understanding to learn new words.

A related concern is that in some experiments children can learn the meaning of a new word by using syntactic cues to determine the English word it corresponds to. Pinker (1994) notes that this use of syntax as a "retrieval cue" does not require any understanding of the implications that syntactic cues have for semantics. To make this point, he gives the example of an experimenter showing children a scene ambiguous between pushing and falling and saying either, "The puppet calls this p . . . " or "The puppet calls this f. . . ." In such a task, children would presumably say "pushing" and "falling" appropriately, by using the sound as a retrieval cue to the relevant English word. But this surely does not show that children can use universal sound-meaning mappings to learn word meanings. By the same token, then, studies in which the child can use syntax to match up a novel word with a pre-existing lexical item do not necessarily show that syntax-semantics mappings play any role in acquisition of a first language.

A final concern has to do with syntactic ambiguity. Some experimenters have found that when children are exposed to a novel lexical Noun Phrase (e.g., "This is zav") describing an animate entity, they will tend to treat the new word as a proper name, as in "This is Fred." Others expose children to a novel adjective (e.g., "This is zav") and find that they construe it as naming a property or subkind, as in "This is red," and still others present children with a novel mass noun (e.g., " This is zav") and find that they construe the word as naming a kind of substance or stuff, as in "This is water." The thing to note about these studies is that the *same* surface string is used to signal each of the different syntactic contexts. In other words, a sentence such as "This is zav" is highly ambiguous.

This has some effect on how we interpret the developmental findings. For instance, in a study by Katz, Baker, and Macnamara (1974) discussed below, children heard a doll described as "this is zav" and tended to interpret "zav" as a proper name. One might be tempted to interpret this as follows: The children knew the word was a lexical Noun Phrase, knew that lexical NPs refer to specific individuals, and inferred that "zav" is a proper name. But this cannot be right, since the word could have been, by virtue of its syntactic frame, an adjective naming a property or a mass noun naming a substance. The actual process must therefore be more complicated than the child exploiting a simple one-to-one mapping from syntactic contexts to aspects of word meaning. Instead the process might be better viewed as one of *convergence*—from the standpoint of the child in the Katz et al. study, the situation had multiple salient interpretations (the word could plausibly refer to a kind of individual or to the specific individual), and so did the surface string (the word could be a lexical Noun Phrase, mass noun, or adjective). But only one interpretation of the situation (the specific individual) matched one of the grammatical interpretations (the Noun Phrase), and this correspondence guided children to the proper name construal. I will return to the question of the precise role of syntax below, in Section V.

A. Nominals

Every language has a distinct grammatical class of nominals; these are used as names, to refer to entities in the world (Bloomfield, 1933; Macnamara, 1982, 1986; Schacter, 1985). In English, nominals fall into three main classes: count nouns, mass nouns, and lexical Noun Phrases (lexical NPs). Count nouns are words like "dog" and "nightmare," which can follow quantifiers such as "a" and "many," and which can be counted and pluralized. Mass nouns are words like "sand" and "advice," which can follow quantifiers such as "much" and "some"—but not "a" and "many"—and which cannot be counted or pluralized. Lexical NPs are words like "Fred" and "she," which are identical syntactically to phrasal Noun Phrases, such as "the dog" or "my cat," as they cannot be modified or quantified at all. (These words are often described as "proper nouns," but this is misleading, as they are not nouns, and the proper/common contrast is semantic, not syntactic.)

One of the major findings in the study of word learning has to do with the acquisition of names for things. When children are exposed to a novel word referring to an unfamiliar object, they tend to interpret the word as referring to that kind of whole object—and not as naming a part of the object, a property of the object, the stuff that the object is made out of, or the activity performed by or on the object (e.g., Au, Dapretto, & Song, 1994; Baldwin, 1989; Macnamara, 1982; Markman & Wachtel, 1988; Soja, Carey, & Spelke, 1991; Taylor & Gelman, 1988; Waxman, 1994). At least at first, the overt syntax of the word appears to play no role in this process. For instance, Waxman and Markow (in press) find that 12- to 13-month-olds behave the same regardless of whether the word is presented as a noun ("See the auto") or as an adjective ("See the auto-ish one")—both nouns and adjectives draw children's attention to the objects, more so than if children are given no word at all ("See this").

Children's early word learning capacities are not, however, limited to the acquisition of names for object kinds. Soja et al. (1991) explored the possibility that young 2-year-olds would be constrained by the ontological category of what a word describes. Children were presented with novel words in either neutral syntax ("This is my blicket"), or informative syntax ("This is a/another blicket" for count noun syntax; "This is some/some more blicket" for mass noun syntax). The words were used to describe objects (e.g., a T-shaped plumbing fixture) or substances (e.g., Nivea cream). Soja et al. found that children extend words referring to solid objects to objects of the same shape, ignoring substance, while extending words referring to nonsolid substances to substances of the same material, ignoring shape. Count-mass syntax had no effect on children's responses. Similarly, Sabrahamyam, Gelman, and Landau (under review) find that even 3-year-olds tend to treat labels for objects as referring to the kind of object and labels for substances as referring to the kind of stuff, regardless of the count-mass status of these labels. These results suggest that children appreciate the ontological distinction between objects and substances prior to the acquisition of syntax, and that this capacity underlies their early acquisition of words.[1]

Even without overt syntactic cues, then, children are capable of learning names for substances. This is consistent with observations of children's spontaneous speech finding early use of substance names, like "water" and "milk." Similarly, it is likely that names for individuals, such as pronouns and proper names, can be learned by children prior to their ability to respond to overt syntactic cues, as some such expressions also appear among their very first words (Nelson, 1973).

Further research on the acquisition of nominals, discussed below, focuses on the role of count-mass syntax and the noun/NP distinction in guiding children to different construals of word meaning.

1. Count Nouns

Using the same design as Soja et al. (1991), Soja (1992) found that once children show productive command of the count–mass distinction, they can use count-mass syntax to infer aspects of word meaning. When taught a mass noun that describes a pile of stuff, they tend to construe it as referring to that kind of stuff (i.e., as having a similar meaning to words like "clay"), but when taught a count noun that describes a pile of stuff, many construe it as referring not to the stuff itself, but to the bounded pile (i.e., as having a similar meaning to words like "puddle" or "pile").

This effect of syntax was limited to the stuff condition. When children were taught count nouns and mass nouns describing a novel object, their interpretation was not affected by the mass noun syntax (i.e., they did *not* construe the mass noun as having the same meaning as words like "wood" or "metal.") This is an interesting asymmetry; count noun syntax can guide children away from construing a word referring to a substance as naming the kind of substance, but mass noun syntax cannot override the tendency to treat a word referring to an object as naming a kind of object. This is consistent with other research on the acquisition of solid-substance names that will be discussed below.

A study by McPherson (1991) explored 2- and 3-year-olds' sensitivity to syntax in a different way, exploiting the ambiguity of the phrase "a little," which can be a quantifier indicating a small amount when used with a mass noun (e.g., "a little water") or a determiner and adjective indicating a small object when used with a count noun (e.g., "a little cup"). Children were taught a word with either count syntax or mass syntax (e.g., "These are vaxes . . . Have you ever seen so many vaxes?" vs. "This is vax . . . Have you ever seen so much vax?"); and shown either objects (small yellow pompons of two different sizes with faces on them) or stuff (tapioca pearls of two different sizes). They then were asked to "Give me a little vax."

McPherson found that children were more likely to choose a small pompon when presented with a count noun than with a mass noun, and more likely to scoop up a small amount of tapioca when presented with a mass noun than with a count noun. This suggests that the count noun syntax biased them toward treating "a little vax" as referring to a small object, while mass noun syntax favored treating the phrase as referring to a small amount, providing further evidence that children are sensitive to the relation between count–mass syntax and aspects of word meaning.

For 2- and 3-year-olds, then, count noun syntax ("This is a zav") guides them to a specific interpretation of the meaning of a word, one that is different from the interpretations they would come to if exposed to other syntactic frames, such as mass noun syntax ("This is some zav"). A question of some interest concerns the precise nature of the semantic correlate of the category "count noun." When children (or adults for that matter) hear a novel word used in count noun syntax, precisely what does this tell them about the meaning of the word?

It is clear from the evidence reviewed above that count noun syntax can inform them that a word refers to an object. One possibility is that this is *all* that count noun syntax maps onto. In other words, by the time children are about $2\frac{1}{2}$ years old, the conceptual correlate of "count noun" is "kind of discrete physical object."[2]

There is some evidence that favors an alternative perspective, which is that, even for young children, the semantic correlate of count noun is "kind of individual," where "individual" is more abstract than "object," including some events (" a race"), bounded substances ("a puddle"), abstract entities ("a joke"), and so on. Kinds of objects tend to be named by count nouns only because objects are salient individuals within the material domain. Several considerations, outlined below, favor this kind-of-individual hypothesis over the kind-of-object proposal (for more detailed discussion see Bloom, 1993; Bloom and Kelemen 1995).

First, most count nouns do not refer to kinds of objects. Some refer to collections ("army," "family," "flock"), others to parts ("finger," "foot," "handle"), and most do not refer to material entities at all ("nap," "idea," "race," "tantrum"). These abstract nouns show up in the spontaneous speech of young children. Nelson (1990, p. 335), for instance, stresses that "many abstract social and cultural concepts . . . are incorporated into the language and presented in passing to children, who pick them up seemingly without effort," and lists some words found in the speech of 20-month-olds, including the count nouns "bath," "breakfast," "friend," "week," and "uncle." In support of this, Nelson, Hampson, and Shaw (1993) analyzed the speech of forty-five 20-month-olds and found that only about half of their nominals referred to basic-level object kinds; many referred to locations ("beach"), temporal entities ("day"), and events ("party").

Similar abstract notions can be found in prelinguistic infants. Studies involving cross-modal matching of numerosity find that 6- to 9-month-olds realize that there is an equivalence between two sounds and two objects, and between three sounds and three objects (Starkey, Spelke, & Gelman, 1990). Six-month-olds are also sensitive to the numerosity of a sequence of distinct actions, such as the jumps of a puppet (Wynn, 1993). Since enumeration requires individuation, these findings suggest that infants possess a notion of "individual" sufficiently abstract to encompass objects, sounds, and actions. Thus, it is possible that such a notion is mapped very early onto the grammatical class of count nouns.

This is not to deny that the proportion of count nouns that name objects is greater in the lexicons of children than of adults (R. Brown, 1957; Macnamara, 1982). But this is likely to have more to do with the life-styles of young children than with inherent limitations in their semantic competence. Children live in a world of cookies and diapers, while adult discourse deals with more abstract entities like faculty meetings and plane reservations.

The precise nature of the count–mass distinction suggests another reason to favor the "kind-of-individual" theory. From the standpoint of semantic theory, the count–mass distinction is quantificational, mapping onto a contrast between entities quantified as individuals versus entities quantified as nonindividuated "stuff." There is no principled linguistic difference between a count noun like "dog" and a count noun like "nap" (Bloom, 1994a;

Gordon, 1988; Jackendoff, 1991). As soon as children start to use count–mass syntax in their productive speech, names for nonobject individuals such as "nap" are marked appropriately as count nouns, just as words like "dog" are (Gordon, 1992). This suggests that there may be no substantive difference between how children and adults understand the semantic implications of the syntactic category "count noun."

A further consideration is empirical, emerging from research exploring how children determine the syntactic categories that words belong to; for instance, how they determine that "dog" is a count noun and "water" is a mass noun. Gordon (1985) found that if preschoolers hear a word used with count noun syntax (e.g., "This is a blicket") they will categorize it as a count noun and if they hear it used with mass noun syntax (e.g., "This is some blicket"), they will categorize it as mass, even if the count noun usage describes a substance and the mass noun usage describes an object. Apparently, the linguistic cues override the object/substance distinction when the child determines whether a new word is count or mass (see also Gathercole, 1986).

These results are sometimes interpreted as showing that the preschooler's understanding of the count–mass distinction is not semantic at all; it is instead "formal" or "distributional" (Levy, 1988; Schlesinger, 1988). But this interpretation is unwarranted, particularly since R. Brown (1957) and Soja (1992) have shown that much younger children are sensitive to count–mass syntax when making semantic inferences. What the results actually suggest is that children's understanding of the count–mass distinction does not reduce to a contrast between objects and nonsolid substances, but is sufficiently abstract to quantify material objects as stuff (perhaps as solid-substance names; see below) and nonsolid substances as individuals (see also Bloom, 1994b; Gordon, 1988).

Finally, there is evidence that children can use count noun syntax to acquire the meanings of words that refer to kinds of nonobject individuals. One such study was mentioned above; recall that Soja (1992) found that when shown a substance named with a count noun, 2-year-olds inferred that the noun extended to other bounded individuals of the same kind; they did not infer that it was a name for the kind of stuff. In other words, they treated it as having a meaning like "puddle," referring to a bounded portion of stuff. In another study (Bloom, 1994a), 3- and 4-year-olds were taught names for a string of bell sounds from a tape recorder, presented in rapid sequence so that they could be construed either as a set of discrete sounds or as undifferentiated noise. They were told either, "These are feps—there really are a lot of feps here" (count noun condition) or "This is fep—there really is a lot of fep here" (mass noun condition). Then children were given a stick and a bell; those who were taught the word as a count noun were asked to "make a fep," while those taught the word as a mass noun were told to "make fep." Even the 3-year-olds tended to make a single sound when asked to make "a fep" and to make a lot of sounds when asked to make "fep," suggesting that they can map count noun syntax onto discrete sounds/actions and mass noun syntax onto continuous sounds/actions.

More recently, Bloom and Kelemen (1995) attempted to teach 4-year-olds, 5-year-olds, and adults novel collective nouns. Subjects were shown an array of unfamiliar objects described either as "These are fendles" or as "This is a fendle." The prediction was that subjects would interpret the plural count noun as an object name, while singular count noun syntax would focus them on the collection as a single individual, on a par with nouns like "army" and "family."

Adults and 5-year-olds were sensitive to the syntactic manipulation, treating the plural count noun as an object name and the singular count noun as a collective noun. This effect was not significant for the 4-year-olds, however. There was an increasing trend with age in the tendency to give the collective interpretation when exposed to a singular count noun. Contrary to the "kind-of-object" theory, however, this was not due to a bias toward construing the word as an object name—errors tended to be evenly divided, with many of the children mistakenly treating the plural count noun as naming the collection. In other words, the failure of the 4-year-olds to learn the collective noun was not due to an across-the-board bias to treat the count noun as naming a kind of object.

These developmental changes could be due to linguistic factors (children are less sensitive to syntactic cues than adults are) or to conceptual factors (children have a different notion of "individual" from adults). One version of the conceptual hypothesis is that the stimuli used in the collection experiment (groups of unrelated objects) were unlikely candidates to be construed as individuals, and children balked at doing so. Real collections described by count nouns have some connection between their elements, either spatiotemporal (as in a bunch of grapes) or more abstract (as in the social relations between members of a family). Ongoing experiments are focusing on the acquisition of names for collections that satisfy certain conceptual criteria for being individuals. The prediction is that if a group of objects is presented in such a way that it "makes sense" as a single entity (in particular, if the group is itself causally potent), even 2- and 3-year-olds should be able to learn a count noun that describes it.

The issues here extend beyond the study of word learning. Count nouns are the linguistic items devoted to picking out kinds of individuals that are central to our understanding of the physical and social world: entities like dogs and cups, families and committees, arguments and jokes. As such, exploring children's understanding of the semantic nature of count nouns might give us some insight into the core of our conceptual system, our "naive ontology" and how it develops.

2. Lexical Noun Phrases

Even prior to acquiring the count-mass distinction, children can use nominal syntax to help acquire aspects of word meaning. In the first study to address the role of syntactic cues since R. Brown (1957), Katz et al. (1974) explored the interaction between syntactic cues and context in the acquisition of names for kinds and individuals. They noted that words describing certain animate beings (and surrogates for animate beings, like dolls) can name either kinds or individuals (e.g., "person" or "Henry"). They speculated that children could use syntax to help learn the meanings of such words. Entities like blocks, however, are not the sorts of things that get their own name. Katz et al. speculated that children would always treat a word describing a block as a name for the kind (e.g., "block"), not the unique individual, regardless of the syntax.

To explore this, they presented children with a novel word occurring either with or without a determiner (e.g., "This is zav" vs. "This is a/the zav"). In a sentence like "This is zav," "zav" can be a lexical NP, while in a sentence like "This is a/the zav," "zav" must be a count noun. For each child, the word was applied either to a doll or to a block. After being taught the word, children were tested to see whether they would extend it to another doll/block (consistent with the kind interpretation) or whether they would restrict it to the original item (consistent with the individual interpretation).

Katz et al.'s predictions were supported: 17-month-old girls (but not boys) were sensitive to syntactic cues when learning the name for the doll, construing "zav" in "This is zav" as a proper name and "zav" in "This is a/the zav" as a name for the kind. In contrast, all of the children applied the kind interpretation for words referring to the block regardless of the syntactic context in which the words were used.

S. A. Gelman and Taylor (1984) replicated this study with slightly older children, changing the methodology and stimuli in certain regards. One change involved using unfamiliar kinds of objects as stimuli; another involved adding a distracter item to the forced choice during testing, so as to control for the possibility of guessing. They found much the same as Katz et al.'s finding: 2½-year-olds were sensitive to the syntax when words named the "animate" entities. They also found that when a lexical NP was used to describe an inanimate object, children tended to choose the distracter item, which is consistent with the view that they were confused by the use of the NP to refer to this sort of object (why would an inanimate thing get its own name?), and were searching for another referent to apply it to.

Hall (1991) manipulated familiarity, using the same methodology as Gelman and Taylor, and found that children were more likely to interpret a lexical NP as a proper name if they already knew the name for the kind of object it refers to. This supports the notion that children have a constraint or principle biasing them against learning more than one name for the same kind of object (Clark, 1987; Markman & Wachtel, 1988).

Liittschwager and Markman (1993) explored the possibility that children in the above studies might have been taking the new word within the "This is zav" sentences as an *adjective* (and thus denoting a subkind or property, as in "This is red"). If so, then their choice of the original item during testing would not be because they were picking out the same individual originally named as "zav," but because they were picking out the object that has the same perceptual properties as this individual. To test this, Liittschwager and Markman showed 3-year-olds an object (such as a bear or shoe), named it ("This is zav" or "This is a zav"), and then moved it to another location and removed a salient property, so that it looked different. Then they took out a second item, also without this property, and placed it next to the first, so that children were facing two objects that looked identical. Children were then asked, "Where's zav?" or "Where's a zav?" If they were learning the lexical NP as a name for the individual, they should point to the moved object, tracking it over space and time, while if they thought the word named a property, they should show no preference in its usage, since the items looked identical. Liittschwager and Markman found that when given sentences such as "This is zav" (but not when given sentences such as "This is a zav"), children chose the same individual they were first shown, consistent with the view that they took the lexical NP as naming an individual, not a property.

Finally, Bloom (1990) explored children's understanding of the relationship between syntax and semantics in a different way, analyzing the spontaneous speech of 1- and 2-year-olds. This analysis tested whether their usage of names for individuals and kinds of individuals was consistent with the syntactic properties of these words. Lexical NPs (like "Fred" and "she") cannot be modified by prenominal adjectives; as a result, phrases like "happy Fred" or "tall she" are ungrammatical. One can only attribute properties to specific individuals with predicates, as in "Fred is happy" or "She is tall." Nouns, in contrast, can appear with both modifiers and predicate adjectives, and thus both "the big dog" and "the dog is big" are acceptable. These syntactic properties of English are not universal; Japanese, for instance, shows a different pattern (Fukui, 1987).

Children honored this syntactic constraint even in their earliest word combinations, suggesting that they: (1) knew which words referred to individuals and which referred to kinds; (2) categorized these words as nouns and NPs appropriately; and (3) had acquired language-particular restrictions on the use of nouns and NPs. These findings provide indirect support for the Katz et al. proposal, showing that the relevant syntax-semantics mappings exist in the minds of young children and apply very early in the process of language development.

3. Mass Nouns

The results from the R. Brown (1957) study show that mass syntax can direct a child toward interpreting a new word as referring to a nonsolid substance, like "water" or "milk" (Soja, 1992; Sabrahmanyam et al., under review). But what about words for *solid* substances, such as "wood"? From a quantificational standpoint these are also nonindividuated entities—one cannot count wood, one must count *pieces* of wood. Wood also passes the "universal grinder" criteria for stuff (Pelletier, 1979); if you grind up wood, you still get wood (compare this with what happens when you grind up a desk).

Solid substances differ from nonsolid substances like water or sand, however. For one thing, they are not malleable or fluid. Moreover, any chunk of solid substance is also, by necessity, a discrete physical object, and so it might require some conceptual work to think about the chunk as a portion of stuff rather than thinking about the chunk as an individual countable entity, as a whole object. Do these considerations make such words harder to learn?

Explorations of children's production (Soja, 1991) and comprehension (Dickinson, 1986; Prasada, 1993) suggest that 2- and 3-year-olds' understanding of English solid-substance names is relatively limited. On the other hand, Soja (1991) found that *adults* rarely use such names when speaking to children, so children's ignorance could be due to the input they receive, not to limitations in their own capacities.

Dickinson (1988) attempted to teach preschoolers new substance names in a set of experiments in which he showed children objects or chunks of objects made of novel solid substances. Children were presented with words in neutral syntax (e.g., "This is the blicket"), count syntax (e.g., "This is a blicket"), mass syntax ("This is some blicket"), or an informative/mass noun condition (e.g., "This is made of blicket"). When the items were objects, the preschoolers were poor at interpreting the words as solid substance names, regardless of the linguistic context (Markman & Wachtel, 1988). Five-year-olds, on the other hand, showed more sensitivity to the linguistic manipulation, giving the substance interpretation over half of the time in the "made of" condition as compared to less than one-fifth of the time in the neutral condition. Dickinson concluded that young children find solid-substance names hard to learn, regardless of the syntax.

Prasada (1993) noted, however, that certain aspects of this study biased against children being able to learn the mass noun as a solid-substance name. In particular, the objects used in Dickinson's study were unfamiliar to the children and there is evidence (see above) that children have a bias to treat new words referring to unfamiliar objects as naming the kind of object. In an experiment using familiar objects, Prasada (1993) found that even 2- and 3-year-olds were capable of learning solid substance names when they were presented with mass syntax and in "made of" constructions, for example, "Give Cookie Monster the thing that is made of sponge." Similarly, Markman and Wachtel (1988) found that children could interpret the word "pewter" in the sentence "This is pewter" as a substance name (or at least as referring to a substancelike property) when the object that it described was familiar and already had a name.

The explanation adopted by Prasada (1993) is primarily linguistic: children have an overriding bias to construe new words as referring to object kinds, thus explaining Dickinson's findings, but there also exist lexical principles that bias against having different words with overlapping reference (mutual exclusivity; Markman & Wachtel, 1988). As a result, using objects with familiar names allowed children to entertain other interpretations of the word's meaning, including the solid-substance construal.

It is unclear, however, whether children's difficulty learning solid substance names for unfamiliar objects can be entirely attributed to an "object-kind" linguistic bias. After all, even 2-year-olds are capable of learning proper names that refer to unfamiliar objects (S. A. Gelman & Taylor, 1984), and slightly older children can learn adjectives for such objects (see below). This suggests that there may be other considerations explaining children's difficulty with names for solid substances. One logical possibility is that young children have no understanding of the referents of these terms, no understanding of the idea of solid stuff—but this seems to be mistaken, as there is evidence that 3-year-olds are actually fairly knowledgeable about certain properties of solid substances, though their understanding does differ in important ways from that of adults (Au, 1994; Massey & Gelman, 1988; C. Smith, Carey, & Wiser, 1985).

Children's problems with solid-substance names may instead be due to their strong bias to treat whole objects as individuals. Note that this bias is not limited to word learning, as it also shows up when children are asked to *count* different sorts of things, like parts and colors (Shipley & Shepperson, 1990). Such a bias would not get in the way of learning proper names, (which refer to specific individuals) or most adjectives (which refer to attributes of individuals), but it would interfere with the learning of solid-substance names, as construing an entity as a portion of stuff is plainly inconsistent with construing it as a single individual. Such a bias may be difficult for children to override, which would lead to their difficulty acquiring solid-substance names.

B. Verbs

Further research concerns the acquisition of verbs. This work has generated considerable controversy, more so than for the domains discussed above. While investigators such as Brown and Katz et al. have argued that syntax can *facilitate* the acquisition of nominal meanings, some scholars have made the stronger claim that syntax plays a central role in the acquisition of verbs, and is perhaps essential for the acquisition of some verb meanings (Gleitman, 1990). This is a provocative and important claim that we will return to below.

Naigles (1990) conducted one of the first studies on the role of syntactic cues in verb learning. She showed 25-month-olds videotaped scenes showing two events: a causal event with two participants, and a noncausal event with a single participant. For instance, a duck would repeatedly push a rabbit into a bending position at the same time that both the rabbit and duck were waving their free arms. Children saw the video as they heard a novel verb in either a transitive context ("The duck is gorping the bunny") or an intransitive context ("The duck and the bunny are gorping"). Then children were shown two new videos simultaneously—one containing just the causal scene (a duck pushing a rabbit, with no arm waving), the other containing just the noncausal scene (the duck and rabbit arm waving, with no pushing)—and were told "Find gorping." The 2-year-olds looked longer at the causal scene when they had heard the transitive verb and longer at the noncausal scene when they had heard the intransitive verb.

Naigles and Kako (1993) conducted further experiments suggesting that, while causation is associated with transitive verb frames, it is not an essential semantic correlate. Two-year-olds who were exposed to a verb in a transitive frame tended to associate the verb to actions of *contact without causation* (as when a frog repeatedly touches the duck, without any effect) more so than those children who were exposed to the verb in only a neutral frame ("Look! Gorping!"). This suggests that hearing a verb used in a transitive frame might inform the child that the verb refers to an action with some property more general than causation, such as "object affectedness" (Gropen et al., 1991).

A different methodology was used by Fisher et al. (1994). Three-year-olds, 4-year-olds, and adults were shown a video depicting an event and given sentences with novel verbs to describe it, for example, "The bunny is nading the elephant" versus "The elephant is daking." The scenes were chosen so that actions in them could be described with existing English words. When subjects were asked what these verbs meant, they tended to give correct translations or paraphrases. For instance, when presented with a video in which the bunny was giving food to the elephant, children would tend to say that "nading" meant "feeding" and "daking" meant "eating," suggesting that their interpretations of the meaning of the words were guided by syntactic cues.

The precise interpretation of the Fisher et al. results is a matter of some disagreement: Pinker (1994) has suggested that they show children can *access* existing lexical items via syntactic structure, but do not support the stronger claim that they can use syntax to *learn* new words (see Section II). In response to this concern, Fisher et al. (1994) conducted a further analysis of those instances where children responded with phrasal descriptions instead of existing English words (e.g., they said "licking it off the spoon" instead of "eating"). An analysis of the 3- and 4-year-olds taken together found that the same effect of syntax held even for these cases, suggesting that while prior lexical knowledge might play some role in children's responses (since they might have accessed these phrasal descriptions only via their knowledge of existing English words), these results cannot be entirely due to direct lexical retrieval.

Other research by Fisher (under review) explored the role of linguistic cues with 3- and 5-year-olds in a different fashion. Children were shown videos depicting novel events and were presented with sentences differing in number of arguments (e.g., "She's pilking" vs. "She's pilking her") and in the type of preposition (e.g., "She's pilking the ball to her" vs. "She's pilking the ball from her"). The subjects were then asked to point to the person performing the action (e.g., "Who's pilking the ball to her?"). Fisher found that 3-year-olds responded to these linguistic manipulations (syntactic in the case of transitive vs. intransitive; lexical in the case of "in" vs. "from") when inferring the agent of the new verb.

An interesting feature of this study was that all the NP arguments were ambiguous feminine pronouns ("she" or "her"), forcing children to use their understanding of the semantic implications of the syntactic parse of the sentence to discover the agent. Fisher speculates that children can use a process of "analogical mapping," in which a sentence structure has its own abstract relational meaning, to determine those aspects of the event relevant to the meaning of the verb (see also Goldberg, 1993).

Other evidence supports some of the premises behind the proposal that syntactic cues are relevant to verb learning. It has long been noted that there are correspondences between verb syntax and verb semantics, some of which are universal (e.g., Jackendoff, 1990; Levin, 1993; Pinker, 1989) and studies of parental speech suggest that the relevant cues to verb meaning are present in the sentences that children hear (e.g., Fisher, Gleitman, & Gleitman, 1991; Naigles & Hoff-Ginsberg, in press). Further, young children are sensitive to the syntactic distinctions required for such an acquisition procedure to work: using preferential looking tasks, Hirsh-Pasek, Golinkoff, Fletcher, DeGaspe Beaubien, and Cauley (1985) found that 17-month-olds are sensitive to word order in English (discriminating between sentences like "Big Bird is tickling Cookie Monster" and "Cookie Monster is tickling Big Bird"), and Hirsh-Pasek et al. (1988) found that 27-month-olds are sensitive to the difference between sentences like "Big Bird is flexing with Cookie Monster" and "Big Bird is flexing Cookie Monster."

Finally, Naigles and her colleagues (Naigles, Fowler, & Helm, 1992;

Naigles, Gleitman, & Gleitman, 1993) have studied the effect of anomalous syntax on children's understanding of the meaning of words that they already know. For instance, they were presented with sentences such as "the zebra brings to Noah" in which the verb "bring" is used in an inappropriate syntactic context. Children tend to focus on the syntactic context, interpreting "bring" as meaning "come" (consistent with the context, but inconsistent with the lexical entry for "bring"). While this research is only indirectly related to the question of whether children can use syntax to acquire the meanings of novel lexical items, it does provide further evidence that they are sensitive to syntax-semantics mappings.

C. Adjectives

Unlike nouns, adjectives appear to draw children's attention toward properties or subkinds. For instance, Taylor and Gelman (1988) presented 2- and 3-year-olds with either a novel noun ("a zav") or a novel adjective ("a zav one") describing an object. They found that children who heard the word as a noun extended the word to objects of the same kind more often than they extended the word to objects that share the same superficial properties, while children who heard it as an adjective gave the opposite response— focusing more on properties, like color, pattern, and texture, and less on object kind (S. A. Gelman and Markman, 1985). L. B. Smith, Jones, and Landau (1992) obtained a similar finding, noting also that the shape bias that exists for count nouns does not apply to the same extent for adjectives. Using a similar design, Waxman and Kosowski (1990) found that nouns focused children on taxonomic categories (following Markman & Hutchinson, 1984), but that adjectives did not.

Other research explores the effect of the noun/adjective contrast on children's hierarchical classification. In a task involving classifying animals and foods, for instance, Waxman (1990) found that nouns facilitated categorization at the superordinate level, but not at the subordinate level (Waxman & Gelman, 1986), while adjectives provided the opposite effect, drawing attention to subordinate kinds.

Some puzzles arise here, as the relationship between the two putative semantic roles of adjectives—adjectives as denoting properties (as viewed by Smith et al., for instance) versus adjectives as denoting subkinds (as viewed by Waxman, for instance)—is unclear. Adjectives do often mark subordinate categories, but there are many exceptions. A typical adjective is "good," but good things are not a meaningful subordinate category within a psychologically natural taxonomy. Conversely, poodles and collies are perfectly good subkinds, but this contrast is marked by nouns, not by adjectives.

It may be that the syntactic category "adjective" is too rough grained to capture the sorts of semantic implications children and adults are sensitive to. Bolinger (1967) distinguishes between predication (as in "The dog is fep") and modification (as in "the fep dog"). Roughly, predication attributes a property to the entity denoted by a Noun Phrase (the specific dog), while modification is "restrictive"; it picks out a subclass of the kind of entity referred to by a noun (the category of dogs). One might tentatively suggest that the results from the property studies are tapping children's sensitivity to adjectives-as-predicates, while those from the subkind studies are tapping children's sensitivity to adjectives-as-modifiers. In support of this, Prasada (under review) presents evidence suggesting that 2- and 3-year-olds are sensitive to the rather subtle semantic differences between modificational and predicative usages of adjectives. He found that children are more likely to give the adjective a "restrictive" interpretation when it appears prenominally, as a modifier, than when it appears as a predicate.

A final issue concerns cross-linguistic differences. Waxman, Senghas, and Benveniste (under review) report a series of experiments that explore the interpretation of novel adjectives and novel nouns by monolingual French and Spanish speakers, and they compare this to previous research with English children. The relevant finding for the purposes here is the contrast between children learning Spanish, in which the noun can be omitted if it is recoverable from the discourse, with those learning English, in which the noun cannot usually be omitted. If there are six mugs and one wants to refer to a specific mug, one would say, "el grande" ("the big") in Spanish, but, "the big mug" or "the big one" in English. Waxman et al. found that exposure to a novel adjective does not focus English-speaking children on object kinds, but it does for Spanish-speaking children. In contrast, nouns focused both the English children and the Spanish children on object kinds. These findings support the claim that, while nouns have a universal semantic correlate, there exists more flexibility in the interpretation of other syntactic categories, as the result of cross-linguistic differences in aspects of syntax such as nominalization and argument omission.

D. Prepositions

Landau and Stecker (1990) explored whether the syntactic contrast between nouns and prepositions can cue young children toward the distinction between words referring to objects and words referring to spatial relations. Children were shown a novel object placed on a box and were told either, "This is a corp" (count noun syntax) or "This is acorp the box" (preposition syntax). In the count noun condition, both 3-year-olds and adults generalized the application of the word to objects of the same shape regardless of location, while in the preposition condition, they generalized the word to objects in the same location (or class of locations), regardless of object shape. More recently, Landau (in press) has found that English-speaking children are sensitive to prepositional syntax when learning words that map onto spatial notions not present in English, such as the Tzeltal relational marker "lechel," which is used to denote a wide flat object that is lying flat (P. Brown, 1993).

Such results can be taken to support the proposal by Landau and Jackendoff (1993) that there is a universal distinction between the semantics of count nouns, which denote objects and other individuals, and prepositions, which only denote certain limited classes of spatial relationships (see also Talmy, 1985). In contrast, Choi and Bowerman (1991) reject the view that children initially map spatial words (like "on" or "lechel") onto an antecedentally constrained set of nonlinguistic spatial concepts. On the basis of data from children learning English and Korean, they argue that children's semantic representation of space is itself strongly influenced by the language that they learn. In particular, Bowerman (in press) suggests that the constrained inferences about the meanings of prepositions by English children in the studies by Landau and her colleagues are not innate; they are learned at an earlier stage of language development. This issue is a matter of current debate, possibly to be resolved by more cross-linguistic research with younger children.

E. Number Words

A final domain where syntactic cues might apply is that of number words, words like "two" and "three" and "ten." Traditional theories explain the acquisition of such words through association, where the child observes (for example) three things, hears the word "three," and links the word with his or her understanding of threeness (Mill, 1843/1973). More recent accounts implicate innate number-specific principles. R. Gelman and Gallistel (1978) posit that children observe certain principles of the number system in natural language; they realize that number words are in a stable order, that they are used in one-to-one correspondence with entities during counting, and that the final item in the string denotes the cardinality of the set counted, and thus children map the string of number words onto a corresponding set of numerical concepts that honors the same principles.

An alternative theory is proposed by Wynn (1992). Wynn found that children go through a lengthy stage in which they know that number words refer to numerosities, but do not know which numerosities they refer to. For instance, a child might know that "three" is a number word (and not an object name or the name of a property that individual objects possess) but be unable to correctly respond when shown two dogs and three dogs and asked, "Can you show me the three dogs?" This cannot be explained by the associationist or counting principle theories, but is consistent with the proposal that children use linguistic cues to determine the general semantic class to which number words belong, and then use other means (such as the counting principles) to determine the precise meaning of such words. Under this account, the developmental stage found by Wynn is the period in which children have learned the semantic class of some words through linguistic information but have not yet successfully applied other mechanisms to acquire their exact meanings.

This hypothesis gains support from an analysis of parent–child speech, exploring both adult usage of number words and children's own usage (Bloom & Wynn, under review). Both adults and children used these words in different linguistic contexts from adjectives and other quantifiers. In particular, number words were used only with count nouns (distinguishing them from quantifiers like "some" and "the," and from most adjectives), they were never used with modifiers like "too" or "very" (distinguishing them from quantifiers like "most," "many," and "few" and adjectives like "big"), and never followed adjectives within the NP (distinguishing them from adjectives). These properties might suffice to inform children about the semantic class that these words belong to—that they are precise quantifiers over specific numerosities. This evidence is indirect (what one would need to clinch the issue is a study in which children were actually taught novel number words through syntactic cues) but provides some suggestion that syntax might underlie lexical acquisition in this domain.

III. THE ORIGIN OF CHILDREN'S KNOWLEDGE OF SYNTACTIC CUES TO WORD MEANING

Where does the ability to determine aspects of word meaning through syntactic cues come from? Many scholars have argued that it is acquired through observation of contingencies between the meanings of words and the syntactic categories they belong to. For instance, R. Brown (1957, p. 26) suggests that, "Human beings are generally adept at picking up imperfect probabilistic implications, and so it may be the case that native speakers detect the semantic nature of the parts of speech of their language." And Katz et al. (1974, p. 472), in their study of children's sensitivity to the difference between "zav" and "a zav," state that, "we can effectively eliminate the possibility that they [the children] are determined by nature to notice definite and indefinite articles on the grounds that many languages, like Latin, do not have them." They propose that children notice the correlation between words without determiners and words that refer to animate beings, and thus learn that this context (e.g., "This is_____") signals that the word is a proper name.

There are two general classes of correlational theories that have been proposed. One is that children first learn the nature of *words* (that they refer, the sorts of entities they refer to, etc.), and then gradually come to realize that different parts of speech carry their own special semantic implications (e.g., Nelson, 1988). The other is that they start off with a general bias to assume that words name kinds of whole objects but must (as in the proposal above) learn the semantic basis of different parts of speech by noting correlations; they notice that count nouns refer to objects, that prepositions refer to spatial relationships, and so on (e.g., R. Brown, 1957).

Such correlational theories are supported by the existence of cross-linguistic differences. Some languages do not have a distinct class of adjectives, for instance, while others lack a morphological count-mass contrast. Furthermore, it is plainly true that the surface realization of these syntactic categories must be acquired; it is an arbitrary fact about English that verbs are sometimes marked with "-ing," or that determiners precede nouns. Thus *some* learning must be going on.

Other investigators have defended a more nativist theory, one in which there exist innate syntax-semantics mappings (e.g., Bloom, 1993; Gleitman, 1990; Pinker, 1989). One source of support for this is that although some variation exists, there do appear to be universal constraints on grammatical structure and on the relationship between cognition and grammar (Bybee, 1985; Chomsky, 1981; Greenberg, 1966; Pinker, 1989; Talmy, 1985). Knowledge of syntactic constraints shows up early in language development (e.g., Crain, 1991), with children obeying abstract principles that do not appear to be learnable on the basis of the input that they receive. Furthermore, as noted above, a sensitivity to mappings from syntax to semantics also emerges early in development, for both nominals (Bloom, 1990; Katz et al., 1974) and verbs (Gleitman, 1990). This is all consistent with the nativist view that children initially possess both grammatical categories and mappings from these categories to semantic structure, and can use these mappings at the onset of language development.[3]

One prediction of this view is that as soon as children start to learn words they should be capable of encoding them as belonging to distinct syntactic and semantic categories; they should not be limited to learning words that refer to kinds of objects. This is in contrast to theories such as that by Waxman (1994), in which it is proposed that children start off with a general expectation that words refer to object categories. The developmental evidence favors the nativist view on this point. Although object names are common in child language, there never appears to be a point at which this is all that they know. On the contrary, even very young children understand names for specific people, actions, and substances, among other things (Bloom, 1990; Huttenlocher and Smiley, 1987; Nelson, 1973; Nelson et al., 1993).

If the mappings are innate, however, why are children unable to use them at the outset of language acquisition (see Waxman & Markow, in press, on

12- and 13-month-olds)? And once they do start to use syntactic cues, why are they less reliant on them than adults are?

One answer is that even if children initially possess syntactic categories and an understanding of their semantic properties, they still must learn the surface realizations of these categories (that in English, verbs can be marked by "-ing," and so on). Only once these are acquired can children determine the syntactic categories of new words and use this information to infer aspects of their meanings. Thus, even if all the mappings discussed above are innate, one must expect some period during which children are unable to apply them (for discussion of how these surface realizations of syntactic categories might be learned, see Pinker, 1984). In addition, there may be some limited cross-linguistic variation in the semantic correlates of a syntactic category (Waxman, 1994); if so, then this, too, must be learned.

Other considerations could make children less capable of using syntactic cues even once they understand the relevant language-particular aspects of syntax. For one thing, conceptual limitations might play some role. Dickinson (1988), for instance, found that older children were better than younger ones in using linguistic information to learn a solid-substance name describing an unfamiliar object. It might be that both the younger and the older children were aware of the semantic implications of mass noun syntax, but that the developmental differences are conceptual. In particular, the younger children might have found it difficult to override the bias to think of a whole object as an individual. As suggested in Section IIA3, effective learning of solid-substance names might await conceptual development in children's ability to naturally think about certain entities as stuff.

A similar example is from Bloom and Kelemen (1995) in which the 5-year-olds and adults, but not the 4-year-olds, construed a singular count noun ("a fendle") as referring to a collection of five objects. This difference might be because younger children found it hard to construe the set of objects as a single individual, as it lacks the conceptual and perceptual coherence that real collections usually possess. Adults are more flexible, we can construe just about *any* set of objects as an individual, and so we follow the syntactic cues. One example of this flexibility concerns the learning of names for modern art. An adult is capable of construing (for instance) several pieces of fiberglass as a single individual once we know that the pieces were arranged with the intent that they be an artwork. By virtue of our understanding of this intention, the collection gains psychological coherence—it becomes real because someone intends it to be real (Bloom, in press-a; see also Levinson, 1989). It is an open question whether young children have the same capacities in this domain.

A different explanation for the adult/child differences is that children might weigh syntax less heavily than adults do when inferring the meaning of a word. In the Bloom and Kelemen study, it is possible that although children know that a phrase with a singular count noun denotes a single individual (including, potentially, a collection of objects), they tend not to pay as much attention to this syntactic information as adults do. This is fully consistent with the nativist view, since any theory assuming that people can attend to more than one source of information in the course of word learning has to admit the possibility of developmental change in the relative importance given to information from these different sources.

More specifically, there are multiple cues that conspire to direct a language learner toward a particular meaning—including cues such as the inferred intention of the language user, perceptual salience, lexical principles such as mutual exclusivity, and mappings from syntactic structure to conceptual categories. The difficulty in weighing such cues can be illustrated with an example from Bloom and Kelemen (1995). Imagine that there is a novel object on a table with a salient part and someone points to the part, saying, "Look at the fendle." The person is pointing to the part and so most likely intends to refer to it; also the syntax of the word is compatible with this interpretation, since a part is a possible individual and the count noun "fendle" can refer to a kind of individual. On the other hand, we are biased to favor construing the whole object, not the part, as the individual, and the fact that we have no prior name for the whole object means that there is no mutual exclusivity restriction biasing against the whole object interpretation. Perhaps the person *meant* to refer to the whole object but was just pointing to the wrong place?

In more normal circumstances, cues to word meaning (syntax, ostension, principles of lexical contrast) will converge, just as different cues in visual perception tend to converge. In cases like the one above, however, they will clash, and children and adults might behave in different ways. Perhaps child/adult differences in sensitivity to syntactic cues will reduce to the fact that children are less driven by linguistic cues and more sensitive to contextual and perceptual factors, perhaps because they simply have less experience with the language and are therefore more swayed by perceptual experience. If so, this might be not particularly revealing from a developmental standpoint, since adults learning a second language might behave in the same way.

In sum, there are arguments that favor a nativist view of the origin of syntax-semantics mappings. This theory is consistent with the existence of universals of syntax and semantics, and is supported by evidence from language acquisition that very young children possess both the capacity to use aspects of syntax to determine aspects of word meaning and the capacity to use word meanings to infer syntactic category. Even children's first words fall into a wide range of semantic categories, falsifying the claim that they initially assume that all words refer to kinds of objects. The existence of developmental differences can be explained in terms of processes, such as conceptual change and differential sensitivity to syntactic cues, that are quite consistent with such a nativist view.

A final point. Everyone agrees that some learning must occur in order for the child to exploit syntactic cues to word meaning, from as little as learning the surface realization of syntactic categories to as much as learning that nouns refer to entities and verbs refer to events. But regardless of how much is learned, there is something quite suspect in claiming that the learning process is *correlational*. There are good reasons to doubt, for instance, that children learn that transitive verbs refer to causal events by noting the correlation between words that are transitive verbs and words that name causal events. Such a theory would predict that children could just as well have learned that count nouns, or prepositions or determiners, name causal events. It would thus entail that the syntax of a language (which words are nouns and adjectives, the number of NP arguments a verb has, etc.) is entirely unrelated to the semantics of a language (which notions a word expresses, the number of participants within a described event, etc.). Children merely notice certain arbitrary correlations between syntax and semantics, and use this knowledge to help them learn words.

This is an implausible perspective on natural language. It is unlikely to be an accident, for instance, that events are named with verbs, that names for people are nominals, or that the number of NP arguments of a verb is related to the number of participants in the event denoted by the verb. These mappings are part of the universal mechanisms through which language allows us to communicate, to refer to events and things, to express predicate-argument relations, and so on. Although there is good reason to believe that principles of syntax are not entirely reducible to principles of semantics (Chomsky, 1981), it is uncontroversial that a rich interface exists between these two levels of mental representation (Williams, 1983). In light of this, even if some aspects of syntax-semantics mappings are learned, these are not likely to be picked up by observing arbitrary correlations of language use.

IV. WHAT ROLE DO SYNTACTIC CUES PLAY IN WORD LEARNING?

The experiments reviewed in Section II show that children can use syntax to learn aspects of the meanings of words. But how important is syntax? Is syntax necessary in order for word learning to succeed?

It is clear enough that syntax is not sufficient to learn the meaning of a word; at best it can help children learn aspects of the meaning of a word. For one thing, the relationship between the syntax of a word and its meaning is not entirely predictable—there is some limited variation both within and across languages. Certain words that are count nouns in French are mass nouns in English; some verbs that appear in the double-object dative structure in English do not appear in the same syntactic context in Dutch. And near-synonyms within a language (e.g., "clothes," a mass noun, and "garments," a plural count noun) can belong to different syntactic categories. This arbitrariness is sharply constrained, but it does exist (Bloom, 1994a; Pinker, 1989, 1994).

More generally, grammar draws relatively crude distinctions, picking out ontological kinds (individual vs. stuff; property vs. event, etc.) and subtypes of events (e.g., events with one participant vs. events with two participants). Word meanings are infinitely more fine grained. Children have to learn the difference between "cup" and "spoon" (both count nouns), "good" and "evil" (both adjectives), "five" and "six" (both quantifiers of precise numerosity), and "loving" and "hating" (both verbs with identical argument structures). At best, then, syntax can aid the child in determining the general class of meaning that the word belongs to. But it cannot entirely solve the problem of word learning (Gleitman, 1990; Grimshaw, 1994; Pinker, 1994).

Is syntax *necessary?* At least some words can be acquired without the aid of overt syntax cues. As noted above, 12- and 13-month-olds can acquire some object names while ignoring syntax, failing to distinguish between adjectives and nouns when learning these labels (Waxman & Markow, in press). Similarly, two-year-olds can learn substance names prior to an understanding of count–mass syntax (Soja et al., 1991). Certainly adults can do the same. If one points to a substance and says "zoop," an adult will construe the word as a substance name, while if one points to an object and says "zoop," the kind-of-object interpretation will be dominant. Thus overt syntactic cues cannot be essential for the acquisition of all word meanings.

A. Is Syntax Ever Necessary? The Case of Verbs

Of course, the fact that children can learn some words without syntactic cues does not mean that they can learn all words without syntactic cues. In particular, as Gentner (1982) argues, nouns might differ from verbs in certain important regards. Some nouns refer to objects, which are salient entities in the environment, highly accessible through perception and ostension. Many verbs, however, describe arbitrary and socially defined relationships between entities, with some cross-linguistic variation as to the sorts of meanings they encode (Pinker, 1989).[4]

Gleitman (1990) presents an extended argument that syntax is central to the acquisition of verbs. Part of this argument is an attack on the associationist premise that children learn verbs by associating them with events that occur at the same time the verbs are used. One problem is that the necessary spatiotemporal contingencies do not appear to exist—parents do not use the verb "opening" just when there is opening going on, for instance (Gleitman & Gillette, in press). Another is that events are inherently ambiguous: if Fred is handling something to Mary and the verb "blicking" is used, it could (among other things) mean "giving," but it could also mean "receiving." Its meaning depends crucially on the perspective one takes. Gleitman argues that linguistic cues can provide this perspective, through the contrast between sentences such as "Fred is _____ the thing to Mary" versus "Mary is _____ the thing from Fred."

Gleitman also discusses children's acquisition of abstract verbs, such as "know" and "think," arguing that syntax provides the child with aspects of the meanings of such words that observation clearly cannot. Along the same lines, Landau and Gleitman (1985) provide the fascinating case study of a blind child who acquired the meanings of the verbs "look" and "see" with little difficulty—clearly for *this* child and *these* words, an associationist theory is inadequate.

These facts—the failure to find spatiotemporal contingencies between verbs and the events they refer to, the ambiguity inherent in any situation, the early acquisition of abstract verbs, and the fact that severe deficits in perceptual abilities do not affect certain aspects of verb learning—pose severe problems for associationist theories of word learning. Given the existence of universal syntax-semantics mappings, and evidence that children can use them, Gleitman (1990) posits that "semantically relevant information in the syntactic structures can rescue observational learning from the sundry experiential pitfalls that threaten it" (p. 48).

Pinker (1994) agrees that an associationist theory cannot explain the process of verb learning and that sensitivity to syntactic cues might play some role in helping children in learning new words. But he argues that there exist other mechanisms, neither syntactic nor associationist, that are much more important. Consider nominals such as "electron" and "Moscow." These words could not be learned through association, but syntax would also be of little help; from the standpoint of grammar, there is no difference between "electron" and "dog," "Moscow" and "Mars." Similar examples exist for verbs. For instance, children somehow learn the difference between different verbs of cognition such as "liking," "loving," and "hating." For the reasons outlined by Gleitman, it is implausible that they do so through an associationist procedure, but syntax also would not help, as such verbs are syntactically identical.

Pinker argues that nonsyntactic mechanisms (for instance, the child's ability to infer the intention of adult language users) might solve some of the problems raised by Gleitman. In particular, although children do not hear verbs at the same time as they witness the events that the verbs denote, it is likely that they can *infer* the intended event from their understanding of the rest of the utterance and the context in which it is used. If an adult looks at the window and asks the child to open it, and if the child can pick up from the context the precise intent that the adult is intending to express, she may be able to figure out what "open" means, even if the word is not uttered at the same time as an act of opening.

Nevertheless, while Pinker's arguments suggest that there exist alternatives to syntax as a theory of verb learning, the possibility still remains that without the aid of syntax, children might not be able to learn the meanings of some verbs. There is no direct evidence on this issue: It is clear that children can learn *some* verb meanings with minimal syntactic structure, just by hearing (for example) "This is blicking" (e.g., Behrend, 1990; Fisher et al., 1994; Forbes and Farrar, 1993; Gropen et al., 1991). But even here the child has syntactic information that the new word is a verb, from the "-ing" morphology.

Thus, two questions arise. First, can a child learn a word referring to a kind of event without *any* syntactic cues as to its syntactic category (e.g., just by hearing, "Look! Blick!")? Second, is it possible to learn certain less accessible verb meanings, such as mental state verbs and verbs in which the subject is not an agent ("receiving"), without information about the full syntactic frames that such verbs normally appear in (e.g., just by hearing, "Look! Blicking!")? These are questions to be resolved by further research.

V. CONCLUSION: THE PROPER PLACE OF SYNTACTIC CUES WITHIN A THEORY OF EARLY LANGUAGE DEVELOPMENT

Both Pinker and Gleitman are drawn to the notion of syntax as a "zoom lens," which serves to draw the child to the relevant aspects of an event, determining whether it should be construed as giving or receiving, thinking or standing, walking or moving. (Their disagreement is over the precise nature of the procedure and how important it is.) The zoom lens metaphor is similar to Brown's notion of syntax as "a filter selecting for attention probably relevant features of the nonlinguistic world." This idea is attractive, and explains the effect of syntax in the verb experiments described above, most of which present children with a scene, give them a sentence, and see if the syntax of the sentence determines which aspect of the scene they think the verb refers to.

In certain regards, however, this is an unrealistic way to think about the role of syntax in word learning. As noted above, most of the time a verb is used the scene is not going on and vice versa; thus, if syntax is going to play a role in actual word learning outside the laboratory, it has to be able to affect children's construals of scenes that are not present in perception. Furthermore, at least when one moves outside the domain of verbs, the syntax is often as ambiguous as the scene. Perhaps a more realistic perspective is that syntax is one important informational source as to the meanings of words, one that works in concert with information obtained from other inferential mechanisms (such as perceptual and conceptual salience, an understanding of the intention of others, an ability to understand discourse, within-lexicon constraints, and so on). The child's task in word learning, then, is to integrate these different sources of information, and from them to infer the most plausible candidate for the word's meaning.

The above discussion draws us toward a (somewhat speculative) summary of the development of syntactic cues to word meaning and their role as part of a theory of word learning (Bloom, in press-a);

1. Prior to the age of about 18 months, children learn the meanings of some words, including names for kinds of objects, kinds of substances, and individual people. Two processes underlie this acquisition: children have the capacity to grasp the intentionality of other language users, and use this capacity to determine the reference of words they hear (e.g., Baldwin, 1991; Macnamara, 1982), and they possess a set of distinct abstract conceptual categories that word meanings must fall into; these categories include "kind of individual," "event," and "property" (Bloom & Kelemen, 1995). At this early stage, overt syntactic cues play no role in word learning.

2. Having acquired the meanings of some words, children use an innate understanding of the relationship between meaning and grammar to determine their syntactic categories, through semantic bootstrapping (see endnote 3). They use this process to generate syntactic parses of some of the sentences they are exposed to, and then apply specialized procedures to learn language-specific aspects of word order and morphology (Pinker, 1984).

3. At this point, syntactic cues can facilitate word learning, as children can use their syntactic and morphological knowledge to syntactically categorize novel words prior to learning their meaning, and use this syntactic information to help figure out what these words mean. The contrasts between nouns and NPs, and between different types of verb argument structures, are acquired very early, and thus help children younger than 2 learn words like "Fred" and "dog," "sleep" and "kick." Other distinctions, such as the contrast between count nouns and mass nouns, emerge somewhat later. More speculatively, it is possible that it is only after this sensitivity to syntactic cues emerges that children become capable of learning the meanings of certain verbs, such as verbs of cognition and perception.

Acknowledgments

Preparation of this chapter was supported by grants from the Spencer Foundation and from the Sloan Foundation. I am grateful to Terry Au, Cynthia Fisher, Rochel Gelman, Barbara

Landau, Letitia Naigles, Sandeep Prasada, Sandra Waxman, and Karen Wynn for very helpful comments on earlier drafts of this paper.

Endnotes

1. Imai and Gentner (1994) report a modified replication of the Soja, Carey, and Spelke (1991) study with 2-year-olds acquiring Japanese, a language without an overt count-mass distinction. While the Japanese children behaved the same as the English children with regard to names for substances and names for complex objects, they behaved differently with regard to names for *simple* objects (e.g., a kidney-shaped piece of wax). Unlike the English children tested by Soja et al., the Japanese children showed no bias toward projecting the names of simple objects on the basis of shape. This suggests that language-particular syntax might influence how words for simple objects are acquired, even for 2-year-olds, and calls into question Soja et al.'s assumption that the children they tested had not yet been tainted with knowledge of English syntax.
2. Some investigators have made the stronger claim that there exists a shape bias, such that children believe that count nouns that name objects "correspond to categories whose members have similar shapes" (Landau, Smith, & Jones, 1988, p. 316). In support of this, children do tend to favor generalizing object names on the basis of shape more so than on the basis of any other property, such as color and size (e.g., Baldwin, 1989, 1992; Landau et al., 1988; L. B. Smith, Jones, & Landau, 1992), although in certain circumstances they will focus on these other properties (Becker & Ward, 1991; Macario, 1991). The nature of this bias is a matter of some debate, one that unfortunately extends beyond the scope of this chapter (for different perspectives see Bloom, in press-b; Landau, Jones, & Smith, 1992; Soja, Carey, & Spelke, 1992; Ward, 1993).
3. The proposal that some syntax-semantics mappings are innate is also a premise behind the theory of "semantic bootstrapping" (Grimshaw, 1981; Pinker, 1984, 1987), which posits that these mappings allow children to learn the syntactic categories of words and phrases and thus "bootstrap" their way into the syntactic system of natural language.
4. Note that this characterization of verbs is similar to that of superordinate nouns, like "jewelry" and "furniture," as these are often characterized as describing socially arbitrary categories, with no clear perceptual commonalties. This suggests that only a subset of nouns—basic-level object names and substance names perhaps—differ from verbs with regard to their perceptual transparency.

References

Au, T. K. (1994). Developing an intuitive understanding of substance kinds. *Cognitive Psychology, 27,* 71–111.

Au, T. K., Dapretto, M., & Song, Y.-K. (1994). Input vs. constraints: Early word acquisition in Korean and English. *Journal of Memory and Language, 33,* 567–582.

Baldwin, D. A. (1989). Priorities in children's expectations about object label reference: Form over color. *Child Development, 60,* 1291–1306.

Baldwin, D. A. (1991). Infants' contribution to the achievement of joint reference. *Child Development, 62,* 875–890.

Baldwin, D. A. (1992). Clarifying the role of shape in children's taxonomic assumption. *Journal of Experimental Child Psychology, 54,* 392–416.

Becker, A. H., & Ward, T. B. (1991). Children's use of shape in extending new labels to animate objects: Identity versus postural change. *Cognitive Development, 6,* 3–16.

Behrend, D. A. (1990). The development of verb concepts: Children's use of verbs to label familiar and novel events. *Child Development, 61*, 681–696.

Bloom, P. (1990). Syntactic distinctions in child language. *Journal of Child Language. 17*, 343–355.

Bloom, P. (1993). Where do constraints on word meaning come from? In E. Clark (Ed.), *Proceedings of the 24th Annual Child Language Research Forum* (pp. 23–34). Stanford, CA: CSLI.

Bloom, P. (1994a). Semantic competence as an explanation for some transitions in language development. In Y. Levy (Ed.), *Other children, other languages: Theoretical issues in language development* (pp. 41–75). Hillsdale, NJ: Erlbaum.

Bloom, P. (1994b). Possible names: The role of syntax-semantics mappings in the acquisition of nominals. *Lingua, 92*, 297–329.

Bloom, P. (in press -a). Theories of word learning: Rationalist alternatives to associationism. In T. K. Bhatia & W. C. Ritchie (Eds.), *Handbook of language acquisition*. San Diego: Academic Press.

Bloom, P. (in press-b). Intention, history, and artifact concepts. *Cognition.*

Bloom, P., & Kelemen, D. (1995). Syntactic cues in the acquisition of collective nouns. *Cognition, 56*, 1–30.

Bloom, P. & Wynn, K. (under review). Linguistic cues in the acquisition of number words.

Bloomfield, L. (1933). *Language*. New York: Holt.

Bolinger, D. (1967). Adjectives in English: attribution and predication. *Lingua, 18*, 1–34.

Bowerman, M. (in press). Learning how to structure space for language—a crosslinguistic perspective. In P. Bloom, M. Peterson, L. Nadel, & M. Garrett (Eds.), *Language and space*. Cambridge, MA: MIT Press.

Brown, P. (1993). The role of shape in the acquisition of Tzeltal (Mayan) locatives. In E. Clark (Ed.), *Proceedings of the 25th Annual Child Language Research Forum* (pp. 211–220). Stanford, CA: CSLI.

Brown, R. (1957). Linguistic determinism and the part of speech. *Journal of Abnormal and Social Psychology, 55*, 1–5.

Bybee, J. (1985). *Morphology: A study of the relation between meaning and form*. Philadelphia: Benjamin.

Choi, S., & Bowerman, M. (1991). Learning to express motion events in English and Korean: The influence of language-specific lexicalization patterns. *Cognition, 41*, 83–121.

Chomsky, N. (1981). *Lectures on government and binding*. Dordrecht: Foris.

Clark, E. V. (1987). The principle of contrast: A constraint on language acquisition. In B. MacWhinney (Ed.), *Mechanisms of language acquisition* (pp. 1–33). Hillsdale, NJ: Erlbaum.

Crain, S. (1991). Language acquisition in the absence of experience. *Behavioral and Brain Sciences, 14*, 597–650.

Dickinson, D. K. (1986). *The development of children's understanding of materials*. Unpublished doctoral dissertation, Harvard University.

Dickinson, D. K. (1988). Learning names for materials: Factors constraining and limiting hypotheses about word meaning. *Cognitive Development, 3*, 15–35.

Fisher, C. (under review). Structural limits on verb mapping: The role of analogy in children's interpretations of sentences.

Fisher, C., Gleitman, H., & Gleitman, L. R. (1991). On the semantic content of subcategorization frames. *Cognitive Psychology, 23*, 331–392.

Fisher, C., Hall, G., Rakowitz, S., & Gleitman, L. R. (1994). When it is better to receive than to give: Syntactic and conceptual constraints of vocabulary growth. *Lingua, 92*, 333–375.

Forbes, J. M., & Farrar, M. J. (1993). Children's initial assumptions about the meanings of novel motion verbs: Biased and conservative? *Cognitive Development, 8*, 273–290.

Fukui, N. (1987). *A theory of category projection and its implications*. Unpublished doctoral dissertation, Massachusetts Institute of Technology.

Gathercole, V. C. (1986). Evaluating competing theories with child language data: The case of the count-mass distinction. *Linguistics and Philosophy, 6,* 151–190.

Gelman, R., & Gallistel, C. R. (1978). *The child's understanding of number.* Cambridge, MA: MIT Press.

Gelman, S. A., & Markman, E. M. (1985). Implicit contrast in adjectives vs. nouns: Implications for word-learning in preschoolers. *Journal of Child Language, 12,* 125–143.

Gelman, S. A., & Taylor, M. (1984). How two-year-old children interpret proper and common names for unfamiliar objects. *Child Development, 55,* 1535–1540.

Gentner, D. (1982). Why nouns are learned before verbs: Linguistic relativity versus natural partitioning. In S. A. Kuczaj, II (Ed.), *Language development: Vol. 2. Language, thought, and culture* (pp. 301–334). Hillsdale, NJ: Erlbaum.

Gleitman, L. R. (1990). The structural sources of word meaning. *Language Acquisition, 1,* 3–55.

Gleitman, L. R., & Gillette, J. (in press). The role of syntax in verb learning. In T. K. Bhatia & W. C. Ritchie (Eds.), *Handbook of language acquisition.* New York: Academic Press.

Goldberg, A. (1993). Another look at some learnability paradoxes. In E. Clark (Ed.), *Proceedings of the 25th Annual Child Language Research Forum* (pp. 60–75). Stanford, CA: CSLI.

Gordon, P. (1985). Evaluating the semantic categories hypothesis: The case of the count-mass distinction. *Cognition, 20,* 209–242.

Gordon, P. (1988). Count-mass category acquisition: Distributional distinctions in children's speech. *Journal of Child Language, 15,* 109–128.

Gordon, P. (1992). *Object, substance, and individuation: Canonical vs. non-canonical count-mass nouns in children's speech.* Unpublished manuscript, University of Pittsburgh.

Greenberg, J. H. (1966). Some universals of grammar with particular reference to the order of meaningful elements. In J. H. Greenberg (Ed.), *Universals of language* (pp. 73–113). Cambridge, MA: MIT Press.

Grimshaw, J. (1981). Form, function, and the language acquisition device. In C. L. Baker & J. McCarthy (Eds.), *The logical problem of language acquisition* (pp. 165–182). Cambridge, MA: MIT Press.

Grimshaw, J. (1994). Lexical reconciliation. *Lingua, 92,* 411–430.

Gropen, J., Pinker, S., Hollander, M., & Goldberg, R. (1991). Affectedness and direct objects: The role of lexical semantics in the acquisition of verb argument structure, *Cognition, 41,* 153–195.

Hall, D. G. (1991). Acquiring proper names for familiar and unfamiliar animate objects: Two-year-olds' word-learning biases. *Child Development, 62,* 1142–1154.

Hirsh-Pasek, K., Gleitman, H., Gleitman, L. R., Golinkoff, R., & Naigles, L. (1988). *Syntactic bootstrapping: Evidence from comprehension.* Paper presented at the Boston University Conference on Language Development, Boston.

Hirsh-Pasek, K., Golinkoff, R., Fletcher, A., DeGaspe Beaubien, F., & Cauley, K. (1985). *In the beginning: One word speakers comprehend word order.* Paper presented at the Boston University Conference on Language Development, Boston.

Huttenlocher, J., & Smiley, P. (1987). Early word meanings: The case of object names. *Cognitive Psychology, 19,* 63–89.

Imai, M., & Gentner, D. (1994). Linguistic relativity vs. universal ontology: Cross-linguistic studies on the object-substance distinction. *Proceedings of the Chicago Linguistics Society,* pp. 171–186.

Jackendoff, R. (1990). *Semantic structures.* Cambridge, MA: MIT Press.

Jackendoff, R. (1991). Parts and boundaries. *Cognition, 41,* 9–45.

Katz, N., Baker, E., & Macnamara, J. (1974). What's in a name? A study of how children learn common and proper names. *Child Development, 45,* 469–473.

Landau, B. (in press). Multiple geometric representations of objects in language and language learners. In P. Bloom, M. Peterson, L. Nadel, & M. Garrett (Eds.), *Language and space.* Cambridge, MA: MIT Press.

Landau, B., & Gleitman, L. R. (1985). *Language and experience.* Cambridge, MA: Harvard University Press.

Landau, B., & Jackendoff, R. (1993). "What" and "where" in spatial language and spatial cognition. *Behavioral and Brain Sciences, 16,* 217–238.

Landau, B., Jones, S., & Smith, L. B. (1992). Perception, ontology, and naming in young children: Commentary on Soja, Carey, and Spelke. *Cognition, 43,* 85–91.

Landau, B., Smith, L. B., & Jones, S. (1988). The importance of shape in early lexical learning. *Cognitive Development, 3,* 299–321.

Landau, B., & Stecker, D. (1990). Objects and places: Syntactic and geometric representations in early lexical learning. *Cognitive Development, 5,* 287–312.

Levin, B. (1993). *English verb classes and alternations: A preliminary investigation.* Chicago: University of Chicago Press.

Levinson, J. (1989). Refining art historically. *Journal of Aesthetics and Art Criticism, 47,* 21–33.

Levy, Y. (1988). On the early learning of grammatical systems: Evidence from studies of the acquisition of gender and countability. *Journal of Child Language, 15,* 179–186.

Littschwager, J. C., & Markman, E. M. (1993, March). *Young children's understanding of proper versus common nouns.* Paper presented at the biennial meeting of the Society for Research in Child Development, New Orleans, 1993.

Locke, J. (1690/1964). *An essay concerning human understanding.* Cleveland, OH: Meridian.

Macario, J. (1991). Young children's use of color in classification: Foods and canonically colored objects. *Cognitive Development, 6,* 17–46.

Macnamara, J. (1982). *Names for things: A study of human learning.* Cambridge, MA: MIT Press.

Macnamara, J. (1986). *A border dispute: The place of logic in psychology.* Cambridge, MA: MIT Press.

Markman, E. M., & Hutchinson, J. E. (1984). Children's sensitivity to constraints in word meaning: Taxonomic versus thematic relations. *Cognitive Psychology, 16,* 1–27.

Markman, E. M., & Wachtel, G. F. (1988). Children's use of mutual exclusivity to constrain the meaning of words. *Cognitive Psychology, 20,* 121–157.

Massey, C. M., & Gelman, R. (1988). Preschoolers' ability to decide whether a photographed unfamiliar object can move by itself. *Developmental Psychology, 24,* 307–317.

McPherson, L. (1991). "A little" goes a long way: evidence for a perceptual basis of learning for the noun categories COUNT and MASS. *Journal of Child Language, 18,* 315–338.

Mill, J. S. (1843/1973). A system of logic: Ratiocinative and inductive (8th ed.). In J. M. Robson (Ed.), *Collected works of John Stuart Mill.* Toronto: University of Toronto Press.

Naigles, L. (1990). Children use syntax to learn verb meanings. *Journal of Child Language, 17,* 357–374.

Naigles, L., Fowler, A., & Heim, A. (1992). Developmental shifts in the construction of verb meanings. *Cognitive Development, 7,* 403–427.

Naigles, L., Gleitman, L. R., & Gleitman, H. (1993). Children acquire word meaning components from syntactic evidence. In E. Dromi (Ed.), *Language and cognition: A developmental perspective* (pp. 104–140). Norwood, NJ: Ablex.

Naigles, L., & Hoff-Ginsberg, E. (in press). Input to verb learning: Evidence for the plausibility of Syntactic Bootstrapping. *Developmental Psychology.*

Naigles, L., & Kako, E. (1993). First contact in verb acquisition: Defining a role for syntax. *Child Development, 64,* 1665–1687.

Nelson, K. (1973). Structure and strategy in learning to talk. *Monographs of the Society for Research in Child Development, 38* (1–2, Serial No. 149).

Nelson, K. (1988). Constraints on word meaning? *Cognitive Development, 3,* 221–246.

Nelson, K. (1990). Comment on Behrend's "Constraints and Development." *Cognitive Development, 5,* 331–339.

Nelson, K., Hampson, J., & Shaw, L. K. (1993). Nouns in early lexicons: Evidence, explanations, and extensions. *Journal of Child Language, 20,* 61–84.

Pelletier, F. (1979). Non-singular reference: Some preliminaries. In F. Pelletier (Ed.), *Mass terms: Some philosophical problems* (pp. 1–14). Dordrecht: Reidel.

Pinker, S. (1984). *Language learnability and language development.* Cambridge, MA: Harvard University Press.

Pinker, S. (1987). The bootstrapping problem in language acquisition. In B. MacWhinney (Ed.), *Mechanisms of language acquisition* (pp. 399–441). Hillsdale, NJ: Erlbaum.

Pinker, S. (1989). *Learnability and cognition.* Cambridge, MA: MIT Press.

Pinker, S. (1994). How could a child use verb syntax to learn verb semantics? *Lingua, 92,* 377–410.

Prasada, S. (1993). Learning names for solid substances: Quantifying solid entities in terms of portions. *Cognitive Development, 8,* 83–104.

Prasada, S. (under review). Young children's use of structural cues in learning the meanings of novel adjectives.

Sabrahmanyam, K., Gelman, R., & Landau, B. (under review). Shape, material, and syntax: Interacting forces in the acquisition of count and mass nouns.

Schacter, P. (1985). Parts-of-speech systems. In T. Shopen (Ed.), *Language typology and syntactic description: Vol. 1. Clause structure* (pp. 3–61). New York: Cambridge University Press.

Schlesinger, I. M. (1988). The origin of relational categories. In Y. Levy, I. M. Schlesinger, & M. D. S. Braine (Eds.), *Categories and processes in language acquisition* (pp. 121–178). Hillsdale, NJ: Erlbaum.

Shipley, E. F., & Shepperson, B. (1990). Countable entities: Developmental changes. *Cognition, 34,* 109–136.

Smith, C., Carey, S., & Wiser, M. (1985). On differentiation: A case study of the development of the concepts of size, weight, and density. *Cognition, 21,* 177–237.

Smith, L. B., Jones, S. & Landau, B. (1992). Count nouns, adjectives, and perceptual properties in children's novel word interpretations. *Developmental Psychology, 28,* 273–286.

Soja, N. N. (1991). *Young children's difficulty with solid substance words.* Unpublished manuscript, Northeastern University.

Soja, N. N. (1992). Inferences about the meanings of nouns: The relationship between perception and syntax, *Cognitive Development, 7,* 29–45.

Soja, N. N., Carey, S., & Spelke, E. S. (1991). Ontological categories guide young children's inductions of word meaning: Object terms and substance terms. *Cognition, 38,* 179–211.

Soja, N. N., Carey, S., & Spelke, E. S. (1992). Perception, ontology, and word meaning. *Cognition, 45,* 101–107.

Starkey, P., Spelke, E. S., & Gelman, R. (1990). Numerical abstraction by human infants. *Cognition, 36,* 97–127.

Talmy, L. (1985). Lexicalization patterns: semantic structure in lexical forms. In T. Shopen (Ed.), *Language typology and syntactic description: Vol. 3. Grammatical categories and the lexicon* (pp. 57–179). New York: Cambridge University Press.

Taylor, M., & Gelman, S. (1988). Adjectives and nouns: Children's strategies for learning new words. *Child Development, 59,* 411–419.

Ward, T. B. (1993). Processing biases, knowledge, and context in category formation. In D. Medin (Ed.), *Psychology of learning and motivation* (Vol. 29, pp. 257–282). San Diego: Academic Press.

Waxman, S. R. (1990). Linguistic biases and the establishment of conceptual hierarchies: Evidence from preschool children. *Cognitive Development, 5,* 123–150.

Waxman, S. R. (1994). The development of an appreciation of specific linkages between linguistic and conceptual organization. *Lingua, 92,* 229–257.

Waxman, S. R., & Gelman, R. (1986). Preschoolers' use of superordinate relations in classifications and language. *Cognitive Development, 1,* 139–156.

Waxman, S. R., & Kosowski, T. (1990). Nouns mark category relations: Toddlers' and preschoolers' word learning biases. *Child Development, 61,* 1461–1490.

Waxman, S. R., & Markow, D. (in press). Words as an invitation to form categories: Evidence from 12- to 13-month infants. *Cognitive Psychology.*

Waxman, S. R., Senghas, A., & Benveniste, S. (under review). A cross-linguistic examination of the noun-category bias: Evidence from French- and Spanish-speaking preschool-aged children.

Williams, E. (1983). Semantic vs. syntactic categories. *Linguistics and Philosophy, 6,* 423–446.

Wynn, K. (1992). Children's acquisition of the number words and the counting system. *Cognitive Psychology, 24,* 220–251.

Wynn, K. (1995). Origins of numerical knowledge. *Mathematical Cognition, 1,* 35–60.

CHAPTER 6

The Development of External Symbol Systems: The Child as a Notator

Kang Lee
Annette Karmiloff-Smith

I. INTRODUCTION

All cultures in the world, primitive or civilized, use language to communicate, and all cultures have extended their spoken communication by developing various forms of external symbol or notation systems (Goody, 1986; Lasswell, Lerner, & Speier, 1979; McLuhan, 1962; Olson, 1994), for example, numbers, alphabetical letters, ideograms, maps, musical notations, and pictorial signs. The invention and use of external symbols such as numbers and letters are considered to be the core impetus in the history of the advancement of human civilization. Not only do notation systems enhance communication between people of the same time period, but they also operate across generations. They thus accelerate the accumulation of knowledge and play a crucial role in advancing human intelligence. For this reason, anthropologists and archaeologists often examine notation systems (or artifacts bearing notations), to unveil the level of knowledge development of a primitive culture (Donald, 1991; Mead, 1979). By doing so, they are able to explore the genesis of knowledge and civilization.

It is for very similar reasons that cognitive developmentalists study the development of notation systems in children. Children of all cultures and time periods are exposed to many notation systems from their own culture

Perceptual and Cognitive Development
Copyright © 1996 by Academic Press, Inc. All rights of reproduction in any form reserved.

(and sometimes of other cultures, too). In many cultures, children are taught to become notators, that is, users of these culturally bounded tools, so that later, as adults, they will use them to inherit former knowledge, produce new knowledge, and pass knowledge on to the next generation.

Notation systems differ from spoken language in important ways. First, they communicate information and ideas in a visual form. Second, they leave a permanent trace and therefore become independent of their creators. Third, unlike the acquisition of a native tongue, which is normally an effortless process, learning to use external symbol can often be arduous. Biological, cognitive, and cultural factors all play an essential part in the process of notational acquisition. Moreover, children's notation systems are not simply a passive copy representing the external world. Rather, children use and adapt notations to serve many different functions, for instance, to communicate with others and to communicate with oneself (e.g., the use of notations as external memory aids). For these reasons, research on the development of notations provides us with a unique insight into the child's evolving mind.

The development of notation systems in children is a classic topic of research in cognitive development. After the seminal work of Vygotsky (1962, 1978) and Luria (1928/1978) on the development of reading, writing, and drawing, interest in the more general issue of the child as a notator was slow to develop. Recently, however, this area of research has seen an up-surge of interest in children's capacity to produce and to "read" notations of different symbol systems, as well as their capacity to invent new ones (Bialystok, 1992; Bolger & Karmiloff-Smith, 1990; Brenneman, Massey, Machado, & Gelman, 1994; Cohen, 1985; DeLoache, 1989a; Ferreiro & Teberosky, 1979; Karmiloff-Smith, 1979, 1990, 1992; Landau & Gleitman, 1985; Liben & Downs, 1989; Tolchinsky-Landsmann & Karmiloff-Smith, 1992, 1993; Tversky, Kugelmass, & Winter, 1991).

Symbolization is a vast area of research that obviously exceeds the scope of this chapter. We therefore focus on the major forms of notation systems widely used in most modern cultures in the world, for example, drawings, written language, number notation, maps, scale models, and photographs. We mainly discuss the cognitive constraints on children's use of various external symbol systems. In addition, our discussions point to theoretical issues related to the development of notation use in children. Finally, we explore future directions of research in this area.

II. SYMBOLIZATION AND NOTATION

Symbolization has two basic elements: the signifier and the signified, with between them a "stand for" relationship. The signifier (or system of signifiers) has been referred to by various terms, for example, "symbol," "sign," and "notation." Although these terms have been discussed for centuries (Todorov, 1982), no consensus has been reached as to their precise meanings. Different theorists and researchers ascribe different meanings to each term. At times the same term is used entirely differently by different individuals. For example, in Peirce's (1965–1966) semiotic theory, the term "symbol" refers to a specific set of signifiers. The relationship between this particular set of signifiers and the signified is arbitrarily established, for example, the English word "cow" and the animal, cow, to which the word refers. By contrast, de Saussure and Piaget use the term "symbol" to refer to what Pierce refers to as an "icon," that is, a signifier that bears common properties with the signified (Krampen, 1991). The purpose of this review is obviously not to discuss, nor, alas, to settle, the disagreement in the usage of the terms. However, to avoid unnecessary confusions, it is important to clarify from the outset how terms will be used in the context of the present review.

Where relevant, we avoid the term "symbol" and use the term "notation" to refer only to those signifiers that satisfy three major principles, as follows: First, notations have the property of what we call "creator independence," that is, they exist independently of their creator and of the actions of the creator. In other words, notations continue to exist when the creator is no longer present or her action ceases to exist. Thus, words in *spoken* language and hand and fingers gestures in sign language are not considered "notations," although they are of course symbolic (Mandler, 1983). Second, notations have the property of what we call "location independence." That is, they leave a trace, exist for an extended period of time, and are accessible to anyone at any time, provided no external force prevents this from occurring. Third, notations have the property of what we call "time independence," that is, they do not have temporal constraints. Hence, dreams and music, although symbolic, are not considered notations. These three criteria—creator, location, and time independence—result in a domain of inquiry that includes the major forms of notations such as drawings, written language, numbers, maps, scale models, and pictures.

III. CONSTRAINTS ON THE DEVELOPMENT OF DRAWING

Children's drawing has been one of the main topics of developmental psychology since the late nineteenth century (Golomb, 1974, 1981, 1992; Harris, 1963; Krampen, 1991). Research into children's drawing has been conducted mainly from one of four approaches. The first focuses on the development of artistic skills (Arnheim, 1966, 1969, 1974; Kellogg, 1969). The second approach was pioneered by Piaget and Luquet and views children's drawing as a direct reflection of the state of their cognitive development (Luquet, 1913, 1927; Piaget & Inhelder, 1948/1956). The third approach is a psychodynamic one that emphasizes the projective significance of children's drawing (Machover, 1949, 1953). For example, Machover (1953) has argued that children's inner emotional world can be revealed through examining their drawings. The fourth approach, which is of direct relevance to the present review, deals with the symbolic function of drawing. Krampen (1991) coined the term "developmental semiotics" to refer specifically to this area. The main concern of developmental semiotics is how children use drawings as symbols to represent both the objective world around them and the subjective world inside them. In the past, the first three approaches dominated this field of inquiry. Only recently has the semiotic approach received the attention of researchers. In this review, we will use both direct and indirect evidence to explore developmental semiotics.

Whatever the culture, children's drawing activity begins at around 2 years of age. Evidence suggests that the use of drawing as a means of symbolizing begins almost as soon as children start to scribble. Moreover, many studies have shown that toddlers do not simply scribble. They often vocalize while scribbling, as if they were giving a running commentary on their output. In other words, toddlers' scribbling is already an index of their attempts to establish a symbolic link between the product of drawing and an external referent. For example, in a case study of his 2-year-old son, J. Matthews (1983) reported that the child produced continuous overlapping spirals while simultaneously commenting, "It's going around the corner." As the paint lines vanished under additional layers of paint, he remarked, "It's gone now." Such data highlight two aspects of these early attempts. First, early drawings represent the rudiments of what one might call "symbolic notation in intention" and, even though very primitive in nature, they show how a number of meanings become associated internally with external scribbles in a condensed, somewhat ambiguous manner. Second, many things are amalgamated into an as-yet undifferentiated whole, that is, the action of drawing and the accompanying verbal commentary. This so-called "action-representation" (Matthews, 1983) does not qualify as a genuine symbolic activity, since "a graphic symbol must sustain its meaning after the motor action has ceased" (Golomb, 1992, p. 11). Rather like spoken language, these early drawing activities only have real-time meaning and thus fail to meet our three principles for notations: creator, location, and time independence.

Toddlers come one step closer to genuine notations when they give names to their scribbles. However, Golomb (1974) found that often toddlers' scribbles are not intentional during the actual act of drawing. Rather, toddlers tend to give meanings to their scribbles post factum. The meanings are stimulus driven. That is, meaning is attributed only after they have seen the final product. Further, the symbolic relation between the drawing and the ascribed meaning often ceases to exist shortly after production, thereby violating both the creator-independence and time-independence principles. In this sense, the symbolic function of drawing and its use as a notation is still not yet dissociated for the child.

As younger children's scribbling repertoire grows (Kellogg, 1969), their drawings begin to communicate certain meanings independent of the notator. They then start to meet our creator-independence principle. Drawings of a person, a car, a horse, or a building begin to actually resemble a person, a car, a horse, or a building. However, the symbolic function of young children's drawing remains limited. As yet, intention outstrips drawing skills. Only a restricted number of graphic units exist in the young child's drawing repertoire (Goodnow, 1977). For example, the human figure is represented solely by the use of repeated circles. But factors other than drawing skills per se play a very important role in constraining young children's use of drawing as a means of notation. These involve a number of cognitive constraints.

The two most common cognitive constraints discussed in the literature on the symbolic relation between a drawing and the represented object are the "canonicality constraint" and the "transparency constraint." Canonicality refers to young children's tendency to make formulaic drawings that represent the common characteristics of the class of the object rather than the unique features of the particular object being drawn (Freeman, 1980). Note that canonical representations do have some notational advantages in that children's general-purpose representations at this stage make their drawings highly recognizable. They thus meet the creator-independence principle, but this is done at the price of losing the specificity of the to-be-represented object. Such findings have been documented in many studies (Barret & Light, 1976; Cox, 1989; Davis, 1983a, 1983b; Freeman & Janikoun, 1972; Goodnow, 1977; Ives & Rovet, 1979). For example, Ives and Rovet (1979) found that between 2 and 12 years of age many children automatically adopt a front view when asked to draw a man and an owl, whereas they adopt a side view when asked to draw a horse, a car, and a boat.

Canonicality persists even when the child is asked to copy an object presented in a noncanonical orientation. Freeman and Janikoun (1972) asked 5- to 9-year-old children to draw a copy of the cup that was presented in front of them with its handle hidden from view. They found that, up to 7 years of age, children included the cup's handle in their drawings even though it was not visible to them. More interesting, although children included the nonvisible handle, they omitted the picture of a flower on the cup even though this was very visible and a unique feature that could have been used to identify the particular cup. Further studies indicate that when asked to draw a transparent mug with its handle facing backward, even more children draw the mug in the canonical orientation (Davis, 1984; Freeman, 1980). This points to children's strong tendency to represent and draw the *class* of an object, rather than the *specific* object to be copied.

Although it is clear that context and the communicative purpose of the drawing task may play an important role in increasing the number of non-canonical drawings (Davis, 1985), this does not hold in all cases. For example, Light and Simmons (1983) used a communication-game paradigm that gave special emphasis to the necessity to take account of the viewer's orientation. Despite this, 5- to 6-year-olds failed to show a significant increase in noncanonical drawings. Davis (1983a) found that the communication condition actually increased children's tendency toward canonicality. On the other hand, while replicating Freeman and Janikoun's findings, Davis (1983b) reported a differential effect of context on 4-year-olds versus 5- to 6-year-olds when asked to draw two cups. Five- and 6-year-old children tended to abandon the canonical drawing of a cup with its handle hidden provided the noncanonically oriented cup was paired with a canonically oriented cup in a copying task. By contrast, 4-year-olds persisted in drawing both cups with their handles visible, despite the fact that one was turned away from the viewer.

Instructions given in a drawing task also affect the canonicality of children's drawing. Davis (1983a) asked 4- to 7-years-olds to draw an empty glass, a glass fully filled with milk, a glass half filled with milk, and a glass with a little milk, under two different instructions: (1) to show "exactly how it looks"; or (2) to show "how much milk there is in the glass." The first condition yielded similar results to those of other studies. In the second condition, more children produced a line representing the level of milk than in the first one. Levels of milk were appropriately represented. This indicates that provided the goal is made explicit, young children can represent in their drawings specific information about a particular object. Nonetheless, the impact of the canonicality constraint on young children's spontaneous drawing is rather robust.

The second constraint, the transparency constraint, is closely related to, but different from, canonicality. Many studies have reported that children tend to draw what they know about an object rather than precisely what they see. For instance, a smaller human figure is drawn inside a bigger human figure to represent a pregnant woman (Golomb, 1992, p. 67; Thomas & Silk, 1990, p. 9); a profile of a human face is drawn with two eyes visible, giving rise to a Picasso-like drawing; "people in a house" are represented by superimposing human figures on the drawing of a house (Golomb, 1992, p. 112; Krampen, 1991, p. 55). This phenomenon has been labeled "intellectual realism" by some researchers and considered a deficit or error (Luquet, 1927; Piaget & Inhelder, 1948/1956). However, from the viewpoint of national development, this might be considered an important advancement, setting it apart from canonicality (Freeman, 1980). In the case of the transparency constraint, children are actually engaged in representing specific information about a particular object rather than general information about a class of objects. Although transparency drawings are visually unrealistic and artistically peculiar, they serve the purpose of communicating ideas about a specific object.

Such a view is, however, challenged by Crook (1984, 1985). Crook first asked 5-year-old children to draw a stick pushed through a ball. More than 60% of the children in this condition made transparency drawings in which a line was drawn right across the circle representing the ball. The results replicated the findings of Clark's classic study (1897), in which he suggested that transparency is the result of children's effort to inform. To test this explanation, Crook included four other conditions: (1) two short sticks pushed into a ball in opposite directions and far apart from each other, (2) two sticks pushed into a ball in opposite directions but joined together in the middle; (3) a single stick painted half red and half black and pushed through a ball so that the joint was invisible; (4) a single stick painted one quarter one color and three quarters another color so that the joint could be seen. Crook found that Condition (2) resulted in 20% transparency drawing and Condition (4) 64%. In Conditions (1) and (3), which actually required information about the joint, no transparency drawings were produced. Crook argued that although transparency drawing is indeed more informative, it is not necessarily motivated by communicative intent. Further studies are needed to settle the interpretation of these different results, but it may well be that rather than lacking awareness of the need to communicate information in their drawings, young children have difficulty in coordinating representations of two types of information about one object simultaneously. Transparency drawing may turn out to be more positive cognitively in that it can be viewed as an index of children's notational effort to communicate information about an object.

Just as young children's drawings focus on representing "insideness" and the canonical details of single objects, older children's drawings representing object arrays in depth are constrained by their ideas about representing relations between objects such as "behindness." Studies have shown that up to 7 to 8 years of age, children have difficulty representing one object behind another. Freeman, Eiser, and Sayers (1977) asked children between 5 and 10 years old to draw one apple behind another. While 9- to 10-year-olds had no problem drawing the nearer apple partially occluding the farther one, the majority of children up to 7 to 8 years old drew two apples side by side or vertically one above the other. Similar results were found by Ingram (1983), Light and MacIntosh (1980), Light and Humphreys (1981), and Light and Simmons (1983). Further studies indicate that the similarity between the two objects and the nature of the farther object affect whether or not the child draws the two objects in a partially occluded fashion (Cox, 1981, 1985, 1986, 1989; Light & Foot, 1986). Cox's studies, for instance, showed that two dissimilar objects (e.g., a block and a man) lead children as young as 6 years old to draw more partially occluded objects than is the case for two identical objects.

However, there is consensus in the literature that children younger than 6 years of age still have difficulty producing partially occluded objects, sometimes even when explicit instructions are given (Barret, Beaumont, & Jennett, 1985; Light & Simmons, 1983). Why does partial occlusion pose such difficulties for younger children? Production or knowledge deficiencies (Freeman, 1980; Piaget & Inhelder, 1948/1956) do not appear to be the answer (Cox, 1985; Light, 1985). As with the case of "insideness" in younger children, Light (1985) suggested that lack of partial occlusion should not be considered in terms of failure but rather as the result of their effort to inform. Light and Humphreys (1981) used a pair of differently colored ceramic "piggy bank" pigs. A red pig was placed behind a green one. Results showed that all of 5- and 6-year-old children produced nonoccluded drawings of the two pigs. Some of them were side by side and some were one above the other. About 80% of the nonoccluded drawings clearly conveyed information that the red pig was somehow following the green pig. Light (1985) argued that young children may rely on array-specific information rather than viewer-specific information to depict "behindness," while older children use other strategies.

A more interesting proposal comes from Ingram (1985). He suggested that young children's drawings of occlusion may involve two coding processes: spatial coding and symbolic coding. Spatial coding leads to viewer-specific drawings and symbolic coding leads to so-called "intellectual realism" or, in this particular case, nonocclusion drawings. Ingram argued that both coding processes may be available even to very young children and become integrated between 5 and 7 years of age. According to this model, drawing "behindness" in young children is constrained by the fact that symbolic coding overrides spatial coding. In any case, it is evident: (1) that young children are able to represent "behindness" for notational purposes; and (2) that "behindness" is represented in a nonoccluded manner. More recent studies have shown that at the same developmental period that children depict "insideness" by using transparency, they depict "behindness," not by using transparency but by using nonocclusion (Cox, 1989), suggesting that they process the two situations very differently. This once again bears witness to young children's effort to represent and differentiate specific information about objects in their albeit inadequate drawings.

A third constraint seen in young children's drawings is the "coordination constraint." This is best illustrated by one of the most favored topics in children's drawing: the human figure. Efforts to draw a human figure emerge soon after the child leaves the scribbling stage. The early human figure drawings tend to be peculiar and of a stereotypic nature. The head is disproportionally large. Certain parts of the body are often missing. Arms and legs, if there are any, tend to come out of the head. This type of representation is called the "tadpole figure." There are different explanations as to why some body parts, particularly the torso, are missing in young children's human figure drawing. Gibson (1969) suggested that young children lack a complete body image, but Piaget (1932), Arnheim (1974), and Cox (1989) maintained that young children do have a complete body image but their knowledge about the human body is not as differentiated as that of older children. Therefore, to the younger child, the large circlelike form in a tadpole drawing is an amalgam of both head and/or torso from which the arms and/or legs emerge (Cox, 1989; Goodnow, 1977).

Memory constraints have also been invoked to explain some of the characteristics of children's tadpole drawings. Thus, Freeman (1980) invoked the memory literature on the serial order effect to explain missing body parts in young children's drawings. However, Golomb (1981, 1992) revealed inconsistency between Freeman's model and current data on children's human figure drawing. He opted instead for a simplicity constraint, suggesting that young children's omission or inclusion of body parts is based on the principle of simplicity of forms, that is, the child's "inclination to economize and to represent what she considers the most essential features of her figure" (Golomb, 1992, p. 48). Another constraint involves planning (Thomas & Silk, 1990). When drawing a human figure, young children tend to draw a circle first to represent the head. When the circle takes too much space, other body parts have to compete for limited space, obliging young children either to omit some body parts or to draw them in a peculiar way.

Despite the rich data available on human figure drawing, tighter studies are still needed to opt between these different explanations. It is possible that lack of planning, undifferentiated body drawing and the inclination to achieve simplicity all interact in young children's tadpole drawings.

As children develop into the primary school years, their drawings become increasingly sophisticated. They are able to represent more specific information about the details of objects and human figures, such as feelings (Golomb, 1992) and movement (Golomb, 1992; Goodnow, 1977). Nonetheless, other constraints still obtain. Karmiloff-Smith (1990) reported that children up to 7 or 8 years of age still have difficulty in some circumstances in changing their already-established routines for drawing certain objects. In her study, children between 5 and 11 years of age were asked to draw a man and a house, and then to draw a man and a house that did not exist. She found that for the nonexistent condition, children of all ages changed the shapes and sizes of elements or the shape of the whole (e.g., a triangular house, a square-headed man), and they deleted essential elements (e.g., a leg or an eye of the human figure, the door of a house). However, only children above 8 years of age spontaneously inserted extra elements (e.g., two heads, three legs), changed position or orientation (e.g., door on roof, arm in the place of a leg), or made cross-category insertions (e.g., a house with eyes, a man with wheels instead of legs). Older children seem to be able to move flexibly between different representational categories.

Constraint on children's drawings was further pursued in a problem-solving context by Lee and Karmiloff-Smith (1996). They asked children between 8 and 11 years of age to first solve a simple board puzzle and then to "mark" something down on paper so that another child would be able to solve the puzzle exactly the way they had. First, children of all ages had no problem in representing the pieces of the board puzzle. In fact, they compiled well with Goodman's principles for an adequate notation (Cohen, 1985; Goodman, 1976). For example, the pieces of the board were represented unambiguously. The notations were also consistent, in that when one piece was referred to by its color, the other pieces were all referred to by color also. Very few children cross-referenced, that is, referred to one piece by its color and another by its shape. By contrast, up to 8 to 9 years of age children had difficulty representing the steps of the solution to the task. Even a number of 10- and 11-year-olds experienced problems with representing sequential information. This was not only a production deficiency. When children were presented with a forced-choice task in which they had to choose between pairs of ready-made notations of the solution, one with various types of redundant information and the other with various forms of explicit sequential marking, younger children favored the former, whereas older children (and adults) now opted for explicit sequential marking. Lee and Karmiloff-Smith argued that the differences stem from the 7- to 8 year-olds' desire to represent all the details of referents coupled with their difficulties in translating temporal information into spatial form. By 10 years of age children are starting to surmount these difficulties in their productions, but it is only in forced-choice tasks that the older children perform like adults.

IV. CONSTRAINTS ON WRITTEN LANGUAGE AND NUMBER NOTATION

The literature on written language is so vast that it would have to be the subject of an entire chapter in its own right (see Frith, 1980, and Goswami & Bryant, 1990, for reviews of the field). In this section, therefore, we focus on early development, that is, on preliterate/prenumerate children's sensitivity to and productions of written language and number notation. One important question is whether young children focus solely on the referential/communicative function of written language and numerals or whether, prior to understanding these functions, they analyze the characteristics of different notational systems and differentiate them from drawing.

Goodman (1976) has demonstrated the difficulty in defining differences between drawing and writing/numerals merely in terms of iconicity, that is, a distinction between realistic depiction of reality versus arbitrary links to reality. This is particularly true when exploring the question developmentally. To avoid the iconicity/noniconicity distinction, Tolchinsky-Landsmann and Karmiloff-Smith (1992) proposed three constraints that writing and number notation must meet and that differentiate them from drawing. These are: relative closure constraint, element/string constraint, and referential-communicative constraint.

The first constraint concerns the relative closure of the conventional systems of writing and number notation. Drawing constitutes a comparatively open system because it is always possible to invent and include new elements. By contrast, each different writing or number system across different cultures is relatively closed. Although new combinations of elements are more or less infinite, the *elements* within each writing/number system are finite; invention and inclusion of new elements is exceedingly rare. The distinction is similar to the one made in linguistics between open class categories (e.g., nouns and verbs), which easily admit new members, and closed class categories (e.g., articles and prepositions), which do not.

The element/string constraint also distinguishes drawing from writing and number notation, in that in the latter two cases strings are segmentable into discrete elements and retain separate meanings. In Goodman's terminology, writing and number notation are articulated into characters, and characters must be disjoint (Goodman, 1976). By contrast, it is difficult to define the equivalent of an element, or a segmentable graphic unit, in drawing (see, however, Willats, 1977, and Freeman, 1980, for interesting discussions in this respect).

Finally the referential-communicative constraint points to a formal mapping both from the notation to the referent and from the referent to the notation. For example, in writing, certain marks refer to a limited range of phonological segments and, conversely, given the pronunciation of a phonological segment, its written notation falls within a limited number of alternatives. This dual direction of referential mapping does not hold for drawing and other pictorial depictions.

A number of studies of emergent literacy have shown that the differentiation between drawing and noniconic forms of notation is precocious developmentally. Once this initial distinction is established, children impose a number of formal constraints on what qualifies as writing, for example, linearity, number of elements in a string, and intrastring variety of elements (Lavine, 1977; Ferrerio & Teberosky, 1979). Studies using sorting tasks have shown that preliterate children consider a notation "good for reading" if it contains more than two and less than eight or nine elements, and provided adjacent elements are not identical. Moreover, these constraints appear to be general across different orthographic systems (Tolchinsky-Landsmann, 1990). This precocious differentiation between drawing and writing stands in sharp contrast with the popular view, and with the results of some experimental studies, that young children confound writing with drawing. Indeed, when preliterate children are instructed to "write a letter to a friend" or to "leave a message for another addressee," they often produce drawings (McLane & McNamee, 1991; Sulzby, 1986). This has led researchers to assume that young children do not differentiate between drawing and writing. However, this apparent contradiction between the results of different studies highlights two different aspects of notational competence. The sorting tasks focus children's attention on notation as a domain of knowledge, whereas the message–oriented tasks concentrate on children's use of notational devices as referential-communicative tools (Tolchinsky-Landsmann & Karmiloff-Smith, 1992). These two aspects of notational competence do not develop synchronously.

The distinction between notation as a domain of knowledge and notation as a referential-communicative tool also helps to account for the discrepant findings in studies focused on number notation (Allardice, 1977; Hughes, 1986; Sastre & Moreno, 1976; Sinclair & Sinclair, 1984). Experiments where number notation is used as a referential-communicative tool again indicate that young children frequently resort to drawing when asked to represent number. However, more recent studies show that if young children's attention is drawn to the notations as formal systems, such as in sorting tasks, then children make clear-cut differences between numerals and drawing (Tolchinsky-Landsmann & Karmiloff-Smith, 1992). For the written system preliterate will not accept repeated letters or strings with a single element. By contrast, for number notation prenumerate children allow single and repeated numbers, demonstrating that they clearly differentiate between writing and number notation.

Such distinctions do not hold only in young children's sorting performance. In their productions they also demonstrate that they adhere to different constraints for drawing, writing, and number notation. One way to discover this is to probe children's productions by using a technique similar to the one used in the drawing literature, which we discussed in an earlier section. When asked to produce numerals that "don't exist" or some writing "that doesn't exist," children display similar sensitivity to that displayed in sorting tasks (Tolchinsky-Landsmann & Karmiloff-Smith, 1993). One solution children adopted for the nonexistent task was to violate the relative closure constraint. For example, children produced nonexistent numbers, letters, and words by transgressing intersystem boundaries. They used parts of the drawing system to make nonletters, nonnumbers, and nonwords. They also used elements of the number system to make nonwords and nonletters, and vice versa. Other children violated the element/string constraint. For example, if they had produced a string of different letters for a real word, they used a string of repeated identical letters for a nonword. If they had produced a single numeral for a real number, they offered an overly lengthy string of numbers for a number that "couldn't possibly exist." For nonletters, they deformed the graphic shape by duplicating parts or changing the contour. A few children blurred the boundaries between elements and invented new units by amalgamating two letters or two numerals to produce nonletters and nonnumbers. Finally, slightly older children violated the referential-communicative constraint. For example, for nonwords they announced that they would write "words that cannot be said" or "words that aren't anything"; for nonnumbers they produced multiple zeros.

In sum, when young children use notations as referential-communicative tools, they focus on the *content* that they wish to convey and may use drawing to express that content. But this is a far cry from confounding different notation systems. The studies discussed above suggest that, unlike the view that writing and number notation are derived ontogenetically from drawing (e.g., Vygotsky, 1978), early on children are sensitive to the domain-specific constraints operating on each notational domain (Bialystok, 1986, 1991, 1992; Karmiloff-Smith, 1992; Tolchinsky-Landsmann & Karmiloff-Smith, 1992, 1993).

V. CONSTRAINTS ON CHILDREN'S USE AND UNDERSTANDING OF MAPS

Maps are graphic notation systems for representing space. They take a wide range of forms and serve many functions ranging from indicating routes to representing geopolitics. Psychologists have recently shown interest in studying the development of map reading and map making (Liben & Downs, 1989). Maps are studied by researchers for three rather different purposes: (1) as a means of revealing children's representation of space; (2) as a unique problem-solving task in its own right; and (3) as a symbolic activity per se. Many developmentalists have taken the first approach and used maps to disclose children's spatial representations (e.g., Feldman, 1980; Gauvain & Rogoff, 1986; Hart, 1979; Hazen, Lockman, & Pick, 1978; Landau, 1986; Piaget & Inhelder, 1948/1956; Siegel & Schadler, 1977). The second approach focuses on how children interpret and use maps (e.g., Blades & Spencer, 1986; Blaut, McCleary, & Blaut, 1970; Blaut & Stea, 1971; Spencer & Darvizhe, 1981; Stea & Blaut, 1973). In contrast to these two approaches, a relatively small number of studies have investigated children's map production as a symbolic activity (Bluestein and Acredolo, 1979; Karmiloff-Smith, 1979; Liben & Downs, 1989; Wolf & Gardner, 1985). Nevertheless, results from all three approaches provide both direct and indirect evidence for understanding how children use maps as notations.

Like other notation systems, maps establish a "stand-for" relationship between the map and the real world. According to Bluestein & Acredolo (1979), to understand this relationship, children have to call on two distinct cognitive processes: "semantic interpretation" and "projection/superimposition." The first entails a differentiation between cartographic and pictographic notations and an understanding of how they refer to their real-world counterparts. In the second, projection and superimposition, children have to understand the relationships that obtain between notations and relate these relationships to those that obtain between objects in real space. Liben and Downs (1989) break down the semantic component into several levels. They suggest that the holistic idea that a map is a representation of a place is at a different level from the idea that a notational element on a map represents a landmark in the real world. The authors also point out that the projection/superimposition component is simply part of a bigger picture. Maps take a wide range of forms, of which the typical road map is merely one. A map is not necessarily made easier by including additional information. Some maps contain not only geographic information but also information on population density, income per capita, and distribution of diseases. The understanding of any map, then, calls on general cognitive constraints beyond the map-specific ones.

In order to explore the semantic interpretation and projection/superimposition components of children's use of maps as notations, Liben and Downs (1989) conducted a series of experiments. In one of their tasks, they asked children and adults to identify a series of maps and maplike notations and either accept or reject them as maps. These notations were selected on the basis of cartographic theory. They varied in a number of key characteristics such as medium (photographs vs. drawings), place represented (e.g., local area vs. a planet), spatial scale (small scale to large scale), viewing angle (e.g., aerial view vs. perspective view), color (color vs. black and white), content (topographic vs. thematic maps), technical graphic properties (e.g., hachures vs. contour lines), and presence or absence of verbal labels. They found that children as young as 3 years of age were able to identify some forms of representations as places (e.g., a Chicago aerial photograph). However, they were confused by other types of maps (e.g., a tourist map of Washington, D.C.). Further analyses revealed that both children and adults tended to categorize as maps those notations that contained characteristics such as small-to-medium scale, color, overhead view, and cartographic symbols. However, young children differed from older children and adults in that they rejected as maps notations that were black and white, large scale, and in perspective view, as well as pictures or photographs. It was found that by age 5 and 6, children had formed a rather mature understanding of the types of notations that are maps and those that are not. However, while they had no problem in identifying holistically a map as a representation of places, they experienced great difficulty in interpreting the componential elements of maps. Their difficulty seemed to reside in their inability to maintain an integrated view that both a map as a whole and its elements simultaneously represent places. For instance, one young child interpreted a baseball diamond on the Chicago aerial photograph as a guitar, while maintaining that the photograph was a map of Chicago. Young children also had an overly realistic view about the symbols on a map. For example, some children believed that a road shown in red on a map would actually be red in the real world, and an airport symbolized by an airplane would have only one airplane.

Based on these findings, Liben and Downs (1989) suggested that children as young as 3 share a similar prototypical map concept with adults. In other words, they understand the stand-for relationship between maps and places. However, young children's conception of maps is limited to understanding the holistic level of the stand-for relationship. They have problems in understanding the relationships between a map as a whole and its elements, the relationships between the elements, as well as the relationships between the elements and what they represent.

Besides investigating the development of map concepts, a few studies have extensively examined children's map reading (Blades & Spencer, 1986, 1987, 1989; Bluestein & Acredolo, 1979; Feldman & Acredolo, 1979; Gauvain & Rogoff, 1986; Hazen et al., 1978; Landau & Gleitman, 1985; Liben & Downs, 1992; M. H. Matthews, 1986; Presson, 1982; Scholnick, Fein, & Campbell, 1990; Uttal & Wellman, 1989). Bluestein and Acredolo (1979) presented children between ages 3 and 5 with a maplike representation of a furnished room and asked them to use the map to find a toy hidden by the experimenter in the room. There were two conditions: (1) three types of alignment (the map was aligned with the layout of the room, the map was rotated 180° from the layout of the room, or the map was shown vertically); and (2) reading the map inside or outside the experimental room. In the Aligned–Inside condition, success rates reached 55% at age 3 increasing to 100% at age 5. The Aligned–Outside condition yielded similar results, but with no age difference. By contrast, when the map was not aligned with the room, only a majority of 5-year-olds found the hidden toy successfully in both the Inside and Outside conditions.

The researchers suggested that 3-year-olds assume that maps are always correctly aligned. This was partially supported by the analysis of errors. When they made errors in nonaligned conditions, children tended to search for the hidden toy at the place directly across from the correct location. In other words, they used the map as if it were correctly aligned. The Vertical–Outside condition showed no age effect. However, in a later study, Liben and Downs (1989) pointed out that Bluestein and Acredolo (1979) used the Aligned–Inside as a pretest, and only those children who passed this condition proceeded with the other conditions. This rendered the Aligned–Inside condition incomparable with the other conditions. By extrapolating the original data, Liben and Downs found that an age difference also existed in the Aligned–Outside and Vertical–Outside conditions. Despite this, the major conclusion of the study remains valid, that is, that alignment is a major constraint on young children's map reading.

The alignment constraint also holds in some circumstances for map reading in older children and adults, that is, it is the default assumption for map use. Using a similar paradigm to the Bluestein and Acredolo study, Presson (1982) examined the errors made by older children (between 5 and 8 years of age). He found that some children ignored the landmark position on the rotated map, indicating that they, too, assumed that the map was aligned with the environment that it represented. This error was particularly evident among 5-year-olds. But even adults make such errors. Levine, Marchon, and Harley (1984) investigated adults' reading of "You are here" maps, typically found in shopping malls or public buildings. They found adults tended to assume that places higher up the map were ahead of them in the environment. In sum, topological alignment remains a cognitive constraint even in older children's and adults' map reading, though they are less affected than young children.

A considerable amount of research has been devoted to understanding landmarks. Both Bluestein and Aredolo (1979) and Presson (1982) suggested that when children are successful in nonaligned conditions, they overcome the alignment constraint by using landmarks. To guide their search they extract critical information such as whether the hiding place is close to or far from the landmark on the map. Landmarks are indeed one of the key elements that a map reader has to come to grips with in order to understand their notational function vis-à-vis the real world. Blades and Spencer (1989) asked children between age 3 and 6 to locate a toy hidden in one of four boxes located at the end of a X-shaped layout with one salient landmark. Children were given a map indicating the location of the toy. The maps were rotated for zero°, 90°, 180°, and 270°. In addition to findings similar to those of Bluestein and Acredolo (1979), results showed that non-aligned conditions did not seem to have a significantly different effect on children's performance. Further analyses revealed that this was due to children's use of the landmark as a reference point. For example, when the toy was hidden near the landmark, the success rate was higher than when the toy was hidden in the branch opposite the landmark. Qualitative differences were also found between 3-year-olds and older children. Three-year-olds used a landmark on a map only as a clue to a hiding place, while 4-year-olds began to consider the map as representing a spatial *relationship* to the environment and the landmark a reference point for that relationship.

Uttal and Wellman (1989) conducted a series of experiments that further illustrates the difference between younger and older children. In their study, children first learned the details of a map representing a large space consisting of six small rooms with six different stuffed animals. Children were required to navigate through the large space and identify the animals living in each of the rooms. It was found that children of 4 and 5 years of age were able to formulate an integral representation of the space by map reading. They demonstrated that they had captured the layout of spatial relationships on the map corresponding to the rooms and animals in the environment. The researchers argued that children using a map to aid navigation in space have to know: (1) that a map represents a certain area of space; (2) how the map represents that space; and (3) what information indicates their current position in space. They found preschoolers had trouble with (3) but not with (1) and (2). By contrast, older children were proficient at all three.

Other cognitive constraints contribute to the developmental difference in map reading between younger and older children. For example, Scholnick et al. (1990) found that encoding spatial information, mental rotation, and use of memory codes affect the way in which children read maps. In their study, children between age 4 and 6 were tested on a map task, a placement task, and a mental rotation task. The map task involved the use of a route map to take a toy to certain locations on a board terrain. The placement task required copying the experimenter's placement on one terrain onto the child's terrain. Since both terrains were identical, unlike map reading no transformations of scale or elements were required. Several measures were taken from the placement task: performance on trials in which toys were placed near a landmark (the landmark placement) and performance in trials that required encoding the entire layout of the terrain (the open field placement), performance in trials in which the terrains were aligned or not aligned, and recall of landmarks. The mental rotation task was derived from Thurstone's (1958) Primary Mental Abilities Battery that requires matching a standard figure with a rotated one. Not surprising, older children performed better than younger ones on the map task as well as on other measures, and younger children did better in the landmark placement than in the open field placement. It is more interesting, however, that younger children's map reading was predicted by their performance on the mental rotation task, the alignment/nonalignment conditions, and the landmark placement condition. By contrast, older children's map reading was predicted by their performance in the mental rotation task, recall of landmarks, and open field placement. These results not only again confirm that younger children have problems with alignment and in integrating spatial relationships, but also indicate that other cognitive factors such as mental imagery and spatial memory affect the development of map reading.

In sum, these various studies allow us to conclude that children as young as 3 years understand that maps represent certain things in space and can use them for object searching or finding their way. Second, 3-year-olds are limited in their map reading by the alignment constraint and tend to ignore the orientation of the map. Third, young children are further constrained by their focus on fixed landmarks rather than the spatial relations between them. On the other hand, older children and adults, though using alignment by default, are able to surmount that constraint by extracting from a map not only information about landmarks but also information about spatial relationships between them. The qualitative difference between younger and older children may also reflect young children's limited understanding of the symbolic functions of the elements on maps. Although around 3 years of age children begin to differentiate maps form pictures and photographs (Liben & Downs, 1989), they seem to read the symbols on maps as unrelated to one another or as representing a small portion of space. Finally, different levels of cognitive development (e.g., memory strategies) also affect children's use and understanding of maps.

VI. CONSTRAINTS ON CHILDREN'S USE OF SCALE MODELS

While different researchers have focused on maps, studies on children's use of scale models have been carried out almost single-handedly by DeLoache and her collaborators (DeLoache, 1987, 1989a, 1989b, 1990, 1991; DeLoache, Kolstad, & Anderson, 1991; DeLoache & Marzolf, 1992). Unlike maps, scale models represent real-world spatial relationships in a three-dimensional fashion. DeLoache's work has repeatedly shown that understanding the symbolic function of a scale model is achieved as early as 3 years of age.

In one of her studies, DeLoache (1987) created a miniature model (called "Baby Snoopy's room") of a furnished room (called "Daddy Snoopy's room"). In one condition (the Hide-in-room/Retrieve-in-model condition), children watched an experimenter hiding a big toy dog (Daddy Snoopy) in the room and were asked to find a small toy dog (Baby Snoopy) in the model (Retrieval 1). Children in this condition were also asked to retrieve the big toy in the room (Retrieval 2), to test their memory for the original hiding place. In the other condition (the Hide-in-model/Retrieve-in-room condition), children were asked to find the big toy dog in the room after watching the experimenter hiding the small toy dog in the model. The toys were always hidden somewhere close to the furniture, that is, close to an easily identifiable landmark. In order to test whether the similarity between the items of furniture in the room and the corresponding ones in the model would affect children's performance, DeLoache changed the perceptual features of some items, while keeping the others closely resembling one another. Three-year-olds reached about 80% successful retrievals of the analogous toy (Retrieval 1), while 2-year-olds succeeded in only 15% of cases. Neither condition nor similarity affected this pronounced age difference. By contrast, both groups did equally well in retrieving the original toy (Retrieval 2), ruling out memory as the explanation for the 2-year-olds' failure.

In order to further explore the significant age difference in young children's understanding of scale models, DeLoache (1989a) and DeLoache et al. (1991) varied the levels of similarity between the room and the model in terms of both the hiding place and the overall layout. Children participated in one of the following four conditions: (1) both the layout and the hiding place were highly similar (the High Space-High Place condition); (2) the layout was similar but the hiding place was dissimilar (the High Space-Low Place condition); (3) the layout was dissimilar but the hiding place was similar (the Low Space-High Place condition); (4) both the layout and the hiding place were dissimilar (the Low Space-Low Place condition). While 2-year-olds' performance remained the same as in the previous study, 3-year-olds' successful retrieval dropped to about 20% in both the High Space-Low Place and Low Space-Low Place conditions, while they displayed successful retrieval in both the High Space-High Place and Low Space-High Place conditions. In other words, when the hiding places resemble one another, 3-year-olds have no problem in establishing a direct stand-for relationship between the model and the real world. Their problems arise with respect to spatial *relations* between landmarks. This is not surprising, since it is in fact in line with the results from the map reading studies, which show that 3-year-olds rely on landmarks rather than spatial layout.

These various results suggest that caution should be taken to avoid overestimating 3-year-olds' understanding of the symbolic function of scale models. In fact, Hazen et al. (1978) demonstrated that even 5-year-olds continue to have difficulties in integrating spatial relations between elements when constructing a scale model. Their findings were obtained from a scale model production task, which is more difficult than DeLoache's scale model comprehension task. However, it is clear that the understanding of scale models as symbols representing spatial relationships in the real world is still not fully developed in preschoolers or even in the early school years.

Another interesting phenomenon was observed in children around $2\frac{1}{2}$ years of age (DeLoache, 1987, 1991; DeLoache & Marzolf, 1992). In Experiment 2 of DeLoache's (1987) study, 2-year-olds participated in the model condition described above, together with tasks using colored photographs depicting the hiding place in the room. It transpired that the same children who failed to retrieve the toy in the scale model condition were able to find the toy on the basis of a photograph of its hiding place. A more controlled follow-up study was also conducted (DeLoache, 1991). In Experiment 1 of this study, children of $2\frac{1}{2}$ years of age participated in four conditions: (1) children watched the experimenter hiding the toy in the model and were then asked to find the analogous toy in the room (the Hide-Model condition); (2) the experimenter only pointed to the hiding place in the model (the Point-Model condition); (3) the experimenter hid the toy behind a set of pictures depicting the items of furniture in the room (the Hide–Photo condition); (4) the experimenter pointed to the hiding place in a photo depicting the hiding place. The Hide-Model condition again resulted in very low success rates (25%). Children's performance in the Point-Model condition was similar. By contrast, the Point-Photo condition yielded 78% successful retrieval, closely replicating the 70% success rates in earlier work (De-Loache, 1987). In Experiment 2, two new conditions were added: the wide-range photo condition and the line drawing condition. Again, photos and drawings gave rise to better performance than scale models. A recent study by DeLoache and Marzolf (1992) found $2\frac{1}{2}$-year-olds to be significantly in advance of 2-year-olds in their understanding of the symbolic function of pictures. These various results indicate that two-dimensional photos/pictures suggest a stand-for relationship more readily than scale models, which the youngest children treat as real-world objects in their own right.

Dow and Pick (1992) further examined the different outcomes of photos and scale models. They specifically investigated whether a model or a picture designated as a representation of something else or as an object in its own right would lead to differential results. Children of age $2\frac{1}{2}$ and 3 years participated in five conditions: (1) photo room: a photograph of a full-sized room; (2) photo model: a photograph of a scale model of the room; (3) photo model possession: a photograph of the model described as Little Teddy's room, while the room was described as Big Teddy's; (4) model possession: a model described as Little Teddy's room; and (5) model: described as "just like the big room." Most of DeLoache's findings were replicated. However, some interesting differences also emerged. Children of $2\frac{1}{2}$ years of age were above 60% correct in both the photo room and photo model conditions. These results were significantly higher than performance on the model condition and the two possession conditions that were similar to DeLoache's conditions. The findings again suggest that very young children have difficulty in maintaining an object as an object in its own right and, at the same time, as a representation of something else.

Why is there such a developmental difference between very young children's understanding of photographs and scale models? DeLoache (1989a) proposed a dual representation hypothesis. She argued that scale models, unlike other external symbol systems, represent other objects and, at the same time, are complex, highly salient objects in their own right. To use a model, the child has to create a dual representation, that is, simultaneously representing it as what it is and as what it stands for. Because the scale model is attractive and salient as a three-dimensional object in its own right, it lures young children into representing it solely as an object. It therefore becomes difficult for them to simultaneously represent it as a referent standing for something in the real world (DeLoache & Marzolf, 1992). Pictures and photographs do not embody this constraint.

While the dual representation hypothesis is attractive and probably accounts for some aspects of young children's difficulties, other findings (Dow & Pick, 1992) reveal potential methodological problems in DeLoache's studies. Indeed, in DeLoache's paradigm the model was always designated as Baby Snoopy's room and therefore represented an object in and of itself rather than as a representation of Daddy Snoopy's room. Given that pictures were also presented in the same way, the original results cannot be dismissed. The most interesting finding emerging from all of these studies is almost paradoxical: young children find it easier to deal with more abstract forms of representation such as pictures than with the more concrete forms such as scale models because of their difficulty to dissociate real-world existence from representations thereof.

VII. SUMMARY AND FUTURE DIRECTIONS

Due to space limitations, our review of the development of notational systems has been necessarily selective. We have not, for instance, dealt with musical notation (see Bamberger, 1982, Catan, 1989, and Cohen, 1985, for some interesting studies of children's inventions of musical notation). However, we believe that the review has covered most of the major forms of notation systems that children of all cultures come to understand and use. This chapter has examined studies of the development of children's use and understanding of drawings, written language, number notation, maps, scale models, photographs, and pictures. The studies show that children's understanding and use of notation systems starts early and continues to develop during the early and later school years, depending on the type of notation system and the various functions each one fills.

The many different studies of children's notational competence indicate that around 2 years of age children show some understanding of the stand-for relationship between notations and what they represent. By 3 years of age they are able to use notations to solve problems in the real world, for example, using maps for finding their way. Further, preliterate and prenumerate children are aware of some of the notational differences between written language, number notation, and drawing. Some of the constraints that they impose on numbers and letters already resemble those that exist in the conventional notation systems of the adult world. Children's capacity to make and use notations develops rather rapidly. By 6 to 7 years of age, they have come to grips with most of the fundamental elements of modern conventional notation systems. In some cases (e.g., drawings), their understanding is close to that of adults. Children's notational competence should not be overestimated, however. The studies we have discussed make it clear that the pattern and the pace of the development of notational competence vary from one system to another. The functions and constraints imposed on each system are different, too. Notational competence will undergo numerous changes, because of children's developing cognitive abilities and their expanding experience. Further, some important aspects of notation systems such as representing temporal information in spatial form continue to pose problems well into adolescence.

There are several directions in which future research should be directed. First, more studies are needed of the relationship between cognitive constraints on notational development, on one hand, and conventional, culturally bound constraints on the other. Most studies have hitherto been restricted to children in Western cultures. A further area of interest is children's metacognitive conceptions about the multiple functions and relationships between different notation systems. This would require within-subjects studies that investigate children's understanding and use of different notational systems and how they are interrelated, to complement the cross-sectional studies carried out hitherto. Third, while quite a lot of work has been done on children's understanding of notations, only a few have been devoted to children's notational *productions*. This is of particular theoretical importance because it may reveal constraints not apparent in the comprehension studies. Fourth, although present studies have shown that notation is not simply an externalization of internal representations, no work has yet focused specifically on the relationship between the two. Clearly it is essential to further explore the relationship between the constraints imposed on internal representations and those on external notational systems. Last, but not least, research into the use and understanding of notation in atypical children is of particular interest. This is not only because of its potential practical applications, but also because, with their limited cognitive capacities, atypical children may use notations in a unique way (e.g., idiot savant drawers, hyperlexics), thereby shedding light on what is essential versus nonessential cognitively in the normal course of notational development.

References

Allardice, B. (1977). The development of written representation for some mathematical concepts. *Journal of Children's Mathematical Behavior, 2,* 135–148.
Arnheim, R. (1966). *Toward a psychology of art.* Berkeley: University of California Press.

Arnheim, R. (1969). *Visual thinking*. Berkeley: University of California Press.
Arnheim, R. (1974). *Art and visual perception: A psychology of the creative eye*. Berkeley: University of California Press.
Bamberger, M. (1982). Revisiting children's drawings of simple rhythms: A function for reflection in action. In S. Strauss (Ed.), *U-shaped behavioral growth*. NY: Academic Press.
Barret, M. D., Beaumont, A. V., & Jennett, M. S. (1985). Some children do sometimes do what they have been told to do: Task demands and verbal instructions in children's drawing. In N. H. Freeman & M. Cox (Eds.), *Visual order: The nature and development of pictorial representation*. Cambridge, UK: Cambridge University Press.
Barret, M. D., & Light, P. H. (1976). Symbolism and intellectual realism in children's drawings. *British Journal of Educational Psychology, 46*, 198–202.
Bialystok, E. (1986). Children's concept of word. *Journal of Psycholinguistic Research, 15*, 13–32.
Bialystok, E. (1991). Letters, sounds, and symbols: Changes in children's understanding of written language. *Applied Psycholinguistics, 12*, 75–89.
Bialystok, E. (1992). Symbolic representation of letters and numbers. *Cognitive Development, 7*, 301–316.
Blades, M., & Spencer, C. (1986). Map use by young children. *Geography, 71*, 47–52.
Blades, M., & Spencer, C. (1987). The use of maps by 4-6-year-old children in a large scale maze. *British Journal of Developmental Psychology, 5*, 19–24.
Blades, M., & Spencer, C. (1989). The development of 3- to 6-year-olds' map using ability: The relative importance of landmarks and map alignment. *Journal of Genetic Psychology, 151*, 181–194.
Blaut, J. M., McCleary, G. S., Jr., & Blaut, A. S. (1970). Environmental mapping in young children. *Environment and Behavior, 2*, 335–349.
Blaut, J. M., & Stea, D. (1971). Studies in geographic learning. *Annals of the Association of American Geographers, 61*, 387–393.
Bluestein, N., & Acredolo, L. (1979). Developmental changes in map-reading skills. *Child Development, 50*, 691–697.
Bolger, F., & Karmiloff-Smith, A. (1990). "The development of communicative competence: are notational systems like language?" *Archives de Psychologie, 58*, 257–273.
Brenneman, K., Massey, C., Machado, S. F., & Gelman, R. (1994). *Notating knowledge about words and objects: Preschoolers' plans differ for 'writing' and "drawing."* Unpublished manuscript.
Catan, L. (1989). Musical literacy and the development of rhythm representation: Cognitive change and material media. In A. Gellatly, D. Gogers, & J. A. Sloboda (Eds.), *Cognition and social world*. Oxford: Oxford University Press.
Clark, A. B. (1897). The child's attitude towards perspective problems. In E. Barnes (Ed.), *Studies in education* (Vol. 1). Stanford, CA: Stanford University Press.
Cohen, S. R. (1985). The development of constraints on symbol-meaning structure in notation: Evidence from production, interpretation, and forced-choice judgment. *Child Development, 56*, 177–195.
Cox, M. (1981). One thing behind another: Problems of representation in children's drawings. *Educational Psychology, 1*, 275–287.
Cox, M. (1985). One object behind another: Young children's use of array-specific or view-specific representations. In N. H. Freeman & M. Cox (Eds.), *Visual order: The nature and development of pictorial representation*. Cambridge: Cambridge University Press.
Cox, M. (1986). *Child's point of view*. Hemel Hempstead, England: Harvester Wheatsheaf.
Cox, M. (1989). Children's drawing. In D. J. Hargreaves (Ed.), *Children and the arts*. Philadelphia: Open University Press.
Crook, C. K. (1984). Factors influence the use of transparency in children's drawing. *British Journal of Developmental Psychology, 2*, 213–221.
Crook, C. K. (1985). Knowledge and appearance. In N. H. Freeman & M. Cox (Eds.), *Visual*

order: The nature and development of pictorial representation. Cambridge: Cambridge University Press.

Davis, A. M. (1983a). *Contextual sensitivity in young children's drawing of familiar objects.* Unpublished doctoral dissertation, University of Birmingham.

Davis, A. M. (1983b). Contextual sensitivity in young children's drawings. *Journal of Experimental Child Psychology, 35,* 478–486.

Davis, A. M. (1984). Noncanonical orientation without occlusion: Children's drawings of transparent objects. *Journal of Experimental Child Psychology, 37,* 451–462.

Davis, A. M. (1985). The canonical bias: Young children's drawings of familiar objects. In N. H. Freeman & M. Cox (Eds.), *Visual order: The nature and development of pictorial representation.* Cambridge: Cambridge University Press.

DeLoache, J. S. (1987). Rapid change in the symbolic functioning of very young children. *Science, 238,* 1556–1557.

DeLoache, J. S. (1989a). The development of representation in young children. *Advances in Child Development and Behavior, 22,* 1–39.

DeLoache, J. S. (1989b). Young children's understanding of the correspondence between a scale model and a large space. *Cognitive Development, 4,* 121–129.

DeLoache, J. S. (1990). Young children's understanding of models. In R. Fivush & J. Hudson (Eds.), *What children remember and why.* Cambridge: Cambridge University Press.

DeLoache, J. S. (1991). Symbolic functioning in very young children: Understanding of pictures and models. *Child Development, 62,* 736–752.

DeLoache, J. S., Kolstad, V., & Anderson, K. N. (1991). Physical similarity and young children's understanding of scale models. *Child Development, 62,* 111–126.

DeLoache, J. S., & Marzolf, D. P. (1992. When a picture is not worth a thousand words: Young children's understanding of pictures and models. *Cognitive Development, 7,* 317–329.

Donald, M. (1991). *Origins of the modern mind: Three stages in the evolution of culture and cognition.* Cambridge, MA: Harvard University Press.

Dow, G., & Pick, H. (1992). Young children's use of models and photographs as spatial representations. *Cognitive Development, 7,* 351–363.

Feldman, D. H. (1980). *Beyond universals in cognitive development.* Norwood, NJ: Ablex.

Feldman, D. H., & Acredolo, L. P. (1979). The effect of active versus passive exploration on memory for spatial location in children. *Child Development, 50,* 698–704.

Ferreiro, E., & Teberosky, A. (1979). *Los sistemas de estritura en el desarolla del nino.* Mexico City: Siglo Weintiuno Editores.

Freeman, N. H. (1980). *Strategies of representation in young children: Analysis of spatial skills and drawing processes.* NY: Academic Press.

Freeman, N. H., Eiser, C., & Sayers, J. (1977). Children's strategies in producing three-dimensional relationships on a two-dimensional surface. *Journal of Experimental Child Psychology, 23,* 305–314.

Freeman, N. H., & Janikoun, R. (1972). Intellectual realism in children's drawings of a familiar object with distinct features. *Child Development, 43,* 1116–1121.

Frith, U. (Ed.). (1980). *Cognitive processes in spelling.* London: Academic Press.

Gauvain, M., & Rogoff, B. (1986). Influence of the goal on children's exploration and memory of large-scale space. *Developmental Psychology, 22,* 72–77.

Gibson, E. J. (1969). *Principles of perceptual learning and development.* NY: Appleton.

Golomb, C. (1974). *Young children's sculpture and drawing: A study in representational development.* Cambridge, MA: Harvard University Press.

Golomb, C. (1981). Representation and reality: The origins and determinants of young children's drawings. *Review of Research in Visual Art Education, 14,* 36–48.

Golomb, C. (1992). *The child's creation of a pictorial world.* Berkeley: University of California Press.

Goodman, N. (1976). *Language of art: An approach to a theory of symbols.* Indianapolis: Hackett.

Goodnow, J. (1977). *Children's drawing.* Cambridge, MA: Harvard University Press.

Goody, J. (1986). *The logic of writing and the organization of society.* Cambridge: Cambridge University Press.

Goswami, U., & Bryant, P. (1990). *Phonological skills and learning to read.* Hillsdale, NJ: Erlbaum.

Harris, D. B. (1963). *Children's drawings as measures of intellectual maturity: A revision and extension of the Goodenough draw-a-man text.* New York: Harcourt.

Hart, R. (1979). *Children's experience of place.* New York: Irvington.

Hazen, N. L., Lockman, J. J., & Pick, H. L. (1978). The development of children's representation of large-scale environments. *Child Development, 49,* 623–636.

Hughes, M. (1986). *Children and number: Difficulties in learning mathematics.* Oxford: Blackwell.

Ingram, N. A. (1983). *The representation of three-dimensional spatial relations on two dimensional picture surface.* Unpublished doctoral dissertation, University of Southampton.

Ingram, N. A. (1985). Three into two won't go: Symbolic and spatial coding processes in young children's drawings. In N. H. Freeman & M. Cox (Eds.), *Visual order: The nature and development of pictorial representation.* Cambridge: Cambridge University Press.

Ives, S. W., & Rovet, J. (1979). The role of graphic orientations in children's drawings of familiar and novel objects, at rest and in motion. *Merrill-Palmer Quarterly, 25,* 281–292.

Karmiloff-Smith, A. (1979). Micro- and macro-developmental changes in language acquisition and other representational systems. *Cognitive Science, 3,* 91–118.

Karmiloff-Smith, A. (1990). Constraints on representational change: Evidence from children's drawing. *Cognition, 34,* 1–27.

Karmiloff-Smith, A. (1992). *Beyond modularity: A developmental perspective on cognitive science.* Cambridge, MA: MIT Press.

Kellogg, R. (1969). *Analyzing children's art.* Palo Alto, CA: National Press.

Krampen, M. (1991). *Children's drawings: Iconic coding of the environment.* New York: Plenum Press.

Landau, J. (1986). Early map use as an unlearned ability. *Cognition, 22,* 201–223.

Landau, J., & Gleitman, L. (1985). *Language and experience: Evidence from the blind child.* Cambridge, MA: Harvard University Press.

Lasswell, H. D., Lerner, D., & Speier, H. (1979). Introduction. In H. D. Lasswell, D. Lerner, & H. Speier (Eds.), *Propaganda and communication in world history* (Vol. 1). Honolulu: East-West Center.

Lavine, L. O. (1977). Differentiation of letterlike forms in prereading children. *Developmental Psychology, 13,* 89–94.

Lee, K., & Karmiloff-Smith, A. (1996). Cognitive constraints on notations: Encoding states versus transformations. *Archives de Psychologie, 64,* 3–25.

Levine, M., Marchon, I., & Harley, G. (1984). The placement and misplacement of you-are-here maps. *Environment and Behavior, 16,* 139–157.

Liben, L. S., & Downs, R. M. (1989). Understanding maps as symbols: The development of map concepts in children. *Advances in Child Development, 22,* 145–201.

Liben, L. S., & Downs, R. M. (1992). Developing an understanding of graphic representations in children and adults: The case of GEO-graphics. *Cognitive Development, 7,* 331–349.

Light, P. H. (1985). The development of view-specific representation considered from a socio-cognitive standpoint. In N. H. Freeman & M. V. Cox (Eds.), *Visual order: The nature and development of pictorial representation.* Cambridge, UK: Cambridge University Press.

Light, P. H., & Foot, T. (1986). Partial occlusion in young children's drawings. *Journal of Experimental Child Psychology, 41,* 38–48.

Light, P. H., & Humphreys, J. (1981). Internal spatial relationships in young children's drawings. *Journal of Experimental Child Psychology, 31,* 521–530.

Light, P. H., & MacIntosh, E. (1980). Depth relationships in young children's drawings. *Journal of Experimental Child Psychology, 30*, 79–87.

Light, P. H., & Simmons, B. (1983). The effect of a communication task upon the representation of depth relationships in young children's drawings. *Journal of Experimental Child Psychology, 35*, 81–92.

Luquet, G. H. (1913). *Les dessins d'un enfant.* Paris: Alcon.

Luquet, G. H. (1927). *Le dessin enfantin.* Paris: Alcon.

Luria, A. R. (1978). The development of writing in the child. In M. Cole (Ed.), *The selected writings of A. R. Luria.* New York: M. Sharpe. (Original work published 1928)

Machover, K. (1949). *Personality projection in the drawings of the human figure.* Springfield, IL: Thomas.

Machover, K. (1953). Human figure drawings of children. *Journal of Projective Techniques, 17*, 85–91.

Mandler, J. (1983). Representation. In F. J. Flavell & E. M. Markman (Eds.), *Handbook of child psychology: Vol. 3. Cognitive development.* New York: Wiley.

Matthews, J. (1983). *Children's drawing: Are young children really scribbling?* Paper presented at the British Psychological Society International Conference on Psychology and Arts, Cardiff.

Matthews, M. H. (1986). The influence of gender on the environmental cognition of young boys and girls. *Journal of Genetic Psychology, 147*, 295–302.

McLane, J. B., & McNamee, G. D. (1991). *Early literacy,* Cambridge, MA: Harvard University Press.

McLuhan, M. (1962). *The Gutenberg galaxy.* Toronto: University of Toronto Press.

Mead, M. (1979). Continuities in communication from early man to modern times. In H. D. Lasswell, D. Lerner, & H. Speier (Eds.), *Propaganda and communication in world history* (Vol. 1). Honolulu: East-West Center.

Olson, D. R. (1994). *The world on paper.* Cambridge: Cambridge University Press.

Peirce, C. S. (1965–1966). *Collected papers of Charles Sanders Peirce* (C. Hartshorne, P. Weiss, & A. W. Burks, Eds.) (Vols. 1–4). Cambridge, MA: Harvard University Press.

Piaget, J. (1932). Some drawings of men and women made by children of certain non-European races. *Journal of the Royal Anthropological Institute, 62*, 127–144.

Piaget, J., & Inhelder, B. (1956). *The child's conception of space.* London: Routledge & Kegan Paul. (Original work published 1948)

Presson, C. C. (1982). The development of map-reading skills. *Child Development, 53*, 196–199.

Sastre, G., & Moreno, M. (1976). Representation graphique de la quantite. *Bulletin de Psychologie, 30*, 355–366.

Scholnick, E. K., Fein, G. G., & Campbell, P. F. (1990). Changing predictors of map use in wayfinding. *Developmental Psychology, 26*, 188–193.

Siegel, A. W., & Schadler, M. (1977). Young children's cognitive maps of their classroom. *Child Development, 48*, 388–394.

Sinclair, A., & Sinclair, H. (1984). Preschoolers' interpretation of written numerals. *Human Learning, 3*, 173–184.

Spencer, C., & Darvizhe, Z. (1981). The case for developing a cognitive environmental psychology that does not underestimate the abilities of young children. *Journal of Environmental Psychology, 1*, 21–31.

Stea, D., & Blaut, J. M. (1973). Notes toward a developmental theory of spatial learning. In R. M. Downs & D. Stea (Eds.), *Image and environment.* Chicago, IL: Aldine.

Sulzby, E. (1986). *Emergent writing and reading in 5-6-year-olds: A longitudinal study.* Norwood, NJ: Ablex.

Thomas, G. V., & Silk, A. M. J. (1990). *An introduction to the psychology of children's drawings.* New York: New York University Press.

Thurstone, L. L. (1958). *Manual for the SRA primary mental abilities.* Chicago: Science Research Associates.

Todorov, T. (1982). *Theories of the symbol* (C. Porter, trans.). Ithaca, NY: Cornell University Press.

Tolchinsky-Landsmann, L. (1990). Early writing development: Evidence from different orthographic systems. In M. Spoolders (Ed.), *Literacy acquisition.* Norwood, NJ: Ablex.

Tolchinsky-Landsmann, L., & Karmiloff-Smith, A. (1992). Children's understanding of notations as domains of knowledge versus referential-communicative tools. *Cognitive Development, 7,* 287–300.

Tolchyinsky-Landsmann, L., & Karmiloff-Smith, A. (1993). Las restricciones del conocimiento notacional. *Aprendizaje y Infancia, 26–63,* 19–51.

Tversky, B., Kugelmass, S., & Winter, A. (1991). Cross-cultural and developmental trend in graphic productions. *Cognitive Psychology, 23,* 515–557.

Uttal, D. H., & Wellman, H. M. (1989). Young children's representation of spatial information acquired from maps. *Developmental Psychology, 25,* 128–138.

Vygotsky, L. S. (1962). *Thought and language.* Cambridge, MA: MIT Press. (Original work published 1934)

Vygotsky, L. S. (1978). *Mind in society.* Cambridge, MA: Harvard University Press.

Willats, J. (1977). How children learn to draw realistic pictures. *Quarterly Journal of Experimental Psychology, 29,* 367–382.

Wolf, D., & Gardner, H. (1985). *Broadening literacy: A final report to the Carnegie Corporation.* Cambridge, MA: Harvard Graduate School of Education.

CHAPTER 7

Origins of Quantitative Competence

Kevin F. Miller

I. ORIGINS OF QUANTITATIVE REASONING

Consider the following problems:

    1. A hand places a puppet on a stage. A screen goes up, occluding the puppet. Then the hand places another puppet behind the screen. Finally, the screen drops, revealing one puppet. Is this surprising?

    2. The arrays below show arrays of different kinds of candies. The first two rows show a standard presentation of items differing only in color, arranged in one-to-one alignment. Given this display, would you have just as much to eat if you ate either row?

    ■ ■ ■ ■ ■ ■ ■ ■ ■ ■ ■
    □ □ □ □ □ □ □ □ □ □ □

    A. How about if you (only) changed the alignment of candies, producing the display below?

    ■ ■ ■ ■ ■ ■ ■ ■ ■ ■ ■
    □ □ □ □ □ □ □ □ □ □ □

    B. What if you cut one of the pieces?

    ■ ■ ■ ■ ■ ■ ■ ■ ■ ■ ■
    □ □ □ □ □ □ □ □ □ ◣ ◥

Perceptual and Cognitive Development
Copyright © 1996 by Academic Press, Inc. All rights of reproduction in any form reserved.

C. What if you replaced one row with the same number of noticeably larger pieces, still in one-to-one alignment?

■ ■ ■ ■ ■ ■ ■ ■ ■ ■ ■

☐ ☐ ☐ ☐ ☐ ☐ ☐ ☐ ☐ ☐ ☐

3. Which problem is more difficult?
   A. Collette had 9 trucks. Then Antoine gave her 5 more. How many does she have now?
   B. Collette had some trucks. Then Antoine gave her 5 more. Now she has 14 trucks. How many did she have to begin with?
4. A shepherd has 125 sheep and 5 dogs. How old is the shepherd?
5. A board was sawed into two pieces. One piece was two-thirds as long as the whole board and was exceeded in length by the second piece by 4 feet. How long was the board before it was cut?

Each of these problems could be used to assess some aspect of quantitative reasoning, and most have been used for that purpose. Understanding the quantitative regularities of the world and mastering the cultural tools that mathematics provides is a process that begins in infancy and continues beyond the last graduate statistics course; the continuity of quantitative development makes it a fruitful source for theories of developmental change. In this chapter I describe some of the problems with a simple, definitional model of early mathematical reasoning. Then I discuss the developmental course that leads from the 5-month-old surprised at the example given as Problem 1 (Wynn, 1992a) to the high school student determining that the board described in Problem 5 must be negative 12 feet long (Paige & Simon, 1966).

II. DOES QUANTITATIVE REASONING DEPEND ON A "NUMBER CONCEPT?"

Problem 2A above presents the classic Piagetian conservation-of-number paradigm. Quantitative reasoning played a major role in the Piagetian program of relating cognitive development to children's acquisition of increasingly adequate logical models of the world. Research on children's understanding of number was the first application of the "logico-mathematical" concept of groupings that pervaded all of Piaget's later work (Bideaud, 1992; Flavell, 1963). In Piaget's view, children come to understand the nature of numbers by first constructing an understanding of the logical principles (classification and seriation) on which number is based. Later Piagetian research focused primarily on children's understanding that numerical equivalence could be defined by one-to-one relations between members of two sets. That is, any sets whose items could be paired up in a one-to-one fashion must necessarily have the same number of items. As Russell (1919) had noted, this logical procedure can serve as the basis for a definition of numerosity, because no prior concept of numerosity is required to perform this operation and, indeed, putting the members of two sets in one-to-one alignment doesn't directly tell you how many items are in either set. A simple procedure based on this definition could, in principle, generate the ordered set of positive natural numbers. Imagine going through the world pairing up the elements of all sets. If one set had items left over when all the members of the other set had been matched, you could place the larger set (the one with items left over) to the right of the smaller set. If they matched exactly, you could place them in the same location. Given infinite time and patience and the existence of at least one set of each numerosity, this procedure would suffice to generate the set of positive natural numbers.

Piaget (1965) argued that what is logically definitional should also form the developmental basis for understanding number. Children's understanding of the importance of one-to-one correspondence in determining numerosity can be assessed by the number conservation procedure, in which children are shown (or asked to create) two rows of objects placed in one-to-one alignment, and are questioned as to the effect of numerosity of changes in the spatial arrangement of the objects in the sets.

Piaget drew a distinction between the number concepts they investigated and mundane skills they termed "merely verbal knowledge." This label was applied to the ability of children to perform numerical operations such as counting and calculating in the absence of a fully operational understanding of number. He suggested (Piaget, 1965, pp. 161, 190) that children cannot learn to add or subtract until they achieve this definitional understanding of number, noting that

> it is true that even children who are still at the earlier stages can be taught to repeat formulae such as $2 + 2 = 4$; $2 + 3 = 5$; $2 + 4 = 6$, etc., but there is no true assimilation until the child is capable of seeing that six is a totality, containing two and four as parts, and of grouping the various possible combinations in additive compositions.

This de-emphasis on verbal knowledge was reflected in Piaget's treatment of the role of counting in the development of number. Counting was classified as "merely verbal knowledge" (Piaget, 1965, p. 29) unless it was accompanied by an operational level of performance on the tasks employed to assess number development. This attitude toward counting was further demonstrated by his discussion of a child (Piaget, 1965, p. 63) who gave correct answers on a conservation task as long as she counted the elements involved. Piaget noted that "when, however, she did not count the elements as they were being exchanged, she showed that she was still at the earlier level."

The idea that quantitative reasoning is based on a definitional understanding of what number is has more than a little intuitive force. This view has also had a real impact on mathematics education, where it's common to find assertions such as the following (Copeland, 1984, p. 12): "Children at different stages cannot learn the same content. They cannot learn about number, for example, until they reach the concrete operational stage."

Although this view presents a simple, unified picture of mathematical competence, it manages to simultaneously overestimate and underestimate what young children know about quantity, and to neglect the cognitive tools (such as counting and measuring procedures) and symbolic systems (such as numerals and arithmetic procedures) whose acquisition is central to understanding the course of mathematical development from infancy to adolescence. Well before children can pass number conservation tests, they show real if limited insights into the nature of quantitative invariance. Children old enough to pass such tasks still show surprising limitations in their understanding even of transformations only slightly removed from the traditional conservation paradigm (see Problems 2B and 2C; Miller, 1989). What appears to unify both the early competence and late misunderstandings children show is that practical procedures for counting and measuring have an intimate relation to children's quantitative concepts.

III. MEASUREMENT AND EARLY QUANTITATIVE KNOWLEDGE

Research on children's understanding of quantitative equivalence suggests that preschoolers know both more and less than the conservation-of-number paradigm would suggest. Children's performance on Piaget's conservation-of-number task in the classic conservation-of-equivalence form presented as Problem 2A above is remarkably predictable. Before 4–5 years of age, children typically assert that this transformation leads to an increase in numerosity in the longer array (e.g., Siegler, 1981; Tollefsrud-Anderson, Campbell, Starkey, & Cooper, 1992). Beyond this point, children generally insist that rearrangement per se has no effect on the relative numerosity of two arrays. Conservation of number is typically substantially easier than the conservation tasks Piaget developed for other domains such as length, area, and volume (e.g., Gelman & Baillargeon, 1983). It would be wrong, however, to assume that children who understand that spatial realignment does not affect relative numerosity have the fundamental understanding of quantity that Piaget attributed to them. Some simple variations on the standard number conservation paradigm reveal substantial limits to children's understanding of conservation. Miller (1989) presented children with variations on conservation tasks involving number, length, area, and volume. As one would expect from previous studies, children performed better on number tasks than on transformations involving other quantitative attributes (length, area, volume), with one important limitation. Most children aged 5 years and older correctly judged the results of transformations on stimuli such as those shown in Problem 2 as long as the number of discrete pieces was predictive of the correct answer. Number need not always be a reliable cue to quantity, however, and the transformations shown in Problems 2B and 2C are examples of situations in which numerosity is not a valid cue to overall amount. When presented with the transformation shown in Problem 2B, in which cutting one piece led to more pieces but no change in total amount, 88% of 5-year-olds and 31% of 8-year-olds asserted that a child eating the transformed array would have more to eat than one eating the comparison row; 81% of 5-year-olds and 56% of 8-year-olds incorrectly judged the arrays presented in Problem 2C as being equivalent, although no child in a control condition had difficulty judging the relative size of the individual pieces. It would appear that what 4- to 5-year-olds understand about number conservation problems is the way that transformations on arrays of objects affect numerosity, rather than the effect of these transformations on actual amount.

The tendency to conflate quantity and numerosity is not a phenomenon limited to children. Pelham, Sumarta, and Myaskovsky (1994) reported that when adults are cognitively taxed by concurrent or complex tasks, they tend to use a "numerosity heuristic" that leads them to overinfer quantity or probability from numerical cues in tasks ranging from estimating the areas of geometric figures broken up into varying numbers of pieces or estimating the value of sets of coins. Number clearly has a special status in quantitative reasoning, and the remainder of this chapter will consider the developmental progression in children's ability to perceive and use numerical information in mathematical problem solving.

IV. THE NATURE OF MATHEMATICAL DEVELOPMENT: AN ORGANIZING METAPHOR

If there is not a single, simple number concept that forms the basis for mathematical development, how should the development of numerical reasoning be represented? Wittgenstein (1953/1958, p. 32) provides a useful metaphor in his discussion of the failings of the philosophical models of number that formed the basis for Piaget's psychological description:

> Why do we call something a 'number'? Well, perhaps because it has a—direct—relationship with several things that have hitherto been called number; and this can be said to give it an indirect relationship to other things we call the same name. And we extend our concept of number as in spinning a thread we twist fiber on fiber. And the strength of the thread does not reside in the fact that some one fiber runs through its whole length, but in the overlapping of many fibers.

This metaphor can be applied to the problem of mathematical development, by conceiving the development of mathematical reasoning as the interweaving of a set of "threads" consisting of interacting concepts and representational and algorithmic skills. What, then, are the threads that contribute to the development of quantitative reasoning?

One model of the components of counting skill was proposed by Greeno, Riley, and Gelman (1984), who argued that early mathematical competence could be subdivided into three types, termed *conceptual, procedural,* and *utilization* competence. Conceptual competence, as the term implies, consists of knowledge of mathematical concepts (such as the importance of one-to-one correspondence in defining numerical equality). Utilization competence is the ability to assess task demands in terms of these conceptual constraints. Procedural competence concerns the ability to plan actual courses of action that will fit the constraints imposed by utilization concerns and not violate conceptual understandings.

A similar model of mathematical development emerged from Ferrara and Turner's (1993) factor analysis of a series of preschool counting and number tasks. Ferrara and Turner described individual differences in counting in terms of a three-factor structure, consisting of what they called a *verbal* component (mastering the conventional number–word sequence), an *action* component involving mastering of object–word relations in counting, and a *contextual* component involving knowledge of the goals and applications of counting.

The action component of Ferrara and Turner's analysis roughly corresponds to the procedural competence postulated by Greeno et al., while Ferrara and Turner's contextual component appears to resemble the utilization competence described by Greeno et al. The verbal component of Ferrara and Turner's model has no direct analog in the Greeno et al. model, and conceptual competence per se is not represented in the Ferrara and Turner model.

Both of these models were developed to deal specifically with the cognition demands of counting, but they can be combined and generalized to provide a more general framework for discussing the components of mathematical development. The development of mathematical competence involves the interaction of *symbolic* competence (mastering a set of symbolic tools such as representations of number and arithmetic operations), *algorithmic* competence (mastering the set of algorithms and techniques that are employed by procedures such as arithmetic, measurement, and problem solving), and *conceptual* competence (acquiring mathematical concepts such as understanding the importance of one-to-one mappings for equality of numerosity, or realizing that addition is a commutative operation).

The utility of Wittgenstein's weaving metaphor is most evident in its emphasis on the importance of relations among different threads. Integrating mathematical concepts, symbolic representations, and arithmetical algorithms is a stumbling block to the development of quantitative reasoning that is the source of repeated impasses in mathematical development. Wittgenstein's weaving metaphor implies more than that mathematical competence is the composite of a series of intertwined abilities. Unlike a chain that is axiomatically only as strong as its weakest link, each strand of a woven rope contributes to the overall strength. One might expect that different sources of mathematical knowledge would show the same kind of interacting, compensatory effect in mathematical development, with extensive variation between children and tasks in the contributions made by conceptual, algorithmic, and symbolic structures in the development of mathematical competence.

A similar model for the development of reading was proposed by Stanovich (1980), who argued that fluent reading involves an interaction among higher-level contextual information and lower-level word recognition processes, with children who have difficulty in one set of skills relying more heavily upon the other. In the case of mathematical development, children may well differ in their reliance upon learned algorithms or conceptual understanding in mathematical problem solving. Furthermore, as is discussed below, the organization of symbolic systems may have a major impact on children's acquisition of particular mathematical concepts.

Starting in infancy, young children show an impressive understanding of number well before they are capable of passing conservation tests. Beyond infancy, the mundane procedures children acquire in order to count and calculate—the "merely verbal learning" that Piaget disparaged—play a significant role in mediating mathematical development. At the same time, integrating those procedures with other knowledge about the world remains a problem that emerges at many points in development, from young children unsure about the effects of spatial arrangement on numerosity to adolescents who blithely produce a negative length as the answer to Problem 5 above.

V. INFANT NUMERICAL ABILITIES

Evidence of numerical competence can be found from nearly the moment of birth. Starkey and Cooper (1980) showed that 22-week-old infants are sensitive to number as a dimension of their world, habituating to repeated presentations of sets of either two or three dots, then dishabituating when shown sets of the other numerosity, even when features such as density and relative numerosity are controlled. Antel and Keating (1983) replicated this basic result with infants 21 to 144 hours old. Starkey, Spelke, and Gelman (1983, 1990; Starkey & Cooper, 1980) have shown that infants' ability to match numbers extends beyond particular modalities, with infants looking longer at a dot display corresponding to particular numbers of audible drumbeats, at least in later blocks of trials. Although Moore, Benenson, Reznick, Peterson, and Kagan (1987) failed to replicate this result, Starkey et al. (1990) argued that differences in procedure, particularly large breaks between blocks of trials, could account for these discrepant results.

Cooper (1984) noted that studies such as those described above indicate that infants possess a robust ability to discriminate sets of two items from sets of three items, but do not imply that infants are aware of even the most basic mathematical relations between such sets. Furthermore, infant numerosity discrimination is quite limited in range. The available evidence suggests that, by 10 to 12 months of age, infants are sometimes able to distinguish between sets of three and four items (Cooper, 1984; Strauss & Curtis, 1981), but cannot distinguish between sets of four and five items (Strauss & Curtis, 1981), or between sets of four and six items (Antell & Keating, 1983; Starkey & Cooper, 1980).

Several recent studies suggest that, within these severe numerosity limitations, infants' understanding of number does encompass more than the ability to discriminate between different set sizes. Wynn (1992) presented 5-month-olds with addition and subtraction analogs involving one or two items (Mickey Mouse dolls). In an addition scenario, one item was placed on a stage and a screen was interposed. Then the infants saw an additional item placed behind the screen, following which the screen was dropped to reveal either one object (impossible outcome) or two objects (possible outcome). A subtraction scenario was also presented in which two objects were initially placed behind the screen, one was removed, and the screen was lowered to reveal either one object (possible) or two objects (impossible). In both scenarios, infants looked longer at the impossible than the possible scenarios, implying either a nascent understanding of addition and subtraction or at the very least an ability to integrate numerical information over time.

Baillargeon, Miller, and Constantino (1995) used a similar paradigm with 10-month-olds and found that children of this age could reliably distinguish possible from impossible results of 1 + 1 scenarios but could not do so for 2 + 1 or 1 + 1 + 1 problems. Showing evidence of flexibility within this range of numerosities, infants did not simply expect that addition would lead to an increase in number. When a screen was in place at the beginning of a trial (so infants did not know how many if any objects were behind the screen), infants did not look longer in scenarios in which placing two objects behind the screen resulted in either two or three objects.

Infant numerical abilities are of interest in part because of the knowledge infants lack. Conventional symbols are clearly not part of infants' repertoires, nor are most of the procedures older children acquire. The procedures infants use in numerosity perception are far from clear. Infant numerosity perception is often termed "subitizing." This asserts a continuity with adult number perception processes that have been studied intensively since Jevons (1871) studied his own quantification processes by throwing handfuls of beans over a paper box and reporting his immediate estimate of the number that had actually fallen into the container. Jevons reported that he was error free through sets of four beans, and concluded that the power of numerical discrimination in a single glance ranged up to a limit somewhere between 4 and 5 items. This apparent ability to perceive small numerosities directly was termed "subitizing" by Kaufman, Lord, Reese, and Volkmann (1949). Using very different procedures based on psychophysical techniques, Taves (1941) also argued that there exists a direct mechanism for perceiving numerosity, but estimated the range of this procedure as extending up to seven items.

Although both intuition and the adult data described above suggest that one can automatically perceive small numbers of items in a single mental act without counting individual elements, there are serious problems for the view that there exists a process for perceiving numerosity that is distinct from counting. One obvious problem is the lack of agreement on the range of numerosities for which such a process applies, with estimates of the upper limit ranging from at least 4 to 7 items. A further argument against the view that subitizing involves an automatic process independent of the number of elements perceived is the typical finding that larger arrays take longer to quantify than do smaller arrays (Kaufman et al., 1949; Klahr, 1973; Mandler & Shebo, 1982; Saltzman & Garner, 1948). The fact that, as Saltzman and Garner (1948) described it, "there is no minimum number of objects below which the reaction time remains constant" (p. 240) poses severe difficulty for the idea that subitizing involves an immediate perceptual act.

Thus, suggesting that infant number processing involves subitizing invokes a process whose mechanism is the source of continuing controversy (e.g., Trick, 1992) and whose implication of some sort of automatic, immediate apprehension is far from established. Two intriguing current models of the mechanism behind human number perception attempt to place this ability in the context of two different research literatures, that of object individuation in attention (Trick, 1992) and the literature on numerosity perception by nonhuman animal species (Gallistel & Gelman, 1992). Trick (1992), developed a model of subitizing based on Pylyshyn's (1989) FINST model of attention. The FINST model proposes that the visual system individuates objects by creating mental reference tokens termed "FINSTS" (short for Fingers of INSTantiation). In the FINST model, only a small number of these tokens can be generated, resulting in a limitation in the range and complexity of objects whose numerosity can be perceived. Once FINSTs have been generated, numerosity is perceived via some kind of rapid counting or pattern association on these tokens (see Klahr, 1973, for a similar mechanism). Gallistel and Gelman (1992) proposed that infant numerosity representation utilizes a preverbal counting mechanism based on an accumulator system. This accumulator mechanism, proposed by Meck and Church (1983) to account for rat numerosity perception, is designed to count either fixed-length pulses corresponding to the number of events to be represented or variable-length pulses that accumulate durations or frequencies of events. Supporting the view that a common mechanism underlies both duration and number perception in animals, Meck and Church (1983) found evidence for transfer between specific numerical and duration comparisons predicted by their model. The Gallistel and Gelman adaptation of the accumulator model yields a robust preverbal counting mechanism, one that can count both events and objects, and one that provides accurate preverbal magnitudes for small set sizes, with increasing variability in the representation as set size increases.

These new models of subitizing pose many yet-unanswered questions, among them the extent to which the perceptual features emphasized in the FINST model apply to the numerosity perception of young children, and the extent to which human preverbal numerosity perception involves a common mechanism used for both numerosity and duration perception. Taken as a whole, studies of numerical competence in precounting children indicate that infants under 1 year of age possess an understanding of number that is at once quite flexible and extremely limited. They seem to understand the various ways that placing objects and events together can result in total set sizes of two, but this insight extends only very slowly to larger numerosities.

What is more of a puzzle is what use it could possibly be to infants to have such a limited understanding of number. A numerical epistemology limited to set sizes of one and two clearly is of only limited mathematical utility. At the same time, this early sensitivity to numerosity may solve two problems that are critical to the development of further mathematical competence. First, the fact that infants discriminate sets based on number means that, at least in a limited way, numerosity is a dimension of infants' worlds. Following Quine (1960), any reference to, say, "two bunnies" has an indefinitely large set of potential construals. Early sensitivity to number implies that the mapping between "two" and the duality of rabbits should be high in the child's list of candidate interpretations of this phrase. Biologically based models of cognitive development (e.g., Lorenz, 1971; Marler, 191) argue that learning involves both a general "instinct to learn" that is an essential part of children's innate endowment and specific tendencies to ensure that some kinds of regularities will be noticed. Infants' numerical abilities may make precisely this kind of contribution to later mathematical development, but they may also have a more specific role to play in the next big step in developing mathematical competence. Knowing in some sense that there are two or three items in a set could be a substantial scaffold to children's early counting, by aiding the acquisition of a procedure (counting) that will ultimately extend well beyond the limits of early number perception. Gallistel and Gelman (1992) argue that such nonverbal representations play a more vital role in the acquisition of explicit verbal procedures, providing a necessary foundation for such learning.

VI. COUNTING AND EARLY MATHEMATICAL DEVELOPMENT

It is with the emergence of counting that the interaction of the symbolic, algorithmic, and conceptual threads of mathematical development comes clearly into play. Most of the current controversies on the development of counting concern exactly the question of how these different factors interact in the development of mature, flexible counting.

Counting a set of objects is a complex cognitive and perceptual-motor task, but one whose complexity is obscured by familiarity. Items to be counted must be delineated and distinguished from items that are not to be counted or have already been counted. Items are counted through pairing with some sort of symbolic representation (conventionally a set of number names). Finally, the mathematical consequences of the results of counting must be realized. Competent counting requires mastery of a symbolic system, facility with a complicated set of procedures that require coordinating pointing at objects and designating them with symbols, and the conceptual understanding that some aspects of counting are merely conventional and others lie at the heart of its utility as a means of ascertaining numerosity.

A. Algorithmic versus Conceptual Components of Early Counting

Most research on the development of counting has concerned the relations between the last two components, algorithmic facility and conceptual insight into counting. Views on the relations between them have fallen into two basic positions. One, first advanced by Gelman and Gallistel (1978) and elaborated in later work (Gelman, 1990, 1993; Gelman and Meck, 1986), argues that a nascent understanding of the mathematical basis of counting organizes and motivates children's acquisition of conventional counting procedures. Gelman and Gallistel (1978) described the counting of preschool children in terms of a set of principles that indicate an understanding of the mathematical goals of counting. These principles are as follows: (1) *one-to-one:* there must be a one-to-one relation between counting words and objects; (2) *stable-order:* these counting words must be recited in a consistent, reproducible order; (3) *cardinal:* the last counting word spoken represents the numerosity of the set as a whole (rather than being a property of a particular item); (4) *item irrelevance:* any collection of distinguishable objects can be counted; and (5) *order irrelevance:* objects can be counted in any sequence without altering the outcome. The first three principles define rules for how one ought to go about counting; the last two define circumstances under which such counting procedures should apply.

The opposite position on the relation between conceptual and algorithmic knowledge in the development of counting has been taken by a number of researchers (Briars & Siegler, 1984; Frye, Braisby, Lowe, Maroudas, & Nicholls, 1989; Fuson, 1988; Fuson & Hall, 1983; Siegler, 1991; Sophian, 1988; Wynn, 1990), who claim that conceptual understanding of counting follows (and may be based on) an initial mastery of conventional counting procedures.

Assessing preschool children's understanding of the conceptual foundations for counting is complicated by the fact that their performance is often quite variable in counting as it is in other domains (Siegler, 1994). For example, Fuson (1988, p. 73) found in a study in which children made repeated counts of a large number of sets of objects, that almost 90% of her sample of $3\frac{1}{2}$- to 4-year-old children made word-point errors (in which there is a violation of the one-to-one correspondence between objects and number words), but these errors were made on only 5% of the objects counted. The fact that many children make these errors could be taken to indicate that they fail to understand the importance of the one-to-one principle; alternatively the low error rate (when measured against total objects counted) could be interpreted as an indication that children are attempting to adhere to this principle. The variability of preschoolers' behavior makes the task of inferring principled knowledge from actual behavior a fundamentally ambiguous enterprise.

Children's difficulty in deploying the complex activities involved in counting could conceivably mask a real understanding of the conceptual basis of this activity. One way of circumventing these difficulties involves asking children to judge the adequacy of the counting of another, rather than performing this activity themselves. Gelman and Meck (1983) did exactly this, asking children to judge the accuracy of counting by a puppet who counted either correctly, incorrectly, or unconventionally (e.g., starting from an unusual starting point, but counting all of a set of items). Gelman and Meck reported good performance among 3- to 5-year-olds, finding that 3-year-olds showed perfect acceptance of correct counting, 96% acceptance of unconventional but correct counting, and 67% rejection of real errors, and improvement between 3 and 4 years of age in rejection of true errors.

Two later studies also looked at children's ability to judge the correctness of counting that was either correct, unconventional but correct, or incorrect. Presenting children with a somewhat expanded set of counting strategies to judge, Briars and Siegler (1984) found that 3-year-olds showed an overall level of acceptance of 95% for standard correct counting, 75% acceptance of unconventional but correct counting, and 57% rejection of real errors. Suggesting that some acceptance of unconventional correct counting was due to a blanket acceptance of the puppet's performance, there was an actual decrease between the 3- and 4-year-old groups in children's acceptance of unconventional correct counting. Finally, and most relevant to the relation between counting skill and judgment of another's counting, the children who failed to meet a criterion of 75% correct in rejecting puppet counting errors also failed to meet the same criterion in their own counting. Briars and Siegler concluded that children's own counting activity might form the basis for their judgments of what constitutes successful counting.

Gelman and Meck (1986) argued that children may have been led to assume that the puppet counter in the Briars and Siegler (1984) study was a skilled counter, and therefore tended to assume that its performance was correct. Frye et al. (1989) included a pretask in which the experimenter tried to trick children by falsely labeling common objects. Frye et al. (1989) then asked 3- to 4-year-olds to judge counting strategies, but had the experimenter variously claim that the counting was correct or incorrect, and had children judge whether the counting had been performed correctly or whether there actually were the number of items the experimenter counted. Looking at children's judgments about whether counting had been done correctly, Frye et al. found that children judged standard counting to be correct about 90% of the time, correctly rejected erroneous counting 70–75% of the time for two different error types, but accepted unconventional but correct counting only 45% of the time.

There are also important limits on children's ability to use counting in problem solving. Several studies (Frye et al., 1989; Miller, Smith, Zhu, & Zhang, 1995; Wynn, 1990) have found that children aged 3 years and younger have a great deal of difficulty in using counting to produce sets of a given numerosity, even when that numerosity is well within their counting range.

Taken as a whole, these studies indicate that variations in the context in which children are asked to judge another's counting can have a big effect on the likelihood that preschool children will accept deviations from conventional counting or avoid counting errors that violate the counting principles. The ability of young preschool children to follow counting principles in their own counting and to focus on them in their evaluation of the counting of others is quite vulnerable to variations in experimental paradigm. The magnitude of variability in young children's counting performance and judgments and the complexity of the coordination involved in successful counting make it likely that the interaction between conventional counting and children's understanding of the underlying rules may run in both directions (similar suggestions have been made by Baroody, 192; Fuson, 1988, 1992a; Siegler, 1991). Furthermore, it is unlikely that the extent to which children build their early counting competence on a conceptual understanding of number or the structure that conventional algorithms provide will be constant either across development or between children. Gelman and Cohen (1988), for example, described the performance on a novel counting task of Down's syndrome children, who differed substantially from normal controls in the extent to which they applied counting principles in this new context. Even within the normal range of intelligence, it should not be surprising to find that individual children may differ in their use of conceptual and algorithmic knowledge in weaving counting competence.

The idea that children may vary in the extent to which they build their understanding of counting on mastery of conventional algorithms versus a deeper understanding of the concepts that underpin this procedure is similar to a description of children's learning to read languages such as English. The English alphabet is a roughly phonetic system of writing, yet exceptions to spelling–sound rules abound (e.g., Gleitman & Rozin, 1977). Gough and colleagues (Gough & Hillinger, 1980; Gough, Juel, & Roper-Schneider, 1983; Juel, Griffith, & Gough, 1986) have argued that children differ in the extent to which they rely on spelling–sound relations (termed "cipher" readers) versus memory and other visual cues (termed "code" readers). Skilled readers need to be able both to use spelling–sound correspondence rules to read unfamiliar words and to recognize the many words whose spelling violates those same rules, but children differ in the extent to which they rely on such rules versus recognition of familiar words in the acquisition of reading ability.

Children learning to count face a situation that differs in important ways from that which confronts them in learning to read. The mathematical regularities that underpin counting are both deeper and more consistent than those reflected in an alphabetic writing system such as English; this makes a "cipher" or principle-based strategy more useful in mathematical development than in learning to read. Nonetheless, examples of conventional counting—supporting a "code" approach—also abound in the child's environment, ranging from those presented on educational television to the modeling of peers and parents. The idea that children should take advantage of both sources of information about how to count, and that different children should vary in the extent to which they rely on conventions or principles, is thus not surprising. What has emerged from nearly a decade of controversy about the relations between principles and conventional procedures in early counting is a more complicated description of what seems at first to be a simple alternative.

VII. SYMBOLIC TOOLS FOR MATHEMATICAL REASONING

Research on the development of counting has focused on the relations between algorithmic and conceptual knowledge in early mathematical development. Learning to count also requires mastering a new symbolic system, the number names, which presents children with another potential source of structure in mathematical development. Mathematical systems, along with other cultural systems such as calendars, numbers, and written language have an internal structure that may serve to highlight some aspects of the underlying domains they represent (time, mathematics, and language) and to obscure others.

There is comparatively little research on the symbolic component of mathematical development, in part because symbolic systems are so fundamental to the representation and manipulation of quantity that studying the consequences of these systems generally requires cross-cultural research looking at how differences between symbolic systems are associated with differences in cognition. This section discusses the contribution that these symbolic systems can make to mathematical development, primarily by describing cognitive consequences of variation between languages in the organization of numerical symbols. Effects on arithmetic of symbolic systems for writing numbers are discussed in the next section; some effects of the organization of number names themselves are described here.

The most basic symbolic tool for mathematics is the set of names a language has for numbers. After describing the organization of several number-naming systems, I describe research that demonstrates that the structure of number names has significant, specific effects on children's efforts to master these mathematical tools.

Names for numbers can be (and have been) generated according to a bewildering variety of systems (Ifrah, 1985; Menninger, 1969). The Hindu-Arabic system for representing the positive whole numbers is clearly a base-ten system, with ten basic primitive symbols (the digits 0–9). These may be freely combined, with place order indicating the power of 10 that each digit represents. The Hindu-Arabic system is a useful reference point in describing number-naming schemes for two reasons. First, it is universally used as at least one orthography for writing numbers. Second, it is as consistent and concise as a base-ten system could be.

Figure 1 shows how spoken names for numbers are formed in two languages, English and Chinese, that differ in important ways. Both can be described to a first approximation as a base-ten system, but the languages different in the clarity and consistency with which the base-ten structure is reflected in actual number names.

As the first section of the figure shows, representations for numbers in the range 1–9 consist of an unsystematically organized list. There is no way

Number name formation in Chinese and English

A One to ten

Numeral	1	2	3	4	5	6	7	8	9	10
Chinese[1]	一 (yī)	二 (èr)	三 (sān)	四 (sì)	五 (wǔ)	六 (liù)	七 (qī)	八 (bā)	九 (jiǔ)	十 (shí)
English	one	two	three	four	five	six	seven	eight	nine	ten

B Eleven to twenty

Numeral	11	12	13	14	15	16	17	18	19	20
Chinese	十一 (shí yī)	十二 (shí èr)	十三 (shí sān)	十四 (shí sì)	十五 (shí wǔ)	十六 (shí liù)	十七 (shí qī)	十八 (shí bā)	十九 (shí jiǔ)	二十 (èr shí)
English	eleven	twelve	thirteen	fourteen	fifteen	sixteen	seventeen	eighteen	nineteen	twenty

C Twenty to ninety-nine

Language	Rule	Example
Chinese	Decade unit (two,three,four,five,six,seven,eight,nine)+ten+unit	三十七 (sān shí qī)
English	Decade name (twen,thir,for,fif,six,seven,eight,nine) + "-ty" + unit	thirty seven

FIGURE 1 Number formation in Chinese and English.

to predict that "5" or "five" or "wǔ" come after "4," "four," and "sì," respectively, in the Arabic numeral, English, or Chinese systems. The single exception to this is the Chinese character representations for one, two, and three, which consist of the appropriate number of horizontal strokes. This compositional structure of the written representation does not extend beyond the first three numbers, and is not reflected in the spoken names for these entities.

Above ten, the languages diverge in interesting ways, as Figure 1B demonstrates. The Chinese number–naming system maps directly onto the Hindu–Arabic number system used to write numerals. For example, a word-for-word translation of "shí qī" (17) into English produces "ten seven." English has unpredictable names for "11" and "12" that bear only a historical relation to "one" and "two" (Menninger, 1969). Whether the boundary between 10 and 11 is marked in some way may be significant, because this is the first potential clue to the fact that number names are organized according to a base-ten system. English names for teen numbers beyond twelve do have an internal structure, but this relation is obscured by phonetic modifications of many of the elements from those used in the first decade (e.g., "ten" → "teen," "three" → "thir," "five" → "fif"). Furthermore, the order of formation reverses place value compared with the Hindu-Arabic and Chinese systems (and with English names above 20), naming the smaller value before the larger value.

Above 20, both number-naming systems follow the Arabic numeral structure of naming the larger value before the smaller one. Although Chinese and Arabic numerals are consistent in forming decade names by combining a unit value and the base (ten), English also becomes much more regular in its formation of number names. Number names are consistently formed from a decade unit (e.g., "twen-") + "-ty" + a unit value in the range 1–9. Except for twenty, thirty, and fifty, the names of decades incorporate the corresponding unit name without modification. The only morphological difference between Chinese and English names for numbers in the range 20–99 is that Chinese is consistent in using unit values for decade names (instead of modifying them as English does in using "twen" for the two-tens decade and "thir" for the three-tens decade) and in using the unmodified name for ten to designate decades (instead of the special "-ty" that English uses).

A. Psychological Consequences of Number Names

Although all the number-naming systems reviewed are essentially base-ten systems, they differ in the consistency and transparency with which this structure is reflected in actual number names. Learning to count in any of these systems first requires children to master a relatively large set of symbols (at least 10) whose order is arbitrary. Beyond that, the structure of the languages reviewed differ in ways that may simplify or complicate the child's task of inducing the structure of number names. Several studies comparing English- and Chinese-speaking children demonstrate that the organization of number names does indeed play a significant role in mediating children's mastery of this symbolic system (Miller & Stigler, 1987; Miller et al., 1995). These studies have reported that: (1) differences in performance on counting-related tasks do not emerge until children in both countries begin learning the second decade of number names, sometime between 3 and 4 years of age; (2) those differences are generally limited to the symbolic aspect of counting, rather than affecting children's ability to use counting in problem solving or their understanding of basic counting principles; and (3) differences in the patterns of mistakes that children make in learning to count reflect the structure of the systems they are learning.

Research on children's acquisition of number names (Fuson, Richards, & Briars, 1982; Miller & Stigler, 1987; Siegler & Robinson, 1982) suggests that American children learn to recite the list of number names through at least the teens as essentially a rote-learning task. When first counting above twenty, American preschoolers often produce idiosyncratic number names indicating that they fail to understand the base-ten structure underlying larger number names, often counting "twenty-eight, twenty-nine, twenty-ten, twenty-eleven, twenty-twelve." This kind of mistake is extremely rare for Chinese children, and indicates that the base-ten structure of number names is more accessible for learners of Chinese than it is for children learning to count in English.

The cognitive consequences of the relative complexity of English number names are not limited to obstacles placed in the way of early counting. Speakers of English and other European languages (Fuson, Fraivillig, & Burghardt, 1992; Fuson, 1992b; Séron, Deloche, & Noël, 1992) face a complex task in learning to write Arabic numerals, one which is more difficult than that faced by speakers of Chinese (compare the mapping between name and numeral for "twenty-four" with that for "fourteen" in the two languages). Work by Miura and her colleagues (Miura, 1987; Miura, Kim, Chang, & Okamoto, 1988; Miura & Okamoto, 1989; Miura, Okamoto, Kim, Steere, & Fayol, 1993) suggests that the lack of transparency of base-ten markings in English has conceptual consequences, as well. They have found that speakers of languages whose number names are patterned after Chinese (including Korean and Japanese) are better able than speakers of English and other European languages to represent numbers using base-ten blocks and to perform other place-value tasks. Because school arithmetic algorithms are largely structured around place-value, this indication that the complexity of number names affects the ease with which children acquire this basic concept is a finding with real educational significance. Further discussion of symbolic effects on performance of arithmetic is presented in the next section.

VIII. FROM COUNTING TO ARITHMETIC

The acquisition and use of arithmetic operations again involves mastery and coordination of conceptual, algorithmic, and symbolic components of calculation.

A. Procedural Aspects of Arithmetic

The ability to rapidly and reliably produce the sum or product of two single-digit integers is surely one of the most basic of the skills mastered in the early school years. Two decades of research on the cognitive processes underlying this simple task has shown the variety and ingenuity of the methods that children use in performing simple arithmetic. Furthermore, there is a near consensus across models that children gradually shift from overt use of algorithms for performing simple arithmetic, such as adding by various counting algorithms, to primarily relying on direct retrieval of known answers (e.g., Ashcraft, 1992; Siegler & Shrager, 1984; see Baroody & Ginsburg, 1986, for an exception to this view).

There are a number of ways that one might perform simple arithmetic, and interview studies of children's procedures indicate that young children use most of them. In the case of addition, one could add two numbers by: (1) directly *retrieving* their sum; (2) *reconstructing* the answer based on knowing the answer to a related problem (e.g., adding 6 + 5 by retrieving the sum of 5 + 5 [10] and adding one); (3) *counting-on* from one of the addends a number of counts corresponding to the other addend (e.g., counting 6 + 5 by saying, "7, 8, 9, 10, 11"); or (4) *counting-all* of the addends. In the case of multiplication, one can (1) *retrieve* the answer; (2) *reconstruct* the answer from a known product ("6 × 4 = 24, so 7 × 4 is 4 more"); (3) use *repeated addition* to compute the answer (6 × 4 = "6 + 6 + 6 + 6"); or (4) *count by one of the multiplicands* (6 × 4 = "6, 12, 18, 24"). These procedures vary greatly in the amount of cognitive record keeping involved (Baroody & Ginsburg, 1986; Fuson et al., 1982), and developmental shifts seem to be in the direction of the increasing use of more efficient strategies.

Several interview studies of the strategies children use in performing simple addition (that involving single-digit numbers) have shown both the variety of strategies children use and developmental shifts in favor of increasing use of retrieval of answers without overt strategy use and counting-on from the larger addend. Houlihan and Ginsburg (1981) interviewed first and second graders concerning strategies used for both simple and complex addition problems. For single-digit combinations, excluding indeterminate or inappropriate procedures (the latter category limited to first graders), 5% of trials were direct retrieval, 40% were counting from one to the sum, and 44% were counting-on from one addend to the sum. By second grade, 31% of the trials for which a procedure could be determined were direct retrieval, 3% used counting from one, 52% of trials used counting-on, and 14% involved reconstruction from a known sum. Siegler (1987a) reported a similar developmental progression between kindergarten and second grade from an initial reliance on counting-all to an increasing use of retrieval and counting-on procedures, although he emphasized that children continue to use a mixture of strategies throughout this period. Svenson, Hedenborg, and Lingman (1976) found a similar pattern for Swedish children, with third graders showing direct retrieval on about one-third of trials, and various counting procedures about half of the time. Two longitudinal studies of children's strategy use in addition during the first three years of elementary school, Carpenter and Moser (1984) and Svenson and Sjöberg (1983), both describe a gradual decrease in counting-all procedures, with an increase in direct retrieval and counting-on from one of the addends, usually the larger one.

Siegler (1987a, 1987b, 1988; Siegler & Shrager, 1984) developed the first models for mental arithmetic that explicitly incorporated multiple solution strategies into a working simulation of children's arithmetic performance. Each of these models incorporates a variety of procedures for solving arithmetic problems, including direct retrieval and several backup strategies, including counting for addition and repeated addition in the case of multiplication. Children begin with an initial distribution of associations of varying strengths between each problem and particular answers. An example of a strong initial erroneous association is the counting-based association to problems such as 3 + 4 of the next item in the counting series (5). Answers are retrieved for a given problem as a function of the strength of their association to that problem. Thus, the likelihood that a given answer will be retrieved is a function both of its own strength of association and of the association between other answers and that problem; problems that show "peaked" distributions of associations have one answer that is likely to be retrieved, while retrieval for problems with flatter distributions will produce more variable answers. Problems for which a retrieved answer exceeds a confidence criterion are solved by direct retrieval, while other problems are solved by means of a backup procedure.

Doing arithmetic changes the structure of associations between answers and problems, because answers to a problem (whether produced by retrieval or by backup strategies) are strengthened as associates to that problem. Over time, the distribution of associations is changed as a function of (1) the characteristics of backup strategies (including the errors that they can produce), and (2) the frequency with which problems are presented.

One important cause for the shift from reconstructive to retrieval processes in children's addition may be the interference that occurs when children begin to learn other arithmetic operations on the same numbers. Miller and Paredes (1990) reported a longitudinal study looking at the effects on children's addition of learning to multiply. As children went through the process of learning multiplication, there was a dramatic increase in cross-operation errors (particularly reporting the product rather than the sum in addition problems), and a substantial decrease in the speed with which they were able to perform addition. This finding suggests that as children develop a more complex computational repertoire, the problem of weaving new knowledge and abilities together with previously mastered competence becomes an increasingly prominent challenge in mathematical development.

B. Conceptual Aspects of Arithmetic

An increasing body of literature demonstrates the importance of children's underlying conceptual representation of a problem situation to their ability to successfully use arithmetic to solve problems. Research on the processes children use in solving word problems (Briars & Larkin, 1984; Riley, Greeno, & Heller, 1988) suggests that, particularly at younger grades, children solve word problems by mentally envisioning the transformations described in the world. Problem 3 above presents two word-problem descriptions of the same physical situation. Both are Change problems in Riley et al.'s terminology, but the first proceeds to a final unknown state, while the second begins with an initial unknown state that must be reconstructed from the result. Solving the second version is substantially more difficult than is the first, which is at least partly due to the difficulty children have in reasoning about changes to an initially unknown state.

Children gradually develop problem representations and algorithms that are less tied to specific conceptual representations of the problem situation. The development of such procedures poses its own difficulties to successful problem solving, however, because children will often blithely scan a problem and combine the numbers in ways that are computationally convenient but nonsensical. Problem 4, adapted from Schoenfeld (1988), illustrates this clearly. Either adding or multiplying sheep and dogs produces numbers that are implausible for human ages, although dividing 125 by 5 produces an answer that is entirely reasonable as being the shepherd's age.

American children may be particularly prone to making such assumptions because American mathematical education presents a very impoverished variety of word problems for them to solve. Stigler, Fuson, Ham, and Kim (1986) analyzed the presentation of word problems in four U.S. textbook series and in the textbook series used in the former U.S.S.R. In contrast to the Soviet textbooks, word problems in the U.S. series showed a much smaller variety of problem types and focused on those that students find easier to solve. Thus, the assumption that particular problem wording will be associated with a particular solution strategy may be a more valid conclusion for someone accustomed to dealing with the U.S. mathematics curriculum.

C. Symbolic Effects in Arithmetic

Arithmetic is generally accomplished using Arabic numerals and conventional arithmetic operations. As noted above, Arabic numerals provide a completely consistent base-ten representation of number, a fact that greatly simplifies the application of arithmetic algorithms. To see why this is so, consider the relative difficulty of decomposing into tens and ones components the addition problem presented in Figure 2, which shows (proceeding clockwise from top left) the same addition problem presented in Roman numerals, Arabic numerals, English words, and Chinese characters. Because Arabic numerals present a clear base-ten representation of numbers, this task is trivial and involves merely attending to the numeral written in each decimal place. Roman numerals present a much greater challenge; the first two symbols in the top number represent its tens-place value, while the first symbol in the lower number represents its tens-place value, and the use of addition and subtraction around 5 are required in order to interpret the units values of these numbers. The English alphabetic representation of the same number also presents a complication to decomposing the number into tens- and ones-values, for the first element of the top number (twenty) corresponds to its tens-value, while the first element of the lower number (four) corresponds to the ones-value of that number. The Chinese character representation of the same problem avoids this problem. The top number

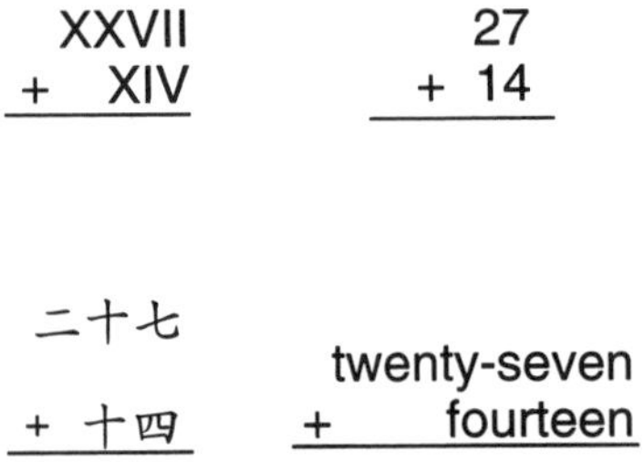

$$XXVII$$
$$+ \ \ XIV$$

$$27$$
$$+ \ 14$$

二十七
$$+ \ 十四$$

twenty-seven
$$+ \ \ \ \ fourteen$$

FIGURE 2   An addition problem presented in four different orthographies: Roman Numerals (*top left*), Arabic numerals (*top right*), English alphabetic writing system (*bottom right*), and Chinese characters (*bottom left*). The top number in Roman numeral notation is literally $10 + 10 + 5 + 2$; the bottom number in this notation is literally $10 + 5 - 1$. The top number in the Chinese character orthography can be read literally as $2 \times 10 + 7$, and the bottom number as $10 + 4$.

can be read literally as "two ten seven" and the lower as "ten four." The tens-place in each number consists of a symbol showing the number of tens (if more than one) and the name for the base (ten), while the final symbol shows the unit-value.

What difference does this make in children's calculation? A dissertation by Paredes (1993) looked at the ability of second through fourth grade American and Chinese children to perform addition with one- and two-digit numbers presented either as Arabic numerals or in the orthography used for writing words in their language (Chinese characters or the English alphabet). As one would expect from other research (Stevenson, Lee, & Stigler, 1986; Geary, Bow-Thomas, Fan, & Siegler, 1993), Chinese children were substantially faster than their American peers at all ages and in all conditions. Where numbers were presented in English word and Chinese character orthographies, children made mistakes that reflected trying to apply algorithms that work well with Arabic numerals to these alternate representations. In the case of English words, the most common mistake for American children with problems such as that shown in Figure 2 (containing a teen number) was to mistakenly combine the units portion of the teen number with the decade portion of the other addend, producing an answer such as 68 for the problem shown. Chinese characters are readily parsed into tens- and ones-place values, but Chinese children had a great deal of difficulty figuring out what to do with the character for 10, which is part of any decade name, providing information that place value gives for Arabic numerals. Chinese children were very likely to resolve this difficulty by treating the top number as though it were 217, resulting in answers such as 231 for the problem shown. Chinese children were quite likely to make this mistake; only the oldest subjects solved as many as half of the problems presented as Chinese characters, compared with success rates ranging from 82–92% for the U.S. subjects. The similarity between Chinese character and Arabic numeral representations of numbers in this case was detrimental to Chinese children, because it facilitated a mistaken transfer of calculation techniques developed for Arabic numerals to a slightly different representation.

IX. MATHEMATICAL REASONING REPRISED

Children use multiple sources of structure in developing quantitative competence. Infants from near the moment of birth attend to number as a feature of their world, but moving from this early, inchoate sensitivity to number to real mathematical sophistication requires developing a repertoire of concepts and abilities that are quite diverse in nature. Making mathematical development possible is the fact that these multiple sources of structure increase the likelihood that different paths will converge on the same ultimate abilities. Children may differ in the extent to which their counting is based on a conceptual understanding of number, the structure that symbolic systems provide, or the conventional models that the social environment makes available to them, but attention to any combination of these factors should result in the same outcome. Early attention to number during infancy could provide important constraints on the kind of counting procedures children might entertain as possibilities. The procedures one acquires for the purpose of counting and calculating provide another important source of structure in the development of mathematical competence, with some features of each entirely conventional (such as the use of a base-ten representation for number) and others fundamental to the success of the procedure. Finally, symbol systems are organized in particular ways that serve to emphasize some mathematical relations, while obscuring others.

The claim that there is substantial convergence in the structure provided by mathematical concepts, conventional algorithms, and symbol systems does not imply that this convergence implies perfect constraint on the development of mathematical competence, as the discussion of students' responses to Problems 4 and 5 noted. The problem of interrelating procedures, concepts, and properly using the structure that symbolic systems can provide is a complex and continuing task, and it is this challenge that provides the continuity in mathematical development from the preschool years to adulthood.

Acknowledgments

Preparation of this chapter was supported by NIMH Grants K02MH01190 and R01MH50222. In addition to the editors, Renée Baillargeon, Judy Deloache, Cynthia Fisher, J. Michael Lake, Gregory Murphy, David Paredes, Alice Penrose, Robert Siegler, and Catherine Smith provided helpful comments on earlier versions of this chapter. Address correspondence to: Kevin F. Miller, Department of Psychology, University of Illinois at Urbana-Champaign, 603 E. Daniel St., Champaign, IL 61820-6267 (electronic mail: kmiller@s.psych.uiuc.edu).

References

Antell, S. R., & Keating, D. (1983). Perception of numerical invariance by neonates. *Child Development, 54,* 695–701.

Ashcraft, M. H. (1992). Cognitive arithmetic: A review of data and theory. Special Issue: Numerical cognition. *Cognition, 44,* 75–106.

Baillargeon, R., Miller, K. F., & Constantino, J. (1995). *10-Month-old infants' intuitions about addition.* Unpublished manuscript, University of Illinois at Urbana-Champaign.

Baroody, A. J. (1992). The development of preschoolers' counting skills and principles. In J. Bideaud, C. Meljac, & J.-P. Fischer (Eds.), *Pathways to number: Children's developing numerical abilities* (pp. 99–126). Hillsdale, NJ: Erlbaum.

Baroody, A. J., & Ginsburg, H. P. (1986). The relationship between initial meaningful and mechanical knowledge of arithmetic. In J. Hiebert (Ed.), *Conceptual and procedural knowledge: The case of mathematics* (pp. 75–112). Hillsdale, NJ: Erlbaum.

Beth, E., & Piaget, J. (1966). *Mathematical epistemology and psychology*. New York: Gordon & Breach.

Bideaud, J. (1992). Introduction. In J. Bideaud, C. Meljac, & J.-P. Fischer (Eds.), *Pathways to number: Children's developing numerical abilities* (pp. 1–17). Hillsdale, NJ: Erlbaum.

Bisanz, J., & LeFevre, J.-A. (1992). Understanding elementary mathematics. In J. I. D. Campbell (Ed.), *The nature and origins of mathematical skills* (pp. 113–136). New York: North-Holland.

Briars, D. J., & Larkin, J. H. (1984). An integrated model of skill in solving elementary word problems. *Cognition & Instruction, 1,* 245–296.

Briars, D., & Siegler, R. S. (1984). A featural analysis of preschooler's counting knowledge. *Developmental Psychology, 20,* 607–618.

Campbell, J. J. D., & Clark, J. M. (1988). An encoding-complex view of cognitive number processing: Comment on McCloskey, Sokol, and Goodman (1986). *Journal of Experimental Psychology: General, 117,* 204–214.

Carpenter, T. P., & Moser, J. M. (1984). The acquisition of addition and subtraction concepts in grades one through three. *Journal for Research in Mathematics Education, 15,* 179–202.

Cooper, R. G. (1984). Early number development: Discovering number space with addition and subtraction. In C. Sophian (Ed.), *The origins of cognitive skills* (pp. 157–192). Hillsdale, NJ: Erlbaum.

Copeland, R. W. (1984). *How children learn mathematics* (Fourth edition). New York: MacMillan.

Durkin, K., Shire, B., Riem, R., Crowther, R. D., & Rutter, D. R. (1986). The social and linguistic context of early number word use. *British Journal of Developmental Psychology, 4,* 269–288.

Ferrara, R. A., & Turner, T. (1993). The structure of early counting competence. *Bulletin of the Psychonomic Society, 31,* 257–260.

Flavell, J. H. (1963). *The developmental psychology of Jean Piaget*. Princeton, NJ: Van Nostrand.

Frye, D., Braisby, N., Lowe, J., Maroudas, C., & Nicholls, J. (1989). Young children's understanding of counting and cardinality. *Child Development, 60,* 1158–1171.

Fuson, K. C. (1988). *Children's counting and concepts of number*. New York: Springer-Verlag.

Fuson, K. C. (1992a). Relationships between counting and cardinality from age 2 to age 8. In J. Bideaud, C. Meljac, & J.-P. Fischer (Eds.), *Pathways to number: Children's developing numerical abilities* (pp. 127–149). Hillsdale, NJ: Erlbaum.

Fuson, K. C. (1992b). Learning addition and subtraction: Effects of number words and other cultural tools. In J. Bideaud, C. Meljac, & J.-P. Fischer (Eds.), *Pathways to number: Children's developing numerical abilities* (pp. 283–306). Hillsdale, NJ: Erlbaum.

Fuson, K. C., Fraivillig, J. L., & Burghardt, B. H. (1992). Relations children construct among English number words, multiunit base-ten blocks, and written multidigit addition. In J. I. D. Campbell (Ed.), *The nature and origins of mathematical skills* (pp. 39–112). New York: North-Holland.

Fuson, K. C., & Hall, J. W. (1983). The acquisition of early number word meanings: A conceptual analysis and review. In H. P. Ginsburg (Ed.), *The development of mathematical thinking* (pp. 49–107). New York: Academic Press.

Fuson, K. C., Richards, J., & Briars, D. J. (1982). The acquisition and elaboration of the number word sequence. In C. J. Brainerd (Ed.), *Children's logical and mathematical cognition* (pp. 33–92). New York: Springer-Verlag.

Gallistel, C. R., & Gelman, R. (1992). Preverbal and verbal counting and computation. *Cognition, 44,* 43–74.

Geary, D. C., Bow-Thomas, C. C., Fan, L., & Siegler, R. S. (1993). Even before formal instruction, Chinese children outperform American children in mental addition. *Cognitive Development, 8,* 517–529.

Gelman, R. (1990). First principles organize attention to and learning about relevant data:

Number and the animate–inanimate distinction as examples. *Cognitive Science, 14,* 79–106.

Gelman, R. (1993). A rational-constructivist account of early learning about numbers and objects. In D. L. Medin (Ed.), *The psychology of learning and motivation* (Vol. 30, pp. 61– 96). San Diego: Academic Press.

Gelman, R., & Baillargeon, R. (1983). A review of some Piagetian concepts. In J. Flavell & E. Markman (Eds.), *Handbook of child psychology: Vol. 3. Cognitive development* (pp. 167–230). New York: Wiley.

Gelman, R., & Cohen, M. (1988). Qualitative differences in the way Down's syndrome and normal children solve a novel counting problem. In L. Nadel (Ed.), *The psychobiology of Down's syndrome* (pp. 51–99). Cambridge, MA: MIT.

Gelman, R., & Gallistel, C. R. (1978). *The child's understanding of number.* Cambridge, MA: Harvard University Press.

Gelman, R., & Meck, E. (1983). Preschoolers' counting: Principle before skill. *Cognition, 13,* 343–359.

Gelman, R., & Meck, E. (1986). The notion of principle: The case of counting. In J. Hiebert (Ed.), *Conceptual and procedural knowledge: The case of mathematics* (pp. 29–57). Hillsdale, NJ: Erlbaum.

Gelman, R., & Meck, E. (1992). Early principles aid initial but not later conceptions of number. In J. Bideaud, C. Meljac, & J.-P. Fischer (Eds.), *Pathways to number: Children's developing numerical abilities* (pp. 171–189). Hillsdale, NJ: Erlbaum.

Gleitman, L. R., & Rozin, P. (1977). The structure and acquisition of reading. I: Relations between orthographies and the structure of language. In A. S. Reber & D. L. Scarborough (Eds.), *Toward a psychology of reading* (pp. 1–53). Hillsdale, NJ: Erlbaum.

Gough, P. B., & Hillinger, M. L. (1980). Learning to read: An unnatural act. *Bulletin of the Orton Society, 30,* 179–196.

Gough, P. B., Juel, C., & Roper-Schneider, D. (1983). Code and cipher: A two-stage conception of initial reading acquisition. In J. A. Niles & L. A. Harris (Eds.), *Searches for meaning in reading/language processing and instruction* (pp. 207–211). Rochester, NY: National Reading Conference.

Greeno, J. G., Riley, M. S., & Gelman, R. (1984). Conceptual competence and children's counting. *Cognitive Psychology, 16,* 94–143.

Houlihan, D. M., & Ginsburg, H. P. (1981). The addition methods of first- and second-grade children. *Journal for Research in Mathematics Education, 12,* 95–106.

Hurford, J. R. (1975). *The linguistic theory of numerals.* Cambridge: Cambridge University Press.

Hurford, J. R. (1987). *Language and number.* Cambridge: Cambridge University Press.

Ifrah, G. (1985). *From one to zero: A universal history of numbers.* New York: Viking.

Jevons, W. S. (1871). The power of numerical discrimination. *Nature, 3,* 281–282.

Juel, C., Griffith, P. L., & Gough, P. B. (1986). Acquisition of literacy: A longitudinal study of children in first and second grade. *Journal of Educational Psychology, 78,* 243–255.

Kaufman, E. L., Lord, M. W., Reese, T. W., & Volkmann, J. (1949). The discrimination of visual number. *American Journal of Psychology, 62,* 498–525.

Klahr, D. (1973). A production system for counting, subitizing, and adding. In W. G. Chase (Ed.), *Visual information processing* (pp. 527–546). New York: Academic Press.

Lorenz, K. (1971). Part and parcel in animal and human societies (1950). In K. Lorenz, *Studies in animal and human behavior* (Vol. 2, pp. 115–195). Cambridge, MA: Harvard.

Mandler, G., & Shebo, B. J. (1982). Subitizing: An analysis of its component processes. *Journal of Experimental Psychology General, 111,* 1–22.

Marler, P. (1991). The instinct to learn. In S. Carey & R. Gelman (Eds.), *The epigenesis of mind* (pp. 37–66). Hillsdale, NJ: Erlbaum.

Mayer, R. E., Lewis, A. B., & Hegarty, M. (1992). Mathematical misunderstandings: Qualitative reasoning about quantitative problems. In J. I. D. Campbell (Ed.), *The nature and origins of mathematical skills* (pp. 137–153). New York: North-Holland.

McCloskey, M., Sokol, S., & Goodman, R. A. (1986). Cognitive processes in verbal-number production: Inferences from the performance of brain-damaged subjects. *Journal of Experimental Psychology: General, 115,* 307–330.

Meck, W. H., & Church, R. M. (1983). A mode of control model of counting and timing processes. *Journal of Experimental Psychology: Animal Behavior Processes, 9,* 320–334.

Menninger, K. (1969). *Number words and number symbols.* Cambridge, MA: MIT Press.

Miller, K. F. (1989). Measurement as a tool for thought: The role of measuring procedures on children's understanding of quantitative invariance. *Developmental Psychology, 25,* 589–600.

Miller, K. F., & Paredes, D. R. (1990). Starting to add worse: Effects of learning to multiply on children's addition. *Cognition, 37,* 213–242.

Miller, K. F., Smith, C. M., Zhu, J., & Zhang, H. (1995). Preschool origins of cross-national differences in mathematical competence: The role of number naming systems. *Psychological Science, 6,* 56–60.

Miller, K. F., & Stigler, J. (1987). Counting in Chinese: Cultural variation in a basic cognitive skill. *Cognitive Development, 2,* 279–305.

Miller, K. F., & Stigler, J. W. (1991). Meanings of skill: Effects of abacus expertise on number representation. *Cognition and Instruction, 8,* 29–67.

Miller, K. F., & Zhu, J. (1991). The trouble with teens: Accessing the structure of number names. *Journal of Memory and Language, 30,* 48–68.

Miura, I. T. (1987). Mathematics achievement as a function of language. *Journal of Educational Psychology, 79,* 79–82.

Miura, I. T., Kim, C. C., Chang, C.-M., & Okamoto, Y. (1988). Effects of language characteristics on children's cognitive representation of number: Cross-national comparisons. *Child Development, 59,* 1445–1450.

Miura, I. T., & Okamoto, Y. (1989). Comparisons of U.S. and Japanese first graders' cognitive representation of number and understanding of place value. *Journal of Educational Psychology, 81,* 109–114.

Miura, I. T., Okamoto, Y., Kim, C. C., Steere, M., & Fayol, M. (1993). First graders' cognitive representation of number and understanding of place value: Cross-national comparisons—France, Japan, Korea, Sweden, and the United States. *Journal of Educational Psychology, 85,* 24–30.

Moore, D., Benenson, J., Reznick, J. S., Peterson, P., & Kagan, J. (1987). Effect of auditory numerical information on infants' looking behavior: Contradictory evidence. *Developmental Psychology, 23,* 665–670.

Paige, J. M., & Simon, H. A. (1966). Cognitive processes in solving algebra word problems. In B. Kleinmuntz (Ed.), *Problem solving: Research, method, and theory.* New York: Wiley.

Paredes, D. R. (1993). *Sources and consequences of developing skill in mental addition: A comparison of U.S. and Chinese grade school children.* Unpublished dissertation, University of Texas at Austin.

Pelham, B. W., Sumarta, T. T., & Myaskovsky, L. (1994). The easy path from many to much: The numerosity heuristic. *Cognitive Psychology, 26,* 103–133.

Piaget, J. (1965). *The child's conception of number* (p. 63). New York: Norton.

Potter, M. C., & Levy, E. I. (1968). Spatial enumeration without counting. *Child Development, 39,* 265–272.

Pylyshyn, Z. (1989). The role of location indexes in spatial perception: A sketch of the FINST spatial–index model. *Cognition, 32,* 65–97.

Quine, W. V. O. (1960). *Word and object.* Cambridge, MA: MIT Press.

Riley, M. S., Greeno, J. G., & Heller, J. I. (1988). Developmental analysis of understanding language about quantities and of solving problems. *Cognition and Instruction, 5,* 49–101.

Russell, B. (1919). *Introduction to mathematical philosophy.* London: George Allen and Unwin, Ltd.

Saltzman, I. J., & Garner, W. R. (1948). Reaction time as a measure of span of attention. *Journal of Psychology, 25,* 227–241.

Saxe, G. B., Guberman, S. R., & Gearhart, M. (1987). Social processes in early number development. *Monographs of the Society for Research in Child Development, 52*(2, Serial No. 216).

Schoenfeld, A. H. (1988). Problem solving in context(s). In R. Charles & E. Silver (Eds.), *The teaching and assessing of mathematical problem solving* (pp. 82–92). Reston, VA: National Council of Teachers of Mathematics.

Séron, X., & Deloche, G. (1987). The production of counting sequences by aphasics and children: A matter of lexical processing? In G. Deloche & X. Seron (Eds.), *Mathematical disabilities: A cognitive neuropsychological perspective* (pp. 171–200). Hillsdale, NJ: Erlbaum.

Séron, X., Deloche, G., & Noël, M. P. (1992). Number transcribing by children: Writing Arabic numbers under dictation. In J. Bideaud, C. Meljac, & J.-P. Fischer (Eds.), *Pathways to number: Children's developing numerical abilities* (pp. 245–264). Hillsdale, NJ: Erlbaum.

Shipley, E. F., & Shepperson, B. (1990). Countable entities: Developmental changes. *Cognition, 34,* 109–136.

Siegler, R. S. (1981). Developmental sequences within and between concepts. *Monographs of the Society for Research in Child Development, 46*(2, Serial No. 189).

Siegler, R. S. (1987a). The perils of averaging data over strategies: An example from children's addition. *Journal of Experimental Psychology: General, 116,* 250–264.

Siegler, R. S. (1987b). Strategy choices in subtraction. In J. A. Sloboda & D. Rogers (Ed.), *Cognitive processes in mathematics* (pp. 81–106). Oxford: Clarendon Press.

Siegler, R. S. (1988). Strategy choice procedures and the development of multiplication skill. *Journal of Experimental Psychology: General, 3,* 258–275.

Siegler, R. S. (1991). In young children's counting, procedures precede principles. *Educational Psychology Review, 3,* 127–135.

Siegler, R. S. (1994). Cognitive variability: A key to understanding cognitive development. *Current Directions in Psychological Science, 3,* 1–5.

Siegler, R. S., & Robinson, M. (1982). The development of numerical understandings. In H. Reese & L. Lipsitt (Eds.), *Advances in child development and behavior* (Vol. 16, pp. 241–310). New York: Academic Press.

Siegler, R. S., & Shrager, J. (1984). A model of strategy choice. In C. Sophian (Ed.), *Origins of cognitive skills* (pp. 229–293). Hillsdale, NJ: Erlbaum.

Sokol, S. M., Goodman-Schulman, R., & McCloskey, M. (1989). In defense of a modular architecture for the number-processing system: Reply to Campbell and Clark. *Journal Experimental Psychology: General, 118,* 105–110.

Song, M., & Ginsburg, H. P. (1987). The development of informal and formal mathematical thinking in Korean and U.S. children. *Child Development, 58,* 1286–1296.

Song, M., & Ginsburg, H. P. (1988). The effect of the Korean number system on young children's counting: A natural experiment in numerical bilingualism. *Child Development, 58,* 1286–1296.

Sophian, C. (1988). Limitations on preschool children's knowledge about counting: Using counting to compare two sets. *Developmental Psychology, 24,* 634–640.

Stanovich, K. E. (1980). Toward an interactive-compensatory model of individual differences in the development of reading fluency. *Reading Research Quarterly, 16,* 32–71.

Starkey, P., & Cooper, R. G. (1980). Perception of numbers by human infants. *Science, 210,* 1033–1035.

Starkey, P., Spelke, E. S., & Gelman, R. (1983). Detection of intermodal numerical correspondences by human infants. *Science, 222,* 179–181.

Starkey, P., Spelke, E. S., & Gelman, R. (1990). Numerical abstraction by human infants. *Cognition, 36,* 97–127.

Stevenson, H. W., Lee, S. Y., & Stigler, J. W. (1986). Mathematics achievement of Chinese, Japanese, and American children. *Science, 233,* 693–699.

Stigler, J. W. (1984). "Mental abacus": The effect of abacus training on Chinese children's mental calculation. *Cognitive Psychology, 16,* 145–176.

Stigler, J. W., Fuson, K. C., Ham, M., & Kim, M. S. (1986). An analysis of addition and subtraction word problems in American and Soviet elementary mathematics textbooks. *Cognition & Instruction, 3,* 153–171.

Strauss, M. S., & Curtis, L. E. (1981). Infant perception of numerosity. *Child Development, 52,* 1146–1152.

Svenson, O., Hedenborg, M., & Lingman, L. (1976). On children's heuristics for solving simple additions. *Scandinavian Journal of Educational Research, 20,* 143–151.

Svenson, O., & Sjöberg, K. (1983). Evolution of cognitive processes for solving simple additions during the first three school years. *Scandinavian Journal of Psychology, 24,* 117–124.

Taves, E. H. (1941). Two mechanisms for the perception of visual numerousness. *Archives of Psychology, 265,* 1–47.

Tollefsrud-Anderson, L., Campbell, R. L., Starkey, P., & Cooper, R. G. (1992). Number conservation: Distinguishing quantifier from operator solutions. In J. Bideaud, C. Meljac, & J.-P. Fischer (Eds.), *Pathways to number: Children's developing numerical abilities* (pp. 151–170). Hillsdale, NJ: Erlbaum.

Trick, L. (1992). A theory of enumeration that grows out of a general theory of vision: subitizing, counting, and FINSTs. In J. I. D. Campbell (Ed.), *The nature and origin of mathematical skills* (pp. 257–299). New York: North-Holland.

Wittgenstein, L. (1953/1958). *Philosophical investigations* (3rd ed.). New York: Macmillan.

Wynn, K. (1990). Children's understanding of counting. *Cognition, 36,* 155–193.

Wynn, K. (1992a). Addition and subtraction by human infants. *Nature, 358,* 749–750.

Wynn, K. (1992b). Children's acquisition of the number words and the counting system. *Cognitive Psychology, 24,* 220–251.

CHAPTER 8

Conversation and Cognition

Michael Siegal

Human conversation can be considered as the culmination of an evolutionary process. Through the use of conversation about mental states, which alerts individuals to others' behavioral intentions and beliefs (i.e., the propositions and statements that others have accepted), humans have adapted to threats to survival and group stability (Dunbar, 1993). Since communication can take place more rapidly in conversation than through direct observation, conversation provides an efficient means to communicate feedback about potentially threatening events that are remote in time and space. The task of understanding conversation is time pressured in that information about mental states must be processed fast enough to keep up with the flow of a speaker's language (Harris, 1996; Leslie, 1994, p. 213). Thus, an awareness of conversational abilities to interpret messages as intended and to resist misleading information is fundamental in investigations of cognition and development, as it is a prerequisite for appraising what speakers know about each other and about the subject domains of their conversations. In this chapter, I review research on conversation in relation to children's knowledge of the mental world in specific domains, such as the domain of food and contamination, and their suggestibility to misleading information.

Perceptual and Cognitive Development
Copyright © 1996 by Academic Press, Inc. All rights of reproduction in any form reserved.

I. CHILDREN AND CONVERSATION: A PARADOX

A. Conversational Awareness in Young Children

Much early childhood socialization involves learning how, when, where, and with whom to converse. As a consequence, young children are quickly prepared to engage in conversation. During the period of their language acquisition, they are socialized by caregivers who make allowance for their early conversational inexperience. According to research carried out in many societies, these adult speakers generally shorten their utterances and do not say more or less than is necessary to sustain conversation; they are clear, relevant, and informative in referring to objects and events in the here and now; and they are concerned to correct truth value in the child's speech rather than errors of syntax (R. Brown & Hanlon, 1970; Cross, 1977; De Villiers & De Villiers, 1978, pp. 192–198; Ferguson, 1977). In this sense, the speech input that children generally receive conforms to the maxims or rules of conversation noted by philosophers of language such as Grice (1975) who have observed that adult conversation is characterized by rules or maxims that enjoin speakers to: Say no more or no less than is required (the maxim of *quantity*). Try to say the truth and avoid falsehood (the maxim of *quality*). Be relevant and informative (the maxim of *relation*). Avoid ambiguity and obscurity (the maxim of *manner*).[1] As Grice has pointed out, these maxims create a "logic in conversation" that involves knowledge of the implications contained in natural language. For example, if a person complains that he has a headache, a friend may respond that there is a drugstore around the corner. The implications are that the walk to the drugstore is short, that the drugstore is open at the time, that it sells tablets to alleviate headaches, and that these tablets are publicly available to be sold to the sufferer if he can pay as a member of the community. To state all this explicitly would be to violate the quantity rule since the implications are likely to be mutually understood among conversationally experienced speakers. Effective communication between speakers and listeners thus involves a common grounding in knowledge of time, location, and community membership that permits a mutual mental representation of contexts for comprehension (Clark, 1992, pp. 60–77; Clark & Brennan, 1991).

By the age of 3 years, the speech habits of children reflect a common grounding and are often in line with conversation as prescribed by the Gricean maxims. They converse fluently with others and demonstrate substantial ability in adjusting speech to the characteristics of listeners such as their age and their access and attention to previous information (Baldwin, 1993; R. Gelman & Shatz, 1977). Moreover, by the age of 3 years, children in Western societies learn as part of the culture to take turns in conversation and to pause until the person has completed his or her message (Broerse & Elias, 1994). They can often interact meaningfully with other children and adults in conversations that are often about their own and others' mental states (Bretherton & Beeghly, 1982; Dunn, 1994; Shatz, 1994; Wellman & Bartsch, 1994).

Nevertheless, the early process of becoming a conversationalist does not prepare preschoolers for specialized settings in which conversational rules are set aside. In communication between adults who are conversationally experienced, it is usually mutually understood in these settings that the rules may be broken to make what Grice refers to as "conversational implicatures." For example, adults know that speakers may be uninformative and state the obvious for purposes of irony (e.g., stating that "It's another sunny day" in referring to the weather of a habitually rainy locality) or that they may be redundant and speak more than is required (e.g., repeatedly asking, "How are you?") to probe an initial answer out of politeness or curiosity in order to establish that this is the respondent's genuine opinion. However, the need to follow the conversational implications of a speaker who has set aside the rules may place the understanding of children who are inexperienced in conversation at risk. Even adults may be misled if a rule is subtly broken and there is a lack of common grounding in communication (e.g., Schegloff, 1987).

B. Culture, Communication, and the Potential for a Clash of Conversational Worlds

This issue emerges frequently in studies of adult cognition in non-Western cultures as well as in studies of cognitive development with children. When investigators study individuals and their culture for the specialized, scientific purpose of determining what they know, the accuracy of their answers depends, in part, on their interpretation of the purpose and relevance of the questions. If they misinterpret questions to mean something else than the speaker intended, they may give answers to what they represent as a very different sort of question. These answers may not reflect the depth of their understanding relevant to the speaker's concerns or—as in the case of persons from some non-Western cultures—may not involve any clear response at all. For example, as I have pointed out elsewhere (Siegal, 1991b), considerable "gratuitous concurrence" has been noted among Aboriginal Australians who attempt to accommodate to the requests of white Australians by feigning nods and muffling sounds. Their answers approximate a "might be" in order that the listener should not be offended (Eades, 1982; Liberman, 1981).

Moreover, there are many cultures where the turn-taking that is so much a part of the conversation of speakers in Western cultures actually becomes an obstacle to effective communication. In his investigation of the Dowayo culture in the Cameroons, Barley (1983, p. 67) writes:

To begin with I was distressed to find that I couldn't extract more than ten words from Dowayos at a stretch. When I asked them to describe something to me, a ceremony, or an animal, they would produce one or two sentences and then stop. I would have to ask further questions to get more information. One day, after two months of fruitless endeavor, the reason struck me. Whereas in the West we learn not to interrupt when somebody else is talking, this does not hold in much of Africa. . . . When listening to someone else talking, a Dowayo stares gravely at the floor, rocks backwards and forwards and murmurs, 'Yes,' 'It is so,' 'Good,' every five seconds or so. Failure to do so leads to the speaker rapidly drying up. As soon as I adopted this expedient, my interviews were quite transformed.

Barley chronicles how both age and covocalization are prerequisites for many conversational exchanges among the Dowayo. Young adults are excluded from the presence of conversations between powerful, learned elders and, within the community of elderly conversationalists, the address "old man" and "grandfather" are liberally employed as terms of respect.

When adults from non-Western cultures are questioned to determine their understanding of Western logic, they may import their own local concerns rather than the scientific concerns of the investigator. For example, when given a syllogism such as "All Kpelle men are rice farmers. Mr. Smith is not a rice farmer. Is he a Kpelle man?," a Kpelle might well reply, "I don't know the man in person. . . . Since I do not know him I cannot answer that question" (Scribner, 1977, p. 490).

Similarly, in specialized settings where well-meaning investigators question children for the scientific purpose of determining what they know, conversations are apt to have some of the characteristics of the relations between powerful and submissive groups of adults who vary in age and cultural background. Ordinarily, as Clark (1992, pp. 3–6) observes, speakers engaged in the cooperative activity of conversation accumulate information through identifying what can be assumed to be given as the common grounding and the new, additional information that the listener does not previously know. They thus adhere to a "new–given contract" about the cooperative use of new and given information. Yet, children who recognize that an adult ordinarily has more knowledge and more power than they do may not identify the novel component in the conversation initiated by the adult questioner and view this to be a breach of the contract. Should they not share an adult speaker's purpose of eliciting knowledge that he or she already possesses, they may be reluctant to accede to such requests and remain silent, or they may respond curtly and switch their answers under repeated questioning in an effort to placate the investigator and bring the conversation to an end, or they may simply attempt to assent to what they believe has been asked in every question.

In this respect, ethnographic research has shown that the methods used by adults to instruct children as to how, when, where, and with whom to converse vary across regions and cultures (Heath, 1983; Ochs, 1983; Schieffelin, 1983, 1986, 1990). The resulting differences in conversational patterns and routines pose a challenge for studies of cognitive development in situations that are located outside middle-class, urban settings in Western countries. Schieffelin (1983) reports that children in the Kaluli culture of New Guinea are not regarded as significant communicators until they produce the "hard speech" of adults who refrain from using simplified language or baby talk in language socialization. To achieve the objective of arming children with speech habits that are well formed and socially appropriate, Kaluli mothers directly instruct children on what to say in conversation by providing model utterances followed by the imperative, "Say like that." Similarly, Rogoff and Mistry (1990) give the example of Mayan culture in which it is inappropriate for children to speak freely to adults. When tested for their ability to recall a story, Mayan children fidget, avoid eye contact and often barely speak. To continue at all, they require considerable prompting and commonly qualify their messages with the word *cha* ("So I have been told") in order to show that they are not claiming a possession of greater knowledge than adults.

Once children do reply, they may import their own relevance. They may interpret questions in a manner different than those intended by the speaker (Beal & Belgrad, 1990; Bonitatibus, 1988; Donaldson, 1978; Hughes & Grieve, 1983; Siegal, 1991a, 1991b, 1995; Siegal & Peterson, 1994). Even Western children can be like the Kpelle and the Maya in their responses. For instance, Labov (1972, pp. 201–240) has documented the effects of the social situation on Black American children's responses to adults' questions about their daily activities and has shown that the more asymmetrical the power relationship, the less willing are children to offer answers freely. Moreover, the tendency to interpret questions in a manner different than intended by a speaker is not restricted to children from minority or disadvantaged groups. For example, to probe for the certainty of children's answers on conservation tasks, Piaget (1929) advocated using countersuggestions ("Another child gave me a different answer. Do you agree?"). However, as Perret-Clermont observes (see Siegal, 1991a, p. 26), children's responses to such suggestions may be based on the presumed answer to the question, "Is he a dumb or smart kid?" rather than referring to any random child.

The potential for a clash of conversational worlds underscores the complexity of the task involved in establishing what children know through using techniques that require a conversational knowledge that children have not yet acquired. Thus, in the case of children and their competence in conversation, a paradox arises. On many occasions, young children communicate well with others. However, in specialized settings such as in testing situations, communication between children and adults who are both

conversationally competent within their own worlds of experience and social interaction may be impaired simply because they do not share the
interpretation of each other's conversational contribution. In order to overcome this obstacle, investigators need to talk to children in an explicit
manner that does not set aside the Gricean maxims and does not require
them to follow the conversational implications of questions.

II. CONVERSATION AND THEORY OF MIND

A. Taking Desires and Beliefs into Account in Predicting Behavior

The need for children to have explicit conversational "enrichment" in questioning is shown in studies that have been carried out on children's theory of
mind (see Taylor, this volume, for a review). In this research, the degree to
which young children can be said to have insight into others' beliefs and
intentions has remained controversial (Flavell, Mumme, Green, & Flavell,
1992; Leslie, 1994; Moses & Flavell, 1990; Perner, 1991; Perner, Leekam, &
Wimmer, 1987; Siegal & Peterson, 1994; Sullivan & Winner, 1993; Wellman
& Bartsch, 1994).

One position is that there is a form of "conceptual limitation" in children's understanding of the critical relation between beliefs and behavior.
For example, Wellman and Bartsch (1988) presented preschoolers with "explicit" false belief tasks in which a story character's desire to find an object
was explicitly mentioned, the object was said to be really in one location,
and the character was said to believe that the object is in another (wrong)
location (e.g., "Jane wants to find her kitten. Jane's kitten is really in the
playroom. Jane thinks the kitten is in the kitchen. Where will Jane look for
her kitten?" Correct answer: kitchen; 3-year-olds' common answer: playroom). Wellman and Bartsch found that 3-year-olds and young 4-year-olds
did poorly on this task and, in a fashion that is reminiscent of Piaget's (1970)
emphasis on egocentrism, proposed that young children do not fully appreciate that desires can be unfulfilled owing to the falsely believed location of
objects. Though they can often determine how behavior follows from beliefs, they weight desires over beliefs when these are in conflict in false belief
tasks. In support of this explanation, Wellman and Woolley (1990) have
reported that, while 2-year-olds and young 3-year-olds fail false belief tasks,
they succeed on tasks that involve predicting behavior on the basis of desires
and Wellman and Bartsch (1994) have reported that 2- and 3-year-olds talk
more about desires than about beliefs.

Presumably children express their desires verbally because they wish
these desires to be met. Yet, their greater talk about desires (i.e., the satisfied
or pleasurable states that would be obtained through achieving a goal) as
compared with beliefs (i.e., the propositions that they and others have

accepted) does not mean that they are without a knowledge of beliefs. Success on explicit false belief tasks requires children to understand and share the purpose and relevance of the questions posed by the experimenter. It is assumed in these tasks that children recognize that the purpose is to test whether children can detect how the beliefs held by others may be initially mistaken and that they follow the implications of the language of test questions such as "Where will a person (with the false belief) look for the object?" to mean "Where will the person look first?" However, children who are inexperienced in conversation may not recognize these implications and thus not display the depth of their understanding of mental states on false belief tasks.

As Fodor (1992) notes, 3-year-olds may approach tests of belief knowledge with a "very simple theory of mind," which consists of this general heuristic: "Predict that the agent will act in a way that will satisfy his desires." In the child's early experience, reliance on this heuristic will often lead to success in their interactions with others and they will have no need to consider the falsity of beliefs. Nevertheless, according to Fodor, children are prompted to discard this heuristic when they realize the possibility that no unique behavioral prediction corresponds to desires. When the outcome of a desire is seen to be ambiguous, they are capable of using a second, more sophisticated heuristic, "Predict that the agent will act in a way that would satisfy his desires if his beliefs were true." The "Selection Processor" theory of mind model proposed by Leslie (1994) incorporates Fodor's observations. It identifies the child's assumption as shown in their pretend behavior that the content of a belief normally reflects relevant current facts about behavior. For example, even 2-year-olds know that two cups without liquid are both empty. But when they are told to pretend that both are full and then see one tipped over, they will say that the other contains the liquid even though both continue to be empty. In their pretence, children focus on the here and now, indicating that pretence is "opaque" in the present tense.

To enable children to consult their memory for information on the false contents of beliefs that may take place in the past or future, Leslie (1994) maintains that help is required in the form of specific questions and contexts. These aids permit the child to resist the "prepotent" tendency to base their belief predictions on a present state of affairs. Without such aids, the purpose may appear to be something more familiar and straightforward that resembles Fodor's first very simple theory of mind heuristic: to test whether children can predict the behavior of others in achieving a goal. The question, "Where will Jane look for her kitten?" may simply be interpreted as "Where does Jane have to look (or go to look) for her kitten in order to find it?" rather than "Where will Jane look first for her kitten?," which is the conversational implication intended by the experimenter who has assumed that the child shares the purpose of the task. Once the question is explicitly formulated to dispense with the need to share the implication, children perform well.

Support for this position comes from the use of explicit questions on explicit false belief tasks. When asked questions such as "Where will Jane look first for her kitten?," Siegal and Beattie (1991, Experiment 2) found that 83% of preschoolers could often correctly predict the consequences of holding a false belief. Leslie (1994; Surian & Leslie, 1995) has replicated this result, reporting that 88% of 3-year-olds passed the "look first" question on such tasks. In both instances, children demonstrated that they understood the meaning of "first" and that they were not using a kind of "dumb strategy" in ignoring beliefs by simply interpreting "first" to mean that they should point to a different location than the one that would allow the story character to fulfill her desires. The children in Siegal and Beattie's research passed a "true belief–look first" task in which they were asked where a story character would look first for her pet when the believed location of the pet corresponded with the real location rather than an alternative one. Leslie reports that children respond correctly when asked to predict the first search strategy of a character who saw that an object had moved locations.

Though a similar pattern of findings has emerged from studies that have used a variety of questioning techniques to prompt a consideration of time and place in children's answers to questions about false beliefs (Lewis & Osborne, 1990; Mitchell & Lacohée, 1991) and from those that have sought to avoid cumbersome forms of questioning (Pratt & Bryant, 1990), the issue has recently been reexamined by Clements and Perner (1994). In their study, children aged between 2 years 5 months and 4 years 6 months were given a story about two mice. One of the mice put some cheese in a blue box to have later when he woke up from sleep. In the meantime, the other mouse found it. She picked up the cheese and put it in a red box to have later for her tea. The children were told that the first mouse was about to wake up. They were asked to answer the question regarding the location of the cheese: "I wonder where he's going to look?" Then they were told, "(The mouse) wants to get the cheese," and asked a second time where the mouse will look. Half the children were asked, "Which box will he open?," and the other half, "Which box will he open first?"

Responses to the first question were analyzed only in terms of the direction of the children's gaze as recorded on videotape rather than in terms of their verbal answers. On this first measure, children above 2 years 11 months responded correctly that the mouse would look in the blue box, whereas, on the second question, fewer children at all ages (though more of the 4-year-olds) answered correctly that the mouse would look in the red box, even when the word "first" was used in the question. Although Clements and Perner maintain that children have only an "implicit" representation of false belief and that they cannot yet explicitly make a verbal judgment of a situation that does not conform to reality, their results can also be explained in terms of conversational theory. In their task, unlike those used by Siegal and Beattie, the children were asked twice to indicate where the mouse would look. This procedure therefore involved repeated questioning in setting aside the Gricean quantity maxim to speak no more or no less than is necessary for effective communication. Having answered the first question correctly, preschoolers who are liable not to recognize the purpose of the experimenter's questions may have been prompted to change their answer on the second question to demonstrate what they perceived was the response that the experimenter was seeking (Poole & White, 1991; Siegal, Waters, & Dinwiddy, 1988). They may in effect be reasoning, "Why would (the experimenter) ask me again? She must want me to change my mind. I'll show her where the mouse has to look to find the cheese." While the Clements and Perner study used a different type of story and form of questioning than that used by Siegal and Beattie and is not directly comparable, Siegal and Peterson (1994, pp. 437–441) have shown that, on tasks similar to that used by Clements and Perner, most 3-year-olds answered correctly on a first trial but frequently erred on a second trial.[2]

Thus, children who can predict the consequences of holding false beliefs may not reveal their knowledge because they do not share the experimenter's purpose in questioning rather than because they weight desires over beliefs. Such results suggest that children's difficulty can be considered in terms of pragmatic factors as opposed to a conceptual limitation in which they cannot conceptualize how another's false belief can lead to an undesired outcome.[3] Explicit questioning techniques that do not require children to follow the conversational implications of questions serve to appraise more accurately whether there is a conceptual limitation in their theory of mind. In this respect, there is a need to avoid complex question structures where the relevant critical information is lost in a remote subordinate clause. For example, the question "When Jane *first* goes to look for her kitten, where will she look?" is less likely to succeed in eliciting children's correct responses on explicit false belief tasks than "Where will Jane look *first* for her kitten?" Nevertheless, very young children might still not be credited with a complete, adultlike understanding of mental states and may not display the same patterns of responses that are shown by adults who themselves do not always take into account the falsity of beliefs in considering behavior (Mitchell, Robinson, Isaacs, & Nye, in press).

B. Conversation, Theory of Mind, and Contamination Sensitivity

Research on children's theory of mind illustrates how their performance can be facilitated by aligning their understanding of the task purpose and relevance with that intended by the experimenter. This understanding should be facilitated in domains where problem solving is clearly related to survival.

Hirschfield and S. A. Gelman (1994, p. 21) characterize a domain as "a body of knowledge that identifies and interprets a class of phenomena assumed to share certain properties and to be of a distinct type" and that "functions as a stable response to a set of recurring and complex problems faced by the organism." Domains serve as guides for describing and explaining the world. In the course of constructing a coherent body of knowledge in a distinctive domain, intelligent learning is selectively channelled by descriptive and explanatory classification criteria.

A key example of a domain related to survival concerns solving problems that are relevant to food and safety. According to an adaptive-evolutionary approach to intelligence (Rozin, 1976a; Rozin & Schull, 1978), organisms in striving for survival and reproductive fitness confront specific problems such as food procurement. Solutions to these problems require an adaptive, specialized intelligence. During the course of evolution, intelligence in specific problem-solving domains becomes more accessible to conscious awareness. For example, the problem of procuring a safe diet involves the intelligence to assist and compete with companions in detecting and extracting foods. It concerns both the foraging and social relational processes that have been viewed by primatologists to influence the evolution of intelligence (Cords, 1992; Milton, 1988). Because food selection in omnivores is fundamental to survival, the problem of recognizing edible foods and possessing an awareness of health-endangering contaminants must be solved early in development. Intelligence in this domain is an adaptive specialization that involves a preparedness for knowing what to identify as safe to eat in the absence of surveillance from caregivers who cannot constantly monitor children's food intake or be vigilant against the deceptions of others.

Rozin (1990) has defined sensory-affective (taste, smell, and appearance), ideational (culturally appropriate or symbolic), and anticipatory (beneficial or dangerous) criteria for classifying a food as edible or inedible. In solving problems in the domain of food and contamination, which is highly relevant to their own concerns (in line with the Gricean maxim of relation), children are constrained to acquire a knowledge of these classification criteria and are apt to recognize that the purpose of questions is to determine their ability to detect edible substances and to reject those that are inedible. Therefore, even 3-year-olds should often be able to distinguish reality from appearance in recognizing that a food that looks edible may be in reality contaminated and to understand the nature of the false beliefs that can arise from this type of health-endangering deception.

1. Evidence for Domain-Specific Knowledge in the Domain of Food and Contamination

In earlier research, children have been directly questioned about their knowledge about the determinants of illness. For example, Kister and Pat-

terson (1980) questioned children in preschool and kindergarten to determine whether they interpret illness to be punishment for naughtiness. The
interviewer said, "Once a boy your age disobeyed his mother. Was that a
nice thing to do? Well, that afternoon, he got a cold (or other ailment). Do
you think he got a cold because he disobeyed his mother? What made him
get a cold? Let's pretend he didn't disobey his mother. Do you think he
would get a cold anyway? Why (not)?" Many children claimed that illness
could result from naughtiness. Similarly, Rozin, Fallon, and Augustoni-
Ziskind (1985) presented 4- to 6-year-olds with substances such as a used
comb and a grasshopper that had been dropped into glasses of juice. Many
of the children indicated their willingness to drink the juice on request. On
this basis, it has been concluded that young children do not understand
contagion and contamination as causes of illness.

Therefore, in response to direct questioning, preschoolers often say, for
example, that they would drink juice that has been in contact with contaminants. However, as noted in these studies, the effects of social pressure are
difficult to evaluate. In studies designed to ascertain whether they believe
that illness is punishment, they may attempt to comply with the suggestion
of an adult interviewer: adults are so powerful that children who are naugh-
ty will inevitably be punished. Under these conditions, they may give a
"play" response that they know is unreal. Moreover, although children may
know that a drink that has been in contact with a foreign substance is
harmful, they may not truly recognize that, in violation of the Gricean
quality rule to be sincere in conversation, a well-meaning experimenter
could directly offer them a contaminated drink to probe for their understanding of the causes of illness. Trust in the authority of the superior adult
can preclude an understanding that the purpose of the questions was to
determine whether they recognize the microscopic basis of contamination.
Barley's (1983, p. 69) studies of the Dowayo are informative on this issue.
The Dowayo claim that the water of a superior is to be respected and can be
safely drunk only if offered and that to drink without the superior's invitation will lead to the water becoming polluted and to disease in the disre-
spectful.

Nonetheless, though young children may harbor fears about the consequences of transgressing an experimenter's authority in their responses to
questions about the causes of illness, they might also be able to voice a
knowledge of the microscopic basis of illness transmission in contexts
where their understanding of the purpose and relevance of questions is
aligned with that intended by the experimenter and they are co-opted to
predict general threats to health. For example, Siegal and Share (1990)
presented 3-year-olds with a naturalistic situation in which a cockroach
accidently is made to fall into a drink of juice. In this setting, they could say
that the drink was not good to consume despite the removal of the cock-

roach, that another child's response that the juice was OK to drink was incorrect, and that a thirsty child should be given a new drink.

By no stretch of the imagination do these results mean that 3-year-olds are as proficient as adults in distinguishing between edible and inedible substances. Nevertheless, such findings suggest the presence of a substantial early knowledge in the food domain that may not be revealed when children do not share the purpose and relevance of questioning. A similar pattern of results has been reported in related research (Au, Sidle, & Rollins, 1993; Kalish, in press; Rosen & Rozin, 1993; Siegal, 1988; Siegal, Patty, & Eiser, 1990; Springer, 1992, Springer & Belk, 1994; see also S. A. Gelman, this volume).

2. Reasoning about Mental States in the Domain of Food and Contamination

An important aspect of a theory of mind that follows from a knowledge of false beliefs and deceptive appearances concerns the critical distinction between a lie and a mistake. Given their early sensitivity to food and contamination and their knowledge that substances that appear fresh may in reality be inedible, young children should be attuned to questions in this domain about problems concerning lies and mistakes. Correct responses on tasks devised to test their understanding would amount to a challenge to the position of Piaget (1932/1977) who maintained that young children regard all false statements as lies and have little or no understanding of lying as deceptive statements intended to mislead others. However, in research on the ability to distinguish between lies and mistakes, young children may not share the scientific purpose for an experimenter's questioning. Should their answers instead reflect their own local concerns, they might after all reason, "Why would an adult go to the trouble to raise the question of lying in a hypothetical protagonist's behavior unless the implication was to use this information in answering the test questions?" or "Why would a grown-up ask me about lying unless he thought that lying had occurred?" If so, preschoolers may be prepared to regard all false statements as lies. Particularly in a setting in which the purpose and relevance of the questioning are not readily apparent, they may infer that an adult would not ask about lying unless he or she thought that lying had taken place and they may be prompted to reply that lying had indeed occurred.

This analysis serves to reinterpret the findings of Wimmer, Gruber, and Perner (1985) who examined the effects produced by the order in which the children were asked questions. They gave 4- and 5-year-olds stories in which a protagonist was said to have the intention of truthfully communicating to a listener information based on a false belief about the location of an object. Half the children who recognized that the character held a false belief were first asked a lexical question, "Did (name of speaker) lie to (name of listener) or did he/she not lie to her/him?," followed by a moral reward question, "What would you give to (name of speaker), a gold star because he/she was nice to (name of listener) or a black point because he/she was nasty to her/him?" For the other half, the moral reward question was presented before the lexical one. Out of 29 children who first said in reply to the lexical question that the protagonist had lied, only 3 switched to evaluating his or her moral behavior positively; however, 22 out of 34 switched from having first evaluated an actor's moral behavior positively to saying in reply to the lexical question that the actor had lied. In fact, the suggestion of lying may have been so powerful that it undermined the viability of a mistake as the implicit alternative that was unstated in the lexical question, leading Wimmer et al.'s children to reverse their initial positive assessment of an actor's behavior.

Similarly, in the research of Strichartz and Burton (1990), adults and children aged 3 to 11 years were required to answer a triple-barrelled test question, "Was (the central story character) telling the truth, something else, or a lie?" The younger children aged 3 to 5 years often disregarded beliefs and intentions in judging all false statements as lies. However, even if the children could keep in mind three possibilities in the question, children who do not recognize that the purpose of the stories is to determine their knowledge about truth, lies, and mistakes may view the situation in terms of their own local concerns. They may regard the purpose as simply to determine whether a child's statement was correct and interpret the test question as simply, "Was (the character) right?" Consistent with this view, Bussey (1992) presented children as young as 4 years with stories about characters who committed misdeeds and then either lied or told the truth about their actions. She found that 4-year-olds distinguished lies from truthful confessions at a level that was above chance, though they were less accurate and less confident of their judgments than were 7-year-olds who scored almost perfectly. Although Bussey's results do not address the issue of children's early ability to distinguish a mistake from a lie, this work suggests that young children are capable of comprehending stories about deception when motives and behaviors are straightforward and described in simple terms.

In view of these concerns, Candida Peterson and I (Siegal & Peterson, in press) examined the extent to which young children distinguish mistakes from lies in the domain of food and contamination where they were asked questions in the form, "Did the protagonist lie or make a mistake?" rather than "Did he (or she) lie?" or "Did he (or she) lie or not lie?" By providing "mistake" as an alternative to "lie," we sought to counter the strong moral connotation of the term "lie" (that can be interpreted to imply that a questioner suspects that lying has occurred) and enable children to indicate that a false statement was not morally reprehensible. Thus their understanding of the purpose of the questioning (i.e., to determine the basis for how a substance could be wrongly regarded as edible) would be facilitated. In contrast to previous research, our hypothesis was that, in the domain of food and safety, they would be likely to recognize whether a false statement was a lie or a mistake.

In an initial investigation, children aged 3 to 5 years were presented with two teddy bears: one who had seen that bread that appeared edible was in reality contaminated with mold and another bear who had not seen the contaminant. Both of the bears were described as having told an uninformed friend that the bread was OK to eat. When asked to identify a bear as lying or mistaken rather than when asked to say whether the bear had lied or not, many children of all ages responded correctly that the bear who had seen the mold lied and that the bear who had not seen the mold made a mistake. In subsequent studies, 3-year-olds often recognized that the bear who told a lie had secret information that the mistaken bear lacked and were able to label this bear as naughtier. As indicated in related research on adults' reasoning about contamination (Occhipinti & Siegal, 1994), 3- and 5-year-olds were also significantly more likely to make the lie–mistake distinction in a setting involving contamination than in other situations that were irrelevant to food or safety and matched for perceived familiarity and danger.

Additional research may show that problems relevant to food and safety may not invariably serve to facilitate performance by means of highlighting the relevance of the task purpose and requirements. Nevertheless, in contrast to food-irrelevant danger stimuli such as snakes (Davey, 1995), a preparedness to adapt intelligent behavior to food safety is in accord with examples from studies of animal learning as well as the rapid human avoidance learning from foods paired with nausea (Revusky & Garcia, 1970; Rozin, 1976b). In this regard, the disgust reaction that occurs from contact with contaminants merits attention as it may lie at the roots of early moral cognition. According to the "ethics of divinity" that predominates in many cultures, the self is seen as a spiritual entity that strives to attain purity and sanctity and to avoid pollution.[4] Even in early childhood, a perpetrator who enacts a deception that exposes individuals to contaminants and jeopardizes their purity and sanctity is liable to be the recipient of moral condemnation. Further research is needed to investigate the extent to which children can transfer their understanding to other contexts, can distinguish between white lies and mistakes using terms that vary in their cultural appropriateness, and can match a reaction to a lie and mistake to an angry and neutral face, respectively, using techniques devised by Ekman (1985, 1994) and Izard (1993).

III. CONVERSATIONAL PROCESSES IN SUGGESTIBILITY AND CHILDREN'S RECOLLECTIONS OF EVENTS

A. Definitional Issues

If children require conversational enrichment in certain knowledge domains to follow the purpose and relevance of experimenters' questions on theory of mind tasks, they might also need such enrichment to enable them to gain an awareness of the information that is appropriate to report on questions about their memory for events. A timely example comes from the burgeoning research on children's suggestibility, and has particular application to their ability to provide reliable eyewitness testimony.

According to Gudjonsson (1986, p. 195), suggestibility can be defined as the extent to which persons "come to accept and subsequently incorporate post-event information" into their recollections of memory. In elaborating on this definition, Ceci, Huffman, Smith, and Loftus (1994, p. 390) have drawn a distinction between "memory-based suggestibility" in which misleading information genuinely alters memory traces and "socially based suggestibility" in which the contents of memory are "deferred" to children's beliefs about what the interviewer wants them to report.

In an extensive review of the literature, Ceci and Bruck (1993, pp. 432–433) have criticized the position that a central or core action in a story or event that involves the child is likely to diminish or even eliminate suggestibility compared with actions that are peripheral (Goodman, Rudy, Bottoms, & Aman, 1990). They claim that many studies do demonstrate genuine "memory-based" suggestibility because children can be misled to provide false reports about critical events that they personally experience. Thus, their failure on memory tests does not only reflect a difficulty in retrieving information (a retrieval deficiency) that has been stored in the original memory trace but a disruption of the original trace itself (a storage failure deficiency).

However, there can be a discrepancy between what adults and children find as central and peripheral issues (Johnson & Foley, 1984; Nelson, 1993b). Even in experiments that deal with child abuse issues, children may retain original details that they do not disclose because of the conversational implications inherent in the format of questioning. These implications convey to children that to respond correctly in experimental settings requires the recognition of what is central to answering the experimenter's questions rather than what is central to the original story details. For example, preschoolers have been asked questions about the personally involving details concerning fictitious events such as, "Did he touch your private parts?" or "How many times did he spank you?" Yet they may answer such questions incorrectly, not because the fictitious events have been stored in their memories, but because the questions themselves imply that these events had taken place. A rationale is needed for children to comprehend the purpose of this line of questioning. Otherwise, those who are inexperienced in the scientific purpose of conversations within experimental settings might reason, "Why would a grown-up ask me these questions unless he thought that these events had happened?" It is notable that adults as well as children are not always completely in agreement as to what constitutes the central, personally involving features of child abuse and that, historically, legal definitions of child abuse have varied within and between cultures (Eekelaar, 1984; Wald, Carlsmith, Leiderman, & Smith, 1983). Even if children in a particular culture do understand that the purpose of questions is to determine whether serious abuse had taken place, they may fail to report abuse or may recant their story, as the consequences of telling may appear to be worse than the consequences of further victimization (Berliner & Barbieri, 1984).

This discrepancy in perceptions of core and peripheral events can jeopardize the common grounding underlying conversations between children and the adults who are seeking to determine what children remember, and has consequences for what children report as remembered. As Bartlett (1932, p. 213) vividly observed, "remembering is not the re-excitation of innumerable fixed, lifeless and fragmentary traces. It is an imaginative reconstruction, or construction, built out of the relation of our attitude towards a whole active mass of organized past reactions or experience, and to a little outstanding detail which commonly appears in image or in language form." When adult or child listeners hear pieces of information that are semantically related, their comprehension and memory reflect a construction of ideas that depends on their knowledge and perception of their environment (Bransford & Franks, 1971; Bransford, Barclay, & Franks, 1972; Nelson, Fivush, Hudson, & Lucariello, 1983).

B. Demonstrations of Suggestibility in Children's Memories

Nevertheless, it has often been maintained, without reference to children's conversational awareness and issues of common grounding and constructive memory, that preschoolers' memories are genuinely more vulnerable than those of older children and adults and that they are more likely to incorporate misleading information in their performance on memory tasks (Ceci & Bruck, 1993).

A series of four studies carried out by Ceci, Ross, and Toglia (1987) surely stands to date as the most extensive demonstration of suggestibility in young children. In a first experiment designed to test the hypothesis that preschoolers' memory is more vulnerable than that of older children to the effects of misleading information, Ceci et al. read children who were aged 3 to 12 years a story about a girl named Loren and her first day at school. In the original story, the children were told that Loren had a stomachache from eating her eggs too fast at breakfast. The story was accompanied by pictures that illustrated the main events. On the following day, the children were met individually, usually by a different experimenter, who presented them with what Ceci et al. termed as either "biased" or "unbiased" information. In the biased condition, the children were provided with information that was inconsistent with the original story details for how and why Loren was sick. They were asked if they remembered a story about Loren who had a headache because she ate her cereal too fast. In the unbiased condition, the children were simply asked if they remembered a story about Loren who was sick from eating her breakfast too fast. Two days after the initial exposure to the story, the children were forced to choose between the original and the biased information in a recognition test in which pictures of the original details (e.g., stomachache) were paired with pictures of the biased information (e.g., headache). There were no significant age differences in the unbiased condition, with most children in all age groups accurately identifying the original information. By contrast, in the biased condition, preschoolers performed significantly worse than the older children. The biased information (e.g., in the form of a headache) appeared to intrude into children's recognition memory, apparently demonstrating their vulnerability to suggestion.

Subsequent experiments using different stories indicated that preschoolers' suggestibility was reduced but not eliminated when a 7-year-old child provided the biased information instead of an adult who may exert a "prestige effect" on responses. To rule out the possibility that both the original and biased information may have co-existed equally in the children's memories but that the biased information may have been chosen because it had been more recently introduced by a second experimenter, a modified recognition procedure was also employed in which the choice was between original and new information that was provided for the first time during the recognition memory test (McCloskey & Zaragoza, 1985). In this instance, suggestibility was also reduced but not eliminated.

The results reported by Ceci et al. are in line with the position of other investigators (e.g., Loftus & Davies, 1984; Yarmey, 1984) concerning the vulnerability of preschoolers' memories to suggestion as compared with the memories of older children and adults. Still, Ceci et al. (1987, p. 47) carefully note that aspects of their research may have been conducive to producing distortion in the children. They proceed to caution that such evidence indicates only that the memories of young children "can be distorted by postevent suggestions, not that they inevitably will be."

Given that memory is a construction of ideas influenced by the knowledge and experience that individuals bring to the task, possibly children may have perceived that the experimenters in the biased conditions of Ceci et al.'s research portrayed the details of the original story, such as those concerning Loren's temporary illness (in setting aside the Gricean quality rule), as unimportant or irrelevant because they themselves did not bother to get them right. Under these conditions, the children may have been prompted to regard the original story details as trivial. Instead of disclosing what they know on tests of their recognition memory, they may have interpreted the biased information in the conversation with the second experimenter to mean that a biased or altogether different alternative was an acceptable, or even a preferred, test choice when compared with the original story details. In their limited conversational experience, young children are apt to be not very proficient at sorting between the relevant and irrelevant details of messages. In comparison, older children and adults are more likely to share the experimenter's scientific purpose that biased information might be presented in order to test for the accuracy of memory for the original stimuli. They are more likely to block the implication in the biased conditions that the original story details are unimportant or irrelevant and to choose the original stimuli on the recognition tests. In studies where the aim is to retain the relevance of these details by making these the focus of conversation, children should be more likely to avoid the effects of suggestibility and to display their original memory of the story details.

According to Kasher (1991), an important property of conversational implicatures is that they are cancelable and can be "countermanded" (e.g., The statement "John read the book and intended to see the movie" implies a causal relationship that is canceled by the expanded statement "John read the book and intended to see the movie, but not necessarily in this order"). In research on children's conditional reasoning, Rumain, Connell, and Braine (1983) demonstrated that many children perform well on such reasoning tasks if the implications that convey a biconditional interpretation are "countermanded" through information that expands on the premises. In these studies, children could reason logically to the extent that differences between the performance of children and adults were mostly nonsignificant.

In a recent investigation that examined the degree to which such implications can be countermanded in studies of children's suggestibility (Siegal & Peterson, 1995), 4- and 5-year-olds heard a story similar to the one about Loren that was used by Ceci et al. (1993). They then were assigned to one of three conditions: unbiased, biased, and "conversationally enriched." Children in the conversationally enriched group were presented with biased information as were the children in the biased condition. In addition, a rationale was presented to cancel the implication that the biased information was relevant to producing an accurate report of the story ("Did the other preschoolers say that they remembered such a story because they were pretending in order to please the grown-up or because that was the real reason Loren was sick?"). As predicted, the memory of the children for original details in the conversationally enriched condition surpassed that of the children in the biased condition and was as accurate as that of the children who had received unbiased information. Nevertheless, the successful performance of the children who were presented with a rationale intended to counteract the implications that flow from the presentation of biased information may have reflected a willingness to refrain from choosing the biased alternative on a recognition test rather than an ability to remember the original story details.

In this regard, Morton, Hammersley, and Bekerian (1985) have proposed a "Headed Records" model designed for retrieving answers to explicit questions. This model concerns the retrieval of individual memory records or "memory units" that are assumed to be stored independently of each other. Each experienced event is stored as a record in a folder with a heading that functions as an "access key." Records attached to headers are searched by consulting the headers with a set of information called a "description." When a match has been found between a description and a heading, the associated record can be retrieved and evaluated. Morton et al. show that a strategic component is necessary to form an effective description of the information needed to gain access to the appropriate record. The processes required for forming descriptions involve the use of components such as temporal modifiers and environmental cues, in other words, time or place. Should two headings match a description, the more recent will be chosen unless a description can be created that discriminates between the alternatives. To formulate such a description spontaneously can be problematic for young children. They are required to learn that access to strategic components can create an appropriate description that leads to the retrieval of the desired record (Morton, 1990; Morton et al., 1985).

According to Morton et al.'s analysis, the results of research on memory distortion (e.g., Loftus, Miller, & Burns, 1978) can be reinterpreted in terms of interference that prevents the formation of descriptions that match with the headers of memory records. Asking subjects to recognize original and misleading information out of the order in which they have been exposed to such information is liable to interfere with matches of descriptions to the relevant header, which may be more remote in time. It impedes their performance on tests of recognition memory even though their memory for the original event has not disappeared but exists in a separate, unretrieved record. This memory can now be retrieved when temporal order is restored.

To investigate children's ability to remember event details when the questions are temporally specific, Peter Newcombe and I (Newcombe & Siegal, in press) presented 120 4- and 5-year-olds with a short story about a little girl, Karen, who was excited about her first day at school. Following Ceci et al.'s method, the critical two details of the story referred to what Karen ate too quickly for breakfast (e.g., cereal) and her ensuing sickness (e.g., a stomachache). The next day, a second experimenter introduced either biased information that was discrepant with the original details (e.g., eggs, headache) or unbiased information about the story. A control group did not receive any information at all. In the test phase one week later, the children were asked to recall the details of Karen's breakfast and illness by pointing to one of three choices that represented original, biased, and novel items. Two test questions were asked in either a specific format that ignored the relevance of the biased information and eliminated the need for children to make sense of this departure from the quality rule (i.e., "Do you remember how Karen was sick when you heard her story for the first time?") or a general, nonspecific format ("Do you remember how Karen was sick when you heard her story?"). The control group was asked only the questions in the nonspecific format.

As hypothesized, few children provided evidence of suggestibility when the questioning was specific. In the terminology of Morton et al.'s model, providing children with temporally specific cues in questions enabled them to create a description that enabled retrieval of the headed record of the original information that was more remote in time. For those children presented with the biased information, the specific questions significantly improved response recognition from 67 to 90%, a figure that did not differ from the 92% success rate achieved by the unbiased group. This pattern of responses was replicated in subsequent research in which children were presented with two items, either original and biased or original and novel, as recognition choices. Thus, the children's memory of the original details could not have merely signified their willingness to refrain from choosing the biased information, since, when provided with a choice between original and novel alternatives, they still chose the original.

This pattern of results addresses another issue in suggestibility research. Brainerd and Reyna (1988) and Howe (1991) have claimed that suggestibility effects such as those shown by Ceci et al. (1987) can be explained in terms of age differences in forgetting. Preschoolers are more "suggestible" than older children and adults because their memories for events are liable to be weaker even after an interval of only a week. Thus, their apparently greater suggestibility is an "epiphenomenon" of a memory trace impairment. According to Brainerd and Reyna, this impairment is not revealed in unbiased conditions that in fact could serve to enhance memory for original details through posing questions that could prompt recall such as "Do you remember the story about Karen who was sick from eating her breakfast too quickly?" Our research showed no differences in memory between children given unbiased information or none at all in a control condition. Indeed, it seems unlikely that there would be age differences over one week in forgetting such simple stories about a child who had a stomachache from eating toast on her first day of preschool, even without the alleged facilitation of information in the unbiased condition.

Further research is needed to determine whether preschoolers display evidence of suggestibility regardless of question format over a longer time interval. However, findings that children are better able to recall the original details of stories and to disregard information that is inconsistent with the original details if provided with specific questions support the position that memories for the original details of events and misleading information coexist (Morton et al., 1985). Regardless of the reason that adults' memory is distorted following exposure to misleading information (for discussion see Loftus, Feldman, & Dashiell, in press), children who are exposed to misinformation in the stories presented by Ceci et al. may not be aware that the purpose and relevance of the test questions are to determine whether they can remember the original story details. Compared with adults, they need to be given specific cues to retrieve the relevant information. Considerable research has now demonstrated that preschoolers are more likely to recall events that have a logical temporal sequence toward achieving an end result such as making a collage or playdough than to recall a sequence that does not have this logical structure (Fivush, Kuebli, & Clubb, 1992). Thus, young children often recall details accurately if provided with support in the form of specific temporal cues in questions and structured contexts (Fivush, 1993).

C. Suggestibility Reconsidered

Despite the considerable research to date, it cannot be concluded that children *as a rule* are more suggestible than adults according to their definition of genuine, memory-based suggestibility. Rather, when considered in terms of conversational processes that can influence children's answers to an investigator's questions, the potential for socially based suggestibility is widespread. It can occur even when there is a strong knowledge base and the events are salient and central but children do not share the purpose and relevance of questioning. In attempts to use Ceci et al.'s (1987) procedure to investigate suggestibility following exposure to misleading information or in related suggestibility research when care has been taken to ensure that there is an equally strong knowledge base and the events are indeed salient, young children are for the most part no less suggestible than older children and adults (e.g., Duncan, Whitney, & Kunen, 1982; Flin, Boon, Knox, & Bull, 1992; Howe, 1991; Marin, Holmes, Guth, & Kovac, 1979; Toglia, Hembrooke, Ceci, & Ross, 1992; Zaragoza, 1991).[5]

To be sure, Ceci et al. (1994) present evidence consistent with the hypothesis that young children's suggestibility is memory based and actually does distort their memory to a greater degree than older children and adults rather than existing as an artifact of their beliefs about what the investigator wants them to report. Two groups of children aged 3–4 and 5–6 years were given lists of events that either really occurred as reported by parents or were fictitiously generated by the experimenter. The children were told to try to recollect whether these events had happened on 7–10 separate occasions that were each separated by an interval of approximately 7–10 days. Both groups of children nearly always correctly recalled the real events. However, on the initial interview the younger children assented to 44% of the false events as opposed to 25% by the older ones. Comparable numbers for the two groups on the final interview were 32 and 36%, respectively. Videotaped interviews of these false assents were often rated as convincing by professionals. Ceci et al. (1994) interpret these results to demonstrate that children, particularly when young, can be easily implanted with false memories. They contend that young children are more likely than older ones to suffer from "source memory errors" in which a memory derived from one source is misattributed to another source and subjects do believe that they saw or heard what was suggested to them (Johnson, Hashtroudi, & Lindsay, 1993; Lindsay, 1990).

Yet, children as young as 3 years have been shown to be adept in distinguishing real from imagined objects and events in a simplified testing procedure where they are asked to sort items into those that are real (can be seen, touched, and acted upon) and those that are not (Wellman & Estes, 1986). Although preschoolers resist, at least in the short term, incorporating mothers' commentaries on events into their own autobiographical memories (Fivush, Hamond, Harsch, Singer, & Wolf, 1991), they may be particularly submissive with unfamiliar adults in testing settings and are unlikely to ask questions spontaneously with the aim of clarifying the procedure (Fivush, 1993). Thus, the suggestibility shown in the Ceci et al. (1994) study may be socially based rather than memory based and reflect considerable gratuitous concurrence, given both the high rate of assenting to any event in a list occurring regardless of whether it was real or not and the particularly low rate of denials by young children (Siegal, 1991b). Moreover, despite rating children's false assents as convincing, professionals themselves are vulnerable to stereotypes of children as naive and innocent and their judgments may be marked by a selective overreliance on what they perceive to be supportive evidence (Faust & Ziskin, 1988; Leippe & Romanczyk, 1989).

Even if children often commit source attribution errors as a result of memory-based suggestibility, there may remain some co-existence of memories for the original story details and the inconsistent or misleading information. Subjects may tacitly remember that they have heard or seen both, despite not recognizing which memory should be matched to the original details and which to the misleading information. But at times, the effects of misleading information on unconscious suggestibility in adult recognition of original details can be reduced by a procedure that requires subjects to identify the source of their memories for each test item (Lindsay, 1990). Similarly, children's recognition is facilitated where there are temporal modifiers in questions that serve to enhance the accessibility of the source or records of the original items through undermining the relevance of the misleading information to choices on memory recognition tasks. The absence of developmental differences in source memory misattributions under conditions when the original and misleading information is salient and children have access to strategic components in memory does not preclude the value of studying memory acceptance in young children; studies of the acceptance of information may demonstrate how new memories are created, especially when there are no prior memories to be retrieved (Loftus & Hoffman, 1989).

Both children and adults may produce suggestible responses in order to sustain a game, for reasons of personal gain, and to avoid embarrassment, especially when under stress (Ceci & Bruck, 1993, pp. 425–429). Compared to adults, young children's recollections of events are often far less complete and depend more on the time since the events occurred and on the format of the memory task and its relevance to previous knowledge and experience (Durkin, 1994; Poole & White, 1993). Yet, at least over relatively short periods of time such as weeks or months, the accuracy of the details that they do report often approaches that of adults (Fivush, 1993; List, 1986). At the same time, young children's reports are vulnerable in that children are motivated to comply to the demands of adults who are perceived as powerful, authority figures. They are more likely than older children and adults to accede to a style of well-intentioned, leading questioning that appears to offer no polite option for denial (e.g., "He was wearing a raincoat, wasn't he?"). In striving to cooperate in unfamiliar experimental procedures when they do not share the purpose for violations of conversational rules, they may be prompted to produce apparently suggestible responses on test questions that, in some circumstances, may not reflect the degree to which they are able to retain the original memories of events. Children's lack of relevant prior knowledge and their failure to utilize strategic memory skills spontaneously, such as employing temporal modifiers and environmental cues, contributes to their inability to organize disparate events into a cohesive whole or to relate one set of events to another. On recognition memory tests, they require explicit questioning that does not depart from the maxims or rules of conversation and is specific to time or place such as, "Do you remember how Karen was sick when you heard the story *for the first time?*"

IV. EXPLAINING THE TRANSITION

Research on the development of a theory of mind and on suggestibility in young children's memories points to a pivotal role for conversation in cognitive development and to the need for young children to be given explicit time and place cues and domain-relevant contexts to ensure that they share the purpose and conversational implications of an experimenter's questions. Older children and adults do not require these cues to the same extent and their performance is more likely to be across domains of knowledge. Neuropsychological and cultural explanations can be proposed to account for this transition.

A. Neuropsychological Changes Accompanying Conversational Awareness

In an evolutionary sense, it can be maintained that the ability to consider others' mental states possesses such adaptive value that a theory of mind deficit could be produced only by an insult to the brain (Whiten, 1991). Under the assumption that the poor theory of mind performance shown by children with autism reflects a neuropsychological deficit (see Endnote 3), Baron-Cohen et al. (1994) have sought to demonstrate that frontal lobe lesions are associated with an impairment in the aspect of possessing a theory of mind that involves the recognition of mental state terms. Their first study compared 15 children with autism with a group of 15 intellectually handicapped children matched for mental age. Each child in the two groups was given a list of mental state (target) words such as "think" and nonmental state (foil) words such as "school" and was asked, "Can the mind do this?" Using a pass criterion of 6 out of 8 possible correct for each of the target and foil words, the children with autism were significantly less likely to˙pass this list than the the mentally handicapped children. In a second study, the same list was then given to healthy normal male volunteers in their early 20s. To determine brain activation in the frontal lobes while subjects heard mental state and nonmental state words similar to those given in the first study, single photon emission computerized tomography was used. Based on previous neurological and animal studies, Baron-Cohen et al. predicted that there would be an increased cerebral blood flow in the orbitofrontal cortex during the mental state term recognition task relative to an adjacent frontal-polar area and relative to a control task in which subjects heard body-related words such as "finger." The prediction was partly confirmed. A significantly increased flow during the mental state task occurred in the right orbitofrontal and frontal-polar cortex areas relative to the left frontal-polar cortex.[6]

These results can be viewed in terms of research on hemispheric specialization and conversational understanding. Thatcher (1992, p. 44) has reported that a surge of right frontal pole growth occurs at 4 years of age and remarks that this surge coincides with children's successful performance on theory of mind tasks. Thatcher's observation fits with the position that theory of mind performance reflects abilities in conversation, since considerable research has shown that the right hemisphere predominates in influencing the interpretation of conversation (Kaplan, Brownell, Jacobs, & Gardner, 1990; Molloy, Brownell, & Gardner, 1990; Zaidel, 1985) and in distinguishing internal emotional states (Cicone, Wapner, & Gardner, 1980). For example, patients with right hemisphere damage (RHD) have difficulty in interpreting indirect requests and commands and rely on the literal meanings of conversation rather than pragmatic cues that involve deriving meaning from contextual information (Foldi, 1987; Weylman, Brownell, Roman, & Gardner, 1989). They also often do not recognize the relevance of the theme of a story in understanding narratives (Schneiderman, Murasugi, & Saddy, 1992).

In a recent study (Siegal, Carrington, & Radel, in press), RHD and left hemisphere damaged (LHD) adult patients were compared in their ability to correctly draw inferences in false belief tasks similar to those employed by Siegal and Beattie (1991). The RHD but not the LHD patients were found to have difficulties similar to those of young children in understanding the conversational implications of test questions (e.g., "Where will Sam look for his puppy?"). Most reported that a central story character would look for a pet in the place where it was really located instead of where the character believed it was located. Removal of the need to infer the questioner's meaning by asking where would the target character "look first" for his or her pet enabled both RHD and LHD subjects to make correct false belief predictions.

However, in contrast to earlier research with children, patients who were incorrect on the false belief test question that required an implication were also often incorrect on the control question ("Where is the puppy really?"). This difference may be attributed to methodological differences between studies. During the story presentation in Siegal and Beattie's (1991) study in which the children were able to answer the control question correctly by stating the real location of the pets, the experimenter referred to miniature figures and to locations inside a doll house. In this study, the patients did not receive the task in the form of a visual presentation. Thus the two locations of the pet—where it was "really" and where it was believed to be—may have been less salient and hence less easily remembered.

In this regard, Moya, Benowitz, Levine, and Finklestein (1986; see also McDonald & Wales, 1986) have reported that RHD subjects are impaired on a number of tasks involving visuospatial abilities and that the recall of the details of verbal passages was moderately correlated with visuospatial ability. Although the tasks used in the present study were simpler than those used by Moya et al., it is likely that some visuospatial ability was required to respond correctly in this study, as each task required subjects to deal with two locations and to predict where the protagonist would look. Recently, Jonides et al. (1993) have argued that one component of working memory, which is essential for language comprehension, is a set of buffers that temporarily store information in either visuospatial or phonological form. Using positron emission tomography scans to measure regional cerebral blood flow in subjects who were engaged in perception and memory tasks, they found that significantly increased activation in areas of the right hemisphere accompany the performance of tasks involving spatial working memory processes. Whereas it is possible that the incorrect responses of the RHD subjects on the false belief task were related to a working memory deficit caused by visuospatial difficulties rather than to pragmatic language difficulties, the fact that the RHD subjects on the "look first" task answered the test and control questions correctly detracts from this explanation. Moreover, the difficulties of RHD patients on language comprehension tasks are not merely restricted to those requiring a representation of spatial information (Delis, Wapner, Gardner, & Moses, 1983).

Thus, a viable explanation for the patients' difficulties in the Siegal et al. study resides once more in the domain of pragmatic language comprehension. The RHD patients may have interpreted the control question "Where is it really?" to mean that they should name the location other than the one they had given in answer to the test question. The patients may have felt that in order to be consistent with their response to the test question, they should indicate that the pet was really in the other location. The wording of the control question may also have indicated to adults that the one location could not be the correct answer to both the test question and the control question.

Sodian, Taylor, Harris, and Perner (1991) and Karmiloff-Smith (1992, pp. 169–170) have speculated that 3-year-olds are constrained by a conceptual deficit with a neuropsychological underpinning. This deficit results in a theory of mind impairment that precludes the ability to understand how actions can lead to deceptive beliefs and outcomes. However, the neuropsychological underpinning may be in the form of a limitation that is pragmatic rather than conceptual and thus can be overcome by conversational enrichment in the form of temporal cues. Fodor (1992) and Leslie (1994) have proposed that an increase in "computation resources" is necessary to answer theory of mind questions without aids. Possibly this increase in processing questions selectively as intended by adult conversationalists may be linked to neurological growth and, in particular, an increasing right hemisphere specialization for the pragmatic interpretation of language.

Neither the Baron-Cohen et al. nor Siegal et al. studies were designed to probe for localization of function within the right hemisphere; this issue is in need of further research. With respect to source attribution errors in remembering the temporal order of items, dysfunction within the frontal lobe may be seen as a prime candidate (Johnson, Hashtroudi, & Lindsay, 1993). It would also be of interest to examine the theory of mind performance of different populations of adult and child patients who have undergone a period of conversational enrichment during rehabilitation.

B. Culture, Conversation, and Mental States

Although at times neglected in studies that have focused on universal processes irrespective of the subject domain, many of children's responses on measures that require conversational understanding plainly reflect processes that are specific to culture and context (Cole, 1985; Gauvain, 1995; Hirschfeld & Gelman, 1994; Tomasello, 1995). As Brothers and Ring (1992) state, any neuroethological theory of the development of social cognition must take into account the plasticity of culturally acquired social judgments.

Inspired by Vygotsky's (1978) writings on the relation between culture and language use, Nelson (1993a, 1993b; see also Bruner, 1991) has proposed a sociocultural account of autobiographical memory that has implications for the role of conversation in research on suggestibility in children's memories and understanding of mental states. Nelson contends that the ability to construct and maintain a story about participation in an event allows the child to accurately remember past events. This ability to employ a "narrative form" in memory emerges at about the age of 4 years (Nelson, 1992). Whereas, at the age of 2 and 3, children are fluent in talking about pretence and mental states in the here and now, language at 4 years has now become a representational system through which children have come to share a wealth of conversational experiences with others in their culture such as parents, peers, and preschool teachers. They are adept at extracting coherent information from stories that have been read to them and are keen to use language to relate their mental states to others in an entertaining way that will capture the attention of listeners. They use their conversation to enter into the social and cultural history of their communities and to reinstate their experiences to themselves and others over time. They thus acquire knowledge that time and place are relevant strategic components of answering questions about memory and mind and become well placed to share the relevance and purpose of an investigator's questions. To provide correct answers on false belief tasks or on memory recognition tests following exposure to biased information, preschoolers may benefit from an experimental, conversational setting that encompasses a "narrative frame" that makes events understandable, highlights strategic memory components of time and place, and precludes source attribution errors.

In their studies of autobiographical memory, Fivush and Hamond (1990) and Nelson (1992, 1993a, 1993b) report that young children are significantly more likely to demonstrate accurate memories if these had previously been discussed in conversations with adults who in their narration elaborated on the source, place, and time of events rather than with adults who emphasized the retrieval of information in the here and now. These interactions contribute to a shared understanding of what is required in response to questions about memory and to a coherent organization of memories that can be retrieved. There may be appreciable cultural differences between the metaphors underlying the conceptualization of the mind as a vehicle for sharing information. Whereas Western cultures are likely to employ the metaphor of the mind as a machine (e.g., "I'm a little rusty today. I've run out of steam"), Japanese culture likens the mind to air or to an atmosphere that has family connotations and is not bounded within the individual person (Kashima, 1994). It can be speculated that use of the family metaphor reflects the choice and success of Japanese methods of transmitting information in schools through collective comprehension activities (Hatano & Inagaki, 1991).

Bauer (1993) points out that this type of analysis raises questions such as whether the development of the narrative form is necessary for autobiographical memory, whether children from non-Western cultures in which memory talk is not permitted are delayed in the development of autobiographical memory, and whether children who experience such memory talk are better at both their recognition and free recall of the past or only the latter. If it is only affecting free recall, perhaps the elaboration provided by narration is one that can be best interpreted in terms of participation effects that influence the style in which children can display their memory of events rather than in terms of memory, per se. However, this interpretation is at variance with the results from a study on the effects of participation on free recall and recognition in 4- and 7-year-olds carried out by Rudy and Goodman (1991). Participating in an event instead of watching had no effect on free recall and in answers to specific questions but, for 4-year-olds, participants were more likely to resist suggestibility in response to misleading questions. Similarly, Chandler and Hala (1994) report a series of theory of mind studies in which preschoolers who are enlisted as active participants succeed well on false belief tasks.

Neisser (1990, p. 337) has observed, following MacIntyre (1984), that participation in conversation is a highly significant cultural practice, as "good conversation requires not just memory but also sensitivity and honesty and intelligence, and occasionally courage as well." Participation that clarifies and explicates the relevance and purpose of questions can take place with parents and siblings. As Grusec and Goodnow (1994, p. 10) note, conversational understanding is central to parent–child relations. In this connection, Dunn (1994) shows that parent–child relations may provide a special focus for the conversational transmission of knowledge of mental states in that the children of parents who engage in "causal talk" about events that are influenced by mental states are more likely to perform well on false belief tasks. Such causal talk must implicitly be based on the principle of "temporal priority," that causes must precede effects and thus are liable to highlight the temporal modifiers necessary to retrieve items in memory. Dunn also notes that performance on false belief tasks is related to shared humor (that is often about disgusting themes), which relies on conversational inferences as well as children's ability to demonstrate "connectedness" in communication through taking into account what others say in their own messages.

Exposure to a greater number of conversational partners may acquaint children with the means to understand the purpose and relevance intended by those who ask questions about memory and mind through experience in organizing their narratives in the manner of a proficient storyteller. In a study that is reminiscent of the finding that geographically nonisolated children succeed more on Piagetian role-taking tasks than do isolated children (Hollos & Cowan, 1973), Perner, Ruffman, and Leekam (1994; see also Lewis, Freeman, Hagestadt, & Douglas, 1994) have reported that children with older siblings do better on false belief tasks than children without. Fivush et al. (1991) have shown that very young children (30- to 35-months-old) who are asked to remember autobiographical events recall different but still accurate details to mothers who have had access to these events and strangers who have not. In some non-Western cultures, this process may be engendered by special forms of teasing between persons of the same or different ages. For example, in Schieffelin's (1986, 1990) account, the Kaluli prefer not to talk about the minds of other persons and maintain that they do not know what is inside.[7] Rather, their speech and behavior is often directed toward predicting and shaping the outcome of a listener's interaction. Teasing is especially used by many conversational partners such as parents, siblings, and cousins as a device of creative and, at times, enjoyable tension to socialize children's behavior particularly with regard to their food habits. Thus, though the means or the focus (on others' mind or behavior) may differ from culture to culture, in conversing with multiple partners, children may be prompted to develop their narrative abilities and to present a coherent, comprehensive account of what they know and remember about others.

V. CONCLUDING REMARKS: TOWARD RESOLVING MORE THAN ONE PARADOX

In recent years, nonverbal techniques such as habituation have been used to investigate cognitive development in infants. In this way, an impressive range of core abilities in understanding the physical world has been shown in young infants (Gelman, 1993; Mehler & Bertoncini, 1988; Spelke, 1994). On these measures, infants cannot misrepresent the questions because none are being asked. Paradoxically, preschoolers have often been observed to fail one verbal task after another immediately after such tasks have been devised to take advantage of the fact that children aged 3 and 4 years now can converse fluently. This paradox has been accompanied by a second that I introduced at the beginning of the chapter: that, although young children are very fluent in conversation, they have difficulty understanding the purpose and relevance of questions in specialized, experimental settings.

Attention to children's conversational understanding with its cultural and neuropsychological underpinnings goes some way toward resolving these two paradoxes. In some domains of understanding, such as number, their difficulties may be conceptual as well as linguistic and require a conceptual restructuring in their thinking. In such instances, their thinking and behavior may be based on prepotent tendencies that are accompanied by a great deal of difficulty in exerting flexibility across contexts and a lack of "inhibitory control" that is required to select the correct alternative from the choices available (Gerstadt, Hong, & Diamond, 1994).

However, in certain key areas, aids in the form of specific adherence to conversational rules can permit the child to resist such tendencies and, for example, to base their belief predictions on something other than the present state of affairs. Once care has been taken to remove the need for them to share the implications of questions, young children are often able to resist suggestibility and can produce a more accurate portrait of memories and beliefs. They may also be aided by a preparedness to learn in certain knowledge domains, such as in the domain of food and contamination.

In this way, the early period in children's cognitive development is one in which the conversational foundations of expressing what they know are put in place. Perhaps this period is necessary and adaptive for children to consolidate a toehold in certain core areas of knowledge that will serve them well in the future.

Acknowledgments

Thanks are due to Terry Au, Rochel Gelman, Peter Newcombe, Robyn Nugent, and Candida Peterson for their helpful comments on an earlier version of this chapter. Preparation of this chapter was facilitated through support from the Australian Research Council.

Endnotes

1. Although the Gricean account of conversation is incomplete and leaves major issues unresolved (for a discussion, see Sperber & Wilson, 1986; Wilson, 1994), the rules proposed by Grice are promissory notes or "conversational rules of thumb," which precede a general theory of collective action (Clark, 1987), and it is widely acknowledged that this framework allows insight into the nature of communication processes (P. Brown & Levinson, 1987; Clark, 1992; Hilton, 1990, 1995; Levinson, 1989).
2. The extent to which this task corresponds to an implicit–explicit distinction is unclear (for a discussion of the several ways in which this distinction has been made, see Durkin, 1994). The children on Clements and Perner's implicit measure were often prompted to possess at least some explicit knowledge through an overt verbal response to a verbal question, though these verbalizations were apparently not of interest to Clements and Perner.

3. Conversational processes might also influence the performance of children with autism whose difficulties on false belief tasks have been often attributed to a specific, neurological deficit (Baron-Cohen, Leslie, & Frith, 1985; Frith, 1989, 1992; Frith, Morton, & Leslie, 1991). Frith and Happé (1994) have now shown that even the minority of children with autism who perform well on theory of mind tasks display a "weak central coherence" in the integration of information. They have difficulty in story comprehension, in filling in conversational gaps, and in recognizing a change in context. Thus, while autistic children may suffer from a neurological deficit, their theory of mind performance might also be seen as an indication of pragmatic difficulties in communication. Deaf children without autism are also limited in their exposure to conversation and perform similarly to children with autism on theory of mind tasks, although possibly for different reasons (Peterson & Siegal, 1995). Initial research has shown that providing either group with conversational enrichment in the form of "look first" questions improves performance but not to the level found in normal children (Eisenmajer & Prior, 1991; Peterson & Siegal, 1995). As parents of children with autism have been found to share some of the same conversational abilities as their offspring (Landa, Folstein, & Isaacs, 1991), the theory of mind performance of children with autism may suffer from both a genetic component and an impoverished conversational environment.

4. Haidt, Koller, and Dias (1993) and Shweder, Mahapatra, and Miller (1987) have shown that an "ethics of divinity" is preeminent in the moral judgments of children in many parts of the world, including such heavily populated representations of humanity as Brazil and India. According to this system of ethics, the self is seen as a spiritual entity that strives to avoid pollution and to attain purity and sanctity. The disgust associated with early contamination sensitivity jeopardizes adherence to this code so that the recognition of deception in this domain may engender an initial awareness of the lie–mistake distinction. Affect and relevance has long been shown to affect judgments of others (Forgas, 1995). Disgust such as that which occurs when deceived about the presence of contaminants can translate into a moral emotion of anger directed toward a protagonist (Nemeroff & Rozin, 1994; Rozin, Lowery, & Ebert, 1994). In this sense, the contamination disgust that is reflected in an early understanding of the lie–mistake distinction may be an initial source of reasoning about health, mental states, and morality.

5. The application of experimental research findings on children's suggestibility to courtroom testimony is controversial and far from straightforward (Davies, 1993; McGough, 1994; Spencer & Flin, 1990). A confident appraisal of children's conversational abilities in this setting awaits further extensive research.

6. In their original report, Baron-Cohen et al. (1994) claimed that the only significant difference occurred in the right orbitofrontal cortex area relative to the left frontal-polar cortex. However, an inspection of the data shows that the difference in right frontal-polar relative to the left frontal-cortex was also significant, $t(11) = 3.78$, $p < .00305$. This figure is significant even at the probability level of $p < .008$ that had been corrected for six pairwise comparisons among cortical areas (.05/6).

7. That the Kaluli prefer not to talk about the mind of course does not mean that their responses on theory of mind tasks would necessarily differ from those of children in other societies. Avis and Harris (1991) suggest that particular cultures might elaborate upon core concepts such as beliefs and desires in distinctive ways.

References

Au, T. K., Sidle, A. L., & Rollins, K. B. (1993). Developing an intuitive understanding of conservation and contamination: Invisible particles as a plausible mechanism. *Developmental Psychology, 29*, 286–299.

Avis, J., & Harris, P. L. (1991). Belief-desire reasoning among Baka children: Evidence for a universal conception of mind. *Child Development, 62*, 460–467.

Baldwin, D. (1993). Infants' ability to consult the speaker for clues to word reference. *Journal of Child Language, 20*, 395–418.

Barley, N. (1983). *The innocent anthropologist: Notes from a mud hut*. Harmondsworth, England: Penguin.

Baron-Cohen, S., Leslie, A. M., & Frith, U. (1985). Does the autistic child have a theory of mind? *Cognition, 21*, 37–46.

Baron-Cohen, S., Ring, H., Moriarty, J., Schmitz, B., Costa, D., & Ell, P. (1994). Recognition of mental state terms: Clinical findings in children with autism and a functional neuroimaging study of normal adults. *British Journal of Psychiatry, 165*, 640–649.

Bartlett, F. C. (1932). *Remembering*. Cambridge: Cambridge University Press.

Bauer, P. J. (1993). Identifying subsystems of autobiographical memory: Commentary on Nelson. *Minnesota Symposia on Child Psychology, 26*, 25–38.

Beal, C., & Belgrad, S. L. (1990). The development of message evaluation skills in young children. *Child Development, 61*, 705–712.

Berliner, L., & Barbieri, M. K. (1984). Children's testimony. *Journal of Social Issues, 40*, 125–137.

Bonitatibus, G. (1988). What is said and what is meant in referentail communication. In J. W. Astington, P. L. Harris, & D. R. Olson (Eds.), *Developing theories of mind* (pp. 326–338). Cambridge: Cambridge University Press.

Brainerd, C. J., & Reyna, V. F. (1988). Memory loci of suggestibility development: Comment on Ceci, Ross, and Toglia (1987). *Journal of Experimental Psychology: General, 117*, 197–200.

Bransford, J. D., Barclay, J. R., & Franks, J. J. (1972). Sentence memory: A constructive versus interpretive approach. *Cognitive Psychology, 3*, 193–209.

Bransford, J. D., & Franks, J. J. (1971). The abstraction of linguistic ideas. *Cognitive Psychology, 2*, 331–350.

Bretherton, I., & Beeghly, M. (1982). Talking about internal states: The acquisition of an explicit theory of mind. *Developmental Psychology, 18*, 906–921.

Broerse, J., & Elias, G. (1994). Changes in the content and timing of mothers' talk to infants. *British Journal of Developmental Psychology, 12*, 131–145.

Brothers, L., & Ring, B. (1992). A neuroethological framework for the representation of minds. *Journal of Cognitive Neuroscience, 4*, 107–118.

Brown, P., & Levinson, S. C. (1987). *Politeness: Some universals in language usage*. New York: Cambridge University Press.

Brown, R., & Hanlon, C. (1970). Derivational complexity and the order of acquisition in child speech. In J. R. Hayes (Ed.), *Cognition and the development of language* (pp. 155–207). New York: Wiley.

Bruner, J. (1991). The narrative construction of reality. *Critical Inquiry, 18*, 1–21.

Bussey, K. (1992). Lying and truthfulness: Children's definitions, standards, and evaluative reactions. *Child Development, 63*, 129–137.

Ceci, S. J., & Bruck, M. (1993). Suggestibility of the child witness: A historical review and synthesis. *Psychological Bulletin, 113*, 403–439.

Ceci, S. J., Huffman, M. L., Smith, E., & Loftus, E. F. (1994). Repeatedly thinking about a non-event: Source misattributions among preschoolers. *Consciousness and Cognition, 3*, 388–407.

Ceci, S. J., Ross, D. F., & Toglia, M. P. (1987). Suggestibility of children's memory: Psycholegal implications. *Journal of Experimental Psychology: General, 116*, 38–49.

Chandler, M., & Hala, S. (1994). The role of personal involvement in the assessment of early false belief skills. In C. Lewis & P. Mitchell (Eds.), *Children's early understanding of mind: Origins and development* (pp. 403–425). Hove, England. Erlbaum.

Cicone, M., Wapner, W., & Gardner, H. (1980). Sensitivity to emotional expressions and situations in organic patients. *Cortex, 16,* 145–158.

Clark, H. H. (1987). Relevance to what? *Behavioral and Brain Sciences, 10,* 714–715.

Clark, H. H. (1992). *Arenas of language use.* Chicago: University of Chicago Press.

Clark, H. H., & Brennan, S. E. (1991). Grounding in communication. In L. B. Resnick, J. M. Levine, & S. Behrens (Eds.), *Perspectives on socially shared cognition* (pp. 127–149). Washington, DC: American Psychological Association.

Clements, W. A., & Perner, J. (1994). Implicit understanding of belief. *Cognitive Development, 9,* 377–395.

Cole, M. (1985). The zone of proximal development: Where culture and cognition create each other. In J. V. Wertsch (Ed.), *Culture, communication, and cognition: Vygotskian perspectives* (pp. 146–161). New York: Cambridge University Press.

Cords, M. (1992). Social versus ecological intelligence. *Behavioral and Brain Sciences, 15,* 151.

Cross, T. G. (1977). Mothers' speech adjustments: The contribution of selected child listener variables. In C. Snow & C. A. Ferguson (Eds.), *Talking to children: Language input and acquisition* (pp. 151–188). Cambridge: Cambridge University Press.

Davey, G. (1995). Preparedness and phobias: Specific evolved associations or a generalized expectancy bias? *Behavioral and Brain Sciences, 18,* 289–297.

Davies, G. (1993). Children's memory for other people: An integrative review. *Minnesota Symposia on Child Psychology, 26,* 123–157.

Delis, D. C., Wapner, W., Gardner, H., & Moses, J. A. (1983). The contribution of the right hemisphere to the organization of paragraphs. *Cortex, 19,* 43–50.

De Villiers, J. G., & De Villiers, P. A. (1978). *Language acquisition.* Cambridge, MA: Harvard University Press.

Donaldson, M. (1978). *Children's minds.* Glasgow: Fontana.

Dunbar, R. I. M. (1993). Co-evolution of neocortex size, group size and language in humans. *Behavioral and Brain Sciences, 16,* 681–735.

Duncan, I. M., Whitney, P., & Kunen, S. (1982). Integration of visual and verbal information in children's memories. *Child Development, 53,* 1215–1223.

Dunn, J. (1994). Changing minds and changing relationships. In C. Lewis & P. Mitchell (Eds.), *Children's early understanding of mind: Origins and development* (pp. 297–310). Hove, England: Erlbaum.

Durkin, K. (1994). The lure and language of implicit memory: A developmental perspective. In N. Ellis (Ed.), *Implicit and explicit learning of languages* (pp. 523–548). London: Academic Press.

Eades, D. (1982). You gotta know how to talk . . . Information seeking in South-East Queensland Aboriginal Society. *Australian Journal of Linguistics, 2,* 61–82.

Eekelaar, J. (1984). *Family law and social policy* (2nd ed.). London: Weidenfeld & Nicolson.

Eisenmajer, R., & Prior, M. (1991). Cognitive linguistic correlates of 'theory of mind' ability in autistic children. *British Journal of Developmental Psychology, 9,* 351–364.

Ekman, P. (1985). *Telling lies.* New York: Norton.

Ekman, P. (1994). Strong evidence for universals in facial expressions: A reply to Russell's mistaken critique. *Psychological Bulletin, 115,* 268–287.

Faust, D., & Ziskin, J. (1988). The expert witness in psychology and psychiatry. *Science, 241,* 31–35.

Ferguson, C. (1977). Baby talk as a simplified register. In C. Snow & C. A. Ferguson (Eds.), *Talking to children: Language input and acquisition* (pp. 209–235). Cambridge: Cambridge University Press.

Fivush, R. (1993). Developmental perspectives on autobiographical recall. In G. S. Goodman & B. L. Bottoms (Eds.), *Child witnesses: Understanding and improving testimony* (pp. 1–24). New York: Guildford.

Fivush, R., & Hamond, N. R. (1990). Autobiographical memory across the preschool years:

Toward reconceptualizing childhood amnesia. In R. Fivush & J. Hudson (Eds.), *Knowing and remembering in young children* (pp. 223–248). New York: Cambridge University Press.

Fivush, R., Hamond, N. R., Harsch, N., Singer, N., & Wolf, A. (1991). Content and consistency in young children's autobiographical recall. *Discourse Processes, 14,* 373–388.

Fivush, R., Kuebli, J., & Clubb, P. A. (1992). The structure of events and event representation: A developmental analysis. *Child Development, 63,* 188–201.

Flavell, J. H., Mumme, D. L., Green, F. L., & Flavell, E. R. (1992). Young children's understanding of different types of beliefs. *Child Development, 63,* 960–977.

Flin, R., Boon, J., Knox, N., & Bull, R. (1992). Children's memories following a five month delay. *British Journal of Psychology, 83,* 323–336.

Fodor, J. (1992). A theory of the child's theory of mind. *Cognition, 44,* 283–296.

Foldi, N. S. (1987). Appreciation of pragmatic interpretations of indirect commands: Comparison of right and left hemisphere brain-damaged patients. *Brain and Language, 31,* 88–108.

Forgas, J. P. (1995). The affect infusion model (AIM): Review and an integrative theory of mood effects on judgments. *Psychological Bulletin, 117,* 39–66.

Frith, U. (1989). *Autism: Explaining the enigma.* Oxford: Blackwell.

Frith, U. (1992). Cognitive development and cognitive deficit. *Psychologist, 3,* 13–19.

Frith, U., & Happé, F. (1994). Autism: Beyond the theory of mind. *Cognition, 50,* 115–132.

Frith, U., Morton, J., & Leslie, A. M. (1991). The cognitive basis of a biological disorder: Autism. *Trends in Neuroscience, 14,* 433–438.

Gauvain, M. (1995). Thinking in niches: Sociocultural influences on cognitive development. *Human Development, 38,* 25–45.

Gelman, R. (1993). A rational-constructivist account of early learning about numbers and objects. *Psychology of Learning and Motivation, 30,* 61–95.

Gelman, R., & Shatz, M. (1977). Appropriate speech adjustments: The operation of conversational constraints on talk to two-year-olds. In M. Lewis & L. A. Rosenblum (Eds.), *Interaction, conversation, and the development of language* (pp. 27–61). New York: Wiley.

Gerstadt, C. L., Hong, Y. J., & Diamond, A. (1994). The relationship between cognition and action: Performance of children $3\frac{1}{2}$–7 years old on a Stroop-like day-night test. *Cognition, 53,* 123–153.

Goodman, G. S., Rudy, L., Bottoms, B., & Aman, C. (1990). Children's concerns and memory: Issues of ecological validity in the study of children's eyewitness testimony. In R. Fivush & J. Hudson (Eds.), *Knowing and remembering in young children* (pp. 249–284). New York: Cambridge University Press.

Grice, H. P. (1975). Logic and conversation. In P. Cole & J. L. Morgan (Eds.), *Syntax and semantics: Vol. 3. Speech acts* (pp. 41–58). New York: Academic Press.

Grusec, J. E., & Goodnow, J. J. (1994). Impact of parental discipline methods on the child's internalization of values: A reconceptualization of current points of view. *Developmental Psychology, 30,* 4–19.

Gudjonsson, G. (1986). The relationship between interrogative suggestibility and acquiescence: Empirical findings and theoretical implications. *Personality and Individual Differences, 7,* 195–199.

Haidt, J., Koller, S. H., & Dias, M. G. (1993). Affect, culture, and morality, or is it wrong to eat your dog? *Journal of Personality and Social Psychology, 63,* 613–628.

Harris, P. L. (1996). Desires, beliefs, and language: The role of conversation. In P. Carruthers & P. K. Smith (Eds.), *Theories of Theories of Mind* (pp. 200–220). Cambridge: Cambridge University Press.

Hatano, G., & Inagaki, K. (1991). Sharing cognition through collective comprehension activity. In L. B. Resnick, J. M. Levine, & S. Teasley (Eds.), *Perspectives on socially shared cognition* (pp. 331–348). Washington, DC: American Psychological Association.

Heath, S. B. (1983). *Ways with words.* New York: Cambridge University Press.

Hilton, D. J. (1990). Conversational processes and causal explanation. *Psychological Bulletin,* *107,* 65–81.

Hilton, D. J. (1995). The social context of reasoning: Conversational inference and rational judgment. *Psychological Bulletin, 118,* 248–271.

Hirschfield, L. A., & Gelman, S. A. (Eds.). (1994). *Mapping the mind: Domain specificity in cognition and culture.* New York: Cambridge University Press.

Hollos, M., & Cowan, P. A. (1973). Social isolation and cognitive development: Logical operations and role-taking abilities in three Norwegian social settings. *Child Development, 44,* 630–641.

Howe, M. L. (1991). Misleading children's story recall: Forgetting and reminiscence of the facts. *Developmental Psychology, 27,* 746–762.

Hughes, M., & Grieve, R. (1983). On asking children bizarre questions. In M. Donaldson, R. Grieve, & C. Pratt (Eds.), *Child development and education.* Oxford: Blackwell.

Izard, C. (1993). Four systems for emotion activation: Cognitive and noncognitive processes. *Psychological Review, 100,* 68–90.

Johnson, M. K., & Foley, M. A. (1984). Differentiating fact from fantasy: The reliability of children's memory. *Journal of Social Issues, 40,* 33–56.

Johnson, M. K., Hashtroudi, S., & Lindsay, D. S. (1993). Source monitoring. *Psychological Bulletin, 114,* 3–28.

Jonides, J., Smith, E. E., Koeppe, R. A., Awh, E., Minoshima, S., & Mintun, M. A. (1993). Spatial working memory in humans as revealed by PET. *Nature, 363,* 623–625.

Kalish, C. W. (in press). Preschoolers' understanding of germs as invisible mechanisms. *Cognitive Development.*

Kaplan, J. A., Brownell, H. H., Jacobs, J. R., & Gardner, H. (1990). The effects of right hemisphere damage on the pragmatic interpretation of conversational remarks. *Brain and Language, 38,* 315–333.

Karmiloff-Smith, A. (1992). *Beyond modularity: A developmental perspective on cognitive science.* Cambridge, MA: MIT Press.

Kasher, A. (1991). On the pragmatic modules: A lecture. *Journal of Pragmatics, 16,* 381–397.

Kashima, Y. (1994). Cultural metaphors of the mind and the organization. In A.-M. Bouvy, F. J. R. van de Vijver, P. Boski, & P. Schmitz (Eds.), *Journeys into cross cultural psychology* (pp. 351–363). Amsterdam: Swets & Zeitlinger.

Kister, M. C., & Patterson, C. J. (1980). Children's conceptions of the causes of illness: Understanding of contagion and use of immanent justice. *Child Development, 51,* 839–849.

Labov, W. (1972). *Language in the inner city: Studies in the black English venacular.* Philadelphia: University of Pennsylvania Press.

Landa, R., Folstein, S. E., & Isaacs, C. (1991). Spontaneous narrative-discourse performance of parents of autistic children. *Journal of Speech and Hearing Research, 34,* 1339–1345.

Leippe, M. R., & Romanczyk, A. (1989). Reactions to child (versus adult) witnesses. *Law and Human Behavior, 13,* 103–132.

Leslie, A. M. (1994). Pretending and believing: Issues in the theory of ToMM. *Cognition, 50,* 211–238.

Levinson, S. C. (1989). A review of relevance. *Journal of Linguistics, 25,* 455–472.

Lewis, C., Freeman, N. H., Hagestadt, C., & Douglas, H. (1994). Narrative access and production in preschoolers' false belief reasoning. *Cognitive Development, 9,* 397–424.

Lewis, C., & Osborne, A. (1990). Three-year-olds' problems with false belief: Conceptual deficit or linguistic artifact? *Child Development, 61,* 1514–1519.

Liberman, K. (1981). Understanding Aborigines in Australian courts of law. *Human Organization, 40,* 247–255.

Lindsay, D. S. (1990). Misleading suggestions can impair eyewitnesses' ability to remember event details. *Journal of Experimental Psychology: Learning Memory, and Cognition, 16,* 1077–1083.

List, J. A. (1986). Age and schematic differences in the reliability of eyewitness testimony. *Developmental Psychology, 22,* 56–57.

Loftus, E. F., & Davies, G. H. (1984). Distortions in the memory of children. *Journal of Social Issues, 40,* 51–67.

Loftus, E. F., Feldman, J., & Dashiell, R. (in press). *The reality of illusory memories.* Cambridge, MA: Harvard University Press.

Loftus, E. F., & Hoffman, H. G. (1989). Misinformation and memory: The creation of new memories. *Journal of Experimental Psychology: General, 118,* 100–104.

Loftus, E. F., Miller, D. G., & Burns, H. J. (1978). Semantic integration of verbal information into visual memory. *Journal of Experimental Psychology: Learning Memory, and Cognition, 4,* 19–31.

MacIntyre, A. (1984). *After virtue* (2nd ed.). Notre Dame, IN: University of Notre Dame Press.

Marin, B. V., Holmes, D. L., Guth, M., & Kovac, P. (1979). The potential of children as eyewitnesses. *Law and Human Behavior, 3,* 295–305.

McCloskey, M., & Zaragoza, M. (1985). Misleading post-event information and memory for events: Arguments and evidence against memory impairment hypothesis. *Journal of Experimental Psychology: General, 114,* 1–16.

McDonald, S., & Wales, R. (1986). An investigation of the ability to process inferences in language following right hemisphere brain damage. *Brain and Language, 29,* 68–80.

McGough, L. S. (1994). *Child witnesses: Fragile voices in the American legal system.* New Haven, CT: Yale University Press.

Mehler, J., & Bertoncini, J. (1988). Development—A question of properties, not change? *International Social Science Journal, 40,* 121–135.

Milton, K. (1988). Foraging behaviour and the evolution of primate intelligence. In R. W. Byrne & A. Whiten (Eds.), *Machiavellian intelligence.* Oxford: Clarendon Press.

Mitchell, P., & Lacohée, H. (1991). Children's early understanding of false belief. *Cognition, 39,* 107–127.

Mitchell, P., Robinson, E. J., Isaccs, J. E., & Nye, R. M. (in press). Contamination in reasoning about false belief: An instance of realistic bias in adults but not children. *Cognition.*

Molloy, R., Brownell, H. H., & Gardner, H. (1990). Discourse comprehension by right-hemisphere stroke patients: deficits of prediction and revision. In Y. Joanette & H. H. Brownell (Eds.), *Discourse ability and brain damage: Theoretical and empirical perspectives* (pp. 113–130). New York: Springer-Verlag.

Morton, J. (1990). The development of event memory. *The Psychologist, 1,* 3–10.

Morton, J., Hammersley, R. H., & Berkerian, D. A. (1985). Headed records: A model for memory and its failures. *Cognition, 20,* 1–23.

Moses, L. J., & Flavell, J. H. (1990). Inferring false beliefs from actions and reactions. *Child Development, 61,* 929–945.

Moya, K. L., Benowitz, L. I., Levine, D. L., & Finklestein, S. (1986). Covariant defects in visuospatial abilities and recall of verbal narrative after right hemisphere stroke. *Cortex, 22,* 381–397.

Neisser, U. (1990). Learning from the children. In R. Fivush & J. Hudson (Eds.), *Knowing and remembering in young children* (pp. 331–346). New York: Cambridge University Press.

Nelson, K. (1992). Emergence of autobiographical memory at age 4. *Human Development, 35,* 172–177.

Nelson, K. (1993a). Events, narratives, memory: What develops? *Minnesota Symposia on Child Psychology, 26,* 1–24.

Nelson, K. (1993b). The psychological and social origins of autobiographical memory. *Psychological Science, 4,* 7–14.

Nelson, K., Fivush, R., Hudson, J., & Lucariello, J. (1983). Scripts and the development of memory. In M. T. H. Chi (Ed)., *Trends in memory development research: Contributions to human development* (Vol. 9, pp. 12–20). Basel: Karger.

Nemeroff, C., & Rozin, P. (1994). The contagion concept in adult thinking in the United States: Transmission of germs and of interpersonal influence. *Ethos, 22,* 158–186.

Newcombe, P. A., & Siegal, M. (in press). Where to look first for suggestibility in children's memories. *Cognition.*

Occhipinti, S., & Siegal, M. (1994). Reasoning about food and contamination. *Journal of Personality and Social Psychology, 66,* 243–253.

Ochs, E. (1983). Cultural dimensions of language acquisition. In E. Ochs & B. B. Schlieffelin (Eds.), *Acquiring conversational competence* (pp. 185–191). London: Routledge & Kegan Paul.

Perner, J. (1991). *Understanding the representational mind.* Cambridge, MA: MIT Press.

Perner, J., Leekam, S. R., & Wimmer, H. (1987). Three year olds' difficulty with false belief: The case for a conceptual deficit. *British Journal of Developmental Psychology, 5,* 125–137.

Perner, J., Ruffman, T., & Leekam, S. R. (1994). Theory of mind is contagious: You catch it from your sibs. *Child Development, 65,* 1228–1238.

Peterson, C. C., & Siegal, M. (1995). Deafness, conversation and theory of mind. *Journal of Child Psychology and Psychiatry, 36,* 459–474.

Piaget, J. (1929). *The child's conception of the world.* London: Routledge & Kegan Paul.

Piaget, J. (1932/1977). *The moral judgement of the child.* Harmondsworth, England: Penguin.

Piaget, J. (1970). Piaget's theory. In P. H. Mussen (Ed.), *Carmichael's manual of child psychology* (Vol. 1, pp. 703–731). New York: Wiley.

Poole, D. A., & White, L. T. (1991). Effects of question repetition on the eyewitness testimony of children and adults. *Developmental Psychology, 27,* 975–986.

Poole, D. A., & White, L. T. (1993). Two years later: Effects of question repetition and rentention interval on the eyewitness testimony of children and adults. *Developmental Psychology, 29,* 844–853.

Pratt, C., & Bryant, P. (1990). Young children understand that looking leads to knowing (so long as they are looking into a single barrel). *Child Development, 61,* 946–961.

Revusky, S. H., & Garcia, J. (1970). Learned associations over long delays. In G. H. Bower (Ed.), *The psychology of learning and motivation: Advances in research and theory* (Vol. 4, pp. 1–84), New York: Academic Press.

Rogoff, B., & Mistry, J. (1990). The social and functional context of children's remembering. In R. Fivush & J. A. Hudson (Eds.), *Knowing and remembering in young children* (pp. 197–222). New York: Cambridge University Press.

Rosen, A. B., & Rozin, P. (1993). Now you see it . . . now you don't: The preschool child's conception of invisible particles in the context of dissolving. *Developmental Psychology, 29,* 300–311.

Rozin, P. (1976a). The evolution of intelligence and access to the cognitive unconscious. In J. M. Sprague & A. N. Epstein (Eds.). *Progress in psychobiology and physiological psychology* (Vol. 6, pp. 245–280). New York: Academic Press.

Rozin, P. (1976b). One-trial acquired likes and dislikes in humans: Disgust as a US, food predominance, and negative learning predominance. *Learning and Motivation, 17,* 180–189.

Rozin, P. (1990). Development in the food domain. *Developmental Psychology, 26,* 555–562.

Rozin, P., Fallon, A., & Augustoni-Ziskind, M. (1985). The child's conception of food: the development of contamination sensitivity to "disgusting" substances. *Developmental Psychology, 21,* 1075–1079.

Rozin, P., Lowery, L., & Ebert, R. (1994). Varieties of disgust faces and the structure of disgust. *Journal of Personality and Social Psychology, 66,* 870–881.

Rozin, P., & Schull, J. (1988). The adaptive-evolutionary point of view in experimental psychology. In R. Atkinson, R. J. Herrnstein, G. Lindzey, & R. D. Luce (Eds.), *Handbook of experimental psychology* (pp. 503–546). New York: Wiley.

Rudy, L., & Goodman, G. S. (1991). Effects of participation on children's reports: Implications for children's testimony. *Developmental Psychology, 27,* 527–538.

Rumain, B., Connell, J., & Braine, M. D. S. (1983). Conversational processes are responsible for reasoning fallacies in children as well as adults: *If* is not the biconditional. *Developmental Psychology, 19,* 471–481.

Schegloff, E. A. (1987). Some sources of misunderstanding in talk-in-interaction. *Linguistics, 25,* 201–218.

Schieffelin, B. B. (1983). Talking like birds: Sound play in a cultural perspective. In E. Ochs & B. B. Schlieffelin (Eds.), *Acquiring conversational competence* (pp. 177–184). London: Routledge & Kegan Paul.

Schieffelin, B. B. (1986). Teasing and shaming in Kaluli children's interactions. In B. B. Schieffelin & E. Ochs (Eds.), *Language socialization across cultures* (pp. 165–181). New York: Cambridge University Press.

Schieffelin, B. B. (1990). *The give and take of everyday life: Language socialization of Kaluli children.* New York: Cambridge University Press.

Schneiderman, E. I., Murasugi, K. G., & Saddy, J. D. (1992). Story arrangement ability in right brain-damaged patients. *Brain and Language, 43,* 107–120.

Scribner, S. (1977). Modes of thinking and ways of speaking: Culture and logic reconsidered. In *Thinking: Readings in cognitive science* (pp. 483–500). Cambridge: Cambridge University Press.

Shatz, M. (1994). Theory of mind and the development of social-linguistic intelligence in early childhood. In C. Lewis & P. Mitchell (Eds.), *Children's early understanding of mind: Origins and development* (pp. 311–329). Hove, England: Erlbaum.

Shweder, R. A., Mahapatra, M., & Miller, J. (1987). Culture and moral development. In J. Kagan & S. Lamb (Eds.), *The emergence of morality in young children* (pp. 1–83). Chicago: University of Chicago Press.

Siegal, M. (1988). Children's knowledge of contagion and contamination as causes of illness. *Child Development, 59,* 1353–1359.

Siegal, M. (1991a). A clash of conversational worlds: Interpreting cognitive development through communication. In L. B. Resnick, J. M. Levine, & S. Behrens (Eds.), *Perspectives on socially shared cognition* (pp. 23–40). Washington, DC: American Psychological Association.

Siegal, M. (1991b). *Knowing children: experiments in conversation and cognition.* Hove, England: Erlbaum.

Siegal, M. (1995). Becoming mindful of food and conversation. *Current Directions in Psychological Science, 6,* 177–181.

Siegal, M., & Beattie, K. (1991). Where to look first for children's knowledge of false beliefs. *Cognition, 38,* 1–12.

Siegal, M., Carrington, J., & Radel, M. (1996). Theory of mind and pragmatic understanding following right hemisphere brain damage. *Brain and Language,* **53**(1), 40–50.

Siegal, M., Patty, J., & Eiser, C. (1990). A re-examination of children's conceptions of contagion. *Psychology and Health, 4,* 159–165.

Siegal, M., & Peterson, C. C. (1994). Children's theory of mind and the conversational territory of cognitive development. In C. Lewis & P. Mitchell (Eds.), *Children's early understanding of mind: Origins and development* (pp. 427–455). Hove, England: Erlbaum.

Siegal, M., & Peterson, C. C. (1995). Memory and suggestibility in conversations with young children. *Australian Journal of Psychology, 47,* 38–41 (Special issue on Developmental Psychology).

Siegal, M., & Peterson, C. C. (in press). Breaking the mold: A fresh look at children's answers to questions about lies and mistakes. *Developmental Psychology.*

Siegal, M., & Share, D. L. (1990). Contamination sensitivity in young children. *Developmental Psychology, 26,* 26, 455–458.

Siegal, M., Waters, L. J., & Dinwiddy, L. S. (1988). Misleading children: Causal attributions for inconsistency under repeated questioning. *Journal of Experimental Child Psychology, 45,* 438–456.

Sodian, B., Taylor, C., Harris, P. L., & Perner, J. (1991). Early deception and the child's theory of mind: False trails and genuine markers. *Child Development, 62,* 468–483.

Spelke, E. (1994). Initial knowledge: Six suggestions. *Cognition, 50,* 431–445.

Spencer, J. R., & Flin, R. (1990). *The evidence of children: The law and the psychology.* London: Blackstone.

Sperber, D., & Wilson, D. (1986). *Relevance.* Oxford: Blackwell.

Springer, K. (1992). Early beliefs about the cause of illness: Evidence against immanent justice. *Cognitive Development, 7,* 429–443.

Springer, K., & Belk, A. (1994). The role of physical contact and association in early contamination sensitivity. *Developmental Psychology, 30,* 864–868.

Strichartz, A. F., & Burton, R. V. (1990). Lies and truth: A study of the development of the concept. *Child Development, 61,* 211–220.

Sullivan, K., & Winner, E. (1993). Three-year-olds' understanding of mental states: The influence of trickery. *Journal of Experimental Child Psychology, 56,* 135–148.

Surian, L., & Leslie, A. (1995). *Competence and performance in false belief understanding.* Paper presented at the Biennial Meeting of the Society for Research in Child Development, Indianapolis, IN.

Thatcher, R. W. (1992). Cyclic cortical reorganization during early childhood. *Brain and Cognition, 20,* 24–50.

Toglia, M. P., Hembrooke, H., Ceci, S. J., & Ross, D. F. (1992). *Children's resistance to misleading postevent information: When does it occur?* Paper presented at the Annual Convention of the American Psychological Society, San Diego.

Tomasello, M. (1995). Commentary on Gauvain. *Human Development, 38,* 46–52.

Vygotsky, L. S. (1978). *Mind in society: The development of higher psychological processes.* Cambridge, MA: Harvard University Press.

Wald, M., Carlsmith, M., Leiderman, P. H., & Smith, C. (1983). Intervention to protect abused and neglected children. *Minnesota Symposia on Child Psychology, 16,* 207–231.

Wellman, H. M., & Bartsch, K. (1988). Young children's reasoning about beliefs. *Cognition, 30,* 239–277.

Wellman, H. M., & Bartsch, K. (1994). Before belief: Children's early psychological theory. In C. Lewis & P. Mitchell (Eds.), *Children's early understanding of mind: Origins and development* (pp. 427–455). Hove, England: Erlbaum.

Wellman, H. M., & Estes, D. (1986). Early understanding of mental entities: A reexamination of childhood realism. *Child Development, 57,* 910–923.

Wellman, H. M., & Woolley, J. D. (1990). From simple desires to ordinary beliefs: The early development of everyday beliefs. *Cognition, 35,* 245–275.

Weylman, S. T., Brownell, H. H., Roman, M., & Gardner, H. (1989). Appreciation of indirect requests by left- but not right-brain-damaged patients: The effects of verbal context and conventionality of wording. *Brain and Language, 36,* 580–591.

Whiten, A. (Ed.). (1991). *Natural theories of mind.* Oxford: Blackwell.

Wilson, D. (1994). Relevance and understanding. In G. Brown, K. Malmkjaer, A. Pollitt, & J. Williams (Eds.), *Language and understanding* (pp. 37–58). Oxford: Oxford University Press.

Wimmer, H., Gruber, S., & Perner, J. (1985). Young children's conception of lying: Moral intuition and the denotation and connotation of "to lie." *Developmental Psychology, 21,* 993–995.

Yarmey, A. D. (1984). Age as a factor in eyewitness testimony. In G. L. Wells & E. F. Loftus (Eds.), *Eyewitness testimony: A psychological perspective* (pp. 142–154). New York: Cambridge University Press.

Zaidel, E. (1985). Language in the right hemisphere. In D. F. Benson & E. Zaidel (Eds.), *The dual brain: Hemispheric specialization in humans* (pp. 205–231). New York: Guilford.

Zaragoza, M. S. (1991). Preschool children's suggestibility to memory impairment. In J. Doris (Ed.), *The suggestibility of children's recollections: Implications for eyewitness testimony* (pp. 27–39). Washington, DC: American Psychological Association.

CHAPTER 9

A Theory of Mind Perspective on Social Cognitive Development

Marjorie Taylor

I. INTRODUCTION

The state of research on social cognitive development has changed dramatically over the past decade. As recently as 1988, research in this area was accurately described in the following way: "There is a wealth of research on the first year of life, research that beautifully documents the nature of infants' social behavior, their fine-tuned responsiveness to the behavior and moods of other people (see, for example, Stern, 1985). There is also a flourishing tradition of research on the capability (and incapability) of school-aged children to take the perspective of others, and on their developing ideas about friendship, authority, and justice (Damon, 1977; Selman, 1980; Youniss, 1980). Between these two fields of research, in the period of the transition from infancy to childhood, there is a relatively unexplored area" (Dunn, 1988, p. 4). After making this general observation, Dunn noted a couple of exceptions, including the work of "a small group of psychologists interested in young children's 'theories of mind.'"

Theory of mind has evolved from being a small special interest topic to a major research enterprise that has been described as currently dominating work on social cognitive development (Flavell & Miller, in press). According to Moses and Chandler (1992), "this new material constitutes some

Perceptual and Cognitive Development
Copyright © 1996 by Academic Press, Inc. All rights of reproduction in any form reserved.

three or four thousand new published pages . . . words like 'deluge' and 'maelstrom,' that we are sometimes guilty of bandying about much too casually, actually do seem to fit" (p. 276). As most theory of mind research has been done with 3-, 4-, and 5-year-olds, social cognitive development during the preschool period is no longer "an unexplored area." In this review, I focus on how and why theory of mind research and research influenced by theory of mind ideas have arguably become some of the most exciting and prominent work in the area of social cognitive development. The first section of this chapter provides a brief history and overview of some of the empirical findings in this area. Then I discuss how this body of work has influenced four important and active areas of social cognitive research: children's understanding of emotion, the development of self, social cognition in infancy, and autism. A final section presents some speculations about the future.

II. THE DEVELOPMENT OF A THEORY OF MIND

Theory of mind researchers share an interest in children's understanding of mental states such as belief and desire. Researchers in this area assume mental states have connections with each other (e.g., perceiving is related to knowing), with events in the real world (e.g., a belief that milk is in the refrigerator), and with one's own actions and the actions of other people (e.g., a person who believes milk is in the refrigerator will look for it there). One point of disagreement is whether children's understanding of mental states is an organized causal-explanatory system with the characteristics that are claimed to define theories or is a less structured collection of information about mental life (Campbell & Bickhard, 1993; Goldman, 1993a; Gopnik & Wellman, 1992). However, many researchers believe that knowledge about the mind, whether this knowledge constitutes a theory in the strict sense of the word or simply a collection of insights is one the most fundamental domains of human understanding (Wellman & Gelman, 1992). As Forguson and Gopnik (1988) point out, "It is difficult to overestimate the extent to which our commitment to CS (common-sense) psychology is implicated in our everyday lives as adults. Our ability to make cooperative plans; our deeply ingrained practice of blaming, excusing, and justifying behavior; our ability to predict what others will do under various conditions; our ability to influence others' behaviors (e.g., to cajole, entreat, persuade, bribe, motivate, etc.) all depend on attributing beliefs, expectations, knowledge, wants, fears, wishes, motives, strategies and the like to others and using these attributions in 'practical reasoning'" (p. 227). Given this account of how knowledge about the mind plays a crucial role in social understanding, theory of mind development in children should be closely related to moral, social, and communicative development (Leekam, 1993) and have great significance for children's everyday interactions with other people and their close relationships with friends and family members (Dunn, 1994).

Although Piaget (1926) was interested in children's understanding of the mind, the current wave of research on this topic began with Premack and Woodruff's (1978) speculations regarding the chimpanzee's understanding of mind. Premack and Woodruff defined "theory of mind" in the following way: "In saying that an individual has a theory of mind, we mean that the individual imputes mental states to himself and to others (either to conspecifics or to other species as well). A system of inferences of this kind is properly viewed as a theory, first, because such states are not directly observable, and second, because the system can be used to make predictions, specifically about the behavior of other organisms" (p. 515). Premack and Woodruff claimed that chimpanzees were capable of imputing mental states to others because their subject, Sarah, was able to demonstrate her understanding of the mental states underlying a situation shown in a videotape (e.g., a human struggling to get out of a locked cage) by choosing the photograph from an array that depicted the correct solution to the problem (e.g., the picture of keys). Premack and Woodruff concluded that an understanding of behavior based on imputing mental states to others is "not a sophisticated or advanced act, but a primitive one" (p. 525) and raised the issue of whether young children could be described as having a theory of mind.

Premack and Woodruff's analysis was immediately criticized on the basis that Sarah's responses did not necessarily demonstrate an awareness of mental states (J. Bennett, 1978; Dennett, 1978; Pylyshyn, 1978). These authors suggested that a truly convincing demonstration of mental state awareness would require the subject to take into account another person's incorrect belief about a situation. A test involving false belief was considered to be crucial because a prediction based on a person's true belief could be made by assessing the actual state of the world rather than the person's mental representation. In contrast, a prediction based on a person's false belief is unambiguously derived from the person's mental representation of the state of the world, rather than from what is actually true.

This methodological issue was, in part, responsible for a surge of research on the development of an understanding of false belief in young children. According to Moses and Chandler (1992), there is a conceptual reason, as well as the methodological one, for the special emphasis that has been given to the study of false belief in the theory of mind literature. The possibility that beliefs can be false is inseparable from what it means to have a belief (Davidson, 1984; Moses & Chandler, 1992; Perner, 1991a). More generally, mastery of false belief has been taken as evidence that children understand that individuals can represent the same object or event in different ways, making false belief tasks a kind of litmus test for having a representational theory of mind (see Chandler, 1988, for a critique). Thus, research on children's understanding of false belief is the logical starting place for this review.

A. Children's Understanding of False Belief

The story begins with Wimmer and Perner's (1983) experiments investigating children's ability to predict another person's behavior on the basis of his or her false belief about the location of an object. In the "unexpected location" task, a child watches as an object is placed in one location by a puppet who leaves the scene and then returns after the object has been moved to another location. When asked where the puppet will search for the object, most 3-year-olds answer that the puppet will search where the object currently is located, failing to take into account the puppet's false belief. The insight that the puppet will look where s/he last saw the object rather than at its current location develops during the preschool years, with 3-year-olds rarely succeeding at this task, and 5-year-olds doing quite well. In another version of a false belief task, the child is shown a box that turns out to have surprising contents (e.g., pencils in a Smarties box). When asked to predict what another person who had not looked into the box would think was inside, most young preschoolers base their judgments on what they know is inside, rather than on the appearance of the box, indicating that they have difficulty attributing a false belief about the contents of the box to another person (Perner, Leekam, & Wimmer, 1987).

The unexpected location and unexpected contents tasks have been scrutinized by researchers interested in the possibility that the routine failure of 3-year-olds was due to some factor other than an inability to reason about false belief. The results of this research indicate that under some conditions, even young 3-year-old children show some understanding of false belief (e.g., Bartsch & Wellman, 1989; Chandler & Hala, 1994; C. Lewis, 1994; Siegal & Beattie, 1991). For example, 3-year-old children are able to *explain* behaviors by referring to false beliefs, although they have difficulty *predicting* them (Bartsch & Wellman, 1989). Providing temporal cues in the test questions (e.g., "Where will Maxi look *first* for the chocolate") has improved the performance of 3-year-olds in some studies (C. Lewis & Osborne, 1990; Siegal & Beattie, 1991; but see Moses & Flavell, 1990). In other experiments, helping children with the memory requirements of the task (e.g., asking children to select a picture of what they believe is in an unopened box instead of requiring them to report their initial belief verbally) has resulted in the majority of 3-year-olds being able to later report their former false belief (P. Mitchell & Lacohee, 1991). Three-year-olds also show improved performance if the salience of the true state of affairs is reduced (Zaitchik, 1991), and if the experimenter goes over the sequence of events in the false belief story twice before asking the test question (C. Lewis, 1994).

Naturalistic observations provide additional evidence that young children have some grasp of false belief before they would be expected to pass the unexpected change and location tasks. For example, 3- and even 2-year-old children spontaneously carry out deceptive acts and seem to be aware of the subsequent false beliefs held by their unwitting victims (e.g., Dunn, 1991; Dunn & Munn, 1985; Reddy, 1991). However, attempts to elicit deception in children under 4 years of age in the laboratory have met with mixed success. Chandler and colleagues (Chandler, Fritz, & Hala, 1989; Hala, Chandler, & Fritz, 1991) found that many 3-year-olds and some 2-year-olds will act deceptively to trick an experimenter about the location of a hidden treasure and seem to understand that their actions will create a false belief in the other person (see also Avis & Harris, 1991; Sullivan & Winner, 1993). However, in other studies, 3-year-olds required heavy prompting in order to deceive and performed poorly on false belief questions related to deception (Peskin, 1992; Ruffman, Olsen, Ash, & Keenan, 1993; Russell, Mauthner, Sharpe, & Tidswell, 1991; Sodian, 1991; Sodian, Taylor, Harris, & Perner, 1991). This second set of studies has been criticized, in turn, for the complexity of the tasks, which could disguise young children's ability to demonstrate their false belief understanding in the context of deception (Chandler & Hala, 1994).

Overall, the results of research on false belief indicate that 3-year-olds are limited in their ability to reason about false belief and may overlook the most obvious seeming cues. In contrast, by five years of age children have overcome almost all difficulties with experimental tasks. They are better able to understand what is being asked, they can follow the story lines, and they are not distracted by problems due to salience. The shift from 3 to 5 years of age in children's ability to answer questions about false belief has been replicated in dozens of studies, including some in which very simple tasks were used (e.g., Moses & Flavell, 1990; Wellman & Bartsch, 1988).

The developmental changes that are observed on false belief tasks— failure on many tasks at three years of age and mastery around 5 years of age[1]—have been interpreted as evidence that children develop a general understanding of representation during the preschool years (Perner, 1991a). On this view, although young children are aware of internal psychological states from an early age, they initially have a nonrepresentational understanding of them. In the case of belief, this means that contact with objects or events in the world is thought of as reliably linked with beliefs, which are understood as direct and accurate reflections of reality. As children develop a representational understanding of belief, they become aware that beliefs are not simple reflections of reality, but can change over time and can vary among different individuals as a function of experience. The results showing that under some conditions 3-year-old children perform well on false belief tasks are interpreted as evidence of a transitional period in development in which children are beginning to understand that belief, as well as other mental states, involve representations of reality (Gopnik & Wellman, 1994). This account of the false belief findings is consistent with the results of studies by Flavell and colleagues who have found that the period from 3 to 5 also shows development in the related ability to report that an object can simultaneously look like one type of thing, but actually be something quite different (Flavell, Flavell & Green, 1983; Flavell, Green, & Flavell, 1986). According to Flavell (1988), children's difficulty with the appearance–reality distinction stems from their tendency to conceptualize mental representations of stimuli and the stimuli themselves as in one-to-one correspondence, an interpretation that dovetails neatly with Perner's claims about children's difficulty understanding that a belief can be false.

Although the conceptual deficit interpretation is currently the dominant point of view in the literature, there are alternative interpretations of the false belief data. For example, C. Lewis (1994) argues that all the studies that demonstrate some understanding of false belief in children under 4 years of age have employed procedures that have helped children grasp the narrative about a person having a false belief in the way intended by the experimenter. Lewis ties mastery of false belief to the developing ability to integrate a set of premises into a coherent story line (see also Carrithers, 1991, for a discussion of narrativity and theory of mind).

Fodor's (1992) hypothesis that an understanding of mind is innate is another alternative to the conceptual deficit account. Fodor explains the developmental differences in performance on false belief tasks in terms of a shift in the heuristics children use for predicting actions in terms of beliefs and desires. The younger child opts for a heuristic that is simple computationally, although it is not always reliable (i.e., people act in ways to satisfy their desires), whereas older children are able to manage a computationally more complex but more reliable heuristic (i.e., people act in ways that would satisfy their desires if their beliefs were true). However, both older and younger children are operating within what Fodor called a VSTM (very simple theory of mind) that differs from an adult theory only in the number of "intentional psychological objects" (i.e., beliefs and desires in VSTM vs. beliefs, desires, hopes, suspicions, etc., in the more elaborated theory).

As Fodor's analysis suggests, the false belief results are best understood within the context of successes and failures on tasks investigating the development of children's understanding of other mental states. In fact, several explanations that have been proposed to account for the false belief data (e.g., in terms of information processing demands, logical complexity, narrativity) lose their force when experimental findings regarding other mental states are taken into account (Gopnik, 1993). Clearly, it is important to consider the overall pattern of research findings, and avoid interpreting the results for any one mental state in isolation. With this point in mind, I will briefly review research assessing children's understanding of desiring, perceiving, pretending, intending, and knowing.

B. Children's Understanding of Other Mental States

Before children readily invoke the possibility of another person having a false belief when predicting his or her behavior, they are mentalistic creatures. Three-year-olds understand the distinction between mental entities and physical objects or events in the real world (Estes, Wellman, & Woolley, 1989; Wellman & Estes, 1986), they talk about mental states (Bartsch & Wellman, 1995; Shatz, Wellman, & Silbur, 1983), and they prefer mentalistic descriptions of events to behavioristic ones (Lillard & Flavell, 1990). The results of false belief studies have sometimes been interpreted in terms of children's general understanding of mind, but mental states differ from each other and false belief may not even be particularly representative of other mental states (Goldman, 1993a). For example, unlike other mental states such as desire, false belief, in principle, cannot be directly perceived in a first-person fashion because it is only after the fact that a belief is known to be false. The distinctions among various kinds of mental states make some easier to grasp than others and, thus, research investigating these distinctions helps to address questions such as how children first achieve particular insights about the nature of mental life and the developmental role of certain kinds of experiences.

1. Desiring

In contrast to children's protracted development of knowledge about false belief, an understanding of desire as a mental state that influences people's behavior seems to be in place very early. By 2 years of age, children talk about their desires in ways that make reference to their own mental states and the mental states of other people (Bartsch & Wellman, 1989, 1995). In addition, young children make explicit distinctions between their own desires and the desires of other people (Flavell, Flavell, Green, & Moses, 1990; Wellman, 1990), understand the relation between desire and actions (Wellman & Woolley, 1990), are able to report their own past desires (Gopnik & Slaughter, 1991), and understand the emotional consequences of unfulfilled and fulfilled desires (Hadwin & Perner, 1991; Stein & Levine, 1989; Yuill, 1984). This impressive early understanding of desire is closely related to an early understanding of emotion. Talk about desires and feelings go together (Bartsch & Wellman, 1995) and children's understanding of the emotional reactions of other people develops along with the ability to assess another person's desires.

Perner (1991a) has argued that children's good performance on desire tasks does not reflect an understanding of representation because children base their judgments on knowledge about the objective desirability of different objects or situations (e.g., candy is desirable). However, Bartsch and Wellman's (1995) analyses of speech samples from ten children in the CHILDES database (MacWhinney & Snow, 1990) shows that even 2-year-olds understand that people can differ in their desires and that the same object can be desirable to one person and undesirable to another (see also Flavell, Mumme, Green, & Flavell, 1992). According to Bartsch and Wellman (1995), 2-year-olds initially understand desire in terms of subjective connections to external objects. An understanding of desire as based on mental representations of objects or situations as being a certain way (i.e., the insight that people desire the object as it is represented, which might be different from the object as it is in reality) develops during the preschool years.

The task of accounting for children's early understanding of desire has been part of the impetus for developing a taxonomy of mental states and identifying the insights that each type requires (Gopnik & Slaughter, 1991; Perner, 1991a; Wellman, 1990). Desire and belief differ in several ways that could potentially influence children's understanding. For example, some authors have accounted for children's early understanding of desire by referring to Searle's (1984) distinction between mental states that have a "mind-to-world" direction of fit (e.g., belief) and mental states that have a "world-to-mind" direction of fit (e.g., desire) (Johnson, 1988; Perner, 1991b). The idea is that there might be something inherently easier to grasp about the possibility of changing the world to correspond to the mind (e.g., actually getting the cookie that you have been wanting) than the possibility of changing the mind to correspond to the world (e.g., realizing that your shoes are under the bed, not in the closet where you thought they were). Desire might also be easier for children to understand because, unlike belief, there is no concept of misrepresentation involved (i.e., past desires are not incorrect in the way that past beliefs can be) (e.g., Perner, 1991a) or because desire is associated with more intensely felt phenomenology than belief (Pillow, 1988). Although there are different accounts of how desire differs from belief, there is some consensus that knowledge about desire develops before knowledge about belief and that "desire psychology" (Wellman, 1990) provides a basis for later developing insights about the mind.

2. Perceiving

Research on the development of psychological knowledge about perception has a long history (Flavell, Botkin, Frye, Wright, & Jarvis, 1968; Piaget & Inhelder, 1948/1956). In the past, work on this topic focused on perspective taking, the ability to consider how objects or events are perceived and understood from the point of view of another person (for reviews see Flavell, 1978, 1992; Newcomb, 1989). In contrast to Piaget's description of preschool children as expecting everyone to have the same point of view as themselves, Flavell and colleagues showed that even 3-year-old children are quite accomplished when asked to report what people can and cannot see ("level 1" perspective taking), although they have difficulty reporting how something looks to another person ("level 2" perspective taking) (Flavell,

1978; Lempers, Flavell, & Flavell, 1977; Masangkay et al., 1974). Perner (1991a) describes Flavell's work on the level 1–level 2 distinction as "the first to split the monolithic notion that Piagetian egocentrism rules throughout early childhood into a more refined and theoretically interesting view of young children's understanding of the mind" (p. 277).

Perspective taking is involved in many theory of mind tasks, but in contrast to past work in this area, errors are attributed to the limitations of children's knowledge about the mind rather than to egocentrism (i.e., the tendency to attribute one's own perspective to another person). In fact, as predicted by the theory of mind framework, children are as likely to make errors when asked to report their own perspective as when asked to report the perspective of another person (e.g., Wimmer & Hartl, 1991). Research on children's understanding of perception within a theory of mind framework has investigated children's knowledge about a variety of topics, such as the understanding that lines of sight are always straight (Flavell, Green, Herrera, & Flavell (1991), that distance affects vision (Flavell, Flavell, Green, & Wilcox, 1980), and that vision involves incoming information to the eyes rather than emissions from the eyes (Cottrell & Winer, 1994). Flavell, Green, and Flavell (1990) have shown that 3-year-olds are able to assess their auditory perceptions, as well as their visual ones (e.g., children correctly reported hearing an object but not seeing it and seeing an object but not hearing it). Yaniv and Shatz (1988) also found that young preschoolers had no difficulty identifying their percepts from different sense modalities. Some understanding of perception seems to be present from a very early age, as evidenced by infants' joint attention and social referencing abilities (see Section IIIC).

According to Gopnik, Slaughter, and Meltzoff (1994), early-developing psychological knowledge about perception might serve as a model for children's later-developing understanding of belief. Gopnik et al. point out that perceiving is conceptually similar to believing because both perceiving and believing have a mind-to-world direction of fit and can potentially involve misrepresentation. In a series of experiments, they showed that 3-year-olds are better able to understand cases of perceptual misrepresentation than false belief, and that children who were given practice and feedback in reporting percepts and past desires showed improvement in their mastery of false belief. These results support the hypothesis that children's developing understanding of mental states such as perception and desire contributes to their understanding of belief.

3. Pretending

The first signs of spontaneous pretense occur very early (12 months) and by 3 or 4 years of age, many children create their own elaborate fantasies involving imaginary people and animals (Singer & Singer, 1990; Taylor, Cartwright, & Carlson, 1993). Children's comprehension of pretend play in others also is impressive, even at age 2 (Harris & Kavanaugh, 1993; Harris, Kavanaugh, & Meredith, 1994). For example, in one task, 2-year-old children watched as a teddy bear poured pretend tea over the head of a toy pig. When asked to dry off the pig, the children had no difficulty understanding that the pig that needed to be dried was the one that had been soaked with imaginary tea (Harris & Kavanaugh, 1993).

For some time there has been speculation that the early-developing ability to engage in and comprehend pretend play is conceptually related to the later-developing understanding of false belief (Leslie, 1987, 1988). More recently, research on individual differences in children's understanding of false belief has converged on experience with pretense as potentially an important contributing factor (Jenkins & Astington, 1993; Perner, Ruffman, & Leekam, 1994; Taylor & Carlson, 1995). However, the role of pretense in theory of mind development is controversial. According to Fodor (1992), young children's ability to pretend is evidence that they have some grasp of false belief. He argues that pretending would be impossible if the child were incapable of understanding false belief, because pretending involves acting as if something is true (e.g., a broom is a horse), when one actually believes it to be false (e.g., the broom is not a horse). Other researchers do not consider pretense to be equivalent to false belief, but instead adopt an intermediate position in which pretense and false belief are conceptually related and pretending plays an important role in theory of mind development. For example, Leslie (1987, 1988) interprets children's understanding of pretense as demonstrating that young preschoolers understand it is possible to have a representation of the world that does not correspond to reality. As Leslie points out, "pretending in the vicinity of 2-year-olds does not lead to disaster" (p. 22). The 2-year-old who sees her mother pretend a banana is a telephone does not become confused about either bananas or telephones because she is capable of representing a pretend version of what her mother is doing (i.e., speaking into a telephone), what her mother is actually doing (i.e., speaking into a banana), and the relation between the two. Leslie describes acts of pretense as involving a decoupling mechanism whereby a copy is made of a primary sensory-based representation for the purpose of pretense. This is the same processing mechanism at work when children represent false belief; thus Leslie claims that cognitive capabilities required for false belief are in place by age 2, as evident by acts of pretending. What is beyond the understanding of the 2-year-old, according to Leslie, is the causal relation between mental states such as beliefs and situations in the world.

Other researchers have questioned these interpretations of children's early-developing ability to pretend and argue that too much conceptual sophistication is credited to young pretenders. For example, both Lillard (1994) and Harris (1994) claim young children understand pretending as a social activity, without necessarily realizing that pretense is based on mental representation. Lillard (1993, 1994) has shown that most 4- and many 5-year-olds tend to claim that a person is pretending when s/he is acting appropriately (e.g., jumping like a kangaroo), even when the person is described as not thinking about the pretend entity (e.g., not thinking about a kangaroo, not knowing that kangaroos hop, and/or not knowing anything about kangaroos). On the basis of these results, Lillard claims that children do not initially conceptualize pretending as involving the mind at all, but instead understand pretending as a kind of action. Thus, it is wrong to interpret children's ability to pretend as demonstrating a precocious understanding of mental representation.

Similarly, Harris (1994) argues that children's insight into pretense stops at the behavioral level and need not extend to understanding other minds. He suggests that 2-year-olds are able to follow pretense stipulations because they: (1) have an understanding of what is causally possible in reality; (2) observe a deviation of these causal properties (e.g., witness mother "pouring" nothing into a cup); and (3) fill in the gaps with their own imagination and mark the event as make-believe, quarantined from the world of reality. According to Harris (1994), false belief is a different matter, because with false belief the child must not only stipulate a nontruth proposition (as in pretense), but also must stipulate a "serious" nontruth proposition in the face of a competing, truthful one. He claims that children later acquire an understanding of these different truth commitments of the false believer and the pretend player through more accurate simulation of different points of view. Although this account points to differences between children's understanding of pretense and their understanding of false belief, Harris gives children's imagination a central role in their ability to predict and explain human behavior (see Section IIIB).

Perner, Baker, and Hutton (1994) interpret children's ability to pretend as demonstrating an impressive ability to understand counterfactuals (Au, 1992), but also claim early acts of pretense do not demonstrate any true understanding of mental representation. In support of this line of argument, Perner et al. have demonstrated that 3-year-old children tend not to differentiate the knowledge conditions that underlie acts of pretending and actions based on false belief. For example, 3-year-olds are likely to report incorrectly that a person who suggested "Sally" as a name for a boy doll dressed in female clothing was pretending the doll was a girl, even though the person did not know the doll was actually male. Perner et al. describe children's understanding of false belief and pretense as closely related, but do not credit young preschoolers with a true understanding of either one. They refer to "prelief" as the mental state underlying all acting-as-if behaviors for young children. "If pretense is the mental state that underlies pretend acting-as-if, and if false belief underlies mistaken acting-as-if, then prelief is the mental state that underlies acting-as-if without differentiation as to whether the acting-as-if is a case of pretense or a mistake" (p. 265). Although this point of view does not credit children with a full understanding of the representational nature of pretense, children's conceptual understanding of pretending is enmeshed with their understanding of false belief.

Despite the persuasive writings and interesting empirical findings of Lillard, Perner, and Harris, the relation between children's ability to produce and understand pretense and their understanding of the mind remains unclear. The results of several recent experiments challenge the view that children do not understand that pretense is based on mental representation (e.g., Dockett & Smith, 1995; Gerow & Taylor, 1995; Hickling, Wellman, & Gottfried, 1995). Perner et al.'s ideas about "prelief" are inconsistent with the results of research by Golomb and Kuersten (1992) who have shown that young children are surprised when an experimenter acts as if she has mistaken a pretend situation for a real one (e.g., the experimenter takes a bite out of a playdough cookie while on a pretend picnic). Fodor (1992) dismisses the view that belief and pretense are undifferentiated, pointing out that "presumably even young children know the difference between acting as if P *because one is pretending that P* and acting as if P because *one believes that P*. Only a demented creature would *really* try to make a phone call with a banana" (p. 290). Along with desiring and perceiving, pretending has not been ruled out as a mental state that is understood at an early age and that plays an important role in children's later-developing knowledge about the mind (see Lillard, in press, for a thoughtful review of this issue).

4. Intending

Infants have goals and direct their actions to bring about their goals, that is, they act intentionally, by at least 16 months and possibly much earlier (Frye, 1991; Piaget, 1952; Willats, 1984). By 2 years of age, children use the language of intention, saying things like "I don't mean to," and "on purpose" (Dunn, 1991). However, theory of mind researchers differ in the extent that they credit young children with the ability to recognize intentions as mental states underlying their own actions and the actions of other people. Some theorists group intentions with desire and pretense as mental states that children understand early on (Forguson & Gopnik, 1988), citing evidence that 3-year-old children are able to distinguish intentional from nonintentional actions (Shultz & Wells, 1985). Other researchers suggest that children's ability to distinguish intentional from nonintentional actions could be due to the use of a matching strategy (i.e., actors are associated with goals that are matched to actual outcomes) without any need to conceptualize intention as a mental state (Astington, 1991; Perner, 1991b).

According to Moses (1993), intention and belief are usually so intertwined that it is difficult to imagine an intention divorced from a particular belief state. For example, a child intends to get a cookie and so opens a box because she believes a cookie is inside. It does not seem possible that a child could intend to get a cookie and then produce an action to bring about that goal without any sort of belief about the location of a cookie. It also is crucial that the intentions be consistent with the beliefs, a situation that does not hold for desire (e.g., the child could want a cookie while believing that there are none to be had) (Moses, 1993). Moses argues that if an intention is unfulfilled, then the beliefs underlying it must have been false. According to this view, intention could not be fully understood by children before they understand belief. In a set of experiments, Moses found that 3-year-old children were quite accurate in their reports of a person's unfulfilled intentions and showed considerable understanding of the false beliefs that accompanied them. These results support Moses's claims about the interdependence of belief and intention, and challenge Perner's (1991b) view that 3-year-olds have a nonrepresentational understanding of intention. In addition, this research adds to a growing body of evidence that, under the right supportive conditions, 3-year-old children have some capacity to reason about belief.

5. Knowing

According to Perner (1991a), there are three aspects to our understanding of what it means to have knowledge: (1) in contrast to information that is *believed,* information that is *known* must be factually correct; (2) the person who knows a piece of information must have had access to an information source; and (3) the person who knows is able to act successfully (e.g., if you know where your book is, you are able to find it). Perner suggests that before children acquire a representational theory of mind during the late preschool period, they tend to focus on (1) and (3) with little thought given to the importance of information sources. Research on children's comprehension of mental verbs such as "know" and "guess" supports this hypothesis (Johnson & Wellman, 1980; Moore, Bryant, & Furrow, 1989; Wellman & Johnson, 1979) because the results indicate that most 3-year-olds and some 4-year-olds understand "know" as acting correctly (e.g., finding a toy in a hidden spot), even if the person had no prior access to the relevant information (e.g., found the toy because of a lucky guess).

Perner's claim also suggests children might not understand the conditions that result in having knowledge and might not attend to the details of events in which new information is acquired. The results of studies investigating children's attention to and understanding of information sources are somewhat mixed, but, in general, although young children are able to report the state of their own knowledge (Povinelli & deBlois, 1992; Wimmer, Hogrefe, & Perner, 1988), they often cannot answer direct questions about why they do or do not know and have difficulty using perceptual access as the basis for deciding what other people know (Perner & Ogden, 1988; Taylor, 1988). For example, in a study by Wimmer et al. (1988), most 3-year-olds and some 4-year-olds could not reliably assess whether another person knew what was in a box as a function of whether the person had looked inside (also see Lyon, 1993). Some task conditions pose fewer difficulties for young children (Pillow, 1989; Pratt & Bryant, 1990), but the bulk of the evidence suggests 3-year-olds often do not know much about the relation between perceiving and knowing.[2] Although, by 4 or 5 years of age, children are able to use perceptual access as the basis for judging the knowledge of another person, they are limited in their ability to judge the knowledge of others in at least two ways: (1) they tend not to realize that a person who has perceptual access to information might not interpret it correctly if the information is ambiguous or uninformative (Chandler & Helm, 1984 ; Taylor, 1988; but see also Perner & Davies, 1991); and (2) they tend not to attribute knowledge to another person on the basis of inference (Sodian & Wimmer, 1987).

Children's lack of attention to events in which knowledge is acquired is also evident in their answers to questions about their own knowledge acquisition. In research by Gopnik and Graf (1988), children learned about the contents of a drawer by looking inside, being told about the contents by the experimenter, or figuring out the contents from a clue. When asked how they had learned about the drawer's contents, 3-year-old children had difficulty identifying the source of their knowledge, often claiming, for example, they had been told the information when in fact they had inferred it. Research by O'Neill and her colleagues (O'Neill, Astington, & Flavell, 1992; O'Neill & Gopnik, 1991) shows that young children also are limited in their understanding of the relation between the modality of sensory experience and the acquisition of knowledge (e.g., touching does not provide information about color).

Although, by 5 years of age, children are able to report *how* they learned the target information, research by Taylor, Esbensen, and Bennett (1994) indicates they have trouble answering questions about *when* the learning event took place. Four- and 5-year-old children claimed to have always known novel information that had just been taught to them by an experimenter. These results suggest young children are able to report the content of information they have learned before they are able to recall or understand much about how the learning took place. Overall, young preschoolers are quite limited in their conception of what it means to know a given piece of information (for review see Montgomery, 1992).

C. Summary

Although, at 3 years of age, children's performance in some studies shows a limited or rudimentary grasp of false belief, their ability to reason about false belief is clearly nowhere near that of the typical 5-year-old who has mastered the notion that a belief about the world is not always accurate and who readily makes use of this understanding in experimental situations. In contrast, there is evidence that children develop an early understanding of mental states such as desiring and perceiving, and possibly pretending and intending. The earlier-developing insights might provide a model for children to think about more difficult concepts such as false belief. An adultlike understanding of what it means to have knowledge might be one of the latest developments in the preschooler's understanding of mind. Accounts of theory of mind development are moving away from an exclusive focus on false belief in recognition that "the interdependent nature of our mentalistic concepts will constrain the way we describe children's knowledge of the mind at different points in development. That is, what we say about children's understanding of any one mentalistic concept will have ramifications for what we are entitled to say about the rest" (Moses, 1993, p. 2).

III. THE INFLUENCE OF THEORY OF MIND RESEARCH

Initially, theory of mind research was focused somewhat narrowly on the development of certain insights about mental life during the preschool period (e.g., the understanding of false belief); however, the theory of mind enterprise has expanded to the point where it now offers a conceptual framework for thinking more broadly about the development of social cognition and for integrating at least some of the diverse topics included in this area. Any move toward integration is an important contribution to this literature, because the scope of research in the domain of social cognition is extraordinarily broad. In fact, it is possible to find books on social cognition in childhood with largely nonoverlapping contents because sometimes the emphasis in this research is on the "social" (e.g., Higgins, Ruble, & Hartup, 1983) and sometimes on the "cognition" (e.g., Flavell & Ross, 1981). Also, as M. Bennett (1993) has pointed out, some of the research has its roots in the social cognitive study of adults that has dominated social psychology for two decades, while other social cognitive work in developmental psychology comes out of a Piagetian tradition (1929, 1932). The new perspective gained from theory of mind research has the potential to help overhaul and organize the laundry list of research topics that make up the field of social cognitive development. Of course not all current social cognitive research falls neatly into a theory of mind framework. Yet, interest in the development of knowledge about the mind extends beyond the borders of those interested in false belief and is influencing much of the recent empirical and theoretical work on social cognition. Here, I briefly describe a few of the ways theory of mind ideas and findings have influenced four areas of social cognitive research: children's understanding of emotion, the development of self, social cognition in infancy, and the social cognitive development of autistic children.

A. Children's Understanding of Emotion

Children's understanding of emotion is an important and active research area in the field of social cognitive development (for reviews see Harris, 1989; Meerum Terwogt & Harris, 1993; Saarni & Harris, 1989). Some of the issues addressed in recent research include the recognition of emotional expressions (Bullock & Russell, 1984; Caron, Caron, & Myers, 1982; Gnepp, 1983; Haviland & Lelwica, 1987; Russell & Bullock, 1986), the use of emotion words (Bretherton & Beeghly, 1982; Brown & Dunn, 1991; Dunn, Bretherton, & Munn, 1987; Ridgeway, Waters, & Kuczaj, 1985; Smiley & Huttenlocher, 1989; Wellman, Harris, Banerjee, & Sinclair, 1995), children's knowledge of the emotions associated with different situations (Barden, Zelko, Duncan, & Masters, 1980; Borke, 1971; Harris, Olthof, Meerum Terwogt, & Hardman, 1987), children's understanding of mixed emotions (Harter, 1983; Harter & Buddin, 1987, Harter & Whitesell, 1989), children's understanding of social rules for emotional expression and control of emotional expression (Cole, 1986; Harris & Gross, 1988; Harris, Olthof, & Meerum Terwogt, 1981; Saarni, 1984, 1989), and children's attempts to change other people's emotions (Dunn, Kendrick, & MacNamee, 1981).

One of the most striking influences of the theory of mind perspective on the study of emotion has been the development of a mentalistic alternative to the view that children's understanding of emotions is based primarily on their knowledge of the situations that are associated with particular emotions (Borke, 1971; Chandler & Greenspan, 1972; Gnepp & Chilamkurti, 1988; Gnepp & Gould, 1985; Harris & Olthof, 1982; Harris et al., 1981; Saarni, 1979). According to the situation theory of emotional understanding, children 6 years of age and younger identify and conceptualize emotion primarily with respect to their knowledge about the links between situations and the emotional expressions these situations typically elicit.

The situation theory of emotions is based on research in which children were asked questions about the relation between situations and emotions (e.g., Borke, 1971) and about how they knew when they were happy, angry, or afraid (Harris et al., 1981). Borke showed that 3- and 4-year-old children have some knowledge about the situations that typically elicit emotions such as happiness and sadness. In her studies, 4-year-old children were able to select the appropriate facial expression from an array of pictures that showed how someone would feel in the situations described in the stories (e.g., they picked a sad face for a story about losing a pet), and even 3-year-olds were aware of the link between being happy and certain situations (e.g., they picked a happy face for a story about a birthday party). Harris et al. showed that when children are asked how they identify their own emotions, 6-year-olds often refer to situations (e.g., I'm happy when it is my birthday), whereas 11- and 15-year-olds referred more frequently to mental states (e.g., If you are happy then you think everything is fine). These results were interpreted as suggesting that preschoolers conceptualize emotions in terms of the situations that elicit them rather than as internal mentalistic experiences. It is not until about 10 years of age that children are described as having shifted to a mentalistic understanding of emotions.

Theory of mind research showing that young children understand mental states such as desire seems inconsistent with the view that preschool children have no conception of the internal mentalistic components of emotional experience. The perspective gained from theory of mind research raised the question of how young children might take into account the ways that people's desires and beliefs affect their appraisals of emotional situations. More generally, emotion research and theory of mind research have come together in studies that explore the relations between children's understanding of emotions and their understanding of mental states such as desire, belief, and intention.

At the age that children first start to verbalize their own desires and the desires of other people they also talk about feelings, both their own and the feelings of other people (Dunn et al., 1987). They are influenced by the amount of talk about desires and feelings in their families (Dunn et al., 1987) and they practice this type of talk in their pretend play (Wolf, Rygh, & Altshuler, 1984). By 3 years of age, children understand the simple relation between desire and emotion. They realize that a person who gets what he or she desires will be happy and a person who does not get what he or she wants will be unhappy (Stein & Levine, 1989; Wellman & Banerjee, 1991; Yuill, 1984).

Other emotions or emotional situations require some ability to take people's belief states as well as their desires into account. One needs only to consider a person's desire for a bike to know that she is happy when she gets one for her birthday. However, the emotion of surprise entails a violation of expectation and thus requires some ability to reason about belief. A person who believed she was going to get a blue bike would be surprised if she received a red one. Happiness or sadness might be combined with the surprise, depending on her color preferences.

To examine children's understanding of these relations, Wellman and Bartsch (1988) told children stories that involved protagonists who either were given or were not given something that they thought or did not think they would receive or something they wanted or did not want. Subjects were asked to rate the happiness and the surprise of the protagonist for each type of story. Four-year-olds linked happiness with desire and surprise with belief, as expected by the theory of mind findings suggesting that 4-year-olds are able to reason about both desire and belief. Three-year-olds were able to understand the link between desire and happiness, but not between belief and surprise (Perner & Hadwin, 1989; Wellman & Banerjee, 1991). However, when asked to explain rather than predict an emotional reaction, some 3-year-olds, as well as the majority of 4-year-olds, made reference to belief when accounting for surprise or curiosity. This result is consistent with theory of mind research showing that 3-year-olds are better able to make reference to beliefs when explaining a person's actions than when predicting them (Bartsch & Wellman, 1989).

In other research investigating children's understanding of the relation between emotion and mental states, MacLaren and Olson (1993) found that 5-year-olds understood that an object was surprising if it violated expectations, regardless of whether it was a pleasant or disappointing surprise. Three-year-old children in this study tended to equate surprise with a good outcome, whether expected or not, instead of considering whether the identity of the object violated the person's expectations. Harris, Johnson, Hutton, Andrews, and Cooke (1989) investigated the ability of children aged 3 to 7 years to coordinate belief and desire when predicting emotions. Children in their study observed a toy monkey remove candy from a candy box and replace it with stones. A hungry bear was given the box and children were asked to judge if the bear would be happy to get the box. A majority of 6-year-olds and about half the 4-year-olds accurately predicted that the bear would be happy even though in reality the box contained rocks, demonstrating their understanding that beliefs must be taken into account when predicting emotional reactions. The 6-year-olds were also able to justify their predictions by referring to the false beliefs of the story character. These results indicate that the ability to predict and explain emotion with reference to mental states is well established by 5 or 6. Overall, the results of these studies demonstrate a well-developed understanding of the relation between mental states and emotion in young children (e.g., even 2- and 3-year-olds seem to understand the link between desire and emotion); and suggest that the situation theory of emotions underestimates young children's understanding of emotions.

One implication of the situation theory of emotional understanding is that young children would be predicted to have difficulty with the distinction between one's actual felt emotion and the emotion displayed in one's expression and behavior (Harris & Olthof, 1982). If children 6 years old and younger do not conceptualize emotion as an inner mental experience, they might not consider the possibility of a mismatch between the emotion a person feels and what they express on their face. Children this age would be expected to be less aware of display strategies involving emotion (e.g., you are supposed to smile when you open a present even if you do not like the present) than are older children. These predictions follow from the situation view of young children's emotional understanding in which internal states play no part. The results of research in which children were asked about the possibility of misidentifying emotions (Harris et al., 1989) and studies in which children were asked to select the appropriate facial expression for situations in which hiding one's true feelings would be important (Saarni, 1979) have shown the predicted developmental shift in performance from 6 to 10 years of age.

Harris, Donnelly, Guz, and Pitt-Watson (1986) were puzzled by the discrepancy between the theory that 6-year-old children do not understand the discrepancy between real and apparent emotion and the results of several theory of mind studies demonstrating the ability of even 4-year-olds to distinguish appearance and reality in the case of objects such as a fake rock (e.g., Flavell et al., 1983). Harris et al. suspected that the difference in performance might be due to the more complex nature of the emotion tasks (see also Harris & Gross, 1988). Flavell and colleagues have used extremely simple tasks in which the appearance and reality of the stimulus objects were explicitly labeled. In contrast, the emotion tasks have typically required children to figure out both the apparent and real emotions from the cues in the story and to appreciate that the person in the story might decide to hide his or her real emotions.

To test this hypothesis, Harris et al. (1986) told children stories in which a character was explicitly described as wanting to hide an emotion and the reason for wanting to hide his or her true feelings was explicitly stated. Under these task conditions, 6-year-olds had no difficulty distinguishing real and apparent emotion and understanding that the apparent emotion would result in an observer having a false belief about the story character's true feelings. However, the performance of most of the 4-year-olds did not differ from chance. When Gross (1989) tried an even simpler task involving physical instantiations of both the real and the apparent emotion (a happy mask on a sad face), 4-year-old children were capable of distinguishing appearance and reality. Perhaps they would also succeed with posed emotional expressions if the apparent and real emotions were explicitly labeled as in Flavell's appearance–reality tasks with physical objects.

In summary, theory-of-mind-related predictions about the developmental sequence for accurate reporting of different types of emotional responses have been tested in several studies. The results support the hypothesis that children's understanding of different emotions is closely related to the types of mental states they entail (e.g., surprise entails belief) and involves some appreciation of the mental states underlying the situations that would be likely to elicit a particular emotion. The research on real and apparent emotion influenced by theory of mind ideas, together with the research investigating the relations between belief–desire states and emotion, argue against the situation theory of emotions by demonstrating that young children have a more mentalistic understanding of emotions than previously believed. Preschoolers do not conceive of emotions solely in terms of behaviors or situations (Harris & Gross, 1988; Wellman et al., 1995).

B. Development of Self

Current topics addressed in research on the development of self include the origins of self knowledge (Butterworth, 1992; Meltzoff, 1990), development of self-recognition (Amsterdam, 1972; Berenthal & Fisher, 1978; Brooks-Gunn & Lewis, 1984; M. Lewis & Brooks-Gunn, 1979), self-conscious emotions (Amsterdam & Greenberg, 1977; Amsterdam & Levitt, 1980; M. Lewis, Sullivan, Stanger, & Weiss, 1989; Stipek, Gralinski, & Kopp, 1990), a developmental taxonomy of self (R. W. Mitchell, 1994; Stern, 1985); the content of self-knowledge at different points in development (Bullock & Lutkenhaus, 1990; Cicchetti & Beeghly, 1990; Eder, Gerlach, & Perlmutter, 1987; Livesly & Bromley, 1973), assessments of one's own abilities (Stipek & MacIver, 1989; Taylor et al., 1994), knowledge of social categories (Fagot & Leinbach, 1993), continuity in the child's sense of self (Povinelli, Landau, & Perilloux, 1995), comparative issues regarding self-development (Gallup, 1977, 1985, Marino, Reiss, & Gallup, 1994; Parker, Mitchell, & Boccia, 1994; Povinelli, 1987, 1989), and the development of self in atypical populations (Cicchetti, 1991; Gallup, McClure, Hill, & Bundy, 1971; Hobson, 1990a; Priel & de Schonen, 1986).

Research on these topics is active and the findings are important for a broad understanding of social cognitive development. However, within the theory of mind framework, there is one issue regarding the self that has been particularly central, namely, the relation between the development of self-knowledge and the development of knowledge about other people. Do we experience our own psychological states directly and then use knowledge of self to simulate the psychological experiences of others or does knowledge about the self have to be inferred in much the same way as knowledge about other people? According to the main point of view within theory of mind research (i.e., the "theory theory"), understanding of self and others develop together as children acquire a theory of mind (Gopnik, 1993; Gopnik & Wellman, 1994). This point of view contrasts with Piagetian theory in which it is assumed that understanding of self is achieved more directly and is used as the basis for understanding other people. Simulation theory (e.g., Harris, 1992), which is currently the main alternative to "theory theory," also gives special status to children's understanding of their own mental states.

1. The Theory Theory

Proponents of the theory theory position argue that children's knowledge of the mind constitutes an organized causal-explanatory system with the defining characteristics of theories (e.g., Gopnik & Wellman, 1994). On this view, children's understanding of the mind is a coherent body of abstract theoretical constructs that are used to explain and predict behavior. The exact nature or content of the theory evolves as children mature. The theory theory account of children's knowledge about the mind makes at least two claims about children's knowledge of self (Gopnik & Wellman, 1992, 1994). The first claim concerns the types of errors children make when asked about their own mental states. According to theory theory, the process underlying the discovery of one's own psychological states does not differ in kind from the process underlying the discovery of the psychological states of other people. Thus, the prediction is that children develop knowledge about the self and other people in parallel. Children who have limited understanding of other people's mental states should be limited in the same ways and to the same extent in their understanding of their own mental states.

This prediction has generally been supported by the results of research comparing the ability of young children to report their own former false beliefs and their ability to answer questions about the current false beliefs of other people (Gopnik & Astington, 1988). In the "representational change" task, children are shown the kinds of stimuli used in standard false beliefs tasks, but instead of being asked about the current false belief of another person, they are asked about their own former false belief (e.g., "when you first saw the box, before you looked inside, did you think there were Smarties or pencils inside?"). Children under 4 years of age have difficulty reporting their own former false beliefs, claiming, for example, to have known that a Smarties box contains pencils even before they looked inside the box. The timetables for mastery of the representational change task and the standard false belief task are quite similar. Three-year-old children have as much difficulty reporting their own past false beliefs as the false beliefs of other people. In addition, Gopnik and Slaughter (1991) have shown that the mental states that are the least problematic for children to identify in other people also are easiest to identify in the self. Three-year-old children in their study could most easily report their own past pretences, past images, and past perceptions. Past desires and past intentions were somewhat more difficult and former false beliefs were the most difficult of all.

The second related claim of theory theory concerns the accuracy of children's reports of their own mental states. If knowledge about one's own mental state has to be inferred rather than being directly perceived, the possibility of error is much more likely and the kinds of errors that are made will result from the general theory children hold. Thus, according to theory theory, there is no reason to expect young children's reports of their own mental states to be particularly accurate. In fact, young children frequently exhibit a striking lack of insight about their own mental states. In addition to their difficulty reporting their own former false beliefs, 3-year-old children often cannot identify the source of their own knowledge, (Gopnik & Graf, 1988; Povinelli & deBlois, 1992), and are unaware of their own learning (Taylor et al., 1994). These errors seem inconsistent with the widely held assumption that people know their own minds, but follows from the view that one's own mental states have to be inferred from one's general knowledge about mental states. In perhaps the strongest statement of this position, Gopnik (1993) describes as an illusion the commonsense belief that people have direct and reliable experience of their own psychological states. She compares our impression of first-person direct knowledge of our own mental states to the impression that experts have of the immediacy of their own specialized knowledge. For example, knowing what move to make in a chess game is derived from extensive experience with the game, but chess experts sometimes report that they directly perceive their next move (see Goldman, 1993a, for a critique of this analogy).

2. Simulation Theory

According to the simulation theory, direct first-person experience of psychological states is not an illusion. "Having psychological beliefs does not depend on having a theory of mind at all. These beliefs are instead simply a consequence of having a mind of a particular sort, a mind that gives rise to psychological experiences" (Goldman, 1993b, p. 3). Along with the idea that psychological states are immediately perceived is the idea that our own experience is used to help understand the experience of others, a notion of perspective taking as simulation (Goldman, 1989; 1992; Gordon, 1992; Harris, 1991). On this view, young children directly experience their own mental states and use knowledge of their own minds as the basis for making inferences about the mental states of others (Harris, 1991; Johnson, 1988). More specifically, children imagine themselves as being in the situation of another person and then attribute the intentions, thoughts, and emotions they experience as a result of this simulation as corresponding to the actual psychological states of the other person.

At first glance, children's poor performance on representational change tasks seems inconsistent with simulation theory, which predicts that children should understand their own mental states earlier than the mental states of other people. However, Harris (1991) argues that a comparison of children's performance on the representational change task and the standard false belief task is not a good test of this prediction (see also Chandler & Carpendale, 1993; Goldman, 1993a). The problem with the representational change task is that the false belief in question does not correspond to the child's *current* mental state. As mentioned earlier, false belief is one mental state that cannot, in principle, be directly experienced. If experienced at all, belief is necessarily experienced as true. It is only later with additional information that children realize a previously held belief is false (Bartsch & Estes, 1993). According to Harris, the problems of 3-year-olds on the representational change task, as well as on the standard false belief task, reflect inadequate simulation (i.e., the failure to adjust default settings, such as equating the other's belief with the child's current true belief) rather than the limitations of their theory of mind. Although Harris's point is well taken, young children are not *always* accurate in their report of current mental states. Light and Nix (1983) found that children had as much difficulty reporting their own current visual perspective of a display (when their own perspective did not correspond to a canonical view in which the objects in the display were optimally in view) as reporting the perspectives of other people. Light and Nix interpreted their results as showing that children do not use their own perspective as the basis for their judgments about the perspective of other people. Instead, children did not seem to understand the concept of perspective, an interpretation that is consistent with the theory theory position.

In summary, Gopnik and Wellman (1992) present a convincing case for theory theory's account of the overall pattern of findings in the theory of mind literature. Young children often cannot answer direct questions about their own mental states and there is an interesting parallel between children's ability to report their own former false beliefs and their ability to report the false beliefs of other people.[3] In addition, theory theory accounts for the successes children have in their reports for some types of mental states and the types of explanations children give for their responses in theory of mind tasks. On the other hand, there is some evidence that children talk about their own mental states earlier and more often than the mental states of other people (Bartsch & Wellman, 1995). The debate between theory theory and simulation theory and the empirical work stimulated by this controversy are important new contributions to the literature on the development of self. The debate is ongoing; thus, questions concerning the status of self-knowledge are likely to be an important focus of future theory of mind research.

C. Social Cognition in Infancy

By 4 or 5 years of age, the achievements of children in the development of social understanding are truly remarkable. Children this age routinely attribute the behavior of themselves and other people to unobservable mental states, they are aware of the conditions that lead to beliefs, they realize that people often misrepresent the world, and that people's actions and emotions are based on their representations of reality rather than reality itself. They have an abstract understanding of human behavior that is thoroughly mentalistic. For Wellman (1993), the rate at which children develop an adultlike theory of mind is comparable to the extremely rapid developmental rate of language acquisition. In fact, just as the recognition of young children's word learning wizardry (Carey, 1978) led to research on innate linguistic knowledge, a growing appreciation for the scope and sophistication of preschoolers' understanding of mind gives credibility to the idea that infants might be richly endowed with innate knowledge, constraints, and/or predispositions that jump-start theory of mind development (Fodor, 1987; Hobson, 1991; Leslie, 1987). The argument is that children could not be expected to acquire an understanding of mind so quickly, accurately, and similarly across cultures (Avis & Harris, 1991) if newborns were social-cognitive blank slates (Wellman, 1993).

The current focus in the theory of mind literature is shifting from the achievements of 4- and 5-year-old children to the search for the origins of these abilities. There are a wealth of behaviors to choose from because infant social cognition, along with other infancy research, has been flourishing since the theoretical and methodological advancements of the 1970s. Some of the findings of research on infant social cognition have shown that babies prefer the sights and sounds of people over most other kinds of perceptual stimuli (Sherrod, 1981), are able to make fine discriminations between faces (Nelson, 1987) and voices (DeCasper & Fifer, 1980; DeCasper & Spence, 1986), are able to detect the cross-modal relation between voices and faces (Spelke, 1976), and can differentiate a person who intends to communicate and one who does not (Trevarthen, 1977). In contrast to Piagetian theory in which preschool children are described as having little understanding of the distinction between animate and inanimate objects, recent research has shown that 3- and 4-year-olds can make this distinction quite clearly when properly interviewed (R. Gelman, Spelke, & Meck, 1983) and even infants show some understanding (Brazelton, Koslowski, & Main, 1974; Frye, Rawling, Moore, & Myers, 1983; Golinkoff, Harding, Carlson, & Sexton, 1984). For example, infants can use information about both the way an object moves and the kind of material it is made of to distinguish between animate and inanimate objects (R. Gelman, Durgin, & Kaufman, 1995) and can discriminate animate-biological motion from random motion (Bertenthal, Profitt, Spetner, & Thomas, 1985). These results show that from a very early age, infants are aware that other people are significant objects in their lives. However, the pressing issue for theory of mind researchers is to identify the kinds of knowledge or behaviors that are most directly related to a developing awareness of mental life.

For Meltzoff and Gopnik (1993), theory of mind development is rooted in infants' ability to imitate. When newborns imitate the facial expressions of other people, they demonstrate an innate ability to map the behaviors of other people onto internal proprioceptive sensations and motor plans for carrying out the actions observed in others (Meltzoff & Moore, 1977, 1983, 1989). Meltzoff and Gopnik argue that this ability provides a starting point for social cognition because it allows infants to immediately appreciate the correspondence between themselves and other people. In addition, Meltzoff and Gopnik point out that proprioceptive sensations are similar in some ways to internal mental states. Newborns' innate ability to recognize the relation between another person's behavior and the infant's own proprioceptive sensations and behavior could be the basis for an early grasp of similar relations between behavior and mental states. The infant's understanding of body and mind are not easily separated and, quite possibly, it is knowledge of the body that leads to discovery of the mind (Meltzoff & Gopnik, 1993). Thus, the ability of newborns to imitate facial expressions is not only an indicator of social knowledge, it is also a mechanism for developing deeper insights about the social world of other people.

Other researchers have looked beyond early imitative behaviors for evidence that infants understand something about the intentions, perceptions, or other type of internal mental states of other people. Increasingly, researchers have become interested in intentionality, a characteristic of mind that is truly fundamental to the whole notion of mentality (Gopnik, 1993). Intentionality, in the philosophical sense, has a more general meaning than the everyday understanding of *intending,* one of the mental states discussed earlier. Intending concerns the distinction between actions that are done according to plan versus actions that are accidental. The notion of intentionality transcends ideas about particular mental states and how children's insights about them develop. Intentionality refers to a property of all mental states, namely, that they are about or directed toward some content (Brentano, 1874/1960). Thoughts, desires, and beliefs are about objects or events. Carey (1991) describes intentionality, the directedness or aboutness of mental states, as a foundational concept intrinsic to any folk psychology.

How and when do infants demonstrate some rudimentary grasp of this general understanding about mental states? A number of related abilities start to emerge at 9 months of age, which could be interpreted as candidates for the first glimmerings of intentionality (Adamson & Bakeman, 1985; Bakeman & Adamson, 1984; Bates, 1979; Bretherton et al., 1981; Lempers et al., 1977; Stern, 1985; Trevarthen & Hubley, 1978). These abilities include social referencing, joint attention, intentional communication, and the imitation of novel actions.

1. Social Referencing

Social referencing is usually described as the infant's use of another person's emotional reaction to an ambiguous object or event as the basis for his or her own appraisal of the object or event (for review see Feinman, 1992). For example, Klinnert, Campos, Sorce, Emde, and Svejda (1983) found that when 12-month-old infants were confronted with a strange new toy, they approached the toy if their mothers looked happy and moved away from the toy (toward their mothers) if the mothers looked fearful. These results could be explained as demonstrating infants' understanding that the mothers are expressing an emotional reaction to a strange toy, but it is also possible that infants react in a general way to their mothers' positive or negative expressions via "mood contagion" and do not relate the expression to anything in particular.

The results of research by Hornik, Risenhoover, and Gunnar (1987) render the mood contagion hypothesis less probable. They found that 12-month-olds selectively avoided or played with toys that the mothers reacted to with disgust or delight. Thus, children in this study did not demonstrate a general tendency to avoid or play with toys as a function of their mothers' expression, as would be predicted by the mood contagion hypothesis. Instead, their avoidance or approach was specific to the target toy that was the object of their mothers' emotional reactions (see also Feiring, Lewis, & Starr, 1984; Walden & Ogan, 1988). Moreover, Moses, Baldwin, and Tidball (1995) have found that infants show a differential reaction to a target toy based on the parents' positive or negative reactions, even when the infant is attending to a different toy at the time that the parent reacts to the toy. For example, 12-month-olds reacted more positively to a toy when it had been the target of the parent's positive affect, even though, at the time of the parent's emotional expression, the infant and the parent had been attending to different toys.

The hypothesized relation between social referencing skills and later theory of mind development is controversial. Moore and Corkum (1994) argue that early-developing social referencing skills do not reflect the social cognitive understanding that others have assumed must guide such behaviors. Even Bretherton (1991), who in general believes infants exhibit an early understanding of mind, does not consider the case for a full understanding of intentionality on the basis of social referencing data to be conclusive. Baldwin and Moses (1994) have meticulously teased apart the alternative explanations for social referencing behavior and conclude that what appears to be an infant's attempt to seek information about a strange object could be interpreted more parsimoniously as attachment behavior. Although Baldwin and Moses do not believe infants actively seek information, they credit them with some understanding of intentionality in that, having seen the parent's emotional expression, the infant understands that the parent has an internal emotional state and that the emotion is about a specific object.

2. Joint Attention

When infants see an adult turn to look in a given direction, the infants tend to look where the adult is looking, an ability known as joint attention. In the first published demonstration of joint attention, an experimenter and infant sat face to face and the experimenter looked to one side and then to the other side. All the infants between 11 and 14 months followed the experimenter's gaze (Scaife & Bruner, 1975). If there does not seem to be an interesting object to look at in the direction of the adult's gaze, the infant looks back at the adult, as if to check the adult's focus of attention (Butterworth & Cochran, 1980). There is some variability in the reports of the age that joint attention is first demonstrated (for review see Moore & Corkum, 1994), but joint attention seems to be firmly established by 12 months of age. By 18 months of age, infants are capable of coordinated joint attention with an age mate, as well as a more competent communicative partner such as their mother (Bakeman & Adamson, 1984) and they are accurate in locating the object of an adult's attention (Butterworth & Cochran, 1980).

The infant's ability to follow the adult's gaze has been interpreted as demonstrating that infants are able to conceptualize another person as looking at something in the same way that they themselves look at something (Baron-Cohen, 1991, Bretherton, 1991; Reddy, 1991). Moore and Corkum (1994) have argued against a social cognitive interpretation of infants' joint attention skills by pointing out that the same behaviors can be explained in terms of instrumental conditioning. Infants learn that when they turn their heads in the same direction as an adult head turn, they will be rewarded with an interesting visual event. This alternative explanation loses its parsimony, however, when one considers Moore and Corkum's finding that infants cannot learn to look in the opposite direction of the adult's head turn. Eleven-month-olds followed the gaze of an adult even when the experimenter reinforced them for looking in the opposite direction.

3. Intentional Communication

Toward the end of the first year, infants begin to show clear signs of producing and comprehending communicative gestures (Lempers et al., 1977; Leung & Rheingold, 1981; Murphy, 1978). By 14 months, infants check to see if their communicative partner has followed their point (Bretherton et al., 1981). If a partner does not respond to an infant's gesture he or she reproduces it, often increasing the gesture's intensity (Bates, 1979). According to Bretherton (1991), the ability of preverbal infants to intentionally communicate is clear evidence that they are able to attribute mental states to other people and to themselves and that one mind can communicate with another mind through the use of signals. Baron-Cohen (1995) also argues for a mentalistic analysis of early communication skills. However, other theorists have suggested alternative explanations (Baldwin & Moses, 1994; Butterworth, 1991; Perner, 1991a).

Although a mentalistic interpretation of nonverbal communication is controversial, the understanding of mind reflected in children's word learning skills is undeniable. In a series of recent studies, Baldwin (1991, 1993) has shown that by at least 18 months, and possibly earlier, infants are able to overcome obstacles to identifying the referent of a new word by taking the adult's direction of gaze into account. For example, infants map a new word to the correct referent, even when the adult produces the word as the infant looks at an object that is different from the one being labeled (Baldwin, 1993). Infants also map verbs onto the appropriate actions, even though the new word is typically heard after the action has just happened or when it is about to happen, rather than when it is currently happening (Tomasello & Kruger, 1992). Tomasello, Kruger, and Ratner (1993) observes that "some very powerful skills of perspective-taking are clearly at work here, as children in these situations must understand the adult's intentions in a way that allows them to determine the adult's focus of attention outside the immediate perceptual context" (p. 498). The ease with which children learn new words suggests they understand the intentionality of language and can use the cues in the environment to understand the word's referent.

4. Imitation of Novel Actions

According to Tomasello, Kruger, and Ratner (1993), one of the important differences between humans and other animals is that human beings are capable of learning from each other by taking the other person's perspective into account. Tomasello et al. refer to this type of knowledge acquisition as "cultural learning." The first evidence of cultural learning occurs at about 9 months when infants begin to initiate novel actions performed by another person to perform a particular goal (Abravonal & Gingold, 1985; Masur & Ritz, 1984; Meltzoff, 1988a, 1988b). (Imitative learning is distinguished from earlier behaviors such as the imitative abilities of newborns because no new information is learned in the earlier acts of imitation.) Tomasello et al. cite Meltzoff's (1988b) demonstration of 14-month-olds learning to bend over to turn on a light with their foreheads by watching an adult model this behavior as one of the best examples of this type of cultural learning. According to Tomasello et al. (1993), the ability to reproduce an adult's behavior in an appropriate context requires an understanding of intentionality, because otherwise the infant would not be able to identify the parts of the adult's behavior that were relevant for bringing about the desired outcome. Tomasello et al. also mention social referencing and joint attention as abilities emerging at 9 months, along with imitative learning, which together demonstrate infants' understanding of people as intentional agents.

5. Summary

Theory of mind research has increased our appreciation of the scope of social cognitive knowledge characteristic of preschoolers. Some authors have proposed that the ability to comprehend and predict the behavior of another person has an innate, biological, and modular basis (Baron-Cohen, 1995; Baron-Cohen & Ring, 1994; Leslie, 1994). If infants are not endowed with an innate knowledge of people, then an account of the innate knowledge they *do* have that allows them to learn about people so efficiently is required (Carey, 1985). Consequently, researchers have scrutinized the abilities of infants that could reflect or promote an understanding of mind. This perspective derived from theory of mind research has moved the study of infant imitation to a more central position in the literature on social cognition in infancy. In addition, there are a variety of important social cognitive skills, including social referencing, the ability to establish joint attention, intentional communication, and the ability to imitate novel actions, that begin to emerge at 9 months of age. Although in their earliest manifestations it is unclear whether an understanding of intentionality underlies these behaviors, by 18 months it is difficult to deny that the infant has an understanding of intentionality. According to Wellman (1993), the evidence suggests that in the second year, infants "may well understand three foundational intentional aspects of persons: a simple but intentional understanding of desire, of perception, and of emotion. That is, they come to see themselves and others as attending to the world, seeking to attain things or experiences from it, and reacting to it affectively" (pp. 21–22).

D. Social Cognition in Autistic Children

Autistic children are known to show severe deficits in social competence (Wing & Gould, 1979), communication skills (Attwood, Frith, & Hermelin, 1988; Schopler & Mesibov, 1983; Mundy, Sigman, Ungerer, & Sherman, 1986), and pretend play (Baron-Cohen, 1988; Ungerer & Sigman, 1981, for review see Frith, 1989). Autistics seem to interpret behavior in a literal fashion, failing to understand distinctions based on intentions, feelings, or beliefs (Frith, 1989). This observation has led to the hypothesis that autistic individuals fail to develop an understanding that people have minds and that mental states are related to behavior. The theory of mind hypothesis about autism has been supported by the results of several studies demonstrating difficulties and delays in autistic children's performance on theory of mind tasks compared with the performance of language-delayed, retarded, or average children. More specifically, these studies have shown that autistic children have difficulty understanding false belief (Baron-Cohen, 1988; Baron-Cohen, Leslie, & Frith, 1985; Perner, Frith, Leslie, & Leekam, 1989), deception (Russell et al., 1991), desire (Harris & Muncer, 1988), the connection between visual access and having knowledge (Baron-Cohen & Goodhart, 1994; Leslie & Frith, 1988; Perner et al., 1989), and the distinction between mental and physical entities (Baron-Cohen, 1989). Only a minority of autistic children with mental ages of up to almost 13 years are able to demonstrate the understanding of mind typical of the average 4-year-old (Perner et al., 1989).

The claim that the deficit in autism is specific to an understanding of mind, rather than a more general failure to understand social relations, to process verbal information, or to cooperate in an experimental setting, has been supported in several experiments. For example, in an experiment by Baron-Cohen, Leslie, and Frith (1986), autistic children, mentally retarded children, and average preschoolers were asked to put a set of pictures in sequence and tell the story in the pictures. When the story involved a mechanical sequence of events (a balloon floating away and bursting when getting stuck in a tree), autistic children outperformed both the mentally retarded and average control subjects. In contrast, when the sequence of events involved a false belief (a child opens a box where he previously put some candy and finds the box empty), even the mentally retarded children were able to sequence the pictures and tell the story in a more coherent fashion than the autistic children.

In other research, autistic children had little difficulty when given a variety of social cognitive tasks that did not require an understanding of mental states (Baron-Cohen et al., 1986). In addition, autistic children are able to perform well when the task can be solved without reference to mental states. For example, unlike average children, autistic children are better able to report their own prior false beliefs than to attribute a false belief to another person (Naito, Komatsu, & Fuke, 1994; Perner et al., 1989). This asymmetry in task performance has been explained as reflecting the tendency of autistic children to regard an utterance as a description of an event rather than expression of belief (Roth & Leslie, 1991). On this view, autistic children solve the representational change task by recalling what they said when they were asked about the contents of the box, without conceptualizing their previous statement in terms of false belief.

The hypothesis that autistic people have a profound and specific deficit in their understanding of mind contrasts with earlier views interpreting the core symptoms of autism as reflecting a profound disturbance in affective development (Hobson, 1990b; Kanner, 1943). According to the theory of mind hypothesis, the primary deficit is cognitive, which in turns leads to disturbances in affective development. Although the debate over the cognitive and affective roots of autism is ongoing (Leslie & Frith, 1990), the theory of mind hypothesis has generated a great deal of new information about autism that is shedding light on both normal and atypical social-cognitive development (for reviews see Baron-Cohen, 1995; Baron-Cohen, Tager-Flusberg, & Cohen, 1993). For autism researchers, the relation between the many impairments that have been identified in autistic children becomes more obvious when autism is thought of as a specific deficit in children's understanding of mental states and mental life. Frith (1989) observes that "several seemingly unrelated features of Autism would suddenly fit together like long-lost pieces in a jig-saw puzzle" (p. 173). Perhaps theory of mind research with normal children will ultimately help identify early diagnostic criteria for autism.

For theory of mind researchers, it has been helpful to study the behavior of autistic children because the findings can be used in the development and testing of theories about normal development. For example, research with autistic children has helped to distinguish two alternative accounts of children's developing understanding of representation. Zaitchik (1990) has shown that young children have difficulty understanding pictorial representations (e.g., photographs) as well as mental ones (e.g., belief), which suggests that children's difficulty with false belief might reflect a general difficulty understanding the nature of representation. However, the finding that autistic children show a clear dissociation in their performance on the two kinds of tasks (i.e., they understand pictorial representation much better than mental representation) supports the alternative view that understanding of mental states is domain specific, but develops in parallel with understanding of nonmental representation (Leslie & Thaiss, 1992). According to Tager-Flusberg, Baron-Cohen, and Cohen (1993), "Without the study of autism it is debatable whether the field would have been focusing on the significance of joint-attention in the development of a theory of mind, for example, or would have considered the modularity of a theory of mind in neuropsychological terms. Indeed, even the link between theory of mind and pretend play owes much to the associated deficits uncovered in autism" (p. 8).

IV. FINAL THOUGHTS AND SPECULATIONS

The growing interest in children's development of theories about mental life is part of a general trend in many areas of cognitive psychology to view theory development as a crucial part of the representation of knowledge and conceptual structure (R. Gelman, 1990; S. A. Gelman, this volume; G. L. Murphy & Medin, 1985; Wellman & Gelman, 1992). According to Murphy and Medin, concepts are coherent to the extent that they fit into people's naive theories about the world. In this review, I have described how concepts such as belief and desire fit into the child's developing theory of mind and how theory of mind provides a conceptual framework for exploring issues related to children's understanding of emotion, the development of self, social cognition in infancy, and the social-cognitive development of autistic children. It should be noted that this review is selective in that some important topics in theory of mind research have not been covered (e.g., comparative work with other species, cross-cultural issues) or have been only briefly mentioned (e.g., neurological theories about theory of mind development), and the list of topics described as influenced by theory of mind research is not exhaustive (e.g., the animate–inanimate distinction, moral development; see Premack & Premack, 1994). For other recent reviews of the theory of mind literature see Astington (1995), Bartsch and Wellman (1995), and Flavell and Miller (in press). It also is true that some areas of social-cognitive research have not been substantially influenced by theory of mind ideas (e.g., children's understanding of race and gender) and there are many critics of this approach to the study of social-cognitive development. For example, theory of mind research has been described as too focused on the cognition of the individual instead of social-cognitive interaction and participation (e.g., Forrester, 1993) and as misleading about the processes involved in acquiring social knowledge (Hobson, 1991; Russell, 1992). Even the name has its problems. After all, "theory of mind" is a phrase that has been described as "a minefield of philosophical and theoretical debate" (Leekam, 1993, p. 26). However, for many developmental psychologists, there is little doubt of the importance of theory of mind research.

In this review I have focused on early childhood, the developmental period in which theory of mind development has been most thoroughly studied. In general, the emphasis on the preschool period is shifting to infancy with the search for the origins of children's understanding of mind. Theory of mind development after the preschool period remains largely unexplored territory, although a few researchers have speculated about the developments that occur after the watershed preschool period (Chandler, 1987; Wellman, 1990) and some intriguing research has been conducted with older children (Fabricus, Schwanenflugel, Kyllonen, Barclay & Denton, 1989; Flavell, Green, & Flavell, 1995; Pillow, 1989).

According to Wellman (1990), it is after the preschool period that expectations about behavior based on belief–desire psychology are integrated with more specific theories about individuals and social categories. This observation is consistent with the results of studies showing that 4-year-old children have difficulty integrating predictions about behavior based on their understanding of mind with predictions based on more specific theories about the self, other individuals, or social categories (Taylor, Cartwright, & Bowden, 1991). When older children and adults try to predict or understand another person's behavior, belief–desire psychology is supplemented with personal information about the particular individual's personality traits and background history. Wellman (1990) speculates that the process of integrating belief–desire psychology with specific knowledge about an individual is also at work in the development of older children's understanding of themselves. He writes, "our understanding of ourselves partakes of and is limited by our framework belief–desire psychology, but it provides a detailed instantiation of the framework theory in a specific self-story, an autobiography. Self-theories constitute specific theories framed by the dictates of naive framework psychology—a specific coherent construal of one's own beliefs, desires, traits, history of perceptions, and memories" (pp. 297–298).

Perhaps it will be research with school-aged children that first integrates theory of mind findings with areas of social cognition such as children's developing knowledge of social categories based on gender, race, and age. Although to date, research and theorizing on social category knowledge has had little contact with the theory of mind literature, both areas have been influenced by the general trend in cognitive science to understand individual concepts as embedded in theories (e.g., S. A. Gelman, this volume; S. A. Gelman & Coley, 1991; S. A. Gelman, Collman, & Maccoby, 1986; Hirschfeld, 1994; Rothbart & Taylor, 1992). One of the challenges for the future will be to better understand how children integrate their knowledge about individual differences in behavior based on social category membership, as well as more idiosyncratic variables such as special knowledge about the self or well-known others, with their general explanatory understanding based on belief–desire psychology.

Acknowledgments

I am very grateful to Lou Moses, Angel Lillard, Susan Gelman, Stephanie Carlson, Bonnie Esbensen, and Rochel Gelman for their comments on a previous draft of this chapter. I also thank Terry Au and Andrew Meltzoff for helpful suggestions.

Endnotes

1. Sometimes the research findings get simplified into a three to four shift, with 4-year-olds showing complete mastery of the tasks that 3-year-olds routinely fail. The data typically do not show a stagelike discontinuity of this sort, but a more gradual increase throughout the preschool years in the percentage of children getting the right answers.

2. Their difficulty seems specific to internal mental states rather than all internal states. Perner and Ogden (1988) found that 3- and 4-year-olds had no difficulty imputing hunger (an internal but nonmental state) to another person on the basis of access to food, although they had difficulty attributing knowledge to another person on the basis of perceptual access to the relevant information.
3. However, as Dittrich and Lea (1993) point out, the parallel development of two abilities is not conclusive evidence of their common causation.

References

Abravonal, E., & Gingold, H. (1985). Learning via observation during the second year of life. *Developmental Psychology, 21,* 614–623.

Adamson, L. B., & Bakeman, R. (1985). Affect and attention: Infants observed with mothers and peers. *Child Development, 56,* 582–593.

Amsterdam, B. K. (1972). Mirror self-image reactions before age two. *Developmental Psychobiology, 5,* 297–305.

Amsterdam, B. K., & Greenberg, L. G. (1977). Self conscious behavior of infants. *Developmental Psychobiology, 10,* 1–6.

Amsterdam, B. K., & Levitt, M. (1980). Consciousness of self and painful self-consciousness. *Psychoanalytic Study of the Child, 35,* 67–83.

Astington, J. W. (1991). Intention in the child's theory of mind. In D. Frye & C. Moore (Eds.), *Children's theories of mind* (pp. 157–172). Hillsdale, NJ: Erlbaum.

Astington, J. W. (1995). *The child's discovery of mind.* Cambridge, Massachusetts: Harvard University Press.

Attwood, A. H., Frith, U., & Hermelin, B. (1988). The understanding and use of interpersonal gestures by autistic and Down's syndrome children. *Journal of Autism and Developmental Disorders, 18,* 241–257.

Au, T. (1992). Counterfactual reasoning. In G. R. Semin & K. Fiedler (Eds.), *Language, interaction, and social cognition* (pp. 194–213). London: Sage.

Avis, J., & Harris, P. L. (1991). Belief–desire reasoning among Baka children: Evidence for a universal conception of mind. *Child Development, 62,* 460–467.

Bakeman, R., & Adamson, L. B. (1984). Coordinating attention to people and objects in mother–child and peer–infant interaction. *Child Development, 55,* 1278–1289.

Baldwin, D. (1991). Infants' contribution to the achievement of joint reference. *Child Development, 62,* 875–890.

Baldwin, D. (1993). Infants' ability to consult the speaker for clues to word reference. *Journal of Child Language, 20,* 395–418.

Baldwin, D. (1995). Understanding the link between joint attention and language. In C. Moore & P. Dunham (Eds.), *Joint attention: Its origins and role in development* (pp. 131–158). Hillsdale, NJ: Erlbaum.

Baldwin, D., & Moses, L. J. (1994). Early understanding of referential intent and attentional focus: Evidence from language and emotion. In C. Lewis & P. Mitchell (Eds.), *Children's early understanding of mind: Origins and development* (pp. 133–156). Hillsdale, NJ: Erlbaum.

Barden, R. C., Zelko, F. A., Duncan, S. W., & Masters, J. C. (1980). Children's consensual knowledge about the experiential determinants of emotion. *Journal of Personality and Social Psychology, 39,* 968–976.

Baron-Cohen, S. (1988). Social and pragmatic deficits in autism: Cognitive or affective? *Journal of Autism and Developmental Disorders, 21,* 37–46.

Baron-Cohen, S. (1989). Perceptual role-taking and protodeclarative pointing in autism. *British Journal of Developmental Psychology, 7,* 113–127.

Baron-Cohen, S. (1991). Precursors to a theory of mind: Understanding attention in others. In A. Whiten (Ed.), *Natural theories of mind: Evolution, development, and simulation of everyday mindreading* (pp. 233–252). Oxford: Blackwell.

Baron-Cohen, S. (1995). *Mindblindness: An essay on autism and theory of mind.* Cambridge, MA: MIT Press.

Baron-Cohen, S., & Goodhart, F. (1994). The "seeing-leads-to-knowing" deficit in autism: The Pratt and Bryant probe. *British Journal of Developmental Psychology, 12,* 397–401.

Baron-Cohen, S., Leslie, A. M., & Frith, U. (1985). Does the autistic child have a "theory of mind"? *Cognition, 21,* 37–46.

Baron-Cohen, S., Leslie, A. M., & Frith, U. (1986). Mechanical, behavioural, and intentional understanding of picture stories in autistic children. *British Journal of Developmental Psychology, 4,* 113–125.

Baron-Cohen, S., & Ring, H. (1994). A model of the mindreading system: Neuropsychological and neurobiological perspectives. In C. Lewis & P. Mitchell (Eds.), *Children's early understanding of mind: Origins and development* (pp. 183–207). Hillsdale, NJ: Erlbaum.

Baron-Cohen, S., Tager-Flusberg, H., & Cohen, D. J. (1993). *Understanding other minds: Perspectives from autism.* New York: Oxford University Press.

Bartsch, K., & Estes, D. (1993). Are false beliefs representative mental states? Commentary on A. Gopnik, How we know our own minds: The illusion of first-person knowledge of intentionality. *Behavioral and Brain Sciences, 16,* 30–31.

Bartsch, K., & Wellman, H. M. (1989). Young children's attribution of action to beliefs and desires. *Child Development, 60,* 946–964.

Bartsch, K., & Wellman, H. M. (1995). *Children talk about the mind.* New York: Oxford University Press.

Bates, E. (1979). Intentions, conventions, and symbols. In E. Bates, L. Benigni, I. Bretherton, L., Camaioni, & V. Volterra (Eds.), *The emergence of symbols* (pp. 69–140). New York: Academic Press.

Bennett, J. (1978). Beliefs about beliefs. Commentary on D. Premack & G. Woodruff, Does the chimpanzee have a theory of mind? *Behavioral and Brain sciences, 4,* 558–560.

Bennett, M. (1993). Introduction. In M. Bennett (Ed.), *The child as psychologist* (pp. 1–25). New York: Harvester Wheatsheaf.

Bertenthal, B. I., & Fischer, K. W. (1978). Development of self-recognition in the infant. *Developmental Psychology, 14,* 44–50.

Bertenthal, B. I., Proffitt, D. R., Spetner, N. B., & Thomas, M. A. (1985). The development of infant sensitivity to biomechanical motions. *Child Development, 56,* 531–543.

Borke, H. (1971). Interpersonal perception of young children: Egocentrism or empathy? *Developmental Psychology, 5,* 263–269.

Brazelton, T., Koslowski, B., & Main, M. (1974). The origins of reciprocity: The early mother–infant interaction. In M. Lewis & L. Rosenblum (Eds.), *The effect of the infant on its caregiver* (pp. 49–76). New York: Wiley.

Brentano, F. (1874/1960). The distinction between mental and physical phenomena. In R. M. Chisholm (Ed.), *Realism and the background of phenomenology* (pp. 39–61). New York: Free Press.

Bretherton, I. (1991). Intentional communication and the development of mind. In D. Frye & C. Moore (Eds.), *Children's theories of mind: Mental states and social understanding* (pp. 49–76). Hillsdale, NJ: Erlbaum.

Bretherton, I., Bates, E., McNew, S., Shore, C., Williamson, C., & Beeghly-Smith, M. (1981). Comprehension and production of symbols in infancy: An experimental study. *Developmental Psychology, 17,* 728–736.

Bretherton, I., & Beeghly, M. (1982). Talking about internal states: The acquisition of an explicit theory of mind. *Developmental Psychology, 18,* 906–921.

Brooks-Gunn, J., & Lewis, M. (1984). The development of early visual self-recognition. *Developmental Review, 4,* 215–239.

Brown, J. R., & Dunn, J. (1991). "You can cry, mum": The social and developmental implications of talk about internal states. *British Journal of Developmental Psychology, 9,* 237–256.

Bullock, M., & Lutkenhaus, P. (1990). Who am I? Self-understanding in toddlers. *Merrill-Palmer Quarterly, 36,* 217–238.

Bullock, M., & Russell, J. A. (1984). Preschool children's interpretation of facial expressions of emotion. *International Journal of Behavioral Development, 1,* 193–214.

Butterworth, G. (1991). The ontogeny and phylogeny of joint visual attention. In A. Whiten (Ed.), *Natural theories of mind: Evolution, development, and simulation of everyday mindreading* (pp. 223–231). Oxford: Blackwell.

Butterworth, G. (1992). Origins of self-perception in infancy. *Psychological Inquiry, 3,* 103–111.

Butterworth, G., & Cochran, E. (1980). Towards a mechanism of joint visual attention in human infancy. *International Journal of Behavioral Development, 3,* 253–272.

Campbell, R. L., & Bickhard, M. H. (1993). Knowing levels and the child's understanding of mind. Commentary on A. Gopnik, How we know our own minds: The illusion of first-person knowledge of intentionality. *Behavioral and Brain Sciences, 16,* 33–34.

Carey, S. (1978). The child as word learner. In M. Halle, J. Bresnan, & A. Miller (Eds.), *Linguistic theory and psychological reality* (pp. 263–293). Cambridge, MA: MIT Press.

Carey, S. (1985). *Conceptual change in childhood.* Cambridge, MA: MIT Press.

Carey, S. (1991). Knowledge acquisition: Enrichment or conceptual change? In S. Carey & R. Gelman (Eds.), *The epigenesis of mind* (pp. 257–292). Hillsdale, NJ: Erlbaum.

Caron, R. F., Caron, A. J., & Myers, R. S. (1982). Abstraction of invariant face expressions in infancy. *Child Development, 53,* 1008–1015.

Carrithers, M. (1991). Narrativity: Mindreading and making societies. In A. Whiten (Ed.), *Natural theories of mind: Evolution, development, and simulation of everyday mindreading* (pp. 305–318). Oxford: Blackwell.

Chandler, M. J. (1987). The Othello effect: Essay on the emergence and eclipse of skeptical doubt. *Human Development, 30,* 137–159.

Chandler, M. (1988). Doubt and developing theories of mind. In J. W. Astington, P. L. Harris, & D. R. Olson (Eds.), *Developing theories of mind* (pp. 387–413). New York: Cambridge University Press.

Chandler, M. J., & Carpendale, J. (1993). The naked truth about first-person knowledge. Commentary on A. Gopnik, How we know our own minds: The illusion of first-person knowledge of intentionality. *Behavioral and Brain Sciences, 16,* 36–37.

Chandler, M. J., Fritz, A. S., & Hala, S. (1989). Small-scale deceit: Deception as a marker of two-, three-, and four-year-olds' early theories of mind. *Child Development, 60,* 1263–1277.

Chandler, M. J., & Greenspan, S. (1972). Ersatz egocentrism: A reply to H. Borke. *Developmental Psychology, 7,* 104–106.

Chandler, M. J., & Hala, S. (1994). The role of person involvement in the assessment of early false belief skills. In C. Lewis & P. Mitchell (Eds.), *Children's early understanding of mind: Origins and development* (pp. 403–426). Hillsdale, NJ: Erlbaum.

Chandler, M. J., & Helm, D. (1984). Developmental changes in the contribution of shared experience to social role-taking competence. *International Journal of Behavioral Development, 1,* 145–156.

Cicchetti, D. (1991). Fractures in the crystal: Developmental psychopathology and the emergence of self. *Developmental Review, 11,* 271–287.

Cicchetti, D., & Beeghly, M. (1990). *The self in transition: Infancy to childhood.* Chicago: University of Chicago Press.

Cole, P. M. (1986). Children's spontaneous control of facial expression. *Child Development, 57,* 1309–1321.

Corkum, V., & Moore, C. (1994). *The origins of joint visual attention in infants.* Unpublished manuscript. Dalhousie University.

Cottrell, J. E., & Winer, G. A. (1994). Development in the understanding of perception: The decline of extramission perception beliefs. *Developmental Psychology, 30,* 218–228.

Damon, W. (1977). *The social world of the child.* San Francisco: Jossey-Bass.

Davidson, D. (1984). *Inquiries into truth and interpretation.* Oxford: Oxford University Press.

DeCasper, A. J., & Fifer, W. P. (1980). Of human bonding: Newborns prefer their mothers' voices. *Science, 208,* 1174–1176.

DeCasper, A. J., & Spence, M. J. (1986). Prenatal maternal speech influences newborns' perception of speech sounds. *Infant Behavior and Development, 9,* 133–150.

Dennett, D. C. (1978). Beliefs about beliefs. Commentary on D. Premack & G. Woodruff, Does the chimpanzee have a theory of mind? *Behavioral and Brain Sciences, 4,* 568–570.

Dittrich, W. H., & Lea, S. E. G. (1993). Intentionality, mind and folk psychology commentary on A. Gopnik, How we know our minds: The illusion of first-person knowledge. *Behavioral and Brain Sciences, 16,* 39–41.

Dockett, S., & Smith, I. (1995). *Children's theories and their involvement in complex shared pretense.* Poster presented at the Biennial Meeting of the Society for Research in Child Development, Indianapolis, IN.

Dunn, J. (1988). *The beginnings of social understanding.* Cambridge, MA: Harvard University Press.

Dunn, J. (1991). Understanding others: Evidence from naturalistic studies of children. In A. Whiten (Ed.), *Natural theories of mind: Evolution, development, and simulation of everyday mindreading* (pp. 51–61). Oxford: Blackwell.

Dunn, J. (1994). Changing minds and changing relationships. In C. Lewis & P. Mitchell (Eds.), *Children's early understanding of mind: Origins and development* (pp. 297–310). Hillsdale, NJ: Erlbaum.

Dunn, J., Bretherton, I., & Munn, P. (1987). Conversations about feeling states between mothers and their young children. *Developmental Psychology, 23,* 132–139.

Dunn, J., Kendrick, C., & MacNamee, R. (1981). The reaction of first-born children to the birth of a sibling: Mothers' reports. *Journal of Child Psychology and Psychiatry, 22,* 1–18.

Dunn, J., & Munn, P. (1985). Becoming a family member: Family conflict and the development of social understanding in the second year. *Child Development, 56,* 480–492.

Eder, R. A., Gerlach, S. G., & Perlmutter, M. (1987). In search of children's selves: Development of the specific and general components of the self concept. *Child Development, 58,* 1044–1050.

Estes, D., Wellman, H. M., & Woolley, J. D. (1989). Children's understanding of mental phenomena. In H. Reese (Ed.), *Advances in child development and behavior* (Vol. 22, pp. 41–87). New York: Academic Press.

Fabricus, W. V., Schwanenflugel, P. J., Kyllonen, P., Barclay, C. R., & Denton, S. M. (1989). Developing theories of mind: Children's and adults' concepts of mental activities. *Child Development, 60,* 1278–1290.

Fagot, B. I., & Leinbach, M. D. (1993). Gender role development in young children: From discrimination to labeling. *Developmental Review, 13,* 205–224.

Feinman, S. (Ed.). (1992). *Social referencing and the social construction of reality in infancy.* New York: Plenum.

Feiring, C., Lewis, M., & Starr, M. D. (1984). Indirect effects and infants' reaction to strangers. *Developmental Psychology, 20,* 485–491.

Flavell, J. H. (1978). The development of knowledge about visual perception. In C. B. Keasey (Ed.), *Nebraska Symposium on Motivation* (Vol. 25, pp. 43–76). Lincoln: University of Nebraska Press.

Flavell, J. H. (1988). The development of children's knowledge about the mind: From cognitive connections to mental representations. In J. W. Astington, P. L. Harris, & D. R.

Olson (Eds.), *Developing theories of mind* (pp. 244–270). New York: Cambridge University Press.

Flavell, J. H. (1992). Perspectives on perspective-taking. In H. Beilin & P. Pufall (Eds.), *Piaget's theory: Prospects and possibilities*, Hillsdale, N.J.: Erlbaum.

Flavell, J. H., Botkin, P. T., Fry, C. L., Wright, J. W., & Jarvis, P. E. (1968). *The development of role-taking and communication skills in children.* New York: Wiley.

Flavell, J. H., Flavell, E. R., & Green, F. L. (1983). Development of the appearance–reality distinction. *Cognitive Psychology, 15,* 95–120.

Flavell, J. H., Flavell, E. R., Green, F. L., & Moses, L. J. (1990). Young children's understanding of fact beliefs versus value beliefs. *Child Development, 61,* 915–928.

Flavell, J. H., Flavell, E. R., Green, F. L., & Wilcox, S. A. (1980). Young children's knowledge about visual perception: Effect of observer's distance from target on perceptual clarity of target. *Developmental Psychology, 16,* 10–12.

Flavell, J. H., Green, F. L., & Flavell, E. R. (1986). Development of knowledge about the appearance–reality distinction. *Monographs of the Society for Research in Child Development, 51,* No. 1 (Serial No. 212).

Flavell, J. H., Green, F. L., & Flavell, E. R. (1990). Developmental changes in young children's knowledge about the mind. *Cognitive Development, 5,* 1–27.

Flavell, J. H., Green, F. L., & Flavell, E. R. (1995). Young children's knowledge about thinking. *Monographs of the Society for Research in Child Development, 60* No. 1 (Serial No. 243).

Flavell, J. H., Green, F. L., Herrera, C., & Flavell, E. R. (1991). Young children's knowledge about visual perception: Lines of sight must be straight. *British Journal of Developmental Psychology, 9,* 73–87.

Flavell, J. H., & Miller, P. H. (in press). Social cognition. In D. Kuhn & R. Siegler (Eds.), *Cognition, perception, and language* Vol. II of W. Damon (Gen. Ed.), *Handbook of child psychology.*

Flavell, J. H., Mumme, D. L., Green, F. L., & Flavell, E. R. (1992). Young children's understanding of different types of beliefs. *Child Development, 63,* 960–977.

Flavell, J. H., & Ross, L. (1981). *Social cognitive development.* New York: Cambridge University Press.

Fodor, J. A. (1987). *Psychosemantics: The problem of meaning in the philosophy of mind.* Cambridge, MA: Bradford Books/MIT Press.

Fodor, J. A. (1992). A theory of the child's theory of mind. *Cognition, 44,* 283–296.

Forguson, L., & Gopnik, A. (1988). The ontogeny of common sense. In J. W. Astington, P. L. Harris, & D. R. Olson (Eds.), *Developing theories of mind* (pp. 226–243). New York: Cambridge University Press.

Forrester, M. A. (1993). *The development of young children's social-cognitive skills.* Hillsdale, NJ: Erlbaum.

Frith, U. (1989). *Autism: Explaining the enigma.* Cambridge: Blackwell.

Frye, D. (1991). The origins of intention in infancy. In D. Frye & C. Moore (Eds.), *Children's theories of mind* (pp. 15–38). Hillsdale, NJ: Erlbaum.

Frye, D., Rawling, P., Moore, C., & Myers, I. (1983). Object–person discrimination and communication at 3 and 10 months. *Developmental Psychology, 19,* 303–309.

Gallup, G. G., Jr. (1977). Self-recognition in primates: A comparative approach to the bidirectional properties of consciousness. *American Psychologist, 32,* 329–338.

Gallup, G. g., Jr. (1985). Do minds exist in species other than our own? *Neurosciences and Biobehavioral Review, 9,* 631–641.

Gallup, G. G., Jr., McClure, M. K., Hill, S. D., & Bundy, R. A. (1971). Capacity for self recognition in differentially reared chimpanzees. *Psychological Record, 21,* 69–74.

Gelman, R. (1990). First principles organize attention to and learning about relevant data: Number and the animate–inanimate distinction as examples, *Cognitive Science, 14,* 79–106.

Gelman, R., Durgin, F., & Kaufman, L. (1995). Distinguishing between animates and inanimates: Not by motion alone. In D. Sperber, D. Premack, & A. J. Premack (Eds.), *Causal cognition: A multidisciplinary debate* (pp. 150–184). Oxford: Clarendon.

Gelman, R., Spelke, E. S., & Meck, E. (1983). What preschoolers know about animate and inaminate objects. In D. Rogers & J. A. Sloboba (Eds.), *The acquisition of symbolic skills* (pp. 297–326). New York: Plenum.

Gelman, S. A., & Coley, J. D. (1991). Language and categorization: The acquisition of natural kind terms. In S. A. Gelman & J. P. Byrnes (Eds.), *Perspectives on language and thought: Interrelations in development* (pp. 146–196). Cambridge: Cambridge University Press.

Gelman, S. A., Collman, P., & Maccoby, E. E. (1986). Inferring properties from categories versus inferring categories from properties: The case of gender. *Child Development, 57,* 396–404.

Gerow, L., & Taylor, M. (1995). *Children's understanding of pretense as based on mental representation.* Poster presented at the Biennial Meeting of the Society for Research in Child Development, Indianapolis, IN.

Gnepp, J. (1983). Inferring emotions from conflicting cues. *Developmental Psychology, 19,* 805–814.

Gnepp, J., & Chilamkurti, C. (1988). Children's use of personality attributions to predict other people's emotional and behavioral reactions. *Child Development, 59,* 743–754.

Gnepp, J., & Gould, M. E. (1985). The development of personalized inferences: Understanding other people's emotional reactions in light of their prior experiences. *Child Development, 56,* 1455–1464.

Goldman, A. (1989). Interpretation psychologized. *Mind and Language, 4,* 161–185.

Goldman, A. (1992). In defense of the simulation theory. *Mind and Language, 7,* 104–119.

Goldman, A. I. (1993a). Competing accounts of belief–task performance. Commentary on A. Gopnik, How we know our minds: The illusion of first-person knowledge. *Behavioral and Brain Sciences, 16,* 43–44.

Goldman, A. I. (1993b). The psychology of folk psychology. *Behavioral and Brain Sciences, 16.* 15–28.

Golinkoff, R., Harding, C. G., Carlson, V., & Sexton, M. E. (1984). The infant's perception of causal events: The distinction between animate and inanimate objects. In L. P. Lipsett & C. Royce-Collier (Eds.), *Advances in infancy research* (Vol. 3). (pp. 145–151) Norwood, NJ: Ablex.

Golomb, C., & Kuersten, R. (1992). On the transition from pretense play to reality: What are the rules of the game? In C. Golomb (Chair), *The pretense–reality distinction in imaginative behavior.* Symposium conducted at the Annual Meeting of the American Psychological Association, Washington, DC.

Gopnik, A. (1993). How we know our minds: The illusion of first-person knowledge of intentionality. *Behavioral and Brain Sciences, 16,* 1–14.

Gopnik, A., & Astington, J. W. (1988). Children's understanding of representational change and its relation to the understanding of false belief and the appearance–reality distinction. *Child Development, 59,* 26–37.

Gopnik, A., & Graf, P. (1988). Knowing how you know: Young children's ability to identify and remember the sources of their beliefs. *Child Development, 59,* 1366–1371.

Gopnik, A., & Slaughter, V. (1991). Young children's understanding of changes in their mental states. *Child Development, 62,* 98–110.

Gopnik, A., Slaughter, V., & Meltzoff, A. (1994). Changing your views: How understanding visual perception can lead to a new theory of mind. In C. Lewis & P. Mitchell (Eds.), *Children's early understanding of mind: Origins and development* (pp. 157–182). Hillsdale, NJ: Erlbaum.

Gopnik, A., & Wellman, H. M. (1992). Why the child's theory of mind really is a theory. *Mind and Language, 7,* 145–171.

Gopnik, A., & Wellman, H. M. (1994). The theory theory. In L. Hirschfield & S. Gelman (Eds.), *Domain specificity in cognition and culture* (pp. 257–293). New York: Cambridge University Press.

Gordon, R. (1992). The simulation theory and the theory theory. *Mind and Language, 7*(1/2), 11–35.

Hadwin, J., & Perner, J. (1991). Pleased and surprised: Children's cognitive theory of emotion. *British Journal of Developmental Psychology, 9,* 215–234.

Hala, S., Chandler, M., & Fritz, A. S. (1991). Fledging theories of mind: Deception as a marker of three-year-olds' understanding of false belief. *Child Development, 62,* 83–97.

Harris, P. L. (1989). *Children and emotion.* Oxford: Blackwell.

Harris, P. L. (1991). The work of the imagination. In A. Whiten (Ed.), *Natural theories of mind* (pp. 283–304). Oxford: Blackwell.

Harris, P. L. (1992). From simulation to folk psychology: The case for development. *Mind and Language, 7*(1/2), 120–144.

Harris, P. L. (1994). Understanding pretense. In C. Lewis & P. Mitchell (Eds.), *Children's early understanding of mind: Origins and development* (pp. 235–260). Hillsdale, NJ: Erlbaum.

Harris, P. L., Donnelly, K., Guz, G. R., & Pitt-Watson, R. (1986). Children's understanding of the distinction between real and apparent emotion. *Child Development, 57,* 895–909.

Harris, P. L., & Gross, D. (1988). Children's understanding of real and apparent emotion. In J. W. Astington, P. L. Harris, & D. R. Olson (Eds.), *Developing theories of mind* (pp. 295–314). New York: Cambridge University Press.

Harris, P. L., Johnson, C. N., Hutton, D., Andrews, G., & Cooke, T. (1989). Young children's theory of mind and emotion. *Cognition and Emotion, 3,* 379–400.

Harris, P. L., & Kavanaugh, R. D. (1993). Young children's understanding of pretense. *Monographs of the Society for Research in Child Development, 58*(1, Serial No. 231).

Harris, P. L., Kavanaugh, R. D., & Meredith, M. C. (1994). Young children's comprehension of pretend episodes: The integration of successive actions. *Child Development, 65,* 16–30.

Harris, P. L. & Muncer, A. (1988). *Autistic children's understanding of beliefs and desires.* Paper presented at the British Psychological Society Developmental Section Conference, Coleg Harlech, Wales.

Harris, P. L., & Olthof, T. (1982). The child's concept of emotion. In G. Butterworth & P. Light (Eds.), *Social cognition: Studies of the development of understanding* (pp. 188–209). Chicago: University of Chicago Press.

Harris, P. L., Olthof, T., & Meerum Terwogt, M. (1981). Children's knowledge of emotion. *Journal of Child Psychology and Psychiatry, 22,* 247–261.

Harris, P. L., Olthof, T., Meerum Terwogt, M., & Hardman, C. E. (1987). Children's knowledge of the situations that provoke emotion. *International Journal of Behavioral Development, 10,* 319–344.

Harter, S. (1983). Children's understanding of multiple emotions: A cognitive-developmental approach. In W. F. Overton (Ed.), *The relationship between social and cognitive development* (pp. 147–194). Hillsdale, NJ: Erlbaum.

Harter, S., & Buddin, B. (1987). Children's understanding of the simultaneity of two emotions: A five-stage developmental acquisition sequence. *Developmental Psychology, 23,* 388–399.

Harter, S., & Whitesell, N. (1989). Developmental changes in children's emotion concepts. In C. Saarni & P. L. Harris (Eds.), *Children's understanding of emotions* (pp. 81–116). New York: Cambridge University Press.

Haviland, J. M., & Lelwica, M. (1987). The induced affect response: 10-week-old infants' responses to three emotional expressions. *Developmental Psychology, 23,* 97–104.

Hickling, A., Wellman, H. M., & Gottfried, G. M. (1995). *Preschoolers' understanding of others' mental attitudes toward pretend happenings.* Unpublished manuscript, University of Michigan.

Higgins, E. T., Ruble, D. N., & Hartup, W. W. (Eds.). (1983). *Social cognition and social development: A sociocultural perspective.* New York: Cambridge University Press.

Hirschfield, L. A. (1994). Is the acquisition of social categories based on domain-specific competence or on knowledge transfer? In L. A. Hirschfield & S. A. Gelman (Eds.), *Mapping the mind: Domain specificity in cognition and culture.* (pp. 201–233). Cambridge: Cambridge University Press.

Hobson, R. P. (1990a). On the origins of self and the case of autism. *Development and Psychopathology, 2,* 163–181.

Hobson, R. P. (1990b). On acquiring knowledge about people, and the capacity to pretend: A response to Leslie (1987). *Psychological Review, 97,* 114–121.

Hobson, R. P. (1991). Against the theory of 'theory of mind.' *British Journal of Developmental Psychology, 9,* 33–51.

Hornik, R., Risenhoover, N., & Gunnar, M. (1987). The effects of maternal positive, neutral, and negative affective communications on infant responses to new toys. *Child Development, 58,* 937–944.

Jenkins, J. M., & Astington, J. W. (1993). *Cognitive, linguistic, and social factors associated with theory of mind development in young children.* Paper presented at the Biennial Meeting of the Society for Research in Child Development, New Orleans.

Johnson, C. N. (1988). Theory of mind and the structure of conscious experience. In J. W. Astington, P. L. Harris, & D. R. Olson (Eds.), *Developing theories of mind* (pp. 47–63). New York: Cambridge University Press.

Johnson, C. N., & Wellman, H. M. (1980). Children's developing understanding of mental verbs: Remember, know, and guess. *Child Development, 51,* 1095–1102.

Kanner, L. (1943). Autistic disturbances of affective contact. *Nervous Child, 2,* 217–250.

Klinnert, M. D., Campos, J. J., Sorce, J. F., Emde, R. N., & Svejda, M. (1983). Emotions as behavior regulators: Social referencing in infancy. In R. Plutchik & H. Kellerman (Eds.), *Emotion: Theory, research and experience* (Vol. 2) (pp. 57–86). New York: Academic Press.

Leekam, S. (1993). Children's understanding of mind. In M. Bennett (Ed.), *The child as psychologist* (pp. 26–61). New York: Harvester Wheatsheaf.

Lempers, J. D., Flavell, E. R., & Flavell, J. H. (1977). The development in very young children of tacit knowledge concerning visual perception. *Genetic Psychology Monographs, 95,* 3–53.

Leslie, A. M. (1987). Pretense and representation: The origins of "theory of mind." *Psychological Review, 94,* 412–426.

Leslie, A. M. (1988). Some implications for mechanisms underlying the child's theory of mind. In J. W. Astington, P. L. Harris, & D. R. Olson (Eds.), *Developing theories of mind* (pp. 19–46). New York: Cambridge University Press.

Leslie, A. M. (1994). TOMM, ToBy, and agency: Core architecture and domain specificity. In L. A. Hirschfeld & S. A. Gelman (Eds.), *Mapping the mind: Domain Specificity in cognition and culture* (pp. 119–148). Cambridge: Cambridge University Press.

Leslie, A. M., & Frith, U. (1988). Autistic children's understanding of seeing, knowing, and believing. *British Journal of Developmental Psychology, 4,* 315–324.

Leslie, A. M., & Frith, U. (1990). Prospects for a cognitive neuropsychology of autism: Hobson's choice. *Psychological Review, 97,* 122–131.

Leslie, A. M., & Thaiss, L. (1992). Domain specificity in conceptual development: Neuropsychological evidence from autism. *Cognition,* 225–251.

Leung, E. H. L., & Rheingold, H. L. (1981). Development of pointing as social gesture. *Developmental Psychology, 17,* 215–220.

Lewis, C. (1994). Episodes, events, and narratives in the child's understanding of mind. In C. Lewis & P. Mitchell (Eds.), *Children's early understanding of mind: Origins and development* (pp. 457–480). Hillsdale, NJ: Erlbaum.

Lewis, C., & Osborne, A. (1990). Three-year-olds' problem with false belief: Conceptual deficit or linguistic artifact? *Child Development, 61,* 1514–1519.

Lewis, M., & Brooks-Gunn, J. (1979). *Social cognition and the acquisition of self.* New York: Plenum.

Lewis, M., Sullivan, M. W., Stanger, C., & Weiss, M. (1989). Self development and self-conscious emotions. *Child Development, 60,* 146–156.

Light, P., & Nix, C. (1983). "Own view" versus "good view" in a perspective-taking task. *Child Development, 54,* 480–483.

Lillard, A. S. (1993). Young children's conceptualization of pretend: Action or mental representational states? *Child Development, 64,* 372–386.

Lillard, A. S. (1994). Making sense of pretence. In C. Lewis & P. Mitchell (Eds.), *Children's early understanding of mind: Origins and development* (pp. 211–234). Hillsdale, NJ: Erlbaum.

Lillard, A. S. (in press). Pretend play and the child's theory of mind. In O. Saracho & B. Spodek (Eds.), *Play in early childhood education.* New York: SUNY Press.

Lillard, A. S., & Flavell, J. H. (1990). Young children's preference for mental state versus behavioral descriptions of human action. *Child Development, 61,* 731–741.

Livesly, W. J., & Bromley, D. B. (1973). *Person perception in childhood and adolescence.* London: Wiley.

Lyon, T. (1993). *Young children's understanding of desire and knowledge.* Unpublished doctoral dissertation, Stanford University.

MacLaren, R., & Olson, D. (1993). Trick or treat: Children's understanding of surprise. *Cognitive Development, 8,* 27–46.

MacWhinney, B., & Snow, C. (1990). The child language data exchange system: An update. *Journal of Child Language, 17,* 457–472.

Marino, L., Reiss, D., & Gallup, G. G., Jr. (1994). Mirror self-recognition in Bottlenose Dolphins (*Tursiops truncatus*): Implications for comparative study of highly dissimilar species. In S. Parker, R. Mitchell, & M. Boccia (Eds.), *Self-awareness in animals and humans: Developmental perspectives* (pp. 380–391). New York: Cambridge University Press.

Masangkay, Z. S., McCluskey, K. A., McIntyre, C. W., Sims-Knight, J., Vaughn, B. E., & Flavell, J. H. (1974). The early development of inferences about the visual percepts of others. *Child Development, 45,* 357–366.

Masur, E., & Ritz, E. (1984). Patterns of gestural, vocal, and verbal imitation performance in infancy. *Merrill-Palmer Quarterly, 30,* 369–392.

Meerum Terwogt, M., & Harris, P. L. (1993). Understanding of EZmotion. In M. Bennett (Ed.), *The child as psychologist: An introduction to the development of social cognition* (pp. 62–110). New York: Harvester Wheatsheaf.

Meltzoff, A. N. (1988a). Infant imitation and memory: Nine-month-olds in immediate and deferred tests. *Child Development, 59,* 217–225.

Meltzoff, A. N. (1988b). Infant imitation after a one week delay: Longterm memory for novel acts and multiple stimuli. *Developmental Psychology, 24,* 470–476.

Meltzoff, A. N. (1990). Foundations for developing a concept of self: The role of imitation in relating self to other and the value of social mirroring, social modeling, and self practice in infancy. In D. Cicchetti & M. Beeghly (Eds.), *The self in transition* (pp. 139–163). Chicago: University of Chicago Press.

Meltzoff, A. N., & Gopnik, A. (1993). The role of imitation in understanding persons and developing a theory of mind. In S. Baron-Cohen, H. Tager-Flusberg, & D. J. Cohen (Eds.), *Understanding other minds: Perspectives from autism* (pp. 335–366). Oxford: Oxford University Press.

Meltzoff, A. N., & Moore, M. K. (1977). Imitation of facial and manual gestures by human neonates. *Science, 198,* 75–78.

Meltzoff, A. N., & Moore, M. K. (1983). Newborn infants imitate adult facial gestures. *Child Development, 54,* 702–709.

Meltzoff, A. N., & Moore, M. K. (1989). Imitation in newborn infants: Exploring the range of gestures imitated and the underlying mechanisms. *Developmental Psychology, 25,* 954–962.

Mitchell, P., & Lacohee, H. (1991). Children's early understanding of false belief. *Cognition, 39,* 107–128.

Mitchell, R. W. (1994). Multiplicities of self. In S. Parker, R. Mitchell, & M. Boccia (Eds.), *Self-awareness in animals and humans: Developmental perspectives* (pp. 81–107). New York: Cambridge University Press.

Montgomery, D. E. (1992). Young children's theory of knowing: The development of a folk epistemology. *Developmental Review, 12,* 410–430.

Moore, C., Bryant, D., & Furrow, D. (1989). Mental terms and the development of certainty. *Child Development, 60,* 167–171.

Moore, C., & Corkum, V. (1994). Social understanding at the end of the first year of life. *Developmental Review, 14,* 349–372.

Moses, L. J. (1993). Young children's understanding of belief constraints on intention. *Cognitive Development, 8,* 1–25.

Moses, L. J., Baldwin, D., & Tidball, G. (1995). *Social referencing versus social receptiveness: Infants' use of others' attentional cues to clarify the reference of emotional displays.* Unpublished manuscript, University of Oregon.

Moses, L. J., & Chandler, M. J. (1992). Travelers guide to children's theories of mind. *Psychological Inquiry, 3,* 286–301.

Moses, L. J., & Flavell, J. H. (1990). Inferring false beliefs from actions and reactions. *Child Development, 61,* 929–945.

Mundy, P., Sigman, M., Ungerer, J., & Sherman, T. (1986). Defining the social deficit of autism: The contribution of non-verbal communication measures. *Journal of Child Psychology and Psychiatry, 27,* 657–669.

Murphy, C. M. (1978). Pointing in the context of a shared activity. *Child Development, 49,* 371–380.

Murphy, G. L. & Medin, D. L. (1985). The role of theories in conceptual coherence. *Psychological Review, 92,* 284–316.

Naito, M., Komatsu, S., & Fuke, T. (1994). Normal and autistic children's understanding of their own and others' false belief: A study from Japan. *British Journal of Developmental Psychology, 12,* 403–416.

Nelson, L. A. (1987). The recognition of facial expression in the first two years of life: Mechanisms of development. *Child Development, 58,* 889–909.

Newcomb, N. (1989). The development of spatial perspective taking. In H. W. Reese (Ed.), *Advances in child development and behavior* (Vol. 22) (pp. 203–249). San Diego: Academic Press.

O'Neill, D. K., Astington, J. W., & Flavell, J. H. (1992). Young children's understanding of the role that sensory experiences play in knowledge acquisition. *Child Development, 63,* 474–490.

O'Neill, D. K., & Gopnik, A. (1991). Young children's ability to identify the sources of their beliefs. *Developmental Psychology, 27,* 390–397.

Parker, S., Mitchell, R., & Boccia, M. (Eds.). (1994). *Self-awareness in animals and humans: Developmental perspectives.* New York: Cambridge University Press.

Perner, J. (1991a). *Understanding the representational mind.* Cambridge, MA: MIT Press.

Perner, J. (1991b). On representing *that:* The asymmetry between belief and intention in children's theory of mind. In D. Frye & C. Moore (Eds.), *Children's theories of mind: Mental states and social understanding* (pp. 139–156). Hillsdale, N.J.: Erlbaum.

Perner, J., Baker, S., & Hutton, D. (1994). Prelief: The conceptual origins of belief and pretence. In C. Lewis & P. Mitchell (Eds.), *Children's early understanding of mind: Origins and development* (pp. 261–286). Hillsdale, NJ: Erlbaum.

Perner, J., & Davies, G. (1991). Understanding the mind as an active information processor: Do young children have a "copy theory of mind"? *Cognition, 39,* 51–69.

Perner, J., Frith, U., Leslie, A. M., & Leekam, S. R. (1989). Exploration of the autistic child's theory of mind: Knowledge, belief, and communication. *Child Development, 60,* 689–700.

Perner, J., & Hadwin, J. (1989). *Children's cognitive theory of amotion.* Paper presented at the meeting of the Society for Research in Child Development, Kansas City, MO.

Perner, J., Leekam, S. R., & Wimmer, H. (1987). Three-year-olds' difficulty understanding false belief: Representational limitation, lack of knowledge or pragmatic misunderstanding. *British Journal of Developmental Psychology, 5,* 125–137.

Perner, J., & Ogden, J. E. (1988). Knowledge for hunger: Children's problem with representation in imputing mental states. *Cognition, 29,* 47–61.

Perner, J., Ruffman, T., & Leekam, S. R. (1994). Theory of mind is contagious: You catch it from your sibs. *Child Development, 65,* 1228–1238.

Peskin, J. (1992). Ruse and representation: On children's ability to conceal their intentions. *Developmental Psychology, 28,* 84–89.

Piaget, J. (1926). *The language and thought of the child.* New York: Harcourt.

Piaget, J. (1929). *The child's conception of the world.* London: Routledge & Kegan Paul.

Piaget, J. (1932). *The moral judgment of the child.* London: Kegan Paul.

Piaget, J. (1952). *The child's concept of number.* New York: Norton.

Piaget, J., & Inhelder, B. (1948/1956). *The child's conception of space.* New York: Norton.

Pillow, B. (1988). The development of children's beliefs about the mental world. *Merrill Palmer Quarterly, 34,* 1–32.

Pillow, B. (1989). Early understanding of perception as a source of knowledge. *Journal of Experimental Child Psychology, 47,* 11–129.

Povinelli, D. J. (1987). Monkeys, apes, mirrors, and minds: The evolution of self-awareness in primates. *Human Evolution, 2,* 493–509.

Povinelli, D. J. (1989). Failure to find self-recognition in Asian elephants (*elephas maximus*) in ˙contrast to their use of mirror cues to discover hidden food. *Journal of Comparative Psychology, 103,* 122–131.

Povinelli, D. J., & deBlois, S. (1992). Young children's (*Homo sapiens*) understanding of knowledge formation in themselves and others. *Journal of Comparative Psychology, 106,* 228–239.

Povinelli, D. J., Landau, K. R., & Perilloux, H. K. (1995). *Self-recognition in young children using delayed versus live feedback: Evidence of a developmental asynchrony.* Unpublished manuscript, University of Southwestern Louisiana.

Pratt, C., & Bryant, P. E. (1990). Young children understand that looking leads to knowing (so long as they are looking into a single barrel). *Child Development, 61,* 973–982.

Premack, D., & Premack, A. J. (1994). Moral belief: Form versus content. In L. A. Hirschfield & S. A. Gelman (Eds.), *Mapping the mind: Domain specificity in cognition and culture* (pp. 149–168). New York: Cambridge University Press.

Premack, D., & Woodruff, G. (1978). Does the chimpanzee have a theory of mind? *Behavioral and Brain Sciences, 1,* 515–526.

Priel, B., & de Schonen, S. (1986). Self-recognition: A study of a population without mirrors. *Journal of Experimental Child Psychology, 41,* 237–250.

Pylyshyn, Z. W. (1978). When is attribution of beliefs justified? Commentary on D. Premack & G. Woodruff, Does the chimpanzee have a theory of mind? *Behavioral and Brain Sciences, 4,* 592–593.

Reddy, V. (1991). Playing with others' expectations: Teasing and mucking about in the first year. In A. Whiten (Ed.), *Natural theories of mind: Evolution, development, and simulation of everyday mindreading* (pp. 143–158). Oxford: Blackwell.

Ridgeway, D., Waters, E., & Kuczaj, S. (1985). Acquisition of emotion-descriptive language: Receptive and productive vocabulary norms for ages 18 months to 6 years. *Developmental Psychology, 21,* 901–908.

Roth, D., & Leslie, A. M. (1991). The recognition of attitude conveyed by utterance: A study of autistic and preschool children. *British Journal of Developmental Psychology, 9*, 315–330.

Rothbart, M., & Taylor, M. (1992). Category labels and social reality: Do we view social categories as natural kinds? In G. R. Semin & K. Fiedler (Eds.), *Language, interaction, and social cognition* (pp. 11–36). London: Sage.

Ruffman, T., Olson, D. R., Ash, T., & Keenan, T. (1993). The ABC's of deception: Do young children understand deception in the same way as adults? *Developmental Psychology, 29*, 74–87.

Russell, J. (1992). The theory-theory: So good they named it twice? *Cognitive Development, 7*, 485–519.

Russell, J., & Bullock, M. (1986). On the dimensions preschoolers use to interpret facial expressions of emotion. *Developmental Psychology, 22*, 96–102.

Russell, J., Mauthner, N., Sharpe, S., & Tidswell, T. (1991). The "windows task" as a measure of strategic deception in preschoolers and autistic subjects. *British Journal of Developmental Psychology, 9*, 331–349.

Saarni, C. (1979). Children's understanding of display rules for expressive behavior. *Developmental Psychology, 15*, 424–429.

Saarni, C. (1984). An observational study of children's attempts to monitor their expressive behavior. *Child Development, 55*, 1504–1513.

Saarni, C. (1989). Children's understanding of strategic control of emotional expression in social transactions. In C. Saarni & P. L. Harris (Eds.), *Children's understanding of emotion* (pp. 181–208). New York: Cambridge University Press.

Saarni, C., & Harris, P. L. (Eds.). (1989). *Children's understanding of emotion*. Cambridge: Cambridge University Press.

Scaife, M., & Bruner, J. (1975). The capacity for joint attention in the infant. *Nature, 253*, 265–266.

Schopler, E., & Mesibov, G. B. (1983). *Autism in adolescents and adults*. New York: Plenum.

Searle, J. (1984). *Minds, brains, and science*. Cambridge, MA: Harvard University Press.

Selman, R. L. (1980). *The growth of interpersonal understanding*. New York: Academic Press.

Shatz, M., Wellman, H. M., & Silber, S. (1983). The acquisition of mental verbs: A systematic investigation of the first reference to mental state. *Cognition, 14*, 301–321.

Sherrod, L. R. (1981). Issues in cognitive-perceptual development: The special case of social stimuli. In M. E. Lamb & L. R. Sherrod (Eds.), *Infant social cognition* (pp. 11–36). Hillsdale, NJ: Erlbaum.

Shultz, T. R., & Wells, D. (1985). Judging the intentionality of action-outcomes. *Developmental Psychology, 21*, 83–89.

Siegal, M., & Beattie, K. (1991). Where to look first for children's knowledge of false beliefs. *Cognition, 38*, 1–12.

Singer, D. G., & Singer, J. L. (1990). *The house of make-believe: Children's play and the developing imagination*. Cambridge, MA: Harvard University Press.

Smiley, P., & Huttenlocher, J. (1989). Young children's acquisition of emotion concepts. In C. Saarni & P. L. Harris (Eds.), *Children's understanding of emotion* (pp. 27–49). New York: Cambridge University Press.

Sodian, B. (1991). The development of deception in young children. *British Journal of Developmental Psychology, 9*, 173–188.

Sodian, B., Taylor, C., Harris, P. L., & Perner, J. (1991). Early deception and the child's theory of mind. *Child Development, 62*, 468–483.

Sodian, B., & Wimmer, H. (1987). Children's understanding of inference as a source of knowledge. *Child Development, 58*, 424–433.

Spelke, E. (1976). Infants' intermodal perception of events. *Cognitive Psychology, 8*, 553–560.

Stein, N. L., & Levine, L. J. (1989). The causal organization of emotional knowledge: A developmental study. *Cognition and Emotion, 3*, 343–378.

Stern, D. (1985). *The interpersonal world of the child.* New York: Basic Books.

Stipek, D. J., Gralinski, J. H., & Kopp, C. B. (1990). Self-concept development in the toddler years. *Developmental Psychology, 26,* 972–977.

Stipek, D. J., & MacIver, D. (1989). Developmental change in children's assessment of intellectual competence. *Child Development, 60,* 521–538.

Sullivan, K., & Winner, E. (1993). Three-year-olds' understanding of mental states: The influence of trickery. *Journal of Experimental Child Psychology, 56,* 135–148.

Tager-Flusberg, H., Baron-Cohen, S., & Cohen, D. (1993). An introduction to the debate. In S. Baron-Cohen, H. Tager-Flusberg, & D. J. Cohen (Eds.), *Understanding other minds: Perspectives from autism* (pp. 3–9). Oxford: Oxford University Press.

Taylor, M. (1988). The development of children's ability to distinguish what they know from what they see. *Child Development, 58,* 424–433.

Taylor, M., & Carlson, S. (1995). Children who create imaginary characters. In K. S. Rosengren & C. Johnson (Chairs), *Uses of magic and fantasy in childhood.* Symposium conducted at the Biennial Meeting of the Society for Research in Child Development, Indianapolis, IN.

Taylor, M., Cartwright, B. S., & Bowden, T. (1991). Perspective taking and theory of mind: Do children predict interpretive diversity as a function of differences in observers' knowledge? *Child Development, 62,* 1334–1351.

Taylor, M., Cartwright, B. S., & Carlson, S. M. (1993). A developmental investigation of children's imaginary companions. *Developmental Psychology, 29,* 276–285.

Taylor, M., Esbensen, B. M., & Bennett, R. T. (1994). Children's understanding of knowledge acquisition: The tendency for children to report they have always known what they have just learned. *Child Development, 65,* 1581–1604.

Tomasello, M., & Kruger, A. C. (1992). Joint attention on actions: Acquiring verbs in ostensive and nonostensive contexts. *Journal of Child Language, 19,* 311–334.

Tomasello, M., Kruger, A. C., & Ratner, H. H. (1993). Cultural learning. *Behavioral and Brain Sciences, 16,* 495–511.

Trevarthen, C. (1977). Descriptive analyses of infant communicative behavior. In H. R. Schaffer (Ed.), *Studies in mother–infant interaction* (pp. 227–270). London: Academic Press.

Trevarthen, C., & Hubley (1978). Secondary intersubjectivity: Confidence, confiding, and acts of meaning in the first year. In A. Lock (Ed.), *Action, gesture, and symbol: The emergence of language* (pp. 183–230). New York: Cambridge University Press.

Ungerer, J., & Sigman, M. (1981). Symbolic play and language comprehension in autistic children. *Journal of the American Academy of Child Psychiatry, 20,* 318–37.

Walden, T. A., & Ogan, T. A. (1988). The development of social referencing. *Child Development, 59,* 1230–1240.

Wellman, H. M. (1990). *The child's theory of mind.* Cambridge, MA: MIT Press.

Wellman, H. M. (1993). Early understanding of mind: The normal case. In S. Baron-Cohen, H. Tager-Flusberg, & D. J. Cohen (Eds.), *Understanding other minds: Perspectives from autism* (pp. 10–39). Oxford: Oxford University Press.

Wellman, H. M., & Banerjee, M. (1991). Mind and emotion: Children's understanding of the emotional consequences of beliefs and desires. *British Journal of Developmental Psychology, 9,* 119–124.

Wellman, H. M., & Bartsch, K. (1988). Young children's reasoning about beliefs. *Cognition, 30,* 239–277.

Wellman, H. M., & Estes, D. (1986). Early understanding of mental entities: A reexamination of childhood realism. *Child Development, 57,* 910–923.

Wellman, H. M., & Gelman, S. A. (1992). Cognitive development: Foundational theories of core domains. In M. R. Rosenzweig & L. W. Porter (Eds.), *Annual review of psychology* (Vol. 43, pp. 337–375). Palo Alto, CA: Annual Reviews.

Wellman, H. M., Harris, P. L., Banerjee, M., & Sinclair, A. (in press). Early understanding of emotion: Evidence from natural language. *Cognition and emotion.*

Wellman, H. M., & Johnson, C. N. (1979). Understanding mental processes: A developmental study of "remember" and "forget." *Child Development, 50,* 79–88.

Wellman, H. M., & Woolley, J. D. (1990). From simple desires to ordinary beliefs: The early development of everyday psychology. *Cognition, 53,* 245–275.

Willats, P. (1984). The stage IV infant's solution of problems requiring the use of supports. *Infant Behavior and Development, 7,* 125–134.

Wimmer, H., & Hartl, M. (1991). Against the Cartesian view on mind: Young children's difficulty with own false beliefs. *British Journal of Developmental Psychology, 9,* 125–138.

Wimmer, H., Hogrefe, G. J., & Perner, J. (1988). Children's understanding of informational access as a source of knowledge. *Child Development, 59,* 386–396.

Wimmer, H., & Perner, J. (1983). Beliefs about beliefs: Representation and constraining function of wrong beliefs in young children's understanding of deception. *Cognition, 13,* 103–128.

Wing, L., & Gould, J. (1979). Severe impairments of social interaction and associated abnormalities in children: Epidemiology and classification. *Journal of Autism and Developmental Disorders, 9,* 11–30.

Wolf, D. P., Rygh, J., & Altshuler, J. (1984). Agency and experience: Actions and states in play narratives. In I. Bretherton (Ed.), *Symbolic play: The development of social understanding* (pp. 195–217). Orlando, FL: Academic Press.

Yaniv, I., & Shatz, M. (1988). Children's understanding of perceptibility. In J. W. Astington, P. L. Harris, & D. R. Olson (Eds.), *Developing theories of mind* (pp. 93–108). New York: Cambridge University Press.

Youniss, J. (1980). *Parents and peers in social development: A Sullivan–Piaget perspective.* Chicago: University of Chicago Press.

Yuill, N. (1984). Young children's coordination of motive and outcome in judgments of satisfaction and morality. *British Journal of Developmental Psychology, 2,* 73–81.

Zatchik, D. (1990). When representations conflict with reality: The preschoolers' problem with false beliefs and "false" photographs. *Cognition, 35,* 41–68.

Zatchik, D. (1991). Is only seeing really believing? Sources of true belief in the false belief task. *Cognitive Development, 6,* 91–103.

Models of
Development

Developmental Cognitive Neuroscience: A Biological Perspective on Cognitive Change

Mark H. Johnson
Rick O. Gilmore

In this chapter we illustrate the ways in which taking a biological perspective can inform, extend, and change our thinking about perceptual and cognitive development. Our aim is not to write a comprehensive review of the emerging field of developmental cognitive neuroscience (Johnson, 1993; Johnson, in press), but rather to illustrate the field's general approach by discussing a subset of topics in which the approach has been taken with some success.

I. WHY TAKE A COGNITIVE NEUROSCIENCE APPROACH TO DEVELOPMENT?

Until recently, the majority of theories of perceptual and cognitive development were generated without recourse to evidence from the brain. Indeed, some authors have argued strongly for the independence of cognitive level theorizing from considerations of the neural substrate. Evidence from the brain was thought to be distracting or irrelevant in some cases, hopelessly complex in others. We begin this chapter by arguing that while the brain's complexity has not diminished, our understanding of its function has improved significantly. Accordingly, we believe that the time is now ripe for exploring the interface between cognitive development and brain develop-

Perceptual and Cognitive Development
Copyright © 1996 by Academic Press, Inc. All rights of reproduction in any form reserved.

ment, and, further, that the interchange of information between these two fields is essential for the continued growth of both. The integration of information from biology and cognitive development sets the stage for a more comprehensive psychology and biology of change than was thought possible previously, and the field that embodies this synthesis we call developmental cognitive neuroscience.

By the term "cognitive neuroscience" we include not only evidence about brain development, such as that from neuroanatomy, brain imaging, and the behavioral or cognitive effects of brain lesions, but also evidence from ethology. Ethology, a science pioneered by Tinbergen, Lorenz, and others in the 1940s and 1950s, concerns the study of a whole organism within its natural environment (Lorenz, 1965; Tinbergen, 1951). We shall see that ethology is a powerful complement to neuroscience, and that the two fields combined can change the way that we think about critical issues in perceptual and cognitive development.

In general, insights from biology have begun to play a more central role in informing thinking about perceptual and cognitive development for a number of reasons, which we outline below.

A. New Methodologies

A range of powerful new methods and tools will be becoming more widely available to cognitive neuroscientists over the next five years or so. These techniques permit questions to be asked about the biological basis of cognitive and perceptual development more directly than can be posed at present.

One set of tools relates to neuroimaging—the generation of "functional" maps of brain activity based on either changes in cerebral metabolism, blood flow, or electrical activity. Some of these imaging methods, such as positron emission tomography (PET), are of limited utility for studying transitions in cognitive development in normal infants because of their invasive nature (requiring the intravenous injection of radioactively labeled substances) and their relatively coarse temporal resolution (on the order of seconds). In contrast, two techniques currently being developed may be readily applied to development in normal children: high-density event-related potentials (HD-ERP) and functional magnetic resonance imaging (F-MRI). HD-ERP is a method of recording from the scalp the electrical activity of the brain. With a high density of electrodes, one can apply algorithms that infer the position and orientation of the sources of electrical activity for the particular pattern of brain waves being generated. Some of the assumptions necessary for the successful use of these algorithms are actually more likely to be true of infants than adults. For example, lower levels of skull conductance and fewer cortical convolutions may improve the accuracy and interpretability of HD-ERP results in infants relative to adult subjects. On the other hand, functional-MRI allows the noninvasive measurement of cerebral blood flow (Raichle & Malinkrodt, 1987; Kwong et al., 1992), with the prospect of millimeter spatial resolution and temporal resolution on the order of seconds, using MRI machines commonly available in modern medical facilities. Once this technique has been further developed with adults, there appear to be no major barriers, other than distracting noise and vibration levels, preventing its application with children and infants.

A second useful tool for linking brain development to behavior is the marker task. This method involves the use of a specific behavioral task, which has been linked to one or more particular brain regions in adult primates by neurophysiological, neuropsychological, or brain imaging studies, and preferably by two or three of these methods. By studying the development of performance on the task at different ages and in different contexts, the researcher gathers evidence for determining whether and how the observed behavioral change is accounted for by known patterns of brain development. In this chapter, we survey several lines of inquiry that illustrate the marker task approach. For example, the exploration of the development of infant visual attention employs experimental methods and theoretical notions adapted from extensive studies with adults (Posner, 1980; Posner & Cohen, 1980). Similarly, the use of variants of the delayed response task in infants and monkeys of various ages typifies the strengths of the marker task: the pattern of findings often converges across experiments and between subject pools on an explanation of the phenomenon in question that is more comprehensive than would have been possible otherwise. In each of the examples that follow, we discuss how the use of specific marker tasks has made simpler the task of drawing empirical predictions and formulating theory.

There are weaknesses to using the marker task approach, of course. One must be concerned about generalizing findings from one task to others, and about the interpretability of results between subject pools that differ significantly. The design of a task that is sufficiently limited in its demands as to give interpretable results, and yet sufficiently demanding to call upon "interesting" cognitive capacities, can also be a challenge. Moreover, since different brain regions may support the same task at different ages (Goldman, 1971), the task of interpreting results is made more complex. Nevertheless, the marker task approach is a useful methodology that promises to provide insight into the development of neurocognitive systems.

Beyond neuroimaging and the marker task, there are techniques in molecular genetics that allow the lesioning of particular genes from the genome of an animal (mainly in rodents so far). A recent example of this is the deletion of the alpha-calcium calmodulin kinase II gene, which results in rats being unable to perform certain learning tasks when adults (Silva, Paylor, Wehner, & Tonegawa, 1992; Silva, Stevens, Tonegawa, & Wang, 1992). This method opens new vistas in the analysis of genetic contributions to cognitive and perceptual change in animals, and may be particularly fruitful when applied to well-studied animal models of development such as visual imprinting in chicks and song learning in passerine birds.

B. Well-Studied Animal Models

A number of animal models of behavioral development have reached a stage where some of the principles discovered may be applicable to aspects of human development (Blass, 1992). One example discussed in this chapter is the work of Horn and collaborators on the neural basis of visual imprinting in the chick (see Horn, 1985; Johnson, 1991, for reviews). This line of research has implicated particular regions of the chick brain in visual imprinting, and has identified electrophysiological, neuroanatomical, and molecular correlates of this process. A neuronal network model of one of these brain regions has been developed, allowing the computational analysis of such phenomena as sensitive periods for learning (O'Reilly & Johnson, 1994). Further, the dissociation of neural systems underlying components of filial preference behavior in the chick has been used to argue for a similar dissociation in the development of face recognition in human infants (Johnson & Morton, 1991; Morton & Johnson, 1991). Consequently, while homologies between species must be made with great care, well-studied animal models increasingly provide useful theoretical and empirical insights into cognitive development in humans.

C. Clinical Utility

Clearly, theories that incorporate and reveal relationships between brain structures and cognitive functions will be useful in understanding the effects of early brain injury or genetic disorder on cognitive development. Later in this chapter we discuss evidence derived from infants with focal damage to the cerebral cortex. Beyond its clinical utility, this line of evidence can also contribute to the development of theories about functional specification, critical periods, and plasticity in the brain. Thus, there is a two-way interaction between clinical evidence and theories in developmental cognitive neuroscience.

D. Mutual Dependence of Development and Cognitive Neuroscience

This chapter specifically focuses on the benefits of taking a cognitive neuroscience approach to development, but the case for a developmental approach to cognitive neuroscience is at least as strong (see Johnson, 1993, for examples). The human adult brain and the mind it sustains is composed of a complex series of hierarchical and parallel systems that have proven difficult to analyze in an exclusively "top-down" manner. An alternative approach studies how these neurocognitive systems emerge and become integrated during development in a fashion similar to the "synthetic psychology" advocated by Braitenberg (1984). This approach may be particularly useful in understanding how later-developing neurocognitive systems are hierarchically arranged on top of existing ones (Johnson, 1992).

No doubt there will still be some readers unconvinced by our somewhat abstract arguments for the merits of a cognitive neuroscience approach to development. Since, after all, the "proof of the pudding is in the eating," we now review some current examples of the developmental cognitive neuroscience approach, and illustrate the ways in which it has led to modifications and reconceptualizations of existing cognitive theories.

II. THE DEVELOPMENT OF SPECIES AND FACE RECOGNITION

A. Introduction

Since the human infant is relatively immobile, with the exception of eye and head movements, for the first 8 months of life, the bulk of what infants learn during this period probably occurs through passive exposure to stimuli. Clearly, socially relevant stimuli such as the speech and faces of caregivers are especially salient to infants, and learning about them particularly important. The fundamental importance of socially salient stimuli has fueled debate about the mechanisms that underlie infants' ability to recognize faces (see Maurer, 1985; Nelson & Ludemann, 1989, for reviews). A recent survey of the literature on the development of face recognition in human infants (Johnson & Morton, 1991; Morton & Johnson, 1991) revealed two apparently contradictory bodies of evidence: while the prevailing view, and most of the evidence, supported the contention that it takes the infant about 2 or 3 months to learn about the arrangement of features that compose a face, one study (Goren, Sarty, & Wu, 1975) suggested that newborns around 10 minutes old would track by means of head and eye movements a facelike pattern further than various "scrambled" face patterns.

Since the newborn study by Goren and colleagues (1975) remained controversial for methodological reasons, Johnson, Dziurawiec, Ellis, and Morton (1991) attempted to replicate it with minor changes to improve the methodology. As in the original study, newborn infants around 30 minutes old were required to track different stimuli. This procedure differs markedly from that employed by other investigators. Rather than having the infant view one or more stimuli in static locations and measuring the length of time spent looking at the stimuli, in the Goren et al. (1975) procedure the dependent measure is how far the infant will turn its head and eyes in order to keep a moving stimulus in view. The stimulus is moved slowly away from the midline and the angle at which the infant disengages its eyes from the stimulus is recorded. In the first study, three of the four stimuli used in the original Goren et al. study were used; a schematic face pattern, a symmetric "scrambled" face, and a blank face outline stimulus. Johnson, Dziurawiec, Ellis, and Morton (1991) were unable to replicate preferential head turning to follow the face pattern, but like others (Maurer & Young, 1983), did successfully replicate the effect using a measure of eye movements (see Figure 1).

In a second experiment the set of stimuli was expanded to include a pattern composed of the configuration of high-contrast areas that compose a face, but without the features of a face, as well as a pattern that had facial features but in the wrong arrangement. The former pattern might be effective if the tracking response were triggered by the appropriate spatial arrangement of high-contrast "blobs" (somewhat similar to a defocused image of a face). The results of this, and several other experiments (for review see Johnson & Morton, 1991), indicated that there is no consistent difference in newborn preferences between the detailed schematic face and the facelike three blobs. While the information necessary to elicit the preferential track-

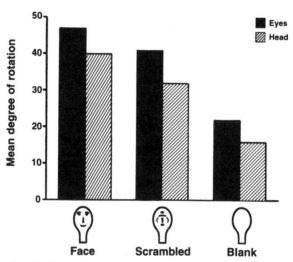

FIGURE 1   Results from Johnson, Dziurawiec, Ellis, and Morton (1991) study showing newborn preferences for facelike stimuli when measured by the extent of eye and head tracking of a slowly moving pattern. A preference for the face stimulus was found using the eye movement measure, but was not revealed by head movements.

ing may be not specific to the details of face features, it may be specific to the arrangement of elements that compose a face. To date, no single unidimensional psychophysical variable, such as spatial frequency, has been able to account for the preferences observed (Johnson & Morton, 1991; Morton, Johnson, & Maurer, 1990).

The newborn studies provided evidence in support of a nativistic account of infant face recognition, but many studies using more conventional infant testing methods, such as preferential looking, had indicated that a preference for face patterns over others was not found until 2 or 3 months after birth (for reviews see Maurer, 1985; Nelson & Ludemann, 1989). For example, Maurer and Barrera (1981) used a sensitive infant control procedure, in which the infant viewed a series of singly presented static stimuli, and established that while 2-month-olds looked significantly longer at a facelike pattern than at various scrambled face patterns, 1-month-olds had no such preference. Johnson, Dziurawiec, Bartrip, and Morton (1992) replicated this result and extended the original findings by including in the stimulus set the "defocused" face arrangement stimulus used in the newborn studies earlier. The results replicated entirely the previous findings: the face was looked at longer than any of the other stimuli by 10-week-olds, but a group of 5-week-olds showed no preference. This latter evidence was consistent with the claim that infants gradually construct representations of faces as a result of repeated exposure to them over the first few months of life (Gibson, 1969). Clearly, these apparently contradictory findings raised a problem for existing theories of the development of face recognition that involved only one process. In order to shed some light on the issues, Johnson and Morton (1991) turned to evidence from two areas of biology: ethology and brain development.

B. Biology

Perhaps one of the most extensively studied examples of perceptual learning in behavioral development is filial imprinting in precocial birds. Imprinting is the process by which young precocial birds such as chicks recognize and develop an attachment for the first conspicuous object that they see after hatching (for reviews see Bateson, 1966; Bolhuis, 1991; Johnson & Bolhuis, 1991; Sluckin, 1972). While imprinting has been reported in the young of a variety of species including spiny mice, guinea pigs, chicks, and ducklings, only in precocial species (those that are mobile from birth) can we measure it using the conventional measure of preferential approach.

The domestic chick can be thought of as the "laboratory rat" of development (Andrew, 1991), since it has proved to be an ideal species for addressing many developmental questions. The chick is also ideally placed in terms of being readily accessible to the molecular biologist and geneticist, as well as being the simplest vertebrate to show cognitive abilities of interest to the psychologist such as object recognition (Horn, 1985; Johnson, 1991; O'Reilly & Johnson, 1994). In the laboratory, chicks will imprint onto a variety of objects such as moving colored balls and cylinders. Even a few hours of exposure to such a stimulus results in strong and robust preferences for it over novel stimuli. Thus, in the absence of a mother hen, the learning is relatively unconstrained: virtually any conspicuous moving object larger than a matchbox will do. Under most circumstances this initial training object will come to be preferred over any other.

Visual imprinting has been localized to a particular region of the chick forebrain, known as the intermediate and medial part of the hyperstriatum ventrale (IMHV) (for reviews see Horn, 1985; Horn & Johnson, 1989). Lesions to IMHV placed before or after training on an object severely impair preference for that object in subsequent choice tests, but do not affect several other types of visual and learning tasks (Johnson & Horn, 1986, 1987; McCabe, Cipolla-Neto, Horn, & Bateson, 1982). Similar-sized lesions placed elsewhere in the chick forebrain do not result in significant impairments of imprinting preference (Johnson & Horn, 1987; McCabe et al., 1982).

In the laboratory a wide range of objects such as red boxes and blue balls are as effective for imprinting as more naturalistic stimuli such as a moving stuffed hen. However, in the wild, precocial birds such as chicks invariably imprint on their mother, and not on other passing objects. These observations raise the question concerning what mechanisms ensure that this plasticity in the chick brain is constrained such that it encodes information about conspecifics, and not about the characteristics of other objects present in its early visual environment.

An answer to this issue arose from a series of experiments in which striking stimulus-dependent effects of IMHV lesions were found (Horn & McCabe, 1984). While groups of chicks trained on an artificial stimulus such as a red box were severely impaired by IMHV lesions placed either before or after training, groups of chicks trained on a stuffed hen were only mildly impaired. Other neurophysiological manipulations also turned out to show differences between the hen-trained and box-trained birds (see Table 1). For example, administration of the neurotoxin DSP4, which depletes forebrain levels of the neurotransmitter norepinephrine, resulted in a severe impairment of preference in birds trained on the red box, but only a mild impairment in birds trained on the stuffed hen (Davies, Horn, & McCabe, 1985). In contrast, levels of plasma testosterone correlate with preference for the stuffed hen, but not preference for the red box (Bolhuis, McCabe, & Horn 1986).

These results led Johnson and Horn (1988) to seek experimental evidence for an earlier suggestion (Hinde, 1961) that naturalistic objects such as hens

TABLE 1   Differential Effects of Neurophysiological Treatments on Preferences
of Box-Trained and Hen-Trained Chicks

	Effect on preference for stimulus	
Treatment	Stuffed fowl	Red box
Administration of testosterone	Increases	No effect
Depletion of noradrenaline	No effect	Impairs
Spontaneous activity in IMHV	No correlation	Significant correlation
Bilateral IMHV lesions	Little effect	Strong effect

may be more effective at eliciting attention in young chicks than are other objects. These authors conducted a series of experiments in which dark-reared chicks were presented with a choice between an intact stuffed hen and a variety of test stimuli created from cutting up and jumbling the pelt of a stuffed hen. Johnson and Horn (1988) concluded that chicks have a spontaneous tendency to attend toward characteristics of the head and neck region of the hen. While this untrained preference seemed to be specific to the correct arrangement of features of the face/head, it was not specific to the species. For example, the head of a duck was as attractive as that of a hen.

The results of these and other experiments led to the proposal that there are two independent neural systems that underlie filial preference in the chick (Horn, 1985; Johnson, Bolhuis, & Horn, 1985). The first is a specific predisposition for the young chick to orient toward objects resembling conspecifics. In contrast to nonspecific color and size preferences in the chick (Johnson & Bolhuis, 1991), the predisposition system appears to be specifically tuned to the correct spatial arrangement of elements of the head and neck region. While the stimulus configuration triggering the predisposition is not species or genus specific, it is sufficient to pick out the mother hen from other objects the chick is likely to be exposed to in the first few days after hatching. The neural basis for this predisposition is currently unknown, but the optic tectum, the homologue of the mammalian superior colliculus, is a likely candidate. The second system acquires information about the objects to which the young chick attends and is supported by the brain region IMHV. In the natural environment, it was argued, the first system ensures that the second system acquires information about the particular individual mother hen close by. Biochemical, electrophysiological, and lesion evidence all support the conclusion that the two systems have largely independent neural substrates (for review see Horn, 1985). For example, while selective lesions to IMHV impair preferences acquired through exposure to an object, they do not impair the predisposition (Johnson & Horn, 1986).

There are, of course, a number of different ways that the predisposition could constrain the information acquired by the IMHV system. For example, the information in the predisposition could act as a sensory "filter" or template through which information had to pass before reaching the IMHV system. This possibility, and a variety of other alternatives, have been rejected on the basis of recent experiments (Bolhuis & Johnson, 1990; Bolhuis, Johnson, Horn, & Bateson, 1989; Johnson & Bolhuis, 1991). The evidence available at present is consistent with the view that the two systems influence the preference behavior of the chick independently, that is, there is no internal informational exchange between them. Instead, it appears that the input to the IMHV system is selected simply as a result of the predisposition biasing the chick to orient toward any henlike objects in the environment. Given that the species-typical environment of the chick includes a mother hen in close proximity, and that the predisposition includes adequate information to pick the hen out from other objects in the early environment, the input to the learning system will be highly selected.

Turning back to the human infant, several authors have argued, on the basis of neuroanatomical and neurophysiological data, that visually guided behavior in the newborn infant is largely mediated by subcortical structures such as the superior colliculus and pulvinar, and that it is not until 2 or 3 months of age that cortical circuitry comes to dominate subcortical circuits (Atkinson, 1984; Bronson, 1974; Johnson, 1990). Consistent with these arguments is the position that visually guided behavior in human infants, like that in domestic chicks, is based on activity in at least two distinct brain systems. Since these systems have distinct developmental time courses, they may differentially influence behavior in infants of different ages.

C. Face Processing in Human Infants

The biological evidence led Johnson and Morton (Johnson & Morton, 1991; Morton & Johnson, 1991) to propose a two-process theory of infant face preferences analogous to that in chicks. The first process consists of a system accessed via the subcortical visual pathway that underlies the preferential tracking in newborns, but whose influence wanes during the second month of life. The second process depends on cortical maturity and exposure to faces, and begins to influence infant orienting preferences from 2 to 4 months of age.

Johnson and Morton (1991) argue that the newborn subcortical preferential orienting system biases the input set to developing cortical circuitry. This circuitry is configured in response to a certain range of input, before it itself gains control over behavior around the third month of life. Once this occurs, the cortical system has enough experience with faces to ensure that it continues to acquire further information about them. Like in the chick, the proposal is that a specific, early-developing brain circuit acts in concert with the species-typical environment to bias the input to later-developing brain circuitry.

One source of evidence that the preferential orienting toward faces found in newborn infants is primarily mediated by subcortical neural circuitry concerns its developmental time course. Although it is not feasible to test older infants with exactly the same procedure as used with newborns, since they will track all patterned stimuli to the maximal extent, Johnson, Dziurawiec, Ellis, and Morton (1991) devised an equivalent situation in which the infant was still required to track, by means of head and eye turning, similar stimuli. In this procedure the infant was rotated in relation to the stimulus rather than the opposite (for details of procedure see Johnson, Dziurawiec, Ellis, & Morton, 1991, Experiment 3). Using this procedure, groups of 4-week-olds, 6-week-olds, 3-month-olds, and 5-month-olds were tested with similar stimuli to those discussed earlier. These experiments revealed that the preferential tracking of faces declines sharply between 4 and 6 weeks after birth. The time course of this response is similar to that of other newborn responses thought to be mediated by subcortical circuits, such as prereaching (von Hofsten, 1984). It has been suggested that the disappearance of these early reflexlike behaviors in the second month of life is due to inhibition by developing cortical circuits (see, e.g., Muir, Clifton, & Clarkson, 1989). This would also seem to be a plausible explanation for the decline observed in the tracking of faces. Thus, not only is it unlikely that the newborns have adequate cortical functioning to support the preferential tracking of faces, but this behavior declines at the same age as other behaviors thought to be subcortically mediated.

Why should the tracking task be so sensitive to newborns' preferences, whereas standard testing procedures with static stimuli are ineffective? One reason is that the peripheral visual field feeds more directly into the subcortical pathway, whereas the fovea feeds mainly into the cortical pathway. In a tracking task such as that described with newborns, the stimulus is continually moving out of the central visual field and toward the periphery. It has been suggested that this movement into the temporal field initiates a saccade to refoveate the stimulus in newborns (for details see Bronson, 1974; Johnson, 1990). This consistent movement toward the periphery would not necessarily arise with static presentations, and therefore preferences will rarely be elicited. Thus, the tracking task may more effectively tap into the capacities of subcortical structures such as the superior colliculus than the conventional infant testing procedures such as preferential looking at static stimuli.

Clearly, none of the above arguments brings us any closer to specifying in detail the neural implementation of newborn preferential tracking, and a number of different possibilities remain open, including the superior colliculus, pulvinar, deeper layers of the cortex, and any combination of these.

Probably only direct methods, such as neuroimaging, will enable further progress to be made on this issue. Nevertheless, given the evidence for the preferential tracking of faces in newborns, how are we to account for the large body of evidence showing no preference for faces until 2 or 3 months of age?

Evidence from neuroimaging and brain damage in human adults, and from single-unit recording in nonhuman primates, indicate that the recognition of individual faces is supported by particular regions of the cerebral cortex (for review see Farah, 1990). Preliminary PET evidence indicates that 2-month-old infants show differential bilateral activation in the temporal lobes following passive exposure to faces (de Schonen, Deruelle, Mancini, & Pascalis, 1993). Indirect evidence that the later-developing ability to recognize individual faces is mediated by this cortical circuitry concerns its developmental onset at 2 or 3 months of age.

More direct evidence for the onset of cortically mediated face processing has been obtained by using an infant version of a task that has been used in both the monkey single-cell recording and in studies of prosopagnosia (Johnson & Vecera, 1993; Vecera & Johnson, 1995). These studies build upon the findings from several laboratories that have reported the existence of cells responsive to face stimuli within the superior temporal sulcus (STS) of the macaque cortex (Perrett, Rolls, & Caan, 1982). There is evidence that these cells become sensitive to faces as a result of experience (Rolls, 1989). Beyond responding to faces and particular views of faces, there is a finer level of processing within STS. Cells that are responsive to views of the head also process information concerning eye gaze direction. For example, Perrett and Mistlin (1990) report that 64% of cells in the macaque responding to the head were also responsive to eye gaze. In particular, neurons that were sensitive to frontal views of the head responded to direct eye gaze, while cells that preferred profile views responded to an averted eye gaze (Perrett & Mistlin, 1990; Perrett et al., 1985).

These findings with nonhuman primates converge with findings from humans. Prosopagnosia in patients typically results from temporo-occipital lesions, although the exact neuropathology is debated. These patients are characterized by their inability to recognize or identify individual faces, and recent evidence suggests that they also have difficulty in processing the direction of another individual's eye gaze. Campbell, Heywood, Cowey, Regard, and Landis (1990) examined the performance of both STS lesioned monkeys and two prosopagnosic patients on discriminating eye gaze direction. Monkeys were presented with two faces, one with direct eye gaze and one with averted eye gaze, and were rewarded for choosing the averted eyes. Following STS lesions the monkeys were impaired at this task, but not in several other face recognition tasks. Similarly, the prosopagnosic patients were unable to choose which of two faces was looking directly at them. These patients, however, performed normally on a control task designed to test perceptual processing. In an independent study, M. J. Farah (unpublished observations, 1990) found a similar eye gaze impairment for her prosopagnosic patient L.H.; again, this patient performed normally on a control task similar to that used by Campbell et al. (1990). These results are consistent with the results of Perrett and his colleagues: If STS, or the homologous area in humans, contains neurons for both facial identity and eye gaze direction, then lesions to this area should result in deficits in both. As the studies above demonstrate, prosopagnosic patients have difficulty with both face recognition and the detection of eye gaze direction.

Given that direction of eye gaze is an aspect of face processing directly linked to cortical processing, we can use it as a "marker task" for cortical face processing in infants. Studies investigating eye gaze sensitivity in infants suggest that 3-month-old infants are insensitive to direct eye contact, that is, these infants do not seem to be able to discriminate between a direct and an averted eye gaze (Bloom, 1974; Samuels, 1985). In contrast to these results with 3-month-olds, Lasky and Klein (1979) found that 5-month-olds fixated a face more when the individual maintained direct eye contact, as opposed to no eye contact (i.e., an averted gaze). These infants also smiled more when the individual maintained a direct eye gaze. Taken together, these findings suggest that sensitivity to the direction of eye gaze may emerge between 3 and 5 months of age.

Vecera and Johnson (1995; Johnson & Vecera, 1993) have tested a group of 4-month-old infants with pairs of life-size photographs of a face that differed in their direction of eye gaze (straight on, 15° averted, 30° averted). Their results suggest that, while some infants preferred to look at the averted gaze, and others at the straight-on gaze, they all showed consistent and strong preferences. This indicates that 4-month-old infants can distinguish between direct and averted eye gazes, even when the difference between the two is as slight as 15°, and is consistent with the development of sensitivity to eye gaze, a "marker" for cortical face processing, developing between 3 and 4 months of age.

Finally, Carey (this volume) describes a number of changes in face processing that result from familiarity with this class of stimuli. Undoubtedly, these effects of expertise will have neural concomitants. There is considerable evidence that cortical circuits retain a certain degree of plasticity even into adult years. Presumably, this cortical plasticity remains sufficient to allow subtle changes in visual information processing as a result of prolonged training.

D. How Biological Evidence Shaped the Cognitive Theory

The biological evidence considered by Johnson and Morton (1991) informed and constrained the development of the psychological theory these authors proposed in a number of ways.

Evidence from the development of the brain ruled out the theory that infants have full face recognition abilities from birth, since many aspects of face recognition appear to be mediated by cortical circuits, and the cortex is relatively immature in the newborn infant. Evidence from neuroscience also generated the notion of two comparatively independent systems. Neurophysiological manipulations in the chick initially revealed the two systems, and anatomical evidence from primates (including humans) indicated the possibility of different developmental time course for cortical and subcortical systems in the human infant.

Ethological considerations influenced the psychological theory by forcing a consideration of the crucial role of the external environment in supporting the development of cognitive systems. The two-process theory holds that the external environment guarantees the presence of conspecifics and their faces (except in laboratory rearing situations). The cognitive mechanisms proposed cannot be understood in isolation of the environment in which they have evolved to operate. Johnson and Morton (1991) developed the notion of a "species-typical" environment, which is composed of aspects of the environment that a species' nervous system has evolved to expect. A similar notion has been developed by Greenough, Black, and Wallace (1987). Aspects of brain development that depend on species-typical environmental input, while not innate in the classical sense of "genetic," should be distinguished from those that are related to learning.

Another factor relating to support from the external environment concerns the nature of the neural representations. Representations in the brain are only partial, in the sense that only some aspects of the entity being represented are captured. When seriously considering the natural environment of the chick or infant it becomes apparent that the content of representations about conspecifics can be minimal and still be adaptive. The neural representation has to be merely sufficient to frequently pick out faces, for example, from other commonly occurring stimuli. In the case of the chick, the representation that triggers appropriate orienting responses may be as minimal as three high-contrast blobs in the correct arrangement for eyes and beak/mouth. This minimal specification is sufficient given the species-typical environment.

The preceding discussion has shown that an integration of biological evidence with behavioral findings has shed new light on the ability of infant animals to identify and learn about the faces of caregivers. The enriched understanding of imprinting and face recognition phenomena emerged because biological data informed cognitive theories, and behavioral findings helped to constrain the search for plausible neural mechanisms. In the next section, we explore a second, related set of problems in which the combination of biological and behavioral evidence is enriching our understanding of the mechanisms that govern visual orienting and attention.

III. VISUAL ORIENTING AND ATTENTION

A. Introduction

Over the first 6 to 8 months of life, the human infant's primary method of gathering information involves shifts of eye gaze and attention. These shifts of attention allow the infant to select particular aspects of the external world for further study and learning. For example, simply by shifting the head and eyes infants can ensure that they are exposed to faces more than to other stimuli. In addition, most of what we have learned about the mental life of the infant has come from tasks in which some measure of looking behavior, such as preferential looking or habituation to a repeatedly presented stimulus, is used. Despite the importance of shifts of attention in early infancy, however, little is known about the mechanisms that underlie these aspects of cognition.

B. Biology

There is now a substantial literature on the neural basis of visual attention that comes from neuropsychological and neuroimaging studies of human adults, as well as single-cell recording and lesion studies in nonhuman primates (see Posner & Petersen, 1990, for review). Rather than review this large body of evidence, we will present one account that focuses on the neural pathways involved in visual orienting (Schiller, 1985). While several cortical circuits other than those discussed by Schiller are likely to be important, especially in covert shifts of attention (see, e.g., Johnson, 1994), this framework has been a useful one in which to explore questions concerning the development of visual orienting.

Schiller (1985) proposes, largely on the basis of nonhuman primate studies, that four pathways are involved in the control of eye movements in the primate brain (see Figure 2):

1. A pathway from the retina to the superior colliculus thought to be involved in the generation of eye movements toward simple, easily discriminable stimuli, and fed mainly by the peripheral visual field. This pathway corresponds to the *subcortical pathway* mentioned in the previous section.

2. A cortical pathway that goes to the superior colliculus from the primary visual cortex and also via the middle temporal area (MT), which may be involved in the smooth tracking of moving stimuli, and in the perception of motion. For convenience we refer to this pathway as the *MT pathway.*

3. A cortical pathway where both broad-band and color-opponent streams of processing converge in the frontal eye fields (FEF), which we refer to as the *FEF pathway.* This cortical circuit may be involved in more

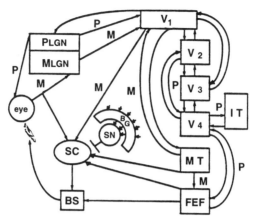

FIGURE 2   A schematic representation of the model proposed by Schiller for the neuro-anatomical pathways thought to underlie oculomotor control in primates. LGN, Lateral geniculate nucleus; SC, superior colliculus; SN, substantia nigra; BG, basal ganglia, BS, brain stem; FEF, frontal eye fields; M, magnocellular stream; P, parvocellular stream; V_1–V_4, visual cortex; IT, inferotemporal cortex; MT, medial temporal cortex. Used with permission from Johnson (1990). Copyright © 1990 by the Massachusetts Institute of Technology.

complex scanning patterns and the temporal sequencing of eye movements within complex arrays.

4. An inhibitory input to the colliculus from several cortical areas via the substantia nigra and basal ganglia, which we refer to as the *inhibitory pathway*. This pathway plays a role in suppressing the response of the colliculus to new stimuli impinging on the peripheral visual field. Recent evidence indicates that this pathway is integrally involved with pathway (3).

Clearly, this scheme has no developmental component. However, information concerning the pre- and postnatal development of the cortical regions implicated in Schiller's model could be used to generate a developmental account of visual orienting.

During prenatal development the mammalian cortex is laid down in an inside-out manner: cells born last in the proliferative zone migrate past their older relatives to form the upper layers (for reviews see Nowakowski, 1987; Rakic, 1988). While all the neurons have reached their adult locations prior to birth in humans, the inside-out pattern of growth continues into the first postnatal months in the form of an increase in myelination, and increases in the length and order of branching of dendrites. Note that this postnatal "tail" of the inside-out development is not evident by other measures such as synaptic density (Huttenlocher, 1990). For example, Becker, Armstrong, Chan, and Wood (1984) reported that the mean total length of dendrites for pyramidal cells in layer III is only about 30% of the maximum at birth, while in layer V the equivalent figure is about 60% of maximum. Furthermore, a higher degree of dendritic branching is found in layer V than in layer III. This layer-wise pattern of development has also been quantitatively described in human motor cortex (e.g., Marin-Padilla, 1970).

What constraints does the inside-out pattern of growth provide, and how can they be related to behavioral changes? Clearly, it is difficult to quantify the extent of myelination or dendritic aborization that would allow "functional" information processing or transmission. Further, it is unlikely that functional activity in neural circuitry is an all-or-none phenomenon. Rather, it is more likely that functional activity would gradually emerge in developing neural tissue. However, the inside-out pattern of growth allows us to make statements about the *sequence* of development of layers in the cortex. Thus, while we cannot say that a particular layer is functional at a particular age, we can argue that the layer will be more capable of supporting patterns of activity similar to that found in the adult than more superficial layers at a given point in development.

This differential developmental sequence is useful in combination with a second characteristic of the cortex: that particular layers show particular patterns of inputs and outputs. For example, outputs from the primary visual cortex to the three cortical pathways mentioned earlier come from different layers of this structure (see Johnson, 1990, for details).

We are now in a position to put together the three pieces of information reviewed above: (1) the primary visual cortex is a gateway through which flows the majority of visual input to the cortical pathways involved in oculomotor control; (2) neural pathways that control eye movements depart from different layers of the primary visual cortex; and (3) some aspects of the postnatal growth of human cortex proceed in an "inside-out" pattern. The combination of these three factors allows us to predict the *sequence* of availability of the cortical pathways. If we can predict the sequence these pathways become available, then we can also make predictions about the sequence in which aspects of visual orienting and attention they mediate should appear. In the next section we summarize Johnson's (1990) proposal for describing several phases of the development of visually guided behavior, with each transition caused by the onset of functional activity in one or other of the cortical pathways initially outlined by Schiller (1985).

C. Human Behavior

The "inside-out," layer-wise pattern of cortical development means that in the newborn human infant only the deeper layers of the primary visual cortex may be capable of performing computations on visual input (for details see Johnson, 1990). Since the outputs to the FEF and MT pathways (see Figure 2) depart from the middle and upper layers, these pathways are assumed not to be processing information at the time of birth. However, evidence from visually evoked potentials suggests that information is entering the primary visual cortex. Accordingly, a pathway that departs from the deepest layer of the primary visual cortex and makes contact with the superior colliculus could have some influence over the activity of the subcortical pathway. Thus, while most of the newborn's visual behavior can be accounted for in terms of processing in the subcortical pathway, some information processing probably occurs in the deeper layers of the primary visual cortex at birth.

Due to the continuing maturation of the primary visual cortex upward from the deeper layers, over the first few weeks of life the output to the inhibitory pathway becomes functional. As mentioned earlier, this pathway is involved in suppressing the response of the colliculus to new stimuli impinging on the peripheral visual field. Consequently, the infant will no longer respond as readily to stimuli presented within its peripheral visual field. This behavioral phenomenon, often known as "obligatory attention" is reported to be particularly prevalent in infants around 1 month of age. Such infants will appear to "lock on" to a particular stimulus for as long as several minutes. Distracting stimuli placed to one side or the other of the stimulus have little or no effect on the direction of gaze.

According to the Johnson (1990) account, by 2 months of age, further maturation of the primary visual cortex results in an output from the middle layers of the primary visual cortex to the MT pathway. This pathway has been associated with the ability of primates to track a moving object smoothly with their eyes. From 2 months of age infants start to show periods of smooth tracking intermingled with the saccadic tracking patterns found in younger infants (Aslin, 1981). They also become more sensitive to stimuli placed in the central visual field, which is indicative of increasing cortical control over eye gaze.

Finally, Johnson (1990) argues that the maturation of the upper layers of the primary visual cortex around 3 to 4 months of age enables the output from these layers to the FEF pathway. Neurophysiological studies in primates and neuropsychological studies on human adults with brain damage have led to the proposal that this pathway is involved in the ability to make anticipatory eye movements and the ability to make organized sequential scanning patterns toward familiar objects.

One information-processing consequence of these neural pathways coming "on-line" may be illustrated by focusing on the transitions in orienting behavior that occur between 2 and 4 months of age. Over the first month or two of the infant's life its visually guided behavior is highly automatic. For example, in a task where the infant tracks a moving object with its eyes, the eye movements rarely anticipate the movement of the stimulus, even if they are able to follow it smoothly (Aslin, 1981). Simultaneously with the onset of the latest developing of the pathways controlling orienting, the FEF pathway (Figure 2), the eye movements of the infant start to reach the target of the moving stimulus before the stimulus itself does. That is, saccades begin to become increasingly predictive.

Evidence from other tasks supports the idea that the ability to make predictive (anticipatory) eye movements does not emerge until 3 or 4 months. Haith and his collaborators (Haith, Hazan, & Goodman, 1988) conducted a study in which $3\frac{1}{2}$-month-old infants viewed one of two series of slides that appeared either on the right- or on the left-hand side of the infant, either alternating with regular interstimulus intervals (ISI) or with an irregular alternation pattern and ISI (Haith et al., 1988). The regular ISI generated more stimulus anticipations, and reaction times to make an eye movement were reliably faster than in the irregular series. The authors argue that infants of this age are able to develop expectancies for noncontrollable spatiotemporal events. Robinson, McCarty, and Haith (1988) report that they were unable to obtain these effects strongly in infants of 6 and 9 weeks old. These results are consistent with the idea that between 9 and 15 weeks the ability to make anticipatory eye movements may emerge.

With the increasing development of parietal and frontal lobes, infants show increasing evidence of being able to shift gaze on the basis of endogenous (cognitive) factors (Johnson, 1994). For example, while 4-month-olds can be trained to use a central cue stimulus to predict the spatial location in which a target stimulus will appear, 2- and 3-month-olds cannot (Johnson, Posner, & Rothbart, 1991). Thus, at this stage the infant is able to use information acquired at an earlier point in time to guide its eye movements. Even later in development Posner and Rothbart (1990) have argued that an "anterior attention system" develops, which allows the infant even greater regulation of its own behavior.

Orienting behavior in the infant may thus be characterized in terms of the emergence of successively more predictive stages of hierarchical control. First of all, there is a transition from a purely input-driven (automatic) system to a system capable of making some predictive eye movements following training on many similar trials. Then, a further transition occurs to a system able to control eye movements on the basis of more cognitive factors, such as learning about associations between stimuli. Finally, there may be a further transition of control to an attention system solely concerned with focusing on internal processes and states.

D. How the Biology Shaped the Cognitive Theory

There are a number of ways in which the neurobiological evidence constrained and informed the systems-level account put forward by Johnson

(1990). First, consideration of the neurobiological evidence led to the postulation that there are multiple, partially independent systems involved in infant visual orienting. Previous theories of infant visual orienting had postulated only one or two mechanisms underlying the behavior (e.g., Cohen, 1988). Second, the evidence from neuropsychology and single-cell recordings suggested some of the information processing characteristics of these pathways, allowing inferences to be made from neural circuitry to cognitive functions. Third, evidence from developmental neuroanatomy at the cellular level was used to make predictions about the sequence of development of components of visual orienting.

In summary, evidence concerning the pre- and postnatal growth of cortical regions thought to underlie the processes involved in visual orienting has been useful in formulating a theory of infant orienting behavior. In particular, changes in the characteristic patterns of visual orienting of infants at various ages have been linked to the emergence of specific pathways that govern one or more aspects of orienting responses. Since the interpretation of visual orienting responses plays a central role in understanding infant cognition, an improved understanding of these processes is important for explaining how perceptual processes affect cognitive development in general. Similarly, in the next section, we will explore a line of research that examines how the development of a particular brain region might be closely linked to the emergence of a high-level cognitive ability, working memory.

IV. PREFRONTAL CORTEX AND WORKING MEMORY

A. Introduction

The ability to maintain information in memory over short periods of time and to use it appropriately to carry out action is a crucial feature of rational thought. This characteristic ability has been termed working memory (Baddeley, 1986), and it undoubtedly plays a role in many aspects of cognitive development, from language learning to problem solving. In this section, we review evidence that implicates a specific region of frontal cortex, the principal sulcus, in tasks that require one form of working memory. Specifically, we will examine recent studies that have explored the relationship between this region of the brain and performance on several delayed-response tasks that require the maintenance of information about locations in space over delays of several seconds. These studies are interesting from a developmental perspective because they are closely related to tasks used by Piaget (1954) to study the emergence of object permanence in infants. In particular, it has been argued (Diamond, 1991) that the maturation of frontal cortical areas during the last half of the human infant's first year of life accounts for both Piaget's observations about object permanence and a variety of other findings in related tasks that implicate working memory.

B. Evidence from Biology

The region of the frontal lobe anterior to the primary motor and premotor cortex, commonly called the prefrontal cortex, accounts for almost one-third of the total cortical surface in humans (Brodmann, 1909, 1912) and is considered by most investigators to be the locus of control for many abilities central to higher-level cognition. The greater magnitude of frontal cortex in humans relative to other species has been taken as evidence that this area of the brain is the substrate for cognitive abilities of the highest order. Extensive clinical (Milner, 1982) and experimental observations of the effects of injury to this region have also supported the notion that prefrontal cortex subserves important aspects of cognition (for reviews see Fuster, 1989; Goldmann-Rakic, 1987). The particular forms of cognitive processing that have been consistently linked to frontal cortex pertain to the planning or carrying out of sequences of action, the maintenance of information "on-line" during short temporal delays, and the ability to inhibit a set of responses that are appropriate in one context but not another.

For example, adult monkeys who are shown a food target being hidden in one of two hiding wells within their reach are able to remember the location of the reward and retrieve it despite intervening delays of 10 s or more and the presence of an opaque screen that prevents continuous fixation on the hiding location. However, adult monkeys in whom the principal sulcus, a region of dorsolateral prefrontal cortex, has been ablated bilaterally are unable to choose accurately between the food wells in which they have only seconds before seen the reward hidden (Goldman & Rosvold, 1970; Goldman, Rosvold, Vest, & Galkin, 1971; Goldman-Rakic, 1987). This severe performance deficit occurs when the delay between food hiding and retrieval is only 1–2 s, but is not observed when the monkey is permitted to retrieve the reward immediately. If the hiding location on the current trial is identical to the one from the immediately preceding trial, the monkey will usually retrieve the object on the first reach. If the side of hiding changes on the current trial, however, the monkey often reaches first to the location where the object was successfully retrieved on the previous trial. This pattern of performance has been interpreted as revealing a deficit in both memory for the currently hidden location and in the ability to inhibit an incorrect reach to the last rewarded location. Similar performance deficits have been shown when the prefrontal cortical regions are temporarily disabled by local cooling (Fuster, 1989) or when the number of hiding locations is increased (Passingham, 1985).

These results are similar to those observed by Diamond and Goldman-Rakic (1989) who tested monkeys with a modification of this task employed by Piaget (1954) in studies of infants' perceptions of object permanence. In the object permanence task, subjects are shown an object hidden at location A and are permitted to retrieve it. After a predetermined number of successful retrievals at location A (usually three), the object is then hidden at location B. Infant monkeys failed to retrieve the hidden object at location B when the delay between hiding and retrieval was 2 s or more. Animals with lesions to the parietal cortex, a brain region closely associated with spatial processing, did not show this performance deficit; nor did lesions to the hippocampal formation, a region known to be crucial for other memory-related tasks, impair monkey performance on (Diamond, Zola-Morgan, & Squire, 1989). These studies strongly suggest that the principal sulcus region plays a central role in delayed-response tasks that require the maintenance of spatial information over temporal delays.

Further evidence comes from several studies in which chronically implanted electrodes showed specific prefrontal cell responses during delayed-response tasks (for reviews see Fuster, 1989; Goldman-Rakic, 1987). Using this technique, Funahashi, Bruce, and Goldman-Rakic (1989, 1990) have demonstrated that neurons in the principal sulcus have specific patterns of activity during a delayed-response task. In this task, rhesus monkeys were trained to fixate a central spot while a brief cue appeared in one of eight locations in the visual periphery. The monkeys were rewarded for maintaining fixation throughout a variable delay period of 1–5 s, and for making an eye movement to the location where the cue had appeared once the central fixation stimulus had turned off. Funahashi et al. (1989, 1990) recorded neurons in the principal sulcus and in the frontal eye fields, a brain region implicated in the volitional control of eye movements (see Section III,C). They found evidence that specific neurons were maintaining a representation of the cued location during the delay period. Sixty percent of the neurons in the principal sulcus were active during the task; 30% of the cells recorded were differentially active during the delay period; and 80% of the cells active during the delay period had receptive fields that coded the direction of the cue and subsequent eye movement. The results from frontal eye field neurons were similar: 71% of the cells recorded showed activity above baseline during some portion of the task; 55% of the cells were differentially active during the delay period; and 32% of the delay cells were sensitive to the direction of the cue and subsequent eye movements. Funahashi et al. (1989, 1990) argued that these results reflect the common function of the prefrontal cortex in delayed-response tasks in both the visual and motor domains, specifically the maintenance of information during short delay periods about spatial locations important for later action. Subsequent results by Wilson et al. (1993) showed that configural cues such as shape could signal spatial saccade goals to trained monkeys and that different populations of memory cells were selectively active in the prefrontal cortex of these animals when spatial versus configural information was relevant.

Studies with adult human patients with frontal lobe lesions and preliminary neurobiological data from human infants support many of the primate findings. Frontal lobe lesions cause impairment in the learning of stylus mazes (Canavan, 1983; Corkin, 1965; Milner, 1965), a task that requires spatial memory, and in performance on the Wisconsin Card Sort (Milner, 1963) in which subjects tend to make perseverative sorting errors long after the sorting category has changed. Adult patients with bilateral frontal damage show impaired performance in delayed-response and delayed-alternation tasks (Freedman & Oscar-Berman, 1986; Pribram, Ahumada, Hartog, & Roos, 1964).

Developmental evidence that links maturation in frontal cortical regions to the emergence of working memory abilities comes from studies (Diamond & Goldman-Rakic, 1986, 1989) that showed that infant monkeys failed in object retrieval tasks in ways similar to frontally lesioned monkeys, but that older, unlesioned monkeys succeeded in the tasks and showed an ability to withstand longer delays with age. Evidence linking this change in behavior to brain maturation comes from studies that show that while prefrontal projections to other cortical regions and the basal ganglia have reached their adult targets and distributions in the monkey by 2 weeks *before* birth (Goldman-Rakic, 1981), prefrontal afferents and efferents myelinate later than other cortical areas (Yakovlev & Lecours, 1967). Furthermore, in a series of EEG studies with normal human infants (Bell, 1992a, 1992b; Bell & Fox, 1992; Fox & Bell, 1990), increases in frontal EEG responses have been shown to correlate with the ability to respond successfully over longer delays in delayed-response tasks.

C. Human Behavior

These findings from biology closely relate to behavioral results first observed by Piaget (1954) a generation ago. Using the object permanence task described previously, Piaget observed that infants younger than $7\frac{1}{2}$ months fail to accurately retrieve a hidden object after a short delay period if the object's location is changed from one where it was previously and successfully retrieved. Infants of this age make a particular perseverative error. They often reach to the hiding location where the object was found on the immediately preceding trial. This characteristic pattern of error, called A not B, was cited by Piaget (1954) as evidence for the failure of infants to understand that objects retain their existence or permanence when moved from view. Between $7\frac{1}{2}$ and 9 months, infants begin to succeed in the task at successively longer delays of 1–5 s (Diamond, 1985). However, their performance is unreliable; infants continue to make the A not B error up to about 12 months if the delay between hiding and retrieval is incremented as the infants age (Diamond, 1985).

Several authors have challenged Piaget's assertion (Baillargeon, 1987; Diamond, 1991; Spelke, Breinlinger, Macomber, & Jacobsen, 1992) that the concept of object permanence emerges between 7 and 8 months. Baillargeon's experimental results have shown that by using habituation measures, infants as young as $3\frac{1}{2}$ months may demonstrate knowledge about the permanence of objects that disappear behind a moving obstruction. Spelke and colleagues (1992) have offered evidence that infants as young as 4 months of age demonstrate knowledge about the continuity and motion of objects by dishabituating to "impossible" displays. Similarly, using the neurobiological evidence cited previously and the results of numerous empirical studies, Diamond has argued that it is the ability to demonstrate an understanding of object permanence by reaching for the hidden object that emerges over this time period, not the understanding itself (see Spelke & Hermer, this volume), which emerges several months earlier. In Diamond's (1991) view, the emergence of the ability to demonstrate knowledge about an object's permanence results from the maturation of prefrontal cortical regions between the ages of 5 and 12 months. These regions are thought to subserve the infant's ability to carry out plans of action over temporal delays and to inhibit contextually inappropriate responses.

The evidence for this position is as follows. Infants younger than $7\frac{1}{2}$ months fail to retrieve hidden objects when any delay whatsoever is imposed between hiding and retrieval. In this sense, human infants behave like the adult monkeys with prefrontal lesions and infant monkeys, as discussed previously. Human infants of this age make similar retrieval errors in both the A not B task, in which the side of hiding is switched after several repeated hidings on one side, and in an object retrieval task when the side of hiding is varied randomly (Diamond & Doar, 1989). This suggests Piaget's observations about object permanence reflect the state of development of one or more underlying neural mechanisms common to performance on both the object permanence and retrieval tasks. Since successful performance on these tasks requires both memory for the most recently hidden location and the inhibition of an incorrect reach to the last rewarded location, the underlying neural mechanism must subserve both behaviors in some fashion. Extensive neurobiological evidence implicates the prefrontal cortex in spatial working memory performance, and dissociations of this region frequently reveal patterns of behavior in which the inhibition of inappropriate responses is impaired. Consequently, the "maturational state" of the prefrontal cortex seems to be a critical factor in determining an infant's behavior on delayed-response tasks.

It may not be the only factor, however. The prefrontal cortex is highly interconnected with other regions of the brain whose developmental time courses and specific functions are still poorly understood (Goldman-Rakic, 1987). Consequently, it may be premature to claim that the immaturity of the prefrontal cortex is the sole or primary determinant of infant failures in delayed response tasks. For example, a dissociation has been observed between studies that rely on actual object retrieval measures on delayed-response tasks and those that rely on looking responses (Diamond, 1985, 1990). If young infants performing the A not B task are permitted to stare at the hiding location during the delay, they are able to retrieve the object after the delay period (Cornell, 1979; Diamond, 1985; Fox, Kagan, & Weiskopf, 1979). If their fixation is interrupted, they fail. On rare occasions, an infant will reach to the incorrect location while looking to the correct location. These findings have led some observers to suggest that there may be differences in the strength or persistence of internal representations for hidden objects that depend on the type of response required (Munakata, McClelland, Johnson, & Siegler, 1994).

This prospect raises questions about the exact role of the principal sulcus in delayed-response tasks. If the principal sulcus is the exclusive site of domain-independent spatial working memory, and it does not sufficiently mature in human infants until the age of $7\frac{1}{2}$ months, then infants younger than this age should not be able to perform versions of the object permanence or delayed response tasks that involve only eye movements. Results from Gilmore and Johnson (1995) call this view into question, however. We found that 6-month-old infants performing an oculomotor delay task similar to that used with macaques (Wilson et al., 1993) showed evidence that they remembered the location of a briefly presented peripheral cue for delays as long as 5 s. Further, infants were able to use configural information, such as an object's shape or color, to predict the location of a subsequent visual reward after several intervening seconds. Similarly sophisticated visual memory abilities have been found using versions of the object permanence task in which looking, not reaching, is the dependent measure. In one such experiment, infants as young as 5 months (Lecuyer, Abgueguen, & Lemarie, 1992) can perform the task. Finally, evidence from Munakata and colleagues (1994) indicates that the failures in object retrieval by younger infants seem closely tied to the ability to integrate visual information with motor commands, not strictly on the ability to generate means–ends sequences in general (Diamond, 1990). Infants who had been trained to retrieve a toy by pulling on a towel or pushing a button were more likely to retrieve the toy when it was in view or behind a transparent screen than when it was hidden behind an opaque screen.

Taken as a whole, these results imply that the development of an infant's capacity to represent, maintain in memory, and use spatial information to drive simple motor behavior such as eye movements may precede the emergence of the ability to utilize this information in reaching toward objects. Moreover, since neurobiological evidence implicates the principal sulcus in delayed-response tasks that require either looking or reaching responses (Funahashi et al., 1989, 1990; Goldman-Rakic, 1987), failures by infants younger than $7\frac{1}{2}$ months may not simply be the result of immaturities in prefrontal cortex, but may also reflect the state of development of other cortical regions, such as parietal cortex, that are also involved in performance of these tasks (Gnadt & Andersen, 1988).

D. How Biology Has Shaped the Cognitive Theory

The neurobiological and neuropsychological evidence we have presented supports a new interpretation of Piaget's observations regarding the development of object permanence. Specifically, performance on the object permanence task is seen to be closely related to the ability to perform delayed-response tasks in general. Extensive neurobiological evidence implicates the principal sulcus in the performance of delayed-response tasks, and although the precise function of prefrontal cortex is not yet clear, the development of performance on delayed-response tasks is closely related to the state of maturation of this region of the brain. Thus, we can begin to view Piaget's notion of object permanence in more general psychological terms as a marker for the state of an infant's working memory capacity and in more particular biological detail as a reflection of the state of development of the infant cortex.

Taking a neurobiological approach to this set of problems provides developmental psychology with tools to move beyond the use of rigid stages to describe behavioral consistencies (Case, 1985), and thereby to understand the *processes* of change more thoroughly. It might be tempting to reinterpret the biological findings in discrete, stagelike terms, by arguing simply that the prefrontal cortex is "immature" prior to $7\frac{1}{2}$ months, and once it "matures" at $7\frac{1}{2}$ months, working memory capacities come into operation. However, the neurobiological and behavioral evidence points in another direction. Delayed-response tasks (and the object permanence task in particular) tap multiple interacting and possibly overlapping neural systems that are still poorly understood, and the available evidence suggests that brain change is continuous, not discrete. Thus, the emergence of the ability to reach for hidden objects is unlikely to be the result of a discrete change to a single neural system. Instead, the development of working memory capacities as indexed by object permanence tasks is a gradual process, first indicated in behavior by habituation and preferential looking measures, later by the oculomotor delay paradigm and visual versions of the object permanence task, and still later by performance in object retrieval (Munakata et al., 1994). Thus, the ability to respond to the persistence of objects in time and space appears to emerge gradually, first in simpler responses, later in more complex ones. A complete understanding of this pattern of results, and the mechanisms of neural and cognitive change that drive them, demands investigation of the function and maturation of the multiple brain regions and pathways that underlie the infant's expanding capacity to demonstrate object permanence.

To illustrate this notion, consider that the information about the location of an occluded object may be maintained in one location useful for making both looking and reaching responses, or this information may be distributed into systems that maintain internal representations in a form particular to looking or reaching (Munakata et al., 1994). In either case, developmental differences in the pathways that underlie these behaviors may explain why one form of response precedes the other. In short, a biological perspective, and in particular an ethological one, helps researchers to resist the notion of a unitary object permanence concept that emerges at some prespecified developmental stage, but instead to explore how patterns of brain development contribute to the emergence of behaviors and capacities consistent with the continuous and gradual development of object permanence.

V. FUTURE DIRECTIONS

The evidence reviewed in this chapter has been presented in support of the basic claim that an integrated exploration of the role of biological factors in cognitive development is not merely possible but actually shows promise. That promise stems both from the use of new experimental methods and analytical tools, for example, neuroimaging and computational modeling, and from the pairing of more traditional experimental methods and theoretical approaches with data derived from biology. Clearly, the topics we have reviewed have been selective. In the final section we briefly review a number of other areas and approaches that we think hold promise for the developmental cognitive neuroscience approach.

A. Neurocomputational Modeling

Computational models that rely on neurally inspired architectures and mechanisms are, we believe, likely to become of central importance for understanding the computational consequences of aspects of brain development. Parallel distributed processing (PDP) is an approach (McClelland & Rumelhart, 1986; Rumelhart & McClelland, 1986) that attempts to model complex learning systems using massively parallel, interconnected sets of simple processing units that are loosely inspired by the architecture and characteristics of the brain. In this framework, inputs to the system consist of patterns of activation that are presented to a set of simple processing units connected to other units through variable connection weights. The system's output likewise consists of a subset of simple processing units that receive projections from elsewhere in the network. The system can be "trained" to produce a specific distribution of output patterns for a specific input using one of several learning rules that determine how each weight in the network is to be adjusted. In this sense, the network "learns" appropriate responses by making appropriate weight adjustments based on signals presented from outside the network.

The PDP framework specifies change mechanisms through its learning algorithms, and global processing changes emerge from the nonlinear interaction of the system's simple processing units. The changing patterns of responses the network makes during training can be examined for insights into the patterns of developmental change that might occur in the biological system. Moreover, the PDP approach is interactionist (McClelland, 1994). It emphasizes that complex behavior can emerge from a simple, parallel processing architecture that is presented with information that has intrinsic regularity. Currently, the approach is only loosely based on neurobiology. However, a number of recent models have attempted to study the computational properties of particular neural circuits (Churchland & Sejnowski, 1992), and their postnatal development in more detail. For example, Parisi (this volume) describes an approach that involves the use of genetic algorithms with artificial neural networks to explore how selection pressures at an evolutionary scale might have contributed to shaping the structure and function of behavior in biological networks. Another example of this approach utilizes the information on chick imprinting discussed in Section II.

O'Reilly and Johnson (1994) have constructed a biologically plausible connectionist model based on the characteristics of the cytoarchitectonics (see Figures 3 and 4) of the IMHV region of the chick brain implicated in visual imprinting. With this model, O'Reilly and Johnson (1994) successfully simulated a range of behavioral phenomena associated with imprinting in the chick. One example concerned the extent of reversibility of imprinted preferences. Lorenz (1937) originally claimed that an imprinted preference was irreversible. However, there is now strong evidence that imprinted preferences can be reversed by prolonged exposure to a second object, although a representation of the original object is retained (Bolhuis, 1991).

O'Reilly and Johnson explored how the model would behave in the same situation as had been presented to chicks in reversibility experiments. The network was trained on a stimulus for either 100 or 125 epochs, before being trained on a second stimulus (with no features overlapping the first) for a variable amount of time. After 100 epochs of training on the first stimulus, 150 epochs of training on the second stimulus resulted in a reversal of preference. Similar to results in chick experiments, the strength of the

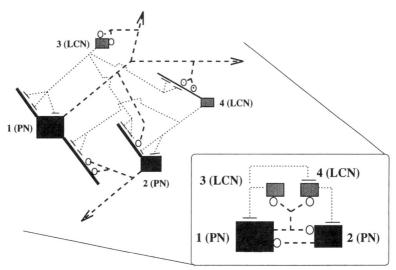

FIGURE 3   Schematic drawing that summarizes the circuitry of the IMHV region in the chick brain. The dendrites are thick solid lines, while the axons are represented as dashed lines for the principal neurons (PNs), and dotted lines for the local circuit neurons (LCNs). Excitatory contacts between the PNs and the LCNs are represented by open circles, while inhibitory synapses from LCNs to the PNs are represented by flat bars. Important features of this architecture are the reciprocal inhibitory connectivity between LCNs and the PNs, and reciprocal excitatory connections between the PNs and the LCNs. Both of these features are used in the simplified model to produce hysteresis in the activation state of IMHV.

preference for the second object increased with further training on it. That the network displayed reversibility is not surprising, as many networks continue to adapt their weights as inputs change. However, unlike many networks that display a catastrophic level of interference from subsequent learning (McCloskey & Cohen, 1989), this model retained a relatively intact preference for the initial stimulus over a novel, untrained one.

Training the network for just 25 more epochs on the first stimulus (125 total) resulted in no reversal of preference following training on a second stimulus, even when trained for as many as 900 epochs on the second stimulus. This phenomenon is strikingly similar to the "self-terminating" sensitive period described for the chick (Bateson, 1966).

An analysis of why the model produces these effects indicated that the hysteresis produced by a combination of the particular circuitry of the model (derived from the patterns of neural connection in IMHV) and the Hebbian learning rule (Hebb, 1949) were the critical factors. Aside from enabling a better understanding of behavioral phenomena, the value of such network models is that they allow precise predictions to be made. For example, the model demonstrated clearly that the length of training on the

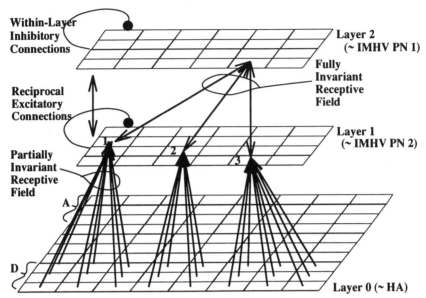

Within-Layer Inhibitory Connections

Layer 2 (~ IMHV PN 1)

Fully Invariant Receptive Field

Reciprocal Excitatory Connections

Layer 1 (~ IMHV PN 2)

Partially Invariant Receptive Field

Layer 0 (~ HA)

Figure 4   Three-layer network architecture used for the simplified model of IMHV used by O'Reilly and Johnson (1994) to demonstrate various imprinting phenomena. Layer 0 represents the main source of input to IMHV from the hyperstriatum accessorium (HA). Layer 1 represents IMHV type 2 principal neurons (PN 2), and layer 2 represents IMHV type 1 principal neurons (PN 1) and their patterns of interconnectivity. The inhibition of PNs by LCNs is implicitly represented by inhibition between cells within layers 1 and 2.

first stimulus will determine the extent of training needed to obtain a reversal of preference to a second stimulus. Further, a point will be reached at which no amount of training on a second stimulus will reverse preference from the first object. These predictions are yet to be tested in a systematic way in the chick.

There are other issues in developmental cognitive neuroscience that computational modeling can help address in a direct and unique fashion (Bates & Elman, 1992; Parisi, this volume). What is the time course of development? What forms can neural representations take and why? How do brain regions gain functional specificity (Miller, Keller & Stryker, 1989; Zipser & Andersen, 1988)? What are the limits of plasticity? What is the importance of typical versus atypical information in the learner's environment? Is immaturity "useful" or adaptive in some way, and if so, how (Elman, 1991)? What are the computational and functional consequences of synaptic proliferation and pruning (Changeux, 1985; Edelman, 1987)? These questions are only beginning to be addressed, but computational models will be central to the answers.

B. Sensory Deficits, Lesions, Developmental Disorders, and Cortical Plasticity

Evidence obtained from congenitally deaf subjects, and from studying the cognitive development of infants following early brain damage, has contributed to an emerging reconceptualization of plasticity in the cerebral cortex. Cortical plasticity is coming to be viewed less as a specialized response to injury and more as a reflection of the natural state of the infant's brain early in life. The question of interest, therefore, becomes not so much identifying the specialized mechanisms of recovery and compensation following damage, but rather attempting to understand the plasticity latent in the cortex of the normally developing infant. The limits of this plasticity can be ascertained by studying subjects who suffered altered or impoverished sensory input early in life.

Neville and colleagues (Neville, 1991) have used event-related potentials (ERPs) to examine cortical plasticity related to intersensory competition. Evidence from visual and spatial tasks in deaf subjects suggests that cortically mediated visual processing is different among subjects reared in the absence of auditory input. Specifically, the congenitally deaf seem more sensitive to events in the peripheral visual field than are hearing subjects. ERPs recorded over classical auditory regions, such as the temporal lobe, are two or three times larger for deaf than for hearing subjects following peripheral visual field stimulation. Thus, the pattern of early sensory experience can have a major influence on the allocation of functions to cortical regions, in this case, by apparently enlarging the area of cortex devoted to visual processing. Furthermore, Neville (1991) has argued, cognitive experiences can also shape the pattern of cortical specialization.

ERP studies reveal greater activation of areas of the left hemisphere in normal hearing subjects during a word reading task. In contrast to this, deaf subjects do not show this lateralization (Neville, 1990). A group of subjects that had learned sign language as their first language, but who were not themselves deaf, showed the lateralization found in the normal-hearing subjects. This pattern of results suggests that it is not the acquisition of sign language per se that gives rise to lack of left hemisphere activation. Rather, the difference may index the activity of processes involved in either phonological or grammatical decoding. Consistent with this interpretation, the lateralization effect was found in deaf signers when they were presented with signed gestures. These findings suggest that the left hemisphere becomes specialized for language regardless of the modality involved, and that the specialization may develop in association with the acquisition of grammatical competence.

Not only can plasticity in a single region of cortex depend both on sensory and cognitive experiences, but several regions of cortex appear able to support similar functions. This has been established by studying subjects who have suffered brain lesions commonly due to strokes during the first year of life. In a recent review of this topic, Stiles and Thal (1993) argued that, while injury to a wide range of cortical areas appears to produce an initial impairment in aspects of language acquisition, by school age these deficits are often very mild. Since presumably several cortical structures play a role in language acquisition, damage to one or more of these structures can be compensated for by the others in certain cases. However, some other functions, such as spatial cognition, do not show the same degree of recovery of function, suggesting the possibility that the extent of cortical plasticity may depend on the form of information processing displaced by brain injury. For example, spatial analysis, as measured by drawing tasks, appears to be impaired by injury to fewer brain regions, but may be less easily recovered from.

A number of developmental disorders that affect cognition such as autism (Frith, 1989) and Williams syndrome (Bellugi, Marks, Bihrle, & Sabo, 1988) also provide us with ways to examine the limits of brain plasticity. As well as being of potential clinical benefit, the study of such disorders can contribute to our knowledge of normal neurocognitive development by revealing the range of possible outcomes when normal developmental paths are disturbed. For example, while autistic individuals commonly have severe deficits in social cognition (such as aspects of language, face recognition, and "theory of mind") (Frith, 1989), they can be at or above normal levels of performance in other domains. In contrast, Williams syndrome individuals suffer from severe deficits in many aspects of cognition, but are comparatively spared in face recognition and language capabilities (Bellugi et al., 1988).

C. Concluding Remarks

We have illustrated how evidence from neurobiology and ethology can provide new insight into some of the central problems of perceptual and cognitive development. Despite the power and usefulness of the approach, or perhaps because of it, we wish to clarify two potential sources of misunderstanding concerning the use of biological evidence. The first concerns the interpretation of biological data. In marshaling evidence that links the emergence of a perceptual or cognitive capacity to the functioning of a specific brain region or pathway, one might be tempted to create a more rigid or static description than the data actually warrant. Since brain maturation is a continuous process, claims about the state of development of one brain region are more accurately characterized as statements about the development of that region relative to other regions. Moreover, the relative states of maturation are themselves subject to continuous modification.

Similarly, there is dramatic variability in the level of neural and cognitive development between individuals of the same age. For example, the age at which infants first show evidence of stereopsis varies from 2 to 5 months (Held, 1985). The broad variability between and within individuals makes it extremely difficult, and often unproductive, to characterize neurocognitive development in terms of stages with fixed temporal parameters. However, evidence from neurobiology does allow us to make predictions about the *sequence* of events at the cognitive level (Johnson, 1990).

This leads us to our second cautionary remark. The mammalian brain shows remarkable plasticity during development, especially so during infancy. The effort to understand how specific brain changes correlate with behavioral change by no means represents a strict biological determinism. While there are clear limits to our cognitive abilities and some of these limits no doubt have neural correlates, our understanding of the brain is still too premature to say with certainty how a particular brain injury, anomaly, or alteration in infancy will ultimately affect behavior.

With these two points in mind, we view the progress made thus far with optimism. Our understanding of face and kin recognition, visual attention, and working memory has been extended significantly, and the promise of new methodological tools gives developmental cognitive neuroscience the potential to illuminate even more challenging questions in the years ahead.

Acknowledgments

Financial assistance from the National Science Foundation (Grant DBS-9120433) to the first author and graduate fellowship support from NIMH Grant MH19102-04 to the second author are gratefully acknowledged.

References

Andrew, R. J. (1991). *Neural and behavioural plasticity: The use of the domestic chick as a model.* Oxford: Oxford University Press.

Aslin, R. N. (1981). Development of smooth pursuit in human infants. In D. F. Fisher, R. A. Monty, & J. W. Senders (Eds.), *Eye movements: Cognition and visual perception* (pp. 31–51). Hillsdale, NJ: Erlbaum.

Atkinson, J. (1984). Human visual development over the first six months of life. *Human Neurobiology, 3,* 61–74.

Baddeley, A. (1986). *Working memory.* Oxford: Oxford University Press.

Baillargeon, R. (1987). Object permanence in very young infants. *Cognition, 20,* 191–208.

Bates, E. A., & Elman, J. L. (1992). *Connectionism and the study of change* (CRL Tech. Rep. No. 9202). San Diego: University of California.

Bateson, P. P. G. (1966). The characteristics and context of imprinting. *Biological Review, 41,* 177–220.

Becker, L. E., Armstrong, D. L., Chan, F., & Wood, M. M. (1984). Dendritic development on human occipital cortex neurones. *Brain Research, 315,* 117–124.

Bell, M. A. (1992a). A not B task performance is related to frontal EEG asymmetry regardless of locomotor experience. [Special issue: Proceedings of the Eighth International Conference on Infant Studies, Miami, FL]. *Infant Behavior and Development, 15,* 307.

Bell, M. A. (1992b). Electrophysiological correlates of object search performance during infancy. [Special issue: Proceedings of the Eighth International Conference on Infant Studies, Miami, FL]. *Infant Behavior and Development, 15,* 3.

Bell, M. A., & Fox, N. A. (1992). The relations between frontal brain electrical activity and cognitive development during infancy. *Child Development, 63,* 1142–1163.

Bellugi, U., Marks, S., Bihrle, A. M., & Sabo, H. (1988). Dissociation between language and cognitive functions in Williams Syndrome. In D. Bishop & K. Mogsford (Eds.), *Language development in exceptional circumstances* (pp. 177–189). New York: Churchill Livingstone.

Blass, E. (1992). Linking developmental and psychobiological research. *Society for Research in Child Development Newsletter,* pp. 3–10.

Bloom, K. (1974). Eye contact as a setting event for infant learning. *Journal of Experimental Child Psychology, 17,* 250–263.

Bolhuis, J. J. (1991). Mechanisms of avian imprinting: A review. *Biological Reviews, 66,* 303–345.

Bolhuis, J. J., & Johnson, M. H. (1990). Sensory templates: mechanism or metaphor? *Behavioral and Brain Sciences, 14,* 349–350.

Bolhuis, J. J., Johnson, M. H., Horn, G., & Bateson, P. P. G. (1989). Long-lasting effects of IMHV lesions on the social preferences of domestic fowl. *Behavioral Neuroscience, 103,* 438–441.

Bolhuis, J. J., McCabe, B. J., & Horn, G. (1986). Androgens and imprinting. Differential effects of testosterone on filial preferences in the domestic chick. *Behavioral Neuroscience, 100,* 51–56.

Braitenberg, V. (1984). *Vehicles: Experiments in synthetic psychology.* Cambridge, MA: MIT Press.

Brodmann, K. (1909). *Vergleichende Lokalisationslehre der Grosshirnrinde in ihren Prinzipien dargestellt auf Grund des Zellenbaues.* Leipzig: Barth.

Brodmann, K. (1912). Neue Ergebnisse über die vergleichende histologische Lokalisation der Grosshirnrinde mit besonderer Berücksichtigung des Stirnhirns. *Anatomischer Anzeiger, 41* (Suppl.), 157–216.

Bronson, G. W. (1974). The postnatal growth of visual capacity. *Child Development, 45,* 873–890.

Campbell, R., Heywood, C. A., Cowey, A., Regard, M., & Landis, T. (1990). Sensitivity to eye gaze in prosopagnosic patients and monkeys with superior temporal sulcus ablation. *Neuropsychologia, 28,* 1123–1142.

Canavan, A. G. M. (1983). Stylus-maze performance in patients with frontal lobe lesions: Effects of signal valency and relationship to verbal and spatial abilities. *Neuropsychologia, 21,* 375–382.

Case, R. (1985). *Intellectual development: A systematic reinterpretation.* New York: Academic Press.

Changeux, J. P. (1985). *Neuronal man: The biology of mind.* New York: Pantheon.

Churchland, P. S., & Sejnowski, T. J. (1992). *The computational brain.* Cambridge, MA: MIT Press.

Cohen, L. B. (1988). An information processing approach to infant cognitive development. In L. Weiskrantz (Eds.), *Thought without language* (pp. 211–228). Oxford: Clarendon.

Corkin, S. (1965). Tactually-guided maze-learning in man: Effects of unilateral cortical excisions and bilateral hippocampal lesions. *Neuropsychologia, 3,* 339–351.

Cornell, E. (1979). The effects of cue reliability on infants' manual search. *Journal of Experimental Child Psychology, 28,* 81–91.

Davies, D. C., Horn, G., & McCabe, B. J. (1985). Noradrenaline and learning: the effects of noradrenergic neurotoxin DSP4 on imprinting in the domestic chick. *Behavioral Neuroscience, 99,* 652–660.

de Schonen, S, Deruelle, C., Mancini, J., & Pascalis, O. (1993). Hemispheric differences in face processing and brain maturation. In B. de Boysson-Bardies, S. de Schonen, P. Jusczyk, P. MacNeilage, & J. Morton (Eds.), *Developmental neurocognition: Speech and face processing in the first year of life* (pp. 149–163). Dordrecht: Kluwer.

Diamond, A. (1985). The development of the ability to use recall to guide action, as indicated by infants' performance on AB̄. *Child Development, 56,* 868–883.

Diamond, A. (1990). The development and neural bases of memory functions, as indexed by the AB̄ and delayed response tasks, in human infants and infant monkeys. *Annals of the New York Academy of Sciences, 608,* 267–317.

Diamond, A. (1991). Neuropsychological insights into the meaning of object concept development. In S. Carey & R. Gelman (Eds.), *The epigenesis of mind: Essays on biology and cognition* (pp. 67–110). Hillsdale, NJ: Erlbaum.

Diamond, A., & Doar, B. (1989). The performance of human infants on a measure of frontal cortex function, the delayed response task. *Developmental Psychobiology, 22,* 271–294.

Diamond, A., & Goldman-Rakic, P. S. (1986). Comparative development in human infant rhesus monkeys on Piaget's AB task: Evidence for dependence on dorsolateral prefrontal cortex. *Neuroscience Abstracts, 12,* 742.

Diamond, A., & Goldman-Rakic, P. S. (1989). Comparison of human infants and infant rhesus monkeys on Piaget's AB̄ task: Evidence for dependence on dorsolateral prefrontal cortex. *Experimental Brain Research, 74,* 24–40.

Diamond, A., Zola-Morgan, S., & Squire, L. R. (1989). Successful performance by monkeys with lesions of the hippocampal formation on AB̄ and object retrieval, two tasks that mark developmental changes in human infants. *Behavioral Neuroscience, 103,* 526–537.

Edelman, G. M. (1987). *Neural Darwinism.* New York: Basic Books.

Elman, J. L. (1991). *Incremental learning, or the importance of starting small* (CRL Tech. Rep. No. 9101). San Diego: University of California.

Farah, M. J. (1990). *Visual agnosia.* Cambridge: MA: MIT Press.

Fox, N. A., & Bell, M. A. (1990). Electrophysiological indices of frontal lobe development. In A. Diamond (Ed.), *The development and neural bases of higher cognitive functions* (pp. 677–698). New York: New York Academy of Sciences.

Fox, N., Kagan, J., & Weiskopf, S. (1979). The growth of memory during infancy. *Genetic Psychology Monographs, 99,* 91–130.

Freedman, M., & Oscar-Berman, M. (1986). Bilateral frontal lobe disease and selective delayed response deficits in humans. *Behavioral Neuroscience, 100,* 337–342.

Frith, U. (1989). *Autism.* Oxford: Blackwell.

Funahashi, S.., Bruce, C. J., & Goldman-Rakic, P. S. (1989). Mnemonic coding of visual space in the monkey's dorsolateral prefrontal cortex. *Journal of Neurophysiology, 61,* 331–349.

Funahashi, S., Bruce, C. J., & Goldman-Rakic, P. S. (1990). Visuospatial coding in primate prefrontal neurons revealed by oculomotor paradigms. *Journal of Neurophysiology, 63,* 814–831.

Fuster, J. M. (1989). *The prefrontal cortex* (2nd ed.). New York: Raven.

Gibson, E. J. (1969). *Perceptual learning and development.* New York: Appleton.

Gilmore, R. O., & Johnson, M. H. (1995). Working memory in infancy: Six-month-olds' performance on two versions of the oculomotor delayed response task. *Journal of Experimental Child Psychology, 59,* 387–418.

Gnadt, J. W., & Andersen, R. A. (1988). Memory related motor planning activity in posterior parietal cortex of macaque. *Experimental Brain Research, 70,* 216–220.

Goldman, P. S. (1971). Functional development of the prefrontal cortex in early life and the problem of neuronal plasticity. *Experimental Neurology, 32,* 366–387.

Goldman, P. S., & Rosvold, H. E. (1970). Localization of function within the dorsolateral prefrontal cortex of the rhesus monkey. *Experimental Neurology, 27,* 291–304.

Goldman, P. S., Rosvold, H. E., Vest, B., & Galkin, T. W. (1971). Analysis of the delayed alternation deficit produced by dorsolateral prefrontal lesions in the rhesus monkey. *Journal of Comparative and Physiological Psychology, 77,* 212–220.

Goldman-Rakic, P. S. (1981). Development and plasticity of primate frontal association cortex. In F. O. Schmitt, F. G. Worden, S. G. Dennis, & G. Adelman (Eds.), *The organization of cerebral cortex* (pp. 69–97). Cambridge, MA: MIT Press.

Goldman-Rakic, P. S. (1987). Development of cortical circuitry and cognitive function. *Child Development, 58,* 601–622.

Goren, C. C., Sarty, M., & Wu, P. Y. K. (1975). Visual following and pattern discrimination of face-like stimuli by newborn infants. *Pediatrics, 56,* 544–549.

Greenough, W. T., Black, J. E., & Wallace, C. E. (1987). Experience and brain development. *Child Development, 58,* 539–559.

Haith, M. M., Hazan, C., & Goodman, G. S. (1988). Expectation and anticipation of dynamic visual events by 3.5-month-old babies. *Child Development, 59,* 467–479.

Hebb, D. O. (1949). *The organization of behavior.* New York: Wiley.

Held, R. (1985). Binocular vision: Behavioral and neuronal development. In J. Mehler & R. Fox (Eds.), *Neonate cognition: Beyond the blooming, buzzing confusion.* Hillsdale, NJ: Erlbaum.

Hinde, R. A. (1961). The establishment of parent–offspring relations in birds, with some mammalian analogies. In W. H. Thorpe & O. L. Zangwill (Eds.), *Current problems in animal behavior* (pp. 175–193). Cambridge: Cambridge University press.

Horn, G. (1985). *Memory, imprinting, and the brain: An inquiry into mechanisms.* Oxford: Clarendon.

Horn, G., & Johnson, M. H. (1989). Memory systems in the chick: Dissociations and neuronal analysis. *Neuropsychologia, 27* (Special issue: Memory), 1–22.

Horn, G., & McCabe, B. J. (1984). Predispositions and preferences. Effects on imprinting of lesions to the chick brain. *Brain Research, 168,* 361–373.

Huttenlocher, P. R. (1990). Morphometric study of human cerebral cortex development. *Neuropsychologia, 28,* 517–527.

Johnson, M. H. (1990). Cortical maturation and the development of visual attention in early infancy. *Journal of Cognitive Neuroscience, 2*(2), 81–95.

Johnson, M. H. (1991). Information processing and storage during filial imprinting. In P. G. Hepper (Eds.), *Kin Recognition* (pp. 335–357). Cambridge: Cambridge University Press.

Johnson, M. H. (1992). Cognition and development: Four contentions about the role of visual attention. In D. J. Stein & J. E. Young (Eds.), *Cognitive science and clinical disorders* (pp. 43–60). San Diego: Academic Press.

Johnson, M. H. (Ed.). (1993). *Brain development and cognition: A reader.* Oxford: Blackwell.

Johnson, M. H. (1994). Visual attention and the control of eye movements in early infancy. In C. Umilta & M. Moscovitch (Eds.), *Attention and performance XV: Conscious and nonconscious information processing* (pp. 291–310). Cambridge, MA: MIT Press.

Johnson, M. H. (in press). *Developmental cognitive neuroscience: An introduction.* Oxford: Blackwell.

Johnson, M. H., & Bolhuis, J. J. (1991). Imprinting, predispositions and filial preference in the chick. In R. J. Andrew (Ed.), *Neural and behavioral plasticity* (pp. 133–156). Oxford: Oxford University Press.

Johnson, M. H., Bolhuis, J. J., & Horn, G. (1985). Interaction between acquired preferences and developing predispositions during imprinting. *Animal Behaviour, 33,* 1000–1006.

Johnson, M. H., Dziurawiec, S., Bartrip, J., & Morton, J. (1992). The effects of movement of internal features on infants' preferences for face-like stimuli. *Infant Behavior and Development, 15,* 129–136.

Johnson, M. H., Dziurawiec, S., Ellis, H. D., & Morton, J. (1991). Newborns' preferential tracking of face-like stimuli and its subsequent decline. *Cognition, 40,* 1–19.

Johnson, M. H., & Horn, G. (1986). An analysis of a predisposition in the chick. *Behavioral Brain Research, 20,* 108–109.

Johnson, M. H., & Horn, G. (1987). The role of a restricted region of the chick forebrain in the recognition of individual conspecifics. *Behavioural Brain Research, 23,* 269–275.

Johnson, M. H., & Horn, G. (1988). The development of filial preferences in the dark-reared chick. *Animal Behaviour, 36,* 675–683.

Johnson, M. H., & Morton, J. (1991). *Biology and cognitive development: The case of face recognition.* Oxford: Blackwell.

Johnson, M. H., Posner, M. I., & Rothbart, M. (1991). The development of visual attention in infancy: Contingency learning, anticipations and disengaging. *Journal of Cognitive Neuroscience, 3,* 335–344.

Johnson, M. H., & Vecera, S. P. (1993). Cortical parcellation and the development of face processing. In B. de Boysson-Bardies, S. de Schonen, P. Jusczyk, P. MacNeilage, & J. Morton (Eds.), *Developmental neurocognition: Speech and face processing in the first year of life* (pp. 93–102). Dordrecht: Kluwer.

Kwong, K. E., Belliveau, J. W., Chesler, D. A., Goldberg, I. E., Weisskoff, R. M., Poncelet, B. P., Kennedy, D. N., Hoppel, B. E., Cohen, M. S., Turner, R., Cheng, H. M., Brady, T. J., & Rosen, B. R. (1992). Dynamic magnetic resonance imaging of human brain activity during primary sensory stimulation. *Proceedings of the National Academy of Sciences, 89,* 5675–5679.

Lasky, R. E., & Klein, R. E. (1979). The reactions of five-month old infants to eye contact of the mother and of a stranger. *Merrill-Palmer Quarterly, 25,* 163–170.

Lecuyer, R., Abgueguen, I., & Lemarie, C. (1992). 9- and 5-month-olds do not make the AB error if not required to manipulate objects. [Special issue: Proceedings of the Eighth International Conference on Infant Studies, Miami, FL.] *Infant Behavior and Development, 15,* 514.

Lewis, T. L., Maurer, D., & Blackburn, K. (1985). The development of young infants' ability to detect stimuli in the nasal visual field. *Vision Research, 25,* 943–950.

Lorenz, K. (1937). The companion in the bird's world. *Auk, 54,* 245–273.

Lorenz, K. (1965). *Evolution and the modification of behavior.* Chicago: University of Chicago Press.

Maratsos, O. (1982). Trends in the development of early imitation in infancy. In T. G. Bever (Eds.), *Regression in mental development: basic phenomena and theories* (pp. 81–101). Hillsdale, NJ: Erlbaum.

Marin-Padilla, M. (1970). Prenatal and early postnatal ontogenesis of the human motor cortex: a Golgi study. I. The sequential development of the cortical layers. *Brain Research, 23,* 167–183.

Maurer, D. (1985). Infants perception of facedness. In T. M. Field & N. Fox (Eds.), *Social perception in infants* (pp. 73–100). Norwood, NJ: Ablex.

Maurer, D., & Barrera, M. (1981). Infants' perception of natural and distorted arrangements of a schematic face. *Child Development, 47,* 523–527.

Maurer, D., & Young, R. E. (1983). Newborns' following of natural and distorted arrangements of facial features. *Infant Behavior & Development, 6,* 127–131.

McCabe, B. J., Cipolla-Neto, J., Horn, G., & Bateson, P. P. G. (1982). Amnesic effects of bilateral lesions placed in the hyperstriatum ventrale of the chick after imprinting. *Experimental Brain Research, 48,* 13–21.

McClelland, J. L. (1994). The interaction of nature and nurture in development: A parallel distributed processing perspective. In P. Bertelson, P. Eelen, G. d'Ydewalle (Eds.), *International Perspectives on Psychological Science: Vol. 1. Leading Themes* (pp. 57–88). Hillsdale, NJ: Erlbaum.

McClelland, J. L., & Rumelhart, D. E. (Eds.). (1986). *Parallel distributed processing: Explorations in the Microstructure of Cognition: Vol. 2. Psychological and biological models.* Cambridge: MA: MIT Press.

McCloskey, M., & Cohen, N. J. (1989). Catastrophic interference in connectionist networks: the sequential learning problem. In G. H. Bower (Ed.), *Psychology of learning and motivation* (Vol. 24, pp. 109–164). San Diego: Academic Press.

Miller, K. D., Keller, J. B., & Stryker, M. P. (1989). Ocular dominance column development: Analysis and simulation. *Science, 245,* 605–615.

Milner, B. (1963). Effects of different brain lesions on card sorting. *Archives of Neurology, 9,* 90–110.

Milner, B. (1965). Visually-guided maze-learning in man: effects of bilateral hippocampal, bilateral frontal, and unilateral cerebral lesions. *Neuropsychologia, 3,* 317–338.

Milner, B. (1982). Some cognitive effects of frontal-lobe lesions in man. *Philosophical Transactions of the Royal Society of London, 298,* 211–226.

Morton, J., & Johnson, M. H. (1991). CONSPEC and CONLERN: A two-process theory of infant face recognition. *Psychological Review, 98,* 164–181.

Morton, J., Johnson, M. H., & Maurer, D. (1990). On the reasons for newborns' responses to faces. *Infant Behavior and Development, 13,* 99–103.

Muir, D. W., Clifton, R. K., & Clarkson, M. G. (1989). The development of a human auditory localization response: A U-shaped function. *Canadian Journal of Psychology, 43,* 199–216.

Munakata, Y., McClelland, J. L., Johnson, M. H., & Siegler, R. S. (1994). *Now you see it, now you don't: A gradualistic framework for understanding infants' successes and failures in tasks of object permanence* (Parallel Distributed Processing and Cognitive Neuroscience Tech. Rep. PDP.CNS.94.2). Pittsburgh, PA: Carnegie Mellon University.

Nelson, C. A., & Ludemann, P. M. (1989). Past, current and future trends in infant face perception research. *Canadian Journal of Psychology, 43,* 183–198.

Neville, H. J. (1990). Intermodal competition and compensation in development: Evidence from studies of the visual system in congenitally deaf adults. In A. Diamond (Eds.), *The development of the neural bases of higher cognitive functions* (pp. 71–91). New York: New York Academy of Sciences.

Neville, H. J. (1991). Neurobiology of cognitive and language processing: Effects of early experience. In K. R. Gibson & A. C. Petersen (Eds.), *Brain maturation and cognitive development: Comparative and cross-cultural perspectives* (pp. 355–380). Berlin: de Gruyter.

Nowakowski, R. S. (1987). Basic concepts of CNS development. *Child Development, 58,* 568–595.

O'Reilly, R., & Johnson, M. H. (1994). Object recognition and sensitive periods: A computational analysis of visual imprinting. *Neural Computation, 6,* 357–389.

Passingham, R. E. (1985). Memory of monkeys (*Maccaca mulatta*) with lesions in prefrontal cortex. *Behavioral Neuroscience, 99,* 3–21.

Perrett, D. I., & Mistlin, A. J. (1990). Perception of facial characteristics by monkeys. In W. C. Stebbins & M. A. Berkley (Eds.), *Comparative perception: Vol. 2. Complex signals* (pp. 187–215). New York: Wiley.

Perrett, D. I., Mistlin, A. J., Potter, D. D., Smith, P. A. J., Head, A. S., Chitty, A. J., Broennimann, R., Milner, A. D., & Jeeves, M. A. (1986). Functional organisation of visual neurones processing face identity. In H. D. Ellis, M. A. Jeeves, F. Newcombe, & A. Young (Eds.), *Aspects of face processing* (pp. 187–198). Dordrecht: Nijhoff.

Perrett, D. I., Rolls, E. T., & Caan, W. (1982). Visual neurones responsive to faces in the monkey temporal cortex. *Experimental Brain Research, 47,* 229–238.

Piaget, J. (1954). *The construction of reality in the child.* New York: Basic Books.

Posner, M. I. (1980). Orienting of attention. *Quarterly Journal of Experimental Psychology, 32,* 3–25.

Posner, M. I., & Cohen, Y. (1980). Attention and the control of movements. In G. E. Stelmach & J. Roguiro (Eds.), *Tutorials in motor behavior* (pp. 243–258). Amsterdam: North-Holland.

Posner, M. I., & Peterson, S. E. (1990). The attention system of the human brain. *Annual Review of Neuroscience, 13,* 25–42.

Posner, M. I., & Rothbart, M. K. (1990). *Attentional mechanisms and conscious experience* (Tech. Rep. No. 90-17). Eugene: University of Oregon, Institute of Cognitive & Decision Sciences.

Pribram, K. H., Ahumada, A., Hartog, J., & Roos, L. (1964). A progress report on the neurological processes disturbed by frontal lesions in primates. In J. M. Warren & K. Akert (Eds.), *The frontal granular cortex and behavior* (pp. 28–55). New York: McGraw-Hill.

Raichle, M. E., & Mallinkrodt, M. E. (1987). Circulatory and metabolic correlates of brain function in normal humans. In V. B. Mountcastle, F. Plum, & S. R. Geiger (Eds.), *Handbook of physiology—The nervous system* (pp. 643–674). Bethesda, MD: American Physiological Association.

Rakic, P. (1988). Instrinsic and extrinsic determinants of neocortical parcellation: A radial unit model. In P. Rakic & W. Singer (Eds.), *Neurobiology of neocortex* (pp. 5–27). New York: Wiley.

Robinson, N. S., McCarty, M. E., & Haith, M. M. (1988, April). *Visual expectations in early infancy.* Poster presented at the VIIth International Conference on Infant Studies, Washington, D.C.

Rolls, E. (1989). Functions of neuronal networks in the hippocampus and neocortex in memory. In J. H. Byrne & W. O. Berry (Eds.), *Neural models of plasticity: Experimental and theoretical approaches* (pp. 240–265). San Diego: Academic Press.

Rumelhart, D. E., & McClelland, J. L. (Eds.). (1986). *Parallel distributed processing: Explorations in the microstructure of cognition: Vol. 1. Foundations.* Cambridge, MA: MIT Press.

Samuels, C. A. (1985). Attention to eye contact opportunity and facial motion by three-month old infants. *Journal of Experimental Child Psychology, 40,* 105–114.

Schiller, P. H. (1985). A model for the generation of visually guided saccadic eye movements. In D. Rose & V. G. Dobson (Eds.), *Models of the visual cortex* (pp. 62–70). Chicester, England: Wiley.

Silva, A. J., Paylor, R., Wehner, J. M., & Tonegawa, S. (1992). Impaired spatial learning in alpha-calcium calmodulin kinase II mutant mice. *Science, 257,* 206–211.

Silva, A. J., Stevens, C. F., Tonegawa, S., & Wang, Y. (1992). Deficient hippocampal long-term potentiation in alpha-calcium calmodulin kinase II mutant mice. *Science, 257,* 201–206.

Sluckin, W. (1972). *Imprinting and early learning* (2nd ed.). London: Methuen.

Spelke, E. S., Breinlinger, K., Macomber, J., & Jacobsen, K. (1992). Origins of knowledge. *Psychological Review, 99,* 605–632.

Stiles, J., & Thal, D. (1993). Linguistic and spatial cognitive development following early focal brain injury: Patterns of deficit and recovery. In M. H. Johnson (Eds.), *Brain development and cognition: A reader* (pp. 643–664). Oxford: Blackwell.

Tinbergen, N. (1951). *The study of instinct.* New York: Oxford University Press.

Vecera, S., & Johnson, M. H. (1995). Eye gaze detection and the cortical processing of faces: Evidence from infants and adults. *Visual Cognition, 2,* 101–129.

von Holfsten, C. (1984). Developmental changes in the organisation of prereaching movements. *Developmental Psychology, 20*, 378–388.

Wilson, F. A. W., O'Scalaidhe, S. P., & Goldman-Rakic, P. S. (1993). Dissociation of object and spatial processing domains in the primate prefrontal cortex. *Science, 260*, 1955–1958.

Yakovlev, P. I., & Lecours, A. (1967). The myelogenetic cycles of regional maturation of the brain. In A. Minokowski (Eds.), *Regional development of the brain in early life* (pp. 3–70). Philadelphia: Davis.

Zipser, D., & Andersen, R. A. (1988). A back-propagation programmed network that simulates response properties of a subset of posterior parietal neurons. *Nature, 331*, 679–684.

CHAPTER 11

Computational Models of Developmental Mechanisms

Domenico Parisi

I. NEW TOOLS FOR THE STUDY OF DEVELOPMENT

This chapter is dedicated to an illustration of what some recent computational models have to offer as tools for conceptualizing and analyzing phenomena and mechanisms of development. The models are those of neural networks, genetic algorithms, and artificial life. Neural networks are computational models of behavior that are explicitly inspired by the structure and manner of functioning of the nervous system (Rumelhart, McClelland, & PDP Research Group, 1986). Genetic algorithms are attempts at reproducing in a computer the phenomena of evolution by natural selection (Holland, 1975). Artificial life aims at simulating in a computer, or otherwise artificially recreating, all biological phenomena, both real and possible (Langton, 1992).

These models are especially promising from the point of view of the study of development because change is perhaps the central phenomena with which they are concerned. For any capacity that the artificial system must exhibit, it is not the case that the researcher directly programs the capacity in the computer. The researcher is limited to a set of decisions concerning the initial conditions of the system and its environment. Starting from these conditions the artificial system is expected to spontaneously

Perceptual and Cognitive Development
Copyright © 1996 by Academic Press, Inc. All rights of reproduction in any form reserved.

evolve, develop, or learn until the final desired capacity is reached. The process and the mechanism(s) of development from the initial to the final state are what these models want primarily to study.

In addition to being based on the method of computer simulation, sharing a biological inspiration, and being centrally interested in change and development, neural networks, genetic algorithms, and artificial life have in common a tendency to draw their conceptual tools from the same source, the theory of complex dynamic or adaptive systems. A complex dynamic system is a system constituted by a large number of relatively simple entities that interact locally among themselves and with the external environment. The global behavior of the system emerges in generally unpredictable ways from these highly nonlinear local interactions. Since a complex system can be conceptualized as a point in a multidimensional space (with each dimension of the space representing a parameter of the system) and the system changes by changing the values of its parameters, the dynamics of change can be viewed as a trajectory of the point in space. Mathematics, physics, and computer science have developed various mathematical and formal tools for analyzing the properties of these systems and their dynamics.

The use of computer simulation as the research methodology and the sharing of a common conceptual framework create new possibilities for the study of change and development using these new tools. Changes in behavior occur at various levels and temporal scales and as a function of different causes. Furthermore, different types of change interact in complex ways (cf. Section II). This makes the study of development a difficult research topic. Different types of change tend to be studied by different disciplines (e.g. psychology, developmental biology, evolutionary biology) using different concepts and methods. It is difficult to compare the results obtained by the various disciplines and almost impossible to study the interactions among different types of change.

Neural networks, genetic algorithms, and artificial life models offer a unified theoretical and methodological framework for studying different types of change and their different causes and, what is especially important, for observing and analyzing within one and the same simulation the interactions that occur among changes at various levels and at various time scales.

Computer simulations almost necessarily imply a simplification with respect to the phenomena that are simulated. In this respect simulation is like theory making. Theories simplify the phenomena they are intended to explain. The problem is not simplification by itself but the ability of simulations and theories to identify the important dimensions of phenomena and their underlying mechanisms. Unlike theories, however, simulations are also experimental laboratories where one can manipulate variables, make predictions on the effects of these manipulations, and observe the (simulated) effects that are actually obtained.

Furthermore, unlike real laboratories, simulations make it possible to study not only real phenomena but also possible phenomena, that is, phenomena that are known not to exist (cf. the definition of artificial life above). Although simulations should ultimately reflect reality if they must advance our scientific knowledge, the analysis of simulated phenomena that are known not to occur in reality (possible phenomena) can be a powerful, although more indirect, method for understanding reality. However, "possible" should not mean "arbitrary." Even simulations of possible phenomena must not depart from basic mechanisms known to obtain in reality.

II. TYPES OF CHANGE

Within the discipline of psychology the term "development" refers to the changes that occur in the behavior of an individual organism during its lifetime or, even more specifically, to the incremental changes that occur during the so-called developmental age of the individual. Changes in the morphology of the body or in internal organs and systems (e.g., the nervous system) tend to be entrusted to other disciplines such as genetics, developmental biology, and neurobiology.

Even with these restrictions, developmental changes in the individual require complex study if one wants to go beyond description and try to identify underlying mechanisms and causes. Two classes of causes are generally recognized. One class is the unfolding of developmental instructions that constitute the individual's inherited genotype. The changes that are mainly due to this first type of cause are called maturation. The other class of causes that determine developmental changes are the environment and the particular experience each individual has with its particular environment. The changes in behavior that predominantly result from this second type of causes are called learning.

Maturation and learning interact in complex ways to produce the observed developmental changes. However, although almost all observed changes have both a genetic and an experiential basis, there is no denying that in development we experience two different "sources of information"—the inherited genotype and the environment—that determine how an organism behaves and the changes that occur in its behavior at successive developmental points. Both classes of causes must be independently clarified in order for their interactions to be analyzed.

This poses a challenge to the discipline of psychology because (developmental) psychology has a tendency to stop at the birth of the individual organism without going further back in time to what has occurred to the individual's ancestors (Charlesworth, 1992). Historically, psychology has taken full responsibility for the study of learning and of the role of experience and the environment in determining behavior and development but it has left to other disciplines, mainly genetics, developmental biology, and evolutionary biology, the study of the genetic causes of development. The genetic causes of development are both proximal and remote. The proximal genetic causes are the inherited set of genes (genetics). The remote genetic causes are those relative to the evolutionary history that has resulted in that set of genes (evolutionary biology). Whereas developmental changes due to learning reflect the particular environment and experience of the particular individual, the genetic causes of development reflect the past history of the population to which the individual organism belongs. Therefore, a complete and satisfying account of development must reconstruct this evolutionary history in order to understand what are the genetic bases of the development of a particular species of organisms, avoiding the two opposite strategies of simply ignoring these bases or "postulating" them on the basis of the observed behavior.

For the human species, a further level of complexity is introduced by the existence of another class of changes, cultural changes. (In other species cultural change and cultural transmission appear much less important.) Cultural changes, like evolutionary changes, tend to occur at the level of the population (society), but, unlike evolutionary changes, they are transmitted extracorporally. Cultural changes are organism-caused changes in both the social and nonsocial (artifacts) environment of the individual and of successive generations of individuals. Since the nature of the environment influences how the individual behaves because of learning, an account of development cannot ignore cultural change.

It is not only the case that behavior changes at various time scales and in dependence of various types of causes. It also happens that the various types of change interact in complex ways. Learning and maturation interact to produce the observed developmental changes. Evolution and development also interact reciprocally because evolved genotypes direct development and developmental sequences constrain the evolutionary changes that can occur. Cultural change is made possible by both evolution and development and it, in turn, influences development and, quite likely, evolution. Because these different types of changes interact in complex ways, none can be understood without taking the others into account.

A final element of complexity in the study of development is that only with difficulty can it be confined to behavior. Changes in behavior (in the individual or in the population) are accompanied by changes in the nervous system and in the genetic material (ignoring other changes in other systems of the body). The changes at these various levels are interrelated (cf. Section IIIB1). As we have remarked at the beginning of this section, psychology tends to restrict its attention to behavior and behavioral development but it is not clear that behavior or behavioral development can be really understood without also considering the neural and the genetic level.

On the basis of what has been said so far, the study of development emerges as a formidable research task. It is for this reason that the unified conceptual and methodological framework that is offered by the new modeling tools of neural networks, genetic algorithms, and artificial life is of particular interest. First, these modeling tools can be equally applied to all types and levels of change using a uniform set of concepts and methods. Second, by including different types and levels of change in the same simulation, these tools can make the study of the interactions among different types and levels possible.

In the sections that follow we describe various simulations with the objective not to offer in-depth analyses of particular behaviors and capacities but to illustrate how neural networks, genetic algorithms, and artificial life models can be applied to the study of the various types of change and their interactions. We omit discussion of cultural change because of limited space and because little work has been done on simulations of cultural change. Although there is a biological emphasis in the new computational models, we should not forget that their underlying conceptual framework, that is, the theory of complex dynamic systems, is abstract and general enough to allow these models to go beyond biology to try to capture (simulate) cultural change and the role of cultural transmission in development.

III. THE EVOLUTION OF A POPULATION OF NEURAL NETWORKS

One phenomenon that may occur rarely in reality but can be usefully analyzed using simulations is pure evolutionary change, which takes place in successive generations of a population of organisms but is not apparent during the life of an individual organism. All the behavioral capacities that are exhibited by an individual are congenital (already present at birth); these behavioral capacities have only to wait for the appropriate environmental stimulation to become expressed in actual behavior. But the behavior of a particular individual, that is, the way the individual reacts to environmental stimuli, is identical in all stages of life. This may apply to few real populations but it can be a useful scenario for the study of "pure" evolutionary change.

If a population of organisms reproduces selectively on the basis of some criterion of fitness and, furthermore, reproduction involves some mechanism for increasing the variability of the population (e.g., genetic mutations or sexual reproduction), some change in the behavior exhibited by individuals of successive generations is likely to be observed. Since behavior is completely controlled by the genes, what changes is the nature of the genetically inherited information. Organisms behave in individually different ways, but the typical (average) behavior of each generation tends to be different from the behavior of preceding and successive generations because of changes in inherited genotypes.

Consider a population of organisms that live in an environment having certain properties. Each organism is modeled by a neural network that controls the organism's behavior in the environment. A neural network is a set of units linked by unidirectional connections. Activation is imposed from outside on some of the units (input units) and it encodes in a quantitative way some current property of the environment. The activation spreads to other units (hidden units) through the connections until it reaches the output units. The activation on the output units encodes some motor behavior. The activation of all the units, except the input units, which are activated from outside, is computed by summing all the excitations and inhibitions arriving to the unit (net input of the unit) and then mapping this value into the activation level of the unit using some (usually) nonlinear function. Excitations come from connected units when the connection has a positive coefficient (weight). Inhibitions come from units with a negative coefficient on the connection. At each time step (spreading of the activation) the network is informed about some property of its local environment and it responds by generating a motor response. The simulation algorithm controls the entire process. It executes the motor behavior of the organism in the environment and it updates the sensory input to the organism at the next time step.

The initial population is composed of randomly generated networks. Hence, each individual will tend to be different from any other individual. The networks can have the same architecture (connectivity pattern among the units) and randomly generated weights on the connections or both the architecture and the weights can be randomly generated. Given the architecture and the weights, each network will respond in a particular way to environmental stimuli. The performance of each individual network is evaluated in terms of a criterion of fitness. For example, if the environment contains food elements and the networks are informed about the position of these elements (input), they will respond by moving in the environment (output) in such a way that the number of food elements reached in a given amount of time (number of spreadings of activation through the network) varies from one individual network to another. This number represents the fitness of the individual.

Reproduction is a function of fitness. Individuals that have more fitness tend to leave more offspring (copies of the network of the parent) than individuals with less fitness. Hence, the next generation will be composed of networks that are copies of the best networks of the preceding generation. Furthermore, offspring are not exact copies of their parents. Random mutations are applied to some of the features of the parent's network (e.g., to some of the weights or to some aspects of the network architecture), and an offspring is generated by combining two complementary parts of two parent networks (sexual reproduction). Therefore, offspring will tend to be similar but not identical to their parents. This added variability will yield individuals that behave either more efficiently than their parents (more fit individuals) or less efficiently (less fit individuals). Selective reproduction will favor the former individuals rather than the latter ones when it is their turn to reproduce.

The two mechanisms of selective reproduction and constant addition of variability (through mutations or sexual recombination) will generally result in an evolutionary increase in average fitness across generations. The individuals of later generations are more likely to respond efficiently to environmental input than the individuals of earlier generations. Figure 1 shows the increase in the average number of food elements reached during life by 100 successive generations of individuals in a population that reproduces selectively and is subject to mutations (but not to sexual recombination).

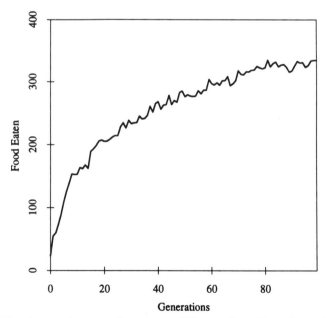

FIGURE 1   Increase in average fitness across 100 generations. Fitness is number of food elements reached by an organism that is informed about the position of food and can displace itself in space. (After Nolfi, Elman, & Parisi, 1994. Copyright © 1994 by the Massachusetts Institute of Technology.)

A. Fitness and Behavior

An increase in fitness across generations necessarily presupposes some change in the behavior of individuals of successive generations. But the relation between behavior and fitness is not a direct one. While fitness may "increase," behavior "changes." And this change can be qualitative and in stages, not only quantitative. Furthermore, the same fitness can be obtained by very different behaviors, and a more or less regular increase in fitness can be the result of complex changes in the underlying behavior. Therefore, how behavior changes evolutionarily in successive generations should be examined independently from an increase in fitness and it should be an important topic of research by itself. For example, evolutionary changes in behavior can be compared with how behavior changes in the individual to identify similarities and differences.

To exemplify the complex relation that may exist between fitness and behavior, consider a population of organisms each of which lives alone in a bidimensional environment containing a single object. Each organism is situated in the center of the environment and cannot move. However, the organism has a two-segment arm that can be moved. The fitness criterion is the total number of time units during the life of the organism in which the end point of the arm (the "hand") coincides with the object. (All the locations of the environment are at reaching distance from the organism.) The organism also has a movable "eye" with a restricted visual field. When the object or the hand (or both) are within the visual field, they are perceived. Otherwise, nothing is perceived.

The organism is modeled by a neural network. The input units of the network encode sensory information about the location of the object and/or the hand if they are within the visual field. Otherwise, all input units have zero activation. The output units encode two distinct motor behaviors: movements of the eye (and, therefore, of the visual field) and movements of the arm. At the beginning of each epoch of life (an epoch is a sequence of a certain number of spreadings) everything is randomly decided: the position of the object in the environment, the position of the arm, and the orientation of the visual field. The organism is free to move both eye and arm in response to environmental stimuli for a certain number of epochs. Its goal (fitness) is to move the arm so that the hand reaches the object and stays there. Fitness is measured as total number of cycles in which hand and object coincide.

This evolutionary task is more complex than the previous one of approaching food. In order to move the arm to reach the object the organism must know where the object is located. But to perceive where the object is located the eye must be moved and positioned so that the object falls within the visual field. Furthermore, in order to move the hand to a specified position (the location of the object) the organism must also know where the hand is currently located. Hence, the hand must also be kept within the visual field. (Notice that no proprioceptive information about the position of arm or hand is available to the organism.) Therefore, the task involves the coordination of two motor abilities, moving the arm and moving the eye, in such a way that at any given time two types of sensory input may be received, one informing the organism about the location of the object and the other informing the organism about the location of the hand.

Figure 2 shows the increase in the fitness of the average individual for each of 500 successive generations. Clearly, evolution succeeds in creating a complex initially nonexistent sensorimotor ability.

The increase in fitness shown in Figure 2 is more or less linear. However, if we examine more closely how the behavior of these organisms changes across the 500 generations, we observe a more complex picture of evolutionary stages. The global capacity to reach the object by coordinating eye and arm is gradually constructed by successively acquiring various component subcapacities (Di Sano, Cecconi, & Parisi, 1993).

At the beginning, given the random assignment of connection weights to the initial population, the organisms tend either to move both eye and arm in a stereotypical manner that is insensitive to input or to respond more or less randomly to input. The first capacity that tends to emerge evolutionarily is the capacity to stop the eye when the object happens to be within the visual field in order to continue to perceive the object. This is easier than keeping the hand within the visual field because the object is fixed, while the

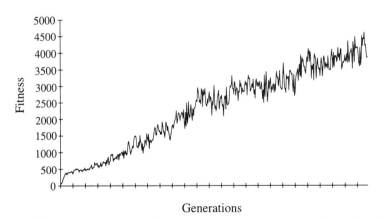

Generations

FIGURE 2   Increase in average fitness across 500 generations. Fitness is number of time units spent with hand on object, by an organism that can move an arm to reach the object and an eye to perceive where the object and its hand are currently located (Di Sano, Cecconi, & Parisi, 1993).

hand moves. Furthermore, the hand not only moves but it is moved by the organism itself. Hence, the capacity to keep the hand in sight depends on the emergence of two subcapacities, the capacity to track a moving object (which by itself is more difficult than keeping a fixed object in sight) and the capacity to coordinate the tracking movements of the eye with the movements of the arm. It is interesting that the evolutionary increase in the capacity to keep the hand in sight is accompanied by a decrement in the already-evolved capacity to keep the object in sight. In some sense, these two isolated subcapacities are in competition. In order to track the hand the organism must in some cases abandon the object from sight.

The next capacity that emerges is a better coordination between eye and arm movements so that the organism becomes able to keep both object and hand simultaneously in sight. Finally, there is improvement in the capacity to generate the fine movements that allow the hand to reach the object while both are in sight and in the capacity to keep the hand on the object once the object has been reached by the hand.

Notice that an organism is rewarded, that is, its fitness is increased, only when its hand is on the object. The capacity to keep the object or the hand in sight, by themselves, are not rewarded. However, these subcapacities are useful preadaptations for the rewarded capacity to reach the object. An organism that succeeds in keeping the object or the hand or, even better, both in sight, is more likely to end up with its hand on the object (and, therefore, to leave offspring) than an organism that perceptually ignores where the object or its hand or both are currently located.

This analysis shows that computational models of evolution can be used to study how capacities are evolutionarily acquired. Rather than concentrating on the final capacity or on the conditions that make its acquisition more or less efficient, the focus of the research is directed on the stages, sequences of stages, mechanisms of passage from one stage to the next one, which are observed during the course of evolution.

Simulations of the evolution of populations of neural networks allow a further level of analysis beyond the level of fitness and the level of behavior. Evolving organisms modeled as neural networks can be examined from the point of view of the organization of their "nervous system." Consider the simulation of eye/hand coordination described above. All the organisms have the same network architecture, which includes a single layer of ten hidden units. We can examine how a network becomes internally, that is, neurally, organized in order to be able to do the task. And we can find in the organization at the neural level a correspondence with the organization at the behavioral level.

To do this we "lesion" each of the ten hidden units separately and observe the changes (deficits) in behavior that result from each lesion. Lesioning a unit means that the unit is eliminated together with all its connections and, therefore, the contribution of the unit to the network's performance is completely canceled. If one applies this lesioning method to the neural network of the best individual of the last generation (which tends to have a high fitness on the task), the following results can be observed. The effects of the lesions are assessed by observing how lesioning each unit affects the performance of the network on each of the behavioral subcapacities we have distinguished. On the basis of this analysis, which simulates brain damage, the ten hidden units appear to group themselves in three main classes. Class A units are those units whose lesioning determines little or no fitness loss and no changes in the various behavioral capacities. When Class B units are lesioned, there is a decrease in the capacity to keep both the object and the hand in sight. The two separate subcapacities are not damaged but their coordination is. The reduced coordination appears to be determined by a paradoxical increase in the capacity to keep either the object or the hand separately in sight. Class C unit lesioning determines a decrease in the capacity to generate the fine movements that allow the hand to reach the object when both the hand and the object are in sight. Notice that these behavioral deficits observed after lesioning single units do not authorize us to assume that specific capacities are represented locally in these single units rather than in a distributed manner over a set of units. However, apparently the analysis of capacities and subcapacities at the behavioral level finds a correspondence in the organization of the network at the neural level.

B. Evolutionary Change at Other Levels

In the preceding section we saw that evolutionary change in artificial organisms can be analyzed at two levels: the level of fitness and the level of behavior. In this section we will extend our analysis of evolutionary change to two further levels: the level of the nervous system and the level of the genotype.

In the simulations described above, individual networks have different connection weights but the same network architecture. Therefore, what evolves is the matrix of connection weights. The network architecture remains constant throughout evolution. But anything can evolve provided that: (1) it varies from one individual to another; (2) it is inherited; and (3) it is subject to mutations and/or sexual recombination at reproduction. We will now discuss simulations in which not only the connection weights but also the network architectures are subject to selective pressure, and, therefore, they too tend to evolve.

Another feature of the preceding simulations was that the genetic information inherited from parent to offspring, that is, the genotype, was a literal description of the phenotypical network. If we understand development, here, to mean the mapping from genotype to phenotype, (as is usual in developmental biology), such mapping was quite simple and direct. In populations of real organisms the genotype/phenotype mapping is much more complex and indirect. More specifically, while the simulations described a linear mapping, that is, a single feature of the genotype corresponded to one and only feature of the phenotype, and vice versa, in reality more complex mappings tend to be nonlinear. A particular feature of the genotype plays a role in determining many different features of the phenotype and a single phenotypical feature is determined by many genotypical features.

Consider a population of networks in which the inherited genotype specifies not only the connection weights of the offspring network within a fixed network architecture but also the network architecture itself. Furthermore, the network architecture is indirectly specified in the inherited genotype. The phenotypical network that actually controls the behavior of the organism in the environment cannot simply be "read" in the inherited genotype but is the result of the execution of genotypical developmental instructions that interact among themselves and with their products in complex ways to yield the phenotypical network.

Contrary to most work on neural networks, which views network architectures as purely topological structures in which all that counts is the pattern of connectivity among units, it is assumed, here, that networks are physical objects in physical space. If networks are considered simply as topological structures, the location of units in space is irrelevant. All that counts is which unit is connected with which unit. On the contrary, if networks are viewed as physical objects the location of units in space, as we will see in a moment, is critical for deciding what the network architecture is going to be.

The execution of the instructions contained in the genotype brings about a process of neural growth (Nolfi & Parisi, 1992, 1995b). Each of a set of units is positioned in a given location in physical (bidimensional) space and it grows branching axons. If a branch of the axon from unit A ends up on unit B, a connection between the two units is established. Otherwise, that branch will remain nonfunctional. It is clear, therefore, that the final network architecture (connectivity) will depend on the spatial location of the units and on the parameters that control the growth of the branching axon from each unit. [Neural growth is restricted to the growth of neurites from already-existing neurons in this model. Other models that include a cell division stage (Belew, 1993; Cangelosi, Parisi, & Nolfi, 1994; Wilson, 1987) can be the basis of more complex genotype/phenotype mappings. Furthermore, neural development can include cell and neurite death in addition to cell and neurite growth.]

The genotype is a long sequence of 0s and 1s, which encodes a set of parameters for each of a given number of network units. The parameters include the following:

1. whether the genetic material concerning a given unit will be expressed or not, that is, whether the corresponding unit will be part of the phenotypical network
2. the spatial coordinates of the unit in the physical space of the network
3. the branching parameters of the axon of the unit (e.g., branching angle, length of branching segments)
4. the weights of the connections departing from the unit
5. the type of the unit (input unit, hidden unit, output unit, what information is encoded by the input and output units)

When all the instructions (parameters) concerning all the units have been executed, a network is obtained that includes both a functional and a nonfunctional component. The functional component (functional network) is that portion of the total network that connects the input units to the output units and, therefore, actually controls the behavior of the organism. (Notice that by appropriately restricting the angle of branching of the axons so that axons necessarily go north, one can guarantee that only feedforward functional networks are generated.) The nonfunctional component includes all the neural branchings that do not establish connections between units and, in addition, those units and groups of interconnected units that are not part of the input-to-output circuit. This nonfunctional component plays no role in determining the organism's behavior.

Figure 3 shows both the total neural structure that develops as a consequence of executing all the instructions contained in the genotype and the functional network that actually controls the organism's behavior.

Given this more complex framework, an organism can be described at four distinct levels. We can determine: (1) what is the genotype inherited by

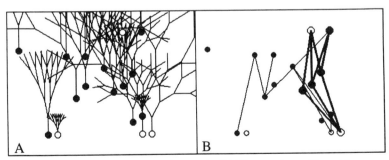

FIGURE 3   Development of a neural network. (A) The growing and branching process of axons. (B) The resulting neural network after removal of nonconnecting branches. Isolated or nonfunctional units and connections are represented by small circles and thin lines. Functional units and connections are represented as large circles and thick lines. The bottom layer contains sensory units, the upper layer motor units, and the remaining layers internal or hidden units. (Nolfi & Parisi, 1995a. Copyright © 1995 by Springer-Verlag.)

the organism; (2) what is the neural network constructed by executing the genotype; (3) what is the behavior this neural network generates in response to environmental input; and (4) what is the fitness obtained by the organism with that behavior. We can compare organisms at each of these levels and analyze evolutionary change accordingly.

1. Complex Relations among Levels

A number of important points can be made on the basis of this fourfold description of organisms. Each level is complexly related to the other levels. The levels are organized in a causal hierarchy. The genotype determines the network, the network determines the behavior, the behavior determines the fitness (see Figure 4). But the causal relation is not one-to-one. Two individuals can have the same neural network but different genotypes, or the same behavior but different neural networks, or the same fitness but different behaviors. In other words, one cannot infer from an organism's appearance at a higher level in the hierarchy the organism's makeup at a lower level.

The inverse relation from lower to higher levels is also complex. In the simulations described above a particular genotype can result in one and only one phenotype (network). Hence, the genotype/phenotype mapping is deterministic. But it is possible to include some context sensitivity in the execution of the developmental instructions contained in the genotype (Wilson, 1987) and this would make it unfeasible to infer (predict) which phe-

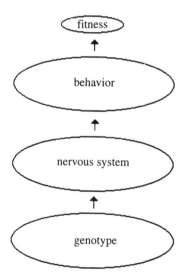

FIGURE 4   Four levels at which an individual organism can be described and compared with other organisms. Arrows indicate the causal relationships within the hierarchy of levels.

notypical network (higher level) would result given a particular genotype (lower level). In addition, whether the genetic material concerning a given network unit will be expressed or not may not be under complete genetic control, as in the present model, but it may partially depend on environmental stimuli (Nolfi, Miglino, & Parisi, 1994). This would add phenotypical plasticity to the model (cf. Section VB2).

As to the higher levels, that is, the behavior and the fitness level, the mapping is already nondeterministic. Given a particular network, the behavior that is exhibited by an organism endowed with that network depends on both the network and the particular local environment in which the individual happens to live. And the same applies to the relation between behavior and fitness. Two individuals can respond in the same way to environmental input, that is, they can have the same behavior, but one individual can end up with a higher fitness if it lives in a more food-rich environment than the other individual.

A further element of complexity in the relations among levels is represented by the following: in the individual, the causal relation is from lower to higher levels, but in the population, the causal relation is from the highest level (fitness) to all lower levels. In fact, if and how each level changes evolutionarily depends on the fitness level. A potential change in genotype, neural network, or behavior may be retained in the population only if it results in an increase at the fitness level or, at least, in no change in fitness (neutral evolution).

2. Functional and Nonfunctional Components

The notion of a functional and nonfunctional component can be generalized from the neural level to the genetic level and to the behavioral level. As will be recalled, at the neural level a distinction has been made between the functional network and the nonfunctional network. The functional network is that portion of the network generated by the genotype that actually maps input into output and therefore controls the behavior of the organism in the environment. The nonfunctional network is the additional neural structure that is also generated by the genotype but plays no role in controlling the organism's behavior.

A similar distinction between a functional and a nonfunctional component can be made at the genetic level. The genotype specifies the parameters for a certain number of units. The first of these parameters (see Section IIIB) specifies whether the genetic material concerning the particular unit will be expressed or not, that is, whether the unit will be generated during development or not. Hence, while there is a maximum number of units in a network, the actual number of units in a particular network is likely to be less than this maximum number because some units may not develop. This means that a particular genotype will be made up of two components, a functional component and a nonfunctional component. The functional component contains the genetic information (parameters) concerning the units that will develop and the nonfunctional component contains the information concerning the nondeveloping units. In the same way that only the functional network is responsible for the actual behavior exhibited by the organism, similarly only the functional component of the genotype is responsible for the actual network (phenotype) that is constructed on the basis of the genotype.

The same distinction between a functional component and a nonfunctional component applies at the behavioral level. To understand this point it is necessary to clarify a special property of neural networks that live in an environment (ecological networks). Ecological networks (Parisi, Cecconi, & Nolfi, 1990) differ from classical connectionist networks in that ecological networks partly determine with their output their own input. In classical nonecological networks it is the researcher who decides what the next input to the network is going to be. More specifically, there is generally no (environmentally mediated) causal relation between the network's output at cycle N and the network's input at cycle N + 1. The situation is different for ecological networks. Ecological networks partly determine with their motor output the next sensory input. By acting on an independent, structured environment, ecological networks change with their (motor) behavior either the environment itself or their relation to the environment. In both cases, they are likely to influence the next environmental input. For example, by turning right instead of left at cycle N, the network causes the sensory input from the nearest food at cycle N + 1 to be at a certain angle rather than at a different angle.

It has been shown that ecological networks exploit this freedom to self-select their own input (Nolfi & Parisi, 1993). In fact, individual networks tend to move in the environment in such a way that they are exposed only to a subset of all possible inputs. And different networks choose different subsets. For example, one network may tend to approach food always from the right, while another network chooses to approach food from the left.

Because of this phenomenon of self-selection of input, it is possible to distinguish between a functional component and a nonfunctional component even at the behavior level. The neural network of a particular organism specifies a motor output for all possible sensory inputs but, in actuality, a particular organism will move in the environment in such a way that only a subset of all possible sensory inputs will be actually experienced by the network. One can determine what this functional behavioral component is by observing the organism while it spontaneously behaves in the environment. The nonfunctional behavioral component (i.e., how the organism responds to inputs that spontaneously would not be encountered) can be ascertained by doing laboratory experiments with the organism, that is, by exposing the organism to stimuli decided by the researcher and recording the organism's response.

As in the case of the genetic level and the neural level, it is only the functional behavioral component that determines the next higher level of the organism, that is, the organism's fitness. The fitness of an individual depends on how the individual reacts to the input actually experienced during its life (functional behavioral component), not on how it would react to inputs that are not experienced (nonfunctional component).

We conclude that a more correct description of the relationships between successive hierarchical levels of the organism is that of Figure 5, which shows explicitly that it is only the functional component of each level that has a causal influence on what the organism looks like or does at the next higher level.

It would be a mistake, however, to think that the nonfunctional components that are present at each level of an organism have no role to play. In fact, while these nonfunctional components have no influence on the individual organism, they can be very important from an evolutionary point of view, that is, they can influence future evolutionary change at the population level. Although the nonfunctional components do not influence the individual organism, still, each organism carries in its body/behavior both functional and nonfunctional components. If the nonfunctional components

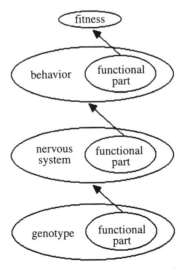

FIGURE 5   This figure more correctly shows that only the functional component at each level has a causal influence on the next higher level.

were simply eliminated, evolutionary change would be quite different from what is observed.

If a single mutation changes the genetic parameter that specifies whether a particular unit in an organism's phenotypical network will develop or not (cf. Section IIIB), and the parameter's value happens to be transformed by the mutation from negative to positive, then a whole new piece of neural structure is suddenly added to the organism's network. This new piece of neural structure was already there, hidden in the genotype but ready to develop and be used. Or, a mutation can transform a piece of nonfunctional neural structure into a component of the functional network. This may change the organism's functional network and, as a consequence, the organism's behavior and fitness.

The general implication is that there may be evolutionary changes in the nonfunctional components at all levels (genetic, neural, and behavioral) that can remain hidden with respect to the functional components and, therefore, for a period of time (number of generations) may play no role in determining the course of the observed evolutionary change at the higher levels. However, as a consequence of a single mutation this hidden change can suddenly become visible and can produce abrupt change at the higher levels. Changes can accumulate for generations in the nonfunctional components at the lower levels, while remaining invisible and without effects. At a certain point, a further small change no different from the other changes that have accumulated can tip the balance and make all the accumulated changes produce a sudden "stagelike" visible change (Miglino, Nolfi, & Parisi, in press).

If one accepts the notion that at each level there is evolutionary change that only in part becomes visible at the next higher level, then one can predict that one should observe less and less change from one generation to the next as one ascends from the lowest level (the genetic level) to the highest level (the fitness level). In other words, when comparing individuals of successive generations one should find that individuals are likely to be different at the genetic level, less likely at the neural level, even less likely at the behavioral level, and rather unlikely at the fitness level.

To test this hypothesis, all the successive ancestors of the best individual of the last generation in the simulation described in this section were examined at all four levels to determine how different each individual was at each level with respect to its parent. The analysis consisted of a set of parent/offspring comparisons from the founder of the lineage in the first generation to the last descendant, that is, the best individual of the last generation. The results are shown in Figure 6. An individual is likely to differ from its parent at the genetic level but progressively less likely to be different as one ascends the hierarchy of levels. At the fitness level, it is rare that a mutation results in a change in fitness from parent to offspring.

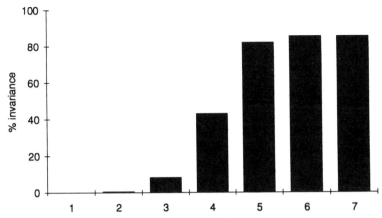

FIGURE 6   Offspring are less and less different from parents as one ascends the hierarchy from the genetic level to the fitness level. The figure shows the percentage of parent/offspring invariance at the total genetic level (1), at the functional genetic level (2), at the total network level (3), at the functional network level (4), at the total behavior level (5), at the functional behavior level (6), at the fitness level (7).

A hierarchical system with complex mapping from one level to the next and both functional and nonfunctional components at each level tends to produce preadaptations (or, better, exaptations; Gould, 1991) and to give a "punctuated equilibria" shape to evolutionary change. Accumulated change at lower levels that is not selected for at the fitness level and, therefore, is adaptively neutral, generates structure that only in later evolutionary stages is co-opted for some function (exaptations). This becoming functional of some previously adaptively neutral structure tends to be sudden and results in long periods of stasis in fitness followed by abrupt fitness increases (Figure 7; see also Miglino et al., in press).

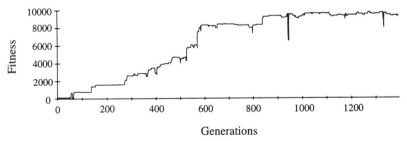

Generations

FIGURE 7   Evolutionary curve of fitness for organisms with a complex hierarchy of levels and both functional and nonfunctional components at each level. The curve has a "punctuated equilibria" shape with long periods of fitness stasis followed by abrupt changes in fitness.

IV. MATURATION

The phenotypical network discussed in Section IIB was said to be the result of a process of neural growth. The network architecture was not directly encoded in the genotype but it emerged as the collective result of the execution of many complexly interacting developmental instructions contained in the genotype. This captures an important aspect of development in that development is viewed as a complex, nonlinear mapping from genotype to phenotype.

Another perhaps even more crucial aspect of development, however, is absent from the simulations described above. Development is a process that takes place in time. Development is change that occurs during the life of an individual organism and it consists of a succession of states of the living organism. In contrast, the temporal nature of (individual) development was ignored in the simulations of the preceding sections, which concentrated on evolutionary change rather than on change in the individual. In this section we describe simulations that view development as change in the individual. The study of development as change in the individual is an important topic in itself and it is also a necessary step if we want to examine the interactions between development and evolution.

Although we spoke of neural growth in the simulations of Section IIB, there was actually no temporally spaced process of neural growth or development. In fact, there was no change in either the nervous system or the behavior of an individual organism during its life. Neural growth was instantaneous. In this section we describe simulations in which the process of neural growth takes time and actually extends for a long period during the life of the individual (developmental age). Since the neural network that underlies the behavior of the organism in the environment changes in successive epochs of life, the organism's behavior also changes. Therefore, we can observe and analyze both neural development and behavioral development.

It still remains true, however, that the changes in nervous system/behavior that occur in these individuals during their life are entirely determined by the inherited genotype. No role is played in these changes by the environment in which the organism lives, by the particular experience of the organism in that environment, or by changes in the organism that are caused by that experience (learning). In other words, what is studied by simulations such as those described in this section is more properly called maturation than development. If one believes that maturation is always influenced by the environment and interacts with learning, then these simulations should be considered as simulations of possible rather than real phenomena of development, much as the simulations of "pure evolutionary change" described in the preceding sections. (For the interaction between maturation and learning, cf. Section VB2.)

To transform the preceding simulations of atemporal development into simulations in which development (or maturation) is a temporal process taking place during the life of the individual, it is necessary to introduce only a small change in the parameters specified by the genotype. As will be remembered, one of the parameters contained in the genotype of the preceding simulations dictated for each network unit whether the unit would actually develop or not. We can modify this parameter by changing it from a "unit development" parameter into a "unit development time" parameter. Instead of specifying *whether* a unit will develop or not, the parameter now specifies *when* a unit is going to develop. The total lifetime of an organism is divided up into a certain number of epochs (each epoch being a certain number of cycles, or spreadings of activation from the sensory to the motor units) and the parameter specifies at which epoch a particular unit will develop, that is, when it will grow its branching axon. In other words, it is not the case, as in the preceding simulations, that all network units develop at the same time (at birth or conception) but rather that different units may develop at different times. To allow for dormant, that is, nondeveloping, units (which from the previous simulations we know are important), the parameter can take values that go beyond the total maximum lifetime of an individual. When this happens the corresponding unit does not develop at all.

By modifying the genotype in this way we obtain organisms that change both their nervous system and their behavior during their life (Nolfi & Parisi, 1992, 1995a). They develop or, better, mature. An organism begins its life with a small neural network that results from the axonal growth of those units of its genotype that have a development time parameter that specifies epoch 0 (birth). The individual lives and behaves in the environment (and possibly accumulates fitness) on the basis of this initial network. Then there is neural development. Additional units can grow their branching axons at later epochs and this will result in an observable growth of the individual's neural structure. Consequently, the individual's behavior will also change. This is behavioral development.

The effects of neural/behavioral development can be observed in the changes in fitness that occur during an individual's life. Figure 8 shows the number of food elements captured in successive epochs of life by individuals belonging to successive generations. It is clear that evolution results in genotypes that support a process of individual development leading from lower to higher levels of the capacity to find food.

What is critical from the point of view of the relation between development and evolution is that an individual's fitness is assessed at all developmental stages. Although the fitness of the individual can vary from epoch to epoch because the individual changes, the individual's reproductive chances depend on its total fitness summed over all ages. This poses an interesting question: Why is there such a thing as development? If development implies

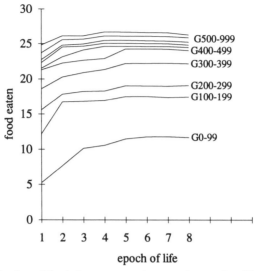

FIGURE 8   Number of food elements eaten in successive epochs of life across a certain number of generations. Evolution creates individuals that grow and are able to eat more food while they grow. (Nolfi & Parisi, 1995a. Copyright © 1995 by Springer-Verlag.)

the existence of early phases in the individual's life in which the individual is able to obtain less fitness, why is development not progressively eliminated by evolution and the individual born as an already-mature, adult organism?

We know from Figure 8 that in the simulations we are describing an individual obtains less fitness when it is "young" than when it reaches "adulthood." It would not be impossible for evolution to completely get rid of development. Genotypes that include network units that develop later in life could be progressively eliminated and the population would eventually include only genotypes with units that develop at birth. In other words, organisms would be born as mature individuals. We know that this is not true in most natural populations. And this is not what is actually observed in our simulations. Figure 9 shows the average epoch in which development in individual organisms ends as a function of generation. (Development ends when the genotype does not contain any more instructions for developing units.) Development appears to constitute a stable feature in this population.

So, why is development evolutionarily maintained? There can be many, not necessarily alternative, answers to this question (cf. Section VB2). One possible answer is that development represents a chance for evolution to explore new evolutionary possibilities efficiently. This is why evolution is interested in development and does not kill development off. After a rea-

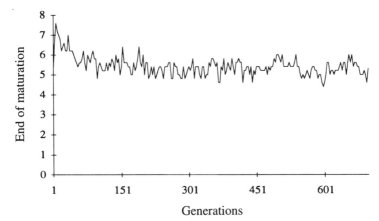

FIGURE 9   Age in which development ends across generations. After an initial decrease, the age of maturation stabilizes at around five epochs (Nolfi & Parisi, 1992).

sonably good adaptation has been reached new mutations are likely to be deleterious. Hence, it would be nice to have a method for exploring novelties without incurring the risk of deleterious mutations. Development can be a solution to this problem. Development allows the evolutionary conservation of mutations that operate later in an individual's life and that tend to have little effect on the individual's global fitness. The initial stages of development have the greatest influence on an organism's fitness. Mutations tend to operate later on and to be relatively noninfluential from the point of fitness. If these later mutations prove to be nondeleterious and useful, they may become evolutionarily anticipated in development and incorporated in a new adaptation. To realize this method that allows the exploration of novelties, while reducing the concomitant risk, evolution needs development, that is, genotypes that map into gradually constructed phenotypes and cause the individual organism to change during its life because of intrinsic reasons.

Some (simulated) facts support this analysis. Figure 10 shows that the functional network of an individual tends to develop early in life, while later development tends to be restricted to the nonfunctional component of the individual's network. As we know (cf. Section IIIB2), the nonfunctional component is where hidden evolutionary changes tend to occur, that is, changes that do not necessarily map into higher levels and, eventually, into fitness. Therefore, the individual is shielded from the risk of negative mutations because most mutations are adaptively neutral. But such hidden changes can suddenly become visible if proven useful and then tend to be anticipated in development in subsequent generations. Figure 11 shows the

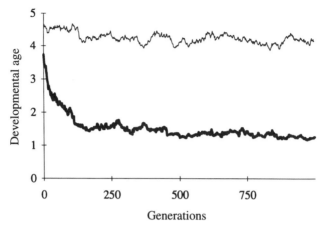

FIGURE 10   Age of development of units of functional (thick line) and nonfunctional (thin line) subnetworks across generations. The portion of the network of an organism that actually controls the organism's behavior (functional subnetwork) tends to mature earlier than the portion that is nonfunctional. (Nolfi & Parisi, 1995a. Copyright © 1995 by Springer-Verlag.)

percentage of posticipations and anticipations for adaptive and neutral mutations. While adaptively neutral mutations are equally likely to appear either earlier or later in the development of individuals of subsequent generations, adaptive mutations tend to appear earlier rather than later, that is, to be evolutionarily anticipated in development.

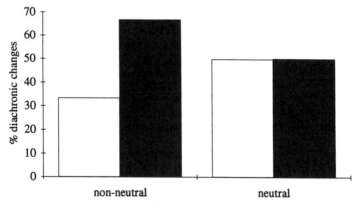

FIGURE 11   Percentage of posticipations (empty bars) and anticipations (filled bars) for adaptive and neutral mutations in the lineage of the best individual of the last generation. (Nolfi & Parisi, 1995a. Copyright © 1995 by Springer-Verlag.)

V. LEARNING

Most work using neural networks is dedicated to learning. Learning is change that occurs in an individual network and that is due to the experience of the particular network with the particular environment (input, teaching input). Neurally, this change consists of modifications of the connection weights of the network or changes in network architecture (network pruning or building). Behaviorally, learned changes are changes in how the network responds to the input at successive stages of learning. In principle, the same kinds of neural and behavioral changes can occur both in evolution and in learning, although there is a tendency to believe that changes in network architecture are more common in evolution and changes in connection weights are more common in learning.

The difference between evolutionary change and change caused by learning concerns (1) the entities in which change occurs, and (2) the mechanism of change. Evolutionary change occurs in populations of organisms, from one organism to its offspring or from one generation to the successive one. In purely evolutionary change the individual organism does not change. Change caused by learning, on the other hand, takes place in the individual organism and, as such, is not transmitted to other organisms, in particular to the individual's offspring. (But learned changes can be transmitted from one organism to another culturally though not genetically if an organism learns by imitating the behavior of another organism; cf. Section VB1.)

Another difference between evolutionary change and change caused by learning is in the mechanism of change. Evolutionary change is caused by selective reproduction and by the various devices that add variability to the population (e.g., mutations and sexual recombination). The network architectures and the connection weights that are appropriate for exhibiting a certain ability are selected from a constantly maintained population of variants. Change caused by learning, on the other hand, occurs in the network architecture and/or in the connection weights of a single network because of some process of internal adjustment of the individual network to environmental input.

A. Learning without Evolution

Research on learning in neural networks is generally not interested in studying the relation between learning and evolution. A typical connectionist simulation begins with a single network with a fixed network architecture and a random assignment of connection weights. The network architecture is not the result of a process of evolution but is arbitrarily decided by the researcher. The randomly generated weight matrix exemplifies a "tabula rasa" conception of learning according to which learning is experience writing on a blank slate. In these conditions it is impossible to analyze predispositions and constraints that evolution can create with respect to learning. Also, since the network that learns is an isolated individual and not a member of a reproducing and evolving population of individuals, it is impossible to examine any effects the learning occurring in the individual can have on the evolution of the population to which the individual belongs. In nature, organisms that learn are part of evolving populations. Therefore, much current research on learning in neural networks must be considered as a study of possible rather than real phenomena.

Another limitation of much current work on neural network learning is that it is nonecological. The actual conditions in which organisms learn and the type of experience they have in their environment are not considered. The "experience" of a neural network during learning, that is, the inputs and the teaching inputs of the network, is decided arbitrarily by the researcher and is not the spontaneous result of the actual interactions between the organism and its environment (cf. Section IIIB2 above). Notwithstanding these limitations, many interesting aspects of learning can be investigated with simulations that ignore evolution and use nonecological neural networks.

An example is the series of simulations of Rumelhart and McClelland (1986) and Plunkett and Marchmann (1991, 1993) on the learning of the past tense of English verbs. A neural network is taught using the back-propagation procedure to generate the appropriate past tense form as output on being given the verb stem as input. The back-propagation procedure consists in gradually changing the connection weights of a network in such a way that the discrepancy (error) between output and an externally provided teaching input (correct output) is progressively reduced (Rumelhart, Hinton, & Williams, 1986). In the past tense simulations the teaching input, that is, the correct past tense of the verb, is provided by the researcher, which shows the nonecological nature of these simulations. In any case, the task to be learned is not easy because English language includes various categories of verbs or stem/past tense mappings (*work/worked; hit/hit; ring/rang; go/went*) and the different categories have different type and token frequencies. Children learn to produce the correct past tense forms over many years and at a certain stage they make overregularization errors (e.g., *hitted* instead of *hit*).

In addition to reproducing various aspects of the actual learning of past tense by children, these simulations demonstrate two general properties of a neural network account of learning. (For a criticism of the past tense simulations, see Pinker & Prince, 1988.) One is its power, which goes well beyond classical associationism because of the distributed character of neural representations. No entity is internally represented by a single element in a neural network but all entities are represented by a large collection of network's elements. The representation takes the form of a pattern of quantitative values over these elements. Hence, the same collection of elements can represent many different entities by varying the pattern of its quantitative values. In the past tense simulations the same set of connection weights incorporate the knowledge necessary to respond correctly with respect to all four classes of stem/past tense mappings. The distributed character of neural representations explains the intrinsic tendency of neural networks to generalize, their capacity to respond to partial or degenerated input, and their robustness when damaged.

The other general property of neural network learning that is demonstrated by the past tense simulations is that such learning can result in systems that exhibit rule-governed behavior but do not incorporate or follow explicit rules. Alternative accounts of past tense performance assume a dual system with a rule-based component to account for regular mappings and an association-based component for the irregular mappings (Pinker, 1991). In general, rules are prominent in symbol manipulation accounts of learning and behavior. The past tense simulations show that behavior we find useful to describe as incorporating rules (e.g., "to make the past tense of *work,* add *ed* to the stem") may be generated by systems that cannot be said to actually contain rules. Hence, a complete description of these systems requires that we go beyond the vocabulary of rules and adopt a more quantitative vocabulary that is similar to the vocabulary of neurobiology (Johnson & Gilmore, this volume).

The past tense simulations, however, are also representative of how neural network learning can be used if one is specifically interested in development. Most work on neural network learning is focused on the final performance that can be obtained and on the best training conditions necessary to obtain that performance. People who study development, on the other hand, are more interested in how behavior changes during training and in how behavioral change depends on the particular training regime. (Section IIIA makes the same point with respect to evolutionary change.) Plunkett and Marchmann (1991, 1993) exemplify this developmental approach to neural network learning by manipulating training conditions (e.g., type and token frequency of various types of verbs at various stages of training) and by analyzing aspects of past tense performance at various stages of learning. They show that neural networks can not only learn the same abilities that humans learn but that the course of learning may be similar in networks and in humans. (For another example, applied to the balance scale task of In-helder and Piaget, 1958, and Siegler, 1981, see McClelland, 1989. Bates and Elman, 1993, Karmiloff-Smith, 1992, McClelland, 1992, and Plunkett and Sinha, 1992, discuss in more general terms how connectionist learning can shed light on development.)

If one is really interested in development, however, learning in neural networks should be studied within an evolutionary context. Development is change that occurs in the individual organism as a consequence of both the experience of the individual organism and the inherited result of the past experiences of the population to which the individual belongs. Therefore, learning should be studied as it occurs in individual networks that are part of evolving populations of networks.

Consider a population of networks that reproduce selectively on the basis of some criterion of fitness. The evolutionary changes are reflected in the inherited genotype that determines the initial state of the individual. If the individual learns during its life, the learning that occurs will be influenced by this initial state. The capacity itself will be learned but a predisposition to learn (or not to learn) that capacity may be genetically inherited. Furthermore, the inherited genotype that results from evolution can influence the changes that occur during an individual's life not only as initial state but as a continuing influence that determines genetically based change (maturation). Changes that result from maturation will interact with changes caused by learning.

1. Learning and Evolution

Learning in neural networks is influenced by the network's initial state, for example, by the randomly selected set of connection weights that are initially assigned to the network. Two networks that are subject to the same learning experience (same sequence of inputs paired with the same teaching inputs) but are initially assigned two different randomly generated sets of weights are likely to have different learning outcomes (Kolen & Pollack, 1990).

Studying learning within an evolutionary context, Belew, McInerney, and Schraudolph (1991) have simulated the evolution of a population of organisms with a fixed network architecture but different weight matrices. During life each individual was taught a nonecological task using backpropagation. (The task was to recognize whether an input pattern was symmetrical or not.) The criterion for reproduction (fitness) was the amount learned by each individual during its life. Each individual inherited its initial weight matrix from its parent with the addition of some mutations (reproduction was agamic, not sexual), whereas the changes in weights due to learning were not inherited. In a succession of generations the task was learned progressively more rapidly. Evidently, evolution was able to select increasingly better initial weight matrices. Individuals of later generations were born with an inherited initial state that predisposed them to learn the symmetry task. Learning was not writing on a blank slate (a randomly generated weight matrix) but it was writing on a slate that was predisposed to receive a particular written message.

In other simulations it was not the initial weight matrix that was inherited but the network architecture. Miller, Todd, and Hegde (1989) had evolving populations of networks learn various tasks in various simulations. At the beginning of life (learning) each network was assigned a random set of connection weights and the networks that learned the particular task better had more chances to generate offspring than those that learned less well. The networks of the initial generation were assigned a randomly generated network architecture. But from the second generation on, the network architecture was inherited. Therefore, what a parent network transmitted to its offspring was not an initial weight matrix, as in the preceding simulation, but a particular network architecture (with mutations). In this simulation there was also an evolutionary increase in the ability to learn. Hence, the networks of the later generations were born with an innate predisposition to learn the particular task. This innate predisposition was incorporated in the particular network architectures that were inherited by the individuals of the later generations, rather than in the initial weight matrices as in the preceding simulation.

The influence of evolution on learning via genetic inheritance of predispositions to learn (or predispositions not to learn) can also be demonstrated when the evolutionary task and the learning task are different tasks. In the simulations just described individual networks are selected for reproduction on the basis of their learning performance. Hence, evolutionary fitness and learning performance are the same thing. In other simulations the capacity that evolves in the population and the capacity that is learned by individual networks during life are different capacities. For example, networks can be selected for reproduction on the basis of their capacity to find food (cf. Section III). The network's input for this (evolutionary) task is location of food and the output is a motor action. In addition, the same networks individually learn during life to predict what the next sensory input from food will be when a currently planned motor action is actually executed. The input for this (learning) task is a planned motor action and the output is a prediction of the action's expected sensory consequences. The hidden units are shared by the two tasks.

By using distinct evolutionary and learning tasks it is possible to demonstrate that the changes caused by learning and those caused by evolution are not independent, although they occur at different time scales, in different types of entities (individuals vs. populations), and because of different mechanisms of change. The relation between evolution and learning appears to be reciprocal: evolution influences learning and vice versa. The locus of the influence of evolution on learning is the inherited genetic information that is the current end result of evolution and at the same time constitutes the initial state of learning. The locus of the influence of learning on evolution is the fitness of the individual that is affected by learning and at the same time determines the course of evolution.

Individuals with an evolved (inherited) capacity to find food learn during their life to better predict the consequences of their actions than individuals without this inherited capacity (see Figure 12). They do not already possess the capacity to predict at birth but they learn that capacity better than randomly generated individuals if given the appropriate learning experience. In other words, what is inherited is not a (congenital) ability to predict but only a predisposition to learn the ability. (A tendency to have certain expectations with respect to the environment could also be congenital, of course.) Apparently, evolution selects not only points in multidimensional space (cf. Section I) which incorporate good congenital performances on some task, but also points situated in subregions of multidimensional space where learning trajectories lead to particularly good performances (predispositions to learn).

Evolved genetic information can create predispositions to learn in more indirect ways. For example, individuals can inherit a congenital tendency to remain in proximity to other individuals (e.g., their parents) if this allows them to learn by imitating the behavior of these other individuals and the learned behavior increases their fitness. Figure 13 shows the spatial distribution of a population of organisms at the beginning of evolution and after twenty generations. At the beginning of evolution individuals move ran-

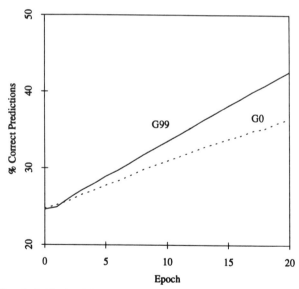

FIGURE 12   Individuals of the last generation (G99), which are born with an inherited (evolved) capacity to find food, learn to predict changes in sensory input from food as a consequences of their motor actions better than individuals of the first generation (G0), which are born without this inherited capacity (Nolfi, Elman, & Parisi, 1994.) Copyright © 1994 by the Massachusetts Institute of Technology.

A 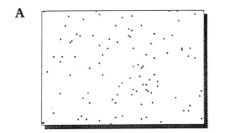   B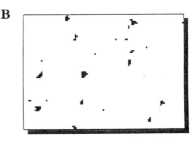

FIGURE 13   (A) Spatial distribution of organisms at the beginning of evolution. (B) Spatial distribution after twenty generations. The population evolves a genetically inherited tendency for individual organisms to aggregate spatially in order to be able to learn from others (Denaro & Parisi, 1994).

domly and do not create spatial aggregations. After twenty generations individuals tend to move in such a way that spatial aggregations of individuals are formed.

What is genetically inherited is the connection weights of a neural network with sensory input encoding the location of the nearest conspecific and output units encoding motor behavior allowing the individual to displace itself in space. However, the fitness that determines the reproductive chances of an individual is not how the individual reacts to this sensory input. Each individual has a second neural network with fixed architecture and a set of connection weights that are randomly assigned at birth. The fitness of an individual is how much the individual learns a nonecological task with this second network. The individual learns by imitating other individuals, that is, by taking the output of other individuals to the same input as its teaching input (Denaro & Parisi, 1994; Hutchins & Hazelhurst, 1995). However, an individual can imitate another individual only if it finds itself near the other individual. Therefore, there is an evolutionary pressure to stay near conspecifics in order to be able to learn from them. The result of such a pressure is shown in Figure 13. Here, an innate predisposition to learn is realized as a genetically inherited tendency to move in space in such a way that the individual is exposed to the appropriate learning experience (Johnson & Gilmore, this volume).

Simulations with separate evolutionary and learning tasks show not only that evolution can influence learning by creating predispositions to learn but also that learning can influence evolution. This influence of learning on evolution can be demonstrated in a strictly Darwinian (non-Lamarckian) context in which none of the changes caused by learning are inherited. This notwithstanding, the evolution of the capacity to find food has an accelerated course in a population of networks that also learn during their life to predict the consequences of their actions (see Figure 14). This can be ex-

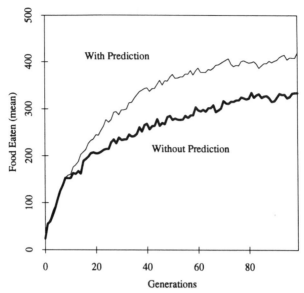

FIGURE 14   Better evolutionary increase in fitness (capacity to find food) in a population of networks that also learn during life to predict the consequences of their own actions compared with a population of networks that do not learn (Nolfi, Elman, & Parisi, 1994. Copyright © 1994 by the Massachusetts Institute of Technology).

plained by considering that: (1) evolution depends on fitness; (2) fitness depends on behavior; and (3) behavior is modified by learning. If the individuals that learn better than others tend to have more fitness, this opens the way for an influence of learning on evolution. The individuals that learn better than others are likely to be points located in favorable subregions of multidimensional space, that is, subregions that contain many points with high fitness. These subregions are those that will be explored by mutations in the next generation. Therefore, learning acts as a third mechanism that favors evolution (besides selective reproduction and the addition of variability through mutations and sexual recombination) in that it allows selection to base its decisions not only on the fitness of the individuals of the current generation but also on the predicted fitness of the offspring of these individuals (Hinton & Nolan, 1987; Parisi, Nolfi, & Cecconi, 1992).

Another explanation for the positive influence of learning on evolution relates to the fact that in many cases learning appears to benefit the average fitness of the population more than the fitness of the best individuals in the population (Nolfi, Elman, & Parisi, 1994). In populations that evolve but do not learn there is only one strategy being selected for reproduction: to have an inherited genotype that results in high fitness. On the other hand, in populations that both evolve and learn there are two distinct strategies: to have an inherited genotype that either results in high fitness or does not result in high fitness by itself but supports a good learning performance that in turn results in high fitness. Hence, learning can increase the number of individuals that have high fitness in the population.

2. Learning and Maturation

Little work has been done on how changes during an individual's life that are genetic in origin (maturation) interact with changes that are due to the particular experience of the individual (learning), but this remains a critical topic of future research if we are to really understand development.

Elman (1993) has done some connectionist simulations that clearly demonstrate the importance of these interactions. A neural network learns by back-propagation to predict the next word in a continuous text. The input to the network is the current word. The output is a prediction of what the next word will be. Elman (1990, 1991) has shown that by learning this task a network eventually incorporates in its internal organization much sophisticated linguistic knowledge that is acquired as a result of language learning, such as grouping of words (or, better, internal distributed representations of words) in useful classes and representing the syntactic structure of sentences. (Elman's prediction task might be an ecological task that children actually do in learning language if one assumes that children try to predict the next word in the sentences spoken by adults around them. The word subsequently heard functions as teaching input for back-propagation learning.)

To predict the next word in a text it is not sufficient to consider the current word but one must keep some memory trace of the words that have preceded the current word in the text. To this purpose Elman has introduced in his networks what he calls "context units" (see also Jordan, 1986). The activation value of each unit at cycle N is copied in one of these context units. Then, at cycle N + 1, the pattern of activation values of the context units is passed as input to the hidden units through distributed connections with learnable weights, together with the new input pattern. Hence, at each cycle the network responds (makes a prediction about the next word in the text) on the basis of both the current word and this cumulative memory trace of the preceding words (or, better, of the internal representations of the preceding words). The trace is cumulative because the memory mechanism is recursive and concerns an indefinite number of past words.

With this more sophisticated network architecture the task can be learned. However, the task remains a difficult one especially if the text includes long sentences. In fact, if a text that includes both short and long sentences is presented from the beginning of training, a network may not learn appropriately. A solution can be found if the training is divided up into phases and sentences of increasing length are presented as training material in successive phases. With this externally imposed training "diet" the networks do learn.

"Motherese" notwithstanding, however, children appear to be exposed to all kinds of language, in particular to both short and long sentences, from the beginning. How can they learn in these conditions? Elman suggests and tests through simulations an *internal* training "diet" hypothesis. The training text includes sentences of all lengths from the beginning, but the memory system of the network undergoes intrinsic changes during training. More specifically, during a first phase of training the memory span of the network is only two or three words. This is obtained by imposing a zero activation value to all context units each two or three cycles. Hence, only a memory trace of the last two/three words is kept by the network in these conditions. In successive phases of training, the memory span is increased to three/four, four/five, and so on, preceding words. In these conditions, the task can be learned. What appears to be taking place is that the system (the network, the child) is internally filtering the input in such a way that, although the objective input is of a certain type (and, as such, unlearnable), the effective input is graduated so that it becomes learnable. The network first learns short-term sequential contingencies in the text and then increasingly longer ones.

The key to this type of network-controlled solution might be the intrinsic (maturational) changes that are taking place in the memory system of the network. We can hypothesize that the inherited genotype of these networks includes developmental instructions that cause a progressive increase in the memory span of the network. This could be tested with simulations of the evolution of populations of networks with inherited genotypes of the type described in Section IV. As will be recalled, these genotypes specify a "unit development time" parameter for each of the network's units with the result that individual networks mature during their life. If a network's fitness depends on the amount learned in the text prediction task during life, we can expect the genotype of successful individuals to include maturational instructions for increasing the linguistic memory span of these individuals in successive epochs of life.

One term that is often used to denote the interaction between maturation and learning is phenotypical plasticity. An organism is said to exhibit phenotypical plasticity if the developmental instructions contained in its genotype do not form a closed system but are open to the external environment and to the individual's experience in the environment. Therefore, the outcome of development depends on these instructions but also on the environment/experience of the individual.

Phenotypical plasticity can be simulated with the developmental model described in Section IV. In that model one instruction contained in the genotype specified the epoch during the life of the individual in which a particular network's unit was to develop, that is, to grow its branching axon. Hence, neural and behavioral development were completely specified genetically and there was no phenotypical plasticity. However, we can modify the model and assume that what is specified in the genotype is only a threshold for growing a branching axon, whereas it depends on the environment/experience of the individual if and when this threshold is reached and the particular unit can actually grow its axon. The model assumes that the variability in the activation level of each network's unit in a succession of cycles is measured and the unit grows its branching axon only if this variability exceeds the genetically specified threshold (Nolfi et al., 1994).

Neural networks representing organisms that can develop either infrared sensors or light sensors or both were used in the simulations. (The neural network controls a small robot with a circular body, sensors distributed at the periphery of the body, and two wheels whose speed is separately controlled by the robot's nervous system.) A population of such organisms lives in an environment that in alternate generations allows the stimulation of only the infrared sensors to detect obstacles (dark environment) or of both the infrared and the light sensors (lighted environment). It turns out that individuals with different sensors, different structure of the nervous system, and different behavior develop in the two different environments (see Figures 15 and 16). Furthermore, the type of individuals that develop in each of the two environments are more effective in terms of fitness if tested at the end of life in the same environment in which they have developed than if tested in the other environment (Figures 17 and 18).

We conclude this section by referring to Elman's suggestion (Elman, 1993) that in the type of maturation/learning interaction he has explored with

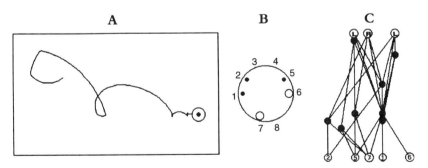

FIGURE 15 An evolved genotype developing in a lighted environment. (A) The path followed by the organism to reach the target (circle). (B) Sensors that have developed in the organism. Large empty circles represent light sensors. Small filled circles represent wall (obstacle) infrared sensors. (C) The organism's nervous system. Bottom-layer circles represent sensory neurons (numbers correspond to center figure). Upper-layer circles labeled L and R represent the motor neurons controlling the left and the right wheel, respectively, of the robot. The remaining layers represent internal neurons. (Nolfi, Miglino, & Parisi, 1994. Copyright © 1994 IEEE.)

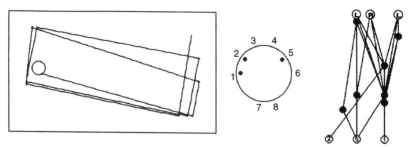

FIGURE 16 The same genotype of Figure 15 developing in a dark environment. (Nolfi, Miglino, & Parisi, 1994. Copyright © 1994 IEEE.)

his simulations there may lie another possible answer to the question: Why development? Development (maturation) may exist (in some animal species) because it makes learning possible. Individuals are not born as mature adults because in such case they could not filter the environmental input impinging on them. Less mature nervous systems can accomplish the important function of input filtering (e.g., through initially limited memory span), thereby making it possible to realize some otherwise impossible learning. In other simulations (Cecconi & Parisi, 1994) it has been shown that an initial period of reproductive immaturity in the life history of a population of organisms disappears evolutionarily if nothing useful happens during immaturity but is maintained if during immaturity the individual

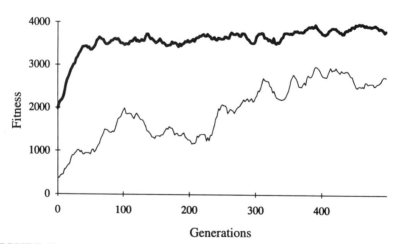

FIGURE 17 Fitness of the best individuals of successive generations that are tested in a lighted environment at the end of life. The thick curve represents the fitness of individuals that have developed in a lighted environment. The thin curve represents the fitness of individuals that have developed in a dark environment. (Nolfi, Miglino, & Parisi, 1994. Copyright © 1994 IEEE.)

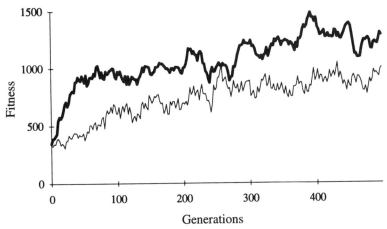

FIGURE 18   Fitness of the best individuals tested in a dark environment. The thick curve refers to individuals that have developed in a dark environment, the thin curve to individuals that have developed in a lighted environment. [Less fitness is in general obtained in a dark than in a lighted environment (cf. Figure 17) because there is less sensory information in the dark than in the lighted environment.] (Nolfi, Miglino, & Parisi, 1994. Copyright © 1994 IEEE.)

can learn some capacity that may increase its fitness as an adult. Furthermore, as it has been shown in this section, development can be used by evolution to produce plastic phenotypes that are adapted to the particular environment in which the individual organism happens to develop. These are all mechanisms through which evolution can create and maintain development.

VI. CONCLUSION

We have presented a certain number of computational models for simulating and analyzing changes in behavior that can occur in populations of organisms (evolution) or in individual organisms (maturation and learning). Since the same methodology (computer simulation) and the same theoretical framework (complex dynamic or adaptive systems) are adopted in developing and testing these models, these models not only can be used to deal with the various types of change separately at various levels (genetic, neural, behavioral), but they can help us analyze the important interactions that occur among different types of change. In particular, by using these models, one can analyze how evolution can create predispositions for learning, how learning can influence evolution, how evolution can result in genotypes that dictate changes during life (maturation), and how these maturational changes can interact with learned changes. (As already suggested, cultural change and its interaction with the other types of change can also be studied using these models.)

The basic model used in the simulations described in this chapter has been the neural network, a computational tool for analyzing structure and change in brain and behavior. However, neural networks have been viewed in this chapter in the perspective of artificial life, a perspective rather different from that of classical connectionism. Artificial life requires us to view neural networks as ecological networks, that is, as neural networks that live in an independent environment. By interacting with their environment neural networks partly determine their own input and can also change the external environment. Furthermore, the perspective of artificial life requires us to view neural networks as the nervous system of organisms that contain also an inherited genotype. The inherited genotype is the result of a process of evolution that can be modeled using a genetic algorithm. The inherited genotype dictates the main properties of the neural network. The process of mapping from the inherited genotype to the phenotypical neural network is development. However, the phenotypical network or, more precisely, the succession of phenotypical networks that constitutes development, is also influenced by the environment in which the organism lives and by the experiences of the individual in that environment. The environment of some organisms (humans) is radically changed by the organisms themselves and the changes are transmitted from one generation to the next, creating a second (cultural) inheritance mechanism besides the genetic inheritance mechanism (Boyd & Richerson, 1985).

All these properties of neural networks viewed in an artificial life perspective are crucial for studying all types of change that occur in organisms and in populations of organisms (and not only purely learned changes, as in classical connectionism) and, above all, the critical interactions among different types of change.

References

Bates, E., Elman, J. L. (1993). Connectionism and the study of change. In M. H. Johnson (Ed.), *Brain development and cognition*. Cambridge, MA: Blackwell.

Belew, R. K. (1993). Interposing an ontogenetic model between genetic algorithms and neural networks. In C. L. Giles, S. J. Hanson, & J. D. Cowan (Eds.), *Neural information processing systems 5*. San Mateo, CA: Morgan Kaufmann.

Belew, R. K., McInerney, J., & Schraudolph, N. N. (1991). Evolving networks: using the genetic algorithm with connectionist learning. In C. G. Langton, C. Taylor, J. D. Farmer, & S. Rasmussen (Eds.), *Artificial life II*. Reading, MA: Addison-Wesley.

Boyd, R., & Richerson, P. J. (1985). *Culture and the evolutionary process*. Chicago: University of Chicago Press.

Cangelosi, A., Parisi, D., & Nolfi, S. (1994). Cell division and migration in a "genotype" for neural networks. *Network, 5,* 497–515.

Cecconi, F., & Parisi, D. (1994). *Learning during reproductive immaturity in evolving populations of neural networks* (Rep. No. 94-05). Rome: Institute of Psychology, CNR.

Charlesworth, W. R. (1992). Darwin and developmental psychology. Past and present. *Developmental Psychology, 28,* 5–16.

Denaro, D., & Parisi, D. (1994). *Imitation and cultural transmission in populations of neural networks* (Rep. No. 94-06). Rome: Institute of Psychology, CNR.

Di Sano, S., Cecconi, F., & Parisi, D. (1993). *Eye-hand coordination in neural networks* (Rep. No. 95-04). Rome: Institute of Psychology, CNR.

Elman, J. L. (1990). Finding structure in time. *Cognitive Science, 14,* 179–211.

Elman, J. L. (1991a). Distributed representations, simple recurrent networks, and grammatical structure. *Machine Learning, 7,* 195–225.

Elman, J. L. (1993). Learning and development in neural networks: The importance of starting small. *Cognition, 48,* 71–99.

Gould, J. L. (1991). Exaptation: a crucial tool for an evolutionary psychology. *Journal of Social Issues, 3,* 43–65.

Hinton, G. E., & Nolan, S. J. (1987). How learning can guide evolution. *Complex Systems, 1,* 495–502.

Holland, J. J. (1975). *Adaptation in natural and artificial systems.* Ann Arbor: University of Michigan Press.

Hutchins, E., & Hazelhurst, B. (1995). How to invent a lexicon: the development of shared symbols in interaction. In N. Gilbert & R. Conte (Eds.), *Artificial societies: the computer simulation of social life.* London: UCL.

Inhelder, B., & Piaget, J. (1958). *The growth of logical thinking from childhood to adolescence.* New York: Basic Books.

Jordan, M. I. (1986). *Serial order: a parallel distributed processing approach* (Rep. No. 8604). San Diego: University of California, Institute for Cognitive Science.

Karmiloff-Smith, A. (1992). Nature, nurture, and PDP: preposterous developmental postulates? *Connection Science, 4,* 253–269.

Kolen, J. F., & Pollack, J. B. (1990). Backpropagation is sensitive to initial conditions. *Complex Systems, 4,* 269–280.

Langton, C. G. (1992). Artificial life. In L. Nadel & D. Stein (Eds.), *1991 Lectures in complex systems.* Reading, MA: Addison-Wesley.

McClelland, J. L. (1989). Parallel distributed processing: implications for cognition and development. In R. G. M. Morris (Ed.), *Parallel distributed processing: implications for psychology and neurobiology.* New York: Oxford University Press.

McClelland, J. L. (1992). *The interaction of nature and nurture in development: a parallel distributed processing perspective* (Rep. No. PDP.CNS.92.6). Pittsburgh, PA: Carnegie-Mellon University, Department of Psychology.

Miglino, O., Nolfi, S., & Parisi, D. (in press). Discontinuity in evolution: how different levels of organization imply pre-adaptation. In R. K. Belew & M. Mitchell (Eds.), *Plastic individuals in evolving populations.* Reading, MA: Addison-Wesley.

Miller, G. F., Todd, P. M., & Hegde, S. (1989). Designing neural networks using genetic algorithms. In J. D. Schaffer (Ed.), *Proceedings of the Third International Conference on Genetic Algorithms.* San Mateo, CA: Morgan Kaufmann.

Nolfi, S., Elman, J. L., & Parisi, D. (1994). Learning and evolution in neural networks. *Adaptive Behavior, 3,* 5–28.

Nolfi, S., Miglino, O., & Parisi, D. (1994). Phenotypic plasticity in evolving neural networks. In D. P. Gaussier & J.-D. Nicoud (Eds.), *From perception to action.* Los Alamitos, CA: IEEE Press.

Nolfi, S., & Parisi, D. (1992). *Growing neural networks* (Rep. No. 92-3). Rome: Institute of Psychology, CNR.

Nolfi, S., & Parisi, D. (1993). Self-selection of input for improving performance. In G. A. Bekey (Ed.), *Neural networks and robotics.* New York: Kluwer.

Nolfi, S., & Parisi, D. (1995a). Evolving neural networks that develop in time. In F. Moràn, A. Moreno, J. J. Moreno, & P. Chacon (Eds.), *Advances in artificial life.* New York: Springer.

Nolfi, S., & Parisi, D. (1995b). "Genotypes" for neural networks. In M. A. Arbib (Ed.), *Handbook of brain theory and neural networks*. Cambridge, MA: MIT Press.

Parisi, D., Cecconi, F., & Nolfi, S. (1990). Econets: neural networks that learn in an environment. *Network, 1,* 149–168.

Parisi, D., Nolfi, S., & Cecconi, F. (1992). Learning, behavior, and evolution. In F. Varela & P. Bourgine (Eds.), *Toward a practice of autonomous systems*. Cambridge, MA: MIT Press.

Pinker, S. (1991). Rules of language. *Science, 253,* 530–535.

Pinker, S., & Prince, A. (1988). On language and connectionism: analysis of a parallel distributed processing model of language acquisition. *Cognition, 28,* 73–193.

Plunkett, K., & Marchmann, V. (1991). U-shaped learning and frequency effects in a multi-layered perceptron: implications for child language acquisition. *Cognition, 38,* 43–102.

Plunkett, K., & Marchmann, V. (1993). From rote learning to system building. *Cognition, 48,* 21–69.

Plunkett, K., & Sinha, C. (1992). Connectionism and developmental theory. *British Journal of Developmental Psychology, 10,* 209–254.

Rumelhart, D. E., Hinton, G. E., & Williams, R. (1986). Learning internal representations by error propagation. In D. E. Rumelhart, J. L. McClelland, & PDP Research Group, *Parallel distributed processing: Explorations in the microstructure of cognition* (Vol. 1). Cambridge, MA: MIT Press.

Rumelhart, D. E., & McClelland, J. L. (1986). On learning the past tense of English verbs. In J. L. McClelland, D. E. Rumelhart, & PDP Research Group. *Parallel distributed processing: Explorations in the microstructure of cognition* (Vol. 2). Cambridge, MA: MIT Press.

Rumelhart, D. E., McClelland, J. L., & PDP Research Group. (1986). *Parallel distributed processing: Explorations in the microstructure of cognition* (Vol. 1). Cambridge, MA: MIT Press.

Siegler, R. S. (1981). Development sequences between and within concepts. *Monographs of the Society for Research in Child Development, 46*(Whole No. 189).

Wilson, S. W. (1987). The genetic algorithm and biological development. In *Proceedings of the Second International Conference on Genetic Algorithms*. Hillsdale, NJ: Erlbaum.

CHAPTER 12

Activity-Dependent Processes in Perceptual and Cognitive Development

Linda B. Smith
Donald B. Katz

The central philosophical question behind research in cognitive development is the origins of knowledge. The two classic philosophical answers are those of the British Empiricists who put the origins of knowledge in perception and those of the nativist-rationalists who place them in the innate structures of mind that interpret percepts. Virtually all contemporary theory rejects these two extremes in favor of their "interaction." But what is this interaction and what does it mean for the role of experience and perception in knowledge? Despite nods to interactionisms, the dominant theory in contemporary cognitive development is decidedly rationalist (e.g., Carey & Gelman, 1991; Spelke, 1990). Innate skeletal knowledge structures or "principles" are hypothesized that are either triggered by or guide the interpretation and selection of environmental "inputs" (R. Gelman, 1993; Markman, 1992).

The traditional rationalist perspective is being increasingly challenged, however: by philosophers such as M. Johnson (1987) and van Gelder (1992), by neuroscientists such as Freeman and Skarda (1985) and Edelman (1987), by linguists such as Lakoff (1987), by cognitive and computational psychologists such as Barsalou (1993) and Bates and Elman (1993), and by developmental psychologists such as Thelen and Smith (1994). These challenges

Perceptual and Cognitive Development
Copyright © 1996 by Academic Press, Inc. All rights of reproduction in any form reserved.

413

push for a fundamental reformation of the nature of perceiving, knowing, and developmental process.

In this chapter, we review the recent empirical advances that lie behind these challenges. We begin by considering the traditional view, which segregates timeless knowledge structures from the real-time processes of perceiving. We then consider new data about perceptual categories in the brain as activity-dependent processes. We then turn to the data on perceptual and category development in infants and young children and find parallel phenomena that suggest that perceiving and knowing in children are also made and maintained by activity.

I. WHAT IS KNOWLEDGE?

Traditional theories in cognitive psychology concentrate on the stability of cognition, how it is that people perform the same cognitive act over and over despite varying local circumstances. For example, each time a person encounters a frog, whether in a pond or in a comic strip, the encountered object is understood to be the same kind of thing, a frog. Traditional theory explains this stability by positing stable knowledge structures. According to this view, the reason that people understand the frog in the pond and the frog in the comic strip to be the same sort of thing is that in both cases they access a single representation, a concept of frog.

Figure 1 portrays an act of knowing in this view: a sensory event makes contact with the concept of frog and it is at the instant of contact—when perceiving activates permanent knowledge stores—that the individual may be said to "know" that it has seen a frog. In this traditional view, knowledge is like the entries in an encyclopedia. An act of knowing consists of reading the right entry. Traditional empiricist and rationalist views share these assumptions; they differ only in whether perception is seen as a major author of the entries.

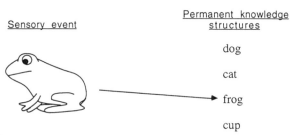

Sensory event

Permanent knowledge structures

dog

cat

frog

cup

FIGURE 1   An act of knowing in the traditional view: A sensory event contacts a knowledge structure.

The central challenge to the encyclopedia view of knowledge is the variability of cognition (e.g., R. Gelman & Greeno, 1989; Goldfield, 1993; Jones & Smith, 1993; Lakoff, 1987; Siegler, 1989). For example, when we encounter two frogs on two different occasions, we do not think *exactly* the same thing. Barsalou (1987) demonstrated this empirically; he found that when people read the word *frog* in isolation, they do not think "eaten by humans." But when *frog* is read in the context of French restaurant, they do think about people eating frogs. The precise nature of a cognitive act, understanding "frog," depends on the context. In brief, knowing is adaptively variable. It is not exactly like taking down the same old encyclopedia entry and using it in unmodified form time after time.

The fact of variability does not show that the traditional view is wrong. As Medin and Ortony (1989) wrote about Barsalou's results "care has to be taken not to equate instability in outputs or behavior with underlying or internal instability. Might it be that our underlying concepts are in fact stable . . . and that the apparent instability is an artifact of the processes that operate on these stable representations?" (p. 191). Medin and Ortony suggest the traditional solution to the stability-variability problem: stability has one cause and variability another. Their solution is summarized by the cartoon in Figure 2. There is a single stable concept of frog that is activated each time we encounter a frog and is the reason that there is a global similarity across each of these encounters. There are also real-time processes

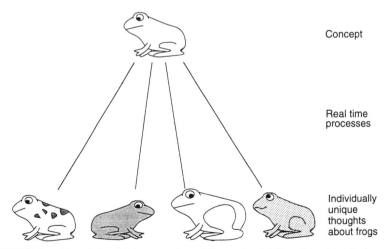

Concept

Real time
processes

Individually
unique
thoughts
about frogs

FIGURE 2   The relationship between the stability and variability of cognition in the traditional view of knowledge as representations.

that take the context-specific input and use it to access, adjust, and combine knowledge representations to fit the particular task at hand.

II. PERCEIVING AND KNOWING IN THE BRAIN

Several remarkable discoveries in neurophysiology and neurodevelopment argue against the solution to stability and variability presented in Figure 2. These findings suggest, instead, that stability and variability are the joint products of the real-time activity of complex dynamic systems. We review four of these recent advances in knowledge in this section.

A. Multimodal Processes

The traditional view of the mammalian brain is of a highly modular device in which sensory information is transmitted along parallel, modality-specific, "labeled lines" (Bullock & Horridge, 1965; Mountcastle, 1980). A central problem in this traditional view is explaining the unity of perception: How is it that sights, sounds, and felt actions are bound into a single experience? The traditional solution to this binding problem has been to assume that the diverse sensory streams are merged and integrated in the association areas of the cortex, at the top of the hierarchy of brain functioning. Recent neurophysiological evidence suggests that this view is wrong (see Damasio, 1989a; Ettlinger & Wilson, 1990; Thelen & Smith, 1994, for reviews). Although there is the primary organization of separate modalities, there is also rich interconnectivity in phylogenetically old and early-maturing systems as well as in phylogenetically new and late-maturing systems.

Research by Meredith and Stein (1987; Stein & Meredith, 1991) on the cat superior colliculus provides one example of the fundamentally multimodal nature of brain functioning. The superior colliculus is a major site involved in the integration of visual, auditory, and somatosensory space (Kandel, Schwartz, & Jessel, 1991; Stein & Arigbede, 1972). Textbooks describe the layers of the superior colliculus as exhibiting topographically organized responses to the location of the distal stimulus in space, with separate but connected topographic maps for each modality. Thus, the superior colliculus may bind modality-specific information about space by mapping the modality-specific topographic "representations" to each other.

Meredith and Stein's results suggest that this textbook understanding of the superior colliculus is not quite right: the coordination of sights, sounds, and touches is less a mapping of one kind of representation to the other than an intermeshing and integration of visual, auditory, and somatosensory inputs into a single multimodal pattern. Specifically, they found that the deep-layer topographic map of visual space in the cat superior colliculus is composed primarily of *multisensory neurons*, neurons that fire in response to auditory and somatic stimulation as well as visual stimulation. Indeed, two-thirds of these deep-layer cells accept corresponding spatial inputs from two or more modalities (Meredith, Clemo, & Stein, 1991). Given that individual units in the so-called modality-specific topographies respond to inputs from two or three modalities, Meredith and Stein argue that there are not just three aligned maps but also multimodal maps.

These findings have profound implications for how we understand sensory intercoordination. Put most boldly, brain activity that corresponds to seeing does not involve vision alone; rather, seeing depends on auditory and somatic events as well as visual ones. These results also suggest profound new ideas about what it means to know something, ideas very different from those depicted in Figure 1. The multisensory neurons in the cat's superior colliculus project to the brain centers that control the orientation of head, ear, and eyes. Thus, the cat "knows" to look toward sounds, not because it has a knowledge structure that is accessed when it hears something, but because in the *real-time* processes of perceiving, auditory events directly alter what one sees and where one looks. In the cat's multimodal map of space, knowing is created in the moment in the simultaneous influences of the modality-specific inputs on each other (Meredith, Wallace, & Stein, 1992).

B. Multimodal Forces on Development

The multimodal interconnectivity in the brain offers new insights into developmental process, insights that turn classic developmental puzzles upside-down. The traditional developmental question (like the traditional neuroscience question) has been the binding problem; given the separate modalities, how do infants come to perceive a unitary world? Consistent with traditional views of binding in the brain, Piaget (1952) placed intersensory coordination in the higher processes and proposed that infants slowly developed mappings from one modality to another. The current developmental evidence (like the current neurophysiological evidence) shows Piaget to be wrong. There is clear evidence of a kind of unity of the senses in newborns (Lewkowicz & Turkewitz, 1980; Mendelson & Haith, 1976) and compelling evidence of well-coordinated senses in slightly older infants (see reviews in Meltzoff, 1990; Rose & Ruff, 1987; Spelke, 1984). The contemporary *developmental* question is thus better reversed; instead of asking how development binds the senses, we might ask how early intersensory interactions make development.

The value of asking this second question is illustrated by Knudsen's (1984) work on the development of the optic tectum in barn owls. The optic tectum, as a homolog of the superior colliculus, is involved in the localization of sensory events, Knudsen found that the organization of auditory space in the optic tectum depends on visual experience. Altered auditory input (an ear plug in one ear that systematically distorts the binaural cues to location) leads to changes in responsivity of cells in the optic tectum and adaptively appropriate behavioral changes *if* there is concurrent visual and auditory input (Knudsen, 1984). If there is no visual information (e.g., the owl is in the dark), there is no reorganization. If the owl wears prisms that realign the visual world, auditory space is reorganized to fit visual space.

This visually guided reorganization of auditory space can, in adulthood, be seen in purely auditory nuclei (the inferior colliculus) only a few synapses "downstream" of the cochlea. Although this finding awaits further exploration, it is likely that reciprocal connectivity between the optic tectum and inferior colliculus drives the changes in the latter structure (Brainerd & Knudsen, 1993). In brief, vision appears to educate the localization of sound in the developing barn owl at many levels of the neural system.

These findings add to Meredith and Stein's by showing how multimodal processes may be calibrated through the act of perceiving, and in addition provide potential evidence pertaining to the importance of reciprocal connectivity as a basis for brain organization (see Section III below). They are similar to findings in other domains also showing intersensory interactions as a causal force in developmental process (e.g., Gottlieb, Tomlinson, & Radell, 1989; Lickliter, 1990; West & King, 1987).

C. Activity-Dependent "Structures"

Virtually all introductory psychology textbooks include a picture like that in Figure 3 of the brain, showing a homunculus lying across the somatosensory cortex. This little man has a large head, large hands, and a very large tongue representing the spatial organization of neural responsivity to tactile stimulation across the body. Textbook characterizations of this somatosensory map present it as highly stable, a hard-wired given in the perceptual repertoire. It is seductively easy to point to this structure as the cause, as the explanation, of why we are more sensitive to tactile stimulation at some parts of our bodies than at others. In this view, our fingertips are more sensitive than our elbows *because* there are more cortical cells devoted to a fingertip than to an elbow. Recent research has shown that this understanding is wrong. We are more sensitive to touch on our fingertips than our elbows and we have more cortical cells devoted to fingertips than elbows because we use our fingertips more than our elbows.

In an elegant series of experiments, Merzenich and colleagues (1984) have shown that the somatosensory homunculus is malleable, not set, even in mature organisms. In their studies of adult New World monkeys, they found that the size of the region in the somatosensory cortex responsive to a particular body area changes with experience, and changes fast. In the New

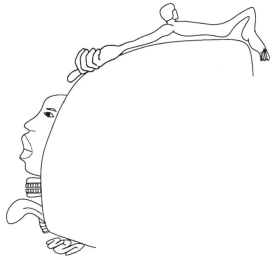

FIGURE 3   The map of responsitivity to stimulation across the somatosensory cortex.

World monkey (as in all primates) the area devoted to the hands and digits is large, with each digit delineated from the next. However, within hours of being deprived of sensory stimulation from one digit (by either cutting the nerve or amputating the digit), the homoncular map changes (Merzenich et al., 1984). The new map that emerges "represents" the new reality of one fewer digit; cells that had been deprived of stimulation become responsive to tactile stimulation on the adjacent finger.

Furthermore, such changes in the homunculus do not require traumatic alterations such as the loss of a finger; they also emerge as the consequence of relatively small changes in use. Monkeys who learn to perform a task requiring the fine discrimination of stimulation at one site evolve larger cortical areas devoted to that site (Recanzone, Merzenich, Jenkins, Grajski, & Dinse, 1992). Monkeys who have two digits sutured together so that they move and explore the world as one develop a cortical organization that conjoins responsivity to the two (S. A. Clark, Allard, Jenkins, & Merzenich, 1988). These studies have also shown that reorganization depends critically on active manual exploration and discrimination. If, for example, monkeys actively make fine discriminations to secure food, then the perceptual experiences engender larger cortical areas for the digits involved. If, however, the monkeys passively receive the very same stimulation, there is little reorganization.

Again, these results challenge old ideas about what knowledge is. Knowing in the somatosensory cortex is an *ongoing product* of perceiving and acting, a self-organizing event in time that depends on the immediate history of its own activity. Merzenich's results are all the more profound because this fluidity of organization is not a unique function of the representation of the hand, or even of the somatosensory cortex; dynamic maintenance of cortex has been documented in a variety of sensory regions and species (e.g., Kaas, 1991; Pons et al., 1991; Singer, 1990).

D. Dynamic Categories

Knowledge that is the ongoing product of perceiving and the history of perceiving will be both stable and variable. It will be stable to the degree that the experienced world does not change; but it will be adaptively variable and reorganize when the experienced world does change. In a remarkable series of experiments, Freeman and colleagues (Freeman, 1981, 1991; Skarda & Freeman, 1987) showed how olfactory categories are stable and variable in just this way. They studied how groups of neurons in the olfactory bulb of rabbits respond to categories of smells. They found that different inhalants did not map to any single neuron or even group of neurons but rather to the spatial pattern of the amplitude of waves across the entire olfactory bulb. However, there was no permanent one-to-one relation between odor category and pattern of activity. Each time the rabbit sniffed a particular odorant *under the same conditions,* that odorant produced the same global pattern of activity. But the pattern of activity in the olfactory bulb that corresponded to a particular odor changed with context, the rabbit's state, and the rabbit's history. The changes in patterns of activity corresponding to particular odorants were particularly dramatic after new experiences. For example, in one study, rabbits were conditioned to associate the scent of sawdust with a particular reinforcement. After this learning there was a new characteristic pattern of olfactory bulb activity associated with the scent of sawdust. When, however, the rabbits were taught to recognize the odor of banana, a new characteristic pattern emerged *for sawdust* as well as for banana. The rabbits' behavioral response to sawdust still looked the same as in the prebanana period. But that apparent stability in outward behavior—the categorization of sawdust before and after training about bananas—did not rest on a constant underlying structure or a constant state of brain activity. Learning about a new smell reorganized the patterns of activity corresponding to known smells.

The fact that the pattern of activity to a single odor changes when other odors are learned directly opposes traditional ideas about representation in the brain. Since Hubel and Wiesel's (1963) discovery of cortical cells responsive to particular line orientations and motions, it has seemed likely that representation in the brain consists of fixed structures that respond to particular kinds of events in the world. If these patterns of response are stable and context *in*sensitive, then these internal patterns of activity might be said to *stand for,* that is, to represent in the classic sense, events in the world. This kind of stability and context sensitivity does not appear to characterize the olfactory bulb in rabbits. The waves of neuronal firing in the olfactory bulb in response to the smell of sawdust do not *stand for* sawdust. Rather, the pattern of activity that emerges when sawdust is smelled depends on the immediate sensory input and the idiosyncratic history of smells experienced *up to that moment in time.*

E. Summary: Activity-Dependent Processes

The findings about intersensory organization, the somatosensory homunculus, and olfactory categories are examples of activity-dependent neural and developmental processes in which knowledge resides in the real-time processes of perceiving. In this way, knowing in the brain seems fundamentally not like that depicted in Figures 1 and 2. These findings emphasize the activity-dependent nature of all biological processes, including development. As Gottlieb (1991a, 1991b) concluded, there may be *no* predetermined epigenesis at any level: "To the extent that it is now recognized that activity is likely involved in all aspects of neural and behavioral development, there is quite possibly no nonexperiential component in such development, and this extends to the genetic level as indicated by the newly introduced term *activity-dependent expression*" (1991b, p. 33). These results also illustrate Oyama's (1985) powerful arguments about the pointlessness of all forms of nature–nurture debates that ignore the dynamic status of living organisms in which causality between internal and external events is mutual, complexly interdependent, and continuous.

III. SELF-MODIFYING SYSTEMS

Computer simulations of the activity-dependent developmental processes suggested by the advances in neuroscience are appearing with increasing frequency (e.g., Bienenstock & von der Malsburg, 1987; Dehaene, Changeux, & Nadal, 1987; Yao & Freeman, 1990). Since these are of potential theoretical importance to cognitive developmentalists, we briefly review one example of such theorizing, Edelman's Theory of Neuronal Group Selection (1987). We chose to present Edelman's model over others for three reasons: first, the model in its simplest form is easily understood and does not require detailed knowledge of neural tracts and brain areas; second, Edelman has specifically applied his model to human cognition and development; and third, Thelen and Smith (1994) offered an extension of this model in their dynamic systems account of human development.

Edelman's theory starts by recognizing that the brain at birth is the product of evolutionary process and the developmental processes of embryology. Thus, at birth, the brain is a complex system made up of many *heterogeneous, overlapping, interacting, and densely connected* subsystems (or, in Edelman's terms, neuronal groups). Development occurs through a self-organizing selectionist and actively dependent process; active connections are maintained and strengthened.

Reeke and Edelman (1984) built a simple computational device to illustrate the core ideas of the theory. The device's task was to learn to recognize all varieties of the letter A, *from mere experience of seeing A's.* Figure 4 provides a schematic illustration of their device. There is no teacher; the device self-educates itself through the interaction of two subsystems as they *simultaneously* process the same physical stimulus. In the feature-analysis subsystem, line detectors are excited by corresponding patterns of stimulation. In the tracing subsystem, information about shape is gained through the movements involved in tracing the letter. The developmental power is in the coupling of these two independent processes in real time. At the same time that the feature analyzer is analyzing features, the shape tracer is extracting a global description of shape. The outputs of these two heterogenous processes, at every step in real time, are mapped onto each other.

In Reeke and Edelman's device, there are actually four mappings being accomplished simultaneously in real time. One mapping, the feature analysis map, maps an input letter to a list of features. The second mapping, the tracing map, maps the input letter to the action sequences of a continuous tracing of the letter. The third and fourth mappings are what Edelman calls the re-entrant maps; they map the activities in the two subsystems to each other. Thus, two independent mappings of the stimulus to internal activity take *qualitatively different* glosses on the perceptual information and through their re-entrant connections, by being correlated in real time, they educate

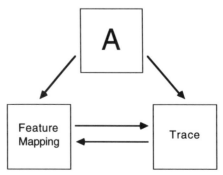

FIGURE 4   Two coupled systems in Reeke and Edelman's (1984) model of category learning.

each other. Reeke and Edelman's simulation successfully taught itself to recognize A's and B's from merely seeing them. In a more complex instantiation of these basic ideas, Edelman (1987) also modeled Merzenich's findings about reorganization in the somatosensory cortex.

The importance of Edelman's theory is that it offers a new conceptualization of the role of perceiving in knowing, one that unifies immediate perceptual experience, the recent history of perceptual experience, the lifetime developmental history of the individual, and the evolutionary history of the species. All these time scales are unified in the behavior *at each moment in real time*. We can see this by thinking about how the activity of each subsystem in Reeke and Edelman's model of letter recognition embody, at once, the influence of all time scales. For example, the activity of the feature subsystem, at each moment in time, t_n, depends on: (1) the sensory input to that system at that time; (2) the activity of the feature subsystem in the just preceding moment in time, t_{n-1}; (3) the activity of the tracing system in the just preceding moment in time, t_{n-1}; (4) the connection strengths between (and within) the subsystems, which embody the developmental history of the individual; and (5) the organization (and fact of) the coupled subsystems themselves, which embody the evolutionary history of the species. In this way, the pattern of activity across the coupled neuronal groups unites in a single moment, real time, developmental time, and evolutionary time. The activity of the system is *always* dependent on *all* of these and is not coherently divisible into what is learned and what is innate, nor into what is constant and what is variable.

Edelman's conception may be the most large-scale, intuitively understandable attempt to join activity dependence in the brain with learning and development. As we have mentioned, however, it is not the only recent model to do so. Changeux and Dehaene have recently explained performance in several tasks, including the A-not-B task, with models that learn under similar principles to those suggested by Edelman (Dehaene & Changeux, 1992; Dehaene et al., 1987). In addition, Freeman has modeled his data on the rabbit olfactory system (Yao & Freeman, 1990). Other theorists treating massive interactions and self-organization as tools for learning in dynamic and connectionist modeling include (but are not limited to) Crick and Koch (1990), Damasio (1989b), Sompolinsky and Kanter (1986), and Tsuda (1991).

Edelman (1987) used the basic ideas of his model to reinterpret selected results from human perceptual development, including Kellman and Spelke's (1983) findings that young babies do not perceive separate objects as separate unless the separate objects are seen moving independently relative to one another. Kellman and Spelke obtained their results in experiments in which 4-month-olds were habituated to a rod whose top and bottom were visible but whose center was occluded by a box as illustrated in Figure 5. Kellman and Spelke investigated various habituation displays: the rod moved; the block moved; the rod and block moved together; no movement. The test displays, also illustrated in Figure 5, consisted of a single rod or the two pieces of a rod, and across experiments these test displays either oscillated or were stationary. The question was whether the infant perceived a single unitary rod or two rod pieces as more different from the habituating event. The results were unambiguous; broken rods were perceived as different and unitary rods as similar only when test objects moved and only when the ends of the habituation rod had moved in common translation behind the occluder. Early in development, the boundary of an object, whether there is one object or two, is defined by motion.

Spelke (1990) interpreted these results in line with the framework in Figure 1: The sensory experiences engendered by common motion contacted the knowledge structures that defined unitary perceptual objects. Indeed, Spelke suggested that these results are consistent with innate knowledge structures that define distinct objects in terms of *represented principles* of motion. However, the evidence does not demand this conclusion; the use of motion cues by infants could be no more innate nor indicative of a pregiven knowledge structure than is the somatosensory homunculus.

Thelen and Smith (1994) proposed a Reeke and Edelman-like model to

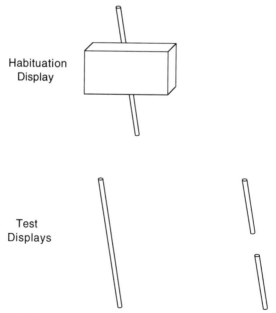

FIGURE 5   Habituation and test events in Kellman and Spelke's (1983) experiment.

explain Kellman and Spelke's results. Their model, illustrated in Figure 6, is made up of two hypothetical coupled and interacting subsystems: the what subsystem maps the static properties of objects (colors, line segments) to internal activity and the where subsystem maps tracking movements to internal activity. Thelen and Smith showed how object segregation could emerge *in task,* in the time-locked cross-relations of perceived edges, textures, and movements. They also showed how generalized expectations about the unitary nature of the objects (and the developmentally later use of static cues to segregate objects) could emerge from repeated experiences of the kinds presented in the experiment, that is, experiences of objects moving.

Thelen and Smith's developmental account is reminiscent of earlier system approaches to development (Bertanfly, 1968; Waddington, 1956; Werner, 1957) and an example of a resurgence of this form of theorizing in developmental psychology (Bates & MacWhinney, 1987; Fogel, 1993; Goldfield, 1993; Oyama, 1985; Saltzman & Munhall, 1992; Thelen, 1989; Tucker & Hirsh-Pasek, 1993).

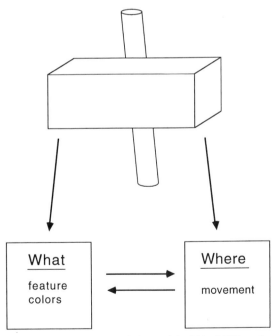

FIGURE 6   Two coupled systems in Thelen and Smith's (1994) explanation of Kellman and Spelke's (1983) results.

IV. ACTIVITY-DEPENDENT DEVELOPMENT: INFANTS AND CHILDREN

In this section, we present a necessarily selective sampling of the relevant developmental literature. Notably absent from our review but pertinent are the extensive literatures on the role of experience in speech perception (e.g., Cooper & Aslin, 1989; Jusczyk, 1992) and attention to prosodic cues (e.g., Fernald & Kuhl, 1987; Kemler-Nelson, Hirsh-Pasek, Jusczyk, & Wright Cassidy, 1989), motor development (e.g., Thelen & Ulrich, 1991), interactions between perception and action systems (Adolph, Eppler, & Gibson, 1993a, 1993b; Bingham, Schmidt, Turvey, & Rosenblum, 1991; Gibson, 1988), and the changes in perceptual learning that emerge with expertise (e.g., Biederman & Shiffrar, 1987; Gibson & Walk, 1956; K. E. Johnson, 1992; Mervis, Johnson, & Scott, 1993; Peron & Allen, 1988). We chose to present here findings from the developmental literature that most closely parallel the recent advances in the biology of knowing.

A. Auditory Effects on Visual Behavior

Shortly after birth, newborns look in the direction of sound (Mendelson & Haith, 1976; Wertheimer, 1961). With development, subtle sound properties and their relation to visual events take control of visual attention such that infants *look* at the visual event that matches what they *hear*. For example, given two visual displays of bouncing balls, 4-month-olds look at the display that is in temporal synchrony with the sound of a bouncing ball (Spelke, 1979). Given faces making vowel sounds, 4-month-olds look at the face that matches the vowel sound they hear (Kuhl & Meltzoff, 1982). The specific kinds of auditory and visual events that control looking behavior develop to involve fine details of temporal synchrony and rhythm (Lewkowicz, 1994) and highly complex correlations such as those that exist between emotional voices and emotional faces (Walker-Andrews, 1988; Walker-Andrews & Lennon, 1991). As Morrongiello (1994) concluded in her review of this literature, *where* infants look is controlled by *what* they hear; all that changes is the complexity of the controlling correspondences. Most developmentalists' interest in the auditory control of looking has been in terms of its use as an experimental paradigm through which sensitivity to various cross-modal correspondences can be documented. However, the phenomenon itself provides a cogent example of what activity-dependent and cascading developmental process might look like.

The presence of sound may also control the depth and kind of visual processing that occurs. There is clear evidence from adult studies that sight–sound correspondences serve *both* to bring visual targets into foveal view and to speed visual processing and object identification (Perrot, Saberi,

Brown, & Strybel, 1990). There is some suggestive evidence from new-borns. Castillo and Butterworth (1981; see also Butterworth, 1981) reported that newborns made more eye movements to spatially coincident sounds and sights than to a sound alone or to sights and sounds presented on contralateral sides. Moreover, infants habituated more rapidly to the visual stimulus spatially coincident with sound than to the visual event alone or to the visual event spatially separated from the sound. In other words, babies seemed to learn about a visual event faster when it was spatially joined with a sound (see Morrongiello, 1994, on this point). The facilitated visual processing that appears to result from temporally and spatially unified visual and auditory events is precisely the kind of phenomenon expected by Edelman's theory.

Some recent findings concerning the effects of naming on children's visual attention to objects also illustrate how auditory control over visual attention may contribute to a self-organizing developmental process. In the first study of this kind, Baldwin and Markman (1989) examined 10- to 14-month-old children's visual attention to objects in the context of: (1) an adult naming the object; (2) an adult talking to another adult; or (3) an adult pointing to the object. They found that infants *looked at* the object more in the context in which it was being named. Baldwin and Markman interpret the data as showing that children this age possess knowledge that names are labels for objects, but acknowledge that given the distinctive prosodic properties of naming (particularly in speech to children, e.g., Fernald, 1984; Jusczyk, 1992), the results could also be due to a direct auditory effect on visual attention.

This second possibility is supported by findings of Roberts (1994; Roberts & Jacobs, 1991; see also Waxman & Hall, 1993). In their study of 13- to 15-month-olds, Roberts and Jacobs found that naming objects and a musical recording of children's songs had the same beneficial effects on children's looking behavior. However, the ideas that sounds and naming organize visual attention may both be correct. From an activity-dependent view of developmental process, it makes sense that an effect of naming on looking might grow out of an effect of sound on looking: If children begin looking at what they hear, and if they acquire from that activity new couplings between hearing and looking such that their looking is controlled by increasingly subtle complex "matches" to what they hear, then they might *develop* attention to concrete objects in the context of naming.

If hearing and seeing interact so strongly in the control of visual attention and if these interactions are causal forces in developmental process, then the uncoupling of seeing and hearing should change the developmental trajectory. From the view of development as a self-organizing system, such uncoupling need not lead to an ultimately different outcome nor necessarily to cognitive deficits. But if the processes of change are driven by interactions among the sensory systems, then alterations to one sensory modality, or the loss of input from a modality, should cause the system to reorganize and alter the causal sequence of events that is development. Recent research on visual attention in the deaf provides intriguing support for these ideas. Profoundly deaf individuals develop both in the context of the loss of species-typical experiences associated with hearing and in the context of altered visual experiences, especially those associated with the complex visuospatial nature of sign language.

Neville and her associates have provided strong evidence in support of the conclusion that growing up deaf leads to different outcomes in *visual processing*. In one study, she found that event-related potentials (ERP) in response to peripheral visual events were two to three times larger for deaf than for hearing subjects; the ERPs did not differ for visual events presented in the fovea (Neville, Schmidt, & Kutas, 1983). Moreover, she showed that deaf adults responded faster than hearing subjects in tasks requiring detection of movement in the periphery but again did not differ from hearing subjects in the detection of movement presented to the fovea. There are two differences in deaf individuals' experiences that may be relevant to this outcome. First, it may be the lack of auditory input per se that fosters heightened peripheral sensitivity. Second, it may be the altered visual experiences engendered by sign language that foster the changes in visual processing. Neville and Lawson (1987) provided information about the role of these two aspects of deaf individuals' experiences by studying hearing adults who were the children of deaf parents and who had learned sign language at an early age. These hearing adults' sensitivity to motion was comparable to that of typically hearing adults who do not know sign language; that is, there was no heightened sensitivity to the detection of motion in the peripheral visual field. This result suggests that it is the *loss of auditory* experiences that in some way causes the heightened *visual* sensitivity in the periphery.

How might the lack of auditory experience alter the development of visual attention? Neville (1990) points to the competition between visual and auditory processes in typical neural development and suggests that the loss of audition allows for the increased growth and activity of the visual sensory system, which in turn results in heightened sensitivity to peripheral motion. Another and compatible possibility is that the lack of auditory input presents the developing deaf child with a different attentional task and, in performing this altered task, heightened peripheral sensitivity develops (see Dittmar, Berch, & Warm, 1982, for related ideas and results). This idea makes sense when one thinks about hearing individuals' typical use of sound to monitor events outside their immediate direction of gaze. Without such auditory information to keep track of potentially relevant events around them, deaf children may develop an alternative solution: heightened sensitivity to events in the periphery in order to shift attention to those events should new information present itself there. (See Arbib, 1972; Posner & Cohen, 1980; Posner & Rothbart, 1980, for further discussions of potential links between peripheral vision and the control of eye movements.)

Quittner and colleagues (Katz & Mitchell, 1993; Mitchell & Quittner, 1996; Quittner, Smith, Osberger, Mitchell, & Katz, 1995) have also reported evidence suggesting a role for auditory input in the development of visual attentional processes. Using a continuous visual performance task in which no sounds were involved, 6- to 14-year-old children were asked to respond to certain sequences of (foveated) visual events but not to respond to others. Quittner et al. found that profoundly deaf children showed a substantially poorer performance at all age levels, such that the oldest deaf children performed more poorly than 6-year-old hearing children. However, deaf children who had received a cochlear implant and had used it for at least one year "caught up" with the developmental trajectory of hearing children. A cochlear implant digitizes sound and stimulates the cochlea at different points, thus providing direct input about acoustic events. This stimulation may directly influence the development of visual processing. In a longitudinal study, Quittner et al. (1995) found that the gains in visual processing occurred in the first 18 months after implant—more rapidly than postimplant changes in language and speech processing, which occur 2 to 3 years after implant. These results suggest a powerful developmental effect of auditory input on visual attentional processes: Children who develop without auditory input show deficits in visual selective attention and when such children are "made to hear" through an auditory prosthesis, they show rapid and substantial gains in visual processing.

Studies of deaf individuals' visual performance also demonstrate the activity-dependent nature of development within a modality, and the effects of fluency in a visual language on visual processing. Right-handed hearing individuals are better at detecting motion in the left visual field but better at processing language (e.g., written words) in the right visual field. Neville and Lawson (1987) found, in contrast, that deaf adults who had learned sign language early showed a right-visual-field advantage for detecting *motion and words* (see Corina, Kritchevsky, & Bellugi, 1992, for a related result). For deaf individuals, language and the detection of motion are coupled activities. Thus, the reorganization reported by Neville and Lawson is precisely the kind expected by an activity-dependent developmental process in which development itself is powered by the activity of perceiving.

B. Self-Locomotion and Spatial Orientation

If, as the results of Merzenich, Knudsen, and Freeman suggest, knowledge emerges in the activity of perceiving and *changes* with changes in perceptual experience, then the onset of self-produced movements should be a powerful force on perceptual and cognitive development. Infants who sit just looking have different perceptual experiences than infants who can reach, grasp toys, and bring them to their mouths. Once infants can reach, for example, they can *provide themselves* with new multimodal experiences involving vision, haptic exploration, and proprioceptive input from self-movement. Bushnell and Boudreau (1993) have specifically suggested that the development of haptic sensitivities is a consequence of exploratory activity.

These ideas suggest that dramatic changes in cognition should occur when infants begin to self-locomote. Self-locomotion drastically alters the nature of perceptual experiences, recruiting new couplings of heterogeneous processes and yielding new kinds of time-locked multimodal experience. The importance of self-produced movement in perceptual development has been long known (e.g., Gibson, 1969; Held & Hein, 1963). We specifically review here recent evidence from the research program of Bertenthal and Campos (1990) who have shown in a variety of studies how the onset of self-locomotion forces qualitative shifts in perception and cognition.

In one study, Bertenthal, Campos, and Barrett (1984) examined the role of self-locomotion on infants' ability to correctly adjust their spatial responses when their own location changed. Three groups of same-age infants were tested: infants who could crawl, infants who could not crawl but had extensive experience in a walker, and infants who could neither crawl nor had walker experience. The task involved training infants to anticipate an interesting event in one location. After training, the infant was moved to the opposite side of the room. The question was whether infants would turn their head in the proper allocentric direction. Infants with crawling and walker experience turned to the objectively correct location, even though it meant turning in the opposite direction relative to their own body. Infants without self-locomotion experience turned egocentrically, not taking account of their changed position relative to the interesting event. These results suggest that the experience of moving oneself about in space educated processes of judging where objects are relative to where the self is (see Acredolo, 1985; Acredolo, Adams, & Goodwyn, 1984, for related results; see Thelen & Smith, 1994, for a fuller theoretical account).

Another developmental phenomenon that appears critically related to the onset of self-locomotion is the A-not-B error (Bertenthal & Campos, 1990; Thelen & Smith, 1994). This hide-and-seek task was invented by Piaget (1952) to study the development of the object concept. In the task, the experimenter hides a tantalizing object in location A, for example, under a bucket on the right, while the infant watches. After some time, usually several seconds, the infant is allowed to search for the object. After several such experiences, there is the critical test trial: the experimenter hides the object in a new location, location B, under a bucket on the left. Children between the ages of 7 and 12 months often fail to search in the new location (B) and search instead in the first location (A). The frequency of failure decreases steadily with age during this period and at each age increases regularly with the length of the delay between the hiding of the object and the moment when the infant is allowed to search (Diamond, 1990; Wellman, Cross, & Bartch, 1986).

Bertanthal et al. (1984) and Kermoian and Campos (1988) showed that success in this task was also related to the self-locomotory status of the infant. Infants who crawled or used walkers were more successful at younger ages than children who did not yet self-locomote. Bertenthal and Campos (1990) showed further that it is the experience in self-locomotion and not some developmental correlate of when children begin self-locomoting that promotes success in the A-not-B task. They experimentally provided noncrawling children with experience in a walker and found measurably improved performance in the A-not-B task for these children. More critically, Kermoian and Campos (1988) showed that not all forms of self-locomotion are associated with increased success in this task. Infants who were belly crawlers were no better than nonlocomoting infants, no matter how long they had been crawling in this manner. This fact makes sense if it is *the multimodal experiences* engendered by self-movement that cause developmental change. Belly crawlers move with their head and faces close to the floor and may not get the varied visual experience of viewing spatial locations (and their changed relations to self and other objects) as a function of movement.

C. Word Learning

Thus far we have reviewed evidence from human perceptual development and multimodal interactions that closely parallel the findings on the dynamic nature of perceptual processes in the brain. Here, we consider evidence on children's changing novel word interpretations that presents intriguing similarities to Freeman's findings about the nonstationariness of olfactory categories in rabbits. The findings on word learning also serve as a transition to the next section on the role of perceptual processes in conceptual development.

Word learning is a form of category learning and one that young children do quite well. Indeed, young children add new words to their vocabulary so fast that many have concluded that they must learn words from hearing them used just once in context (Carey, 1982; Markman, 1989). But this poses a perplexing problem; how, for example, from seeing one chair and hearing it called *chair* can a child know what other objects are also called *chair?*

Studies of novel word interpretation attempt to answer this question by presenting children with a novel object, naming the object with a novel name, and then asking the children what other objects are also called by this name. One robust finding in these tasks is that children as young as 24 months principally name objects by their shape (e.g., Imai, Gentner, & Uchida, 1994; Jones, Smith, & Landau, 1991; Landau, Jones, & Smith, 1988; L. B. Smith, Jones, & Landau, 1992; Soja, Carey, & Spelke, 1991). This finding is so robust that some have conjectured that it represents innate "ontological" knowledge about categories (e.g., Soja et al. 1991).

Landau et al. (1988), in contrast, hypothesized that this shape bias is learned in the course of learning words. Consistent with this idea, Jones, Smith, Landau, and Gershkoff-Stowe (1992) showed in a longitudinal study that the shape bias emerged in individual children between 18 and 24 months and emerges *after* the individual child has more than fifty object names in his or her productive vocabulary. This fact suggests that children must learn a number of object names before a generalized attention to shape in naming develops.

Further research has shown the shape bias to be developmentally nonstationary, highly context dependent, and continually changing as a consequence of word learning. Jones and Smith (1993) summarized the results across a variety of novel word interpretation studies with the developmental curves in Figure 7. The studies they summarized examined children's performances at a variety of ages and in tasks involving novel adjectives ("a daxy one") as well as novel nouns (Landau, Jones, & Smith, 1992; L. B. Smith et al., 1992), studies that asked children only to make "likeness" judgments and not to interpret novel words (e.g., Smith et al., 1992) and studies that challenged the shape bias by putting glittery colors (Smith et al., 1992) or eyes (Jones et al., 1991) on the objects. The results across these studies show that the shape bias changes with development, becoming more robust, more specific to count nouns, and more context dependent.

The continually changing nature of children's novel word interpretations suggests that the shape bias does not result from a fixed knowledge structure. Rather, the data suggest that each word learned is both a product of a complex system created by the history of prior words learned and a causal force that changes the system and thus future novel word interpretations. This pattern of development is thus like the dynamic olfactory categories in rabbits found by Freeman: both sets of results suggest "a mind in motion" constantly changing itself to fit the whole of its experiences.

The direction of development in Figure 7 is also noteworthy because it is toward increasing variability and increasing context sensitivity, a direction seemingly at odds with the traditional view of development as toward increasingly abstract and stable representations. However, it is a developmental direction consistent with Barsalou's example, of *frog* and *French restaurant* presented at the beginning of this chapter. Intelligent behavior, the

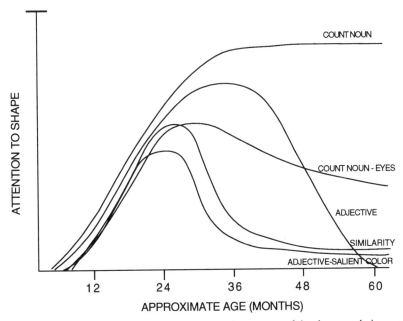

FIGURE 7 Jones and Smith's (1993) theoretical summary of developmental changes in the strength of shape bias.

product of development, may not be best viewed as doing (or thinking) the same thing over and over.

In an important recent study, Imai, Gentner, and Uchida (1994) showed that 3- and 5-year-old children also do not "do" the "same thing" each time they categorize, but rather adjust their responses in what are likely to be adaptively smart ways. They presented children with pictures of well-known objects such as those in Figure 8. In one condition, the children were asked what object "went with" the cake and they chose the functionally relevant gift. In another condition, the children were asked what object would have the "same name" as the picture of cake in a pretend "dinosaur" language and they chose the same-shaped hat as most likely to have the same name. Finally, all the children knew that both the cake and pie were desserts and for eating. These results tell us that children's cognitions are adaptively variable. When seeing the picture of cake, the children did not open and use without modification a single encyclopedic entry; they did not think just one kind of thought. Rather, they adjusted what they attended to and thought about to fit the task at hand.

Lakoff (1987) used the concept of *mother* to argue that all human cognition is adaptively variable in this way. By Lakoff's analysis, people possess

FIGURE 8   Simplified drawing of the kinds of stimuli sets by Imai, Gentner, and Uchida (1994).

at least the following conflicting models of *mother:* (1) the birth model, the person giving birth is the mother; (2) the genetic model, the female who contributed the genetic material is the mother; (3) the nurturance model, the female who nurtures and raises a child is the mother; and (4) the marital model, the wife of the father is the mother. Lakoff points to sentences such as *I was adopted* and *don't know who my real mother is and I'm not a nurturant person so I don't think I could be a real mother to any child* to show that people know all these models and use them despite the fact they do not agree and do not pick out the same person as the mother. Moreover, people use these models creatively in such metaphors as "Necessity is the mother of invention" and "We all want our boyfriends to mother us."

Lakoff (1987) uses this example to argue against the model of knowing in Figures 1 and 2: the traditional model can be retained only if we: (1) pick one definition of mother as the single represented knowledge structure and let the others be context-dependent variants and the products of real-time processes; or (2) posit that all definitions of mother are represented and that real-time processes select the appropriate one. Either way, the bulk of the work in knowing *mother* will lie in the context-dependent processes, not in the stable knowledge structures. According to Lakoff, the multiple and conflicting meanings of mother are not problematic if knowledge is viewed as embodied—a *living* process that is creative and variable because it emerges in the interactions of multiple disjunctive glosses on the same reality.

V. CONCEPTUAL DEVELOPMENT

Developmental psychologists traditionally pit the perceptual, context-dependent, and variable against the conceptual, context-independent, and stable, with the former being immature and the latter mature (see, e.g., Keil, 1989; L. B. Smith & Heise, 1993). The findings about development that we have reviewed here suggest that such a partition, like the traditional partition between nature and nurture, may not capture the full complexity of cognition or developmental process. In this section, we briefly consider recent theoretical arguments and findings suggesting that higher mental functioning may be a direct consequence of perceiving.

A. Embodied Concepts

M. Johnson (1987) has presented compelling arguments that even abstract and scientific concepts have their origins and continued meaning in bodily experience, in perceiving and acting. As one example, Johnson cites our generalized experience of *physical containment* as one important force on people's thinking. He notes how statements such as *I don't want to leave any relevant data out of my argument* are based on and understood in terms of our authentic experiences with real containers. There is no physical presence of data in an argument, but people *construe* an argument to be like a container and "data" to be like things that can be put in or taken out. This idea, that our most abstract forms of knowing emerge in the mundane of everyday perceiving and acting, is one with a long tradition in developmental psychology and one with contemporary support. Johnson's ideas share much, for example, with Piaget's (1952) theory of sensorimotor development, which places the origins of number, reciprocity, and classification in the activities of infants and children in their daily lives. R. Gelman's (1972; R. Gelman & Gallistel, 1978) elegant work on the origins of number concepts in children's counting is consistent with these ideas (see also Ascher, 1991; Fuson, 1988), as are recent cross-cultural analyses of the body-centered nature of human counting systems. Also particularly consistent with Johnson's ideas are Mandler's (1988, 1992) detailed theoretical analyses of the origins of the concepts of animate and inanimate in perceived motion.

B. The Perceived Products of Behavior

The development of spatial classification provides another possible example of the activity-dependent origins of abstract ideas. People commonly display their knowledge of object categories by grouping objects in space—by, for example, putting all the boxes close together in one pile and all the balls close together in another pile. Such spatial classifications are symbolic behaviors in that nearness is used to *stand for* similarity and farness to *stand for* dissimilarity. The use of space to represent similarities was recognized by Inhelder and Piaget (1964) as an indicator of higher intellectual functioning and is a widely used measure of intellect in standardized tests. Young children seem to discover spatial classification on their own in that they spontaneously classify objects—use space to indicate perceived similarities and differences—at around 18 months of age (e.g., Gopnik & Meltzoff, 1987; Sugarman, 1983).

Namy, Smith, and Gershkoff-Stowe (under review) suggested how children might discover the symbolic use of space to represent similarity in their spontaneous play with objects. They found that 18-month-old children who did not yet spontaneously classify objects on their own could be made to do so if they were given play experiences that promoted interaction with only one kind of object while rejecting the other. For example, children were given a transparent shape sorter into which only one kind of object fit. In this task, the children thus played with that one kind of object and ignored all other kinds. This experience caused the children in a different subsequent task to spatially classify, to make multiple spatial groups of like objects. Namy et al. suggest that the original practical desire of playing with one kind of object led to like objects being gathered together in close spatial proximity (on the table or in the bottom of the transparent shape sorter). They suggest further that *seeing* like objects gathered together gave the children the idea of using space to represent likeness and difference. In this way, the symbolic use of space to classify may have emerged from the external *physical* products of behavior and the re-entrant mapping of these perceived products onto internal activity. Several other lines of research also suggest that explicitly realized symbols that are concrete products of behavior may be important forces on cognitive development; these include research on young children's use of scale models as explicit symbols (DeLoache, 1992), the role of measurement in the development of concepts of quantity (Miller & Baillargeon, 1990), and the role of writing and learning to spell in phonological development (Treiman, 1993).

C. Cognitive Redescriptions

The suggestion that young children take the external products of their own activity as inputs into their cognitive system and in so doing alter the cognitive system is a classic one in theories of development (see, e.g., Luria, 1976; Vygotsky, 1962). It is also a key idea in Karmiloff-Smith's (1992) theory of developing cognition. She has suggested that cognition moves forward by "redescribing" its own internal activities. A. Clark and Karmiloff-Smith (in press) specifically suggested that such redescriptional processes are one way of getting symbol-like cognitions out of dynamic processes.

Karmiloff-Smith's basic idea can be illustrated by an example borrowed from Varela, Thompson, and Rosch (1991, p. 101). Varela et al. wrote:

> For many years biologists considered protein sequences as being instructions coded in the DNA. It is clear, however, that DNA triplets are capable of

predictably specifying an aminoacid in protein if and only if they are embedded in the cell's metabolism, that is, in the thousands of enzymatic regulations in a complex chemical network. It is only because of the emergent regularities of such a network as a whole that we bracket out the metabolic background and thus treat triplets as codes for aminoacids.

In other words, there is for DNA triplets (in a particular context) sufficient stability that those DNA triplets can be treated as symbolic units, "genes." Although these "genes" do not really exist and are not independent of the substratum from which they emerge, they are useful theoretical constructs for the scientists who think about DNA triplets and the processes associated with them.

Similarly, although "symbolic representations" may not exist in any sense, they may be useful constructs to the scientists who think about cognition *and* for ordinary people who think about their own cognitions and perceive the outward consequences of those internal processes. Indeed, we speculate that the cognitive redescriptions to which Karmiloff-smith refers may occur *only* through the perception and re-entrance of the externally realized products of ones own behavior, as in Namy et al.'s proposals about spatial classification. Words and language learning may be particularly critical here. Words are externally realized symbols that can be, just like the products of children's play with objects, re-entered or reperceived and associated with the internal activity that gives rise to them. Gentner (1989; see also Gentner & Rattermann, 1991) and also Gasser and Smith (1991; see also L. Smith & Sera, 1992; L. B. Smith, 1993) have offered independent accounts of the development of similarity that posit a form of "re-entrance" or "redescription" through the learning of words.

VI. CONCLUSION: THE ORIGINS OF KNOWLEDGE

In light of the evidence reviewed here, the two classic philosophical answers to the origins of knowledge are clearly both wrong. The activity-dependent processes seen in neural development an in perceptual and cognitive development suggest neither a tabula rasa nor innate ideas. In one way, this hardly seems newsworthy, since it has become commonplace to give lip service to interactionism. However, to date, there has been little earnest attention paid to the processes of self-organization, to the history of "interactions" that make development and knowledge. The advancing discoveries reviewed here suggest that the time is ripe for the serious study of developmental process and for the final retirement of the old "saws" of learned and innate. The activity-dependent processes of living organisms suggest that knowing is the dynamic product of a moment in time—a product that integrates immediate sensory input, current internal activity, and the developmental and evolutionary history of the organism.

Acknowledgments

The writing of this chapter was supported by a Lilly Fellowship to L. Smith. We thank Joan Stiles, Joe Steinmetz, Esther Thelen, Rochel Gelman, and Terry Au for comments and discussions.

References

Acredelo, L. P. (1985). Coordinating perspectives on infant spatial orientation. In R. Cohen (Ed.), *The development of spatial cognition* (pp. 115–140). Hillsdale, NJ: Erlbaum.

Acredelo, L. P., Adams, A., & Goodwyn, S. W. (1984). The role of self-produced movement and visual tracking in infant spatial orientation. *Journal of Experimental Child Psychology, 38,* 312–327.

Adolph, K. E., Eppler, M. A., & Gibson, E. J. (1993a). Development of perception of affordances. In C. Rovee-Collier (Ed.), *Advances in infancy research.* (Vol. 8, pp. 51–98). Norwood, NJ: Ablex.

Adolph, K. E., Eppler, M. A., & Gibson, E. J. (1993b). Crawling versus walking infants perception of affordances for locomotion on slopes. *Child Development, 64,* 1158–1174.

Arbib, M. A. (1972). *The metaphorical brain.* New York: Wiley.

Ascher, M. (1991). *Ethnomathematics: a multicultural view of mathematical ideas.* Pacific Grove, CA: Brooks/Cole.

Baldwin, D. A., & Markman, E. M. (1989). Establishing word–object relations: A first step. *Child Development, 60,* 1291–1306.

Barsalou, L. W. (1987). The instability of graded structure: Implications for the nature of concepts. In U. Neisser (Ed.), *Concepts and conceptual development: Ecological and intellectual factors in categorization* (pp. 101–140). New York: Cambridge University Press.

Barsalou, L. W. (1993). Flexibility, structure, and linguistic vagary in concepts: Manifestations of a compositional system of perceptual symbols. In A. C. Collins, S. E. Gathercole, & M. A. Conway (Eds.), *Theories of memories* (pp. 29–101). London: Erlbaum.

Bates, E., & Elman, J. (1993). Connectionism and the study of change. In M. H. Johnson (Ed.), *Brain development and cognition* (pp. 623–642). Cambridge, MA: Blackwell.

Bates, E., & MacWhinney, B. (1987). Competition, variation and language learning. In B. MacWhinney (Ed.), *Mechanisms of language acquisition.* Hillsdale, NJ: Erlbaum.

Bertanfly, L. von (1968). *General system theory.* New York: Braziller.

Bertenthal, B. I., & Campos, J. J. (1990). A systems approach to the organizing effects of self-produced locomotion during infancy. In C. Rovee-Collier & L. P. Lipsitt (Eds.), *Advances in infancy research* (Vol. 6, pp. 1–60). Norwood, NJ: Ablex.

Bertenthal, B., Campos, J., & Barrett, K. (1984). Self-produced locomotion: An organizer of emotional cognitive, and social development in infancy. In R. Emde & R. Harmon (Eds.), *Continuities and discontinuities* (pp. 175–210). New York: Plenum.

Biederman, I., & Shiffrar, M. M. (1987). Sexing day-old chicks: A case study and expert systems analysis of a difficult perceptual-learning task. *Journal of Experimental Psychology: Learning, Memory, and Cognition, 13,* 640–645.

Bienenstock, E., & von der Malsburg, C. (1987). A neural network for invariant pattern recognition. *Europhysics Letters, 4*(1), 121–126.

Bingham, G. P., Schmidt, R. C., Turvey, M. T., & Rosenblum, L. D. (1991). Task dynamics and resource dynamics in the assembly of a coordinated rhythmic activity. *Journal of Experimental Psychology: Human Perception and Performance, 17,* 359–381.

Brainerd, M. S., & Knudsen, E. I. (1993). Experience-dependent plasticity in the inferior colliculus: A site for visual calibration of the neural representation of auditory space in the barn owl. *Journal of Neuroscience, 13,* 4589–4608.

Bullock, T. H., & Horridge, G. A. (1965). *Structure and function in the nervous systems of invertebrates* (Vol. 1). San Francisco: Freeman.

Bushnell, E. M., & Boudreau, J. P. (1993). Motor development in the mind: The potential role of motor abilities as a determinant of aspects of perceptual development. *Child Development, 64*, 1005–1021.

Butterworth, G. (1981). The origins of auditory–visual perception and visual propriation in human development. In R. Walk & H. Pick (Eds.). *Intersensory perception and sensory integration* (pp. 37–70). New York: Plenum.

Carey, S. (1982). Semantic development: The state of the art. In E. Wanner & L. R. Glietman (Eds.), *Language acquisition: The state of the art* (pp. 347–389). Cambridge: Cambridge University Press.

Carey, S., & Gelman, R. (1991). *The epigenesis of mind*. Hillsdale, NJ: Erlbaum.

Castillo, M., & Butterworth, G. (1981). Neonatal localization of a sound in visual space. *Perception, 10*, 331–338.

Clark, A., & Karmiloff-Smith, A. (in press). The cognizer's innards: A psychological and philosophical perspective on the development of thought. *Mind and Language*.

Clark, S. A., Allard, T., Jenkins, W. M., & Merzenich, M. M. (1988). Receptive fields in the body-surface map in adult cortex defined by temporally correlated inputs. *Nature, 332*, 444.

Cooper, R. P., & Aslin, R. N. (1989). The language environment of the young infant: Implications for early perceptual development. *Canadian Journal of Psychology, 43*, 247–265.

Corina, D. P., Kritchevsky, M., & Bellugi, V. (1992). Linguistic permeability of unilateral neglect; Evidence from American Sign Language. *Proceedings of the Cognitive Science Conference*, pp. 384–389.

Crick, F., & Koch, C. (1990). Toward a neurobiological theory of consciousness. *Seminars in Neuroscience, 2*, 263–275.

Damasio, A. R. (1989a). Time-locked multiregional retroactivation: A systems-level proposal for the neural substrates of recall and recognition. *Cognition, 33*, 25–62.

Damasio, A. R. (1989b). The brain binds entities and events by multiregional activation from convergence zones. *Neural Computation, 1*, 123–132.

Dehaene, S., & Changeux, J.-P. (1992). A simple model of prefrontal cortex function in delayed-response tasks. *Journal of Cognitive Neuroscience, 1*, 244–266.

Dehaene, S., Changeux, J.-P., & Nadal, J. P. (1987). Neural networks that learn temporal sequences by selection. *Proceedings of the National Academy of Sciences U.S.A., 84*, 2727–2731.

DeLoache, J. S. (1992). Young children's understanding of models. In R. Fivush & J. Hudson (Eds.), *What children remember and why*. Cambridge: Cambridge University Press, 182–204.

Diamond, A. (1990). Development and neural bases of AB and DR. In A. Diamond (Ed.), *The development and neural bases of higher cognitive functions* (pp. 267–317). New York: National Academy of Sciences.

Dittmar, M. L., Berch, D. B., & Warm, J. S. (1982). Sustained visual attention in deaf and hearing adults. *Bulletin of the Psychonomic Society, 19*, 339–342.

Edelman, G. M. (1987). *Neural Darwinism*. New York: Basic Books.

Ettlinger, G., & Wilson, W. A. (1990). Cross-modal performance: behavioral processes, phylogenetic considerations and neural mechanism. *Behavioural Brain Research, 40*, 169–192.

Fernald, A. (1984). The perceptual and affective salience of mother's speech to infants. In L. Feagans, C. Garvey, & R. Gollinkoff (Eds.), *The origins and growth of communication* (pp. 5–29). Norwood, NJ: Ablex.

Fernald, A., & Kuhl, P. K. (1987). Acoustic determinants of infant preference for motherese speech. *Infant Behavior and Development, 10*, 279–293.

Fogel, A. (1993). *Developing through relationships: Communication self and culture in early infancy.* Cambridge, England: Harvester Press.

Freeman, W. J. (1981). A physiological hypothesis of perception. *Perspectives in Biology and Medicine, 24,* 561–592.

Freeman, W. J. (1991). The physiology of perception. *Scientific American, 264,* 78–85.

Freeman, W. J., & Skarda, C. A. (1985). Spatial EEG patterns, nonlinear dynamics and perception: The neo-Sherringtonian view. *Brain Research Reviews, 10,* 147–175.

Fuson, K. C. (1988). *Children's counting and concepts of number.* New York: Springer-Verlag.

Gasser, M., & Smith, L. B. (1991). The development of a notion of sameness: A connectionist model. In *Proceedings of the 13th Annual Conference of the Cognitive Science Society* (pp. 719–723). Hillsdale, NJ: Erlbaum.

Gelman, R. (1972). The nature and development of early number concepts. In H. W. Reese & L. P. Lipsitt (Eds.), *Advances in child development and behavior* (Vol. 7, pp. 115–167). New York: Academic Press.

Gelman, R. (1993). A rational-constructivist account of early learning about numbers and objects. In D. Medin (Ed.), *Psychology of learning and motivation* (Vol. 30, pp. 61–96). San Diego: Academic Press.

Gelman, R., & Gallistel, C. R. (1978). *The child's understanding of number.* Cambridge, MA: Harvard University Press.

Gelman, R., & Greeno, J. G. (1989). On the nature of competence: Principles for understanding in a domain. In L. B. Resnick (Ed.), *Knowing and learning: Issues for a cognitive science of instruction* (pp. 125–186). Hillsdale, NJ: Erlbaum.

Gentner, D. (1989). The mechanisms of analogical learning. In S. Vosniadou & A. Ortony (Eds.), *Similarity and analogical reasoning* (pp. 199–241). Cambridge, MA: Cambridge University Press.

Gentner, D., & Rattermann, M. J. (1991). Language and the career of similarity. In S. A. Gelman & J. P. Byrnes (Eds.), *Perspectives on thought and language: Interrelations in development.* Cambridge: Cambridge University Press.

Gibson, E. J. (1969). *Principles of perceptual learning and development.* Englewood Cliffs, NJ: Prentice-Hall.

Gibson, E. J. (1988). Exploratory behavior in the development of perceiving, acting, and the acquiring of knowledge. *Annual Review of Psychology, 39,* 1–41.

Gibson, E. J., & Walk, R. D. (1956). The effect of prolonged exposure to visually presented patterns on learning to discriminate them. *Journal of Comparative and Physiological Psychology, 49,* 239–242.

Goldfield, E. C. (1993). Dynamic systems in development: Action systems. In L. B. Smith & E. Thelen (Eds.), *A dynamic systems theory of development: Applications* (pp. 51–70). Cambridge, MA: MIT Press.

Gopnik, A., & Meltzoff, A. N. (1987). The development of categorization in the second year and its relation to other cognitive and linguistic developments. *Child Development, 58,* 1523–1531.

Gottlieb, G. (1991a). Experiential canalization of behavioral development: Results. *Developmental Psychology, 27*(1), 35–39.

Gottlieb, G. (1991b). Epigenetic systems view of human development. *Developmental Psychology, 27*(1), 33–34.

Gottlieb, G., Tomlinson, W. T., & Radell, P. L. (1989). Developmental intersensory interference: Premature visual experience suppresses auditory learning in ducklings. *Infant Behavior and Development, 12,* 1–12.

Held, R., & Hein, A. (1963). Movement produced stimulation in the development of visually guided behavior. *Journal of Comparative and Physiological Psychology, 56,* 872–876.

Hubel, D. H., & Wiesel, T. N. (1963). Shape and arrangement of columns in cat's striate cortex. *Journal of Physiology, 160,* 106–154.

Imai, M., Gentner, D., & Uchida, N. (1994). Children's theories of word meaning: The role of shape in early acquisition. *Cognitive Development, 9,* 45–75.

Inhelder, B., & Piaget, J. (1964). *The early growth of logic in the child.* New York: Norton.

Johnson, K. E. (1992). *The effect of expertise on hierarchical systems of categorization.* Unpublished doctoral dissertation, Emory University, Atlanta, GA.

Johnson, M. (1987). *The body in the mind: The bodily basis of meaning, imagination, and reason.* Chicago: University of Chicago Press.

Jones, S., & Smith, L. B. (1993). The place of perception in children's concepts. *Cognitive Development, 8,* 113–139.

Jones, S., Smith, L., & Landau, B. (1991). Object properties and knowledge in early lexical learning. *Child Development, 62,* 449–516.

Jones, S., Smith, L., Landau, B., & Gershkoff-Stowe, L. (1992, October). *The developmental origins of the shape bias.* Paper presented at the Boston Child Language Conference, Boston.

Jusczyk, P. W. (1992). Developing phonological categories from the speech signal. In C. A. Ferguson, L. Menn, & C. Stoel-Gammon (Eds.), *Phonological development: Models, research, and implications* (pp. 17–64). Timonioum, MD: York Press.

Kaas, J. H. (1991). The formation of cooperative cell assemblies in the visual cortex. *Journal of Experimental Biology, 153,* 177–197.

Kandel, E. R., Schwartz, J. H., & Jessel, T. M. (1991). *Principles of Neural Science* (3rd ed.). New York: Elsevier.

Karmiloff-Smith, A. (1992). Nature, nurture and PDP: Preposterous Developmental Postulates? *Connection Science, 4,* 253–269.

Katz, D. B., & Mitchell, T. V. (1993). *The development of visual selective attention in deaf children.* Poster presented at the meeting of the Society for Research in Child Development, New Orleans.

Keil, F. C. (1989). *Concepts, kinds, and cognitive development.* Cambridge: Cambridge University Press.

Kellman, P. J., & Spelke, E. S. (1983). Perception of partly occluded objects in infancy. *Cognitive Psychology, 15,* 483–524.

Kemler-Nelson, D. G., Hirsh-Pasek, K., Jusczyk, P. W., & Wright Cassidy, K. (1989). How the prosodic cues in motherese might assist language learning. *Journal of Child Language, 16,* 55–68.

Kermoian, R., & Campos, J. J. (1988). Locomotor experience: A facilitator of spatial cognitive development. *Child Development, 59,* 908–917.

Knudsen, E. I. (1984). The role of auditory experience in the development and maintenance of sound localization. *Trends in Neurosciences, 7,* 326–30.

Kuhl, P. K., & Meltzoff, A. N. (1982). The bimodal perception of speech in infancy. *Science, 218,* 1138–1141.

Lakoff, G. (1987). *Women, fire, and dangerous things: What categories reveal about the mind.* Chicago: University of Chicago Press.

Landau, B., Jones, S. S., & Smith, L. B. (1988). The importance of shape in early lexical learning. *Cognitive Development, 3,* 299–321.

Landau, B., Jones, S. S., & Smith, L. B. (1992). Perception, ontology, and naming in young children: Commentary on Soja, Carey, and Spelke. *Cognition, 43,* 85–91.

Lewkowicz, D. J. (1994). Development of intersensory perception in human infants. In D. J. Lewkowicz & R. Lickliter (Eds.), *Development of intersensory perception: Comparative Perspectives.* Hillsdale, NJ: Erlbaum.

Lewkowicz, D. J., & Turkewitz, G. (1980). Cross-modal equivalence in early infancy: Auditory-visual intensity matching. *Developmental Psychology, 16,* 597–607.

Lickliter, R. (1990). Premature visual stimulation accelerates intersensory functioning in bobwhite quail neonates. *Developmental Psychobiology, 23,* 15–17.

Luria, A. R. (1976). *Cognitive development: Its cultural and social foundations.* Cambridge, MA: Harvard University Press.

Mandler, J. (1988). How to build a baby: On the development of an accessible representational system. *Cognitive Development, 3,* 113–136.

Mandler, J. (1992). How to build a baby II: Conceptual primitives. *Psychological Review, 99,* 587–604.

Markman, E. M. (1989). *Categorization and naming in children.* Cambridge, MA: MIT Press.

Markman, E. M. (1992). Constraints on word learning: Speculations about their nature, origins, and domain specificity. *Modularity and constraints in language learning: The Minnesota Symposia of Child Psychology, 25,* 59–101.

Medin, D., & Ortony, A. (1989). Psychological essentialism. In S. Vosniadou & A. Ortony (Eds.), *Similarity and analogical reasoning* (pp. 179–195). New York: Cambridge University Press.

Meltzoff, A. N. (1990). Towards a developmental cognitive science: The implications of cross-modal matching and imitation for the development of representation and memory in infancy. In A. Diamond (Ed.), *The development and neural bases of higher cognitive functions* (pp. 1–25). New York: New York Academy of Sciences.

Mendelson, M. J., & Haith, M. M. (1976). The relation between audition and vision in the human newborn. *Monographs of the Society for Research in Child Development, 41*(4), Serial No. 167).

Meredith, M. A., Clemo, H. R., & Stein, B. E. (1991). Somatopic component of the multisensory map in the deep laminal of the cat superior colliculus. *Journal of Comparative Neurology, 312,* 353–370.

Meredith, M. A., & Stein, B. E. (1987). Multisensory integration in superior colliculus neurons is determined by modality-specific receptive field properties. *Society of Neuroscience Abstracts, 13,* 431.

Meredith, M. A., Wallace, M. T., & Stein, B. E. (1992). Visual, auditory, and somatosensory convergence on output neurons of the cat superior colliculus: multisensory properties of the trecto–reticulo–spinal projection. *Experimental Brain Research, 88,* 181–186.

Mervis, C. B., Johnson, E. K., & Scott, P. (1993). Perceptual knowledge, conceptual knowledge, and expertise: Comments on Jones and Smith. *Cognitive Development, 8,* 139–149.

Merzenich, M. M., Nelson, R. J., Stryker, M. P., Cynder, M. S., Shoppmann, A., & Zook, J. M. (1984). Somatosensory cortical map changes following digit amputation in adult monkeys. *Journal of Comparative Neurology, 224,* 591–605.

Miller, K. F., & Baillargeon, R. (1990). Length and distance: do preschoolers think that occlusion brings things together. *Developmental Psychology, 26,* 103–115.

Mitchell, T. V., & Quittner, A. (1996). A multimethod study of attention and behavior problems in hearing-impaired children. *Journal of Clinical Child Psychology, 25,* 83–96.

Morrongiello, B. (1994). Effects of collocation on auditory–visual interactions and cross-modal perception in infants. In D. J. Lewkowicz & R. Lickliter (Eds.), *The development of intersensory perception: Comparative perspectives* (pp. 235–264). Hillsdale, NJ: Erlbaum.

Mountcastle, V. B. (1980). *Medical physiology* (14th ed.). St. Louis: Mosby.

Namy, L., Smith, L. B., & Gershkoff-Stowe, L. (under review). The discovery of classification by young children.

Neville, H. J. (1990). Intermodal competition and compensation in development: Evidence from studies of the visual system in congenitally deaf adults. *Annals of the New York Academy of Sciences, 608,* 71–91.

Neville, H. J., & Lawson, D. (1987). Attention to central and peripheral visual space in a movement detection task, III. Separate effects of auditory deprivation and acquisition of a visual language. *Brain Research, 405,* 284–294.

Neville, H. J., Schmidt, A., & Kutas, M. (1983). Altered visual-evoked potentials in congenitally deaf adults. *Brain Research, 266,* 127–131.

Oyama, S. (1985). *The ontogeny of information: Developmental systems and evolution.* Cambridge: Cambridge University Press.

Peron, R. M., & Allen, G. L. (1988). Attempts to train novices for beer flavor discrimination: A matter of taste. *Journal of General Psychology, 115,* 403–418.

Perrot, D. R., Saberi, K., Brown, K., & Strybel, T. Z. (1990). Auditory psychomotor coordination and visual search performance. *Perception & Psychophysics, 48,* 214–226.

Piaget, J. (1952). *The origins of intelligence in children.* New York: International Universities Press.

Pons, T. P., Garraghty, P. E., Ommaya, A. K., Kaas, J. H., Taub, E., & Mishkin, M. (1991). Massive cortical reorganization after sensory deafferentation in adult macaques. *Science, 252,* 1857–1860.

Posner, M. I., & Cohen, Y. (1980). Attention and the control of movements. In G. E. Stelmach & J. Requin (Eds.), *Tutorials in motor behavior* (pp. 243–258). Amsterdam: North-Holland.

Posner, M. I., & Rothbart, M. K. (1980). The development of attentional mechanisms. In J. H. Flower (Ed.), *Nebraska Symposium on Motivation.* Lincoln: University of Nebraska Press.

Quittner, A. L., Smith, L. B., Osberger, M. J., Mitchell, T. V., & Katz, D. B., (1995). The impact of audition on the development of visual attention. *Psychological Science, 5,* 347–353.

Recanzone, G. H., Merzenich, M. M., Jenkins, W. M., Grajski, K. A., & Dinse, H. R. (1992). Topographic reorganization of the hand representation in cortical area 3b of owl monkeys trained in a frequency-discrimination task. *Journal of Neurophysiology, 67,* 1031–1056.

Reeke, G. N., Jr., & Edelman, G. M. (1984). Selective networks and recognition automata. *Annals of the New York Academy of Sciences, 426,* 181–201.

Roberts, K. (1994). Categorical responding in 15-month-olds: Influence of the noun-category bias and the covariation between visual fixation and auditory input. *Cognitive Development, 10,* 21–41.

Roberts, K., & Jacobs, M. (1991). Linguistic vs attentional influences on nonlinguistic categorization in 15-month-old infants. *Cognitive Development, 6,* 355–375.

Rose, S. A., & Ruff, H. A. (1987). Cross-modal abilities in human infants. In J. D. Osofsky (Ed.), *Handbook of infant development* (pp. 318–362). New York: Wiley.

Saltzman, E. Z., & Munhall, K. G. (1992). Skill acquisition and development: The roles of state-, parameter-, and graph-dynamics. *Journal of Motor Behavior, 16,* 128–141.

Siegler, R. (1989). Mechanisms of cognitive development. *Annual Review of Psychology, 40,* 353–380.

Singer, W. (1990). The formation of cooperative cell assemblies in the visual cortex. *Journal of Experimental Biology, 153,* 177–197.

Skarda, C. A., & Freeman, W. J. (1987). How brains make chaos in order to make sense of the world. *Behavioral and Brain Sciences, 10,* 161–195.

Smith, L. B., & Sera, M. (1992). A developmental analysis of the polar structure of dimensions. *Cognitive Psychology, 24,* 99–142.

Smith, L. B. (1993). The concept of same. *Advances in Child Development and Behavior, 24,* 215–252.

Smith, L. B., & Heise, D. (1993). Perceptual similarity and conceptual structure. In B. Burns (Ed.), *Advances in psychology—Percepts, concepts, and categories: The representation and processing of information* (pp. 233–272). Amsterdam: Elsevier.

Smith, L. B., Jones, S. S., & Landau, B. (1992). Count nouns, adjectives, and perceptual properties in children's novel word interpretations. *Developmental Psychology, 28,* 273–289.

Soja, N., Carey, S., & Spelke, E. (1991). Ontological categories guide young children's inductions of word meanings: Object terms and substance terms. *Cognition, 38,* 179–211.

Sompolinsky, H., & Kanter, I. (1986). Temporal association in asymmetric neural networks. *Physical Review Letters, 57,* 2861–2864.

Spelke, E. S. (1979). Perceiving bimodally specified events in infancy. *Developmental Psychology, 15,* 626–636.

Spelke, E. S. (1984). The development of intermodal perception. In L. B. Cohen & P. Salapatek (Eds.), *Handbook of infant perception* (pp. 132–158). New York: Academic Press.

Spelke, E. S. (1990). Origins of visual knowledge. In D. N. Osherson, S. M. Kosslyn, & J. M. Hollerbach (Eds.), *An invitation to cognitive science: Visual cognition and action* (pp. 99–128). Cambridge, MA: MIT Press.

Stein, B. E., & Arigbede, T. (1972). Unimodal and multimodal response properties of neurons in the cat's superior colliculus. *Experimental Neurology, 36,* 179–196.

Stein, B. E., & Meredith, M. A. (1991). Functional organization of the superior colliculus. In A. G. Leventhal (Ed.), *The neural basis of visual function* (pp. 85–110). Hampshire, England: Macmillan.

Sugarman, S. (1983). *Children's early thought: Developments in classification.* Cambridge: Cambridge University Press.

Thelen, E. (1989). Self-organization in developmental processes: Can systems approaches work? In M. Gunnar & E. Thelen (Eds.), *Systems in development: The Minnesota Symposia in Child Psychology* (Vol. 22, pp. 77–117). Hillsdale, NJ: Erlbaum.

Thelen, E., & Smith, L. B. (1994). *A dynamic systems approach to the development of cognition and action.* Cambridge, MA: MIT Press.

Thelen, E., & Ulrich, B. D. (1991). Hidden skills: A dynamic systems analysis of treadmill stepping during the first year. *Monographs of the Society for Research in Child Development, 56*(1, Serial No. 223).

Treiman, R. (1993). *Beginning to spell: A study of first grade children.* New York: Oxford University Press.

Tsuda, I. (1991). Chaotic itinerancy as a dynamical basis of hermeneutics in brain and mind. *World Futures, 32,* 167–184.

Tucker, M., & Hirsh-Pasek, K. (1993). Systems and language: Implications for acquisition. In L. B. Smith & E. Thelen (Eds.), *A dynamic systems theory of development: Applications* (pp. 359–381). Cambridge, MA: MIT Press.

van Gelder, T. (1992). *What might cognition be if not computation?* (Cognitive Science Research Rep. No. 75). Bloomington: Indiana University.

Varela, F., Thompson, E., & Rosch, E. (1991). *The embodied mind.* Cambridge, MA: MIT Press.

Vygotsky, L. S. (1962). *Thought and language.* Cambridge, MA: MIT Press.

Waddington, C. H. (1956). *Principles of embryology.* London: Allen & Unwin.

Walker-Andrews. A. S. (1988). Infants' perception of the affordances of expressive behaviors. In C. K. Rovee-Collier (Ed.), *Advances in infancy research* (pp. 173–221). Norwood, NJ: Ablex.

Walker-Andrews, A. S., & Lennon, E. (1991). Infants' discrimination of vocal expressions: Contributions of auditory and visual information. *Infant Behavior and Development, 14,* 131–142.

Waxman, S., & Hall, D. G. (1993). The development of a linkage between count nouns and object categories: Evidence from fifteen-to-twenty-one-month-old infants. *Child Development, 64,* 1224–1241.

Wellman, H. M., Cross, D., & Bartsch, K. (1986). Infant search and object permanence: A meta-analysis of the A-not-B error. *Monographs of the Society for Research in Child Development, 54,* (5 Serial No. 214).

Werner, H. (1957). The concept of development from a comparative and organismic point of view. In D. B. Harris (Ed.), *The concept of development* (pp. 125–148). Minneapolis: University of Minnesota Press.

Wertheimer, M. (1961). Psychomotor coordination of auditory-visual space at birth. *Science, 134,* 1692.

West, M. J., & King, A. P. (1987). Settling nature and nurture into an ontogenetic niche. *Developmental Psychobiology, 20,*. 549–562.

Yao, Y., & Freeman, W. J. (1990). Model of biological pattern recognition with spatially chaotic dynamics. *Neural Networks, 3,* 153–170.

Index